EIGHTH EDITION

Joining Together

Group Theory and Group Skills

David W. Johnson
University of Minnesota

Frank P. Johnson

Boston ■ New York ■ San Francisco
Mexico City ■ Montreal ■ Toronto ■ London ■ Madrid ■ Munich ■ Paris
Hong Kong ■ Singapore ■ Tokyo ■ Cape Town ■ Sydney

This book is dedicated to our parents,
Roger W. Johnson and Frances E. Johnson,
who created the basic group to
which we first belonged.

EDITOR: Arnis Burvikovs
EDITORIAL ASSISTANT: Christine Lyons
MARKETING MANAGER: Tara Whorf
COVER ADMINISTRATOR: Linda Knowles
PHOTO RESEARCHER: Deborah Brown; Liz Wood
COMPOSITION and PREPRESS BUYER: Linda Cox
MANUFACTURING BUYER: JoAnne Sweeney
PRODUCTION ADMINISTRATOR: Deborah Brown
EDITORIAL-PRODUCTION SERVICE: P. M. Gordon Associates, Inc.
ILLUSTRATOR: Drew Dernavich
ELECTRONIC COMPOSITION: Omegatype Typography, Inc.

Library of Congress Cataloging-in-Publication Data

Johnson, David W.
    Joining together : group theory and group skills / David W. Johnson, Frank P.
Johnson.—8th ed.
        p.   cm.
    Includes bibliographical references and index.
    ISBN 0-205-36740-2
    1. Social groups.   2. Leadership.   3. Group relations training.   I. Johnson, Frank P.
(Frank Pierce)   II. Title.

HM716.J64 2002
302.3—dc21

                                                                                        2002024013

PRINTED IN THE UNITED STATES OF AMERICA
10 9 8 7 6 5 4   RRD-VA   07 06 05

Contents

5 Leadership 174

6 Using Power 226

7 Decision Making 274

List of Exercises

Preface

We, the authors, know a great deal about groups. We grew up in one. There are seven children in our family. Frank is the oldest. David is in the middle. We are five years apart in age. Although Frank was very bossy as a child and refused to believe that David was not supposed to clean up his room, our relationship survived. As part of a group of seven children, we raised each other and learned about group dynamics in the trenches of trying to decide as a group who gets the extra piece of pie, who sits by the windows in the car, who decides which game we are going to play, who sweeps and who mops, and whether we go to sleep with the light on or off.

Families are not the only group setting. Within all organizations and social systems, and throughout all walks of life, groups are the key setting in which things get done. The need for knowledge of group dynamics and skills in being part of small groups is more important than ever. Our original reasons for writing *Joining Together* included introducing readers to both (a) the theory and research findings needed to understand how to make groups effective and (b) the skills required to apply that knowledge in practical situations. Expertise in working in groups is based on an integration of such knowledge and skills. *Joining Together* is more than a book reviewing current knowledge in the area of small groups, and it is more than a book of skill-building exercises. The theory and exercises are integrated into an inquiry or experiential approach to learning about the dynamics of small groups. Throughout one's life, choices, opportunities, and successes are created by (a) knowledge of group dynamics and (b) mastery of the skills required to apply that knowledge in practical situations.

What we know about group functioning is dynamic, not static. It is constantly being revised and updated as new insights are translated into revised theoretical explanations for group behavior and new lines of research. Significant advances in the field continue to be achieved. Much has changed since we published the first edition of this book in 1975. Some theories have been disconfirmed in the intervening years. Other theories have been refined or subsumed into new conceptual systems. This book reflects the new developments in theory and research by taking an updated look at what we know about group dynamics. Although the readers of this book are diverse, *Joining Together* remains focused on the characteristic dynamics found in virtually all groups. Examples are used from all walks of life. Because this book is intended to serve as an introduction to the group dynamics, we have maintained a balanced, integrative stance when presenting theories and research findings.

The authors wish to thank many people for their help in writing this book and in preparing the manuscript. We owe much to the social psychologists who have influenced our theorizing and to the colleagues with whom we have conducted various types of laboratory-training experiences. We have tried to acknowledge sources of the exercises included in this book whenever possible. Some of the exercises presented are so commonly used that the originators are not traceable. If we have inadvertently missed giving recognition to anyone, we apologize. Special thanks are extended to our wives, Linda Mulholland Johnson and Jane Miley Johnson, who contributed their support to the development and writing of this book.

Joining Together

1

Group Dynamics

Basic Concepts to Be Covered in This Chapter

In this chapter a number of concepts are defined and discussed. The major ones are listed following. Divide into pairs. Each pair is to (a) define each concept, noting the page on which it is defined and discussed, and (b) ensure that both members of the pair understand the meaning of each concept. Then combine into groups of four. Compare the answers of the two pairs. If there is disagreement, look up the concept in the chapter and clarify it until all members agree on and understand the definition.

Concepts

1. Action research
2. Effective group
3. Group
4. Group dynamics
5. High-performance group
6. Interdependent
7. Kurt Lewin
8. Norms
9. Primary group
10. Recurring-phase theory of group development
11. Reference group
12. Role
13. Sequential-stage theory of group development
14. Status

GROUP DYNAMICS AND ME

Figure 1.1 provides a helpful summary of the nature of group dynamics. The purposes of this book are to:

1. Understand the theory and research on group dynamics.
2. Improve your small group skills.

In order to achieve these purposes, you may wish to think carefully about each of the statements given on page 5.

THE IMPORTANCE OF GROUPS

Although the scientific investigations of group work are but a few years old, I don't hesitate to predict that group work—that is, the handling of human beings not as isolated individuals, but in the social setting of groups—will soon be one of the most important theoretical and practical fields. . . . There is no hope for creating a better world without a deeper scientific insight into the . . . essentials of group life.

Kurt Lewin (1943)

Humans Are Small Group Beings

Our origins are somehow linked with the fate of the Neanderthals. We have never been proud of our extinct predecessors, partly because of their looks. Nevertheless,

Importance of Groups	Nature of Groups	Types of Groups
We are small group beings We live in groups Groups and quality of life	Group orientation Individual orientation	Pseudo Traditional Effective High performance

Group Structure	Stages of Group Development	Basic Elements of Effectiveness
Roles Norms	**Recurring Stages** Task and emotional expressions Depend, pair, fight–flight Affection, inclusion, control **Sequential Stages** Forming Storming Norming Performing Adjourning	Positive interdependence Individual accountability Promotive interaction Social skills Group processing **Field of Group Dynamics** Nature of group dynamics History of group dynamics Kurt Lewin Nature of book

Dynamics of Promotive Interaction

Creating clear, operational, mutual goals members are committed to.
Communicating ideas and feelings accurately and clearly.
Distributed participation and leadership.
Equal access to power based on expertise, access to information.
Decision procedures flexibly matched with situational needs.
Controversy used to promote creative problem solving, critical thinking.
Conflicts are faced, encouraged, and resolved constructively.

Figure 1.1 Nature of group dynamics.

the Neanderthals represent a high point in the human story. Their lineage goes back to the earliest members of the genus *Homo*. They were the original pioneers. Over thousands of years Neanderthals moved out of Africa by way of the Near East into India, China, Malaysia, and southern Europe. In recent times, 150,000 or so years ago, they pioneered glacial landscapes and became the first humans to cope with climates hospitable only to woolly mammoths and reindeer.

There is no anatomical evidence that the Neanderthals were cerebrally inferior to us (the Cro-Magnons). In fact, they had a larger brain than we do. There is no doubt whatever that they were our physical superiors. Their strongest individuals could probably lift weights of half a ton or so. Physically, we are quite puny in comparison. But we gradually replaced the Neanderthals during an overlapping period of a few thousand

Self-Diagnosis

Each of the following seven statements describes an action related to group effectiveness. For each statement mark:

5 = I always behave that way   **2** = I seldom behave that way
4 = I frequently behave that way   **1** = I never behave that way
3 = I occasionally behave that way

WHEN I AM A MEMBER OF A GROUP:

____ **1.** I clarify the group's goals and ensure that the goals are formulated so that members "sink or swim" together and are committed to achieving them.

____ **2.** I facilitate communication by modeling good sending and receiving skills and ensuring that communication among all group members is distributed and two-way.

____ **3.** I provide leadership by taking whatever action is needed to help the group achieve its goals and maintain good working relationships among members, and I encourage all other members to do the same.

____ **4.** I use my expertise and knowledge to influence the other group members to increase their efforts to achieve our mutual goals, and I let myself be influenced by other members who are knowledgeable and have relevant expertise.

____ **5.** I suggest different ways of making decisions (such as majority vote or consensus), depending on the (a) availability of time and resources, (b) size and seriousness of the decision, and (c) amount of member commitment needed to implement the decision.

____ **6.** I advocate my views and challenge the views of others in order to create high-quality and creative decisions.

____ **7.** I face my conflicts with other group members and present the conflicts as problems to be jointly solved. If we are unable to do so, I ask other group members to help us resolve the conflicts constructively.

____ **Total Score**

years. It may have mainly been a matter of attrition and population pressure. As the glaciers from Scandinavia advanced, northern populations of Neanderthals moved south while our ancestors were moving north out of Africa. About 40,000 years ago the two groups met in Europe. We flourished and they vanished about 30,000 years ago.

There are numerous explanations for the disappearance of the Neanderthals. Perhaps they evolved into us. Perhaps we merged through intermarriage. Perhaps there was intergroup competition for food, with the Neanderthals unable to meet our challenge and dying off in marginal areas. Perhaps the Neanderthals were too set in their ways and were unable to evolve and refine better ways to cooperate, whereas we were continually organizing better cooperative efforts to cope with changing climatic conditions. There seems to be little doubt that we were more able to form and maintain cooperative efforts.

During the time we (the Cro-Magnons) overlapped with the Neanderthals, our ancestors developed highly sophisticated cooperative efforts characterized by social organization, group-hunting procedures, creative experimentation with a variety of materials, sharing of knowledge, divisions of labor, trade, and transportation systems. We sent out scouts to monitor the movements of herds of animals we preyed on. The Neanderthals probably did not. We cached supplies and first aid materials to aid hunting parties far away from our home bases. The Neanderthals apparently did not. Neanderthals probably engaged their prey chiefly in direct combat. We developed more efficient ways of hunting, such as driving animals over cliffs, and thereby fundamentally changed our relationship with the rest of the animal kingdom. Instead of behaving like lions and other carnivores and going after young and old and sick animals to weed out the less fit, large-scale game drives wiped out entire herds and perhaps entire species. We developed more sophisticated tools and weapons to kill from a distance such as the spear-thrower and the bow and arrow. The Neanderthals probably did not. The Neanderthals used local materials to develop tools. We were more selective, often obtaining special fine-grained and colorful flints from quarries as far as 250 miles away. This took a level of intergroup cooperation and social organization that Neanderthals did not seem to develop. We improved the tool-making process through experimentation and sharing knowledge. The Neanderthals did not. The Neanderthals used stone almost exclusively for tools. We used bone and ivory to make needles and other tools. We "tailored" our clothes and made ropes and nets. Our ability to obtain more food than we needed resulted in trading and the formation of far-ranging social networks. Status hierarchies, the accumulation of wealth, artistic efforts, laws, and storytelling to preserve traditions followed as more complex forms of cooperation were developed. Whether we replaced or evolved from the Neanderthals, our ingenuity was especially evident in organizing cooperative efforts to increase our standard of living and the quality of our lives. We excelled at organizing effective group efforts.

Humans are small group beings. We always have been and we always will be. As John Donne said, "No man is an island, entire of itself." For 200,000 years humans lived in small hunting and gathering groups. For 10,000 years humans lived in small farming communities. It is only recently, in the past 100 years or so, that large cities have become the rule rather than the exception.

We Live in Groups

def: ubiquitous: Membership in groups is inevitable and <u>ubiquitous</u>. All day long we interact first in one group and then in another. Our family life, our leisure time, our friendships, and our careers are all filled with groups. In fact, if a person from outer space conducted a study of the people of Earth, group membership would probably be the dominant characteristic noted. We are born into a group called the *family*, and we would not survive the first few years of our lives, the first few weeks, or even the first few minutes without membership in this group. It is within our family and peer groups that we are socialized into ways of behaving and thinking, educated, and taught to have certain perspectives on ourselves and our world. Our personal identity is derived from the way in which we are perceived and treated by other members of our groups. We learn, work, worship, and plan in groups. As humans we have an inherent social nature: Our life is filled with groups from the moment of our birth to the moment of our death.

Groups and the Quality of Your Life

As the effectiveness of our groups goes, so goes the quality of our life. **Understanding group dynamics is central to maintaining a viable family.** For thousands of years, family life has been one of the sustaining values of civilization. (Anthropologist Margaret Mead observed that the family is the toughest institution humans have.) Yet the structure of the family has been changing. First, there was the demise of the extended family. Second, there was the demise of the nuclear family. One out of four children today is being raised by a single parent. In order to build and maintain a constructive family life within the diverse demands of modern life, individuals have to have a thorough knowledge of group dynamics and small group skills.

A knowledge of group dynamics is central to effective businesses and industries. During the first half of the twentieth century, mass production made the United States the world leader in manufacturing. In the 1980s and 1990s, companies turned to the high productivity generated by small groups. Ford Industries, for example, formed problem-solving groups to deal with shop floor problems, interface groups to work on problems that cut across work groups, opportunity teams to oversee implementation of new technology and facilities improvements, special project teams to manage specific events such as auto shows, linking teams to deal with issues that require input from several shifts and departments, launch teams to coordinate the process and design needed to launch a successful new project, vendor quality teams to develop ongoing communication with suppliers both inside and outside the company, and resource committees to provide consulting and training on request (Banas, 1988). What makes organizations viable today is their ability to create teams dominated by a culture of learning, continuous improvement, and adaptation (see Chapter 13).

Understanding group dynamics is central to education. The paradigm of teaching is changing from lecture and individual work to cooperative learning (Johnson, Johnson, & Holubec, 1998a, 1998b). Instead of listening to lectures and taking notes, students work in small groups to maximize both their own learning and the learning of their classmates. Cooperative learning typically produces higher achievement, more positive relationships, and greater psychological health than does competitive or individualistic learning (Johnson & Johnson, 1989) (see Chapter 11).

A knowledge of group dynamics is central to the long-term maintenance of psychological health. We are in an epidemic of depression, anxiety, and mental illness (Seligman, 1988). Two major surveys of mental illness in the United States, for example, showed that, contrary to expectations, younger people were much more likely to have had a depressive episode than were older people (Seligman, 1988). The rate of depression over the last two generations has increased roughly tenfold; people are experiencing much more depression now than they did two generations ago, feeling hopeless, giving up, being passive, having low self-esteem, and committing suicide. Being involved in supportive groups prevents the occurrence of psychological problems. The use of supportive and caring groups is the ideal mode of treatment of psychological problems (see Chapter 12).

Knowing group dynamics theory and having small group skills can change your life. It can make you more employable and lead to greater career success. It can improve your friendships. It can lead to more caring and loving family relationships and greater competence as parents. It can promote greater psychological health and increased ability to cope with stress and adversity. **When it comes to group functioning, knowledge does give power.** But knowledge of group dynamics in itself is not sufficient to promote effective functioning—social skills are also required. To promote effective group functioning, you must both know what an effective group is and have the necessary social skills.

Now that the importance of groups is clear, there is a need to understand what is and is not an effective group.

EXERCISE

1.1 *Your Solitary Activities*

1. List everything you do in a typical day from the moment you wake up to the moment you fall asleep.
2. Delete from your list all the activities you perform with groups of people and see what is left.
3. Form a group of three and discuss the results.

EXERCISE

1.2 *Who Am I?*

We are all members of groups. If we are asked to describe who we are, most of us include information about the groups to which we belong. "I'm a student at the University of Minnesota," "I'm a member of the hockey team," "I'm a Johnson," "I'm a male," "I'm an American," and so forth. Membership in groups may be formal ("I'm an employee of IBM"), aspiring ("I want to be rich"), marginal ("Sometimes I'm invited to Ralph's parties, sometimes I'm not"), voluntary ("I'm a Baptist"), and nonvoluntary ("I'm a female"). To a large extent, our memberships define who we are as individuals.

1. We can all describe ourselves in many ways. Write ten different answers to the question "Who am I?" on a sheet of paper. Answer in terms of groups you belong to, beliefs you hold, and your roles and responsibilities.
2. Rank your answers from most important to your sense of self to least important to your sense of self.
3. Form a group of three and share your self-descriptions. Count how many memberships are represented in the triad. Discuss the role of groups in your view of who you are as a person.
4. Count how many group memberships are represented in the class.

EXERCISE

1.3 *Saving the World from Dracula*

The purpose of this exercise is to provide an introduction to group dynamics. A problem-solving situation is used.

1. Form heterogeneous groups of four.
2. The group's task is to formulate a plan to save the world by stopping Count Dracula from initiating a new reign of terror by vampires. Your group is to establish:
   a. How vampires may be destroyed.
   b. How to protect yourself from vampires.
   c. A vampire's strengths and weaknesses that must be overcome and exploited.
   d. When (time of day) vampires may be destroyed.
3. Complete the task by creating a plan and then ranking the items from most important to least important. Read the situation sheet. Your *goal* is to rank items from most important (1) to least important (10) and write out a rationale explaining why you ranked the items as you did.
   a. Working *individually,* rank the items from most important (1) to least important (10). Write out a rationale explaining your ranking.
   b. Working *cooperatively* in your group, rank the items again, coming to a consensus. Write out a rationale explaining the group's ranking. There should be one ranking and rationale from the group.
4. Score your own and your group's ranking (see page 583 in Appendix for answer key):
   a. Compute the absolute difference (ignore plus and minus signs) between your individual ranking and the experts' ranking.
   b. Compute the absolute difference (ignore plus and minus signs) between your group's ranking and the experts' ranking.
   c. A perfect ranking will have a score of zero. The lower your score, the more accurate your ranking. The criteria for success are:

0–20	Excellent
21–30	Good
31–40	Poor
41+	Terrible

5. When the group has solved the problem, answer the following questions:
   a. What is the group's goal?
   b. What were the patterns of communication among group members?
   c. How did leadership emerge in the group? Who provided what types of leadership in your group?
   d. What determined how influential each member was in the group?
   e. What method of decision making was used and how effective was it?

f. Why or why not did members challenge each other's conclusions?

g. What conflicts arose among group members and how were they managed?

h. How do you simultaneously participate in a group and observe the processes the group uses to complete its tasks?

i. What actions by group members helped (and hindered) the team in completing its task?

THE DANGER OF DRACULA

You are a group of scientists who specialize in public health. Your mandate is to prevent epidemics and threats to the general health of the public. Your current concern is the possibility of a proliferation of vampires resulting from the release of Count Dracula from his grave, where he has been trapped for over a hundred years.

Voivode Dracula (1431–1476) was Vlad III, Prince of Wallachia (a province of Romania bordered to the north by Transylvania and Moldavia, to the east by the Black Sea, and to the south by Bulgaria). He was known (a) as a brilliant, courageous, cunning, and clever general who defeated the Turkish army and (b) as Vlad the Impaler for impaling tens of thousands of victims on sharpened stakes. In 1459, on St. Bartholomew's Day, for example, Dracula had 30,000 citizens of the city of Brasov impaled, arranging the stakes in various geometric formations in front of the city. He was also a noted statesman and scholar. His mighty brain, iron resolution, and immense cruelty made him a formidable adversary. Although supposedly he was killed in battle in 1476 by the Turks, it soon became apparent that he had become a vampire. He adopted the title of *count* and terrorized that region of Europe until he was imprisoned in his grave in the late 1800s by a team of English scientists and adventurers. The exact whereabouts of his grave were hidden to prevent any misguided soul from freeing him.

Archaeologists excavating an ancient castle in Transylvania have uncovered Count Dracula's crypt and coffin. When they open the casket they will release Count Dracula once more on the world. Not believing in the danger, the archaeologists are inviting television crews to film the opening, hoping the publicity will help them raise money. You, however, know the truth. Vampires do exist and, once released, Count Dracula will create at least five more vampires a day, each of which will create five more vampires a day. In a very short time, vampires could be terrorizing the whole world. Your group has the responsibility of preventing this world disaster by destroying Count Dracula before he can begin. Your plan must include:

a. The procedures you will use to destroy Dracula.

b. The procedures you will use to protect yourself from Dracula.

c. A description of Dracula's strengths and weaknesses that must be overcome and exploited.

d. When (time of day) Dracula will be destroyed.

Pooling the resources of your group, you have twelve relevant items. **Your task is to rank these items according to their importance for your quest to prevent a reign of terror by Count Dracula,** starting with 1 for the most important item and ending with 12 for the least important one.

How to Destroy Dracula	Protection Procedures	Dracula's Strengths and Weaknesses	When (Time) We Will Destroy Dracula

SAVING THE WORLD FROM DRACULA RANKING SHEET

Rank the following items according to their importance for saving the world from Dracula, from 1 for the most important to 12 for the least important.

	1	2	3	4	2–4	3–4
Item	**Your Ranking**	**Group Ranking**	**Experts' Ranking**	**Individual Difference Scores**	**Group Difference Scores**
1. Oak stake					
2. Diagram/map of Dracula's castle and key to Dracula's crypt					
3. Human ability to cooperate					
4. Table detailing sunrise and sunset in Transylvania					
5. 44-magnum revolver and shells					
6. Branch of wild rose					
7. Sharp ax and several cloves of garlic					
8. Tickets: plane to Budapest, train to Transylvania, car to castle					
9. Collapsible steel cage					
10. Cross, holy water, communion wafers					
11. Two high-intensity flashlights					
12. Herbs mixed by a witch at midnight under a full moon					
Total					

HOW TO CREATE AN EFFECTIVE GROUP

I will pay more for the ability to deal with people than for any other ability under the sun.

John D. Rockefeller

Not all groups are effective. In fact, most groups may be less effective than they should be. To be effective, a group must (a) achieve its goals, (b) maintain good working relationships among members, and (c) adapt to changing conditions in the surrounding organization, society, and world. In order to ensure that the groups you belong to are effective, you must follow a set of guidelines to ensure that the group's goals are achieved, good relationships among members are maintained, and the group adapts to changing conditions (see Table 1.1). These guidelines provide (a) a direction in building an effective group, (b) a framework for diagnosing how well a group is functioning, and (c) a means for motivating group members to improve (compare actual performance with ideal performance (see Table 1.2).

Guideline 1: Establish clear, operational, relevant group goals that create positive interdependence and evoke a high level of commitment from every member. Groups exist for a reason. People join groups to achieve goals they are unable to achieve by themselves. To be effective, the goals must be clear so that all members understand the nature of the goals; must be operational so that members understand how to achieve the goals; must be relevant to members' needs so that they commit themselves to achieve the goals; and must create positive interdependence among members. Group goals and social interdependence are discussed in Chapter 3.

Guideline 2: Establish effective two-way communication within which group members communicate their ideas and feelings accurately and clearly. Communication is the basis for all human interaction and group functioning. Members must send and receive messages effectively in order to exchange information and transmit meaning. Competition among members must be minimized. Two-way communication is required for effective group work. Communication among group members is discussed in Chapter 4.

Guideline 3: Ensure that leadership and participation are distributed among all group members. All members are responsible for providing leadership. The equalization of participation and leadership ensures that all members are involved in the group's work, committed to implementing the group's decisions, and satisfied with their membership. It also (a) ensures that the resources of every member are fully utilized and (b) increases the cohesiveness of the group. Leadership is discussed in Chapter 5.

Table 1.1   **Guidelines for Creating Effective Groups**

1. Establish clear, operational, relevant group goals that create positive interdependence and evoke a high level of commitment from every member.
2. Establish effective two-way communication within which group members communicate their ideas and feelings accurately and clearly.
3. Ensure that leadership and participation are distributed among all group members.
4. Ensure that the use of power is distributed among group members and that patterns of influence vary according to the needs of the group as members strive to achieve their mutual goals.
5. Match the method of decision making with the (a) availability of time and resources, (b) size and seriousness of the decision, and (c) amount of member commitment needed to implement the decision. The most effective way of making a decision is usually by consensus.
6. Encourage structured controversies in which members advocate their views, disagree, and challenge each other's conclusions and reasoning in order to create high-quality, creative decisions.
7. Ensure that members face their conflicts of interests and use integrative negotiations and mediation to resolve them constructively.

Table 1.2   **Comparison of Effective and Ineffective Groups**

Effective Groups	Ineffective Groups
Goals are clarified and modified so that the best possible match between individual goals and the group's goals is achieved; goals are structured cooperatively so that all members are committed to achieving them.	Members accept imposed goals; goals are competitively structured so that each member strives to outperform the others.
Communication is two way, and the open and accurate expression of both ideas and feelings is emphasized.	Communication is one-way, and only ideas are expressed; feelings are suppressed or ignored.
Participation and leadership are distributed among all group members; goal accomplishment, internal maintenance, and developmental change are underscored.	Leadership is delegated and based on authority; participation is unequal, with high-power members dominating; only goal accomplishment is emphasized.
Ability and information determine influence and power; contracts are built to make sure that individuals' goals and needs are fulfilled; power is equalized and shared.	Position determines power; power is concentrated in the authority system; obedience to authority is the rule.
Decision-making procedures are matched with the situation; different methods are used at different times; consensus is sought for important decisions; involvement and group discussions are encouraged.	Decisions are always made by the highest authority; there is little group discussion; members' involvement is minimal.
Structured controversy in which members advocate their views and challenge each other's information and reasoning is seen as the key to high-quality, creative decision making and problem solving.	Disagreement among members is suppressed and avoided; quick compromises are sought to eliminate arguing; groupthink is prevalent.
Conflicts of interest are resolved through integrative negotiations and mediation so that agreements are reached that maximize joint outcomes and leave all members satisfied.	Conflicts of interest are resolved through distributive negotiations or avoidance; some members win and some members lose, or else conflict is ignored and everyone is unhappy.
Interpersonal, group, and intergroup skills are stressed; cohesion is advanced through high levels of inclusion, affection, acceptance, support, and trust; individuality is endorsed.	The functions of group members are stressed; individuality is deemphasized; cohesion is ignored; rigid conformity is promoted.

Guideline 4: Ensure that the use of power is distributed among group members and that patterns of influence vary according to the needs of the group as members strive to achieve their mutual goals. Members' power is based on expertise, ability, and access to information, not on authority or personality characteristics. Group members should form coalitions that help fulfill personal goals on the basis of mutual influence and interdependence. Power is discussed in Chapter 6.

Guideline 5: Match decision-making procedures with the needs of the situation. There are many different ways groups can make decisions. There must be a balance between the availability of time and resources (such as members' skills) and the method of decision making used. Balance is also needed among the size and seriousness of the decision, the commitment needed to put it into practice, and the method used for making the decision. The most effective way of making a decision is usually by consensus (unanimous agreement). Consensus promotes distributed participation, the equalization of power, productive controversy, cohesion, involvement, and commitment. Decision making is discussed in Chapter 7.

Guideline 6: Engage in controversy by disagreeing and challenging each other's conclusions and reasoning, thus promoting creative decision making and problem solving. In order to make effective decisions, members must present the best case possible for each major alternative course of action and subject all other alternatives to critical analysis. **Controversies** (conflicts among opposing ideas and conclusions) promote involvement in the group's work, quality and creativity in decision making, and commitment to implementing the group's decisions. They ensure that minority opinions are accepted and used. Such intellectual conflict results in more creative, effective decisions. Controversy and creativity are discussed in Chapter 8.

Guideline 7: Face your conflicts and resolve them in constructive ways. Group members must face their conflicts of interest (promoted by incompatible needs or goals, scarce resources, and competitiveness) and engage in problem-solving (integrative) negotiations to resolve them. There are five basic strategies to manage conflicts of interest: withdrawal, forcing (distributive, win–lose negotiations), smoothing, compromise, and problem solving (integrative negotiations). The more effective the group, the more frequently conflicts of interest will be valued for their potentially constructive outcomes and resolved through problem-solving negotiations. Where problem-solving negotiations fail, another group member needs to mediate. Even in intergroup and cross-ethnic conflicts, problem-solving negotiations need to be used. When they are resolved constructively, conflicts are an important and indispensable aspect of increasing group effectiveness. Conflicts of interest are discussed in Chapter 9.

If you follow the preceding guidelines, the groups to which you belong will be effective. It will help, however, if you also know the answers to the following questions:

1. What is a group?
2. What are the types of groups?
3. What is the nature of group structure?
4. How do groups develop over time?
5. What is the field of group dynamics?

EXERCISE **1.4** *What Is a Group?*

The definition of a group is quite controversial. The purpose of this exercise is to structure a critical examination of the different definitions. The procedure is as follows:

1. The class forms groups of seven members.
2. Each member receives a sheet containing one of the seven definitions that appear on the following pages. Without interacting with the other group members, each member is to:
   a. Study his or her definition until it is thoroughly understood.
   b. Plan how to teach the definition to the other members of the group.
   c. Give three examples of groups that meet the criterion contained in the definition.

d. Give three examples of two or more people in close proximity who do not meet the criterion contained in the definition.
e. Explain in what way(s) his or her group (doing this exercise) meets the criterion contained in the definition.
Allow ten minutes for this phase of the exercise.
3. Each group meets to derive a single definition of the concept *group*. Up to twenty minutes are allowed for this phase.
4. Each group reads its definition to the entire class.
5. If there is substantial disagreement, the class forms new groups (composed of one member from each of the previous groups). The task of the new group is to arrive at one definition of the concept *group*, each member representing the definition of his or her former group.
6. Each group reads its definition to the entire class.

WHAT IS A GROUP?

Everyone knows that groups exist. Many social scientists think they know exactly what a group is. The trouble is, they do not agree with each other. Following are seven of the most common definitions of the concept *group*.

Goals

Groups exist for a reason. People join groups in order to achieve goals they are unable to achieve by themselves. A **group** may be defined as a number of individuals who join together to achieve a goal. It is questionable whether a group could exist unless there was a mutual goal that its members were trying to achieve. Freeman, as early as 1936, pointed out that people join groups in order to achieve common goals. Other social scientists who have defined *group* this way are Mills and Deutsch:

> To put it simply, they [small groups] are units composed of two or more persons who come into contact for a purpose and who consider the contact meaningful. (Mills, 1967, p. 2)

> A psychological group exists (has unity) to the extent that the individuals composing it perceive themselves as pursuing promotively interdependent goals. (Deutsch, 1949a, p. 136)

Interdependence

A **group** may be defined as a collection of individuals who are interdependent in some way. According to this definition, the individuals are not a group unless an event that affects one of them affects them all. Social scientists who have defined *group* in this way are Cartwright and Zander, Fiedler, and Lewin:

> A group is a collection of individuals who have relations to one another that make them interdependent to some significant degree. As so defined, the term *group* refers to a class of social entities having in common the property of interdependence among their constituent members. (Cartwright and Zander, 1968, p. 46)

By this term [group] we generally mean a set of individuals who share a common fate, that is, who are **interdependent** in the sense that an event which affects one member is likely to affect all. (Fiedler, 1967, p. 6)

Conceiving of a group as a dynamic whole should include a definition of group that is based on interdependence of the members (or better, the subparts of the group). (Lewin, 1951, p. 146)

Interpersonal Interaction

A **group** may be defined as a number of individuals who are interacting with one another. According to this definition, a group does not exist unless interaction occurs. Social scientists who have defined *group* in this way are Hare, Bonner, Stogdill, and Homans.

For a collection of individuals to be considered a group, there must be some interaction. (Hare, 1976, p. 4)

A group is a number of people in interaction with one another, and it is this interaction process that distinguishes the group from an aggregate. (Bonner, 1959, p. 4)

A group may be regarded as an open interaction system in which actions determine the structure of the system and successive interactions exert coequal effects upon the identity of the system. (Stodgill, 1959, p. 18)

We mean by a group a number of persons who communicate with one another often over a span of time, and who are few enough so that each person is able to communicate with all the others, not at secondhand, through other people, but face-to-face. (Homans, 1950, p. 1)

Perceptions of Membership

A **group** may be defined as a social unit consisting of two or more persons who perceive themselves as belonging to a group. According to this definition, the persons are not a group unless they perceive themselves to be part of a group. Social scientists who have defined *group* in this way are Bales and Smith:

A small group is defined as any number of persons engaged in interaction with one another in a single face-to-face meeting or series of such meetings, in which each member receives some impression or perception of each other member distinct enough so that he can, either at the time or in later questioning, give some reaction to each of the others as an individual person, even though it may be only to recall that the other was present. (Bales, 1950, p. 33)

We may define a social group as a unit consisting of a plural number of separate organisms (agents) who have a collective perception of their unity and who have the ability to act and/or are acting in a unitary manner toward their environment. (Smith, 1945, p. 227)

Structured Relationships

A **group** may be defined as a collection of individuals whose interactions are structured by a set of roles and norms. According to this definition, the individuals are not a group unless their interactions are so structured. Social scientists who have defined *group* in this way are McDavid and Harari and Sherif and Sherif:

> A social-psychological group is an organized system of two or more individuals who are interrelated so that the system performs some function, has a standard set of role relationships among its members, and has a set of norms that regulate the function of the group and each of its members. (McDavid & Harari, 1968, p. 237)

> A group is a social unit which consists of a number of individuals who stand in (more or less) definite status and role relationships to one another and which possesses a set of values or norms of its own regulating the behavior of individual members, at least in matters of consequence to the group. (Sherif & Sherif, 1956, p. 144)

Mutual Influence

A **group** may be defined as a collection of individuals who influence each other. Individuals are not a group unless they are affecting and being affected by each other; therefore, the primary defining characteristic of a group is interpersonal influence. Shaw (1976, p. 11) stated, "A group is two or more persons who are interacting with one another in such a manner that each person influences and is influenced by each other person."

Motivation

A **group** may be defined as a collection of individuals who are trying to satisfy some personal need through their joint association. According to this definition, the individuals are not a group unless they are motivated by some personal reason to be part of a group. Individuals belong to the group in order to obtain rewards or to satisfy personal needs. It is questionable that a group could exist unless its members' needs are satisfied by their membership. Social scientists who have defined group in this way are Bass and Cattell:

> We define "group" as a collection of individuals whose existence as a collection is rewarding to the individuals. (Bass, 1960, p. 39)

> The definition which seems most essential is that a group is a collection of organisms in which the existence of all (in their given relationships) is necessary to the satisfaction of certain individual needs in each. (Cattell, 1951, p. 167)

THE NATURE OF GROUPS

It takes two flints to make a fire.
   Louisa May Alcott

In a bus trapped in a traffic jam, six passengers begin to talk to each other, comparing reactions and sharing previous similar experiences. They start to develop a plan of action to get the bus out of the heavy traffic. Is this a group? In Yellowstone National Park it is deep winter. Several cross-country skiers glide through an isolated, snow-covered valley. They are studying winter ecology and photography. Periodically they cluster around a professional photographer as he explains the ways the winter scenes may be photographed. The vacationers admire and discuss the beautiful winter scenery as they photograph it. Is this a group? Do groups exist at all? How do you tell when you are a member of a group?

Barriers to Capitalizing on the Power of Groups

Directions: Consider the following five sources of resistance to using small groups. Rate yourself from 1 to 5 on each source.

Causes of the Missed Opportunities to Capitalize on the Power of Groups

	1————2————3————4————5	
Low	**Middle**	**High**
Not a Concern of Mine	Somewhat a Concern	Consistently and Strongly a Concern

_____ **Belief that isolated work is the natural order of the world.** Such a myopic focus blinds individuals to the realization that no one person could have built a cathedral, achieved America's independence from England, or created a supercomputer.

_____ **Resistance to taking responsibility for others.** Many individuals do not easily (a) take responsibility for the performance of colleagues or (b) let colleagues assume responsibility for their work.

_____ **Confusion about what makes groups work.** Many individuals may not know the difference between effective and ineffective groups.

_____ **Fear that they cannot use groups effectively.** Not all groups work. Most adults have had experiences with ineffective and inefficient committees, task forces, and clubs and know how bad groups can be. When many educators weigh the potential power of learning groups against the possibility of failure, they choose to play it safe and rely on isolated work.

_____ **Concern about the time and effort required to change.** Using groups requires individuals to apply what is known about effective groups in a disciplined way. Learning how to do so and engaging in such disciplined action may seem daunting.

Not every collection of people can be considered a group. The *Oxford English Dictionary* (1989) defines a *group* as a number of persons or things regarded as forming a unit on account of any kind of mutual or common relation or classified together on account of a common degree of similarity. Groups may be contrasted with aggregates. An **aggregate** is a collection of individuals who are present at the same time and place but who do *not* form a unit or have a common degree of similarity. Individuals standing on a street corner, the members of an audience at a play, and students listening to a lecture are aggregates, not groups.

As we have seen, there are many different definitions of the concept *group*. Whereas the definition of small groups usually includes member interaction, a group can involve large numbers of members who have some common characteristic without actually meeting each other (such as a reference group). A community can be a large group. Individuals with the same ethnic heritage can be considered a large group. The social scientists who have tried to define what a group is seem much like the blind men trying to describe an elephant. Each social scientist has taken some aspect of a group and assumed that this aspect reveals the essence of a group. One solution to the profusion of definitions is to combine them all into one definition. A small group may be defined as two or more individuals who (a) pursue common goals, (b) are interdependent, (c) interact with each other, (d) share norms concerning matters of common interest and participate in a system of interlocking roles, (e) influence each other, (f) find the group rewarding, and (g) define themselves and are defined by others as belonging to the group. Not all of these characteristics are equally important, and although it is impossible to gain consensus among social scientists as to which characteristics are most important, the authors prefer the following definition: A **small group** is two or more individuals in face-to-face interaction, each aware of positive interdependence as they strive to achieve mutual goals, each aware of his or her membership in the group, and each aware of the others who belong to the group. Though there may be some groups that do not fully fit this definition, the most commonly recognized examples of groups do.

Based on the preceding definitions, how do you tell the difference between an aggregate and a group? Is an audience at a concert a group? Are the people traveling in the same airplane a group? Are the children waiting in the same line to talk to Santa Claus a group? Are all twenty-one-year-old males in our society a group?

Group Orientation

The **group orientation** focuses on the group as a whole. In explaining the actions of group members, social scientists focus on the influences of the group and the larger social systems of which it is a part. Emile Durkhem (1898, p. 104), arguing that groups were entities different from individuals, stated, "If, then, we begin with the individual, we shall be able to understand nothing of what takes place in the group." He posited that small **primary groups** (small groups characterized by face-to-face interaction, interdependence, and strong group identification such as families and very close friends) are the building blocks of society, and he worked upward from this level to an analysis of social systems in general. He was convinced that a group mind or collective consciousness dominates individual will in many situations. Le Bon (1897) believed that a group mind exists separate from the minds of individual members. Cartwright and Zander (1968) maintained that a group can be emotionally healthy or pathological. Cattell (1951) described groups as possessing different personalities. Lewin (1935), as a Gestalt psychologist, noted that a group cannot be understood by considering only the qualities and characteristics of each member. When individuals merge into a group, something new is created that must be seen as an entity in itself. Changes in one aspect of a group will necessarily lead to changes in the other group features.

Individualistic Orientation

The **individualistic orientation** focuses on the individual in the group. In order to explain the functioning of the group, psychologists focus on the attitudes, cognitions, and personalities of the members. Floyd Allport (1924) argued that groups do not think, feel, or act (only people do) and, therefore, groups are not real and are not deserving of study. He said, "Groups have no nervous systems, only individuals have nervous systems." To Allport, groups are no more than (a) shared sets of values, ideas, thoughts, and habits that exist simultaneously in the minds of several persons or (b) the sum of the actions of each member taken separately. His *coup de grace* was his observation, "You can't stumble over a group." Many social scientists have agreed with Allport and have taken a rather cavalier approach to the attributes that determine whether a collection of people is a group. Groups have also been defined on the basis of individual perceptions of other members (Bales, 1950), individual reward (Bass, 1960), and individual purpose and meaning (Mills, 1967). Much of the research on groups, furthermore, has used individual members as the unit of analysis.

Even though the concept *group* can be defined, not everyone believes that groups exist. One of the more interesting social scientific debates centers on the nature of groups. There are two contrasting positions: the group orientation and the individual orientation.

Solomon Asch (1952) adopted a middle ground by comparing groups to water. He argued that in order to understand the properties of water, it is important to know the characteristics of its elements, hydrogen and oxygen. This knowledge alone, however, is not sufficient to understand water; the combination of hydrogen and oxygen must be examined as a unique entity. Similarly, groups must be studied as unique entities, even though it is important to know the characteristics of the individual members. There is evidence that groups evoke stronger reactions than an individual engaging in the same behavior, and actions by groups and individuals elicit differing preferences for redress (Abelson, Dasgupta, Park, & Banaji, 1998). When individuals are perceived to be part of a cohesive group (as opposed to an aggregate of unrelated individuals), observers express stereotypic judgments about the individuals and infer that their behavior was shaped by the presence of others (Oakes & Turner, 1986; Oakes, Turner, & Haslam, 1991; Wilder, 1977, 1978a). A racial slur by an individual, for example, provokes a different reaction than a racial slur by a group. Social scientists of both the individualistic and group persuasions have generated theories of group functioning and conducted research to validate or disconfirm the theories. Both are represented in this book.

ASPECTS OF GROUPS

In order to understand the nature of groups, it is necessary to understand:

1. The relationship between group structure and group productivity.
2. The nature of group structure.
3. The ways groups develop over time.
4. How the dynamics of the group determine its effectiveness.

CREATING PRODUCTIVE GROUPS

There is nothing magical about working in a group. Some groups are highly effective and achieve amazing things. Some groups are highly ineffective and waste everyone's time. The authors have studied various types of groups for over thirty years. We have interviewed thousands of members in a wide variety of organizations in a number of different countries to discover how groups are being used and where and how groups work best. On the basis of our findings and the findings of other researchers such as Katzenbach and Smith (1993), we have developed a group performance curve to clarify the difference between ineffective and effective groups (Figure 1.2). The curve illustrates that how well any small group performs depends on how it is structured (Katzenbach & Smith, 1993). The performance curve describes four types of groups. It begins with the individual members of the group and illustrates their performance relative to pseudo-groups, traditional work groups, effective groups, and high-performance groups.

Figure 1.2 The group performance curve.

A **pseudogroup** is a group whose members have been assigned to work together but who have no interest in doing so. They believe they will be evaluated by being ranked from the highest performer to the lowest performer. While members talk to each other, they are actually competing. They see each other as rivals who must be defeated, block or interfere with each other's performance, hide information from each other, attempt to mislead and confuse each other, and distrust each other. The result is that the sum of the whole is less than the potential of the individual members. Members would be more productive if they were working alone. The group does not mature because members have no interest in or commitment to each other or to the group's future.

A **traditional work group** is a group whose members are assigned to work together and accept that they have to do so. Members believe that they will be evaluated and rewarded as individuals, not as members of the group. The work is structured so that very little joint work is required. Members interact primarily to clarify how the work is to be done. They seek each other's information but have no motivation to inform their groupmates. Helping and sharing are minimized. Members are accountable as separate individuals, not as members of a team. Some members loaf, seeking a free ride on the efforts of their more conscientious groupmates. The conscientious members feel exploited and do less. The result is that the sum of the whole is more than the potential of some of the members, but the more hard-working and conscientious members would perform better if they worked alone.

An **effective group** is more than the sum of its parts. It is a group whose members commit themselves to the common purposes of maximizing their own and each other's

Types of Groups

Demonstrate your understanding of the different types of groups by matching each definition with the appropriate group. Check your answers with your partner and explain why you believe your answers to be correct.

Type of Group	Definition
____ 1. Pseudogroup	a. A group in which members work together to accomplish shared goals. Members perceive that they can reach their goals if and only if the other group members also reach their goals.
____ 2. Traditional group	b. A group whose members have been assigned to work together but who have no interest in doing so. The structure promotes competition at close quarters.
____ 3. Effective group	c. A group that meets all the criteria for being an effective group and outperforms all reasonable expectations, given its membership.
____ 4. High-performance group	d. A group whose members agree to work together but see little benefit from doing so. The structure promotes individualistic work with talking.

success. Members are assigned to work together, and they are happy to do so. They believe that their success depends on the efforts of all group members. An effective group has a number of defining characteristics. They include positive interdependence that unites members to achieve clear operational goals, two-way communication, distributed leadership, power based on expertise, a decision-making procedure appropriate to the situation; to challenge each other's information and reasoning; and to resolve conflicts constructively. In addition, members hold each other accountable to do their fair share of the work, promote each other's success, appropriately engage in small group skills, and determine how effectively they are working together.

A **high-performance group** meets all the criteria for an effective group and outperforms all reasonable expectations, given its membership. What differentiates a high-performance group from an effective group is the level of commitment members have to each other and to the group's success. Jennifer Futernick, who is part of a high-performance, rapid-response team at McKinsey & Company, calls the emotion binding her teammates together a form of love (Katzenbach & Smith, 1993). Ken Hoepner of the Burlington Northern Intermodal Team (also described by Katzenbach & Smith, 1993) stated: "Not only did we trust each other, not only did we respect each other, but we gave a damn about the rest of the people on this team. If we saw somebody vulnerable, we were there to help." Members' mutual concern for each other's personal growth enables high-performance groups to perform far above expectations and also to have a lot of fun. Unfortunately, high-performance groups are rare. Most groups never achieve this level of development.

EXERCISE

1.5 *Developing an Effective Group*

The purpose of this exercise is to give participants some practice in planning how to develop an effective group. The procedure is as follows:

1. The class forms groups of four.
2. Groups read and discuss the paragraph below and then answer the following questions about the situation:
   a. Which alternative would you choose if you were there?
   b. What kind of people would you want as companions in such a situation?
   c. What should the goals of the group be?
   d. How should leadership be managed?
   e. Who should have the most power in making decisions?
   f. What decision-making procedure should be used?
   g. How should conflicts be managed?
3. Each group decides whether its answers to the above questions are indicative of an effective or an ineffective group.
4. Each group shares its answers with the rest of the class.

SINKING BOAT SITUATION

On a dark summer night, seven persons cling to a swamped and slowly sinking boat on a black tropical sea. They are not alone. A large shark glides below them, and soon, perhaps, there will be more. With fear thick in their salt-swollen throats, the seven are faced with a difficult choice. If they kick in unison, they may be able to fight the fierce current and tides driving them away from the shore and all make it to safety; if they stick together they have an equal chance to survive or drown. If they split up, each going it alone, one or two of the stronger swimmers might make it to safety, but the majority will certainly drown or be devoured by sharks.

1. Which alternative would you choose if you were there?
2. Which alternative would you want your companions to choose?
3. What are the characteristics the group would have to exhibit in order to ensure that everyone survives?

GROUP STRUCTURE

Imagine that you are an ecologist whose career has been dedicated to studying the seven corners of the world. In your studies of six of the corners you have encountered many diverse habitats, from thick rain forests to parched deserts. They all, however, had a set of features in common: topography, weather patterns, plants, animals, and their interconnections. You have observed, for example, that plants and animals have certain territories that comprise an elaborate division of labor and broad symbioses, and that plants and animals adapt over time so that they are uniquely suited to survive and flourish within their habitat. Thus, you expect to find a basic ecological structure within the final, seventh corner of the world.

Now imagine that you are studying small groups. Although there are many diverse types of groups, when you approach a new group you look for the basic features that characterize all groups: a purpose that defines the territory of the group and binds the members together, a definable pattern of communication among members, different members performing different functions that fit into an overall division of labor, procedures for managing conflicts, expectations concerning acceptable and unacceptable behavior by group members, and the adaptation of the group to the organization, society, and culture within which it is based. Once the basic structure has been identified, the nature of interpersonal relations in the group can be understood as clearly as the functioning of an ecosystem.

Like ecosystems, groups have a structure. Observers of groups look beyond the unique features of the group to its basic structure. The **group structure** is a stable pattern of interaction among members. Groups function as members interact. Groups are networks of human relationships, and a group is effective only if members are effective in cooperating with each other. Whenever two or more individuals join together to achieve a goal, a group structure develops. Within any group, no matter which organization, society, or culture it belongs to, there are differentiated roles and integrating norms. The group's roles and norms structure the interaction among group members. Roles differentiate the responsibilities of group members, whereas norms integrate members' efforts into a unified whole. Each is discussed briefly.

Roles: Differentiation Within Groups

Think of a group to which you have belonged and answer this question: Did everyone in the group act the same way or perform the same functions? In all likelihood, your answer is "no." Usually, a considerable degree of differentiation exists within groups, so different members work on different tasks and are expected to accomplish different things. In other words, different group members play different roles. Roles define the formal structure of the group and differentiate one position from another. Formally, a **role** may be defined as a set of expectations defining the appropriate behavior of an occupant of a position toward other related positions. Often such roles are assigned in a relatively formal manner, such as appointing a president, secretary, treasurer, and so on. At other times, individuals drift into various roles on the basis of their interests and skills. Once a role is assumed, however, the member is expected (by other group members) to behave in certain ways and members who conform to their role requirements are rewarded, whereas those who deviate are punished. Roles ensure that the task behaviors of group members are appropriately interrelated so that the group's goals are achieved. The roles are complementary in that one cannot be performed without the other (e.g., the roles of "teacher" and "student"). The expectations that define a role include both rights and obligations. The obligations of one role are the rights of other roles. One of the obligations of being a teacher, for example, includes structuring a learning situation; one of the rights of being a student is to have learning situations structured by the teacher. Within a group, expectations of the obligations of a role can conflict (i.e., role conflict). What a principal and what students expect from a teacher, for example, can be contradictory. Contradictory expectations can create one type of role conflict. There is also a second type.

Imagine that you are Pat Garrett and one of your best friends is Billy the Kid. You are appointed sheriff, and your superiors expect you to fulfill your role by arresting Billy

Group Structure

	Definition	Example
Roles	Expectations defining the appropriate behavior of an occupant of a position toward other related positions.	President, vice president, secretary; summarizer, recorder
Norms	Common beliefs regarding group members' appropriate behavior, attitudes, and perceptions; rules, implicit or explicit, that regulate the behavior of group members.	Promptness, courtesy, reciprocity, responsibility

the Kid. Billy expects you to fulfill your role as friend by leaving him alone. Which role would you want to fulfill if you were Pat Garrett? What would you actually do? Each person is required to fill multiple roles. When the demands of one role are incompatible with the demands of another, **role conflict** exists. Sometimes such role conflict can provide great drama. What Sheriff Pat Garrett illustrated when he shot down his friend Billy the Kid was that roles can powerfully influence our actions, often leading us to act contrary to our private feelings or vested interests. Milgram (1974) provided another example with his famous studies on obedience to authority. In these studies, he placed paid adult subjects in the role of teacher and gave them the responsibility of giving "learners" an electric shock when they committed a memory error. Milgram intended to show that teachers would refuse to comply with the requirements of their role, but although almost all teachers began to express reluctance and show signs of stress as the intensity of the shock increased and the learner cried out in pain, the majority of the teachers continued to administer the shocks. Over 60% of subjects administered the maximum shock (450 volts) to the learner. Even when the teacher was compelled to hold the learner's hand to the shock plate, the figure dropped only to 30%. Milgram's results point out that many people can commit a variety of costly, harmful, and even immoral actions if role pressure is severe enough.

Different social roles are usually associated with different degrees of status. **Status** is generally a function of the degree to which an individual's contribution is crucial to the success (and prestige) of the group, how much power (control over outcomes) that individual has, and the extent to which the person embodies some idealized or admired characteristic (such as being physically attractive). In many subhuman groups (and some human ones) status is determined by physical dominance. Although status and power ordinarily go hand in hand, they need not. Johnson and Allen (1972) separated status and power experimentally. They found that having high status and high power in an organization results in an enhanced self-perception that leads to altruistic behavior but disdain for the worker. But when individuals have high status but low power in an organization that rewards high power, they engage in selfish behavior (they deviate from the prescribed norms in order to increase their own rewards) and have respect for the worker.

Status differences have a number of important effects on group process. High-status individuals are likely to be valued by the group and treated more tolerantly. They are often less affected, therefore, by group norms and peer pressure than lower-status members, in part because they are less likely to expect punishment for their actions (Johnson & Allen, 1972). High-status members, furthermore, have a disproportionately strong impact on group decisions and judgments, whereas those low in status tend to be ignored even when they offer intelligent and creative advice. Torrance (1954) studied the decision making of B-26 combat crews, in which the pilot was the commanding officer, the navigator was a commissioned officer, and the tail gunner was an enlisted man inferior in status to the two officers. He found that when one of the men had the right answer and the other two were mistaken, the pilots were almost always successful in persuading the other two to accept their view (94%), the navigators were not quite as successful (80%), and the tail gunners were much less persuasive (63%). It is not uncommon in decision-making groups for a low-power person to have a critical insight or piece of information and be ignored. Sometimes the tail gunners' opinions were correct, but they were still ignored.

Norms: Integration of Members' Actions

Whereas roles differentiate members' rights and obligations from each other, norms integrate the actions of all group members. Norms are rules, implicit or explicit, established by groups to regulate the behavior of their members. Norms tell group members how to behave, or how *not* to behave, in various situations. The **norms** of a group are the group's common beliefs regarding appropriate behavior, attitudes, and perceptions for members. They are the prescribed modes of conduct and belief that not only guide the behavior of group members but also help group interaction by specifying the kinds of responses that are expected and acceptable in particular situations. All groups have norms, set either formally or informally. A group of students that often parties together, for example, will have common ideas about what is acceptable and unacceptable behavior at a party, that is, about what is expected of everyone. More formally organized groups, such as classes, will have norms about absence, tardiness, accomplishment of assigned work, and appropriate times to speak. In any group, some norms specify the behavior expected of all group members and others apply only to persons in specific roles. In the classroom, for instance, some norms govern both the teacher's and the students' behavior, but others may apply only to the teacher or only to the students. Because norms refer to the expected behavior sanctioned (rewarded or punished) by a group, they have an "ought to" or "must" quality: Group members must not disrupt the group's work, group members ought to participate in discussions, and so on. The norms of any group vary in importance. Those that are less important for the objectives and values of the group usually allow for a greater range of behavior and bring less severe pressures for members to conform than do norms that are highly relevant to group functioning. Because most groups insist on adherence to their norms as a basic requirement for membership, individuals wishing to join or remain in specific groups generally follow these "rules of the game." If they do not, they may soon find themselves on the outside looking in.

For a group norm to influence a person's behavior, the person must recognize that it exists, be aware that other group members accept and follow the norm, and accept and follow it him- or herself. At first a person may conform to a group norm because the group typically rewards conforming behavior and punishes nonconforming behavior. Later the person may internalize the norm and conform to it automatically, even when no other group members are present. A regulation that all members should be on time for group meetings, for example, becomes a norm only to the extent that the individual group member accepts it, sees other group members accepting it, and sees them enforcing the regulation among themselves.

Group norms help a group maintain behavioral consistency among group members. They provide a basis for predicting the behavior of other members and serve as a guide for a member's own behavior. Norms thus help each group member anticipate how the others will behave in repetitive situations, and they reduce ambiguity concerning appropriate behavior within the group. Norms are formed only with respect to matters that have some significance to the group. They may apply to all members or only to certain members. Norms vary in the degree to which they are accepted by the group members. Some norms allow for more deviation than others. Some norms require strict adherence to a rule; others permit a wide range of behavior that is regarded as acceptable.

Norms cannot be imposed on a group but rather develop out of the interaction among members. Norms are social products. This was demonstrated ingeniously by Muzafer Sherif (1936). When a fixed point of light is viewed in total darkness, it appears to move spontaneously, a perceptual phenomenon known as the *autokinetic effect.* Sherif utilized this phenomenon in studying how group norms develop and how group members come to form coherent, shared beliefs about novel events. Sherif led individuals to a totally dark room and turned on a tiny light. He asked participants, first individually and then in groups, to note how much the light moved. When tested in groups, the participants coalesced in their judgments on the amount of movement. Sherif was able to increase or decrease subjects' estimates of movement dramatically if he paid confederates to offer particularly large or small estimates. Once a group decision was made about how much the light was moving, the norm persisted even when the group was not present. Individual participants used the group judgment as a frame of reference to evaluate the perceived movement of the light. Many of the judgments and values of individual group members that seem to be their own are shaped in part by the judgments of other group members.

Another classic study on the impact of group norms on the beliefs and values of group members was conducted by Theodore Newcomb (1943). Born in 1903, Newcomb had studied with Goodwin Watson and Gardner Murphy at Columbia University. He was a pioneer of social psychology and a cofounder of the social psychology program at the University of Michigan. He conducted a number of studies on the impact of the college experience on students, the most famous of which was his classic study of group norms at Bennington College. The students, all females from mostly well-to-do and politically conservative families, lived in a community where most of the faculty and older students were somewhat materialistic and politically liberal. A majority of the Bennington students became progressively more liberal over their careers, but some did not. Newcomb was able to relate the student's ultimate political orientation to the group she identified with—liberal if she thought of herself as primarily a member of the campus community and conservative if her primary identification was with her family. This study served as the basis on which the study of reference groups began. A **reference group** is a group people identify with, compare their attitudes to, and use as a means to evaluate those attitudes.

THE DEVELOPMENT OF GROUPS OVER TIME

In addition to having a structure, groups change over time. The kinds of developmental changes seen in most groups have been described by well over one hundred theories. Most of these theories have taken one of two approaches (Hill & Gruner, 1973; Shambaugh, 1978). **Recurring-phase theories** specify the issues that dominate group interaction that recur again and again. Robert Freed Bales (1965), for example, stated that an equilibrium has to exist between task-oriented work and emotional expressions to build better relationships among group members. The group tends to oscillate between these two concerns, sometimes for more solidarity and sometimes for a more work-oriented focus. Bion (1961) stated that groups focus on the three basic themes of dependence on the leader, pairing among members for emotional support, and fight–flight reactions to a threat to the group. William Schultz (1958) proposed that group development occurs as members concern themselves with three issues—affection, inclusion, and control.

Sequential-stage theories specify the typical order of the phases of group development. Moreland and Levine (1982, 1988) suggested that group members go through predictable stages of membership: prospective member, new member, full member, marginal member, and ex-member. At each stage, the member is concerned about a different aspect of group life. For example, the new member attempts to change the group to meet his or her needs, while the group attempts to mold the new member to fit group needs. The full member engages in role negotiation in order to find a niche that is most comfortable. Worchel, Coutant-Sassic, and Grossman (1992) proposed six stages of group development. There is a stage of discontent, when individuals feel that their present group(s) are not meeting their needs. A precipitating event brings members together. Members begin to identify with the group. Attention then turns to group productivity. Attention shifts to the individual group member who negotiates with the group to expand task efforts to meet personal goals. Finally, the group begins to disintegrate. Outside of group research, Levinger (1980) proposed that there are five stages of close relationships: initial attraction, building a relationship, continuation, deterioration, and ending the relationship. Hopper (1950) proposed that revolutions develop through a series of identifiable stages. There is a preliminary stage in which crime, suicide, travel, and emigration all increase; a popular stage in which the discontent spreads; and an institutional stage in which a new government is established. With all of these theories to choose from, the only conclusion may be that groups follow a pattern of development; there have been frequent attempts to define what those states are, but they still remain unclear.

Probably the most famous sequential-stage theory was formulated by Bruce W. Tuckman (1965; Tuckman & Jensen, 1977). Tuckman reviewed over fifty studies on group development conducted in a variety of settings (mostly therapy and training groups of limited duration). Although the description of the stages the groups went through varied widely on the surface (some studies identifying three stages and others identifying seven or eight), Tuckman found a surprising amount of agreement beneath the diversity. He identified five stages: forming, storming, norming, performing, and adjourning. At each stage groups focus on specific issues, and this focus influences members' behaviors. During the *forming stage,* there is a period of uncertainty in which members try to determine their place in the group and the procedures and rules of the group. During the *storming stage,* conflicts begin to arise as members resist the influence of the group and rebel against accomplishing the task. Members often confront their various differences, and the management of conflict becomes the focus of attention. During the *norming stage,* the group establishes some consensus regarding a role structure and a set of group norms for appropriate behavior. Cohesion and commitment increase. In the *performing stage* the group members become proficient in working together to achieve the group's goals and become more flexible in developing its patterns of working together. In the *adjourning stage* the group disbands. Of all the sequential-stage theories, Tuckman's, with its emphasis on forming, storming, norming, performing, and adjourning, still seems the most useful and creates the most interest.

Virtually all the studies that Tuckman reviewed, however, involved group leaders who were passive and nondirective and who made no attempt to intervene in the group process. In most groups there is a coordinator, team leader, or instructor who tries to ensure that the group functions productively. In applying Tuckman's conclusions to such groups, the authors (with the help of Roger Johnson and a number of other colleagues) identified seven stages of development:

1. Defining and structuring procedures.
2. Conforming to procedures and getting acquainted.
3. Recognizing mutuality and building trust.
4. Rebelling and differentiating.
5. Committing to and taking ownership of the goals, procedures, and other members.
6. Functioning maturely and productively.
7. Terminating.

Each of these stages is discussed in turn.

Defining and Structuring Procedures

When a group begins, the members are usually concerned about what is expected of them and the nature of the group's goals. Group members want to know what is going to happen; what is expected of them; whether they will be accepted, influential, and liked; how the group is going to function; and who the other group members are. Group members expect the coordinator to explain how the group is to function in a way that reassures them that their personal needs will be met. When a group first meets, therefore, the coordinator should describe the procedures to be used, define the group's goals, establish the interdependence among members, and generally organize the group and announce the beginning of the group's work.

Conforming to Procedures and Getting Acquainted

As group members follow the prescribed procedures and interact around the task, they become acquainted with one another and familiarize themselves with the procedures until they can follow them easily. They learn the strengths and weaknesses of the other group members. During this stage, the group members depend on the coordinator for direction and clarification of the goals and procedures of the group. Also during this stage, the coordinator stresses the following group norms:

1. Taking responsibility for one's own performance and the performance of the other members of the group.
2. Providing assistance to other members.
3. Responding to other members in an accepting, supportive, and trustworthy way.
4. Making decisions through consensus.
5. Confronting and solving problems in group functioning. During this stage the goals and procedures of the group are the coordinator's. The group members conform to the prescribed procedures and interact with each other, but they are not personally committed to the group's goals and to each other.

Recognizing Mutuality and Building Trust

The third stage of group development is marked by group members recognizing their interdependence and building trust. A sense of mutuality develops as group members recognize that they sink or swim together. Members begin to take responsibility for each other's performance and appropriate behavior. Trust is built through disclosing one's thoughts, ideas, conclusions, and feelings and having the other group members respond with acceptance, support, and reciprocation of the disclosures. Trust is discussed at length in Chapter 3 and in Johnson (2000).

Rebelling and Differentiating

The fourth stage of group development is marked by group members (a) rebelling against the coordinator and the procedures and (b) differentiating themselves from each other through disagreements and conflicts. On the road to maturity, a group will go through a period (sometimes short, sometimes long) of challenging the authority of the coordinator. This is an ordinary occurrence and should be expected. This swing toward independence contrasts sharply with the dependence demonstrated by members during stage 2. Many group members may believe that participation is a passive process in which they can slip by without doing much work. Group members may wish to test and challenge the coordinator's sincerity and commitment to the procedures. Members may become *counterdependent* and attempt to establish their independence by doing just the opposite of what the group-learning procedures call for. Relationships among group members are often built through a cycle of becoming friendly, establishing independence through disagreement and conflict, and then committing oneself to a relationship. Differentiating is important for group members to establish boundaries and autonomy (Johnson, 1979, 1980a).

The coordinator will encounter both rebellion against the group procedures and conflict among group members as a natural and expected stage of group development.

The coordinator will want to deal with both in an open and accepting way. Some advice for doing so includes:

1. Do not tighten control and try to force conformity to prescribed procedures; reason and negotiate.
2. Confront and problem-solve when members become counterdependent and rebellious.
3. Mediate conflicts among members who are helping the group establish members' autonomy and individuality.
4. Work to help members take ownership of the procedures and commit themselves to each other's success.

Coordinating a group at this stage is like teaching a child to ride a bicycle: One runs alongside to prevent the child from falling, but one must relinquish control so that the child can learn to balance alone.

Committing to the Group's Goals and Procedures

During this stage, dependence on the coordinator and conformity to the prescribed procedures are replaced by dependence on the other members of the group and personal commitment to the collaborative nature of the experience. The shift from the coordinator's group to the members' group that began in the previous stage is finalized in this stage. The group becomes "ours" rather than "the coordinator's." Group norms become internalized, and group members embrace them. Motivation becomes intrinsic rather than extrinsic. Members become committed to the procedures and accept responsibility for maximizing the performance of all group members. Group members also become

Summary of the Coordinator's Role

1. Introduce, define, and structure the group.
2. Clarify procedures, reinforce members for conforming to the procedures, and help members become acquainted.
3. Emphasize and highlight the cooperative interdependence among group members and encourage them to engage in both trusting and trustworthy behaviors.
4. Accept the rebellion by and differentiation among group members as a normal process, and use confrontation and constructive negotiation to help members establish their independence from each other and the prescribed procedures.
5. Help members commit themselves to and take ownership of the group's goals and procedures.
6. Be a consultant to the group, providing needed resources for the group to function effectively.
7. Signal termination and help the members move on to future groups.

concerned about each other's welfare, provide support and assistance (not because the coordinator wants them to but because they care about each other), believe that they can rely on the support and assistance of other group members, and truly become friends.

Functioning Maturely and Productively

As the group achieves maturity, autonomy, and productivity, a group identity emerges. Group members work together to achieve a variety of goals and deal with conflict in constructive ways. They collaborate to achieve the group's goals while ensuring that their relationships with each other are maintained at a high-quality level. The coordinator becomes a consultant to the group rather than a directive leader. The relationships among group members continue to improve, as does the relationship between the coordinator and the members. In the maturely functioning group, all the criteria for effective groups are met. Many groups never reach this stage.

Terminating

The life of every group is finite. The group eventually ends and the members go their separate ways. The more mature and cohesive the group and the stronger the emotional bonds that have been formed among group members, the more potentially upsetting is the termination period. Nevertheless, group members deal with the problems of separating so that they can leave the group experience behind them and move on to new experiences.

Length of Each Stage

Not all stages last the same amount of time. Many groups move very quickly through the first five stages, spend considerable time functioning maturely, and then terminate quickly. The average amount of time groups tend to spend in each stage is presented in Figure 1.3.

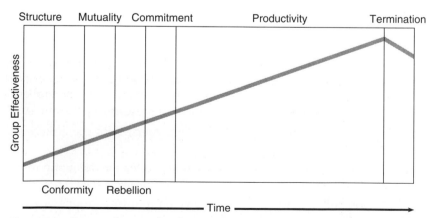

Figure 1.3 Stages of group development.

Conclusion

Both the sequential-stage and the recurring-phase perspectives are useful for understanding group development. They are not contradictory. A group may move through various stages while dealing with basic themes that surface as they become relevant to the group's work. Because the issues underlying the themes are never completely resolved, they can recur later.

EXERCISE

1.6 *Are Groups Beneficial or Harmful?*

There has been some controversy over whether group membership is constructive or destructive. The purpose of this exercise is to structure a critical discussion of the issue.

1. **Assignment to Groups:** Assign participants to groups of four. Each group is to write a short statement summarizing and explaining its position on whether individual or group decision making is more effective.
2. **Assignment to Pairs and Positions:** Divide each group into two pairs:
   a. Pair One takes the position that individuals are superior to groups in making decisions and is given Briefing Sheet One.
   b. Pair Two takes the position that groups are superior to individuals in making decisions and is given Briefing Sheet Two.
3. Review the rules for constructive controversy.
4. Conduct the exercise and monitor participants to ensure that the procedures are skillfully followed.
5. Have participants process their experience.

ARE GROUPS BENEFICIAL OR HARMFUL?

Tasks

1. Make the best case possible for your assigned position. Ensure that it gets a fair and complete hearing.
2. Critically analyze and challenge the opposing positions. Ensure that the information and logic stand up under critical scrutiny.
3. Reach a consensus on the group's best reasoned judgment about the issue.

Procedure

1. **Prepare Positions:** Working with your partner, prepare a persuasive presentation that makes the best case possible for your assigned position. The presentation should have three parts: a thesis statement (your position), a rationale (your information organized in a logically compelling way), and a conclusion (your position). In preparing your presentation, use the overview of social-psychological research, applicable text material, and what you know from other sources. You have ten minutes to prepare (a) a forceful and persuasive three-minute presentation and (b) your arguments for the open discussion. Both members of the pair have to be ready to give the presentation.
2. **Present Positions:** Meet with a person representing the opposing position. Give a three-minute presentation of the best case possible for your position. Be persuasive. Listen to the other person's three-minute presentation; take notes and ask for clarification of anything that is not fully understood.

3. **Advocate, Attack, and Defend Discussion:** Continue to advocate the best case possible for your position. Critically analyze and challenge the opposing position. Point out the shortcomings in its information and logic. Defend your position from the attacks of the opponent. The discussion should focus on theory, research, and facts, not on opinions and impressions. You have ten minutes to discuss the issue.

4. **Reverse Perspectives:** Give a two-minute presentation of the best case possible for the opposing position. Summarize the opposing position (information and logic). The summary should be complete and accurate. Add any additional information you may have that supports the opposing position. Listen to the opponent's presentation of your position and correct anything that is incorrectly understood.

5. **Write a Joint Report:** Drop all advocacy. Reach a consensus on the nature of your best reasoned judgment about the issue. Write one statement summarizing and explaining your joint conclusions on whether individual or group decision making is more effective. The best reasoning from both sides should be synthesized or integrated into your best reasoned judgment. Base your conclusions on theory, research, and facts.

RULES FOR CONSTRUCTIVE CONTROVERSY

1. I am critical of ideas, not individuals. I challenge and refute the ideas of the opposing pair, but I do not indicate that I personally reject the members of the pair.
2. I focus on reaching the best decision possible, not on "winning." I remember that we are all in this together.
3. I encourage everyone to participate and to master all the relevant information.
4. I listen to everyone's ideas, even if I don't agree.
5. I paraphrase or restate what someone has said if it is not clear to me.
6. I first bring out all the ideas and facts supporting both sides, and then I try to put them together in a way that makes sense.
7. I try to understand both sides of the issue.
8. I change my mind when the evidence indicates that I should do so.

BRIEFING SHEET ONE: GROUPS ARE GOOD FOR HUMANS

1. Under most conditions, the productivity of groups is higher than the productivity of individuals working alone.
2. Groups make more effective decisions and solve problems more effectively than individuals working alone.
3. It is through group memberships that the values of altruism, kindness, consideration for others, responsibility, and so forth are socialized in us.
4. The quality of emotional life in terms of friendship, love, camaraderie, excitement, joy, fulfillment, and achievement is greater for members of groups than for individuals acting alone.
5. The quality of everyday life is higher in groups because of the advantages of specialization and division of labor. Our material standard of living, for example—our housing, food, clothing, transportation, entertainment, and so forth—would not be possible for a person living outside of a society.
6. Conflicts are managed more productively in groups. Social influence is better managed in groups. Without group standards, social values, and laws, civilization would be impossible.
7. A person's identity, self-esteem, and social competencies are shaped by the groups of significance to him or her.

8. Without cooperation, social organization, and groups of various kinds, humans would not survive. Humans have a basic social nature, and our survival and evolution are the results of the effectiveness of our groups.
9. Friendship, love, companionship, meaning, purpose, cooperation, and all that is good in life occur in groups.

BRIEFING SHEET TWO: GROUPS ARE NOT GOOD FOR HUMANS

1. People in groups are more likely to take greater risks than they would alone. Groups tend to take more extreme positions and indulge in more extreme behavior than their members would alone.
2. In groups there is sometimes a diffusion of responsibility such that members take less responsibility for providing assistance to someone in need or for rewarding good service.
3. In large groups, individuals can become anonymous and therefore feel freer to engage in rowdy, shocking, and illegal behavior. When one member engages in impulsive and antisocial behavior, others may do likewise. Riots are often initiated and worsened by such modeling effects.
4. Being identified as part of a group may increase the tendency of nonmembers to treat one in impersonal and inhumane ways. It is easier, for example, to drop a bomb on the "enemy" than on a person.
5. Group contagion often gives rise to collective panic.
6. Millions of people have been swept into mass political movements, only to become unhappy victims of the distorted visions of their leaders.
7. Groups often influence their members to conform. One type of conformity, obedience to authority, can cause a person to act in cruel and inhumane ways to others. The identity of the individual can be threatened when conformity is too extreme.
8. It is within groups that injustice, abuse, bullying, stereotypes, scapegoating, and all antisocial actions occur.

THE FIELD OF GROUP DYNAMICS

Close cooperation between theorists and practitioners can be accomplished . . . if the theorist does not look toward applied problems with highbrow aversion or with a fear of social problems, and if the applied psychologist realizes that there is nothing so practical as a good theory.

Kurt Lewin (1951, p. 169)

The Nature of Group Dynamics

The field of group dynamics is a combination of theory, research, and practice. Theory identifies the characteristics of effective groups, research validates or disconfirms the theories, and practical procedures based on the validated theory are implemented in the real world to see if they work. The theory, research, and practical applications of group dynamics all interact and enhance each other (see Figure 1.4). Theory both guides and summarizes research. Research validates or disconfirms theory, thereby leading to its refinement and modification. Practice is guided by validated theory, and applications of

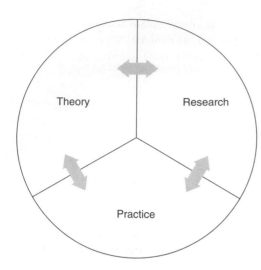

Figure 1.4 Relationship among theory, research, and practice.
Source: D. W. Johnson & R. T. Johnson, *Cooperation and competition: Theory and research* (Edina, MN: Interaction Book Company, 1989). Reprinted with permission of the authors.

the theory reveal inadequacies that lead to refining of the theory, conducting new research studies, and modifying the application. This book emphasizes the interaction among theory, research, and practice.

Group dynamics is the scientific study of behavior in groups to advance our knowledge about the nature of groups, group development, and the interrelations between groups and individuals, other groups, and larger entities. What happens among group members is dynamic, not static. The interaction among group members is characterized by forces such as communication and leadership that are in constant motion and change. Social scientists interested in groups analyze the dynamics within groups by constructing theories and conducting research to test the theories. They then apply the validated theory to real-world situations to see if they work.

History of the Field of Group Dynamics

Group dynamics is a relatively young field, one that is rooted in a wide range of traditionally separate fields. Although the earliest existing philosophical literature contains a great deal of wisdom about the nature of groups, and although the basic assumptions of group dynamics were discussed from the sixteenth through the nineteenth centuries, the field of group dynamics is a twentieth-century development. Interested scientists came from many different disciplines and branches of the social sciences. The field of group dynamics, therefore, is the common property of all the social sciences.

Although its roots go back to the late 1800s, group dynamics gained prominence in the early 1940s. After a worldwide depression, the rise of dictatorships in Europe, and the Second World War, most Americans were worried about the fate of their country and the future of democracy. There was general agreement that they needed a better understanding of how democratic organizations could be made to function more effectively. Scientists had helped win the war, many people said, and now research should improve democracy. The field of group dynamics was thought to have significant potential for doing so. The health of a democratic society was seen as depending on the effectiveness of its component groups. Strengthening the family, the community, and the multitude of groups within our society was viewed as the primary means of ensuring the vitality of our democracy. For Americans, the scientific study of how groups functioned was needed to maintain a democratic form of government and solve current social problems.

The drive to strengthen democracy by using the scientific method to strengthen groups resulted in two interrelated movements within psychology. The *first* was the scientific study of group dynamics. Searching for ways to strengthen democracy, social psychologists (a new group of specialists) (a) developed experimental methods of studying group dynamics and (b) began to conduct studies of group discussion, group productivity, attitude change, and leadership. The *second* movement was the application of group dynamics theory and research to derive methods for training leaders and group members in the social skills needed to promote effective functioning of democratic groups. At the heart of both movements was Kurt Lewin, perhaps the greatest social psychologist who ever lived. He was not the first person, however, to develop theory and conduct research on group dynamics.

In the late nineteenth century, researchers on group dynamics focused on the question "What change in an individual's normal solitary performance occurs when other people are present?" Norman Triplett, an Indiana University psychologist, studied the records of the Racing Board of the League of American Wheelmen. Triplett observed that cyclists' times were faster when they were racing against each other than when they simply raced against the clock. He hypothesized that the presence of other people (i.e., competitors) acts as a stimulant to the performer. If this hypothesis were valid, Triplett reasoned, it would hold for activities other than bicycle racing. Creating an analogy to bicycle racing, Triplett (1898) asked children to wind fishing reels and compared their performance when alone with their performance when another child was present. They performed faster when an audience was present. This experiment was the first attempt to investigate the impact of social interdependence (i.e., competitive versus individual efforts) on a motor performance task.

Triplett's work later resulted in research on social facilitation–impairment (Zajonc, 1965), social interdependence (Johnson & Johnson, 1989), and social loafing (Harkins & Szymanski, 1987). Social facilitation researchers, for example, were interested in the question "Does the impact of an audience differ on simple versus complex tasks?" If you were running a mile, would an audience make you run faster or slower? If you were asked to assemble a complex new machine you had never seen before, would an audience increase or decrease the speed of your work? Allport (1924), Moede (1920), and others found that on simple tasks an audience increased the speed of performance, whereas on complex tasks an audience decreased it.

The second line of research, which became prominent in the late 1920s and 1930s, focused on the question "Are individuals or groups more productive on problem-solving and decision-making tasks?" (Gordon, 1924; Shaw, 1932; Watson, 1928). Overall, the results indicated that groups are more productive than individuals. The descendants of this tradition are the research on social interdependence (Deutsch, 1962; Johnson & Johnson, 1989), jury decision making (e.g., Kerr et al., 1976), minority influence in groups (e.g., Moscovici, 1985a), conformity (e.g., Asch, 1951), and group polarization (e.g., Myers, 1978).

At the end of the 1930s the field of group dynamics advanced rapidly, due largely to the efforts of Kurt Lewin and three sociologists. In the 1930s and 1940s, research on groups was popularized by the pioneering work of Kurt Lewin, who maintained that the behavior of individuals should be understood in terms of the nature of the groups to which they belong (Lewin, 1943, 1948). Sherif (1936) studied the impact of group norms on the perception of an ambiguous stimulus. In an ingenious experiment he demonstrated that the judgments made by individuals were influenced by the judgments of their fellow group members. From 1935 to 1939, Newcomb (1943) conducted his famous field study investigating the impact of social norms concerning political issues on the students at Bennington College. As a result of their interaction, students tended to change their politically conservative attitudes to politically liberal ones. In 1937, W. F. Whyte moved into a Boston slum and began a three-and-a-half-year study of social clubs, political organizations, and racketeering. Whyte (1943) reported in vivid detail the structure, culture, and functioning of the Norton Street gang and the Italian Community Club. His study dramatized the great significance of groups in the lives of individuals and in the functioning of larger social systems.

It was Kurt Lewin more than anyone else who stressed the importance of applying existing knowledge to solving social problems. From 1890 to 1940 there had been a gradual growth in the number of published studies on group behavior from one per year to approximately thirty per year. By the late 1940s, 55 studies were being published annually, and by the end of the 1950s the rate had skyrocketed to about 150. During the 1960s and 1970s the rate of research studies on group dynamics persisted at about 125 per year. Primarily through the influence of Lewin and his associates and students, group dynamics became one of the dominant fields in the social sciences.

By far the most influential study of group dynamics in the late 1930s was that of three psychologists: Lewin, Lippitt, and White (1939). This study made it clear that important social issues could be studied experimentally in the laboratory. The study focused on the influences of different leadership patterns on groups and group members. Groups of ten- and eleven-year-old children met regularly for several weeks under the leadership of an adult, who behaved in one of three ways: democratically, autocratically, or in a laissez-faire manner. The effects of these leadership styles on the behavior of group members were large and dramatic. Severe forms of scapegoating, for example, occurred in the autocratic groups, and at the end of the experiment the children in some of those groups destroyed the things they had constructed.

Following this study, Lewin and his associates began a number of research studies aimed at developing a theory of group dynamics. French (1941) conducted a laboratory experiment comparing the effects of fear and frustration on organized versus unorganized groups. Bavelas (1942) conducted an experiment to determine whether the behavior of leaders of youth groups could be significantly modified through training. When the United States entered the Second World War, Lewin, French, and Marrow (Marrow, 1957) explored group-decision procedures as a means of improving industrial production, and Lewin, Radke, and others (Lewin, 1943; Radke and Klisurich, 1947) conducted a number of experiments on group decision as a means of changing eating habits related to wartime food shortages.

In the 1950s, the research of Bales and his colleagues on small discussion groups clarified the patterning of group members' responses and the nature of roles within a

group (Bales, 1950, 1953; Bales & Slater, 1955). Bavelas (1948) and Leavitt (1951) exam
ined information exchange by imposing network structures on decision-making groups
and observing their effects on productivity. Schachter (1951) researched group reactions
to the opinions of deviates. Deutsch (1949b, 1962) investigated cooperation and com
petition and the nature of trust.

In the 1950s the seeds were planted that ended the group dynamics movement. Fes
tinger's theories of informal social communication (1950) and social comparison (1954)
focused social psychology on the individual (not the group) as the primary unit of analy
sis. Social psychology began to examine how the attitudes, values, personality, and
thoughts of an individual guided and influenced social behavior. This individualistic
trend was accelerated by the emergence of several other theoretical perspectives during
the late 1950s, such as attribution theory (Heider, 1958), cognitive dissonance (Festinger,
1957), and persuasion (Hovland, Janis, & Kelley, 1953).

In the 1960s and 1970s, to most social psychologists the individual appeared to be
a simpler unit than the group on which to base the study of social interaction. Statisti
cal and methodological difficulties in group research moved researchers toward research
on individual variables. Psychologists tended to decompose social variables into smaller
segments rather than integrating them into larger social structures. They preferred to
use single-factor rather than multifactor explanations for behavior. Studies that involved
the systematic observation of groups in naturalistic settings typically were too difficult
and expensive to conduct, analyze, and interpret.

In the 1980s and 1990s, however, the investigation of group dynamics had a resur
gence. Many of the pragmatic, methodological, and statistical difficulties that had
thwarted group research in the 1950s and 1960s were either reduced or largely overcome.
The research on a number of group issues such as cooperation, conflict resolution, dis
tributive justice, intergroup relations, and cross-cultural interaction became major foci
of social psychology (Deutsch, 1985; Johnson & Johnson, 1989; Tjosvold, 1991a; Tjos
vold & Johnson, 1982). In industrial psychology the determinants of work-group pro
ductivity and modes of effective leadership were the focus of considerable research
(Hackman & Oldham, 1980; Tjosvold, 1991b). Clinical psychologists emphasized the
client–therapist dyad and treatment of families as dysfunctional systems (e.g., Johnson
& Matross, 1977; Wolman & Strikcer, 1983). In sociology, research focused on the pos
session and use of power, dominance hierarchies, and group structure (e.g., Berger,
Rosenholtz, & Zelditch, 1980). In Europe, interest was focused on group issues such as
minority influence (Moscovici, 1985a) and intergroup relations (Tajfel, 1981).

In the twenty-first century, interest in group dynamics is on the rise.

KURT LEWIN AND THE FIELD OF GROUP DYNAMICS

At the head of both of the group dynamic movements in the 1940s was one of the most
important psychologists of the twentieth century, **Kurt Lewin.** Lewin was born on Sep
tember 9, 1890, in the tiny village of Mogilno in the Prussian province of Posen (now
part of Poland), where his father owned and operated a general store. In 1910 Lewin
began studying for a doctorate in philosophy and psychology at the University of Berlin.
After finishing his doctoral work in 1914, he entered the kaiser's army as a private and

Kurt Lewin

fought for four years in World War I in the infantry. He left the army as a lieutenant with an Iron Cross and returned to the University of Berlin to teach. There he became part of the Psychological Institute, where Max Wertheimer, Kurt Koffka, and Wolfgang Kohler were formulating their Gestalt theory. Lewin became one of the Gestaltists, but he was never an orthodox follower of their early leaders. His interests were in the area of motivation, and his work was directed more to practical application than to understanding for its own sake. In 1933, as Hitler was rising to power, Lewin migrated to the United States. He subsequently worked at Cornell University, the University of Iowa (where he taught at the Child Welfare Research Station), and the Massachusetts Institute of Technology, where he set up and headed the famous Research Center for Group Dynamics (which later moved to the Institute for Social Research at the University of Michigan). On February 11, 1947, Lewin died unexpectedly of a heart attack.

In his advocacy of the study of group dynamics Lewin was noted for three things: his development of theory, his early championing of the use of experimental methodology, and his insistence that theory and research be relevant to social practice.

Kurt Lewin was above all a theorist. Throughout his career he was concerned primarily with the problem of constructing an empirically based theory of human behavior. Lewin believed that every field of science must be concerned primarily with theory, because it is theory that illuminates the causal structure of the empirical world. Lewin's contributions to theory in group dynamics included (a) an emphasis on building conceptual systems that explained the dynamics observed in groups and (b) creating a field theory analysis of the field (Lewin, 1943, 1948). Borrowing concepts and language from force field physics, Lewin theorized that individuals move through different regions of their life space, being either impelled by forces or drawn by valences that exist along power vectors. Some of the strongest forces and valences an individual experiences stem from groups. With this theoretical orientation, Lewin and his associates and students formulated a wide variety of theories and research programs that defined the field of group dynamics.

Lewin had a genius for thinking of ways to study his ideas experimentally, and he inspired in his students something of this ability. It was Lewin's study of different leadership strategies that proved that complex social phenomena could be studied with experimental methods. Lewin was convinced that the use of experimental methods in researching the dynamics of groups would revolutionize the field, and he was right.

Lewin did not see his commitment to theory as irrelevant to, or in any way incompatible with, his concern for the solution of social problems. He was convinced that the interests of the theorist and the practitioner were inextricably interrelated. He believed that social science theory should do more than advance knowledge—it should also provide guidelines for action. Lewin coined the term **action research** for the use of the scientific method in solving research questions that have significant social value. He urged social scientists to develop theories that could be applied to important social problems.

Lewin saw clearly that practitioners and theorists share a common interest in understanding reality and acting competently. He viewed them as having interdependent tasks: Practitioners identify significant problems to be solved, theorists develop a valid view of reality that contains the keys for solving the problems, and practitioners apply the theory. Practitioners keep theorists in contact with social reality, and theorists provide practitioners with a deeper understanding of the social problems that confront them. Lewin believed that theorists have a special obligation: to provide the kind of theory that can be used in solving social problems. Lewin was a doer, and he wanted to conduct and inspire research that made a difference in the real world of human affairs. He was constantly suggesting ways to bridge the gap between theoretical science and public policies and practices. The particular applications he suggested were infused with democratic values. He had a profound faith in democracy, which to him was much more than just a political system. It was also a way of life, based on mutual participation and continual interaction in decision making for purposeful change.

Kurt Lewin was in his element with an informal seminar group. He was not at his best in a formal lecture, as he was not highly organized. But he had an enthusiasm for psychological analysis that was contagious. His contacts with his students were so strong that sometimes an afternoon discussion would last beyond midnight. Informal group discussions reflected not only Lewin's style of interacting with other people but also his belief in democracy. Given his style of working with groups, his interest in social action, and his concern for democratic decision making, it was not surprising that Lewin turned increasingly to the study of group dynamics in his years in America. Although Lewin did not create the field of group dynamics (it was the result of developments occurring over several decades and in different disciplines), he was the major link between much of the theorizing and much of the practical application in the field. The contents of this book as well as the entire field of group dynamics are heavily influenced by Lewin and his work.

THE NATURE OF THIS BOOK AND HOW TO USE IT

This is not a book that you can read with detachment. It is written to involve you with its contents. By reading this book, you will not only be able to learn the theoretical and empirical knowledge now available on group dynamics, but you will also learn to apply this knowledge in practical ways in the groups to which you belong. Often in the past, group dynamics practitioners did not pay attention to the research literature, and group dynamics researchers neglected to specify how their findings could be applied. Thus, the knowledge about effective groups and the learning of group skills was often divided. In this book we directly apply existing theory and research to the learning and application of effective group skills. As you participate in the exercises, use diagnostic procedures

Keeping a Personal Journal

As you read this book, you will be well advised to keep a journal in which you record what you are learning about group dynamics and about how you behave in group situations. You may also wish to include specific information you have learned about the social psychology of groups, effective behavior in groups, and the extent to which you have developed the group skills you want. A **journal** is a personal collection of writing and thoughts that have value for the writer. It has to be kept up on a regular basis. Entries are evaluated by whether they are valuable to the author, can be shared with others, and reflect significant thinking. Such a journal will be of great interest to you after you have finished this book. You may also wish to include specific information you have learned about group dynamics. *The purposes of the journal are:*

1. To keep track of the activities related to group dynamics.

2. To answer in writing some of the questions that are important for a clear understanding of the book's content (these will often be suggested, but others can be selected by you).

3. To collect thoughts that are related to the book's content (the best thinking often occurs when you are driving to or from school, about to go to sleep at night, and so forth).

4. To collect newspaper and magazine articles and references that are relevant to the topics covered in each chapter.

5. To keep summaries of conversations and anecdotal material that are unique, interesting, or illustrate things related to group dynamics.

(Note: If you publish your journal, as did John Holt, Hugh Prather, and others, all we ask is a modest 10 percent of the royalties.)

Learning Contract

Before beginning the next chapter, we would like to propose a learning contract. The contract is as follows:

> I understand that I will be taking an experiential approach to learning about group dynamics and to developing the skills needed to function effectively in groups. I willingly commit myself to the statements hereunder.

1. I will use the structured experiences in this book to learn from. This means I am willing to engage in specified behaviors, seek out feedback about the impact of my behavior on others, and analyze my interpersonal interactions with other class members in order to make the most of my learning.

2. I will make the most of my own learning by (a) engaging in specified behaviors and being open about my feelings and reactions to what is taking place so that others may have information to react to in giving me feedback and in building conclusions about the area of study; (b) setting personal learning goals that I will work actively to accomplish—which means that I will take responsibility for my own learning and not wait for someone else to "make me grow"; (c) being willing to experiment with new behavior and to practice new skills; (d) seeking out and being receptive to feedback; and (e) building conclusions about the experiences highlighted in the exercises.

3. I will help others make the most of their learning by (a) providing feedback in constructive ways, (b) helping to build the conditions (such as openness, trust, acceptance, and support) under which others can experiment and take risks with their behavior, and (c) contributing to the formulation of conclusions about the experiences highlighted in the exercises.

4. I will use professional judgment in keeping what happens among group members in the exercises appropriately confidential.

Signed: _____

for assessing your current skill levels, and discuss the relevant theory and research provided, you will bridge the gap between theory and practice.

In selecting exercises for this book, we tried to include those that were original, short, relevant to the theory and research being discussed, clear and simple, and easy to prepare. We intended each exercise to be like a supporting actor; it should do its work effectively, unobtrusively, and without upstaging the theory and research being presented. Each exercise is also aimed at promoting the development of group skills. The book defines the skills needed for effective group functioning and provides opportunities for readers to practice the skills for themselves and to receive feedback on their performance.

The purpose of this book is to bring together the theory on group dynamics, the research testing that theory, and structured exercises aimed at building practical group skills and illuminating the meaning of the theory and research presented. The central aim of each chapter is to review the most important theory and research, analyze basic issues in group dynamics, and provide structured skill-building exercises and other in-structional aids. The format of each chapter is based on sound pedagogy and the princi-ples of experiential learning. Most chapters begin with a discussion task involving the concepts presented in the chapter. At the beginning of most chapters is a short diag-nostic instrument that will help you become more aware of your current behavior in the area discussed in the chapter. Also in most chapters is a controversy in which you and your classmates argue different sides of one of the central issues of the chapter. Ex-ercises aimed at developing skills and understanding in the topic of the chapter are then provided. The relevant theory and research are presented. At the end of many of the chapters, there is a procedure for examining the changes in your knowledge and skills.

In using this book, you should diagnose your present knowledge and skills in the areas that are covered, actively participate in the exercises, reflect on your experiences, read the chapters carefully, and integrate the information and experiences into action theories related to group dynamics. You should then plan how to continue your skill- and knowledge-building activities after you have finished the book.

The journal is an important part of this book. It is not an easy part. The entries should be important to you in your effort to make this course useful to youself and, be-cause this is a cooperative course, useful to your fellow participants. You may be sur-prised at how writing sharpens and organizes your thoughts.

YOUR SKILL LEVEL

Before going on, it will be useful for you to assess your current group skill level. Answer the following questions, describing yourself as accurately as you can:

1. How do you see yourself as a group member? What is your style of functioning within groups?
2. What are your strengths in functioning in groups? How do they fit into the way you see yourself as a group member?
3. What situations within groups do you have trouble with and why? How do you feel when faced with them? How do you handle them? How would you like to handle them?
4. In what group skills do you wish to grow and develop? What changes would you like to make in your present group behavior? What new strengths in group behavior would you care to develop? What new group skills would you like to acquire?

SUMMARY

Humans are small group beings. Groups are ubiquitous, and it is inevitable that you now belong to many, many groups. As the effectiveness of your groups goes, so goes the quality of your life. You, therefore, have to have a working knowledge of group dy-namics and the small group skills required to put that knowledge to use in school, at work, during leisure activities, at home, in your neighborhood, and in every other arena of your life. To begin with, you must know what is and is not a group. That is harder than it seems, as social scientists have yet to agree on a single definition. Generally, however, a *small group* is two or more individuals in face-to-face interaction, each aware of positive interdependence as they strive to achieve mutual goals, each aware of his or her membership in the group, and each aware of the others who belong to the group. Group dynamics is the scientific study of behavior in groups. The study of group dynamics has about a one-hundred-year history in North America. All groups have a basic structure that includes roles and norms. Groups develop over time and pass through stages, although there is little agreement as to what those stages are. Their productivity depends on five basic elements (positive interdependence, individual accountability, promotive interaction, appropriate use of social skills, group processing). Not all groups are effective. To be effective, group members have to (a) ensure each other's commitment to clear mutual goals that highlight members' interdependence, (b) ensure accurate and complete communication among members, (c) provide leadership and appropriate influence, (d) flexibly use decision-making procedures that ensure that all alternative courses of action receive a fair and complete hearing and that each other's reasoning and conclusions are challenged and critically analyzed, and (e) resolve their conflicts constructively. One of the most important figures in the field of group dynamics is Kurt Lewin. His work, more than anyone's, shows the interrelationships between knowledge about group dynamics and actual small group skills. The purpose of this book is to bring together the theory on group dynamics, the research testing it, and structured exercises aimed at helping readers master practical group skills. The experiential learning procedures used in creating this integration of theory, research, and practical skills are discussed in the next chapter.

2

Experiential Learning

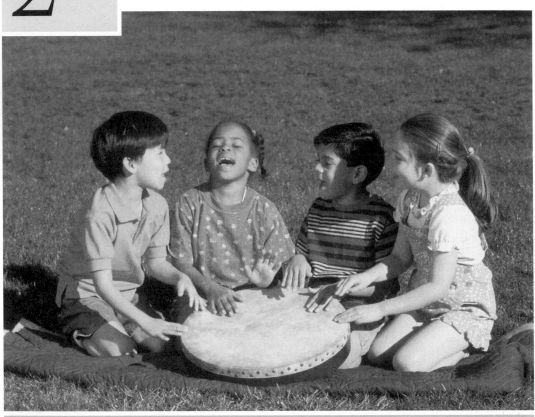

Basic Concepts to Be Covered in This Chapter

In this chapter a number of concepts are defined and discussed. The major ones are listed following. Divide into pairs. Each pair is to (a) define each concept, noting the page on which it is defined and discussed, and (b) ensure that both members of the pair understand the meaning of each concept. Then combine into groups of four. Compare the answers of the two pairs. If there is disagreement, the members look up the concept in the chapter and clarify it until they all agree on the definition and understand it.

Concepts

1. Action theory
2. Content
3. Experiential learning
4. Feedback
5. Participant-observer
6. Procedural learning
7. Process
8. Role playing

PROCEDURAL LEARNING

Knowing is not enough; we must apply. Willing is not enough; we must do.

Goethe

One learns by doing the thing; for though you think you know it, you have no certainty until you try.

Sophocles

The hand is the cutting edge of the mind.

Jacob Bronowski, *Ascent of Man*

Increasing your expertise in group dynamics requires procedural learning. Learning how to implement group dynamics theory and research is very similar to learning how to play tennis or golf, how to perform brain surgery, or how to fly an airplane. It involves more than simply reading material for a recognition level or even a total-recall level of mastery. **Procedural learning** exists when you study group dynamics to:

1. Learn conceptually group dynamics theory and research.
2. Translate your conceptual understanding into a set of group skills.
3. Actually use your group skills.
4. Eliminate errors in using your group skills to move through the initial awkward and mechanical stages of mastery to attain a routine-use, automated level of mastery.

In other words, you must acquire an understanding of group dynamics theory and research, develop a conceptualization of group skills, engage in guided practice to enact the skills and eliminate implementation errors, and persevere in using the group skills so that you can use them appropriately in a more and more automated fashion.

Procedural learning differs from simply learning facts and acquiring knowledge due to a heavier reliance on feedback about performance and the modification of implementation efforts until the errors of performance are eliminated. Procedural learning involves a progressive refinement of knowledge and skill as the procedures are practiced, practiced, and practiced.

✘ It is the procedural nature of mastering group dynamics that makes this book different from most other textbooks. This may seem strange at first. Traditionally, in the United States, we have made a separation between "head" learning and "hand" learning. "Real" classes are supposed to be head learning, whereas "vocational" classes are supposed to be hand learning. Thus, there is a focus on the head and a denial that the hand is present and important. In learning group dynamics, however, you should remember Jacob Bronowski's (1973) observation that it is the hand that drives the subsequent evolution of conceptual understanding. The hand becomes an instrument of vision, revealing the conceptual nature of the procedure being used. To understand you have to "act." True understanding results only from doing. **It is from using group skills that you will gain an understanding of what group dynamics is and how useful it can be.**

Procedural learning is based on experiential learning. The Russian cognitive theorist L. S. Vygotsky stated that learning from experience is the process whereby human development occurs. Your development and continual improvement of group skills depend on your participation in the skill-building exercises included in this book. Those exercises, and the links they provide with the theory and research discussed, are based on experiential learning. In experiential learning the responsibility for your learning lies with you, not with the teacher or instructor. Experiential exercises are structured so that you can experiment with your behavior, try things out, see what works, build skills, and develop action theories out of your own experiences. Appropriate theory is then presented so that you can summarize your learning and build conceptual frameworks within which you can organize what you know. Although experiential learning is a stimulating and involving activity, it is important to remember always that experience alone is not beneficial. You learn from the combination of experience and the conceptualization of your experiences.

In this chapter the nature of action theories and experiential learning is discussed. The procedures through which group skills are learned are presented. In addition, directions for how to conduct a skill-training experience and the ethics of doing so are discussed. First of all, to understand experiential learning you must know what an action theory is.

ACTION THEORIES

Change and growth take place when a person has risked himself and dares to become involved with experimenting with his own life.

Herbert Otto

All humans need to become competent in taking action and simultaneously reflecting on their action in order to learn from it. In integrating thought with action, we plan our behavior, engage in it, and then reflect on how effective we were. When we learn a pattern of behavior that effectively deals with a recurrent situation, we tend to repeat it over and over until it functions automatically. Such habitual behavioral patterns are based on theories of action. An **action theory** is a theory about what actions are needed to achieve a desired consequence in a given situation. All theories have an "if . . . then . . ."

Kurt Lewin and Experiential Learning

The use of experiential procedures to learn about behavior in groups was greatly influenced by Kurt Lewin. When Lee Bradford and Ken Benne were looking for help in training community leaders in leadership and group decision-making skills, they approached Lewin. What resulted was the experiential learning method. One of Lewin's characteristics was to discover valuable concepts and principles by observing his own and other people's experiences. The most trivial event, the most casual comment, might spark a thought in Lewin's mind that would result in a new theoretical breakthrough in the social psychology of groups. Those associating with Lewin never knew when he might make an important discovery, and this produced an excitement rare in a relationship with a colleague or teacher. Students and colleagues learned from Lewin how important it is to examine one's own experiences for potential principles about the way in which groups develop and work. Thus, Lewin's personal style focused on experiential learning.

Much of Lewin's research highlighted the importance of active participation in groups in order to learn new skills, develop new attitudes, and obtain new knowledge about groups. His research demonstrated that learning is achieved most productively in groups whose members interact and then reflect on their mutual experiences. In this way members are able to spark one another's insights and creativity in deriving conclusions about group dynamics. From Lewin, therefore, came an emphasis on studying one's own experiences in order to learn about group dynamics, on discussing mutual experiences to increase mutual learning and creativity, and on behaving democratically in structuring learning situations.

form. An action theory states that in a given situation, if we do x, then y will result. Our theories of action are normative. They state what we ought to do if we wish to achieve certain results. Examples of action theories can be found in almost everything we do. If we smile and say "hello," then others will return our smile and greeting. If we apologize, then the other person will excuse us. If we steal, then we will be punished. If a person shoves us, then we should shove back. All our behavior is based on theories that connect our actions with certain consequences.

In essence we build an action theory. As our behavior becomes habitual and automatic, our action theories become tacit (we are not able to put them into words). When our behavior becomes ineffective, we become aware of our action theories and modify them.

As children we are taught action theories by parents and other socializing agents. As we grow older we learn how to modify our action theories and develop new ones. We learn to try to anticipate what actions will lead to what consequences, to try out and experiment with new behaviors, to experience the consequences, and then to reflect on our experiences to determine whether our action theory is valid or needs modification. Experiential learning is a procedure based on the systematic development and modification of action theories.

We all have many action theories, one for every type of situation we regularly find ourselves in. This does not mean that we are aware of our action theories. An action is usually based on tacit knowledge—knowledge that we are not always able to put into words. Because most of our action theories function automatically, we are rarely conscious of our assumed connections between actions and their consequences. One of the purposes of this book is to help you become more conscious of the action theories that guide how you behave in small group situations, test these theories against reality, and modify them to make them more effective.

GAINING EXPERTISE THROUGH EXPERIENTIAL LEARNING

We shall not cease from exploration
And the end of all our exploring
Will be to arrive where we started
And know the place for the first time.

T. S. Eliot, "Four Quartets"

Aesop tells the story of the lion, the bear, and the fox. The bear was about to seize a stray goat when the lion leaped from another direction on the same prey. The bear and the lion then fought furiously for the goat until they had received so many wounds that both sank down unable to continue the battle. Just then the fox dashed up, seized the goat, and made off with it as fast as he could go, while the lion and the bear looked on in helpless rage. "How much better it would have been," they said, "to have shared in a friendly spirit." The bear and the lion had learned from their direct experience an important lesson in the advantages of cooperation over competition.

We all learn from our experiences. From touching a hot stove we learn to avoid heated objects. By dating we learn about male–female relationships. Every day we have experiences we learn from. Many aspects of group dynamics can be learned only by experience. Hearing a lecture on resisting group pressure is not the same as actually experiencing group pressure. Seeing a movie on how to manage conflict is not the same as facing an angry neighbor who is yelling in your face. Reading a description of leadership is not the same as leading the charge up San Juan Hill. It takes more than listening to explanations to learn group skills.

Experiential learning may be defined as generating an action theory from your own experiences and then continually modifying it to improve your effectiveness. The purpose of experiential learning is to affect the learner in three ways: (1) The learner's cognitive structures are altered, (2) the learner's attitudes are modified, and (3) the learner's repertoire of behavioral skills is expanded. These three elements are interconnected and change as a whole, not as separate parts. Working on any one part in the absence of the other two will be ineffective:

1. Information and knowledge can generate interest in changing but will not bring about change. Knowing a rationale for change is not sufficient for motivating a person to change.
2. Firsthand experience alone will not generate valid knowledge. For hundreds of years, for example, scientists believed that there were four elements in the world—earth, air, fire, and water. Experience with different types of gases and different

types of matter <u>did not generate a correct theory of physics</u>. Besides experience, there must be a theoretical system that the experience tests out and reflection on the meaning of the experience.

3. It takes more than engaging in a new behavior to result in permanent change. <u>New skills may be practiced and mastered but will fade away unless action theories and attitudes also change.</u>

The process of experiential learning can be represented as a four-stage cycle (see Figure 2.1). First, you engage in behavior on the basis of your current action theory. Second, you assess the consequences of your actions through reflection and feedback. Third, you reflect on the effectiveness of your actions and reformulate or refine your action theory. <u>Finally, you implement your revised action theory by engaging in a modified set of behaviors.</u> You repeat this process of continuous improvement until you develop expertise in using group skills. To engage in these four steps, furthermore, you must believe that you are capable of implementing the behaviors specified by the theory, perceive these behaviors as appropriate, and have positive attitudes toward implementing the theory.

The experiential learning process of formulating an action theory, testing it behaviorally, assessing consequences and obtaining feedback, reflecting, and modifying and refining the theory is based on a number of principles that need to be understood and followed. These principles are based on the theorizing of Kurt Lewin (Lewin, 1935; Lewin & Grabbe, 1945).

Principle 1: Effective experiential learning will affect the learner's cognitive structures (action theories), attitudes and values, perceptions, and behavioral patterns. To learn to be a more effective decision maker, for example, the learner must develop (a) a concept of what decision making is (knowledge), (b) an action theory concerning what decision-making behaviors will lead to effective group decision making, (c) positive attitudes toward new decision-making procedures, (d) a perception that the new decision-making

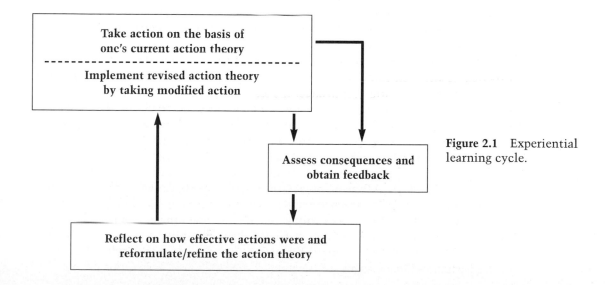

Figure 2.1 Experiential learning cycle.

actions are situationally appropriate and that one is capable of performing them, and (e) the behavioral skills needed to perform the new decision-making actions.

Principle 2: People will believe more in knowledge they have discovered themselves than in knowledge presented by others. Lewin was a great believer in experimental procedures whereby a person behaviorally validates or disproves a theory. He believed that such procedures needed to be introduced into the educational process so that students could test alternative behavioral patterns under controlled conditions. An approach to learning based on inquiry and discovery increases students' motivation to learn and their commitment to implement their conclusions in the future.

Principle 3: Learning is more effective when it is an active rather than a passive process. When a learner can take a theory, concept, or practice and "try it on for size," he or she will understand it more completely, integrate it more effectively with past learning, and retain it longer. Many concepts (such as mathematical procedures) are never really learned until one uses them.

Principle 4: New action theories, attitudes, and behavioral patterns cannot be accepted with a piecemeal approach; one's whole cognitive-affective behavioral system has to change. The three elements are interconnected, and they change as a whole rather than as separate parts. Like any system, a cognitive-affective behavioral system demands coherence, consistency, orderliness, and simplicity. Trying to change part of the system will not be effective. The need for consistency creates resistance to the item-by-item approach to new learning. Only when the whole system changes will the new learning be fully accepted and integrated.

Principle 5: It takes more than information to change action theories, attitudes, and behavioral patterns. Telling people about the desirability of change does not mean that they will change. Providing a rationale for change is not sufficient to motivate people to change. Reading a book or listening to a lecture does not result in mastery and retention of the material, does not promote attitude change, and does not increase social skills. Information does generate interest in learning more about the desired changes.

Principle 6: It takes more than firsthand experience to generate valid knowledge. Lewin stated that thousands of years of human experience with falling bodies did not bring humans to a correct theory of gravity. Besides experience, there must be a theoretical system tested by experience and reflection on the meaning of the experience.

Principle 7: Behavior changes will be temporary unless the action theories and attitudes underlying them are changed. New behavioral skills may be practiced and mastered, but without changes in the person's action theories and attitudes, the new behavior patterns will fade away.

Principle 8: Perceptions of oneself and one's social environment must change before changes in action theories, attitudes, and behavior will take place. Learners must perceive themselves as capable of doing the needed behaviors and must see the behaviors as being appropriate to the situation before they will engage in them. Lewin believed that behavior, action theories, and attitudes are all steered by perception. Your perceptions of yourself and your immediate situation affect how you behave, what you believe, and how you feel.

Principle 9: The more supportive, accepting, and caring the social environment, the freer a person is to experiment with new behaviors, attitudes, and action theories. As the need to justify oneself and protect oneself against rejection decreases, it becomes easier to experiment with new ways of behaving, thinking, and valuing.

Principle 10: In order for changes in behavior patterns, attitudes, and action theories to be permanent, both the person and the social environment have to change. The person's role definitions, the expectations of the person held by colleagues and friends, and the general values of career and social settings all must change if the person is to maintain these changed behaviors, attitudes, and action theories. Team training is more effective than individual training because it changes both individuals and their social environment at the same time.

Principle 11: It is easier to change a person's action theories, attitudes, and behavioral patterns in a group context than in an individual context. The discussion and consensual validation that take place within a group provide a personal commitment and encouragement for change that is not present when only one person is being changed.

Principle 12: A person accepts a new system of action theories, attitudes, and behavioral patterns when he or she accepts membership in a new group. New groups with new role definitions and expectations for appropriate behavior are helpful in educational efforts. A person becomes socialized by internalizing the normative culture of the groups to which he or she belongs. As the person gains membership in a new group, a new normative culture is accepted and internalized.

Experiential learning procedures are especially useful when you want to learn new skills. In the next section we shall review how skills are learned.

LEARNING GROUP SKILLS

For things we have to learn before we can do them, we learn by doing them.

Aristotle

You are not born with group skills, nor do they magically appear when you need them. You have to learn them. Group skills are learned just as any other skill is learned. Learning how to lead a group is no different from learning how to play the piano or throw a football. All skills are learned the same way, according to the following steps:

1. **Understand why the skill is important and how it will be of value to you.** To want to learn a skill, you must see a need for it. You need to know that you will be better off with the skill than without it.
2. **Understand what the skill is, what are the component behaviors you have to engage in to perform the skill, and when it should be used.** To learn a skill, you

1. TRY
2. TRY AGAIN
3. TRY AGAIN
4. TRY AGAIN
5. TRY AGAIN

must have a clear idea of what the skill is and you must know how to perform it. Often it is helpful to observe someone who has already mastered the skill perform it several times while describing it step by step. Apprentices, for example, watch masters of their craft perform the skill over and over again.

3. **Find situations in which you can practice the skill over and over again while a "coach" watches and tells you how well you are performing it.** There are four levels of guided practice. The *first* level consists of practicing successive approximations of the group skill while others provide scaffolding on how to do so. *Scaffolding* is support, in the form of reminders, prompts, and help, that you require to approximate the expert use of the group skills. As you practice the skills again and again, the scaffolding gradually fades until you use the skill by yourself, which is called *soloing*. The *second* level consists of using the group skills while articulating and explaining how to do so to your coach. This ensures that the scaffolding is internalized and that self-monitoring and self-correcting on how to engage in the skill take place. The *third* level is independent practice. You engage in the skill while self-monitoring and self-correcting your efforts. In effect, you give yourself feedback. This solidifies your sense of self-efficacy and commitment to use the skills. *Finally*, you decontextualize your use of the skills by using them in a variety of groups and in a variety of situations. Try practicing the skill for a short time each day for several days until you are sure you have mastered it completely.

4. **Assess how well the skill is being implemented.** The key to assessing how well you engage in the skill is to realize that you can never fail. Rather, your behavior approximates what you ideally wish and, through practice and experiential learning (i.e., progressive refinement), the approximations get closer and closer to the ideal. You have to sweat in practice before you can perform in concert. Short-term failure is part of the process of gaining expertise, and long-term success is inevitable when short-term failure is followed by persistent practice, obtaining feedback, and reflecting on how to implement the group skills more competently. Receiving feedback, furthermore, is necessary for correcting mistakes in learning a skill and for identifying problems you are having. Through feedback you find out how much progress you are making in mastering the skill. Feedback lets you compare how well you are doing with how well you want to do.

5. **Keep practicing until the skill feels real and it becomes an automatic habit pattern.** Most skill development goes through the following steps.

a. Self-conscious, awkward engagement in the skill. Practicing any new skill feels awkward, and group skills are no exception. The first few times someone throws a football, plays a violin, or paraphrases, it feels strange.

b. A feeling of phoniness while engaging in the new skill. After a while the awkwardness passes, and enacting the skill becomes more smooth. Many individuals, however, feel that the skill is unauthentic. Encouragement is needed to move them through this stage.

c. Skilled but mechanical use of the skill.

d. Automatic, routine use in which the skill is fully integrated into your behavioral repertoire and seems like a natural action to engage in. You have to practice long enough to go through the stages of skill development. The more you use a skill, the more natural it feels. It is then, when you apply the skill to real situations, that it will gain the fire and life that may sometimes be lacking when you practice.

6. **Load your practice toward success.** Set up practice units that you can easily master. It always helps to feel like a success as you practice a skill.

7. **Get friends to encourage you to use the skill.** Your friends can help you learn by giving you encouragement to do so. The more encouragement you receive, the easier it will be for you to practice the skill.

8. **Help others learn the skill.** Harvey S. Firestone said, "It is only when we develop others that we permanently succeed." Nothing is completely learned until it is taught to someone else. By helping others learn group skills, you will enhance your own expertise.

In learning most skills there is a period of slow learning, then a period of rapid improvement, then a period in which performance remains about the same (a plateau), then another period of rapid improvement, then another plateau, and so forth. Plateaus are quite common in skill learning. You have to persevere in practicing the skill until the next period of rapid improvement begins.

In order for you to move from awkwardness to the automatic use of skills, sustained practice of the skills over a long period of time has to be encouraged. The goal is to reach the state where you automatically and naturally use small group skills while working with others to achieve mutual goals.

This book is designed to provide you with information about the nature of and the need for the group skills discussed. The behaviors needed to engage in the skills are specified. Questions that test your understanding of the material presented are included in most chapters. You are given instructions for participating in exercises that allow you to practice the skills and receive feedback on how well you are mastering them. It is up to you, after engaging in the exercises, to practice the skills until you feel comfortable performing them. At the end of most chapters, you will be asked to evaluate how well you have mastered the skills.

In short, this book provides you with guidance for increasing your group skills. It is up to you to take advantage of the material and exercises presented and use them in ways that will increase your group skills. The extent of your learning and skill development rests entirely on your commitment to use this book in fruitful ways.

EXPERIENTIAL LEARNING AND MOTIVATION

All men by nature desire to learn.

Aristotle

What motivates you to learn concepts and skills? If someone offered you the opportunity either to earn a great deal of money or to experience a sense of accomplishment and satisfaction from learning a skill, which would you choose? Some educators seem to believe that students must be forced or persuaded into learning; others seem to believe that learning is enjoyable in its own right. What do you believe? Experiential learning stresses the sense of success of accomplishment in learning. Motivation is based on what you see as desirable learning goals and the method you choose to accomplish them. The goal-directed aspect of motivation places an emphasis on your feeling of success or failure in the learning situation. What leads to psychological success in a learning situation? Kurt Lewin and his associates (1944) came up with four factors. They found evidence that you will experience psychological success (as opposed to psychological failure) if:

1. You are able to define your own goals.
2. The goals are related to your central needs and values.
3. You are able to define the paths that lead to the accomplishment of the goals.
4. The goals represent a realistic level of aspiration for you—neither too high nor too low, but high enough to test your capabilities.

You will feel successful when you are encouraged to take as much responsibility for your own behavior as you can handle. You must believe that you are in control of (or at least have some influence over) your learning in order to feel psychological success. Experiential learning offers the opportunity for experiencing success by allowing you to decide what aspects of your experience you wish to focus on, what skills you wish to develop, and how you conceptualize the conclusions drawn from your experience. This is quite different from the traditional lecture approach to learning, in which you are a passive listener and the material being presented is controlled by the instructor. When an instructor decides what material will be presented and how it will be presented without letting learners have any influence over the decision, learners will experience psychological failure no matter how entertaining the presentation is.

Although the primary motivation for learning in experiential situations is psychological success, there are extrinsic factors that will encourage further learning. The approval and support of other learners is an example of extrinsic motivators that facilitate learning without interfering with intrinsic motivators, such as a sense of accomplishment. As you participate in the exercises in this book, your learning will accelerate if other participants give you approval and recognition for successful learning. You should consciously try to give approval to other readers who are seriously trying to increase their group skills. Few influences on our behavior are more powerful than the support and approval of a group of friends or acquaintances. Using such group influences to help individuals learn is one of the most constructive ways of assuring the development of group skills and knowledge.

ROLE PLAYING

Role playing is a tool for bringing patterns of behavior and their consequences into focus by allowing participants to:

1. Experience the situation concretely.
2. Identify effective and ineffective behavior.
3. Gain insight into their behavior.
4. Practice the skills required to manage the situation constructively.

Role playing is a vital training tool for mastering new skills. It can simulate real-life situations, making it possible to try new ways of handling situations without suffering any serious consequences if the methods fail. Within a role-playing situation, an imaginary situation is set up in which individuals act and react in terms of the assumptions they are asked to adopt, the beliefs they are asked to hold, and the characters they are asked to play. The outcome of a role-playing situation is not determined in advance, and the situation is not rehearsed. Initial instructions are given and the actors determine what happens.

When participating in a role-playing exercise, remain yourself and act as you would in the situation described. You do not have to be a good actor to play a role. You only need to accept the initial assumptions, beliefs, background, or assigned behaviors and then let your feelings, attitudes, and behavior change as circumstances seem to require. The role-play instructions describe the point of departure and the beginning frame of reference. You and the situation then take over.

Your experiences in participating in the role play may lead you to change your attitudes and future behavior. You may have emotional experiences that were not expected when the role playing began. The more real the role playing and the more effective the exercise, the more emotional involvement you will feel and the more you will learn.

In role playing, questions may be raised that are not answered in your briefing sheet. When this happens, you are free to make up facts or experiences that apply to the circumstances. Do not make up experiences or facts that do not fit the role. In participat

ing in role playing, you should not consult or look at your role instructions. Once they are used to start the action, you should be yourself. A role player should not act the way he or she feels a person described in the instructions should behave. The role player should act as naturally as possible, given the initial instructions of the role.

In conducting role plays, there are three important points to remember. *First*, help the participants get into the situation and their roles by introducing them in such a way that the players are emotionally involved. Introduce the scene to the role players. *Second*, always discuss the role play when it is finished. How could the conflict have been prevented? How did the characters feel in the situation? Was the solution satisfactory? What other solutions might have worked? *Third*, be sure to "de-role" after the role playing has ended. Some participants will have trouble getting into their role and other participants will have trouble getting out of their role. Announce clearly that the role play is over and that participants should reflect on and analyze the role play, not continue it.

LEARNING HOW TO BE A PARTICIPANT-OBSERVER

What Is a Participant-Observer?

A **participant-observer** is a person who is skilled enough to both participate in group work and observe the group process at the same time (see Figure 2.2). While a group is working, a distinction is commonly made between:

1. **Content:** What is being discussed in order to achieve the group's goals.
2. **Process:** The sequence of group members' actions that take place over time and are aimed at achieving the group's goal.

Ideally, a competent group member actively participates in the group's work while also observing the process being used to achieve the group's goals. To do so, a group member must function on two levels—as participant and as observer. Periodically, the group should stop its taskwork and discuss the process being used. Members continuously improve the group by (a) discussing the quality of the process being used, (b) reflecting on its effectiveness in achieving the group's goals and maintaining effective working relationships among members, and (c) setting goals for improving the process. Such reflection and discussion are aimed at (a) streamlining the group's process to make it simpler (reducing complexity) and (b) eliminating unskilled and inappropriate actions (error-proofing the process). The process a group uses to achieve its goals includes setting clear goals that create interdependence, communicating effectively, providing leadership, using appropriate decision-making procedures, resolving conflicts constructively, and so forth. A person highly skilled in process observation can participate in group work and observe group process at the same time, thus becoming a participant-observer. The steps in developing competence in being a participant-observer are:

> ## Group Processing
>
> Receive feedback
> Analyze and reflect
> Set improvement goals
> Celebrate

1. Observing.
2. Giving and receiving feedback.
3. Reflecting and setting goals for improvement.
4. Modifing behavior in the next group meeting.
5. Repeating the cycle over and over again automatically in every group of which you are a member.

Figure 2.2   Participant-observer.

Learning How to Observe

Learning how to be a participant-observer begins with learning how to observe the process the group is using to achieve its goals. The process includes goal setting, communication, leadership, use of power, decision making, and conflict resolution. Gaining competence in observing involves consciously engaging in formal observation with a wide variety of observation schedules hundreds of times until the observation procedures become internalized and become an automatic habit pattern. Such automaticity is developed by repetition and the use of a variety of procedures.

Observing is aimed at describing and recording behavior as it occurs. From the behavior of group members an observer can make inferences about the group process—the way in which the group is functioning. The problem with observation of groups is the potential for lack of objectivity by the observers (Hastorf & Cantril, 1954). Each

Feedback Checklist

Feedback	Yes	No
Is feedback given?		Was not given or received; start over.
Is feedback generating energy in students?		Students are indifferent; start over.
Is energy directed toward identifying and solving problems so that performance is improved?		Energy used to resist, deny, avoid feedback; start over.
Do students have opportunities to take action to improve performance?		No, students are frustrated and feel like failures; start over.

Constructing an Observation Procedure

Observation procedures are used to answer the question "How often are certain actions or events happening?" Observation forms are used to tally and count the number of times a behavior, action, or event is observed in a specified time period. An example is given below. The form has to be designed so that all potential observers can use it (i.e., age appropriate). A structured (formal) observation form is created in the following way:

1. Define exactly what behaviors, actions, skills, or events are being observed (such as "contributes ideas," "encourages participation," "checks for understanding," "gives group direction"). All observers have to look for the same thing.

2. Determine the time period during which data will be collected. One group may be observed for fifty minutes or each group may be observed for two minutes. Observations may be summarized after one class session or after several class sessions.

3. Enter the actions to be observed in the first column (each action or skill is placed in a separate row; the final row is reserved for the total of the columns).

4. Make an additional column for each member of the group and make a final column to record the total for each row on the form.

5. Make sure that all columns are clearly labeled and wide enough to enter data.

group member is biased in ways that may affect his or her perception and assessment of what is taking place in the group. A solution to the problem of bias is the use of structured coding systems, which require observers to categorize each group behavior into an objectively definable category.

Four steps are usually involved in observation. The *first* step is to prepare for observing. You must decide which member behaviors, actions, and skills are to be observed (the guidelines for creating effective groups in Table 1.1 detail the aspects of the group process to be observed). You choose a member to be an observer. If you are observing more than one group, you must make a sampling plan (describing how long you will observe each group and in what order you will observe the groups). Next, you find or construct an observation form or checklist that specifies observable and countable behaviors reflecting the aspect of group process to be studied. Numerous observation sheets are included in this book. You train the observers to use the selected or created form. You may also use an unstructured procedure to record the frequencies of targeted actions.

Second, you observe and record how often each member performs the specified behaviors. When there is more than one observer, you may be able to focus only on some of the group members. *Third*, you look at how often group members engage in the specified behaviors and then infer how well the group is functioning in that aspect of the group process under observation. The *final* step is to summarize the observations in a clear and useful manner and then present the summary to the group as feedback. The group can discuss the observations and revise the group process to make it more effective.

You report the results of your observations to the other group members as feedback. **Feedback** is information on actual performance that individuals compare with criteria for ideal performance. When feedback is given skillfully, it generates energy, directs the energy toward constructive action, and transforms the energy into action toward improving the performance of the teamwork skills. Member performance improves, and the discrepancy between ideal and real performance decreases. Increased self-efficacy tends to result. Members tend to feel empowered to be even more effective next time. The accompanying checklist may help in assessing the effectiveness of feedback.

The purpose of process observation is to clarify and improve the ways in which the group is presently functioning through an objective assessment of the interaction among members. Information about group process is collected and then openly discussed so that group procedures and members' behavior can be modified in order to improve the group's effectiveness.

By the time you finish this book, you will have developed skills in observing the group process. At first the observation tasks specified in the exercises will seem difficult, but gradually you will find them easier and more helpful as your skills develop. As effective future behavior depends upon awareness of the nature and consequences of current behavior, there is no substitute for direct observation in skill development and in the facilitation of group effectiveness. Any effective group member must be aware of the group process while participating in the group, and it is through observation practice that such skills are developed.

CONDUCTING SKILL-TRAINING EXERCISES

A Typical Skill-Training Session

Before discussing how to conduct a skill-training session, it may be helpful to review the overall structure of a group exercise. A typical session involves the following procedures:

1. Participants are given an introduction by a coordinator, who then conducts a warm-up discussion. The introduction should include the objectives of the session, an outline of what will happen, and a description of the specific skills with which the participants will be concerned during the exercise. The warm-up discussion sets the stage for the exercise, engenders participant involvement, and promotes an emotional connection among participants. The warm-up could take the form of a brief exchange of current feelings among participants or an interesting anecdote about group skills told by the coordinator. The expectations of the participants should be set at this point.

2. The exercise is then conducted.

3. After the exercise is completed, the participants are asked to conceptualize, analyze, and summarize their experience. This step may be structured through discussion questions or data feedback about how each person and the group behaved. The personal learnings of each participant, their application to his or her life, and the theoretical principles into which the participants gained insight as a result of their experience can be focused on.

4. In a general session, participants should talk about the experience and summarize their ideas about their experience. The coordinator should integrate appropriate theory and cognitive frameworks into the participants' statements. The emphasis at this point is upon integrating the important learnings, theory, and research with their experiences.
5. The coordinator should then discuss applying the learnings and skills to the participants' specific life situations.
6. The success of the session in accomplishing its objectives should be evaluated.
7. At the end of the session a sense of closure needs to be provided by the coordinator. This may be achieved by a short, enjoyable, involving experience. Or the coordinator may simply say that the training exercise is over.

Designing a Skill-Training Session

A skill-training program could involve any number and combination of the exercises presented in this book. It could consist of a single exercise or of several exercises drawn from different chapters. It could last a few minutes or several days. Whatever the length of the session and the number of exercises used, the basic design of the training process is the same. The following elements need to be considered when the coordinator designs a skill-training session:

1. The coordinator–participant relationship must be examined. Useful questions to be answered include: What is the purpose of the session? Why is the coordinator conducting it? What is the contract between the coordinator and the participants? What is the relationship between the coordinator and the participants? Your motivation as coordinator, hidden agendas (if any), explicit and implicit assumptions about the session and the participants, and your limitations and competencies should be reviewed. It is also helpful to know the following information about the participants:
   a. *Expectations:* What do the participants hope, believe, or fear will happen or not happen?
   b. *Experience:* What kind of previous training have the participants had?
   c. *Relevance:* How might the learnings be used after the session?
   d. *Relationships:* What are the participants' past and future relationships with each other?
   e. *Needs:* What specific learnings and what general learnings do the participants want or need?
   f. *Vital data:* Sex, age, marital status, general attitudes, physical or emotional problems and pressures, back-home support possibilities, and so on.
   g. *Motivation:* What is the level of the participants' motivation?
   h. *Recruitment:* How were the participants recruited? Did they all voluntarily agree to attend the session?
2. The desired outcomes of the session should be specified; they are usually discussed as objectives or goals. They should specify who is to be trained and what is to be the direction and magnitude of the desired learning. Clearly specified goals are useful when you are deciding upon the components of the session and

its evaluation. All the criteria for clear goals given in Chapter 4 are important when you are stating the session's objectives. Participants should be able to spell out the learnings they will try to achieve.

3. Detail the constraints on the session. These include the time periods available, the location, the facilities, and your range of competencies.

4. Generate a list of alternative exercises and activities that can be used in the skill-training session. These alternatives may include a variety of exercises and theory sessions. This list can be put together from two sources: the desired outcomes of the session and the resources and preferences of the coordinator(s). All the exercises in this book and in *Reaching Out* are possibilities.

5. Make a tentative design for the session. Evaluate it in terms of these questions:
   a. Is it appropriate for accomplishing the desired outcomes?
   b. Are the activities within your range of competencies?
   c. Is there an opportunity for participants to express their needs, expectations, or both?
   d. Does it enable the participants to make the transition from the outside world to the session and back to the outside world?
   e. Does it encourage the transfer of learnings?
   f. Does it have high personal relevance for the participants, and will it enable them to function better in their day-to-day life?
   g. If there is more than one coordinator, does it allow time for you to check signals with each other?
   h. Are high- and low-tension activities appropriately placed within the design?
   i. Are the assumptions about the skills and backgrounds of the participants appropriate?
   j. Does the overall design provide a sense of continuity, appropriate transitions among activities, a good "flow"?
   k. Are participants able to see the relationship between the exercises and the desired outcomes of the session?
   l. Does it allow for a logical flow of experiences?
   m. Does it offer flexibility in case of unexpected and emerging needs?
   n. Is it consistent with the principles of experiential learning?
   o. Is there opportunity for ongoing participant feedback and evaluation?
   p. Are you prepared to recognize and deal with unanticipated learning outcomes?
   q. Are all the necessary materials and facilities available?

6. Make sure you are highly committed to the final design. If there is more than one coordinator, assign responsibilities. Arrange for the materials and facilities.

7. If there is more than one coordinator, assess how you function as a staff. See if any team development needs to take place among the staff before the skill-training sessions begin.

Evaluation

Evaluation is the process of determining how successful—or unsuccessful—a group was in achieving its goal or objective. In the case of a skill-training session, it is the process of gathering evidence about whether the desired outcomes of the session were achieved, what unanticipated learnings were accomplished, how the activities involved in the session contributed to its success or failure, and what the coordinator(s) could do to improve their competencies. In an evaluation there must be a clear operational statement of the desired outcomes, ways to measure how nearly the desired outcomes were achieved and what activities and coordinator behaviors contributed to the session's success or failure, time for the participants to give feedback on the effectiveness of the session, and time following the session for the data to be analyzed and conclusions drawn.

In evaluation it is helpful to know such things as the emotional reactions of the participants (how they feel now), the specific or significant learnings the participants have obviously achieved, the amount of increased participant competence in performing the skills, what future experiences the participants now see the need for, the degree to which the desired outcomes were achieved, the participants' reactions to various parts of the session, and what the coordinator(s) did that was helpful or unhelpful to the participants.

The coordinator(s) can use a variety of data-collection procedures to evaluate a session: interviews, general statements made by the participants, questionnaire responses, observation of how skills were applied, and so on. All sessions do not have to be evaluated at a high level of proficiency, but more than the general impressions of the coordinator(s) should be used. At the very least, the coordinator(s) should be able to direct the same session in the future in a more effective and efficient way.

Helpful Guidelines

In conducting the exercises in this book the coordinator will have a set of general responsibilities. These include:

1. Organizing the materials, procedures, and facilities needed in order to manage the exercise.
2. Introducing, ending, and tying together the experiences involved in the exercise.
3. Keeping time in a task-oriented way in order to prevent the participants from getting sidetracked.
4. Restating and calling attention to the main learnings of the exercise, which include relating the experiences to the theory.
5. Setting a climate of experimentation, acceptance, openness, and warmth so that participants will be encouraged to try out new skills and improve their competencies.
6. Serving as an anchor point by being reliable, knowledgeable, trustworthy, and responsible.
7. Modeling the skills he or she wishes to teach.
8. Following the general outlines of experiential learning.
9. Being enthusiastic about the value of the exercise.
10. Knowing and understanding the material well.
11. Making sure everyone understands the instructions and responsibilities.
12. Being sensitive to the differences in participation, needs, and styles of the participants.

13. Remaining flexible so that the preplanned procedures do not interfere with the participants' learning.
14. Enjoying the exercises and making sure that he or she also learns and benefits from them.

ETHICS OF EXPERIENTIAL LEARNING

All learning activities require a code of ethics, either implicit or explicit. Workers in this field have paid a great deal of attention to the ethics of growth-group leaders but have given little consideration to the ethics of conducting experiential-learning activities. Some of the ethical issues relevant to the types of skill-training exercises included in this book are as follows.

The most serious ethical issue involved in teaching group skills is determining the value and necessity of such cognitive and behavioral changes for the participants. Attempting to teach another person carries with it a responsibility not to work against that person's best interests and needs. In addition, the only way to promote ethical standards in teaching–learning relationships is for the teachers to enforce their code of ethics on themselves and to use good judgment in what they do. As long as a teacher's behavior is based on care, respect, and regard for participants, ethical violations will be minimized. Persons leading experiential-learning activities must therefore develop a personal code of ethics to which they hold themselves accountable. The following points should provoke some thought as to what that personal code of ethics might include.

The Contract: Informed Consent and Mutual Agreement

1. The coordinator's intentions and objectives should be clearly communicated to the participants. The participants should understand that they are going to participate in an experiential exercise in which they will be expected to examine their own behavior and the behavior of others and analyze the behaviors for purposes of learning.
2. The coordinator and participants should easily understand the nature of the contract. They should agree on the number of experiences, the length of each session, and the appropriateness and objectives of each exercise.
3. The point at which the contract is terminated should be clear to both the coordinator and the participants.

The Activities

1. Participation should be voluntary. Advise participants that they can say "no" and sit on the sidelines as the exercise is being conducted.
2. The coordinator should have an explicit reason for conducting the exercise and be prepared to explain the reason clearly.
3. Only exercises the coordinator is competent to direct should be conducted.

4. The coordinator should present relevant theory and research when it is appropriate to the participants' learning and increased effectiveness.
5. The coordinator should be constantly aware of his or her behavior styles and personal needs and deal with them productively. The coordinator should also be aware of the impact of his or her needs and style on the participants.
6. The coordinator should assess all experiences by discussing the participants' feelings and reactions to them and by asking the participants what can be learned from the experiences. Adequate time must be programmed into the design of the session for this purpose.
7. The coordinator should not initiate confrontations between participants, which may damage their future relationship. This does not mean that the coordinator should discourage risk taking in giving feedback, making honest disclosures, or attempting to face conflicts and improve the relationship. It simply means that confrontations should originate with the participants, not the coordinator.
8. If any personal information is revealed, the coordinator should make sure that the possibility of its being used in any way to damage the participants is minimized.
9. Ideally, the coordinator should be able to recognize symptoms of serious psychological stress and make responsible decisions when such problems arise. At the very least, the coordinator should know where emergency psychological services are available.
10. In evaluation, the coordinator should receive feedback that will improve his or her performance. The sessions should be open to scrutiny by competent professionals interested in the effectiveness of experiential learning.
11. The coordinator should conduct follow-up interviews with participants to determine the impact of the sessions on them and to assess their feelings and reactions to the sessions.

The Coordinator's Knowledge, Skills, and Needs

1. **Knowledge:** The coordinator's actions need to be based on empirically validated theory. Folklore, superstition, common sense, fads, popular gimmicks, and personal experiences are not adequate bases for teaching others. The coordinator should thoroughly understand the principles of experiential learning, the steps of skill development, and the knowledge the exercise is designed to teach.
2. **Experience:** The coordinator should have some experience and skill in conducting exercises and helping participants reflect on their own and others' behavior. Knowing the steps of experiential learning is not enough. The coordinator should also have some skills and competencies in applying the principles of experiential learning.
3. **Clear Explanations:** At any time during the exercises, the coordinator should be able to explain the relevant theory and the way in which current activities relate to the theory. The coordinator is free to use intuition when conducting an exercise, but should be able to reconstruct the theory behind his or her intuitive actions.
4. **Self-Awareness:** The coordinator should be aware of his or her personal needs and deal with them productively.

Final Notes

Your ability to conduct and coordinate experiential-learning exercises will improve as you apply the material in this book with intelligence and caution. If you are interested in other skill-building exercises, see Johnson (1991, 2000) and Johnson and Johnson (1997). You do not have to be a skilled teacher to conduct the exercises contained in this book, but constant concern for increasing your knowledge and skills in experiential learning is helpful.

The preceding statements are meant to be guidelines, not rigid rules. The only effective way to enforce ethical standards in educational activities is for the persons conducting the educational problems to enforce their code of ethics on themselves and use good judgment in what they do. Again, as long as a coordinator's behavior is based on care, respect, and regard for the participants, ethical violations will probably be avoided. We hope that the preceding guidelines will help the users of this book build a personal code of ethical conduct.

SUMMARY

To master the field of group dynamics, you must learn the relevant theory and research and master the skills that put that knowledge into action. Such procedural learning results from skill-building experiences as well as academic study. Procedural learning involves a progressive refinement of knowledge and skill as the procedures are practiced, practiced, and practiced. In other words, this book focuses on both head and hand learning.

Experiential learning begins with the formulation of an action theory. Action theories specify what actions are needed to achieve a desired consequence in a given situation. The next step is to take action and engage in the relevant group skills. The success or failure of the actions is assessed. Upon reflection, the action theory is refined and reformulated. Then the group skills are used again in a modified and improved way. This cycle is repeated over and over again as the skills are refined and continuously improved. This continuous improvement process eventually results in expertise in the use of group skills as changes in cognitive understanding, attitudes, and behavioral patterns result. While learning experientially, you experience psychological success. While mastering group skills, furthermore, you need to observe how they are being used by other group members while you fully participate in the group. Such participant-observation enables you to know when to use various group skills and how to help others to do so in order to improve the functioning of the group. In order to learn the group skills discussed in this book, you need to conduct the skill-building exercises competently and ethically.

3

Group Goals, Social Interdependence, and Trust

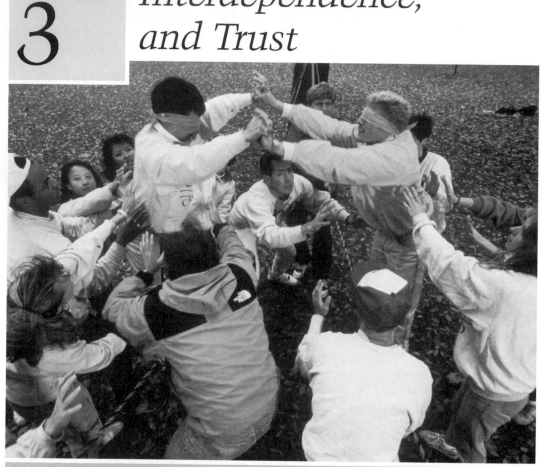

Ch 3-7
Read thoroughly! →

Basic Concepts to Be Covered in This Chapter

In this chapter a number of concepts are defined and discussed. The major ones are listed following. Divide into pairs. Each pair is to (a) define each concept, noting the page on which it is defined and discussed, and (b) ensure that both members of the pair understand the meaning of each concept. Then combine into groups of four. Compare the answers of the two pairs. If there is disagreement, look up the concept in the chapter and clarify it until all the members agree on and understand the definition.

Concepts

1. Competitive efforts
2. Cooperative efforts
3. Distributive justice
4. Equality distribution of benefits
5. Goal
6. Goal structure
7. Group goal
8. Hidden agenda
9. Individual efforts
10. Level of aspiration
11. Merit distribution of benefits
12. Need distribution of benefits
13. Nonoperational goals
14. Operational goals
15. Social interdependence
16. Vision

INTRODUCTION

The honor of one is the honor of all.
The hurt of one is the hurt of all.

> Creek Indian creed

Groups form for a cooperative purpose. Since their beginnings, humans have joined together to cooperate to achieve goals that each member could not achieve alone. Whereas elephants have size and cheetahs have speed, it is our ability to engage in cooperative enterprises to achieve group goals that distinguishes us as a species. Social interdependence defines the ways in which the goals of individuals are related. Social interdependence is the heart of all human interaction, and cooperation is the heart of all small group efforts. To be effective, groups must set goals that all members commit themselves to cooperate in achieving. There are two steps in doing so:

1. Operational goals and the paths to achieving the goals are clearly specified and measurable.
2. Cooperative interdependence is structured among group members.

PKR 5 EXERCIZES
do 1 pg summary   > due 7/11/2006.
1 pg journal entry

69

3.1 Orientations Toward Social Interdependence

This exercise has two purposes: (1) to make you more aware of your orientation toward goal interdependence with others and (2) to make your group more aware of members' orientations toward social interdependence. The procedure is as follows:

1. Working by yourself, complete the following questionnaire.
2. Using the scoring table that follows the questionnaire, determine your score and then determine the group average for each scale.
3. Have a group discussion concerning the orientation toward social interdependence of group members.

SOCIAL INTERDEPENDENCE QUESTIONNAIRE

For each of the following items, indicate your *general* perceptions about each statement. In the appropriate space, write down the number that most accurately describes your attitude.

1 = never	4 = mostly
2 = seldom	5 = always
3 = sometimes	

1. I like to compare myself with others to see who is best.
2. In my situation, people spend a lot of time working by themselves.
3. In my situation, people share their ideas and resources with each other.
4. In my situation, people are motivated to see who can do the best job.
5. In my situation, individuals like to work by themselves.
6. In my situation, individuals learn a lot of important things from each other.
7. In my situation, individuals want to do better than others.
8. In my situation, it bothers individuals when they have to work with each other.
9. In my situation, individuals help each other do a good job.
10. In my situation, individuals are encouraged to outperform each other.
11. In my situation, individuals would rather work alone than work together.
12. In my situation, individuals believe that they are more productive when they work with each other.

Competitive	*Individualistic*	*Cooperative*
1. _____	2. _____	3. _____
4. _____	5. _____	6. _____
7. _____	8. _____	9. _____
10. _____	11. _____	12. _____
Total _____	Total _____	Total _____

3.2 Are Group Goals Necessary?

There has been some controversy over whether group goals are necessary. The purpose of this exercise is to structure a critical discussion of the issue. The procedure is as follows.

1. **Assignment of Positions:** The class forms groups of four. Each group is ultimately to write a report summarizing its position on whether:
   a. Groups cannot function without goals.
   b. Group goals are of no use.

The report is to contain the group's overall conclusions and the facts and rationale supporting its position. The supporting facts and rationale may be obtained from this chapter, the entire book, and outside reading.

2. **Preparation Pairs:** Each group divides into pairs. One pair is assigned the position that groups cannot function without goals and the other pair the position that group goals are of no use. The pairs review the supporting sections of this chapter, the procedure for the exercise, and the rules for constructive controversy (p. 34). Each pair prepares a persuasive "best case" rationale for its assigned position that includes as many facts and research findings as possible. Ten minutes are allowed for this phase.

3. **Presentations:** One member of each pair changes chairs. A "group goals are necessary" person should be seated with a "group goals are unnecessary" person. The "group goals are necessary" person has up to three minutes to present the best case possible for the position, being as forceful and persuasive as possible. The "group goals are unnecessary" person takes notes and asks for clarification of anything that is not fully understood. The "group goals are unnecessary" person then makes a presentation.

4. **Open Discussion** (Refute and Rebut): There is an open discussion of whether group goals are necessary. Each side presents as many facts and research findings as it can to support its point of view. Members listen critically to the opposing position and ask for supporting facts for any conclusions made by the opponent. Participants should ensure that all the facts supporting both sides are brought out and discussed. The guidelines for constructive controversy should be followed. About ten minutes are allowed for this phase.

5. **Perspective Reversal:** Members of each pair change chairs. The "group goals are necessary" person presents in three minutes the best case possible for the "group goals are unnecessary" position. He or she should be as forceful and persuasive as possible and add new arguments or facts if possible. The "group goals are unnecessary" person then presents the best case possible for the "group goals are necessary" position.

6. **Synthesis and Integration:** Participants drop all advocacy and come to their best reasoned judgment as to whether group goals are necessary. The pair of members summarize the information and arguments for each position and come to an agreement. Each pair prepares a short presentation on its conclusion to the rest of the class. Because other groups will have other conclusions, each group may need to explain the validity of its position to the class. About ten minutes are allowed for this phase.

7. **Whole Class Discussion:** The coordinator samples the decisions made by the groups of four by having several of them present their position to the class. The class then discusses similarities and differences among the positions, and the coordinator summarizes what the participants have learned about group goals.

BRIEFING SHEET: GROUPS CANNOT FUNCTION WITHOUT GOALS

Your position is that a group cannot function without having at least one goal that is understood and accepted by several of its members. To support your position, use the rationale given below, any material from this chapter that is applicable, and your outside reading.

Group goals guide the actions of members and allow them to plan and coordinate their efforts. Group goals direct, channel, guide, energize, motivate, and coordinate the behavior of group members. Groups cannot exist unless the activities of their members are directed toward achieving something (a goal). It is the power of goals to influence members to engage in needed behaviors that makes goals essential to an effective group. All in all, groups cannot function effectively or even exist without goals.

BRIEFING SHEET: GROUP GOALS ARE OF NO USE

Your position is that a goal is not useful to a group and is a concept that has no basis in reality. To support your position, use the rationale given below, any material from this chapter that is applicable, and your outside reading.

Group goals are often stated in such vague terms that they could not possibly be effective guides for the actions of members. When asked, many group members cannot accurately describe the group's goals, and thus the goals can have no impact on these persons. Often goals do not determine members' efforts because the goals seem unrelated to what group members actually do. Appraisals of group process, moreover, usually reveal that groups have not achieved their goals, which suggests that the goals are not the true motivators of members' actions. It may even be that groups do not try to accomplish anything; they just exist. All in all, goals are of no use to a group.

WHAT IS A GOAL?

On September 17, 1868, Major George A. Forsyth and fifty handpicked scouts were camped on Beecher's Island (a small island in the dry bed of the Arikaree River) in eastern Colorado Territory. Full-scale war had just erupted with the Indian tribes of the Great Plains. Forsyth and his scouts had left Fort Hays in Kansas to find the enemy, but the Native Americans found Forsyth first. On that morning, the Cheyenne war chief known as Roman Nose led over 700 Cheyenne and Oglala warriors in a dawn attack on Forsyth's camp. Many of Forsyth's men and all his horses were killed or wounded. Forsyth was shot in both legs, and a bullet creased his skull. The men were trapped on the island. By September 25, as a result of stealthy sniping and repeated charges, half of Forsyth's men were casualties. Wondering whether he would live to see another morning, Forsyth lay stretched out beside the rotting carcass of his dead horse. A horrific stench rose from the dead men and animals around him. The overall goal of Forsyth and his scouts was to survive. They did have, however, a number of short-term goals. They had to construct a barrier to protect them from enemy fire. They used the dead horses. Maintaining group unity and support was essential for morale, hope, and an effective defense. Water, shelter, food, and caring for the wounded were problems. Luckily, the weather was mild enough that shelter was not a necessity. They had enough water on the island to survive. After several days, however, the scouts began to eat their horses' decaying flesh.

The situation seemed hopeless. Suddenly, the Indians withdrew. Puzzled, the survivors soon saw why. A company of cavalry was galloping toward the island. Unknown to Forsyth, two of his scouts had slipped through the besieging Indians and traveled to Fort Wallace in Kansas. Captain Louis H. Carpenter, a Civil War comrade of Forsyth's, immediately mounted a company of cavalry for a rescue expedition. Carpenter's troopers were officially known as Company H of the 10th Calvary, but to their Indian foes they were the "buffalo soldiers." Rather than fight these soldiers, Roman Nose decided to withdraw. Over the course of three decades, the buffalo soldiers gained a reputation for being the most professional, experienced, and effective troops on the frontier.

Groups exist for a reason. People join groups in order to achieve goals they are unable to achieve by themselves. The goal may be to build a better mousetrap, to climb a mountain, to get the most pay for the least amount of work, or to apply the material being presented in this book. The essence of a **goal** is that it is an ideal. It is a desired end toward which people are working, a state of affairs that people value. **The goals of individuals are related through social interdependence.** There may be a positive correlation among individuals' goal attainments (i.e., cooperation), a negative correlation among individuals' goal attainments (i.e., competition), or no correlation among individuals' goal attainments (i.e., individualistic efforts). Such **goal structures** specify the type of social interdependence among individuals as they strive to accomplish their goals. They specify the ways in which individuals will interact with each other. Social interdependence is discussed in depth in a later section of this chapter. When a positive correlation exists among individuals' goal attainments, a group goal results. A **group goal** is a future state of affairs desired by enough members of a group to motivate the group to work toward its achievement. Ever since there were two humans on earth, people have joined together to achieve mutual goals and to maximize their joint welfare.

A Joint Vision

Goals are not intellectual, cold, or analytical. Goals enlist the emotions of group members and point them toward coordinated efforts. The more the goal elicits emotions, the more it is a vision. Group members share a vision of what they can accomplish when they work together. A **vision** is an ideal and unique image of the future. The vision clarifies the mission and goals of the group. Stephen Wozniak and Stephen Jobs shared a vision as they invented the Apple computer in a garage. They took their dream from a garage to a multinational computer company. To end world hunger, to prevent the pain and anguish of children dying of cancer, to allow the deaf to hear with an artificial ear, to allow people to live with an artificial heart, to find a drug to prevent the body's rejection of transplanted organs—all are visions that bring tears, laughter, bitter disappointment, determination, hope, depression, enthusiasm, and joy. The vision tells group members what is possible if all work together for a common purpose. It shows members how their values and interests will be served by the accomplishments they are striving for. The goals of the group create a compelling vision that focuses the passion of members and ignites the flame of inspired work. The vision binds members through a shared *emotional* commitment. Group goals breathe life into group members' hopes and dreams and enable them to see the exciting possibilities of their joint efforts.

Do Group Goals Exist?

Do groups have goals or are there only the various individual goals of the group's members? As dry as this question may seem, social psychologists have hotly debated this issue for decades. Emmy Pepitone (1980), for example, insists that group goals can be identified, that they function as an important source of member interdependence in groups, and that they denote a common central focus that is present most of the time and is readily identifiable as an objective reality. She states that group goals provide an aspect of unity, of a common fate, that one cannot readily convey simply by noting the individual goals of group members. Lewin (1944) said that there are situations in which group members do seem to act to maximize joint outcomes or accomplish group goals rather than to maximize their individual outcomes or achieve their individual goals. Both Horwitz (1954) and Pepitone (1952) conducted studies that indicated that group members become motivated to have their group achieve its goal and are personally satisfied when the group does so. The success of the group, rather than their personal gain, seems to be the major source of their satisfaction. More recent studies (Matsui, Kakuyama, & Onglateo, 1987; Mitchell & Silver, 1990) indicate that group goals, compared with individual goals, result in higher group performance, greater goal acceptance, and more cooperation among group members. Numerous other studies have demonstrated that individuals do focus on joint outcomes rather than individual outcomes when they are placed in situations requiring cooperation with others.

Many social scientists, however, believe that a group goal is a combination of the individual goals of all group members. People, therefore, become group members because they have certain goals and motives that they wish to express or fulfill through group membership. Each person brings to the group a wish to satisfy personal goals. These goals are not always clearly known to the member. He or she may be completely aware, partially aware, or totally unaware of his or her goals and motives during a group meeting.

There is no definitive answer to the question whether group goals exist in and of themselves or are simply a reflection of the overlap among the personal goals of the group's members. It is safe to conclude, however, that both group and individual goals exist and that the group goals must be relevant to the individual needs of the members. Group members usually try to achieve both individual and group goals, and the degree to which they accomplish this through the same activities determines how effective the group will be in attaining its goals. The situation is further complicated by the fact that most groups and individuals have several goals, that different members value different goals at different times, and that even the same member places different values on the same goal at different times.

Whether group goals are entities in and of themselves or simply a combination of the individual goals of members, they are important for numerous reasons.

EXERCISE 3.3 *Your Goal-Related Behavior*

This exercise examines goal-related behavior in problem-solving groups. Working by yourself, answer the following three questions. Be honest. Check as many responses to each question as are characteristic of your usual behavior. Then form a triad with two of your classmates, and discuss your answers and why you answered the questions as you did. Develop as much awareness of your behavior in goal-related situations as possible.

1. When I am a member of a group that does not seem to have a clear awareness of what its goals are or how they are to be achieved, I usually:
   _____ Feel uninterested and refuse to attend meetings.
   _____ Ask the designated leader to stop messing around and tell the group what it is supposed to be doing.
   _____ Ignore the situation and be extra nice to the other members.

_____ Propose that members review the group's goals and state that in return they will be told what to do to achieve the goals.

_____ Initiate a group discussion to clarify each member's understanding of the group goals until all group members clearly understand what they are and what actions the group needs to take to accomplish them.

2. When a member of a group that has a clear understanding of its goals seems to have little commitment to accomplishing them, I usually:

_____ Refuse to have anything to do with that member and avoid him or her.

_____ Make fun of the group member until he or she becomes more committed.

_____ Pretend that there is nothing wrong and be nice to the other person.

_____ Propose a compromise in which the person works harder and the group expects less.

_____ Initiate a group discussion in which the group goals are considered and reformulated to make them more relevant to each member's goals.

3. When I am a member of a group that has conflicting opinions on what its goals should be, or that has members with conflicting needs and motives, I usually:

_____ Simply withdraw and wait for them to work out their differences.

_____ Tell the leader to decide who is right and who is wrong and tell the losers to shut up.

_____ Try to smooth over the differences and ask everyone to be nice and keep their differences to themselves.

_____ Propose a 50/50 compromise in which everyone gets half of what he or she wants.

_____ Figure out how much cooperative and competitive behavior exists in the group and give the group feedback based on my observations in an attempt to increase cooperation among its members.

_____ Start a group discussion on the different positions, goals, and motives of group members and seek a solution that is acceptable to everyone.

START WITH GOALS

If a man does not know to which port he is sailing, no wind is favorable.

Seneca

There are two aspects of ensuring members' commitment to the group's goals. The *first* is to ensure that the goals meet the START criteria (see Table 3.1). To be effective, goals need to be specific (so it is clear what needs to be done next), measurable (so progress can be tracked), challenging but achievable, relevant, and aimed at competencies that will be transferred to other situations. The *second* way to ensure members' commitment is to involve group members in the process of forming the goals. When group members participate in setting goals, there tends to be a better match between the group goals and the motives of members and a better understanding of the actions needed to achieve the goals. In addition, involvement leads to ownership of the goals, which leads to commitment. While indifferent to others' goals, individuals seek out opportunities to achieve their own goals and commit considerable energy to doing so. Other factors influencing commitment are how desirable the goal seems (the benefits group members will receive if the goal is accomplished) and the ways in which members will relate to each other in working toward the accomplishment of the goal (some ways of relating are more enjoyable and involving than others).

Table 3.1 **START with Goals**

Goal Characteristic	Definition of Characteristic
S Specific	Goals have to be specific enough so that they are clearly understood and a plan to achieve them can be developed. Specific goals indicate what needs to be done next.
T Trackable and measurable	Members must be able to determine the extent to which they have reached the goals. Goals must be operationalized so that the steps to achieving them are clear and understandable.
A Achievable but challenging	Goals must be challenging enough so that the group has a 50/50 chance of achieving them. Group must be able to achieve the goals if they work hard enough and have sufficient teamwork.
R Relevant	Goals must be relevant to the members' interests and the interests of other stakeholders in the group. Members must see the goals as meaningful and be personally committed to achieving them.
T Transfer	Goals must be aimed at having members take what is learned and transfer it to other situations. Whatever skills members master today should be usable in other situations tomorrow.

EXERCISE

3.4 *Clear and Unclear Goals*

This exercise constructs the behavioral consequences of having clear and unclear goals. Approximately one hour is needed to complete it. The procedure is as follows:

1. Seat the participants in groups of six to eight, formed into circles.
2. Introduce the exercise as focusing upon clear and unclear group goals.
3. Have each group select an observer, who reports to a designated place for instructions. While the observers are being briefed, urge the group members to get acquainted with one another.
4. Give each observer a copy of the observation guide and tell observers that the groups will work on two tasks. The first task will be unclear, the second clear. Their job is to make careful observations of group behavior on the two tasks. The observers then return to their groups but sit outside the circle.
5. Brief all groups as follows: "We are going to study group behavior by working on two brief tasks. Your observer will not participate but will report to you at the end of the second task. Your first task will take about eight minutes. I will give you a warning a minute before the time is up. The task is: List the most appropriate goals to govern the best developmental group experiences in order to maximize social development in a democratic society."
6. While the groups work on the task, the observers should take notes. After seven minutes give the warning and after eight minutes end the discussion.
7. Give the second task: "List as many of the formally organized clubs or organizations that exist in a typical community as you can." State that the groups will have six minutes to work on the task. At the end of five minutes give a one-minute warning and after six minutes end the discussion.
8. Give a copy of the observation guide to all participants. Then have each group discuss its experience, using the information obtained by the observers as its major resource. This discussion should last ten to fifteen minutes.

9. Form clusters by asking one group to pull its chairs in a circle around another group. The inner group becomes group A and the outer group becomes group B. Instruct group A to produce a list of characteristics of clear and unclear goals, with one person recording them on newsprint in two columns. Allow six minutes for this task. Group B is to listen to group A, take notes, and be ready to add to the list. After six minutes, instruct group B to comment on the list and have both groups jointly select the four or five most important characteristics of clear and unclear goals from the list. Give them nine minutes to do so.

10. Groups A and B then change places, with group B now in the center. Group B is told to list behavioral symptoms of each of the characteristics of clear and unclear goals listed on the newsprint, beginning with the most important characteristics. After nine minutes, group A joins the discussion, which should take another six minutes.

11. Each cluster presents its work to the other group. Hold a general discussion on the nature of group goals and their consequences in feeling and behavior, using the material in the following section.

CLEAR AND UNCLEAR GOALS EXERCISE: OBSERVATION GUIDE

During this exercise the groups will work on two tasks. The first task will be unclear, and the second will be clear. Your job as an observer is to make careful notations of group behavior on the two tasks. When you understand the form, return to your group but sit outside the circle.

		First Task	**Second Task**
1. Number of times a member clarified the goal or asked that it be clarified.			
2. Assessment of the "working climate" of the group: Was it cooperative, hostile, pleasant, critical, accepting, and so forth?	At the beginning?		
	At the middle?		
	At the end?		
3. Frequency of verbal behavior not directly related to getting the job done (side conversation, jokes, comments).			
4. Frequency of nonverbal behavior not related to getting the task done (looking around the room, horseplay, bored withdrawal, hostility).			
5. How much progress did the group make in getting the task done? (Make an estimate.)			

CLARITY OF GOALS

To be useful, goals have to be clear. If you have done the preceding exercise, you will have a list of the characteristics of both clear and unclear goals and the behavioral symptoms of groups with clear and unclear goals. Some of the symptoms of unclear goals are a high level of group tension, joking or horseplay, distraction by side issues, and the failure to use good ideas. The importance of clear goals may be seen when groups lose their direction. John DeLorean (Wright, 1979) describes how highly qualified executives at General Motors held numerous pointless meetings where trivial issues were discussed at length. These highly paid executives forgot their true goal of planning for the corporation's future. Latham and Baldes (1975) report the beneficial effects of clear goals. When truck drivers who hauled logs from the woods to the mill were told to "do their best" when loading the logs they carried about 60% of what they could legally haul. When they were later encouraged to reach a goal of 94% of the legal limit, they met this specific goal. In financial terms, this clarification of goals earned the company more than a quarter of a million dollars. Goal accomplishment depends on members' coordinating and synchronizing their actions. To do so, the goal and the actions required to achieve the goal must be clear. Goals become clarified as they are made more specific, operational, workable, measurable, and observable.

OPERATIONAL GOALS

The secret of success is constancy of purpose.

Benjamin Disraeli

Operational goals are goals for which specific steps to achievement are clear and identifiable. **Nonoperational goals** are abstract and ambiguous; the specific steps required to achieve them are not discernible. Broad, long-range goals are often nonoperational and can be related to specific actions only through the formation of subgoals. An example of an operational goal is "Name three qualities of a good group member." An example of a nonoperational goal is "Draw conclusions about the theoretical and empirical findings of qualities of effective actions by a group member."

An operational goal has indicators that will make it evident when it has been achieved. There is no sense in going somewhere if you do not know when you have arrived. The goal "Name three qualities of a good group member" is operational in that when you have listed three items, and if they refer to group membership, you will know that the goal has been reached. The goal "Draw conclusions about the theoretical and empirical findings of qualities of effective actions by a group member" is nonoperational in that it may be difficult to tell when such a goal has been achieved. Whatever indicators are used to tell when a group has accomplished its goals, several of them are better than one, and indicators that are observable, countable, and specific are better than those that are nonobservable, noncountable, and ambiguous. Usually the goal of a problem-solving group will have indicators that reflect both the accomplishment of the goal (profit, new members gained, problems solved) and the maintenance of working relationships among group members (group cohesion, effective communication, effective decision making, high level of trust among members).

There are several advantages for a group in having operational goals. The *first* advantage is in facilitating communication among its members and between the group and other groups. A goal must be stated in such a way that it succeeds in telling what the group intends to accomplish, and this communication is successful when any knowledgeable person can look at the group's behavior or products and decide whether or not the goal has been reached. *Second*, operational goals help guide the group in planning and carrying out its tasks. Operational goals help a group to select and organize the appropriate resources and methods it will need in working on its tasks. *Third*, operational goals help the group evaluate both the group process and the group product. By specifying the criteria for goal accomplishment, the group can evaluate its progress. Fourth, when goals are operational, conflicts about what actions the group members should take are more likely to be solved by rational, analytic processes.

How are clear, operational goals developed? It must be recognized that for most groups, clear goals cannot always be determined in advance, especially if they are to be acceptable to all or most of the members. The first job of any group, therefore, is to modify any stated goal until all the group members understand it and a consensus exists concerning how it is to be operationalized, or put into practice. Through such discussions, commitment to goals is built and the goals become acceptable to the group members. The more time a group spends establishing agreement on clear goals, the less time it needs to achieve them—and the more likely it will be that the members will work effectively for the common outcome.

GROUP GOALS AND LEVEL OF ASPIRATION

Kurt Lewin and his associates developed a theory of level of aspiration to explain how people set goals for themselves and their groups (Lewin, Dembo, Festinger, & Sears, 1944). **Level of aspiration (LOA)** may be defined as the compromise between ideal goals and realistic expectations. The theory generally predicts that individuals enter situations with an ideal outcome in mind (for example, earning a B in this course) but revise their goals upward after success and downward after failure (if they get As on the first two tests, they change their LOA to aspire to an A, but if they get Cs on the first two tests, they change their LOA to aspire to a C). As they gain experience, individuals revise their ideal expectations to match the reality of the situation.

Groups, like individuals, develop levels of aspiration. Alvin Zander conducted a series of studies with populations as diverse as high school boys batting a ball down a runway as a team (Zander & Mcdow, 1963) and United Fund chapters setting their fund-raising goals (Zander, 1971). He demonstrated that groups set goals that are slightly optimistic and revised their goals as feedback about performance levels became available. Groups tended to lower their level of aspiration somewhat less after failure than they raised it after success. In the United Fund study, for example, of the chapters that failed to reach their goal, only 40% lowered their goal for the next year. Of the chapters that succeeded in reaching their goal, 80% raised their goal. Although this optimistic bias is constructive in most circumstances, there are times when it leads to a cycle of failure. When unsuccessful United Fund chapters set overoptimistic goals year after year, the continued failure decreased morale, work enjoyment, and group efficiency. Whereas optimistic goal setting challenges members to work hard to improve performance, the refusal to revise overly idealistic goals in unsuccessful groups can set the stage for future failure and its consequences.

DEALING WITH HIDDEN AGENDAS

The personal goals of the group members can be homogeneous (alike) or heterogeneous (different). Homogeneity of individual members' goals (or consensus about what the group's goals should be) usually helps group functioning, whereas heterogeneity of individual members' goals (or disagreement about what the group's goals should be) usually interferes with group functioning. Individual group members with homogeneous goals are usually happier with the group and its tasks than are members of groups with heterogeneous goals. Heterogeneous goals may easily become **hidden agendas**—personal goals that are unknown to all the other group members and are at cross-purposes with the dominant group goals. Hidden agendas can greatly hinder, and even destroy, group effectiveness. Yet they are present in almost every group. A group, therefore, must both increase consensus among group members on what the group's goals should be and decrease disagreement among different members' goals. Some procedures for doing this are as follows:

1. When you first form a group, thoroughly discuss its goals, even when they are prescribed by superiors or by the constitution of the group. Such a discussion will clarify the members' understanding of the goals and help clear away any misunderstandings concerning the tasks necessary to reach them. During the discussion the group should reword, reorganize, and review the goals until the majority of members feel a sense of ownership toward them.

2. As the group progresses in its activities, remember that it is continuously working on two levels at once: toward the achievement of the group's goals and toward the achievement and satisfaction of the individual members' goals and motives. Look for hidden agendas. Recognizing a group problem is the first step in diagnosing and solving it.

3. Bear in mind that there are conditions under which hidden agendas should be brought to the surface and rectified and conditions under which they should be left undisturbed. The group must make a judgment about the consequences of bringing hidden agendas to the attention of the entire group. One way to tell how willing other group members are to deal with hidden agendas is to initiate a discussion on the subject, taking care not to force anyone to admit his or her own hidden agenda. A statement like this one may be helpful: "I wonder if we've said all that we feel like saying about the issue. Maybe we should take time to go around the table so that any further thoughts can be brought up."

4. Do not scold or pressure the other group members when hidden agendas are recognized. They are present and legitimate and must be worked on in much the same manner that group tasks are handled. Hidden agendas should be given dif-

ferent amounts of attention at different times, depending upon their influence on the group's effectiveness and on the nature of the group and its members.

5. Spend some time evaluating the ability of the group to deal productively with hidden agendas. Each experience the group has should reveal better ways in which to handle agendas more openly. As groups mature, hidden agendas are reduced.

HELPING GROUPS SET EFFECTIVE GOALS

Still the question recurs, "Can we do better?" The dogmas of the quiet past are inadequate to the stormy present. The occasion is piled high with difficulty, and we must rise with the occasion. As our case is new, so we must think anew, and act anew.

Abraham Lincoln, Annual Message to Congress, December 1, 1862

Two methods of helping groups set effective goals are the survey-feedback method and program evaluation and review. The **survey-feedback method** begins with the consultant or leader interviewing the individual members about the goals and priorities of the group as they see them. These interviews are conducted before a periodic meeting of the group (such as annually or semiannually). On the basis of the information collected, and working within the organizational goals, the consultant conducts a group session in which the group sets its goals and priorities for the next six months or year. During this meeting the group plans its short-term goals, defines specific responsibilities for working on the tasks, ranks the tasks and goals in terms of priority to the group, and sets group-development goals for more effective group work. Special attention is paid to

Characteristics of Effective Group Goals

1. The extent to which the goals are operationally defined so that they are measurable and observable. Members need to know what they are supposed to do.
2. The extent to which group members see the goals as being meaningful, relevant, realistic, acceptable, and attainable.
3. The extent to which the goals create positive interdependence among group members.
4. The degree to which both group goals and individual members' goals can be achieved by the same tasks and activities.
5. The extent to which the goals are challenging and offer a moderate risk of failure.
6. How easily the goals can be modified and clarified.
7. How long a group has to attain the goals.

specifying the leadership and membership-role relationships necessary not only for working on the tasks but also for developing ways in which to identify and solve group-relationship problems that might hinder goal achievement.

In program evaluation and review—or the **critical path method**—groups are helped by a consultant to set effective goals by first specifying the end state they want to achieve. Working backward from this final goal, the group then details what must happen immediately before it is achieved, and the tasks and subgoals needed to accomplish it are all spelled out. The group decides which of the activities and subgoals are most critical for final goal accomplishment and allocates resources accordingly. A timetable for accomplishing each subgoal is set. The whole process is then reviewed, and responsibilities are assigned.

3.5 *Plane Wreck*

The purpose of this exercise is to give participants an opportunity to experience cooperation based on a division of labor as well as a joint goal. The procedure is as follows:

1. The class forms groups of three. One member plays the role of observer, another member the role of A, and the third member the role of B.
2. Each group of three needs the following materials:
   a. a blindfold
   b. five or six odd-sized pieces of cardboard
   c. a roll of cellophane tape or masking tape
   d. a piece of rope at least three feet long
3. *The situation:* A and B were flying a plane that suddenly developed engine trouble and crashed on a desert island with no water. They will be rescued in a few days, but they must have water if they are to survive. They have some materials for making a container to hold rainwater. The only problem is that B received a heavy blow on her head and is now both blind and mute. A has badly burned both hands and is not able to use them at all. But they must build the container if they are to live. A rain cloud is quickly approaching, and they must have the container finished before it reaches the island. A few drops are already beginning to fall.
4. The observer ties A's hands behind his back and blindfolds B. B is not to say a word during the entire building process.
5. The observer takes notes on how well the two persons work together. How good are the directions? How well are they carried out? How cooperative are the two persons? What communication problems exist? What could they have done differently?
6. If the container is not finished in twenty minutes, the two persons stop. The group then combines with another group of three, and the two groups discuss the following questions:
   a. How did the person playing A feel?
   b. How did the person playing B feel?
   c. What does the container look like? If it were made of wood and nails instead of cardboard and tape, would it hold water? (If there is a hole in the bottom, the answer is "no.")
   d. What would have improved the cooperation between A and B?
   e. What did you learn about the division of labor in a cooperative task?
7. Each group of six shares its major conclusions and experiences with the rest of the class.

3.6 *Broken Squares*

The purpose of this exercise is to explore the results of cooperation and competition among group members in solving a group problem. The exercise is done in groups of five participants and two observers. Tables that seat five should be used. At least four groups are recommended, but two may do in a pinch. Place the tables far enough apart so that members of one group cannot observe the activities of the other groups. One set of squares is needed for each group of five. (Instructions for making a set of squares may be found in the Appendix on page 584.) Approximately one hour is needed for the exercise. The procedure for the coordinator is as follows:

1. Introduce the exercise as one focusing on how goals are defined by members of a group. State that it will consist of completing a group task involving a puzzle.
2. Hand out the observation instructions to the observers. Within each group, give each participant an instruction sheet and an envelope containing pieces of the puzzle (see the directions for making a set of squares). Half of the groups should receive instructions that they are to act cooperatively and half instructions that they are to act competitively. State that the envelopes are not to be opened until the signal is given. Review the instructions with each group in such a way that cooperative groups do not hear the instructions to the competitive groups and vice versa. Ask if the observers understand their role.
3. Give the signal to begin. The groups are to work until all of them have solved the puzzle. Each group should be carefully timed by its observers. If a group becomes deadlocked for more than twenty-five minutes, this phase of the exercise should be ended.
4. Collect the observation sheets and record the information in the table below. While you are doing this the groups should pair off, a cooperative group with a competitive group, and share and discuss their instructions and experiences with each other. Group observers are to participate fully in this discussion. By the end of the discussion, the groups should have recorded their conclusions about the differences between working in a cooperatively oriented and a competitively oriented problem-solving group.
5. Share the results of the discussions among all the groups. Then present the information gathered by the observers. Using the material in the following section on goal structures, define cooperation and competition and discuss the impact of goal structures on group functioning and effectiveness.

You may conduct this exercise with only one group by leaving out the instructions about cooperative and competitive orientations and the comparison between cooperative and competitive groups. The issue of goal structure can still be discussed profitably.

BROKEN SQUARES EXERCISE: INSTRUCTIONS TO EACH MEMBER OF THE COOPERATIVE GROUP

Each member of your group has an envelope containing pieces of cardboard for forming squares. When the signal is given to begin, the task of the group is to form one square in front of each member. Only parts of the pieces for forming the five squares are in each envelope. The exercise has two goals: your individual goal of forming a square in front of yourself as fast as possible and the group's goal of having squares formed in front of every member as fast as possible. The individual goal is accomplished when you have a completed square in front of you. The group goal is accomplished when all group members have completed squares in front of them.

You are to role play a member of a group whose members are all highly cooperative. To you the group goal is far more important than the individual goal. Your job is to cooperate with the other group members as much as possible in order to accomplish the group goal in the shortest period of time possible. To you the other group members are your partners, and you are concerned with helping them put together a completed square. All members of your group have received the same instructions.

The rules for the exercise are as follows:

1. No talking, pointing, or any other kind of communication is allowed among the five members of your group.
2. No person may ask another member for a piece of the puzzle or in any way signal that another person is to give him or her a puzzle piece.
3. Members may give puzzle pieces to other members.
4. Members may not throw their pieces into the center for others to take; they have to give the pieces directly to one person.
5. Anyone may give away all the pieces of his or her puzzle, even if he or she has already formed a square.
6. Part of the role of the observers is to enforce these rules.

BROKEN SQUARES EXERCISE: INSTRUCTIONS TO EACH MEMBER OF THE COMPETITIVE GROUP

Every person in this group has an envelope that contains pieces of cardboard for forming squares. When the signal is given to begin, your task is to form a square in front of you. Only parts of the pieces for forming the five squares are in each envelope. The exercise has two goals: your individual goal of forming a square in front of you as fast as possible and the group's goal of forming squares in front of every member as fast as possible. The individual goal is accomplished when you have a completed square in front of you. The group goal is accomplished when all group members have completed squares in front of them.

You are to role play a member of a group whose members are all highly competitive. To you the individual goal is far more important than the group goal. Your job is to compete with the other group members to see who can get a complete square in front of himself or herself first. At the end of the exercise group members will be ranked on the basis

Data from Observation Sheets

	Cooperative	Competitive
Number of groups completing the task		
Time for task completion		
Number of times a member gave away a puzzle piece		
Number of times a member took a puzzle piece		
Number of members who cut themselves off from others		
Cooperative behaviors		
Competitive behaviors		

of their speed in completing their square. The member finishing first will be labeled the best person in the group, the person finishing second will be labeled the second best person in the group, and so on, with the last person finishing being labeled the worst person in the group. The other group members are your competitors, and you are concerned with completing your square before they do. If you complete your square and then decide to give a piece of it away, you lose your previous rank in terms of the order of members completing their squares and must start over. All members of your group have received the same instructions.

The rules for the exercise are as follows:

1. No talking, pointing, or any other kind of communicating is allowed among the five members of your group.
2. No person may ask another member for a piece of the puzzle or in any way signal that another person is to give him or her a puzzle piece.
3. Members may give puzzle pieces to other members.
4. Members may not throw their pieces into the center for others to take; they have to give the pieces directly to one person.
5. Part of the role of the observers is to enforce these rules.

BROKEN SQUARES EXERCISE: INSTRUCTIONS FOR OBSERVERS

Your job is part observer, part recorder, and part rule enforcer. Do your best to strictly enforce the rules on the instruction sheet for participants. Then observe and record as accurately as possible the items listed below. The information you record will be used in a discussion of the results of the exercise.

1. Did the group complete the task? _____ Yes _____ No
2. How long did it take the group to complete the task? _____ minutes, _____ seconds
3.

Number of times a group member took a puzzle piece from another member:	Number of times a group member gave a puzzle piece to another member:

4. Number of members who finished their square and then divorced themselves from the struggles of the rest of the group: _____
5. Were there any critical turning points at which cooperation or competition increased?

_____

_____

_____

_____

6. What behaviors in the group showed cooperativeness or competitiveness?

_____

_____

_____

_____

3.7 Cooperative, Competitive, and Individualistic Goal Structures

The purposes of this exercise are (a) to provide an experiential definition of the three goal structures and (b) to direct participants' attention to the contrasting patterns of interaction created by these three structures. (The correct answers are in the Appendix on page 585.) The procedure for the coordinator is as follows:

1. Assign participants to heterogeneous groups of three.
2. Conduct a competitive task experience as follows:
    a. State that the members of each triad are to compete to see who is best in identifying how many squares are in a certain geometric figure. The criterion for winning is simply to identify more correct squares than the other two triad members. Ask the participants to turn their square figure right side up, and tell them to begin.
    b. At the end of four or five minutes, instruct the participants to stop. Ask them to determine who is the winner of each triad, ask the winners to stand, and then have everyone applaud.
    c. Tell the participants to turn away from their triad and, working by themselves, write down (1) how they felt during the competition and (2) what they noticed during the competition. Give them another three or four minutes to do this.
3. Conduct an individualistic task experience as follows:
    a. State that participants are to work individualistically to find as many two-sided figures in a geometric figure as they can. All participants who find 95% of the biangles will receive an evaluation of "excellent," all those who find 90% will receive an evaluation of "good," and so forth. Tell the participants to turn their biangles right side up and begin.
    b. At the end of four or five minutes, ask the participants to stop. Then announce the number of biangles in the figure. Ask the participants to leave their triad and, working

Goal Structure and Interaction Among Group Members

	Goal Structures		
	Cooperative	Competitive	Individualistic
Interaction			
Communication			
Facilitation of others' efforts			
Peer influence			
Utilization of others' resources			
Divergent thinking			
Emotional involvement in task			
Acceptance and support among members			
Trust among members			
Conflict management			
Division of labor			
Fear of failure			

by themselves, describe (1) how they felt and (2) what they noticed during this task. Give them another three or four minutes to do this.

4. Conduct a cooperative task experience as follows:

   a. State that the participants are to re-form their triads and work as a group to identify as many triangles in a geometric figure as they can, making sure that all members of the triad can correctly identify all the triangles. When they are finished, the members of each triad should sign the group's paper to indicate their agreement with the group's answer. All members of the groups finding 95% of the triangles will receive an evaluation of "excellent," all members of the groups finding 90% of the triangles will receive an evaluation of "good," and so forth. Tell the participants to turn their triangle figures right side up and begin.

   b. At the end of nine or ten minutes, tell the participants to stop. Inform them of the number of triangles in the figure. Then ask them to turn away from their triad and, working by themselves, write down (1) how they felt and (2) what they noticed during the cooperative task. Give the participants four minutes to do this.

5. Instruct the participants to share their reactions to the three types of task situations with the other members of their triad. Give them ten or twelve minutes to do so. Then sample the reactions of the triads in a class discussion. Ask the participants to draw conclusions about the reactions of the triads to the three task experiences.

6. Instruct the triads to fill out the table on page 86 on the basis of their experiences in the three goal structures and the comments made by the other triads. In the spaces provided, they should summarize their observations of the interaction that occurred in three task situations.

7. Review with the entire class the conceptual definitions of the three goal structures and discuss their views of the impact of each of these structures on group functioning and productivity.

Goal Structure Exercise: Squares

How did I feel?
What did I notice?

Goal Structure Exercise: Biangles

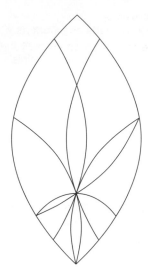

How did I feel?
What did I notice?

Goal Structure Exercise: Triangles

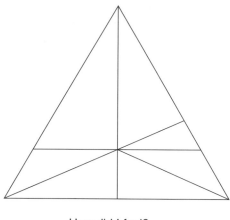

How did I feel?
What did I notice?

EXERCISE 3.8 *Subsistence*

The purpose of this exercise is to observe how unequal resources affect the development of cooperation or competition within a group. The exercise simulates the effects of poverty and affluence in a life-and-death situation. The procedure is as follows:

1. Form groups of seven. One member should volunteer to be the recorder, and another member should volunteer to be the observer. Each group should have five participants, one recorder, and one observer.
2. To play the game contained in this exercise, the group needs a pack of blank 3 × 5-inch index cards to serve as food cards. The group also needs a pack of hunting and gathering cards. Each card should have one of the statements listed on pages 91–92 written on it.
3. The basic procedure of the game is as follows:
   a. Each participant receives three food cards.
   b. The recorder shuffles the hunting and gathering cards and places them in the center of the group.
   c. Each participant draws a card in turn (going counterclockwise), reads it to the group, and receives from or gives to the recorder the required number of food cards.
   d. The day's hunting and gathering is over when every participant has drawn one card. Participants may give any number of food cards to each other. At the end of the day they must give one food card to the recorder. Failure to do so results in death by starvation and dropping out of the game.

    e. After seven rounds the week's hunting and gathering is over. Points are awarded to group members.

    f. The game is played for a minimum of two weeks.

4. The role of the observer is to record the frequency of the behaviors listed on the observation sheet. The frequencies are reported to the group during the concluding group discussion.

5. The role of the recorder is to

    a. Read the Subsistence Instruction Sheet to the group.

    b. Review the rules with participants.

    c. Give each participant three food cards.

    d. Shuffle the hunting and gathering cards and place them in the center of the group.

    e. Distribute and collect food cards on the basis of the cards drawn.

    f. At the end of each round, collect one food card from each participant.

    g. Ensure that each participant announces how many food cards he or she has at the end of each round.

    h. Announce how many participants starved to death and who has the most food cards at the end of each week (seven rounds).

6. When the game is over, discuss the following questions:

    a. Who survived and who died?

    b. How was a cooperative or a competitive strategy decided on?

    c. How did participants feel about the impending death by starvation?

    d. How did the dead feel when they knew others could have saved them?

    e. How did the survivors feel when others died when they had extra food cards?

    f. Who organized the group to create a just distribution of food?

    g. What real-life situations parallel this exercise?

SUBSISTENCE INSTRUCTION SHEET

A severe drought has devastated your world. Because food is so scarce, you have banded together into a hunting and gathering group. It is more efficient for several people to coordinate their hunting and gathering so that more territory may be covered in any one day. There are five members of your hunting and gathering group. The food cards in your hands represent all you have left of your dwindling food supply. Because you are already weakened by hunger, you must eat at the end of each day (round) or die. At that time, you must give up one food card. When you are out of cards, you will die of starvation. A member who does not have one food card at the end of a day (round) is considered to be dead and can no longer participate in the group. Members with only one food card may not talk. Only members with two or more food cards may discuss their situation and converse with each other. You may give food cards to each other whenever you wish to do so.

RULES FOR SUBSISTENCE EXERCISE

1. The game begins when the recorder gives all participants three food cards, shuffles the hunting and gathering cards, and places them in the center of the group.

2. The purpose of the game is to gain points. You receive eight points if at the end of the week of hunting and gathering (seven rounds) you have more food cards than does any other participant in your group. If no one in your group has starved at the end of the week of hunting and gathering, all participants receive five points.

3. The game is played for a minimum of two weeks. At the beginning of each week, all participants begin with three food cards and with all five participants alive.

4. You draw one card during each round. You read it aloud to the group and receive from or give to the recorder the number of food cards indicated.
5. During a round you may give food cards to other participants if you wish to.
6. All participants read the hunting and gathering cards aloud. Only those with two or more food cards, however, may discuss the game with each other. Participants with one or no food cards must be silent.
7. At the end of each round, participants hold up their food cards and announce to the group how many food cards they have.
8. At the end of each round, participants give one food card each to the recorder. This symbolizes the food eaten during the day to stay alive.
9. If a participant cannot give a food card to the recorder at the end of a round, the participant dies of starvation and is excluded from further rounds during that week.
10. At the end of each week of hunting and gathering (seven rounds) the recorder announces who has the most food cards and how many participants starved to death. Points are then awarded.

Subsistence Record Sheet

Name	Round 1	Round 2	Round 3	Round 4	Round 5	Round 6	Round 7

Subsistence Observation Sheet

	Round 1	Round 2	Round 3	Round 4	Round 5	Round 6	Round 7
Number of cards given away							
Number of cards taken away							
Number of people starved							
Cooperative strategy suggested							
Competitive comment							
Other							
Other							

SUBSISTENCE EXERCISE: HUNTING AND GATHERING CARDS

You found no food today.

You made a beautiful shot at what looked like a deer, but it turned out to be a strangely shaped rock. You got no food today.

You shot a bird. You get one food card from the recorder.

Wild dogs chased you, and to get away you threw them one day's food. Give the recorder one food card. If you do not have a food card and if no one will give you one, you die of starvation.

You fell asleep and slept all day. You got no food today.

Excellent shot. You killed a deer worth two days' food. You get two food cards from the recorder.

You met a member of another group and fell in love. To impress your new love, you gave him or her one day's food. Give the recorder one food card. If you do not have a food card, and no one will give you one, you die of starvation.

You shot a snake. You get a food card from the recorder.

Army ants chased you, and to get away you threw them one day's food. Give the recorder one food card. If you do not have a food card and if no one will give you one, you die of starvation.

You shot a lizard. You get one food card from the recorder.

While running away from a lion, you took refuge in a peach tree. You receive one food card from the recorder.

You shot a deer but missed. You got no food today.

Lucky fluke! You shot at a deer and hit a rabbit. You get one food card from the recorder.

While you were hunting, a skunk broke into your hut and ate two days' worth of food. Give two food cards to the recorder. If you do not have two food cards and if no one will give you any, you die of starvation.

While you were hunting, a lion ate you and all your food. Give all your food cards to the recorder and drop out of the game. Since you did not starve, your group's points are not affected. You are reborn the next week.

You found a nest of field mice and hit each one over the head. You get one food card from the recorder.

You found no food today.

You shot a bird. You get one food card from the recorder.

You found a berry bush. Berries are in season. You get one food card from the recorder.

Lucky fluke! You shot at a wild pig and hit a rabbit. You get one food card from the recorder.

Excellent shot. You aimed at a bird you thought was standing on a rock. Your arrow hit the rock, which turned out to be a wild pig. You get two food cards from the recorder.

You found a deer, but a bear scared it away before you could shoot at it. You got no food today.

Excellent shot. Just as you shot at a deer, a wild pig ran in the way and got killed. You receive two food cards from the recorder.

You shot a rabbit. You get one food card from the recorder.

You found no food today. It was probably too hot for anything to be out and around.

You found some wild carrots. You get one food card from the recorder.

You found an apple tree. Birds had eaten almost all of the apples. You get one food card from the recorder.

Excellent shot. You killed a wild pig. You get two food cards from the recorder.

While hunting, you accidentally stepped on a snake and killed it. You receive one food card from the recorder.

> On your way home you fell into a swamp. You lost two days' worth of food to a hungry crocodile. Give two food cards to the recorder. If you do not have them and if no one will give them to you, you die of starvation.
>
> Excellent shot. You killed a deer. You get two food cards from the recorder.
>
> You found some wild lettuce. You get one food card from the recorder.
>
> You shot a rabbit. You get one food card from the recorder.
>
> You shot a bird. You get one food card from the recorder.
>
> You shot an aardvark. You get one food card from the recorder.
>
> While hunting, you found a berry bush. Berries are in season. You get one food card from the recorder.
>
> Best of luck! You found a deer with a broken leg. You killed it with your stone club. You get two food cards from the recorder.
>
> You looked and looked and looked but found no food today.
>
> You shot at a rabbit, but it zigged instead of zagged. You got no food today.
>
> You walked for miles and found nothing to gather or shoot at. You got no food today.

GROUP GOALS AND SOCIAL INTERDEPENDENCE AMONG MEMBERS

Theoretical Orientations

Two are better than one, because they have a good reward for their toil. For if they fall, one will lift up his fellow; but woe to him who is alone when he falls and has not another to lift him up. . . . And though a man might prevail against one who is alone, two will withstand him. A threefold cord is not quickly broken.

Ecclesiastes 4:9–12

Sandy Koufax was one of the greatest pitchers in the history of baseball. He was perhaps the only major-league pitcher whose fastball could be heard to hum. Opposing batters, instead of talking and joking in the dugout, would sit quietly and listen for Koufax's fastball to hum. When it was their turn to bat, they were already intimidated. There was, however, a simple way for Koufax's genius to have been negated: by making the first author of this book his catcher. To be great, a pitcher needs an outstanding catcher (Koufax's great partner was Johnny Roseboro). David is such an unskilled catcher that Koufax would have had to throw the ball much more slowly in order for David to catch it. This would have deprived Koufax of his greatest weapon. Placing Frank at a key defensive position in the infield or outfield, furthermore, would have seriously affected Koufax's success. Sandy Koufax was not a great pitcher on his own. Only as part of a team could Koufax achieve greatness. In baseball and in every other group, it takes a cooperative effort. Extraordinary achievement comes from a cooperative group, not from the individualistic or competitive efforts of isolated individuals.

Understanding the nature of cooperative, competitive, and individualistic efforts begins with theory. At least three general theoretical perspectives have guided research on cooperation—cognitive-developmental, behavioral, and social interdependence (see Figure 3.1). The *cognitive-developmental perspective* is largely based on the theories of Piaget and Vygotsky. The work of Piaget and related theorists is based on the premise

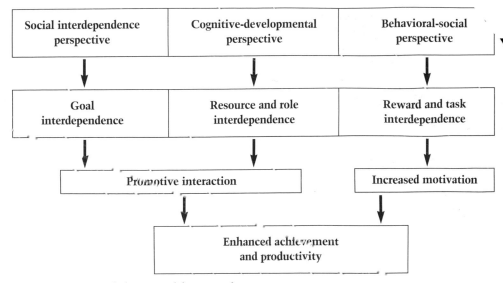

Figure 3.1   General theoretical framework.
Source: D. W. Johnson and R. Johnson, *Cooperation and competition: Theory and research* (Edina, MN; Interaction Book Company, 1989). Reprinted with permission of the authors.

that when individuals cooperate on the environment, sociocognitive conflict occurs that creates cognitive disequilibrium, which in turn stimulates perspective-taking ability and cognitive development. The work of Vygotsky and related theorists is based on the premise that knowledge is social, constructed from cooperative efforts to learn, understand, and solve problems. The *behavioral theory perspective* focuses on the impact of group reinforcers and rewards on productivity. Skinner focused on group contingencies, Bandura focused on imitation, and Homans as well as Thibaut and Kelley focused on the balance of rewards and costs in social exchange among interdependent individuals. Although the cognitive-developmental and behavioral theoretical orientations have their followings, by far the most important theory dealing with cooperation and competition is **social interdependence theory.**

Social Interdependence Theory

Theorizing on *social interdependence* began in the early 1900s, when one of the founders of the Gestalt school of psychology, Kurt Koffka, proposed that groups are dynamic wholes in which the interdependence among members can vary. One of his colleagues, Kurt Lewin, refined Koffka's notions in the 1920s and 1930s, stating that (a) the essence of a group is the interdependence among members (created by common goals) that results in the group being a "dynamic whole," so that a change in the state of any member or subgroup changes the state of any other member or subgroup, and that (b) an intrinsic state of tension within group members motivates movement toward the accomplishment of the desired common goals.

Lewin's students and colleagues conducted research indicating that it is the drive for goal accomplishment that motivates cooperative and competitive behavior. Ovisanki

emonstrated that interrupted tasks were almost always resumed when the sub-
e left free to do as they wished. Lissner (1933), Mahler (1933), and many others
vestigated the conditions under which one activity can substitute for and, hence, release the tension connected with another, interrupted activity. The substitute value was
measured by the amount of decrease in resumption or recall of the interrupted original
activity after a substitute activity had been completed. Helen Block Lewis (Lewis, 1944;
Lewis & Franklin, 1944) demonstrated that cooperative work that is interrupted and not
completed can lead to a persisting force to recall that is not much different from the
pressure to recall induced by interrupted individual work. In other words, if a collabo-
rator completes the original activity, his or her actions substitute for one's own, and the
tension induced by being interrupted before the task was completed is released. From
Lewin's field theory, and from the research of these and other members and colleagues
of Lewin, it may be concluded that it is the drive for goal accomplishment that motivates cooperative, competitive, and individualistic behavior.

In the late 1940s, one of Lewin's graduate students, Morton Deutsch, extended
Lewin's reasoning about social interdependence and formulated a theory of cooperation and competition (Deutsch, 1949a, 1962). Deutsch conceptualized two types of social
interdependence—cooperative and competitive—and individualistic efforts as the absence
of interdependence. Deutsch was born in 1920, graduated from City College of New York
in 1939, and obtained a master's degree from the University of Pennsylvania in 1940. After
serving in the United States Air Force from 1942 to 1945, he entered the doctoral program
in social psychology at MIT to study with Kurt Lewin. Deutsch has received a variety of
professional rewards during his career, including the prestigious Kurt Lewin Memorial
Award for contributions to the solution of social problems through theory and research
and the Gordon Allport Memorial Award for contributions to constructive intergroup relations through theory and research. Following in Lewin's footsteps, Deutsch has become
noted as an outstanding social psychologist because of his commitment to the development of theory about complex social issues, his ability to find ways to study these issues
in a laboratory setting, and his dedication to the solution of social problems. Deutsch's
(1949a) original theory has served as a major conceptual structure for this area of inquiry
for the past forty-five years. His theory and research pioneered future work on social interdependence. Since his initial theorizing, Deutsch has extended his theory of social interdependence to include trust, conflict resolution, and systems of distributive justice. The
progression of his theorizing over the past forty years is one of the seminal works in
the history of psychology. Deutsch's theory was extended and applied to education by the
authors at the University of Minnesota (Johnson, 1970; Johnson & Johnson, 1974, 1989).
Our work has been extended and applied to business and industry (Tjosvold, 1986).

Social interdependence exists when individuals share common goals and each individual's outcomes are affected by the actions of the others (Deutsch, 1949a, 1962;
Johnson & Johnson, 1989). It may be differentiated from **social dependence** (i.e., the outcomes of one person are affected by the actions of a second person but not vice versa)
and **social independence** (i.e., individuals' outcomes are unaffected by each other's actions). There are two types of social interdependence: cooperative and competitive. The
absence of social interdependence and dependence results in individualistic efforts.

There are three ways in which the actions of individuals may be related to the actions of others. One's actions may promote the success of others, obstruct the success

Morton Deutsch

of others, or have no effect at all on the success or failure of others. In other words, individuals may be (Deutsch, 1949a, 1962; Johnson & Johnson, 1989):

1. Working together cooperatively to accomplish shared learning goals. When a situation is structured **cooperatively,** individuals' goal achievements are positively correlated; individuals perceive that they can reach their goals if and only if the others in the group also reach their goals. Thus, individuals seek outcomes that are beneficial to all those with whom they are cooperatively linked.

2. Working against each other to achieve a goal that only one or a few can attain. When a situation is structured **competitively,** individuals work against each other to achieve a goal that only one or a few can attain. Individuals' goal achievements are negatively correlated; each individual perceives that when one person achieves his or her goal, all others with whom he or she is competitively linked fail to achieve their goals. Thus, individuals seek an outcome that is personally beneficial but detrimental to all others in the situation.

3. Working by oneself to accomplish goals unrelated to the goals of others. When a situation is structured **individualistically,** there is no correlation among participants' goal attainments. Each individual perceives that he or she can reach his or her goal regardless of whether other individuals attain or do not attain their goals. Thus, individuals seek an outcome that is personally beneficial without concern for the outcomes of others.

The basic premise of social interdependence theory is that the type of interdependence structured in a situation determines how individuals interact with each other, which, in

Table 3.2 **Social Interdependence Theory**

Process	Cooperative	Competitive	Individualistic
Interdependence	Positive	Negative	None
Interaction pattern	Promotive	Oppositional	None
Outcome 1	High effort to achieve	Low effort to achieve	Low effort to achieve
Outcome 2	Positive relationships	Negative relationships	No relationships
Outcome 3	Psychological health	Psychological illness	Psychological pathology

turn, determines outcomes (see Table 3.2). Positive interdependence tends to result in promotive interaction, negative interdependence tends to result in oppositional or contrary interaction, and no interdependence results in an absence of interaction. In cooperative situations the actions of participants substitute for each other, participants respond positively to each other's effective actions, and members are open to influence by each other. In competitive situations the actions of participants do not substitute for each other, participants respond negatively to each other's effective actions, and they refuse to be influenced by each other. When there is no interaction, there is little substitutability, emotional response, or influence. The relationship between the type of social interdependence and the interaction pattern it elicits is assumed to be bidirectional. Each may cause the other.

Social interdependence to humans is like water to fish. Because we are immersed in it, social interdependence can escape our notice. Whether it is quite personal or so impersonal that we are barely aware of it, we regularly underestimate the role that social interdependence plays in human life. Because we cannot imagine its absence, we often do not consider its presence.

Interaction Patterns

Between 1898 and 1989, over 575 experimental and 100 correlational studies were conducted by a wide variety of researchers in different decades with subjects of different ages, in different subject areas, and in different settings (see Johnson & Johnson, 1989, for a complete list of these studies). One of the issues addressed by this research is the types of interaction patterns found within cooperative, competitive, and individualistic situations.

Positive interdependence creates promotive interaction. **Promotive interaction** occurs as individuals encourage and facilitate each other's efforts to reach the group's goals (such as maximizing each member's learning). Group members promote each other's success by (Johnson & Johnson, 1989):

1. Giving and receiving assistance (both task-related and personal).
2. Exchanging resources and information. Group members seek information and other resources from each other, comprehend information accurately and without bias, and make optimal use of the information provided. There are a number of beneficial results from (a) orally explaining, elaborating, and summarizing information and (b) teaching one's knowledge to others. Explaining and teaching increase the degree to which group members cognitively process and organize information, engage in higher-level reasoning, attain insights, and become personally committed to achieving. Listening critically to the explanations of groupmates provides the opportunity to utilize others' resources.

3. Giving and receiving feedback on taskwork and teamwork behaviors. In cooperative groups, members monitor each other's efforts, give immediate feedback on performance, and, when needed, give each other assistance.

4. Challenging each other's reasoning. Intellectual controversy promotes curiosity, motivation to learn, reconceptualization of what one knows, higher-quality decision making, greater insight into the problem being considered, and many other important benefits (Johnson & Johnson, 1979, 1995b).

5. Advocating increased efforts to achieve. Encouraging others to achieve increases one's own commitment to do so.

6. Mutually influencing each other's reasoning and behavior. Group members actively seek to influence and be influenced by each other. If a member has a better way to complete the task, groupmates usually quickly adopt it.

7. Engaging in the interpersonal and small group skills needed for effective teamwork.

8. Determining how effectively group members are working together and how the group's effectiveness can be continuously improved.

Types of Positive Interdependence

Positive Goal Interdependence: Students perceive that they can achieve their learning goals if and only if all the members of their group also attain their goals. Members of a learning group have a mutual set of goals that they are all striving to accomplish.

Positive Celebration/Reward Interdependence: The group celebrates its success. A joint reward is given for successful group work and members' efforts to achieve.

Positive Resource Interdependence: Each member has only a portion of the information, resources, or materials necessary for the task to be completed, and all members' resources have to be combined in order for the group to achieve its goal.

Positive Role Interdependence: Each member is assigned complementary and interconnected roles that specify responsibilities that the group needs in order to complete a joint task.

Positive Identity Interdependence: The group establishes a mutual identity through a name, flag, motto, or song.

Environmental Interdependence: Group members are bound together by the physical environment in some way. An example is putting people in a specific area in which to work.

Positive Fantasy Interdependence: A task is given that requires members to imagine that they are in a life-or-death situation and must collaborate in order to survive.

Positive Task Interdependence: A division of labor is created so that the actions of one group member have to be completed if the next team member is to complete his or her actions.

Positive Outside Enemy Interdependence: Groups are placed in competition with each other. Group members then feel interdependent as they strive to beat the other groups and win the competition.

Negative interdependence typically results in oppositional interaction. **Opposi-tional interaction** occurs as individuals discourage and obstruct each other's efforts to achieve. Individuals focus both on increasing their own success and on preventing any-one else from being more successful than they are. No interaction exists when indi-viduals work independently, without any interaction or interchange with each other. Individuals focus only on increasing their own success and ignore as irrelevant the ef-forts of others. Each of these interaction patterns creates different outcomes.

Promotive interaction tends to result in a wide variety of outcomes that may be divided into the categories of high effort to achieve, positive relationships, and psy-chological health. Oppositional interaction tends to result in low effort to achieve by most students, negative relationships, and low psychological health, and no interac-tion tends to result in low effort to achieve, an absence of relationships, and psycho-logical pathology.

OUTCOMES OF SOCIAL INTERDEPENDENCE

The fundamental facts that brought about cooperation, society, and civiliza-tion and transformed the animal man into a human being are the facts that work performed under the division of labor is more productive than isolated work and that man's reason is capable of recognizing this truth. But for these facts men would have forever remained deadly foes of one another, irreconcilable rivals in their endeavors to secure a portion of the scarce supply of means of sustenance provided by Nature. Each man would have been forced to view all other men as his enemies; his craving for the satis-faction of his own appetites would have brought him into an implacable conflict with all his neighbors. No sympathy could possibly develop under such a state of affairs. . . .We may call consciousness of kind, sense of com-munity, or sense of belonging together the acknowledgment of fact that all other human beings are potential collaborators in the struggle for survival because they are capable of recognizing the mutual benefits of cooperation.

Ludwig Von Mises (1949)

Within Yosemite National Park lies the famous Half Dome Mountain. The Half Dome is famous for its 2,000 feet of soaring, sheer cliff wall. Unusually beautiful to the ob-server, and considered unclimbable for years, the Half Dome's northwest face was first scaled in 1957 by Royal Robbins and two companions. This incredibly dangerous climb took five days, with Robbins and his companions spending four nights on the cliff, sleep-ing in ropes with nothing below their bodies but air. Even today, the northwest face is a death trap to all but the finest and most skilled rock climbers. Far above the ground, moving slowly up the rock face, are two climbers.

The two climbers are motivated by a shared vision of successfully climbing the northwest face. As they move up the cliff they are attached to each other by a rope (the lifeline). As one member climbs (the lead climber), the other (the belayer) ensures that the two have a safe anchor and that he or she can catch the climber if the climber falls. The lead climber does not begin climbing until the belayer says "go." Then the lead climber advances, puts in a piton, slips in the rope, and continues to advance. The pitons help the belayer catch the climber if the climber falls, and they mark the path up the cliff. The lifeline (i.e., rope) goes from the belayer through the pitons up to the climber. When the lead climber has completed the first leg of the climb, he or she becomes the belayer and the other member of the team begins to climb. The pitons placed by the lead climber serve to guide and support the second member of the team up the rock face. The second member advances up the route marked out by the first member until the first leg is completed and then leapfrogs and becomes the lead climber for the second leg of the climb. The roles of lead climber and belayer are alternated until the summit is reached.

All human life is like mountain climbing. The human species seems to have a *cooperation imperative:* We desire and seek out opportunities to operate jointly with others to achieve mutual goals. We are attached to others through a variety of "lifelines," and we alternate supporting and leading others to ensure a better life for ourselves, our colleagues and neighbors, our children, and all generations to follow. Cooperation is an inescapable fact of life. From cradle to grave we cooperate with others. Each day, from our first waking moment until sleep overtakes us again, we cooperate within family, work, leisure activities, and community by working jointly to achieve mutual goals. Throughout history, people have come together to (a) accomplish feats that any one of them could not achieve alone and (b) share their joys and sorrows. From conceiving a child to sending a rocket to the moon, our successes require cooperation among individuals. The cooperation may be less clear than it is in climbing up a cliff, but it exists nonetheless.

Considerable research based on Deutsch's classic work on cooperation and competition has been conducted during the past thirty years. Working together to get the job done can have profound effects. In trying to understand how cooperation works, and in continually refining our understanding of how to implement cooperation most effectively, we have (a) reviewed over 550 experimental and over 100 correlational research studies conducted during the last 100 years comparing cooperative, competitive, and individualistic efforts and (b) conducted a thirty-five-year program of research that has resulted in over eighty-five published studies. The numerous variables that are affected by cooperation may be subsumed within three broad interrelated outcomes (see Figure 3.2) (Johnson & Johnson, 1989):

1. Effort exerted to achieve.
2. Quality of relationships among participants.
3. Participants' psychological adjustment and social competence.

If research is to have an impact on theory and practice, it must be summarized and communicated in a complete, objective, impartial, and unbiased way. In an age of information explosion, there is considerable danger that theories will be formulated on the basis of small and nonrepresentative samples of available knowledge, thereby resulting in fallacious conclusions that in turn lead to mistaken practices. A quantitative reviewing procedure, such as meta-analysis, allows for more definitive and robust conclusions. A **meta-analysis** is a method of statistically combining the results of a set of independent studies that test the same hypothesis and using inferential statistics to draw conclusions about the overall result of the studies. The essential purpose of a meta-analysis is to summarize a set of related research studies so that the size of the effect of the independent variable on the dependent variable is known.

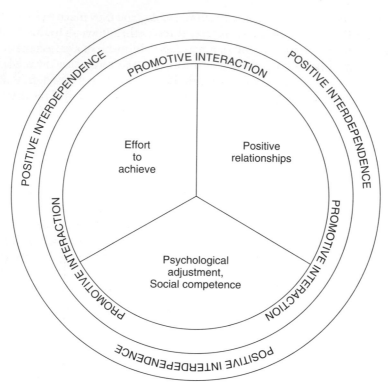

Figure 3.2 Outcomes of cooperation.
Source: D. W. Johnson & R. T. Johnson, *Cooperation and competition: Theory and research* (Edina, MN: Interaction Book Company, 1989). Reprinted with permission of the authors.

Effort to Achieve and Produce

Two heads are better than one.

John Heywood

The investigation of the relative impact of the three types of social interdependence on achievement is the oldest research tradition within American social psychology. Between 1898 and 1989, researchers conducted over 375 experimental studies, with over 1,700 findings on social interdependence and productivity and achievement (Johnson & Johnson, 1989). That does not count the research on social facilitation and other related areas where implicit competition may be found. Because research participants have varied widely in terms of sex, economic class, age, and cultural background, because a wide variety of research tasks and measures of the dependent variables have been used, and because the research has been conducted by many different researchers with markedly different orientations working in different settings and in different decades, the overall body of research on social interdependence has considerable generalizability.

A meta-analysis of all studies (Johnson & Johnson, 1989) found that the average person cooperating performed at about two-thirds of a standard deviation above the average person learning in a competitive (effect size = 0.67) or individualistic situation (effect size = 0.64) (see Table 3.3). Not all the research, however, has been carefully conducted. The methodological shortcomings found in many research studies may significantly reduce the certainty of the conclusion that cooperative efforts produce higher achievement than do competitive or individualistic efforts. When only studies with high internal validity were included in the analysis, the effect sizes were 0.88 and 0.61, respectively. Further analyses revealed that the results held constant when group measures of productivity were included as well as individual measures, for short-term as well as long-term studies, and when symbolic as well as tangible rewards were used.

A number of the studies operationally defined cooperation in a way that included elements of competition and individualistic work. The original jigsaw studies, for example, operationalized cooperative learning as a combination of positive resource interdependence and an individualistic reward structure (Aronson, Blaney, Stephan, Sikes, & Snapp, 1978). Teams-Games-Tournaments (TGT; DeVries & Edwards, 1974) and Student-Team-Achievement Divisions (STAD; Slavin, 1986) operationalized cooperative learning as a combination of in-group cooperation and intergroup competition, and Team-Assisted-Individualization (TAI; Slavin, 1986) is a mixture of cooperative and individualistic learning. When such "mixed" operationalizations were compared with "pure" operationalizations, the effect sizes for the cooperative versus competitive comparison were 0.45 and 0.74, respectively, $t(37) = 1.60$, $p < 0.06$ (Johnson & Johnson,

Table 3.3 **Mean Effect Sizes for Impact of Social Interdependence on Dependent Variables**

Conditions	Achievement	Interpersonal Attraction	Social Support	Self-Esteem
Total Studies				
Coop vs. Comp	0.67	0.67	0.62	0.58
Coop vs. Ind	0.64	0.60	0.70	0.44
Comp vs. Ind	0.30	0.08	−0.13	−0.23
High-Quality Studies				
Coop vs. Comp	0.88	0.82	0.83	0.67
Coop vs. Ind	0.61	0.62	0.72	0.45
Comp vs. Ind	0.07	0.27	−0.13	−0.25
Mixed Operationalizations				
Coop vs. Comp	0.40	0.46	0.45	0.33
Coop vs. Ind	0.42	0.36	0.02	0.22
Pure Operationalizations				
Coop vs. Comp	0.71	0.79	0.73	0.74
Coop vs. Ind	0.65	0.66	0.77	0.51

Note: Coop = Cooperation, Comp = Competition, Ind = Individualistic

Source: D. W. Johnson and R. Johnson, *Cooperation and competition: Theory and research* (Edina, MN: Interaction Book Company, 1989).

1989). The effect sizes for the cooperative versus individualistic comparisons were 0.13 and 0.61, respectively, $t(10) = 1.64$, $p < 0.07$.

Besides higher achievement and greater retention, cooperation, compared with competitive or individualistic efforts, tends to result in more (Johnson & Johnson, 1989):

1. Willingness to take on difficult tasks and persist, despite difficulties, in working toward goal accomplishment. In addition, there is intrinsic motivation, high expectations for success, high incentive to achieve based on mutual benefit, high epistemic curiosity and continuing interest in learning, and high commitment to achieve.
2. Long-term retention of what is learned.
3. Higher-level reasoning, critical thinking, and metacognitive thought. Group members should be able to "sort sense from nonsense" and have the critical-thinking abilities of grasping information, examining it, evaluating it for soundness, and applying it appropriately. Cooperative situations promote a greater use of higher-level reasoning strategies and critical thinking than do competitive or individualistic situations. Cooperative experiences promote more frequent insight into and use of higher-level cognitive and moral reasoning strategies than do competitive or individualistic experiences (effect sizes = 0.93 and 0.97, respectively).
4. Creative thinking (process gain). **Process gain** occurs when new ideas, solutions, or efforts are generated through group interaction that are not generated when persons work individually. In cooperative groups, members more frequently generate new ideas, strategies, and solutions than they would think of on their own.
5. Transfer of learning from one situation to another (group to individual transfer). **Group-to-individual transfer** occurs when individuals who learned within a cooperative group demonstrate mastery on a subsequent test taken individually. What individuals learn in a group today, they are able to do alone tomorrow.
6. Positive attitudes toward the tasks being completed. Cooperative efforts result in more positive attitudes toward the tasks being completed and greater continuing motivation to complete them. The positive attitudes extend to the work experience and the organization as a whole.
7. Time on task. Over thirty studies did in fact measure time on task. They found that cooperators spent more time on task than did competitors (effect size = 0.76) or students working individualistically (effect size = 1.17). Competitors spent more time on task than did students working individualistically (effect size = 0.64). These effect sizes are quite large, indicating that members of cooperative learning groups do seem to spend considerably more time on task than do students working competitively or individualistically.

Because the most credible studies (due to their high methodological quality) and the "pure" operationalizations of cooperative learning produced stronger effects, considerable confidence can be placed in two conclusions about cooperative efforts: They promote more positive cross-ethnic relationships than do competitive or individualistic efforts, and they promote greater effort to achieve than do competitive or individualistic efforts.

Not all research supporting the use of a cooperative goal structure has been experimental. Balderston (1930) conducted a study of group-incentive plans by collecting written descriptions of such plans from a number of companies. In each instance, the pay of all members depended on the productivity of the group as a whole. Balderston found that this method of work doubled the efficiency of the workers, increased their pay about 25%, and reduced their costs substantially compared to the previous situation, in which a flat rate was paid to each individual. The users of group-incentive methods stated that their plans were valuable because they increased cooperation and team spirit among members, reduced monotony on the job, and caused workers to focus on a common goal.

Kurt Lewin often stated, "I always found myself unable to think as a single person." Most efforts to achieve are a personal but social process that requires individuals to cooperate and to construct shared understandings and knowledge. Both competitive and individualistic structures, by isolating individuals from each other, tend to depress achievement and productivity.

Quality of Relationships

A faithful friend is a strong defense, and he that hath found him,
hath found a treasure.

Ecclesiasticus 6:14

We are created not for isolation but for relationships. At heart, we are not a thousand points of separated light but, rather, part of a larger brightness. **Within organizations, caring and committed relationships are not a luxury. They are a necessity.** Organizations increasingly have members who are isolated and unattached to family or peers and members from a variety of ethnic, historical, and cultural backgrounds. Recent national surveys indicate that it is feeling valued, loved, wanted, and respected by others that gives life meaning and purpose, and it is intimate relationships that create happiness. Organizations may focus on building positive relationships among heterogeneous members. There is considerable evidence comparing the impact of cooperative, competitive, and individualistic efforts on interpersonal attraction and social support.

Since 1940, over 180 studies have compared the impact of cooperative, competitive, and individualistic efforts on interpersonal attraction (Johnson & Johnson, 1989). Cooperative efforts, compared with competitive and individualistic experiences, promoted considerable more liking among individuals (effect sizes = 0.66 and 0.62, respectively) (see Table 3.3). The effects sizes were higher for (a) high-quality studies and (b) studies using pure operationalizations of cooperative learning than for studies using mixed operationalizations. The weighted effect sizes for cooperation versus competition and cooperation versus individualistic efforts are 0.65 and 0.64, respectively. When only the methodologically high-quality studies are examined, the effect sizes rise to 0.77 and 0.67. Pure cooperation results in greater effects than do mixtures of cooperative, competitive, and individualistic efforts (cooperative vs. competitive: pure = 0.75 and mixed = 0.48; cooperative vs. individualistic: pure = 0.67 and mixed = 0.36).

Much of the research on interpersonal relationships has been conducted on relationships between white and minority students and between students with and without disabilities (Johnson & Johnson, 1989). There have been over forty experimental studies comparing some combination of cooperative, competitive, and individualistic experiences on cross-ethnic relationships and over forty similar studies on mainstreaming of students with disabilities (Johnson & Johnson, 1989). Their results are consistent. Working cooperatively creates far more positive relationships among diverse and heterogeneous students than does learning competitively or individualistically.

An extension of social interdependence theory is **social judgment theory,** which focuses on relationships among diverse individuals (Johnson & Johnson, 1989). The social judgments individuals make about each other increase or decrease the liking they feel towards each other. Such social judgments are the result of either a process of acceptance or a process of rejection (Johnson & Johnson, 1989). The process of **acceptance** is based on the individuals promoting mutual goal accomplishment as a result of their perceived positive interdependence. The promotive interaction tends to result in frequent, accurate, and open communication; accurate understanding of each other's perspective; inducibility; differentiated, dynamic, and realistic views of each other; high self-esteem; success and productivity; and expectations for positive and productive future interaction. The process of **rejection** results from oppositional or no interaction based on perceptions of negative or no interdependence. Both lead to no or inaccurate communication; egocentrism; resistance to influence; monopolistic, stereotyped, and static views of others; low self-esteem; failure; and expectations of distasteful and unpleasant interaction with others. The processes of acceptance and rejection are self-perpetuating. Any part of the process tends to elicit all the other parts of the process.

The positive relationships among members promoted by cooperative efforts result in a high level of group cohesion. **Group cohesion** may be defined as the mutual attraction among members of a group and the resulting desire to remain in the group. Highly cohesive groups, where members like each other, are characterized by greater ease in setting goals (Festinger, Schachter, & Back, 1950), greater likelihood in achieving those goals (Seashore, 1954; Wolfe & Box, 1988), and greater susceptibility to influence by groupmates (Schachter, Ellertson, McBride, & Gregory, 1951). The impact of group cohesiveness on group performance is stronger for small groups and seems to be driven predominantly by members' commitment to the successful task performance and regulation of their behavior toward that end (Mullen & Cooper, 1994) (see Figure 3.3). Groups become cohesive by formulating and working together on issues that are specific, immediate, and realizable. As cohesiveness increases, absenteeism and turnover of membership decrease, and the following increase: member commitment to group goals, feeling of personal responsibility to the group, willingness to take on difficult tasks, motivation and persistence in working toward goal achievement, satisfaction and morale, willingness to endure pain and frustration on behalf of the group, willingness

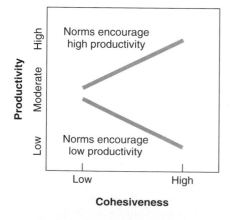

Figure 3.3 The hypothesized link between productivity and cohesiveness.

to defend the group against external criticism or attack, willingness to listen to and be influenced by colleagues, commitment to each other's professional growth and success, and productivity (Johnson & Johnson, 1989; Watson & Johnson, 1972). Cohesiveness within a group, team, department, business, classroom, or school is determined by how well members like each other as people and colleagues.

Positive peer relationships influence the social and cognitive development of students and such attitudes and behaviors as educational aspirations and staying in school (Johnson & Johnson, 1989). Relationships with peers influence what attitudes and values students adopt, whether students become prosocial or antisocial, whether students learn to see situations from a variety of perspectives, the development of autonomy, aspirations for postsecondary education, and whether students learn how to cope with adversity and stress.

Besides liking each other, cooperators give and receive considerable social support, both personally and academically (Johnson & Johnson, 1989). Since the 1940s, more than 106 studies comparing the relative impact of cooperative, competitive, and individualistic efforts on social support have been conducted. Social support may be aimed at enhancing another person's success (task-related social support) or at providing support on a more personal level (personal social support). Cooperative experience promotes greater task-oriented and personal social support than does competitive (effect size = 0.62) or individualistic (effect size = 0.70) experiences. Social support tends to promote achievement and productivity, physical health, psychological health, and successful coping with stress and adversity.

Psychological Adjustment and Social Competence

All for one, one for all.

Alexandre Dumas

The third set of issues researched involve promoting psychological health, self-esteem, and social competencies. **Psychological health** is the ability to develop, maintain, and appropriately modify interdependent relationships with others to succeed in achieving goals (Johnson & Johnson, 1989). To manage social interdependence, individuals must correctly perceive whether interdependence exists and whether it is positive or negative, be motivated accordingly, and act in ways consistent with normative expectations for appropriate behavior within the situation. Four studies have directly measured the relationship between social interdependence and psychological health. The samples studied included suburban high school seniors (Johnson & Norem-Heibeisen, 1977), juvenile and adult prisoners (N. James & Johnson, 1983), step-couples (S. James & Johnson, 1988), and Olympic hockey players (Johnson, Johnson, & Krotee, 1986). The results indicated that (a) working cooperatively with peers and valuing cooperation result in greater psychological health than does competing with peers or working independently and (b) cooperative attitudes are highly correlated with a wide variety of indices of psychological health, competitiveness was in some cases positively and in some cases negatively related to psychological health, and individualistic attitudes were negatively related to a wide variety of indices of psychological health. Cooperativeness is positively related to a number of indices of psychological health, such as emotional maturity, well-adjusted social relations, strong personal identity, ability to cope with adversity, social competencies, and basic trust in and optimism about people. Personal ego strength, self-confidence, independence, and autonomy are all promoted by being involved in cooperative efforts. Individualistic attitudes tend to be related to a number of indices of psychological pathology, such as emotional immaturity, social maladjustment, delinquency, self-alienation, and self-rejection. Competitiveness is related to a mixture of healthy and unhealthy characteristics. Whereas inappropriate competitive and individualistic attitudes and efforts alienate individuals from others, healthy and therapeutic growth depends on increasing individuals' understanding of how to cooperate more effectively with others. Cooperative experiences are not a luxury. They are absolutely necessary for healthy development.

Social interdependence theory has been extended to self-esteem. A process of self-acceptance is posited to be based on (a) internalizing perceptions that one is known, accepted, and liked as one is; (b) internalizing mutual success; and (c) evaluating oneself favorably in comparison with peers. A process of self-rejection may occur from (a) not wanting to be known, (b) low performance, (c) overgeneralization of self-evaluations, and (d) the disapproval of others. Since the 1950s, there have been over eighty studies comparing the relative impact of cooperative, competitive, and individualistic experiences on self-esteem (Johnson & Johnson, 1989). Cooperative experiences promote higher self-esteem than do competitive (effect size = 0.58) or individualistic (effect size = 0.44) experiences. Our research demonstrated that cooperative experiences tend to be related to beliefs that one is intrinsically worthwhile, others see one in positive ways, one's attributes compare favorably with those of one's peers, and one is a capable, competent, and successful person. In cooperative efforts, students (a) realize that they are accurately known, accepted, and liked by their peers; (b) know that they have contributed to their own, others', and group success; and (c) perceive themselves and others in a differentiated and realistic way that allows for multidimensional comparisons based on complementarity of their own and others' abilities. Competitive experiences tend to be related to conditional self-esteem based on whether one wins or loses. Individualistic experiences tend to be related to basic self-rejection.

A number of studies have related cooperative, competitive, and individualistic experiences to perspective-taking ability (the ability to understand how a situation appears to other people) (Johnson & Johnson, 1989). Cooperative experiences tend to increase perspective-taking ability, whereas competitive and individualistic experiences tend to promote egocentrism (being unaware of perspectives other than your own) (effect sizes of 0.61 and 0.44, respectively). Furthermore, individuals who are part of a cooperative effort learn more social skills and become more socially competent than do persons competing or working individualistically. Finally, it is through cooperative efforts that many of the attitudes and values essential to psychological health (such as self-efficacy) are learned and adopted.

An important aspect of psychological health is social competence. **Social skills and competencies tend to increase more in cooperative than in competitive or individualistic situations** (Johnson & Johnson, 1989). Working together to get the job done increases students' abilities to provide leadership, build and maintain trust, communicate effectively, and manage conflicts constructively. Employability and career success depend largely on such social skills. Most modern work occurs within teams. Intelligence and technical expertise are of no use if individuals are not skillful group members. The social skills learned within cooperative learning groups, furthermore, provide the basis for building and maintaining lifelong friendships, loving and caring families, and cohesive neighborhoods.

The higher the level of an individual's psychological pathology (e.g., depression, anger, anxiety), the less able he or she is to develop and maintain caring and committed relationships. The association between antisocial behavior and rejection by the normal peer group, for example, is well documented (Cantrell & Prinz, 1985; Dodge, Coie, & Bakke, 1982; Roff & Wirt, 1984). Inappropriately aggressive behavior leads to rejection by peers (Coie & Kupersmidt, 1983; Dodge, 1983). Rejected children are also deficient in a number of social-cognitive skills, including peer group entry, perception of peer group norms, response to provocation, and interpretation of prosocial interactions (Asarnow & Callan, 1985; Dodge, 1983; Putallaz, 1983). Among children referred to child guidance clinics, 30% to 75% (depending on age) are reported by their parents to experience peer difficulties (Achenbach & Edelbrock, 1981). These difficulties are roughly twice as common among clinic children as among nonreferred youngsters. Moreover, referred children have fewer friends and less contact with them than nonreferred children, their friendships are significantly less stable over time, and their understanding of the reciprocities and intimacies involved in friendships is less mature (Selman, 1981).

RECIPROCAL RELATIONSHIPS AMONG THE THREE OUTCOMES

The reason we were so good, and continued to be so good, was because he (Joe Paterno) forces you to develop an inner love among the players. It is much harder to give up on your buddy, than it is to give up on your coach. I really believe that over the years the teams I played on were almost unbeatable in tight situations. When we needed to get that six inches we got it because of our love for each other. Our camaraderie existed because of the kind of coach and kind of person Joe was.

David Joyner

Each of the outcomes of cooperative efforts (effort to achieve, quality of relationships, and psychological health) influences the others and, therefore, they are likely to be found together (Johnson & Johnson, 1989). *First,* caring and committed friendships come from a sense of mutual accomplishment, mutual pride in joint work, and the bonding that results from joint efforts. The more individuals care about each other, the harder they will work to achieve mutual goals. *Second*, joint efforts to achieve mutual goals promote higher self-esteem, self-efficacy, personal control, and confidence in one's competencies. The psychologically healthier individuals are, the better able they are to work with others to achieve mutual goals. *Third*, psychological health is built on the internalization of the caring and respect received from loved ones. Friendships are developmental advantages that promote self-esteem, self-efficacy, and general psychological adjustment. The healthier people are psychologically (i.e., free of psychological pathology such as depression, paranoia, anxiety, fear of failure, repressed anger, hopelessness, and meaninglessness), the more caring and committed their relationships are. Because each outcome can induce the others, you are likely to find them together. They are a package, with each outcome leading to all three. Together they induce positive interdependence and promotive interaction.

Competitive and Individualistic Efforts

The basic social psychological query is "Under what conditions are cooperative, competitive, and individualistic efforts effective?" The hundreds of studies that have been conducted to try to answer this question indicate that under most conditions, cooperation has more powerful effects on the variables studied than do competitive or individualistic efforts. Under most conditions, cooperative efforts are more effective than competitive and individualistic efforts.

There are conditions under which competition may be used effectively (Johnson, Johnson, & Holubec, 1998b; Stanne, Johnson, & Johnson, 1999). *First*, competition has to take place within the broader context of positive interdependence. The location, boundaries, criteria for winning, and rules of conduct have to all be agreed on and followed if competition is to be constructive. *Second*, the competition should be between groups, not individuals. *Third*, the task has to be appropriate. The task should require well-learned skills to be practiced; well-learned material to be reviewed; or simple, unitary/nondivisible, overlearned tasks to be performed. When tasks are new and/or complex, competition is inappropriate. *Fourth*, competition is appropriate only when competitors are evenly matched in terms of previous performance so that they will believe they have a reasonable chance of winning. If they believe they have no chance of winning or can win with no effort, they exert little effort. *Finally*, competition is appropriate only when it does not matter who wins and who loses. When competition is engaged in for fun and enjoyment, winning is incidental. When winning is considered of great importance, it generates high levels of anxiety that interfere with performance, especially when tasks are new and complex. There is some evidence that on very simple, overlearned, repetitive motor tasks, competition may produce higher achievement than cooperation (Johnson & Johnson, 1989).

It is unclear whether individualistic efforts have any advantage over cooperative efforts. Far more research is needed to clarify the conditions under which competitive or individualistic efforts may have more powerful effects than cooperation.

MEDIATING VARIABLES: THE BASIC ELEMENTS OF COOPERATION

The truly committed cooperative learning group is probably the most productive tool humans have. Creating and maintaining truly committed cooperative groups, however, is far from easy. Individuals fool themselves if they think well-meaning directives to "work together," "cooperate," and "be a team" will be enough to create cooperative efforts among members. **There is a discipline to creating cooperation.** Making teams work is like being on a diet. It does no good to diet one or two days a week. If you wish to lose weight, you have to control what you eat every day. Similarly, it does no good to structure a team carefully every fourth or fifth meeting. The basic elements are a regimen that, if followed rigorously, will produce the conditions for effective cooperation. The **basic components of effective cooperative efforts** are positive interdependence, individual and group accountability, face-to-face promotive interaction, appropriate use of social skills, and group processing.

Positive Interdependence: We Instead of Me

During a football game, the quarterback who throws the pass and the receiver who catches the pass are positively interdependent. The success of one depends on the success of the other. Both have to perform competently to assure their mutual success. If one fails, they both fail.

Positive group interdependence exists when one perceives that one is linked with others in such a way that one cannot succeed unless they do (and vice versa) and/or that one must coordinate one's efforts with the efforts of others to complete a task (Johnson & Johnson, 1989). The discipline of using cooperative groups begins with structuring positive interdependence. Group members have to know that they "sink or swim together"; that is, they have two responsibilities: to maximize their own productivity and to maximize the productivity of all other group members. There are two major categories of interdependence: outcome interdependence and means interdependence (Johnson & Johnson, 1989; Johnson, Johnson, & Holubec, 1998a). When persons are in a cooperative or competitive situation, they are oriented toward a desired outcome, end state, goal, or reward. If there is no outcome interdependence (goal and reward interdependence), there is no cooperation or competition. In addition, the means through which the mutual goals or rewards are to be accomplished specify the actions required by group members. Means interdependence includes resource, role, and task interdependence (which are overlapping rather than independent of each other).

Positive interdependence has numerous effects on individuals' motivation and productivity, not the least of which is to highlight the fact that the efforts of all group members are needed for group success. When members of a group see their efforts as unnecessary for the group's success, they may reduce their efforts (Kerr, 1983; Kerr & Bruun, 1983; Sweeney, 1973). When group members perceive their potential contribution to the group as being unique, they increase their efforts (Harkins & Petty, 1982). When goal, task, resource, and role interdependence are clearly understood, individuals realize that their efforts are required for the group to succeed (i.e., there can be no free riders) and that their contributions are often unique. In addition, reward interdependence needs to be structured to ensure that one member's efforts do not make the efforts of other members unnecessary. If the highest score in the group determined the group grade, for example, low-ability members might see their efforts as unnecessary and contribute minimally, and high-ability members might feel exploited, become demoralized, and therefore decrease their efforts so as not to provide undeserved rewards for irresponsible and ungrateful free riders (Kerr, 1983).

A series of research studies was conducted to clarify the impact of positive interdependence on achievement. The results indicated the following:

1. Group membership in itself does not seem sufficient to produce higher achievement and productivity—positive interdependence is also required (Hwong, Caswell, Johnson, & Johnson, 1993). Knowing that one's performance affects the success of groupmates seems to create "responsibility forces" that increase one's efforts to achieve.

2. Interpersonal interaction is insufficient to increase productivity—positive interdependence is also required (Lew, Mesch, Johnson, & Johnson, 1986a, 1986b; Mesch, Johnson, & Johnson, 1988; Mesch, Lew, Johnson, & Johnson, 1986). Individuals achieved more under positive goal interdependence than when they worked individualistically but had the opportunity to interact with classmates.

3. Goal and reward interdependence seem to be additive (Lew, Mesch, Johnson, & Johnson, 1986a, 1986b; Mesch, Johnson, & Johnson, 1988; Mesch, Lew, Johnson, & Johnson, 1986). Whereas positive goal interdependence is sufficient to produce higher achievement and productivity than do individualistic efforts, the combination of goal and reward interdependence is even more effective.

4. Both working to achieve a reward and working to avoid the loss of a reward produce higher achievement than do individualistic efforts (Frank, 1984). There is no significant difference between working to achieve a reward and working to avoid a loss.

5. Goal interdependence promotes higher achievement and greater productivity than does resource interdependence (Johnson, Johnson, Ortiz, & Stanne, 1991).

6. Resource interdependence by itself may decrease achievement and productivity compared with individualistic efforts (Johnson, Johnson, Stanne, & Garibaldi, 1990; Ortiz, Johnson, & Johnson, 1996).

7. The combination of goal and resource interdependence increases achievement more than goal interdependence alone or individualistic efforts (Johnson, Johnson, Stanne, & Garibaldi, 1990; Ortiz, Johnson, & Johnson, 1996).

8. Positive interdependence does more than simply motivate individuals to try harder; it facilitates the development of new insights and discoveries through promotive interaction (Gabbert, Johnson, & Johnson, 1986; Johnson & Johnson, 1981; Johnson, Skon, & Johnson, 1980; Skon, Johnson, & Johnson, 1981). Members of cooperative groups use higher-level reasoning strategies more frequently than do individuals working individualistically or competitively.

9. The more complex the procedures involved in interdependence, the longer it will take group members to reach their full levels of productivity (Ortiz, Johnson, & Johnson, 1996). The more complex the teamwork procedures, the more members have to attend to teamwork and the less time they have to attend to taskwork. Once the teamwork procedures are mastered, however, members concentrate on taskwork and outperform individuals working alone.

The constructive effects that positive interdependence contribute to cooperative efforts do not mean that it is always advantageous. There are conditions under which positive interdependence may have negative effects on cooperation. Further research is needed to clarify the conditions under which positive interdependence does and does not contribute to the effectiveness of cooperation.

Individual Accountability/Personal Responsibility

After positive interdependence, a key variable mediating the effectiveness of cooperation is a sense of personal responsibility for working to accomplish the group's goals. This involves being responsible for (a) completing one's share of the work and (b) facilitating the work of other group members and minimally hindering their efforts. Personal responsibility is promoted by individual accountability. Certainly lack of individual accountability reduces the feeling of personal responsibility. Members will reduce their contributions to goal achievement when the group works on tasks where it is difficult to identify members' contributions, when there is an increased likelihood of redundant efforts, when there is a lack of group cohesiveness, and when there is lessened responsibility for the final outcome (Harkins & Petty, 1982; Ingham, Levinger, Graves, & Peckham, 1974; Kerr & Bruun, 1981; Latané, Williams, & Harkins, 1979; Moede, 1927; Petty, Harkins, Williams, & Latané, 1977; Williams, 1981; Williams, Harkins, & Latané, 1981). If, however, there is high individual accountability and it is clear how much effort each member is contributing, if redundant efforts are avoided, if every member is responsible for the final outcome, and if the group is cohesive, then the social loafing effect vanishes. The smaller the group, in addition, the greater the individual accountability may be (Messick & Brewer, 1983).

Archer-Kath, Johnson, and Johnson (1994) investigated whether or not positive interdependence and individual accountability are two separate and independent dimensions. They compared the impact of feedback to the learning group as a whole with the individual feedback to each member on achievement, attitudes, and behavior in cooperative learning groups. Students received either individual or group feedback in written graph/chart form only on how frequently members engaged in the targeted behaviors. If individual accountability and positive interdependence are unrelated, no differences should be found in perceived positive interdependence between conditions. If they are related, students in the individual feedback condition should perceive more positive interdependence than students in the group feedback condition. Individual feedback resulted in greater perceptions of cooperation, goal interdependence, and resource interdependence than did group feedback, indicating that positive interdependence and individual accountability are related and that by increasing individual accountability, perceived interdependence among group members may also be increased.

The results of these studies indicated that individual accountability does increase the effectiveness of a group by ensuring that all members achieve and contribute to the achievement of their groupmates.

Promotive (Face-to-Face) Interaction

Promotive interaction may be defined as individuals encouraging and facilitating each other's efforts to complete tasks and to achieve in order to reach the group's goals. Promotive interaction is characterized by students (a) providing each other with efficient and effective assistance, (b) exchanging needed resources such as information and materials and processing information more efficiently and effectively, (c) providing each other with feedback in order to improve their subsequent performance on assigned tasks and responsibilities, (d) challenging each other's conclusions and reasoning in order to promote higher-quality decision making and greater insight into the problems being considered, (e) advocating exerting effort to achieve mutual goals, (f) influencing each other's efforts to achieve mutual goals, (g) acting in trusting and trustworthy ways, (h) being motivated to strive for mutual benefit, and (i) feeling less anxiety and stress (Johnson & Johnson, 1989). The amount of research documenting the impact of promotive interaction on achievement is too voluminous to review here. Interested readers are referred to Johnson and Johnson (1989).

Social Skills

Placing socially unskilled students in a learning group and telling them to cooperate will obviously not be successful. Students must be taught the interpersonal and small group skills needed for high-quality cooperation and be motivated to use them. To coordinate efforts to achieve mutual goals, students must (a) get to know and trust each other, (b) communicate accurately and unambiguously, (c) accept and support each other, and (d) resolve conflicts constructively (Johnson, 2000; Johnson & Johnson, 1997). Interpersonal and small group skills form the basic nexus among individuals, and if individuals are to work together productively and cope with the stresses and strains of doing so, they must have a modicum of these skills. Students need to master and use interpersonal and small group skills to capitalize on the opportunities presented by a cooperative learning situation. Especially when learning groups function on a long-term basis and engage in complex, free exploratory activities over a prolonged period, the interpersonal and small group skills of the members may determine the level of members' achievement and productivity.

In their studies on the long-term implementation of cooperative learning, Marvin Lew and Debra Mesch (Lew, Mesch, Johnson, & Johnson, 1986a, 1986b; Mesch, Johnson, & Johnson, 1988; Mesch, Lew, Johnson, & Johnson, 1986) investigated the impact of a reward contingency for using social skills as well as positive interdependence and a contingency for academic achievement on performance within cooperative learning groups. In the cooperative skills conditions, students were trained weekly in four social skills, and each member of a cooperative group was given two bonus points toward the quiz grade if all group members were observed by the teacher to demonstrate three out of four cooperative skills. The results indicated that the combination of positive goal interdependence, an academic contingency for high performance by all group members, and a social skills contingency promoted the highest achievement. Archer-Kath, Johnson, and Johnson (1994) trained students in the social skills of praising, supporting, asking for information, giving information, asking for help, and giving help. Students received either individual or group feedback in written graph/chart form on how frequently they engaged in the targeted behaviors. The researchers found that giving students individual feedback on how frequently they engaged in targeted social skills was more effective in increasing students' achievement than was group feedback. The more socially skillful students are, the more attention teachers pay to teaching and rewarding the use of social skills, and the more individual feedback students receive on their use of the skills, the higher the achievement that can be expected within cooperative learning groups.

Not only do social skills promote higher achievement, they contribute to building more positive relationships among group members. Putnam, Rynders, Johnson, and Johnson (1989) demonstrated that when students were taught social skills, observed by the teacher, and given individual feedback on how frequently they engaged in the skills, their relationships became more positive.

Group Processing

In order to achieve, students in cooperative learning groups have to work together effectively. Effective group work is influenced by whether or not groups periodically reflect on how well they are functioning and plan how to improve their work processes. A **process** is an identifiable sequence of events taking place over time, and **process goals** refer to the sequence of events instrumental in achieving outcome goals. **Group processing** may be defined as reflecting on a group session to (a) describe what member actions were helpful and unhelpful and (b) make decisions about what actions to continue or change. The purpose of group processing is to clarify and improve the effectiveness of the members in contributing to the joint efforts to achieve the group's goals.

Yager, Johnson, and Johnson (1985) examined the impact on achievement of (a) cooperative learning in which members discussed how well their group was functioning and how they could improve its effectiveness, (b) cooperative learning without any group processing, and (c) individualistic learning. The results indicate that the high-, medium-, and low-achieving students in the cooperation with group processing condition scored higher on daily achievement, postinstructional achievement, and retention measures than did the students in the other two conditions. Students in the cooperation without group processing condition, furthermore, scored higher on all three measures than did the students in the individualistic condition.

Putnam, Rynders, Johnson, and Johnson (1989) conducted a study in which there were two conditions: cooperative learning with social skills training and group processing and cooperative learning without social skills training and group processing. Forty-eight fifth-grade students (thirty-two nonhandicapped and sixteen students with IQs ranging from 35 to 52) participated in the study. In the cooperative learning with social skills training condition, the teacher gave students examples of specific cooperative behaviors to engage in, observed how frequently they engaged in the skills, gave them feedback on how well they worked together, and had them discuss for five minutes how to use the skills more effectively in the future. In the uninstructed cooperative groups condition, students were placed in cooperative groups and worked together for the same period of time with the same amount of teacher intervention (aimed at the academic lesson and unrelated to working together skillfully). Students both with and without disabilities were randomly assigned to each condition. They found that more positive relationships developed between those with and without disabilities in the cooperative skills condition and that these positive relationships carried over to postinstructional free-time situations.

Johnson, Johnson, Stanne, and Garibaldi (1990) conducted a study comparing cooperative learning with no processing, cooperative learning with teacher processing (teacher specified cooperative skills to use, observed, and gave whole class feedback on how well students were using the skills), cooperative learning with teacher and student processing (teacher specified cooperative skills to use, observed, gave whole class feedback on how well students were using the skills, and had learning groups discuss how well they interacted as a group), and individualistic learning. Forty-nine high-ability black American high school seniors and entering college freshmen at Xavier University participated in the study. A complex computer-assisted problem-solving assignment was given to all students. The students in all three cooperative conditions performed better than did those in the individualistic condition. The combination of teacher and student processing resulted in greater problem-solving success than did the other cooperative conditions.

Archer-Kath, Johnson, and Johnson (1994) provided learning groups with either individual or group feedback on how frequently members had engaged in targeted social skills. Each group had five minutes at the beginning of each session to discuss how well the group was functioning and what could be done to improve the group's effectiveness. Group processing with individual feedback was more effective than group processing with whole group feedback in increasing students' (a) achievement motivation, actual achievement, uniformity of achievement among group members, and influence toward higher achievement within cooperative learning groups; (b) positive relationships among group members and between students and the teacher; and (c) self-esteem and positive attitudes toward the subject area.

The results of these studies indicated that engaging in group processing clarifies and improves the effectiveness of the members in contributing to joint efforts to achieve the group's goals, especially when specific social skills are targeted and students receive individual feedback on how frequently and how well they engaged in the skills.

Summary

There is nothing magical about telling individuals to work together as a team. The basic elements that both (a) create cooperative efforts and (b) mediate the relationship between cooperation and outcomes must be vigilantly structured into every group session. The basic elements are positive interdependence, individual accountability, promotive interaction, appropriate use of social skills, and group processing. These elements form a regimen that, if followed rigorously, will produce the conditions for effective cooperation.

THE EVOLUTION OF COOPERATION

Within group efforts cooperation has to evolve (Axelrod, 1984). The pursuit of self-interest by each group member leads to a poor outcome for all. The problem is that although an individual can benefit from mutual cooperation, each one can also do even better by exploiting the cooperative efforts of others. But when the interactions are repeated, both participants attempt to exploit the other, leading to mutual poor outcomes. Exploiting the cooperative efforts of others may pay off when there is a known and limited number of interactions between yourself and the other group members and when you can remain lost in a sea of anonymous others, preventing others from retaliating effectively. Cooperation, however, pays off when:

1. The number of interactions is not fixed in advance. Cooperation requires that individuals have a sufficiently large chance to meet again so that they have a stake in their future interaction. Cooperation is very difficult to establish in one-time encounters. An important way to promote cooperation is to arrange for the same two people to meet each other again, be able to recognize each other, and each recall how the other has behaved until now. This continuing interaction is what makes it possible for cooperation based on reciprocity to be stable. In other words, make the future more important relative to the present. There are two ways of doing this. The *first* is by making the interactions more durable. Prolonged interaction allows patterns of cooperation that are based on

reciprocity to be worth trying and allows them to become established. The *second* is by making the interactions more frequent. The more frequent the interactions, the more important future cooperation is. One way to increase the frequency of interactions is to keep others away. By breaking cooperation into small pieces, the potential gain from competition in any one interaction is small compared to the future gains from continued cooperation.

2. You and the other group members are easily identifiable to each other. That is, because of continuing contact and other factors such as a fixed meeting place, each group member must realize that retaliation is possible. When interaction among group members is durable and frequent, cooperation is the only behavior that makes sense. Improve recognition ability. The ability to recognize the other people from past interactions, and to remember the relevant features of those interactions, is necessary to sustain cooperation. Exploitive behavior must be recognized when it occurs. The scope of sustainable cooperation can be expanded by any improvements in the individuals' ability to recognize each other from the past and to be confident about the prior actions that have actually been taken.

3. Group members emotionally identify with other members and with the group so that they value each other's well-being and want to promote each other's long-term welfare and the long-term success of the group. Group members need to care about each other and about the group. An excellent way to promote cooperation is to teach people to care about the welfare of others. The greater the altruistic motives of the individuals involved, the more stable the cooperation.

4. Group members understand the value of reciprocity, and are able and willing to reciprocate both cooperation and competition. One of the basic principles of cooperation is reciprocation. Follow a tit-for-tat strategy so that both cooperation and competition are reciprocated.

5. The temptation to exploit the cooperative efforts of group members is reduced by:
   a. Changing the payoffs so that competition is too costly to be considered. The short-term incentive for cooperation should ideally be greater than the short-term incentive for competition.
   b. Not being envious. You should be more concerned about how you are doing relative to individualistic and competitive alternatives than about whether another group member is benefiting more than you from the collaboration.
   c. Not being the first to exploit another member's cooperative efforts. It pays to cooperate as long as the other group members are doing so. You will avoid much unnecessary conflict by keeping a clear cooperative orientation.

GOAL STRUCTURES AND THE ALLOCATION OF BENEFITS AMONG GROUP MEMBERS

I am in Birmingham because injustice is here. . . . Injustice anywhere is a threat to justice everywhere. We are caught in an inescapable network of mutuality, tied in a single garment of destiny.

Martin Luther King, Jr., Letter from the Birmingham Jail

Aesop tells a story of a man who had four sons. The father loved them very much, but they troubled him greatly because they were always fighting with each other. Nothing the father said stopped their quarreling. "What can I do to show my sons how wrong it is to act this way?" the father thought. One day he called his sons to him and showed them a bundle of sticks. "Which of you, my sons, can break this bundle of sticks?" he asked them. All the boys tried in turn, but not one of them could do it. Then the father untied the bundle and gave each son a single stick. "See if you can break that," he said. Of course, they could easily do it. "My sons," the father said, "each of you alone is weak— as easy to injure as one of these sticks. But if you will be friends and stick together, you will be as strong as the bundle of sticks."

Individuals join groups because in the long run they are better off being part of the group. The better the group functions, the better off the individual members are; the better off the individual members are, the more they can contribute to the group's efforts; and therefore the better the group functions. Part of the process promoting effective cooperation among members to ensure their individual well-being is the distribution of rewards. The way in which rewards are distributed among group members can have a marked effect on how members behave toward one another in the future and how effective the group is (Deutsch, 1975, 1979). Depending on the circumstances, rewards may be distributed according to merit, equality, or need.

The **equity** or **merit view** of **distributing benefits** has been presented by Homans (1961) as a basic rule of distributive justice and equity theory. In a just distribution, rewards will be distributed among individuals in proportion to their contributions. In other words, those members who contribute the most to the group's success should receive the greatest benefits. It is commonly assumed that when rewards (for example, bonuses, salaries, advancement, grades) are contingent on performance, productivity will increase. Individual incentive plans, however, sometimes run into problems as individuals restrict output out of fear of being rejected by colleagues, intrinsic motivation is replaced with extrinsic motivation, and the negative consequences of competition may surface within the group. There are a number of other problems with the merit approach to distributing rewards within a group. One is that the economic values upon which equity theory is based can have unfortunate effects on group members' views of themselves and each other as well as on the relationships among members. From a utilitarian, economic point of view, group members are of value only to the extent that they contribute to the group's success. Such a view results in depersonalization of both self and others and the attitude that different members have different value. Depersonalization and differential value undermine respect for self and other group members. Members may view their self-worth as being related to the rewards they receive, which in turn are related to the contributions they make to group goal accomplishment. They may view other members in the same way. Thus, if a member contributes little to group success and receives disproportionately small rewards, he or she is viewed as having little personal worth. Diesing (1962) describes such a situation as being alienated from oneself and others.

From the equity point of view, rewards have value only because they are a scarce commodity that one competes with others to obtain. Any intrinsic value is ignored. The utilitarian value of a reward increases with the number of persons who want the reward; the reward becomes a scarce commodity when its supply is far less than the demand for it. The symbolic meaning of the reward may become far more important than its intrinsic value. Children fight over being first in line, not because of the intrinsic value of the position but rather because it symbolizes that they are a winner, superior to those who are positioned behind them. Diesing (1962) describes such a situation as being alienated from one's possessions and creations. Thus, the competition among group members that is fostered by making rewards proportionate to members' contributions may seriously reduce the cohesiveness of the group, cause morale problems, and undermine group effectiveness as trust and communication among members deteriorate.

Group members who are successful under a merit system of distributive justice often misattribute their success to their efforts rather than to their talents. Certain group members have more resource attractors than others. A **resource attractor** is an attribute that tends to attract other resources because it gives the possessor an advantage in competition for these other resources. Examples of resource attractors are ability, training, previous experience, drive, and character. Group members with a large number of resource attractors often get higher rewards than those with few resource attractors and may attribute their success to their worthiness and effort (implying that those who have fewer resource attractors are less worthy and more lazy).

Finally, a frequent result of a merit system is that the group members who are rewarded the most are given the power to distribute future rewards on the basis of their assessment of how much each member is contributing to the group effort. Deutsch (1975, 1979) notes that this allows those who are in power to bias the system of allocation to perpetuate their disproportionate rewards and power even when they are no longer making relatively large contributions to the group's well-being.

An **equality system of distributive justice** rewards all group members equally. If a football team wins the Super Bowl, all members receive a Super Bowl ring. If a learning group completes an assignment at an A level, all members of the group receive an A. To prevent the problems of the merit system, group incentive systems may be used. In most stores, for example, sales clerks are on individual commission systems. What happens when they are switched to a group commission system? Babchuk and Good (1951) decided to find out. Sales were good with the individual incentive program, but the clerks avoided maintenance duties, competed with one another for customers, and suffered low morale. Under the group plan, a sense of teamwork developed and the sales clerks reported a greater feeling of satisfaction. Blau (1954) compared two groups of interviewers in an employment agency. In one, there was fierce competition to fill job openings. In the other, the interviewers worked cooperatively. Members of the competitive group, who were personally ambitious and extremely concerned about productivity, hoarded job notifications rather than posting them so that everyone could see them, as they were supposed to do. This practice eventually was used defensively and so became self-perpetuating. Members of the cooperative group, by contrast, told each other about vacancies and encouraged each other to fill them. The cooperators ended up filling significantly more jobs. Deutsch (1975, 1979) notes that the consequences of an equality system of distributive justice are mutual esteem, equal status, and mutual respect among members. He states that the principle of equality is more congenial to fostering enjoyable personal relationships, group loyalty, and cooperativeness.

The **distribution of benefits according to need** results in a situation in which the group members who are most in need of the benefits receive a disproportionate amount of them. The member who has the largest family may receive the highest monetary bonus, the member who is grieving for the death of her parents may be asked to do the least work, or the member who has the least ability will be given the most support and assistance for completing his assigned tasks. A student who has never received an A might be given the highest grade in the group. Rawls (1971) pointed out that one of the natural duties of members of a group is to help another member who is in need or in jeopardy, providing that one can do so without excessive loss or risk to oneself. The gain to the member who needs help is seen as far outweighing the loss or risk to oneself as well as the loss of that required to assist that person. Such a system of distributive justice emphasizes the confidence and trust members may have in their colleagues' good intentions. Deutsch (1975, 1979) notes that a caring-oriented group will stress responsibility for each other, permissiveness toward members expressing their needs, heightened sensitivity to each other's needs, and support and nurturance of each other's legitimate needs.

Whatever system of distributing rewards a group uses has to be perceived as just by group members. When rewards are distributed unjustly, there may be low morale and high conflict among members, which in turn may decrease productivity. The evidence indicates that before a task is performed, people generally perceive that an equity or competitive reward system is fairest, but after a task is completed, they view a cooperative reward system in which all group members receive the same reward as the fairest (Deutsch, 1979, 1985; Johnson & Johnson, 1983; Johnson, Johnson, Buckman, & Richards, 1986; Wheeler & Ryan, 1973).

SOCIAL INTERDEPENDENCE AND THE REAL WORLD

In real life, all three types of interdependence exist simultaneously and continuously. All individuals within a modern industrial/information-based society need to be able to work cooperatively with peers, superiors, and subordinates; compete for fun and enjoyment; and work autonomously on their own. In most situations, group members will usually have a mixture of cooperative, competitive, and individualistic motives. They may be committed to group goals and work to maximize joint outcomes while at the same time seeking to outperform a peer and to meet personal needs unrelated to the concerns of other members. Frank Pierce, for example, as a division chief for Skidmore Corporation, has a cooperative interest in ensuring a high level of productivity for his division, a competitive interest in being seen as the most productive division head within the company, and an individualistic interest in keeping blocks of time free to write a book on successful management. Within a basketball team, a player may focus on the cooperative goal of ensuring the team wins, the competitive goal of being the best player on the team, and the individualistic goal of perfecting a jump shot. Mixtures of the three types of social interdependence are continually present in any situation. Which one dominates the situation, however, has important implications for individual, group, and organizational productivity, morale, and well-being.

The effectiveness of a group can be easily damaged when an individual dominated by competitiveness joins the group. Kelley and Stahelski (1970) found that several things happen in such a situation. *First,* the cooperative members begin behaving in competitive ways, violating trust, hiding information, and cutting off communication. *Second,* the competitive person sees the formerly cooperative members as having always been competitive. *Third,* the cooperative members are aware that their behavior is being determined by the other's competitive behavior, but the competitive person is not aware of his or her impact on cooperative members. Cooperativeness needs to dominate group life. Effective patterns of interaction among members are usually far easier to destroy than to build.

EXERCISE

3.9 *Your Cohesion Behavior*

How does your behavior affect group cohesion? When you want to increase group cohesion, what do you do? How would you describe your behavior in influencing group cohesion?

The following questions should help you reflect upon how your behavior influences the cohesion of the groups to which you belong. Answer each question as honestly as possible.

1. I try to make sure that everyone enjoys being a member of the group.
   Never 1 : 2 : 3 : 4 : 5 : 6 : 7 : 8 : 9 Always
2. I discuss my ideas, feelings, and reactions to what is currently taking place within the group.
   Never 1 : 2 : 3 : 4 : 5 : 6 : 7 : 8 : 9 Always
3. I express acceptance and support when other members disclose their ideas, feelings, and reactions to what is currently taking place in the group.
   Never 1 : 2 : 3 : 4 : 5 : 6 : 7 : 8 : 9 Always
4. I try to make all members feel valued and appreciated.
   Never 1 : 2 : 3 : 4 : 5 : 6 : 7 : 8 : 9 Always
5. I try to include other members in group activities.
   Never 1 : 2 : 3 : 4 : 5 : 6 : 7 : 8 : 9 Always
6. I am influenced by other group members.
   Never 1 : 2 : 3 : 4 : 5 : 6 : 7 : 8 : 9 Always
7. I take risks in expressing new ideas and my current feelings.
   Never 1 : 2 : 3 : 4 : 5 : 6 : 7 : 8 : 9 Always
8. I express liking, affection, and concern for other members.
   Never 1 : 2 : 3 : 4 : 5 : 6 : 7 : 8 : 9 Always
9. I encourage group norms that support individuality and personal expression.
   Never 1 : 2 : 3 : 4 : 5 : 6 : 7 : 8 : 9 Always

These questions focus upon several ways of increasing group cohesion. Question 1 describes a general attempt to keep cohesion high. Questions 2 and 3 pertain to the expression of ideas and feelings and the support for others expressing ideas and feelings; such personal participation is essential for cohesiveness and for the development of trust. Questions 4 and 8 also focus upon support for, and liking of, other group members. Question 5 refers to the inclusion of other members, and question 6 takes up one's willingness to be influenced by other members. Questions 7 and 9 center on the acceptance of individuality within the group. All these factors are important for group cohesion. Discuss your answers with another group member. Then add all your answers together to get a total cohesion score. Keep your responses to these questions in mind as you proceed through this chapter.

EXERCISE

3.10 The Level of Acceptance in Your Group

What is the level of acceptance in your group? The purpose of this exercise is to provide a way in which the level of acceptance in your group may be assessed and discussed. The procedure is as follows:

1. With the other members of your group, fill out the questionnaire below. Questionnaires should be unsigned so that no one's responses can be identified.
2. Tabulate the results in the summary table that follows the questionnaire.
3. Discuss the conclusions that can be drawn from the results. Consider these two questions:
   a. What is contributing to the present high or low level of acceptance in the group?
   b. How may the level of acceptance in the group be increased?

QUESTIONNAIRE: LEVEL OF ACCEPTANCE

Think about the ways in which the members of your group normally behave toward you. In the parentheses in front of the statements below, place the number corresponding to your perceptions of the group as a whole, using the following scale:

5 = they *always* behave this way
4 = they *typically* behave this way
3 = they *usually* behave this way
2 = they *seldom* behave this way
1 = they *rarely* behave this way
0 = they *never* behave this way

My fellow group members:

1. (——) .... are completely honest with me.
2. .... (——) .... understand what I am trying to communicate.
3. .... (——) .... interrupt and ignore my comments.
4. .... (——) accept me just the way I am.
5. (——) .... tell me when I bother them.
6. .... (——) .... don't understand things I say or do.
7. .... (——) .... are interested in me.
8. .... (——) make it easy for me to be myself.
9. (——) .... don't tell me things that would hurt my feelings.
10. .... (——) .... understand who I really am.
11. .... (——) .... include me in what they are doing.
12. .... (——) evaluate whether I am acceptable or unacceptable.
13. (——) .... are completely open with me.
14. .... (——) .... immediately know when something is bothering me.
15. .... (——) .... value me as a person, apart from my skills or status.
16. .... (——) accept my differences or peculiarities.

(——) Authenticity with me
    (——) Understanding of me
        (——) Valuing of me
           (——) Accepting of me

Total the number of points in each column. Statements 3, 6, 9, and 12 are reversed in the scoring; subtract from 5 the rating given to each before placing the remainder in each column.

Summary Table: Level of Acceptance

Score	Authenticity	Understanding	Valuing	Accepting
0–4	_____	_____	_____	_____
5–8	_____	_____	_____	_____
9–12	_____	_____	_____	_____
13–16	_____	_____	_____	_____
17–20	_____	_____	_____	_____

EXERCISE

3.11 *How Trusting and Trustworthy Am I?*

When you are attempting to build a relationship with someone, there is always the risk that the person will react in a rejecting and competitive way. In order for two group members to trust each other, each has to expect the other to be trustworthy and each has to engage in trusting behavior. This exercise allows you to compare the way you see your trust-building behavior in the group with the way other members see it. The procedure is as follows:

1. Complete the following questionnaire. Score your responses.
2. Then make a slip of paper for each member of your group. Fill out each slip as shown, rating the member from 1 (low) to 7 (high) on how open and accepting you perceive him or her to be.

Member receiving feedback: Edythe
1. Openness and sharing: 3
2. Acceptance, support, and cooperativeness: 6

Base your rating on how you think the person has behaved during the entire time your group has met together.

3. Hand each member his or her slip. If there are six members in your group, you should receive five ratings of yourself, and each of the other members should likewise end up with five slips. Compute an average of how the other members see your behavior by adding all your ratings for openness and dividing up the number of slips and then doing the same with your ratings for acceptance.
4. Discuss with the other group members how similar your perception and their perceptions of your openness and acceptance are. If there is a difference between the two, ask the group to give you more specific feedback about your trust-building behavior in the group. Then discuss how to build trust with others in situations outside the group.

UNDERSTANDING YOUR TRUST ACTIONS QUESTIONNAIRE

The following is a series of statements that describe behavior in a group. Rate each statement as honestly as you can. There are no right or wrong answers. It is important for you to describe your behavior as accurately as possible. Answer between 1 (I never behave that way) and 7 (I always behave that way).

7 = I always behave that way
6 = I almost always behave that way
5 = I frequently behave that way
4 = I behave that way as frequently as not

3 = I occasionally behave that way
2 = I seldom behave that way
1 = I never behave that way

When I Am a Member of a Group:

_____ 1. I offer facts, give my opinions and ideas, and provide suggestions and relevant information to help the group discussion.

_____ 2. I express my willingness to cooperate with other group members and my expectation that they will also be cooperative.

_____ 3. I am open and candid in my dealings with the entire group.

_____ 4. I give support to group members who are on the spot and struggling to express themselves intellectually or emotionally.

_____ 5. I keep my thoughts, ideas, feelings, and reactions to myself during group discussions.

_____ 6. I evaluate the contributions of other group members in terms of whether their contributions are useful to me and whether they are right or wrong.

_____ 7. I take risks in expressing new ideas and current feelings during a group discussion.

_____ 8. I communicate to other group members that I am aware of and appreciate their abilities, talents, capabilities, skills, and resources.

_____ 9. I offer assistance to anyone in the group in order to improve the performance of everyone.

_____ 10. I accept and support the openness of other group members, supporting them for taking risks and encouraging individuality in group members.

_____ 11. I share any materials, books, sources of information, or other resources I have with the other group members in order to promote the success of all members and the group as a whole.

_____ 12. I often paraphrase or summarize what other members have said before I respond or comment.

_____ 13. I level with other group members.

_____ 14. I warmly encourage all members to participate, giving them recognition for their contributions, demonstrating acceptance and openness to their ideas, and generally being friendly and responsive.

SCORING THE TRUST QUESTIONNAIRE

In order to obtain a total score for trusting actions and trustworthy actions, write the score for each item in the appropriate column and then total the scores for each column. Reverse the scoring for the starred questions (If you circled 2, write 6; if you circled 1, write 7; 4 remains the same).

Trusting (Openness and Sharing) Actions	Trustworthy (Acceptance and Support) Actions
_____ 1.	_____ 2.
_____ 3.	_____ 4.
_____ 5.*	_____ 6.*
_____ 7.	_____ 8.
_____ 9.	_____ 10.
_____ 11.	_____ 12.
_____ 13	_____ 14.
_____ **Total**	_____ **Total**

If you have a score of 35 or over, classify yourself as being trusting or trustworthy. If you have a score below 35, classify yourself as being distrustful or untrustworthy.

3.12 *Practicing Trust-Building Skills*

This exercise provides an opportunity to practice trust-building skills. Form a group of six members. Choose one member to be an observer. Complete the following task. Then listen carefully to the report of the observer on the interaction among group members and analyze the dynamics of building trust.

GENETIC TRAITS TASK

Working as a group, estimate the number of people in your school who possess each of the following physical traits. Establish the frequency of occurrence of each trait, first in your group, then in the entire class. Based on the percentage of occurrence of each trait in your group and the class, estimate the number of people in your school who possess each trait.

Trait	Group	Class	School
1. Dimples in the cheeks versus no dimples.			
2. Brown (or hazel) eyes versus blue, gray, or green eyes.			
3. Attached versus free earlobes (an earlobe is free if it dips below the point where it is attached).			
4. Little-finger bend versus no bend (place your little fingers together with your palms toward you; if your little fingers bend away from each other at the tips, you have a little-finger bend).			
5. Tongue roll versus no tongue roll (if you can curl up both sides of your tongue to make a trough, you have it, and it's not contagious).			
6. Hairy versus nonhairy middle fingers (examine the backs of the middle two fingers on your hands and look for hair between the first and second knuckles).			
7. Widow's peak versus straight or curved hairline (examine the hairline across your forehead and look for a definite dip or point of hair extending down toward your nose).			

EXERCISE

Observation Sheet

	1	2	3	4	5	Total
1. Contributes ideas						
2. Describes feelings						
3. Paraphrases						
4. Expresses acceptance and support						
5. Expresses warmth and liking						
Total						

Trusting behaviors = 1 and 2; Trustworthy behaviors = 3, 4, and 5

EXERCISE

3.13 *Open versus Closed Relationships*

Are the relationships among group members open or closed? This exercise gives participants an opportunity to reflect on and discuss this question. The procedure is as follows:

1. Read carefully the information in Table 3.4 on open and closed relationships.
2. Working by yourself, write down the answers to the following questions:
   a. On a scale of 1 (*very closed*) to 10 (*very open*), how open are your relationships with other group members?
   b. Are there relationships in the group you wish to make more open?
   c. Are there relationships in the group you wish to make more closed?
   d. What actions are needed to make a relationship more open?
   e. What actions are needed to make a relationship more closed?
3. Meet as a group and discuss each of the questions. Arrive at a group consensus on the answers to questions (d) and (e).
4. Each group shares its conclusions about open and closed relationships with the rest of the class.

DEVELOPING AND MAINTAINING TRUST

I am afraid to tell you who I am, because, if I tell you who I am,
you may not like who I am, and it's all that I have.

John Powell

An essential aspect of group effectiveness is developing and maintaining a high level of trust among group members. The more members trust each other, the more effectively they will work together (Deutsch, 1962, 1973; Johnson, 1974). Group effectiveness rests on every member's sharing resources, giving and receiving help, dividing the work, and contributing to the accomplishment of mutual goals. Such behaviors will occur when there is trust that everyone else is contributing to the group's progress and not using members' openness and sharing of resources for personal rather than group gain. Group members will more openly express their thoughts, feelings, reactions, opinions, information,

Table 3.4 Open and Closed Relationships

Closed ◄—— ——► Open

	Closed			Open
Content being discussed	The content is of concern to no one (weather talk).	The content consists of technical aspects of work.	The content consists of the ideas and feelings of one person.	The content consists of the relationship between the two persons.
Time reference	No time reference (jokes and generalizations).	Distant past or future being discussed.	Recent past or future being discussed.	The "here and now" being discussed.
Awareness of your sensing, interpreting, feeling, intending	You never listen to yourself and try to ignore, repress, and deny feelings and reactions.		You are constantly aware of what you are sensing, the interpretations you are making, your feelings, and your intentions about acting on your feelings.	
Openness with own ideas, feelings, reactions	Your statements are generalizations, abstract ideas, intellectualizations; feelings are excluded as irrelevant, inappropriate, and nonexistent.		Your personal reactions such as attitudes, values, preferences, feelings, experiences, and observations of the present are stated and focused upon; feelings are included as helpful information about the present.	
Feedback from other people	Feedback from others is avoided, ignored, not listened to, and perceived as being hostile attacks on your personality.		Feedback from others is asked for, sought out, listened to, and used to increase your self-awareness; it is perceived as being a helpful attempt to add to your growth and effectiveness.	
Acceptance of yourself	You believe that once you are known, you will be disliked and rejected; therefore, you hide your real self and try to make the impression you think will be most appreciated by other people.		You express confidence in your abilities and skills; you discuss your positive qualities without bragging and without false modesty; you understand how you have used your strengths in the past to achieve your goals and are confident you will do so again in the future.	
Openness to others' ideas, feelings, reactions	You avoid and disregard others' reactions, ideas, and feelings; you are embarrassed and put off by others' expressions of feelings; you reject other people and try to one-up and better them; you refuse to hear their feedback on their reactions to your behavior.		You listen to and solicit others' reactions, ideas, and feelings; you are interested in and receptive to what others are saying and feeling; you express a desire to cooperate fully with them; you make it clear that you see their value and strengths even when you disagree with them; you ask others for feedback on their perceptions of your behavior.	
Acceptance of other people	You evaluate the other person's actions, communicate that the other is unacceptable, show disregard for the other as a person.		You react without evaluation to the other person's actions, communicate that the other is acceptable, value the other as a person.	

The Elements of Trust

1. You are in a situation where the choice to trust another person can lead to either beneficial or harmful consequences for your needs and goals. Thus, you realize that there is a risk involved in trusting.

2. You realize that whether beneficial or harmful consequences result depends on the actions of another person.

3. You expect to suffer more if the harmful consequences result than you will gain if the beneficial consequences result.

4. You feel relatively confident that the other person will behave in such a way that the beneficial consequences will result.

and ideas when the trust level is high. When the trust level is low, group members will be evasive, dishonest, and inconsiderate in their communications. The development and maintenance of trust is discussed at length in Johnson (2000).

Trust is essential for relationships to grow and develop among group members. In order to build a productive group, members must create a climate of trust that reduces their own and other members' fears of betrayal and rejection and promotes the hope of acceptance, support, and confirmation. Trust is not a stable and unchanging personality trait. Trust is dynamic. It is an aspect of relationships, and it constantly changes and varies. Every action each member takes increases or decreases the trust level of the group.

What is trust and how do you create it? *Trust* is a word everyone uses, yet it is a complex concept and difficult to define. Deutsch (1962) may have developed the best definition. He defined *trust* as including the following elements.

Making a choice to trust another member involves the perception that (a) the choice can lead to gains or losses, (b) whether you will gain or lose depends on the behavior of the other member, (c) the loss will be greater than the gain, and (d) the other member will probably behave in such a way that you will gain rather than lose. Sounds complicated, doesn't it? In fact, there is nothing simple about trust; it is a complex concept and difficult to explain. An example may help. Imagine that you are part of a group analyzing *Hamlet.* You begin to contribute to the discussion, knowing you will gain if you contribute good ideas that other members accept but lose if your ideas are laughed at and belittled. Whether you gain or lose depends on the behavior of other group members. You will feel more hurt if you are laughed at than you will feel satisfaction if your ideas are appreciated. Yet you expect the other group members to consider your ideas and accept them. The issue of trust is captured in the question every group member asks: "If I openly express myself, will what I say be used against me?"

Another example may help. Trust is when you lend your older brother your bicycle. You can gain his appreciation or lose your bike; which one happens depends on him. You will suffer more if your bike is wrecked than you will gain by his appreciation, yet you really expect him to take care of your bike. (Sad experience has led an unnamed person to recommend that you never lend your bike to your older brother!)

Building Interpersonal Trust

In order to work together effectively to achieve a mutual goal, individuals must establish mutual trust. Trust is established through a sequence of trusting and trustworthy actions (see Figure 3.4). If person A takes the risk of being self-disclosing, he may be either confirmed or disconfirmed, depending on whether person B responds with acceptance or rejection. If person B takes the risk of being accepting, supportive, and cooperative, she may be confirmed or disconfirmed, depending on whether person A is disclosing or nondisclosing. To complete tasks and achieve goals, group members are required to disclose more and more of their ideas, thoughts, conclusions, feelings, and reactions to the immediate situations and to each other. Once they do, other group members are required to respond, hopefully with acceptance, support, and cooperativeness. If group members express an opinion and do not get the acceptance they need, they may withdraw from the group. If they are accepted, they will continue to risk disclosing their thoughts and observations and continue to develop their relationships with other members.

Interpersonal trust is *built* through risk and confirmation and is *destroyed* through risk and disconfirmation. Without risk there is no trust, and the relationship cannot move forward. The steps in building trust are:

1. Person A takes a risk by disclosing his thoughts, information, conclusions, feelings, and reactions to the immediate situation and to person B.
2. Person B responds with acceptance, support, and cooperativeness and reciprocates person A's openness by disclosing her own thoughts, information, conclusions, feelings, and reactions to the immediate situation and to person A.

An alternative way in which trust is built is:

1. Person B communicates acceptance, support, cooperativeness toward person A.
2. Person A responds by disclosing his thoughts, information, conclusions, feelings, and reactions to the immediate situation and to person B.

	High Acceptance, Support, and Cooperativeness		Low Acceptance, Support, and Cooperativeness	
High Openness and Sharing	Person A	Trusting Confirmed	Person A	Trusting Disconfirmed
	Person B	Trustworthy Confirmed	Person B	Untrustworthy No risk
Low Openness and Sharing	Person A	Distrusting No risk	Person A	Distrusting No risk
	Person B	Trustworthy Disconfirmed	Person B	Untrustworthy No risk

Figure 3.4 The dynamics of interpersonal trust.

Being Trusting and Trustworthy

In a cooperative group, the crucial elements of trust are openness and sharing on the one hand and acceptance, support, and cooperative intentions on the other. Working cooperatively with others requires openness and sharing, which in turn are determined by the expression of acceptance, support, and cooperative intentions in the group. **Openness** is the sharing of information, ideas, thoughts, feelings, and reactions to the issue the group is pursuing. **Sharing** is offering your materials and resources to others in order to help them move the group toward goal accomplishment. **Acceptance** is the communication of high regard to others and their contributions to the group's work. **Support** is the communication to others that you recognize their strengths and believe in their ability to manage the situation productively. **Cooperative intentions** are the expectations that you are going to behave cooperatively and that every group member will also cooperate in achieving the group's goals.

The level of trust within a group is constantly changing according to members' ability and willingness to be trusting and trustworthy. **Trusting behavior** may be defined as the willingness to risk beneficial or harmful consequences by making oneself vulnerable to other group members. More specifically, trusting behavior involves being self-disclosing and openly accepting and supportive of others. **Trustworthy behavior** may be defined as the willingness to respond to another person's risk-taking in a way that ensures that the other person will experience beneficial consequences. This involves your acceptance of another person's trust in you. Expressing acceptance, support, and cooperativeness as well as reciprocating disclosures appropriately are key aspects of being trustworthy in relationships with other group members. In considering members' trustworthy behavior, you should remember that **accepting and supporting the contributions of other group members does not mean that you agree with everything they say.** You can express acceptance and support for the openness and sharing of other members and at the same time express different ideas and opposing points of view.

Acceptance is probably the first and deepest concern to arise in a group. Acceptance of others usually begins with acceptance of oneself. Group members need to accept themselves before they can fully accept others. **Acceptance is the key to reducing anxiety and fears about being vulnerable.** Defensive feelings of fear and distrust are common blocks to personal functioning and to the development of constructive relationships. Certainly, if a person does not feel accepted, the frequency and depth of participation in the group will decrease. To build trust and to deepen relationships among group members, each member needs to be able to communicate acceptance, support, and cooperativeness.

The key to building and maintaining trust is being trustworthy. The more you accept and support others, the more likely they will disclose their thoughts, ideas, theories, conclusions, feelings, and reactions to you. The more trustworthy you are in response to such disclosures, the deeper and more personal the thoughts others will share with you. When you want to increase trust, increase your trustworthiness.

The major skills necessary for communicating acceptance, support, and cooperativeness involve the expression of warmth, accurate understanding, and cooperative intentions. There is considerable evidence that the expression of warmth, accurate understanding, and cooperative intentions increase trust in a relationship, even when there are unresolved conflicts between the individuals involved (Johnson, 1971; Johnson & Matross, 1977; Johnson & Noonan, 1972). The procedures for communicating feelings such as warmth and for communicating that one is listening and accurately understands what the other is saying are covered in Chapter 4. Cooperative intentions are expressed by comments indicating that you want to work together to achieve a mutual goal.

When you reciprocate self-disclosures, you increase trust and influence the other person to be even more self-disclosing. Reciprocating self-disclosures makes oneself vulnerable to rejection, and the mutual vulnerability resulting when all members actively participate in a group increases members' trust that all members will accept and support the others.

Destroying Trust

For trust to develop, one person has to let down his or her guard and become vulnerable to see whether the other person abuses that vulnerability. Many such tests are necessary before the trust level between two people becomes very high. A series of positive encounters may be necessary before trust is high. **However, it often takes just one betrayal to establish distrust and, once established, distrust is extremely resistant to change.** Distrust is difficult to change because it leads to the perception that despite the other person's attempts to "make up," betrayal will recur in the future.

Creating distrust is not a good idea for several reasons. *First,* when group members do not trust other members to do their share of the work, for example, they will loaf themselves rather than risk looking like a fool who did the bulk of the work (Kerr, 1983). *Second,* when group members cannot trust each other, they often compete simply to defend their own best interests. Such competition is self-defeating in the long run, because it initiates a negative cycle. Distrust creates competition, which creates greater distrust, which creates greater competition. *Third,* distrust creates destructive conflict among group members. But to know how to maintain trust in a relationship, it is important to be aware of the actions that make you look untrustworthy.

There are three types of behavior that will decrease trust in a relationship. The *first* is the use of rejection, ridicule, or disrespect as a response to the other's openness. Making a joke at the expense of the other person, laughing at his disclosures, moralizing about her behavior, being evaluative in your response, or being silent and poker-faced all communicate rejection and will effectively silence the other person and destroy some of the trust in the relationship. The *second* is the nonreciprocation of openness. To the extent that you are closed and the other members are open, they will not trust you. If a group member is open and you do not reciprocate, she will often feel overexposed and vulnerable. The *third* type of behavior that will decrease trust in a relationship is the refusal to disclose your thoughts, information, conclusions, feelings, and reactions after the other person has indicated considerable acceptance, support, and cooperativeness. If a group member indicates acceptance and you are closed and guarded in response, he will feel discounted and rejected.

3.14 *Definitions*

Following are concepts and definitions. Match the correct definition with the correct concept. Find a partner and (a) compare answers and (b) explain your reasoning for each answer.

_____	**1. Openness**	a. The willingness to risk beneficial or harmful consequences by making oneself vulnerable to other group members.
_____	**2. Sharing**	b. The communication to another person that you recognize her strengths and believe she has the abilities she needs to manage the situation productively.
_____	**3. Acceptance**	c. The expectations that you are going to behave cooperatively and that every group member will also cooperate in achieving the group's goals.
_____	**4. Support**	d. The sharing of information, ideas, thoughts, feelings, and reactions to the issue the group is pursuing.
_____	**5. Cooperative intentions**	e. The willingness to respond to another person's risk-taking in a way that ensures that the other person will experience beneficial consequences.
_____	**6. Trustworthy behavior**	f. The communication of high regard for another person and his or her contributions to the group's work.
_____	**7. Trusting behavior**	g. The offering of your materials and resources to others in order to help them move the group towards goal accomplishment.

Reestablishing Trust After It Has Been Broken

How can trust, once lost, be regained? The following guidelines may help. To reestablish trust, group members should:

1. Increase positive outcome interdependence by establishing cooperative goals that are so compelling that everyone will join in to achieve them. Such goals are often referred to as *superordinate goals.*
2. Increase their resource interdependence so that it is clear that no one person has a chance of succeeding on his or her own.
3. Openly and consistently express their cooperative intentions.
4. Reestablish credibility by making certain that their actions match their announced intentions. They must always follow up on their word.
5. Be absolutely and consistently trustworthy in dealing with each other. Acceptance and support of other members are critical.
6. Periodically "test the waters" by engaging in trusting actions and making themselves vulnerable to the other members.
7. Apologize sincerely and immediately when they inadvertently engage in untrustworthy actions.
8. Strive to build a reputation for being tough but fair by:
   a. Initially and periodically responding cooperatively to other members who act competitively (even when they know in advance that the others plan to compete).

b. Using a tit-for-tat strategy that matches the other persons' behavior if the others continue to compete. When the competitors realize that their competitiveness is self-defeating and the best they can hope for is mutual failure, they may start cooperating.

Trusting Appropriately

Trust no one.

The X Files

Trust is not always appropriate. There are times when you will think it inadvisable to disclose your thoughts, feelings, or reactions to another person. There are people you undoubtedly know who would behave in very untrustworthy ways if you made yourself vulnerable to them. To master the skills in building and maintaining trust, therefore, you need to be able to tell when it is appropriate to be trusting and when it is not. A person must develop the capacity to size up situations and make an enlightened decision about whom to trust and when, and how much to trust others. Remember not to reveal yourself so quickly to another person that he or she is overpowered and bewildered. Remember also that there are situations in which trust is inappropriate and destructive to your interests.

Never trusting and *always* trusting are inappropriate. Trust is appropriate only when you are relatively confident that the other person will behave in such a way that you will benefit rather than be harmed by your risk, or when you are relatively sure that the other person will not exploit your vulnerability. In some situations, such as competitive ones, trust is not appropriate. When you have a mean, vicious, hostile boss who has taken advantage of your openness in the past, it is inappropriate to engage in trusting behavior in the present.

Trusting as a Self-Fulfilling Prophecy

Tom joins a new group expecting the members to dislike and reject him. He behaves, therefore, in a very guarded and suspicious way toward the other group members. His actions cause them to withdraw and look elsewhere for a friendly companion. "See," he then says, "I was right. I knew they would reject me." Sue, who joins the same group at the same time Tom does, expects the members to be congenial, friendly, and trustworthy. She initiates warmth and friendliness, openly discloses her thoughts and feelings, and generally is accepting and supportive of the other members. Consequently, she finds her fellow members to be all that she expected. Both Tom and Sue have made a self-fulfilling prophecy.

A **self-fulfilling prophecy** is, in the beginning, a false definition of a situation that evokes a new behavior, one that makes it possible for the originally false impression to come true. The assumptions you make about other people and the way in which you then behave often influence how other people respond to you, thus creating self-fulfilling prophecies in your relationships. People usually conform to the expectations others have for them. If other people feel that you do not trust them and expect them to violate your trust, they will often do so. If they believe that you trust them and expect them to be trustworthy, they will often behave that way. The perception of others as untrustworthy is probably a major source of tensions leading to conflict. The history of labor–management strife, interracial violence, war, and revolution demonstrates the power of distrust. The lack of trust helps create conflict, and conflict can lead to increased distrust. There can be a vicious circle of distrust causing conflict that increases distrust that increases conflict.

In building trust in a relationship, your expectations about the other person may influence how you act toward that person, thus setting up the possibility of a self-fulfilling prophecy. There is a lot to be said for assuming that other people are trustworthy.

Personal Proclivity to Trust

Although trust exists in relationships, not in people, there has been some attempt to measure individual differences in the willingness to trust others. Rotter (1971) developed the Interpersonal Trust Scale to distinguish between people who have a tendency

Helpful Hints About Trust

1. **Trust is a very complex concept to understand and teach to your students.** It may take a while before they fully understand it.

2. **Trust exists in relationships, not in someone's personality.** Although some people are more naturally trusting than others, and although it is easier for some people to be trustworthy than others, trust is something that occurs **between** people, not **within** people.

3. **Trust is constantly changing as two people interact.** Everything you do affects the trust level between you and the other person to some extent.

4. **Trust is hard to build and easy to destroy.** It may take years to build up a high level of trust in a relationship; then one destructive act can destroy it all.

5. **The key to building and maintaining trust is being trustworthy.** The more accepting and supportive you are of others, the more likely they will disclose their thoughts, ideas, theories, conclusions, feelings, and reactions to you. The more trustworthy you are in response to such disclosures, the deeper and more personal the thoughts a person will share with you. When you want to increase trust, increase your trustworthiness.

6. **Trust needs to be appropriate. Never** trusting and **always** trusting are inappropriate.

7. **Cooperation increases trust; competition decreases trust.** Trust generally is higher among collaborators than among competitors.

8. **Initial trusting and trustworthy actions within a group can create a self-fulfilling prophecy.** The expectations you project about trust often influence the actions of other group members toward you.

to trust others and those who tend to distrust. A high truster tends to say, "I will trust a person until I have clear evidence that he or she cannot be trusted." A low truster tends to say, "I will not trust a person until there is clear evidence that he or she can be trusted." High trusters tend to be more trustworthy than low trusters. High trusters, compared with low trusters, are (a) more likely to give others a second chance, respect the rights of others, and to be liked and sought out as friends (by both low- and high-trust people) and (b) less likely to lie and be unhappy, conflicted, or maladjusted.

14 references in Ch3./

SUMMARY

Groups exist for a reason. People join groups to achieve goals they are unable to achieve by themselves. The personal goals of individual group members are linked together by positive interdependence. Group goals result. Group goals direct, channel, motivate, coordinate, energize, and guide the behavior of group members. To be useful, however, group goals have to be clear and operational. The group level of aspiration is continually being revised on the basis of success and failure.

The basis for the group goals is the positive interdependence among group members. Social interdependence theory originated from Kurt Lewin's field theory and was formalized by Morton Deutsch. In the past ninety years, over 600 studies have been conducted. The numerous variables that are affected by cooperation may be subsumed within three broad and interrelated outcomes: effort to achieve, quality of relationships among participants, and psychological health and social competence. Within cooperative groups, as opposed to competitive and individualistic efforts, achievement is higher, committed and caring relationships form, and the self-esteem and social competence required to cope with stress and adversity develop. Each of these outcomes affects the others. The more group members work together to get the job done, the more members care about each other. The more members care about each other, the harder they work to get the job done. The more group members work together to get the job done, the greater their social competencies and psychological health become. The healthier they are psychologically, the harder they will work to get the job done. The more caring and supportive the relationships, the greater the psychological health, and the greater the psychological health, the more caring and support individuals can give to each other. When individuals join in a cooperative effort, the whole Gestalt results. The key elements that power cooperation are positive interdependence, individual accountability, promotive interaction, social skills, and group processing. Finally, there are conditions under which competitive and individualistic efforts are productive. Group members will often have a mixture of cooperative, competitive, and individualistic goals. In both cases, the cooperative goals must dominate.

An essential aspect of ongoing cooperation is the level of trust among members. Trust consists of two parts: being trusting and being trustworthy. Trust is built when a person takes a risk and acts in a trusting way and the other person responds supportively in a trustworthy way. The key to trust, therefore, is being trustworthy.

The cooperative effort to achieve group goals requires frequent, clear, and accurate communication. Group members must be able to communicate and listen clearly and effectively. You will learn how to do this in the next chapter.

Communication
Within Groups

4

Basic Concepts to Be Covered in This Chapter

In this chapter a number of concepts are defined and discussed. The major ones are listed following. Divide into pairs. Each pair is to (a) define each concept, noting the page on which it is defined and discussed, and (b) ensure that both members of the pair understand the meaning of each concept. Then combine into groups of four. Compare the answers of the two pairs. If there is disagreement, look up the concept in the chapter and clarify it until all members agree on and understand the definition.

Concepts

1. Assimilation
2. Authority hierarchy
3. Channel
4. Communication network
5. Defensive communication
6. Effective communication
7. Gatekeeper
8. Group communication
9. Group norms
10. Informal communication network
11. Leveling
12. Message
13. Noise
14. One-way communication
15. Receiver
16. Sender
17. Sharpening
18. Two-way communication

INTRODUCTION AND DEFINITIONS

The brothers Grimm tell a tale about a valiant little tailor who, bothered by flies, swatted at them with a cloth. When he lifted up the cloth, seven flies lay dead under it. "Seven!" the tailor said. "Seven at one blow!" So, proud of his success, he made himself a belt on which he embroidered "Seven in one blow!" Later in the day he met the king, who read the words on the belt. "Seven men at one blow!" the king exclaimed. "This is a mighty warrior indeed!" "If you kill the two evil giants who are murdering and plundering the people of my kingdom, I will give you my only daughter in marriage and half my kingdom as well!" "What a fine offer," the little tailor said. "I am willing to slay your giants." The rest is history.

This breakdown in communication resulted in a little tailor marrying a princess and becoming a king. Not all misunderstandings are as benign. While failures to communicate effectively surround us every day, they more often bring problems and discomfort rather than riches, love, and position. In fact, breakdowns in communication bring such pain and difficulties that a great deal of attention is paid in group dynamics to effective group communication.

In this chapter the nature of effective group communication is defined. To understand group communication, two factors must be discussed: the patterns of group communication and the variables that influence its effectiveness (see Figure 4.1). Group communication can be understood better as a pattern of interaction among members than as a specific set of skills. Investigators use three approaches to examine patterns of

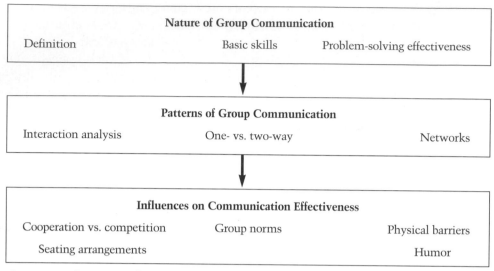

Figure 4.1 The nature of group communication.

group communication: interaction analysis, one- versus two-way communication, and communication networks. The influences on communication effectiveness include physical barriers, seating arrangements, cooperative versus competitive context, group norms, and humor. Each of these topics is discussed in this chapter.

EXERCISE

4.1 *Your Communication Behavior (I)*

What is your communication behavior like in a group? How would you describe your communication actions? Begin a discussion of communication within groups by answering the following questions as honestly as possible:

1. If I as group chairperson were giving a set of instructions and the other group members sat quietly with blank faces, I would
   ____ State the instructions clearly and precisely and then move on.
   ____ Encourage members to ask questions until I was sure that everyone understood what he or she was supposed to do.
2. If the group chairperson gave a set of instructions to the group that I did not understand, I would
   ____ Keep silent and later ask another group member what he or she meant.
   ____ Immediately ask the chairperson to repeat the instructions and answer my questions until I was sure I understood what he or she wanted me to do.
3. How often do you let other group members know when you like or approve of something they say or do?
   Never 1 : 2 : 3 : 4 : 5 : 6 : 7 : 8 : 9 Always
4. How often do you let other group members know when you are irritated or impatient with, embarrassed by, or opposed to something they say or do?
   Never 1 : 2 : 3 : 4 : 5 : 6 : 7 : 8 : 9 Always

5. How often do you check out what other group members are feeling and how they are reacting rather than assuming that you know?

        Never 1 : 2 : 3 : 4 : 5 : 6 : 7 : 8 : 9 Always

6. How often do you encourage other group members to let you know how they are reacting to your behavior and actions in the group?

        Never 1 : 2 : 3 : 4 : 5 : 6 : 7 : 8 : 9 Always

7. How often do you check to make sure you understand what other group members mean before agreeing or disagreeing?

        Never 1 : 2 : 3 : 4 : 5 : 6 : 7 : 8 : 9 Always

8. How often do you paraphrase or restate what other members have said before responding?

        Never 1 : 2 : 3 : 4 : 5 : 6 : 7 : 8 : 9 Always

9. How often do you keep your thoughts, ideas, feelings, and reactions to yourself in group sessions?

        Never 1 : 2 : 3 : 4 : 5 : 6 : 7 : 8 : 9 Always

10. How often do you make sure that the rest of the group knows all the information you have about the current topic of discussion?

        Never 1 : 2 : 3 : 4 : 5 : 6 : 7 : 8 : 9 Always

These questions deal with several aspects of communication in groups that will be discussed in this chapter. Questions 1 and 2 refer to whether communication is one-way (from the chairperson to the rest of the group members) or two-way. Questions 3 and 4 focus on your willingness to give feedback to other group members on how you are receiving and reacting to their messages. Questions 5 and 6 refer to your willingness to ask for feedback about how other group members are receiving and reacting to your messages. Questions 7 and 8 focus on receiving skills, and questions 9 and 10 relate to your willingness to contribute (send) relevant messages about the group's work. Review your answers to these questions and summarize your present communication behavior in a group.

GROUP COMMUNICATION

Communication is the basis for all human interaction and for all group functioning. Through communication, members of groups reach some understanding of one another, build trust, coordinate their actions, plan strategies for goal accomplishment, pool expertise, make persuasive arguments, agree upon a division of labor, promote each member's commitment and effectiveness, and even exchange insults. All cooperative action depends on effective communication, and our daily lives are filled with one communication experience after another. It is through communication that the members interact, and effective communication is a prerequisite for every aspect of group functioning.

Group communication involves multiperson exchange within a small group. Whenever group members see each other, they have a continuous effect on each other's perceptions and expectations of what the others are going to do. Group communication, then, can be defined broadly as any verbal or nonverbal behavior that is perceived by other group members (Johnson, 2000). Communication is much more than just the exchange of words: All behavior conveys some message and is, therefore, a form of communication. **Group communication,** however, is more commonly defined as a message sent by a group member to one or more receivers with the conscious intent of affecting the receivers' behavior. A group member sends the message "It is time to vote" to evoke the response "Everyone in favor raise your right hand." Under this more limited definition, any signal aimed at influencing the receiver's behavior in any way is communication.

This definition of group communication does not mean that there is always a sequence of events in which a group member thinks of a message and sends it, and other group members receive it. Group communication is a process in which members receive, send, interpret, and infer all at the same time—there is no beginning and no end. In addition, all communication involves symbols to which certain meanings are attached. These symbols can be either verbal (all words are symbols) or nonverbal (all expressions and gestures are symbols). Finally, the exchange of ideas and experiences among group members is possible only when they have adopted the same ways of relating a particular nonverbal, spoken, written, or pictorial symbol to a particular experience.

How do you tell when communication is effective and when it is not? **Effective communication** exists among group members when the receivers interpret the sender's message in the same way the sender intended it. If John tries to communicate to the other group members that it is a wonderful day and he is feeling great by saying "Hi" with a warm smile, and if the other group members interpret John's "Hi" and smile as meaning that John thinks it is a beautiful day and he is feeling well, then effective communication has taken place. If group members interpret John's "Hi" and smile as meaning that he wants to initiate a group discussion, then ineffective communication has taken place.

The basic unit of group communication is the group, not the individual (Poole, 1998, 1999; Warriner, 1956). Lewin, Asch, Deutsch, and the other pioneers of social psychology took the primacy of the group as fundamental to group dynamics. Only later did the individual replace the group as the primary unit of analysis, perhaps because of the methodological convenience in conducting controlled laboratory research rather than for theoretical reasons (Steiner, 1974). Since the 1960s, individuals (either interacting with one another or presenting themselves through mass media) have been the favored unit of analysis in studies of group dynamics. Groups and organizations have been viewed as contexts for communication and other aspects of group dynamics rather than as fundamental units in themselves.

The difficulty in creating a theory of group communication is the complexity of understanding a multiperson exchange. In a dyad, communication is a two-way exchange (see Figure 4.2). In a triad, however, there are six lines of communication. In a group of four, there are twelve interactions to keep track of. Creating a conceptual framework

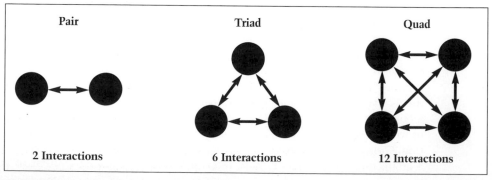

Pair	Triad	Quad
2 Interactions	6 Interactions	12 Interactions

Figure 4.2 Communication in small groups.

Group Environment

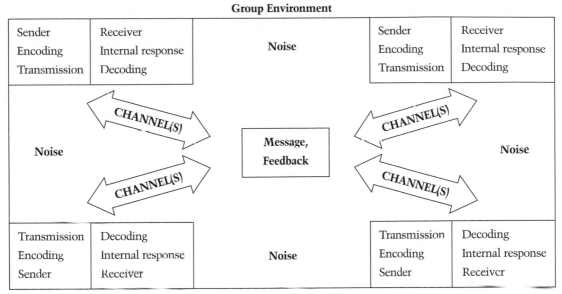

Figure 4.3   The group communication process.

that illuminates the communication in groups of six, ten, twenty, or ninety individuals may be beyond current social science.

In Figure 4.3 the communicator is referred to as the **sender,** and the persons at whom the message is aimed are the **receivers.** The **message** is any verbal or nonverbal symbol that one person transmits to others; it is subject matter being referred to in a symbolic way (all words are symbols). A **channel** can be defined as the means of sending a message to another person: the sound waves of the voice, the light waves that make it possible to see words on a printed page. Because communication is a process, sending and receiving messages often take place simultaneously: A person can be speaking and at the same time paying close attention to the receiver's nonverbal responses.

GROUP ENVIRONMENT

Figure 4.3 represents a model of the process of communication within a small group:

1. The ideas, feelings, and intentions of the sender and the way he or she decides to behave lead him or her to send a message.
2. The sender encodes a message by translating ideas, feelings, and intentions into a message appropriate for sending.
3. The sender transmits the message to the receivers.
4. The message is sent through a channel.
5. The sender perceives any discernible response of the receivers, thus receiving feedback.
6. The receivers decode the message by interpreting its meaning. The receivers' interpretation depends on how well they understand the content of the message and the intentions of the sender.

7. The receivers respond internally to this interpretation of the message.
8. **Noise** is any element that interferes with the communication process. In the sender, noise refers to such things as his or her attitudes and frame of reference and the appropriateness of his or her language or other expression of the message. In the receiver, noise refers to such things as attitudes, background, and experiences that affect the decoding process. In the channel, noise refers to (a) environmental sounds, such as static or traffic, (b) speech problems, such as stammering, and (c) annoying or distracting mannerisms, such as a tendency to mumble. To a large extent, the success of communication is determined by the degree to which noise is overcome or controlled.

Usually communication models portray communication between two individuals because message exchange between two individuals is relatively orderly and meanings are fairly easy to understand. The analysis of communication in dyadic situations is helpful. Dyadic analyses, however, may be misleading, as they do not represent the complexity of group interaction, in which multiple relationships must simultaneously be developed and managed and do not exhaust the interesting possibilities of group communication (Keyton, 1999). In this chapter, therefore, the emphasis is on group (not interpersonal) communication.

SENDING AND RECEIVING MESSAGES

Even though group communication is a multiperson exchange of messages, there are basic sending and receiving skills that all group members must master. These skills are discussed in more detail in Johnson (2000). While this chapter focuses on group communication, it is still helpful to review the communication skills that every group member should master.

Sending Messages Effectively

To send a message effectively, the sender must phrase the message so that it will be comprehended, the sender will have credibility as a sender, and the sender will ask for feedback on how the message is affecting the receiver (Johnson, 1974, 2000):

1. Clearly own your messages by using first-person singular pronouns (I, my). Personal ownership includes clearly taking responsibility for the ideas and feelings that one expresses. People disown their messages when they use phrases such as "most people," "some of our friends," and "our group." Such language makes it difficult for listeners to tell whether the individuals really think and feel what they are saying or whether they are repeating the thoughts and feelings of others.
2. Make your messages complete and specific. Include clear statements of all necessary information the receiver needs to comprehend the message. Being complete and specific seems obvious, but often people do not communicate the frame of reference they are using, the assumptions they are making, the intentions they have in communicating, or the leaps in thinking they are making.
3. Make your verbal and nonverbal messages congruent. Every face-to-face communication involves both verbal and nonverbal messages. Usually these mes-

sages are congruent. The person who is saying that he appreciates your help is smiling and expressing warmth in other nonverbal ways. Communication problems arise when a person's verbal and nonverbal messages are contradictory. If a person says, "Here is some information that may be of help to you" with a sneer on his face and a mocking tone of voice, the meaning you receive is confused by the two different messages being sent.

4. Be redundant. Sending the same message more than once and using more than one channel of communication (such as pictures and written messages as well as verbal and nonverbal cues) will help the receiver understand your messages.

5. Ask for feedback concerning the way your messages are being received. To communicate effectively, you must be aware of how the receiver is interpreting and processing your messages. The only way to be sure is to continually seek feedback about what meanings the receiver is attaching to your messages.

6. Make the message appropriate to the receiver's frame of reference. Explain the same information differently to an expert in the field and a novice, to a child and an adult, to your boss and your coworker.

7. Describe your feelings by name, action, or figure of speech. When communicating your feelings, it is especially important to be descriptive. You may describe your feelings by name ("I feel sad"), by actions ("I feel like crying"), or by figures of speech ("I feel down in the dumps"). Description will help communicate your feelings clearly and unambiguously.

8. Describe others' behavior without evaluating or interpreting. When reacting to the behavior of others, be sure to describe their behavior ("You keep interrupting me") rather than evaluating it ("You're a rotten, self-centered egotist who won't listen to anyone else's ideas").

One of the most important elements in interpersonal communication is the credibility of the sender. **Sender credibility** refers to the receiver's attitude toward the perceived trustworthiness of the sender's statements. Sender credibility depends on (a) reliability as an information source, (b) motives, (c) expression of warmth and friendliness, (d) trustworthiness, (e) expertise, and (f) dynamism. The studies on sender credibility provide little evidence to suggest which of these dimensions is most important. It seems that a highly credible sender is one who is perceived positively in all of these dimensions. A sender low in credibility, on the other hand, is one who is perceived negatively in any one of the dimensions. Unless we appear credible to other group members, they will tend to discount our messages and we will not be able to communicate effectively with them.

The third basic set of skills involves asking for feedback on how your messages were received and then listening carefully to the responses of the other group members. The listening skills are reviewed as receiving skills.

Effective message-sending skills are examined in detail in Johnson (2000), which discusses the basic theory behind sending effective verbal and nonverbal messages and includes specific exercises for developing these skills. All group members should learn and review these skills.

Receiving Messages Effectively

The skills involved in receiving messages focus on giving feedback about the reception and the message in ways that clarify and aid continued discussion. Receiving skills have two basic parts: (a) communicating the intention of wanting to understand the ideas and feelings of the sender and (b) understanding and interpreting the sender's ideas and feelings. Of the two, many theorists consider the first—communicating the intention to understand correctly, but not to evaluate, a message—to be more important. The principal barrier to building effective communication is the tendency of most persons to judge or evaluate the message they are receiving: The sender makes a statement and the receiver responds inwardly or openly with "I think you're wrong," "I don't like what you said," "I think you're right," or "That is the greatest (or worst) idea I have ever heard!" Such evaluative receiving will make the sender defensive and cautious, decreasing the openness of the communication. Though the tendency to give evaluative responses is common in almost all conversations, it is accentuated in situations where emotions are deeply involved. The stronger the feelings, the more likely two group members will evaluate each other's statements from their own point of view only. Thus, it is highly important for the receiver to indicate that he or she wants to understand the sender fully before making an evaluation.

The specific receiving skills are paraphrasing, checking one's perception of the sender's feelings, and negotiating for meaning (Johnson, 2000).

1. Paraphrase accurately and nonevaluatively the content of the message and the feelings of the sender. This is the most basic and important skill in receiving messages. When paraphrasing, it is helpful to restate the sender's ideas and feelings in your own words rather than repeating his or her words exactly, avoid any indication of approval or disapproval, neither add to nor subtract from the sender's message, and indicate that you understand the sender's frame of reference.

2. Describe what you perceive to be the sender's feelings. This description should try to identify those feelings without expressing approval or disapproval and without attempting to interpret them or explain their causes. It is simply saying, "Here is what I understand your feelings to be; am I accurate?"

3. State your interpretation of the sender's message and negotiate with the sender until you both agree on the message's meaning. Often the words contained in a message do not carry the actual meaning. A person may ask, "Do you always shout like this?" and means "Please quiet down." Sometimes, therefore, paraphrasing the content of a message will do little to communicate your understanding of it. In such a case, you must negotiate the meaning of the message. You may wish to begin by saying, "What I think you mean is . . ." If you are accurate, you then reply; if you are inaccurate, the sender restates the message until you can state its essential meaning.

A complete treatment of these basic receiving skills, so important to effective communication, can be found in Johnson (2000), which also contains exercises for developing verbal and nonverbal competence in using them.

4.2 *Who Will Be President of Bewise College?*

The purpose of this exercise is to examine within a task-oriented group the communication patterns, the pattern of information sharing, and the effects of collaboration and competition on group problem solving. The exercise takes about one hour and twenty minutes. Participants are organized into groups of four role players and two observers. Any number of groups may be directed at the same time. The procedure for the coordinator is as follows:

Timetable		Materials	
Activity	Minutes	Item	Number
Introduction to exercise	10	Briefing sheet	1 per student
Briefing of observers	5	Set of data sheets	1 per group
Groups make decision	30	Candidate summary	1 per student
Whole class discussion	15	Observation sheet	1 per observer
Group processing	15		
Conclusions and closure	5		

1. Introduce the exercise as focusing on communication within a problem-solving situation. Review the briefing sheet in a realistic manner to set the stage for the role play.
2. Divide the class into groups of six. Ask two participants to volunteer to be observers, and ask each group to choose the president of Bewise College. Suggest that there is one correct decision. Tell them that they must reach their decision independently of the other groups. Then distribute a briefing sheet, a candidate summary sheet, and one data sheet to each of the four participants. Ensure that the four different data sheets are distributed to different members in each group. **Emphasize that in the exercise, all communication in the group must be verbal.** A participant may read his or her data sheet out loud and may take notes on what other members say, but may not read other members' materials, may not let other group members read his or her data sheet, and may not let other group members read his or her notes.
3. Instruct the observers how to use the Patterns of Communication Observation Sheet. The four participants should read their materials while you are doing so. Distribute copies of the frequency chart and brief observers on how they are used. All observers will need at least six copies of the observation form, so time should be given for them to make their extra copies.
4. Give the signal to begin the group meeting. You may introduce an element of competition by posting groups' solutions in order of completion and by posting the number of minutes used by each group to make their decision.
5. In a whole class discussion, have all the groups share their decision about which candidate to hire and why. After all the groups have reported, review the correct answer, which appears on page 585 in the Appendix.
6. Have participants discuss the nature of communication within their groups. Review the observation sheets. Then ask the group to discuss their experience, using the observations of the observers. Observe the processing of each group, and make notes about what students learned in order to provide examples of what they learned from the experience. Here are some relevant questions for discussion.
   a. What were the patterns of communication within the group?
      1. Who spoke to whom how frequently?
      2. Who talked, how often did they talk, and for how long?
      3. Who triggered whom in what ways?

PATTERNS OF COMMUNICATION OBSERVATION SHEET

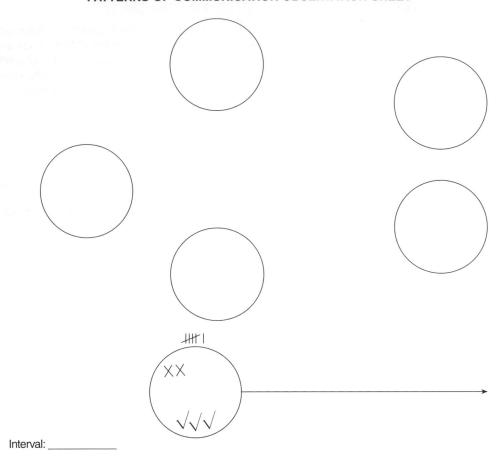

Interval: _____

4. Who interrupted whom?
5. Who encouraged whom to participate?
6. What could have been done to gain more effective participation?
  b. Did all the group members easily obtain the needed information? Did they share their information appropriately, request each other's information, and create the conditions for information sharing?
  c. Were the resources of all group members used? Was everyone listened to?
  d. How cooperative or competitive were the group members?
  e. How did the group make decisions?
  f. What problems did the group have in working together?
  g. What conclusions about small group communication may be drawn from the group's experience?
7. Summarize what the group members have learned, relate it to relevant material in the chapter, and provide closure by complimenting the groups on the quality of their work (regardless of whether they made the right decision).

BEWISE COLLEGE BRIEFING SHEET

1. This is the first meeting of your group.
2. **There is verbal communication only.** The information you bring with you is all in your head. Do not read anyone else's materials and do not let anyone else read yours.
3. Assume that there is a correct decision (there is one candidate you should hire).
4. Assume that all information in your data sheet and candidate summaries is correct.
5. The decision should be made by consensus. All members should agree on the candidate to hire and be able to explain why the candidate chosen will make the best president.
6. You must work on the problem as a group.

Use one sheet for each five-minute interval. Label the circles with the names of the group members; indicate a message from a sender to a receiver with an arrow; when someone sends a message to the entire group, indicate this with an arrow to the center. Indicate the frequency of message sending with tally marks (IIII II). Place an *x* in the member's circle every time he or she interrupts or overrides another group member. Place a check (✓) in the member's circle every time he or she encourages another member to participate.

BEWISE COLLEGE DATA SHEET 1

Your group is a committee consisting of board members, administrators, faculty, and students of Bewise College. Your group has been authorized by the Board of Regents to select a new president of the college from the list of candidates. Each of the represented groups (Board of Regents, administrators, faculty, students) has its own list of requirements for the new president. Insofar as possible, your group is pledged to select a candidate who meets these requirements.

Bewise College was established in 1969. It is located in the heart of an industrial city with a population of about 100,000. In addition to a standard liberal arts curriculum, Bewise College offers a curriculum in which students can receive college credit for work and learning experiences outside the college. There is only one other college in the same city; it is the smallest college in the state, and until 1984 all students attending it were African-Americans.

The new president faces a series of challenges. The Board of Regents sees the need for a president who can raise money to support the college. The college is now in a desperate financial position. The college has been losing money for the past two years. It may have to close if it cannot balance its budget. The college administrators want a president with administrative experience. The college is making budget cuts that will require a strong and experienced administrator to orchestrate.

BEWISE COLLEGE DATA SHEET 2

Your group is a committee consisting of board members, administrators, faculty, and students of Bewise College. Your group has been authorized by the Board of Regents to select a new president of the college from the list of candidates. Each of the represented groups (Board of Regents, administrators, faculty, students) has its own list of requirements for the new president. Insofar as possible, your group is pledged to select a candidate who meets these requirements.

Bewise College was established in 1969. It is located in the heart of an industrial city with a population of about 100,000. In addition to a standard liberal arts curriculum, Bewise College offers a curriculum in which students can receive college credit for work and learning experiences outside the college. Within the state, only Brown College, Samuels College, and Holubec College are larger, which makes Bewise one of the largest colleges in the state. Samuels College is attended primarily by students from wealthy families. Andrews is the smallest college in the state.

The new president faces a series of challenges. The Board of Regents wants a president who can be effective in public relations, creating a positive image of the college within the community, state, and nation. Public relations primarily depend on the president's ability to make powerful public speeches to a wide variety of groups and organizations. The college administrators want an experienced administrator as president. They are very concerned about hiring a president who will not be a competent administrator. The college is launching a comprehensive assessment of the faculty's teaching performance. Administrative experience is needed to manage such a program.

BEWISE COLLEGE DATA SHEET 3

Your group is a committee consisting of board members, administrators, faculty, and students of Bewise College. Your group has been authorized by the Board of Regents to select a new president of the college from the list of candidates. Each of the represented groups (Board of Regents, administrators, faculty, students) has its own list of requirements for the new president. Insofar as possible, your group is pledged to select a candidate who meets these requirements.

Bewise College was established in 1969. It is located in the heart of an industrial city with a population of about 100,000. In addition to a standard liberal arts curriculum, Bewise College offers a curriculum in which students can receive college credit for work and learning experiences outside the college. The students attending Bewise College are primarily minority group members, working-class and lower-income students, the elderly, and dropouts from other colleges and universities.

The new president faces a series of challenges. The faculty wants a president who has teaching experience, because they believe it will make the president sympathetic to the problems of the faculty. In addition, they see the need for a president who comes from a background that would provide insights into the type of student attending Bewise College. Students are dissatisfied with and angry about the quality of teaching at Bewise College. They therefore want a president with an education degree who can judge the teaching ability of faculty and insist on improvements.

BEWISE COLLEGE DATA SHEET 4

Your group is a committee consisting of board members, administrators, faculty, and students of Bewise College. Your group has been authorized by the Board of Regents to select a new president of the college from the list of candidates. Each of the represented groups (Board of Regents, administrators, faculty, students) has its own list of requirements for the new president. Insofar as possible, your group is pledged to select a candidate who meets these requirements.

Bewise College was established in 1969. It is located in the heart of an industrial city with a population of about 100,000. In addition to a standard liberal arts curriculum, Bewise College offers a curriculum in which students can receive college credit for work and learning experiences outside the college. The faculty consists primarily of young and dedicated but inexperienced instructors. Because universities are always larger than colleges, Bewise is smaller than the State University, but it is growing rapidly.

The new president faces a series of challenges. Faculty members are upset with the difficulty in teaching the students at Bewise College and are dissatisfied with the unresponsiveness of the students. They therefore want a president who has had experience in working with the types of students attending Bewise College. The students have stated that the only qualification they will recognize as valid for judging faculty teaching ability is a president with a degree in education. Students also see the necessity of having a president who comes from a background that would provide insights into the types of students attending Bewise College.

BEWISE COLLEGE CANDIDATE SUMMARY SHEET

Name	David Wolcott
Education	Graduated from Andrews College in liberal arts in 1982; master of education in English from Winfield University in 1984; doctorate in political science from Winfield University in 1993.
Employment	Instructor in English at Winfield University, 1984–1988; taught political science at James University, 1988–1997; representative in state legislature, 1990–1992; chairman of the department of political science at James University, 1995–1999; dean of students at James University, 1999 to the present.
Other	Is well known for his scholarship and intelligence.
Name	Roger Thornton
Education	Graduated from Samuels College in science in 1975; master of education in chemistry from Smith University in 1982; doctorate in administration from Smith University in 1986.
Employment	High school chemistry teacher, 1982–1989, high school principal, 1989–1996, school superintendent, 1996 to the present.
Other	Very innovative and efficient administrator; very successful political speaker (the superintendent of schools is elected in his district); his father is vice president of a large bank.
Name	Edythe Constable
Education	Graduated from Brown College with a degree in liberal arts in 1985; master's in accounting from Smith University in 1990; doctorate in administration from Smith University in 1998.
Employment	Insurance agent, 1985–1990; certified public accountant, 1990–1998; vice president of finance, Williams College, 1998 to the present.
Other	Taught accounting in night school for eight years; volunteer director of a community center in a lower-class neighborhood for four years; was highly successful in raising money for the community center; has a competing job offer from a public relations firm for which she has worked part time for two years.
Name	Frank Pierce
Education	Graduated from Smith University with a degree in industrial arts in 1988; master of education in mathematics from Smith University in 1991; doctorate in administration from State University in 1997.
Employment	Neighborhood worker, 1988–1991; coordinator of parent-volunteer program for school system, 1991–1995; assistant superintendent for community relations, 1995 to the present.
Other	Has written a training program for industrial education.
Name	Helen Johnson
Education	Graduated from Brown College with a degree in social studies education in 1986; master of education in social studies from Brown College in 1990.

Employment	Taught basic academic skills in a neighborhood center run by the school system, 1986–1990; chairperson of the student teaching program, Smith University, 1990–1994; dean of students, Smith University, 1996–2000; vice president for community relations and scholarship fund development, Smith University, 2000 to the present; frequently asked to give speeches on Smith University throughout the state.
Other	Grew up in one of the worst slums in the state; has written one book and several scholarly articles. Given award for fund-raising effectiveness.

Name	**Keith Clement**
Education	Graduated with a degree in biology education from Mulholland College in 1987; master's in administration from Mulholland College in 1989.
Employment	Biology teacher in a high school, 1986–1992; consultant in fund-raising, public relations firm, 1992 to the present.
Other	Is recognized as one of the leading fund-raisers in the state; entertaining speaker; has written a book on teaching working-class students; extensive volunteer work in adult education.

EXERCISE

4.3 *Solstice-Shenanigans Mystery*

The purpose of this exercise is to study the way in which information is communicated in problem-solving groups. A mystery situation is used. Each of the accompanying clues should be written on a separate card. (The answers appear on page 585 in the Appendix.)

Timetable		Materials	
Activity	**Minutes**	**Item**	**Number**
Introduction to exercise	5	Deck of clue cards	1 per group
Briefing of observers	5	Observation sheet	1 per group
Groups make decision	20		
Whole class discussion	5		
Group processing	5		
Conclusions and closure	5		

1. Introduce the exercise as focusing on communication within a problem-solving situation. Set the stage for the exercise by announcing that each group has been formed to solve a crime.
2. Assign students to groups of five. One member should volunteer to be an observer. The observer's task is to record the communication patterns of the group, using the Patterns of Communication Observation Sheet (see p. 144).
3. The task of each group is to work cooperatively to solve a crime. Each group is to answer the following questions by consensus:
   a. What was stolen?
   b. How was it stolen?
   c. Who was the thief?
   d. What was the thief's motive?
   e. What time did the crime take place?

3. Each group receives a deck of cards. On each card is written a clue to the mystery. Keeping the cards face down so that the clues cannot be read, one member deals them all out so that each member has several clues.

4. Each group member is to read aloud the clues on his or her cards but must not show the cards to anyone else. Members may take notes but may not look at the cards of other members. All communication in the group is to be verbal.

5. When a group has answered the above five questions concerning the crime, it may wish to answer the following two questions if the other groups are not yet done:
   a. What happened to the other items?
   b. Who was present at the party?

6. Each group is to discuss the communication patterns it used in solving the mystery. Members may use the following questions to structure the discussion:
   a. What were the patterns of communication within the group?
      1. Who spoke to whom how frequently?
      2. Who talked, how often did they talk, and for how long?
      3. Who triggered whom in what ways?
      4. Who interrupted whom?
      5. Who encouraged whom to participate?
      6. What could have been done to gain more effective participation?
   b. Did all the group members easily obtain the needed information? Did they share their information appropriately, request each other's information, and create the conditions for sharing the information?
   c. Were the resources of all group members used? Was everyone listened to?
   d. How cooperative or competitive were the group members?
   e. How did the group make decisions?
   f. What problems did the group have in working together?
   g. What conclusions about small group communication may be drawn from the group's experience?

7. Summarize what the group members have learned, relate it to relevant material in the chapter, and provide closure by complimenting the groups on the quality of their work (regardless of whether they made the right decision).

SOLSTICE-SHENANIGANS MYSTERY CLUES

Mr. Purloin showed great interest in Mrs. Klutz's expensive diamond ring.
Mr. Purloin danced all evening with Ms. Beautiful. Mrs. Klutz was always losing things.
Mrs. Klutz could not find her diamond ring after leaving the party.
The hosts had a big party to celebrate the summer solstice.
The hosts had a painting by Artisimisso.
Artisimisso was a sixteenth-century Italian artist.
Paintings by sixteenth-century Italian artists are quite valuable.
Mr. Avarice was heard to say that he would do anything for a valuable painting.
Mr. Klutz is a dealer in fine art.
Mr. Klutz needed money badly to keep his business from failing.
Mr. Klutz always carried his briefcase with him.
Mr. Avarice is known to be very rich.
All of Artisimisso's paintings are small.
Mrs. Klutz spent most of the evening in a dark corner of the patio with Mr. Handsome.
Ms. Perceptive saw something glitter in a corner of the patio as she was getting ready to leave the party.

Ms. Perceptive admired a painting by Artisimisso when she arrived at the party.
Ms. Perceptive noticed that the picture she admired was not there when she left the party.
Ms. Perceptive left the party at 10:00. Ms. Wealthy brought her dog to the party.
Ms. Wealthy could not find what she had brought to the party.
The neighbors owned three dogs.
The neighbors found four dogs in their backyard after the party.
Mrs. Klutz admired the painting by Artisimisso when she left the party.
Mrs. Klutz left about 9:30. Mr. Handsome was a kleptomaniac.
Mr. Handsome left the party twenty minutes after Mrs. Klutz.
Mr. and Mrs. Klutz left the party together.
Mr. Purloin was a jewel thief.
Ms. Beautiful noticed the painting when she left the party at 9:45.
Ms. Beautiful left the party with Mr. Purloin.
Ms. Wealthy and Mr. Avarice left the party together.
Ms. Wealthy left the party about the time Mr. Klutz did.

EXERCISE

4.4 *Liepz and Bounz*

The following exercise is based on the same principle as Exercise 4.3. Use the same procedures, observation tasks, and discussion tasks used in the mystery exercise. Use six group members (including one observer). The solution is on page 585 in the Appendix. Each of the following pieces of information is to be placed on a card. The cards are randomly distributed among the five group members.

It is five liepz from Farmland to Parker.
It is eight liepz from Parker to Selma.
It is nine liepz from Selma to Muncie.
A liepz is ten bounz.
A liepz is a way of measuring distance.
There are four bounz in a mile.
A hobz is ten skibz.
A skibz is ten jumpz.
A jumpz is a way of measuring time.
There are four jumpz in an hour.
A hobz is a way of measuring time.
A skibz is a way of measuring time.
David jogs from Farmland to Parker at the rate of twenty-five liepz per jumpz.
David jogs from Parker to Selma at the rate of twenty liepz per jumpz.
David jogs from Selma to Muncie at the rate of fifteen liepz per jumpz.

BRIEFING SHEET

Pretend that liepz and bounz are new ways of measuring distance and that hobz, skibz, and jumpz represent a new way of measuring time. David jogs from Farmland through Parker and Selma to Muncie. The task of your group is to determine how many jumpz the entire trip took. You will be given cards containing information related to the task of the group. You may share this information verbally, but do not show your cards to anyone. You have twenty minutes for the task.

COMMUNICATION IN A PROBLEM-SOLVING GROUP

For any problem-solving group to be effective, the members have to obtain the information they need to solve the problem, and they have to put it together in such a way that an accurate or creative solution results. The previous exercises focused on the communication of information within a group. The situation in each exercise can be seen in Figure 4.4.

In most problem-solving groups, some information is shared by everyone, some information is known only to a few members, and each member may have information that no one else in the group knows. Each member is responsible for communicating what he or she knows to the other members of the group. Each member is also responsible for seeking out the information known by the other members. Thus, effective sending and receiving skills are both essential for all group members. What makes the exchange of information problematic is the noise that is usually present in problem-solving groups. Determinants of noise include how a group member is perceived, how much information a group member thinks each of the others has, how trustworthy a member has been in the past, how the messages are formulated and sent, what receiving skills are used, how cooperative the group is, and whether the member believes his or her information will contribute to the group's efforts.

The coordination of information, ideas, experiences, and opinions is an essential part of problem solving in a group. How successful a group is with such coordination depends on the skills of the members in sending and receiving messages and on the group norms about and procedures for communicating. Most important, however, problem-solving effectiveness is determined by the pattern of communication among group members. Three of the views of communication patterns are interaction analysis, one- and two-way communication in authority hierarchies, and communication networks.

INTERACTION ANALYSIS

The patterns of communication among group members are an important aspect of group process to observe and discuss. The interaction among group members may be analyzed through the use of the Patterns of Communication Observation Sheet used in the Bewise College exercise. There are three levels of interaction that may be analyzed.

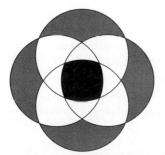

Figure 4.4 Communication of information. The black area represents information known to all group members; the gray areas represent information known to only one group member; the white areas represent information known to two or more members of the group.

The *first* level is the relative frequency and length of communication acts—who talked, how often he or she talked, and how much of the total available time that person used. The *second* level is who communicates to whom. Some persons speak to those they are trying to impress, others to those from whom they want support, and still others to those from whom they expect opposition. Information on this pattern of communication among group members is often helpful in pinpointing conflicts that must be resolved and increasing the group members' understanding of how they are relating to one another.

The *third* level of communication to observe is who triggers whom and in what ways. There are clear patterns of triggering. For example, whenever one member speaks another may always speak next, even if the remarks are not initially directed to him or her. This kind of triggering may reflect either support ("attaboy") or a desire to undo the point ("yeahbut") that has just been made. Schein (1969) quotes a businessman as saying that in group discussions in his company it takes at least three "attaboys" to undo the damage of one "yeahbut." Another type of triggering occurs when one member of a group interrupts other members. Knowing who interrupts whom gives the observer clues as to how members see their own status or power in the group relative to that of other members. Generally, high-authority members feel freer to interrupt low-authority members than vice versa. Interrupting others is one of the more common and more destructive kinds of communication behavior, and observing the patterns of interruption often reveals a great deal about relationships among members.

Many observation systems have been developed to examine group communication. One of the most famous, which is discussed in depth in Chapter 5 is Bales' (1953) equilibrium theory, in which he posited that effective groups must meet both task and socioemotional needs, which involves maintaining a balance between task and socioemotional activity. Bales and his associates developed an observation system known as *interaction-process analysis* (IPA) to analyze the interaction among group members. They concluded that distinct task and socioemotional roles tend to emerge in groups. This led various scholars and practitioners to compile lists of roles in groups. If socioemotional issues are not dealt with periodically, the mounting tension may inhibit the group's ability to make progress toward achieving its goals. In a similar formulation, Homans (1950) analyzed a number of previous case studies and concluded that a group must balance activity in its external system (which deals with achieving its goals and adapting to its environment) with activity in its internal system (which deals with relations among group members and the development of the group). The external and internal systems must stay in balance.

Communication patterns in decision-making and problem-solving groups have been analyzed by Gouran and Hirokawa (1996). They posit that in effective decision making, communication serves two functions—promotive functions (promoting sound reasoning and critical thinking) and counteractive functions (preventing groups from making errors). Thus, communication among group members facilitates the pooling of information, identifying and remedying individual errors, and making persuasive arguments. The effectiveness of decisions tends to increase as group communication focuses on problem analysis, clear and realistic goal setting, and critical and realistic evaluation of information and alternatives.

EXERCISE

4.5 *Transmission of Information*

The objective of this exercise is to compare the effectiveness of one-way and two-way communication. At least ten persons and two observers are required.

Timetable		Materials	
Activity	Minutes	Item	Number
Introduction to exercise	5	Observation sheet 1	1 per student
Briefing of class	10	Observation sheet 2	1 per student
One-way demonstration	10	Summary table 1	1 per student
Two-way demonstration	15	Summary table 2	1 per student
Whole class discussion	20	Summary graph	1 per student
Conclusions and closure	5		

1. Introduce the exercise as an example of information being passed from member to member within a group.
2. Ask ten persons to leave the room. They are to constitute two groups of five members each.
   a. One-Way Communication: Entering the room one by one, each member is to listen to a brief story and repeat it to the next person in his or her own way, without help from other participants or the group's observer. The receiver cannot ask questions or comment. He or she must simply listen to the story and then repeat it to the next person.
   b. Two-Way Communication: Entering the room one by one, each member is to listen to the story and ask questions about it to clarify its meaning and to make sure that he or she knows what the story is about. The person then repeats the story to the next person in the group in his or her own way, without help from other participants or the group's observer; the receiver can ask as many questions as he or she wants. You may wish to record the whole experience so that it can be played back for the participants' benefit.
3. After the ten participants have left the room, pass out copies of the accompanying observation sheets and a copy of "The Story" to the observers. Discuss the use of the observation sheet and read the story aloud. Explain the basic concepts of leveling, sharpening, and assimilation (these are discussed in the section on the effects of one-way communication on a message).
4. Begin the demonstration of one-way communication. Ask the first person to enter the room, read the story once, ask the second person to enter, have the first person repeat the story to the second person, and so on until the fifth person repeats the story to the observers.
5. Begin the demonstration of two-way communication. Ask the first person to enter the room, read the story once, obtain answers to all questions he or she has about the story, ask the second person to enter, have the first person repeat the story to the second person and answer all of the second person's questions, and so on until the fifth person repeats the story to the observers.
6. Reread the original story out loud.
   a. Using the results recorded by the observers and the following summary tables and summary graph, chart the percentages of original details retained correctly in the successive repetitions and compare the one-way and two-way communications.
   b. Discuss the results, incorporating the material in the sections on the characteristics of communication within an authority hierarchy and the effects of one-way communication

on a message. Ask the group for further evidence that leveling, sharpening, and assimilation occurred.

c. Ask what conclusions about one-way and two-way communication can be drawn on the basis of the results of the demonstration.

d. Ask the group what conclusions can be drawn about communication in authority hierarchies.

Other stories can be used in this exercise. Often, the more the cultural background of the story differs from the listener's culture, the more the story is taken in. A story from the Eskimo culture that might be used in this exercise appears below "The Story."

OBSERVATION SHEET: ONE-WAY COMMUNICATION

List in the first column the twenty specific details of the story (these appear in italics in the story). Verify the list when the coordinator reads the story to the first person. As person 1 repeats the story to person 2, note the mistakes in person 1's version by writing the wrong words or phrases in the proper row and column. To help in scoring, use a check mark for details correctly reported and a zero for details left out. Repeat this procedure for the rest of the participants.

Detail	Original Story	Version 1	Version 2	Version 3	Version 4	Version 5
1						
2						
3						
4						
5						
6						
7						
8						
9						
10						
11						
12						
13						
14						
15						
16						
17						
18						
19						
20						

OBSERVATION SHEET: TWO-WAY COMMUNICATION

List in the first column the twenty specific details of the story (these appear in italics in the story). Verify the list when the coordinator reads the story to the first person. As person 1 repeats the story to person 2, note the mistakes in person 1's version by writing the wrong words or phrases in the proper row and column. To help in scoring, use a check mark for details correctly reported and a zero for details left out. Repeat this procedure for the rest of the participants.

Detail	Original Story	Version 1	Version 2	Version 3	Version 4	Version 5
1						
2						
3						
4						
5						
6						
7						
8						
9						
10						
11						
12						
13						
14						
15						
16						
17						
18						
19						
20						

The Story*

A *farmer* in *western Kansas* put a *tin roof on his barn.* Then a *small tornado* blew the roof off, and when the farmer found it *two counties away,* it was *twisted and mangled* beyond repair.

A *friend and a lawyer* advised him that the *Ford Motor Company* would pay him a *good price* for the scrap tin, and the farmer decided he would *ship the roof* up to the company to see *how much* he could get for it. He crated it up in a very *big wooden box* and sent it off to *Dearborn, Michigan,* marking it plainly with his *return address* so that the Ford Company would know where to *send the check.*

*This story by Samuel J. Sackett, the actual title of which is "Tin Lizzie," is included in Botkin (1957). This title should not be mentioned until the end of the exercise.

Twelve weeks passed, and the farmer didn't hear from the Ford Company. Finally, he was just on the *verge of writing them* to find out what was the matter when he *received an envelope* from them. It said, "We don't know what *hit your car,* mister, but we'll have it fixed for you by the *fifteenth of next month.*"

The War of the Ghosts

One night two young men from Egulac went down to the river to hunt seals, and while they were there it became foggy and calm. Then they heard war cries, and they thought, "Maybe this is a war party." They escaped to the shore and hid behind a log. Now canoes came up, and they heard the noise of paddles, and they saw one canoe coming up to them. There were five men in the canoe and they said:

"What do you think? We wish to take you along. We are going up the river to make war on the people."

One of the young men said: "I have no arrows."

"Arrows are in the canoe," they said.

"I will not go along. I might be killed. My relatives do not know where I have gone. But you," he said, turning to the other, "may go with them."

So one of the young men went, but the other returned home.

The warriors went on up the river to a town on the other side of Kalama. The people came down to the water and they began to fight, and many were killed. Presently the young man heard one of the warriors say: "Quick, let us go home. That Indian has been hit." Now he thought, "Oh, they are ghosts." He did not feel sick, but they said he had been shot.

So the canoes went back to Egulac, and the young man went ashore to his house and made a fire. And he told everybody: "Behold, I accompanied ghosts, and we went to fight. Many of our fellows were killed, and many of those who attacked us were killed. They said I was hit, but I did not feel sick."

He told it all, and then he became quiet. When the sun rose he fell down. Something black came out of his mouth. His face became contorted. The people jumped up and cried.

He was dead.

Summary Table: One-Way Communication

Person	Details Correct		Details Incorrect		Details Left Out		Total Details
	Number	Percentage	Number	Percentage	Number	Percentage	
1							
2							
3							
4							
5							

Summary Table: Two-Way Communication

| Person | Details Correct | | Details Incorrect | | Details Left Out | | Total Details |
	Number	Percentage	Number	Percentage	Number	Percentage	
1							
2							
3							
4							
5							

Summary Graph

On this graph, plot the percentages of original details retained correctly in one-way and two-way communication. Connect the one way results with a solid line and the two-way results with a broken line.

4.6 One- and Two-Way Communication

This exercise contrasts the impact of one-way and two-way communication on communication effectiveness. Each participant needs two sheets of paper and a pencil. The coordinator needs copies of the accompanying square arrangements, which are given on page 585 in the Appendix. The coordinator may wish to copy the two summary tables onto a blackboard or a large sheet of paper.

Timetable		Materials	
Activity	Minutes	Item	Number
Introduction to exercise	5	2 sheets of paper	1 per student
Briefing of class	10	Pencil or pen	1 per student
One-way demonstration	10	2 diagrams	1 per class
Two-way demonstration	15	2 summary tables	1 per class
Whole class discussion	20		
Conclusions and closure	5		

1. Introduce the exercise as a comparison of the effectiveness of one-way and two-way communication.
2. Select a sender and two observers (if the group has fewer than seven members, select only one observer). The sender should be a person who communicates well and who speaks clearly and loudly enough to be heard.
3. One-Way Communication: Have the sender sit either with her back to the receivers or behind a screen:
   a. Give the sender the first arrangement of squares, making sure that the group members do not see it. Tell the sender to study the arrangement carefully for two minutes in order to be prepared to instruct the group members on how to draw a similar set of squares on their paper.
   b. Ask the first observer to note the behavior and reactions of the sender during the exercise and to make notes for later comments.
   c. Ask the second observer to make notes on the behavior and reactions of the receivers. Facial reactions, gestures, posture, and other nonverbal behaviors may be observed.
   d. Give the group these instructions: "The sender is going to describe a drawing to you. You are to listen carefully to her instructions and draw what she describes as accurately as you can. You will be timed, but there is no time limit. You may ask no questions of the sender and give no audible response. You are asked to work independently."
   e. Display Table 1 in the front of the room. Then tell the sender to give the instructions for drawing the first arrangement of squares as quickly and accurately as she can. Make sure that there are no questions or audible reactions from the group members.
   f. When the sender has completed giving the instructions for the first square arrangement, record the time it took her to do so in the proper space in Table 2. Ask all members of the group to write down the number of squares they think they have drawn correctly in relation to the preceding square.
4. Two-Way Communication: Instruct the sender to face the group members.
   a. Give the sender the second square arrangement and tell him or her to study the relationship of the squares in this new diagram for two minutes in preparation for instructing the receivers on how to draw it.

Table 1 Accuracy of One- and Two-Way Communication

One-Way Communication			Two-Way Communication		
Correct	Guess	Actual	Correct	Guess	Actual
5					
4					
3					
2					
1					
0					

    b. Ask the first observer to note the behavior and reactions of the sender during the exercise and to make notes for later comments.

    c. Ask the second observer to make notes on the behavior and reactions of the receivers. Facial reactions, gestures, posture, and other nonverbal behaviors may be observed.

    d. Give the group these instructions: "The sender is going to describe another drawing to you. This time she will be in full view of you, and you may ask as many questions as you wish. She is free to reply to your questions or amplify her statements as she sees fit. She is not, however, allowed to make any hand signals while describing the drawing. You will be timed, but there is no time limit. Work as accurately and rapidly as you can."

    e. Display Table 1 in the front of the room. Then tell the sender to give the instructions for drawing the first arrangement of squares as quickly and accurately as she can. Make sure that any receiver who wishes to ask questions does so. Audible reactions from the receivers are permitted.

    f. When the sender has completed giving instructions for the second figure, record the time in the appropriate space in Table 2. Ask the group members to guess the number of squares they have drawn correctly and to record the number on their papers.

5. Score the accuracy of the drawings:

    a. Obtain a median for guessed accuracy on the first drawing by recording the number of group members who guessed zero, the number who guessed one, and so on in Table 1. Find the median number guessed by counting from zero the number of group members guessing each number until you reach half the members of the group. Then record the median in Table 2.

    b. Repeat this method to get the median of accurate guesses for the second drawing.

    c. Show the group members the master drawing for the first set of squares, and point out the relationship of each square to the preceding one. Each square must have

Table 2 Medians for One- and Two-Way Communication

Medians	One-Way	Two-Way
Time elapsed		
Guess accuracy		
Actual accuracy		

exactly the same relationship to the preceding one that appears on the master drawing in order to be counted as correct. When this step has been completed, ask the members to count and record the actual correct number. Have them make a similar count for the second square arrangement.

d. Obtain the median for accuracy for the first and second arrangements and place them in Table 2.

6. Discuss the following questions with the class:

a. What may be concluded from the results in terms of time, accuracy, and level of confidence?

b. What did the observers record during the exercise? How did the behavior of the sender and the group members vary from one situation to the other? What were the group members and the sender feeling during the two situations?

c. How does this exercise compare with situations you find yourself in at work, school, or home? How might you change your behavior in relating to your friends and acquaintances as a result of what you have experienced during this exercise?

COMMUNICATION PATTERNS IN AN AUTHORITY HIERARCHY

Within every organization and in many groups there is an authority hierarchy. An **authority hierarchy** exists when role requirements are established in such a way that different members perform different roles and members performing particular roles supervise the other members to make sure they fulfill their role requirements. If a group, for example, is divided into several committees, each responsible for a different aspect of the group's work, its role structure would look like Figure 4.5. The members are supervised by the committee chairpersons, and the committee chairpersons are supervised by the group chairperson. Within an authority hierarchy, a system of rewards and punishments is usually established so that a supervisor will have some power over the persons he or she is supervising. Although authority hierarchies are established to increase the effectiveness of the group, they can often interfere with its effectiveness by

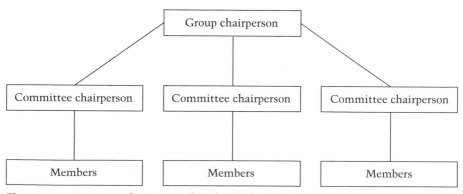

Figure 4.5 A group and its internal authority hierarchy.

undermining necessary processes such as distributed participation and leadership, equalization of power, controversy procedures, and communication.

To organize itself to accomplish its goals, maintain itself in good working order, and adapt to a changing world, a group structures the communication among members by scheduling meetings, requesting reports from group members, setting up conferences among members, and writing summaries of group progress. The communication network thus created determines the amount and type of information a group member will receive from the other members. In any group, communication is selective, a communication network exists, incentives to use the network properly are present, and members are expected to use certain procedures for communicating with each other. Thus, a college seminar will schedule meetings and faculty–student conferences as the communication network, be selective in choosing the material upon which communication will be based, use learning and grades as incentives for participating in the network, and encourage certain procedures (for example, when the instructor talks, students listen). The formal network, incentives, and procedures are established to coordinate members' efforts to accomplish goals. In addition to the formal communication network, in many groups there is an **informal communication network,** which includes patterns of friendship and social contact among group members.

The procedures used within the formal communication network based on an authority hierarchy may be one-way, one-way with feedback, and two-way. In **one-way communication,** a group chairperson gives instructions to the committee chairpersons, who pass them on to the group members. The committee chairpersons are not allowed to communicate with the group chairperson, and the group members are not allowed to communicate with the committee chairpersons. The receivers are passive, and communication effectiveness is determined by how the messages are created and presented. One-way communication tends to take less time than the other two procedures but to be less effective. Though it tends to be less frustrating for the sender, it tends to be far more unsatisfactory for the receivers.

In one-way-with-feedback communication, the chairperson presents the message and the group members give feedback on how well they understand it. The exchange is

completed when the group members indicate to the chairperson that they have received the message correctly. No provision exists for mutual influence or exchange. This procedure tends to be faster than two-way communication and less frustrating for the chairperson, but also less effective and more frustrating for the group members.

Two-way communication is a reciprocal process in which each member may initiate messages and clarify other members' messages. In two-way communication, the chairperson and the other group members freely exchange ideas and information in a productive discussion. Both sending and receiving skills are needed. Feelings of resistance or doubt can be discussed and resolved at the time they are experienced so that they are not potential barriers to commitment. Two-way communication encourages open and candid member interaction, distributed participation and leadership, consensual decision making, and other elements of group effectiveness. Although two-way communication tends to be more time-consuming than the one-way procedures and more frustrating for the chairperson, it tends to be less frustrating for the group members and more effective in the long run. Any goal-directed, problem-solving group that hopes to be effective should use two-way communication.

Even when a two-way communication procedure is encouraged, the authority hierarchy will influence communication among group members. High-authority group members usually do most of the talking, and most of the messages are directed at them. Low-authority members often do not communicate very much with each other during a group meeting, preferring to address their remarks to high-authority members. Because they generally fear evaluation by those with power, members without power take few risks, speak inconsequentially, and avoid frankness in their remarks. High-authority members often hesitate to reveal any of their own limitations or vulnerability, a tendency that also decreases open and effective communication among group members. Thus, several influences push the group's use of communication procedures toward practices that thwart the kind of discussion and problem solving needed for it to function effectively.

How can these tendencies be avoided so that communication within a group is effective? There are two answers to this question. The first is to establish a cooperative group climate that encourages the equal participation of all members. The second is to promote the attitude that all members' ideas and views are of interest. Because communication is interpersonal, furthermore, anything that interferes with the relationships among group members interferes with their communication.

Informal Communication Networks and Gatekeepers

When one-way communication procedures are used in a group, comprehension of messages is often so poor that group members turn to the informal communication network for clarification. Often certain group members are better able to interpret messages from higher-ups. In such cases, other members will seek them out and ask for their help. Such members are called opinion leaders or gatekeepers. A **gatekeeper** is a person who translates and interprets messages, information, and new developments to groupmates. There are two common types of gatekeepers: information gatekeepers (who receive messages from superiors and outside sources or who read, listen, and reflect upon written reports and verbal messages to a greater extent than other group members) and technological gatekeepers (who read more of the theory and research literature in their field and consult more with outside sources than do the other group members).

Gatekeepers frequently serve as translators by taking messages from superiors and rephrasing them in a more understandable form and to clarify the specific meanings they have for different group members. When one-way communication is being used, the original source is often not available for questioning and clarification of messages; group members, therefore, must rely on the gatekeepers. Group members, furthermore, may remember a gatekeeper's interpretation of a message better than the original message. Research on testimony in court cases indicates that people remember initial reports of events they witnessed better than the events themselves (Jones & Gerard, 1967). If the gatekeeper misconstrues the message, errors in understanding are amplified as interpretations are passed from member to member. Even with two-way communication, group members will at times be unable to clarify a message and will use gatekeepers to help them do so.

Effects on the Message of a One-Way Communication Procedure

What happens to information when it is passed through several persons with little or no clarification? The more the message is passed from person to person, the more distorted and changed it tends to become. Communicators attempt to reduce the message to a simple one that has significance for their frame of reference, interests, experience, and tasks. Three psychological processes characterize the communication between persons who are unable to communicate directly with the original source of a message (Allport & Postman, 1945; Bartlett, 1932):

1. **Leveling:** The receiver tends to reduce the amount of information he or she receives by remembering much less of the message than was presented by the sender. The message tends to grow shorter, more concise, and more easily grasped and told. In successive versions, fewer words are used and fewer details are mentioned.
2. **Sharpening:** The receiver sharpens certain parts of the information so that a few high points are readily remembered, while most of the message is forgotten. Sharpening is the selective retaining, perceiving, and reporting of a limited number of details from a larger context. It is the reciprocal of leveling—one cannot exist without the other. Certain points become dominant, and all the others are grouped about them.
3. **Assimilation:** The receiver takes much of the message into his or her own frame of reference and personality. Thus, interpretations and memories of what he or she heard are affected by the receiver's own thoughts and feelings. This process involves not only changing the unfamiliar to some known context, but also leaving out material that seems irrelevant and substituting material that gives meaning in the person's own frame of reference.

Because these three processes are at work whenever one-way procedures are being used, inefficient and ineffective communication usually results. This is true even when gatekeepers supplement the procedure.

EXERCISE

4.7 *Group Observation*

Review the material in the previous sections by taking the Patterns of Communication Observation Sheet (see p. 144) and observing at least two groups of which you are a member: one group in which there is a chairperson (such as a teacher) who dominates the meeting and another group in which free and open discussions are held among members. Observe the communication patterns in both groups and compare them. Write a description of the communication patterns in each group and discuss them with other members of your class.

4.8 *Communication Networks*

The purpose of this exercise is to compare the impact of five different communication patterns on productivity and morale. Each group member is to write down his or her reactions to each experience. Participants need to understand how to play poker.

Timetable		Materials	
Activity	Minutes	Item	Number
Introduction to exercise	5	Deck of cards	1 per group
5 communication networks	30	Paper and pen	1 per student
Group processing	15		
Whole class discussion	10		
Conclusions and closure	5		

1. Introduce the exercise as a structured experience in learning how communication networks affect communication among group members.
2. Assign students to groups of six. One member needs to volunteer to be an observer. The task of the observer is to time how long it takes the group to complete its task and to make notes about the behavior and apparent feelings of the participants.
3. **Chain:** The five participants in each group form a straight line, with everyone facing the same way. Each member receives five cards from a regular deck of playing cards. **No verbal communication is allowed,** but members may write notes to the person in front of or behind them. Members may pass cards to the person in front of or behind them. The group task is to select one card from each member's hand in order to make the highest-ranking poker hand possible. After the group has decided on a poker hand, each member should write an answer to the following questions:
   a. How satisfied are you with the group and its work?
   b. How did you feel?
   c. What did you observe?
4. **Y:** The same task with the same rules is repeated, but this time the group members arrange themselves in a Y formation, with everyone facing toward the center person. Members may pass notes and cards only to the person on their left or right. **No verbal communication is allowed.** After the group has completed the task, each member writes answers to the same three questions.
5. **Circle:** The same task with the same rules is repeated, but this time the group members arrange themselves in a circle. Members may pass notes and cards only to the person on their left or right. **No verbal communication is allowed.** After the group has completed the task, each member writes answers to the same three questions.
6. **Wheel:** The same task with the same rules is repeated, but this time the group members arrange themselves in a wheel, as in Figure 4.6. Members on the outside may pass notes and cards only to the person in the middle; the member in the middle may pass

Figure 4.6 Communication networks.

notes and cards to anyone. **No verbal communication is allowed.** After the group has completed the task, each member writes answers to the same three questions.

7. **Open:** The same task is repeated, this time with the members sitting in a circle. Any member may communicate with anyone else in the group. Members may pass cards and notes to whomever they wish in the group. **No verbal communication is allowed.** After the group has completed the task, each member writes answers to the same three questions.

8. **Group Processing:** Using the reactions group members wrote down after each experience and the observer's impressions, the group discusses and writes down the advantages and disadvantages of each communication pattern.
    a. What were the feelings of the members in the middle of a communication pattern? What were the feelings of those on the fringe?
    b. What communication pattern allowed the group to arrive at a poker hand in the shortest amount of time?
    c. If you were in charge of a company, which communication pattern would you try to use?
    d. How many messages were sent in each communication pattern?
    e. Did each pattern have a leader? For those patterns that did, what position did the leader occupy?

9. **Whole Class Discussion:** Each group shares its conclusions with the rest of the class.

10. Summarize what the group members have learned, relate it to relevant material in the chapter, and provide closure by complimenting the groups on the quality of their work.

COMMUNICATION PATTERNS AND NETWORKS

If a group is to function effectively, its members must be able to communicate easily and efficiently. Communication within the group needs to be arranged so that ideas, knowledge, and other information may flow freely. To this end, a number of studies have been conducted on the physical arrangement of communication networks, that is, on who can communicate with whom and whether the communication is direct or via another group member. More specifically, **communication networks** are representations of the acceptable paths of communication among members of a group or organization. Typically, these studies imposed various communication networks on groups in order to determine their effects. Some of the networks that have been investigated are diagrammed in Figure 4.6. The dots represent individual group members, and the lines represent links in the communication network. The most common procedure for imposing communication networks was first formulated by Alex Bavelas (1948). He suggested placing group members in cubicles connected by slots in their walls, through which written messages could be passed. When all slots are open, every group member can communicate directly with every other member. Other patterns are formed merely by selecting the appropriate slots.

Communication networks have been found to influence the emergence of leadership, the development of organization, the morale of group members, and the efficiency of problem solving (Leavitt, 1951; Shaw, 1964). The member who occupies a central physical position in a communication network usually emerges as the leader of the group. Because the central member has more information, he or she can coordinate group activities. Members who occupy a central position in a communication network are usually more satisfied with the group's work than members who occupy fringe positions. Typically, the morale of a group is higher in decentralized (circle, open) communication networks than in centralized ones (chain, Y, wheel).

When a task is simple and requires only the collection of information, a centralized network is more efficient in terms of speed and lack of errors. But when the task is complex and requires the analysis of information, the decentralized networks are more efficient, as we can see in Table 4.1. The problem with centralized communication networks is that the members in the centralized positions may easily receive more messages than they can handle. Furthermore, any extra demands that must be addressed by a member in a centralized position are likely to interfere with the efficiency of the network.

Table 4.1 **Differences Between Centralized (Wheel, Chain, Y) and Decentralized (Circle, Open) Communication Networks as a Function of Task Complexity**

	Simple Problems	Complex Problems	Total
Time			
Centralized faster	14	0	14
Decentralized faster	4	18	22
Messages			
Centralized sent more	0	1	1
Decentralized sent more	18	17	35
Errors			
Centralized made more	0	6	6
Decentralized made more	9	1	10
No difference	1	3	4
Satisfaction			
Centralized higher	1	1	2
Decentralized higher	7	10	17

Note: Simple problems were symbol, letter, number, and color identification tasks; complex problems were arithmetic, word arrangement, sentence construction, and discussion problems.

Source: M. E. Shaw, Communication networks, in L. Berkowitz (Ed.), *Advances in experimental social psychology*, Vol. 1 (New York: Academic Press, 1964). Reprinted with permission.

EXERCISE

4.9 *Sitting in a Circle*

How a group sits has a great deal of influence on how its members communicate. This exercise focuses on the effects of sitting in a circle. Each group engages in three five-minute discussions. After each discussion, each member writes down several adjectives to describe his or her reactions to the discussion. A different position is to be used for each discussion: (a) a circle in which everyone's back is to the center, (b) a circle with members face to face and a large rectangular table between them, and (c) a circle with members face to face and nothing between them.

After the fifteen minutes of discussion, members compare their reactions to the three positions. What were the differences in feelings? Was there any difference in how productive the discussion was? What effects did the different positions have on the discussion? How was communication affected? The advantage of sitting close together in a circle with nothing between members is that their unobstructed view of one another increases their opportunities to receive and send nonverbal messages. This type of circular seating arrangement also encourages more equal participation because there is no podium or seat at the head of a table to suggest that a particular member should assume leadership.

INFLUENCES ON EFFECTIVENESS OF GROUP COMMUNICATION

There are a number of influences on the effectiveness of group communication. The most powerful is whether the group climate is primarily cooperative or competitive. Other influences on communication effectiveness include group norms, physical setting, seating arrangements, and humor.

EFFECTS OF COOPERATION AND COMPETITION ON COMMUNICATION

Within any group, there tends to be a mixture of cooperative and competitive efforts. In some groups the interactions among members are almost purely cooperative, in other groups interactions are almost purely competitive, and in still other groups interactions are about half cooperative and half competitive. As was discussed in Chapter 3, the more cooperative the interaction among members, the more effective the group tends to be. This is as true for communication as it is for any other aspect of group functioning.

Cooperative Context

Many research studies show that when group members are working cooperatively, communication tends to be more frequent, open, complete, accurate, and honest (Deutsch, 1973; Johnson & Johnson, 1989). Within cooperative situations, individuals typically have a long-term time orientation, with energy focused both on achieving goals and on building good working relationships with others. Cooperators are interested in informing as well as being informed by others. They tend to use both sending and receiving skills more frequently and effectively. In addition, their perceptions of the other person and the other person's actions are far more accurate and constructive. Misperceptions and misunderstandings occur less frequently and are far easier to correct and clarify. The effective communication is influenced by the fact that in cooperative situations individuals trust and like each other and, therefore, are willing to respond helpfully to each other's wants, needs, and requests. Finally, when conflicts occur, group members tend to recognize the legitimacy of each other's interests, and conflicts tend to be defined as mutual problems to be solved in ways that benefit everyone involved. Perhaps the surest way to improve communication effectiveness within a group is to increase the cooperativeness of the group's goals and the positive interdependence among members.

One important aspect of cooperation is social support. Gibb (1961) conducted an eight-year study of communication in groups and identified supportive communication as being promoted by six types of behavior—description, problem orientation, spontaneity, empathy, equality, and provisionalism. Broome and Fullbright (1995), in a study on group productivity, found that the three major barriers to developing a positive, supportive group communication climate were dominance issues (in terms of power and relationships), interpersonal conflict, and personal fears of criticism and reprisal.

Competitive Context

When group members are competing with each other, communication tends to be either lacking or deliberately misleading (Deutsch, 1973; Johnson & Johnson, 1989). Competition, therefore, gives rise to espionage or other techniques for getting information other group members are unwilling to share and "diversionary tactics" to delude or mislead opponents about oneself. Within competitive situations, group members typically have a short-term time orientation and focus their energy on winning. They tend to deny the legitimacy of others' needs and feelings and consider only their own interests. Group members tend to have a suspicious, hostile attitude toward each other that increases their readiness to exploit each other and refuse each other's requests. The very nature of competition influences group members to work to gain an edge toward winning and to fear the possibility of losing. The more intense the competition, the more likely communication will be ineffective.

An important aspect of competition is defensiveness. Gibb's (1961) study primarily focused on defensive communication within groups. **Defensive communication** is behavior that occurs when a person feels threatened or anticipates a threat. Gibb identified six types of behavior that create defensive communication: evaluation, control strategy, neutrality, superiority, and certainty. The use of defensive communication by one group member tends to create similar defensive reactions in others. The more defensive the communication in a group, the more likely it is that members will misperceive the motives, values, and emotions of other members and the less efficient and effective communication tends to be.

EXERCISE

4.10 *Norms and Communication*

The purpose of this exercise is to demonstrate how group norms affect communication among group members. The participating groups must be groups that have worked together for several hours.

Timetable		Materials	
Activity	Minutes	Item	Number
Introduction to exercise	5	Discussion sheet	1 per member
Briefing of observers	5	Observation sheet	1 per observer
Groups make decision	20		
Group processing	15		
Whole class discussion	10		
Conclusions and closure	5		

1. Introduce the exercise as a structured experience in learning how group norms affect communication among group members.
2. Have each group select two observers. The observers need to construct four Patterns of Communication Observation Sheets (see p. 144), making the number of circles on the sheets equal to the number of members in the group they are observing. Explain the use of the observation sheet.
3. Give each group a copy of the discussion sheet and state that the groups have twenty minutes to discuss the topic. Give the signal to begin.
4. **Group Processing:**
   a. Ask the observers to report to their group. Groups are to discuss the communication pattern among their members and how it relates to the group norms they have been listing.
   b. Each group should also discuss how its members feel about the amount of their participation and how it could change group norms so as to gain more widespread participation and more effective communication among members.
   c. Each group should then revise its list of group norms in light of the discussion.
5. Have the groups share their conclusions in a general discussion.
6. Summarize what the group members have learned, relate it to relevant material in the chapter, and provide closure by complimenting the groups on the quality of their work.

DISCUSSION SHEET: WHAT IS A GROUP NORM?

Group norms so that members will know how they are expected to behave and what are the common rules or customs followed by group members. In some groups, for example, members address each other by their last names; in other groups, first names are used. All groups have norms, and usually these norms are eventually followed without conscious thought. Norms can develop so that every member does the same thing (dressing formally for a group meeting) or something different (dressing differently for a group meeting).

Norms are not built from scratch but develop from the values, expectations, and habits that the members bring with them when the group is first formed. "Don't interrupt the chairperson," an expression of respect for authority, is a norm that most persons bring with them into new groups. Norms can also be implied by the setting in which the group meets. Most persons do not sit on the floor in a room that is arranged formally. Most persons do not remain standing when their group is meeting at a beach.

Norms have a powerful influence upon communication within a group. Members seldom examine them or deliberately change them to improve group effectiveness. Usually they simply follow norms without question. This does not mean that norms do not change. Norms do change as expectations of appropriate member behavior change, but this is commonly an unobtrusive process.

What norms have developed in your group? Do you all sense where you are supposed to sit? Do you all sense who should be listened to and who should be ignored? Do you interrupt each other or is politeness a group norm? Are jokes allowed or is the tone of the group serious? How do discussions usually start? How are boredom and frustration generally expressed, if at all? Can certain topics be talked about and should others be avoided? Is the emotional involvement of members supposed to be high or low? In answering these questions, you will become more conscious of the norms that are present in your group.

Spend the next twenty minutes discussing your group norms and listing them on a sheet of paper.

PHYSICAL INFLUENCES ON COMMUNICATION

Physical factors can facilitate or block effective communication within a group. The environment of the meeting place can be a source of stress (Baum, Singer, & Baum, 1982; Halpern, 1995). It can be too hot, cold, impersonal, big, small, noisy, or distracting. On the other hand, many people seek out environments to spend time in because they feel better after spending time in such places as their homes, rooms, or even cubicles in an office (Altman & Churchman, 1994; Carlopio, 1996) and feel rejuvenated and energized by certain places and settings (Hartig, Mang, & Evans, 1991; Herzog & Bosley, 1992).

Temperatures from the mid-60s to the mid-80s are viewed as comfortable, but temperatures outside of this range can reduce productivity. If a room is too hot, physical effects such as exhaustion, aggressiveness, and even physical damage (such as heat stroke) can result. Extreme temperatures are potentially physically harmful. The same is true for noise. While sounds ranging from 0 to 50 decibels generally produce little irritation, sounds over 80 decibels may bother group members. While loud noise can be ignored for a short period of time, in general the louder the noise, the more likely it will produce distraction, irritation, and psychological stress (Cohen & Weinstein, 1981). Group communication may be enhanced if members pay attention to where they meet, the acoustics of the meeting space, the time of day the meeting takes place, the duration of the meeting, and the ventilation, temperature, and lighting in the room.

SEATING ARRANGEMENTS

Seating arrangements are typically taken for granted or unrecognized. They may, however, create a small group ecology (Sommer, 1967). The way group members seat themselves in relation to each other exerts significant influence on their perceptions of status, patterns of participation, leadership activities, and affective reactions (Gardin, Kaplan, Firestone, & Cowan, 1973; Howells & Becker, 1962; R. Myers, 1969; Steinzor, 1950; Strodtbeck & Hook, 1961). Members who believe that they have relatively high status in the group select positions (such as the head of the table) accordingly. Members sitting at the end positions of a rectangular arrangement participate more and are seen as having more influence on the group decision than members seated at the sides (Nemeth & Wachtler, 1974; Riess, 1982; Riess & Rosenfeld, 1980). Members tend to communicate with members facing them rather than with members adjacent to them. Easy eye contact among members enhances frequency of interaction, friendliness, cooperativeness, and liking for the group and its work. The more formal a seating arrangement, the more anxious members may feel. The group's formal leader usually sits at the head of the table, and the member sitting at the head of the table is usually perceived to be the leader.

HUMOR

Humor is an important influence on the effectiveness of communication in groups; it tends to promote cohesiveness and reduce tension (Bloch, Browning, & McGrath, 1983). Smith and Powell (1988) found that group leaders who used self-disparaging humor were perceived to be more effective at relieving tension, better at encouraging member participation, and more willing to share opinions than leaders who used superior-targeted or subordinate-targeted disparaging humor. Dension and Sutton (1990), in a field study of operating room nurses, found that humor served two functions: it reduced tension among surgical team members and it provided variety when standard operating procedures were perceived as boring to the members. Humor was more effective when higher-power members initiated it. Vinton (1989) reported that humor served three purposes in one work group: (a) self-ridiculing jokes signaled to coworkers that one was willing to participate in a friendly, informal relationship, (b) teasing eased working relationships when members worked in cramped quarters, and (c) bantering helped lessen the status differentials that existed among the members. Taken together, these studies indicate that the effectiveness of group communication is enhanced by appropriate and usually self-directed humor.

TAKING A SURVEY

Group effectiveness is enhanced when members have a clear understanding of each other's positions. One way to clarify such information is the survey method. A group survey consists of any member asking for the opinions of all the other members at any time. Each member then states in two or three sentences his or her current position on the topic under discussion. A survey is not a vote, and it does not bind the group members to a fixed position; it is a device to help communication and problem solving within a group.

E X E R C I S E

4.11   *Your Communication Behavior (II)*

How would you now describe your communication behavior in a problem-solving group? What are your strengths in communicating, and in what areas do you still wish to build skills? Now that you have completed the exercises and read the material in this chapter, take twenty minutes or so to write a description of how you see your communication behavior in problem-solving groups. Include a description of the way you formulate and send messages, the receiving skills you use, the way you contribute information and ideas to the group, the way you receive information about group meetings and group business, and so on.

After you have written your description, meet with two persons who know you well and discuss it with them. Is it accurate? Can they add anything? Do they have other ideas that might help clarify your communication behavior?

SUMMARY

Group communication occurs when group members send a message to one or more receivers with the conscious intent of affecting the receivers' behavior. It involves a multi-person exchange within a small group. It is effective when the receivers interpret the sender's message in the same way the sender intended it. There are basic sending and receiving skills that all group members need to master. Sending skills include taking clear ownership for one's messages, making messages complete and specific, ensuring that one's verbal and nonverbal messages are congruent, building in redundancy, obtaining feedback on how the message was received, adapting the message to the receiver's frame of reference, describing one's feelings, and describing others' behavior with evaluation. Receiving skills include paraphrasing accurately and nonevaluatively the content of the message and the sender's feelings, describing one's perception of the sender's feelings, and negotiating the meaning of the message until receiver and sender agree.

While all group members need to master sending and receiving skills, group communication is primarily analyzed according to the patterns of communication among group members and the factors that facilitate its effectiveness. There are three ways that communication patterns may be analyzed:

1. The interaction among members: The patterns of communication in groups are revealed by documenting (a) the length and frequency of each person's communication acts, (b) who speaks to whom, and (c) who triggers communication acts by whom in what ways.
2. The nature of one-way and two-way communication within authority hierarchies: Many groups have authority hierarchies. Within the hierarchy, the pattern of communication may be one-way, one-way with feedback, and two-way. Two-way communication is the most desirable in terms of group effectiveness. It is time-consuming and often frustrating for the chairperson, but it is less frustrating for the group members and much more effective in the long run. One-way communication often results in the creation of informal communication networks with gatekeepers. One-way communication also results in receivers leveling, sharpening, and assimilating the message.

3. The communication network in the group: Communication networks studied include circle, chain, Y, wheel, and open patterns. These patterns influence not only the flow of information in the group, but also who is perceived to be the leader, the way problems are solved and tasks are completed, the satisfaction and morale of group members, and the ease with which simple and complex tasks are completed. The more complex the task, the more open communication patterns are needed.

Many factors influence the effectiveness of communication patterns in groups. Cooperative or competitive communication determines how effective and how defensive the patterns of communication are. The more cooperative the climate, the more effective communication tends to be. Group norms largely determine communication effectiveness. There are also physical barriers to communication effectiveness, including the acoustics of the room, the seating patterns, ventilation, temperature, lighting, and the duration of the meeting. Seating arrangements determine who is perceived to be the leader and who exerts influence. There are times when group members need to know the position of all other members on an issue. This is easily accomplished by taking a survey.

You are now aware of the power and importance of group communication, the variety of patterns group communication may take, and the factors influencing communication effectiveness. The next chapter will discuss the nature of leadership within groups.

5

Leadership

Basic Concepts to Be Covered in This Chapter

In this chapter a number of concepts are defined and discussed. The major ones are listed following. Divide into pairs. Each pair is to (a) define each concept, noting the page on which it is defined and discussed, and (b) ensure that both members of the pair understand the meaning of each concept. Then combine into groups of four. Compare the answers of the two pairs. If there is disagreement, look up the concept in the chapter and clarify it until all the members agree on and understand the definition.

Concepts

1. Charismatic leader
2. Delegating
3. Distributed-actions theory of leadership
4. Influence approach to leadership
5. Initiating structure
6. Leader
7. Leadership styles
8. Machiavellian leadership
9. Maturity
10. Participating
11. Relationship behavior
12. Role position approach to leadership
13. Selling
14. Task behavior
15. Telling
16. Trait approach to leadership

WHAT IS LEADERSHIP?

Who built the seven towers of Thebes?
The books are filled with the names of kings.
Was it kings who hauled the craggy blocks of stone?
In the evening when the Chinese wall was finished,
Where did the masons go?

Bertolt Brecht

What is a leader? What is leadership? Are leaders born or are they made? Does effective leadership originate in a person or in a set of actions and behaviors? All cooperative efforts take leadership. Throughout your life you will lead others and be led by others. Providing leadership and following someone else's leadership pervade all aspects of life, including work, school, play, and citizenship.

The English word *lead* is more than a thousand years old. Its meaning has changed little from its Anglo-Saxon root, *laedare,* "to lead people on a journey." To lead is to guide by influencing the destination and the direction for the group to go. The *Oxford English Dictionary* notes the appearance of the word *leader* in the English language as early as 1300. The word *leadership,* however, did not appear until about 1800. A **leader** is a person who can influence others to be more effective in working to achieve their mutual goals and maintain effective working relationships among members. Individuals may become leaders through a wide variety of activities, such as winning supporters, solving problems, negotiating deals, building coalitions, mending fences among members, uniting rivals, or stirring emotions. Whatever the actions taken, leadership involves social influence. **Leadership** is the process through which leaders exert such

Example of a Leader: Benjamin Franklin

Before Benjamin Franklin reached thirty years of age he had been chosen public printer for the colony of Pennsylvania, founded the famous and influential Junto Club, created and published *Poor Richard's Almanac* (the most widely read publication in America), founded the first circulating library, and been elected grand master of the Freemasons Lodge of Pennsylvania. The next year he inaugurated the first fire-fighting company in Pennsylvania and was chosen clerk of the Pennsylvania Assembly. He was one of the most successful businessmen in the colonies but had enough interest in scholarship and research to be the founder (at age thirty-seven) of the American Philosophical Society. He continued to serve in a variety of leadership posts in politics, the army, science, diplomacy, and education (founding the academy that became the University of Pennsylvania). At eighty he led the group enterprise of writing the Constitution of the United States. A biographer noted, "Nobody could approach him without being charmed by his conversation, humor, wisdom, and kindness" (Fay, 1929).

How would you explain Benjamin Franklin's success as a leader? Was it due to his (pick only one):

____ **1.** Genetic traits?

____ **2.** Style of leadership?

____ **3.** Ability to influence others?

____ **4.** Occupation of positions of authority?

____ **5.** Ability to provide helpful behaviors in diverse situations?

In selecting one of these alternatives, you have decided on a theory of leadership. In this chapter we shall review each of these theories.

influence on other group members. By comparison, the root origin of *manage* is a Latin word meaning "hand," and managers are individuals who "handle" the status quo.

Being a leader, exerting leadership, takes skill. In work, school, or play, you use leadership skills. **Leadership skills** are the sum total of your ability to help the group achieve its goals and maintain an effective working relationship among members. Just as you learn the skills for doing math or science, you learn how to provide leadership. Anyone can learn leadership skills. All it takes is practice, practice, practice. Once learned, leadership skills can be used throughout life.

EXERCISE

5.1 *Who Are Your Heroes?*

Who is your ideal leader? Who does our society consider to be ideal leaders? Everyone has heroes whom they would like to imitate. The strength and dedication of George Washington, the intellect and commitment of Thomas Jefferson, the courage of Harriet Tubman, and the values and determination of Martin Luther King, Jr. may inspire us to wish to be like them. Who is your ideal leader? What qualities does our society believe the ideal leader must have?

Every society has a vision of what constitutes a leader. The ancient Egyptians, for example, attributed three qualities of divinity to their king (Frankfort, Frankfort, Wilson, & Jacobsen, 1949): "Authoritative utterance is in thy mouth, perception is in thy heart, and thy tongue is the shrine of justice." An analysis of leaders in Homer's *Iliad* resulted in four sets of ideal leadership qualities admired by ancient Greeks (Sarachek, 1968): (1) justice and judgment (Agamemnon), (2) wisdom and counsel (Nestor), (3) shrewdness and cunning (Odysseus), and (4) valor and action (Achilles).

1. Working by yourself, complete the following two tables.
2. Form a group of four. Compare answers and reach a consensus about society's views of who leaders are and what characteristics they have.

Who Are Ideal Leaders?

Leaders Society Admires	Leaders I Admire	Leaders We Admire
1.	1.	1.
2.	2.	2.
3.	3.	3.
4.	4.	4.

What Are Qualities of Ideal Leaders?

Qualities Society Admires	Qualities I Admire	Qualities We Admire
1.	1.	1.
2.	2.	2.
3.	3.	3.
4.	4.	4.
5.	5.	5.
6.	6.	6.

EXAMPLE OF A HERO KING

Alfred is the only king in English history who is given the title "the Great." Alfred became king of Wessex in England in 849, a time when the Vikings had conquered the north and the Danes had conquered the east. It appeared that the Vikings and Danes might conquer all of England. Alfred, however, drove the Danes out of the south and west of England and united that part of England as never before. He became famous for courage and skill as a warrior who fought "like a wild boar." He built an efficient army and a navy that patrolled the English Channel, discouraging further invasions and turned the attention of the Vikings and Danes toward the north of France. He then proceeded to repair the ravages of the Danish incursions. He rebuilt churches, imported foreign scholars, founded schools, began the compilation of the English Chronicle, and personally translated a number of books from the Latin, including *Bede's History* (which celebrates the glory of the English people). He is known as a lawgiver and educator who was devoted to the welfare of his people. His code of law was the first to survive in its original form. He hoped for a day when all the youth in England would be devoted to learning. Alfred was the first great statesman to emerge clearly from the mists of early English history. He died in 900 and, largely due to his work, most of the tenth century in England was a golden age of peace and prosperity. Never again was England to have such a king.

5.2 *Personal Leadership Experience Task*

EXERCISE

Write a description of a time in your life when you engaged in your most significant and effective leadership performance that represents your personal standard of excellence as a leader. Describe the details of the situation, including the place where it occurred, when it took place, who was involved, what was your role, what were the results, and what recognition (if any) you received. Also include what you learned about leadership from this experience.

_____

_____

_____

_____

_____

Form a group of four. Compare your descriptions. Write down four conclusions about leadership excellence. Be ready to share your conclusions with the entire class.

OUR CONCLUSIONS ABOUT OUR LEADERSHIP EXPERIENCES

1. _____
2. _____
3. _____
4. _____

5.3 *Controversy: What Is the Nature of Leadership?*

EXERCISE

The five views of leadership can be the basis for an academic controversy. The purpose of the controversy is to analyze the five views of leadership critically. The procedure is as follows:

Step 1   Forming Leadership Groups: Form leadership groups of five. The goals of the group are to:

a. Learn all five views of leadership.
b. Critically analyze each view of leadership.
c. Come to a consensus about the nature of leadership based on group members' best reasoned judgment.
d. Write a summary of the group's conclusions about the nature of leadership.

To achieve these goals, group members need to participate in a structured controversy.

Step 2   Forming Preparation Pairs: In each group members count off from 1 to 5. Each group pairs up with another group. Members of the two groups form preparation pairs. The 1s become a pair, the 2s become a pair, and so forth. Each preparation pair adopts one of the leadership theories.

1s	Genetic traits view of leadership
2s	Style view of leadership
3s	Influence view of leadership
4s	Position view of leadership
5s	Distributed-actions view of leadership

The pairs meet separately to (a) learn their position and (b) prepare a forceful three-minute presentation of their position. Both members must contribute to building a persuasive case for their view of leadership. The **purpose of the presentation** is to persuade the other members of their leadership group to adopt the recommended view as the most valid and reasonable view of leadership. The presentation should include (a) a position statement: "Our view is that a leader is someone who . . ."; (b) a rationale supporting the position containing as many facts and research findings as possible, arranged in logical order to maximize their persuasiveness, and illustrated with a visual drawing: "Because of a, b, and c, you must conclude that . . ."; and (c) a conclusion that is a restatement of the position statement: "Therefore, the most valid view of leadership is . . .".

Each person needs his or her own copy of the presentation. The pairs have about ten minutes for this phase of the exercise.

Step 3   Practicing as Pairs: Each person finds a new partner who has the same number and is prepared to present the same view. A number 1 finds another 1, a number 2 finds another 2, and so forth. The pair members share their presentation plan and their visual. Each person takes something from the other's preparation and adds it to his or her own in order to strengthen the presentation.

PREPARATION FORM

1. "The most valid theory of leadership is:" (the theory assigned to me is):

   _____

2. Because of: (List the reasons why your theory is the most valid view of leadership and then arrange the reasons in the most persuasive order.)

	Reason	Most Persuasive Order
a.		
b.		
c.		
d.		
e.		
f.		

3. Therefore, I have to conclude that the most valid theory of leadership is:

   _____

Step 4   Presenting the Best Case Possible for the Assigned Position: The leadership group of five meets. Each member presents the best case possible for his or her assigned position. The presentation is aimed at persuading the other members to adopt the position as the most valid view of leadership. The other group members should listen carefully, take notes, and ask for clarification of anything that is not fully understood. Each person has about three minutes to present his or her position (fifteen minutes total for a group of five).

MY PRESENTATION

_____ I will give a strong, enthusiastic, sincere appeal for the listeners to agree with me.

_____ I will make eye contact, speak clearly, and use appropriate gestures.

_____ I will keep my presentation within the time limits.

_____ I will create a visual to illustrate my points.

MY ANALYSIS OF THE THEORIES

Persuasive Points	Criticisms
Theory 1:	
Theory 2:	
Theory 3:	
Theory 4:	
Theory 5:	

Step 5   Challenging the Validity of Each Position: The group of five has an open discussion (anyone can speak at any time) in which members:

a. Continue to advocate the best case for their assigned position.
b. Continue to learn the other positions.
c. Challenge the validity of each of the other positions (give them a trial by fire) by critically analyzing (1) the theory, research, and assumptions of each position and (2) the logic of the presentation ("Your position has the following flaws . . .").
d. Defend their own position from the challenges of the other group members ("You are mistaken—my position is valid because . . .).

Each member should present as many facts and research findings as possible to support the group's position. Members should listen critically to the opposing position, asking for facts to support any conclusions made by the opposing pair. Participants should ensure that all the facts supporting both sides are brought out and discussed. The rules for constructive controversy should be followed. About ten minutes should be allowed for this phase.

Step 6   Reversing Perspectives: Each person presents the best case possible for the position of the next higher number (number 1 presents the 2 position, 2 presents the 3 position, 3 presents the 4 position, 4 presents the 5 position, 5 presents the 1 position). Group members need to be as forceful and persuasive as possible in arguing for the opposing position. They expand on the other position, adding new arguments or facts that the advocate did not present. Each member has about two minutes for the presentation (ten minutes total for the group of five).

Step 7   Synthesizing and Integrating the Five Positions: Group members drop all advocacy, synthesize and integrate the best information and reasoning from all five positions, and come to a consensus on their view of leadership. Each writes down his or her best reasoned judgment as to the nature of leadership: (a) the group position, (b) the rationale arranged in a logical order, and (c) a conclusion that is the same as the position. About ten minutes should be allowed for each group for this phase.

GROUP POSITION

1. Our group position is: _____

_____

_____

_____

2. Because of:

a. _____

b. _____

c. _____

d. _____

3. Therefore, you have to conclude that our conclusions are valid.

Step 8   Groups Present Their Positions to the Entire Class: Each leadership group presents its final position to the entire class. Because other groups will have other conclusions, each group may explain the validity of its position to the class.

Step 9   Group Processing: Each leadership group discusses the following:

1. What leadership actions did each member take to help the group effectively advocate and challenge each of the leadership theories?

   a. _____

   b. _____

   c. _____

   d. _____

   e. _____

2. What can each member do to be even more effective next time?

   a. _____

   b. _____

   c. _____

   d. _____

   e. _____

3. What were the most enjoyable parts of arguing about leadership?

   a. _____

   b. _____

   c. _____

4. What did I learn about myself as an arguer?

   a. _____

   b. _____

   c. _____

WHAT IS LEADERSHIP?

There are several different views of leadership. The following questionnaire measures your view. The procedure is:

1. Working by yourself, complete the following questionnaire.
2. Determine your score.
3. Form a group of four members. Compare your scores. Then read the following sections of this chapter.

   The statements listed below reflect various theories of leadership. Read each statement carefully. Using the following scale, indicate the degree to which you agree or disagree with each statement.

   1 = strongly disagree
   2 = disagree
   3 = neither disagree or agree
   4 = agree
   5 = strongly agree

   1. Leaders are born, not made.
      Strongly Disagree   1———2———3———4———5   Strongly Agree

2. Each leader has his or her own style.
   Strongly Disagree   1———2———3———4———5   Strongly Agree
3. The leader in a group is the person who is most able to influence the others.
   Strongly Disagree   1———2———3———4———5   Strongly Agree
4. Whoever has the most authority (power invested in a position) is the leader.
   Strongly Disagree   1———2———3———4———5   Strongly Agree
5. With training, anyone can learn to be a leader.
   Strongly Disagree   1———2———3———4———5   Strongly Agree
6. Great leaders with unique and inborn traits are discovered, not developed.
   Strongly Disagree   1———2———3———4———5   Strongly Agree
7. If you want to be a leader, know your style and go with it.
   Strongly Disagree   1———2———3———4———5   Strongly Agree
8. If you are appointed leader, then you are the leader, because subordinates are sup-posed to obey their superiors.
   Strongly Disagree   1———2———3———4———5   Strongly Agree
9. A leader persuades and inspires members to follow the leader's views of what needs to be done.
   Strongly Disagree   1———2———3———4———5   Strongly Agree
10. Leadership is acting in a way that helps the group achieve its goals and maintain good working relationships among members.
    Strongly Disagree   1———2———3———4———5   Strongly Agree
11. A good predictor of leadership ability is whether or not the person comes from a family of leaders.
    Strongly Disagree   1———2———3———4———5   Strongly Agree
12. To choose who should lead, decide which style of leadership is most effective.
    Strongly Disagree   1———2———3———4———5   Strongly Agree
13. The leader is the person who influences others to do what is best.
    Strongly Disagree   1———2———3———4———5   Strongly Agree
14. A leader makes sure that subordinates do their jobs.
    Strongly Disagree   1———2———3———4———5   Strongly Agree
15. Any member of a group may become a leader by taking actions that help the group complete its goal and maintain effective working relationships.
    Strongly Disagree   1———2———3———4———5   Strongly Agree
16. Leaders are "great persons" who become (or who are) members of elite social groups because of their outstanding inborn traits.
    Strongly Disagree   1———2———3———4———5   Strongly Agree
17. Some leaders are democratic. Some leaders are authoritarian. Every leader has his or her own style.
    Strongly Disagree   1———2———3———4———5   Strongly Agree
18. Leaders are leaders because they influence group members more than group mem-bers influence them.
    Strongly Disagree   1———2———3———4———5   Strongly Agree
19. Leaders are given the authority and power to punish and reward group members.
    Strongly Disagree   1———2———3———4———5   Strongly Agree
20. A leader varies his or her behavior from situation to situation to provide the appropri-ate leadership actions at the appropriate time.
    Strongly Disagree   1———2———3———4———5   Strongly Agree

What Is Leadership: Scoring

Genetic Traits	Style	Influence	Authority	Needed Functions
_____ 1	_____ 2	_____ 3	_____ 4	_____ 5
_____ 6	_____ 7	_____ 8	_____ 9	_____ 10
_____ 11	_____ 12	_____ 13	_____ 14	_____ 15
_____ 16	_____ 17	_____ 18	_____ 19	_____ 20
_____ **Total**	_____ **Total**	_____ **Total**	_____ **Total**	_____ **Total**

The higher the total score for each category, the more strongly you tend to believe in that explanation of leadership. The lower the total score in a category, the less strongly you tend to believe in that explanation of leadership.

TRAIT THEORIES OF LEADERSHIP

Perhaps Benjamin Franklin was one of the greatest leaders of the eighteenth century because he was genetically superior to his contemporaries. Throughout history many people have believed that leaders are born, not made, and that great leaders are discovered, not developed. Especially in times of great social upheaval and trouble, many people have looked for a great leader who has unique inborn traits. This is the "great man" or "great woman" theory of leadership. Royalty, members of elite social classes, older siblings, and early maturers are likely to believe in this approach to leadership. One of the strongest advocates of this theory of leadership was Aristotle, who once stated, "From the moment of their birth, some are marked for subjugation and others for command." There do seem to be individuals who dominate others through the force of their personality, their charisma, what they stand for, or their ability to manipulate others. There also have been historical periods when the prevailing ideology was that leaders are superior to other human beings.

In the early twentieth century there were many strong advocates of the **trait theories of leadership.** Wiggam (1931), for example, concluded that the survival of the fittest and marriage among them produce an aristocratic class that differs biologically from the lower classes. Advocating the social Darwinism that was popular at that time, Wiggam took the position that an adequate supply of superior leaders depended on a proportionately high birth rate among the abler classes. Henry Ford remarked, "The question 'Who should be boss?' is like asking 'Who ought to be the tenor in the quarter?' Obviously, the man who can sing tenor." He was suggesting that the boss is a person who has the natural ability to lead. The historian Thomas Carlyle believed that genius would exert its influence wherever it were found.

Hundreds of research studies have been conducted to identify the personal attributes of leaders. In one of the more interesting ones, Frederick Adams Woods (1913), an early-twentieth-century American historian, examined 386 rulers in fourteen countries in Western Europe who lived between A.D. 1000 and the French Revolution. All of these rulers had absolute power over their kingdoms. Each was classified as strong, weak, or mediocre on the basis of knowledge about his or her intellectual and personal characteristics (which were presumably independent of the strength or weakness of the nation at that time). The condition of each country was also classified as prosperous, declining, or lacking a clear indication of either. (This classification was based on the country's economic and political status, not on its artistic, educational, and scientific development.) Wood found a relationship between the monarchs' personalities and the state of the countries. He summarized his results as follows: "Strong, mediocre, and weak monarchs are associated with strong, mediocre, and weak periods respectively" (p. 246). Although the correlation coefficient was reasonably strong (between +0.60 and +0.70), as with any correlation we cannot infer a direct relationship between cause and effect. However, Wood clearly favored the interpretations that strong leaders cause their countries to flourish.

The typical research studies on trait theories have compared the characteristics of a leader (defined as an individual holding a position of authority, such as the president of the United States) with the characteristics of a follower (defined as an individual not holding a position of authority, such as a low-level government employee). The findings of these studies are somewhat contradictory and inconclusive. Bird (1940) analyzed the results of twenty studies that had considered seventy-nine leadership traits. He found little consistency in the results from one study to another. Of the seventy-nine traits, fifty-one made a difference in only one study each. High degrees of four traits—intelligence, initiative, sense of humor, and extroversion—were identified often enough in leaders for Bird to consider them "general traits of leadership." Mann (1959) reviewed 125 studies of leadership and personality characteristics representing over 700 findings (see Table 5.1). He concluded that intelligence and personal adjustment seem to be correlated with leadership.

There may be leaders who are more intelligent than nonleaders, yet it is evident that many of the most intelligent people never obtain positions of leadership. Intelligence

Table 5.1 **Percentage of Significant Relationships Reported in a Positive or Negative Direction for 125 Studies, Representing 751 Findings on the Relationship of Various Personality Characteristics and Leadership**

Personality Factors and Number of Studies of Each	Number of Findings	Percent Yielding Sig. Positive Relationship	Percent Yielding Sig. Negative Relationship	Percent Yielding Neither
Intelligence, 28	(196)	46% (91)	1%* (1)	53% (104)
Adjustment, 22	(164)	30% (50)	2%* (2)	68% (112)
Extroversion, 22	(119)	31% (37)	5% (6)	64% (76)
Dominance, 12	(39)	38% (15)	15% (6)	46% (18)
Masculinity, 9	(70)	16% (11)	1%* (1)	83% (58)
Conservatism, 17	(62)	5% (3)	27% (17)	68% (42)
Sensitivity, 15	(101)	15% (15)	1%* (1)	84% (85)

*Rounded upward.

Source: R. Mann, A review of the relationship between personality and performance in small groups, *Psychological Bulletin, 56,* 241–270, 1959. Reprinted with permission.

may have been a prerequisite for Benjamin Franklin's type of leadership, but it is doubtful whether Franklin or John Adams or George Washington possessed the highest IQ of their period (Cox, 1926). A follow-up study of 1,000 highly intelligent children from California showed that in twenty-five years relatively few of them had become famous leaders (Terman & Odor, 1947). None had attained high political office or the presidency of a corporation or college. Only 5% were in *Who's Who,* and only 13% were in *American Men of Science.* Despite the finding that leaders are better adjusted psychologically than nonleaders, many leaders (such as Adolf Hitler) have showed signs of being emotionally disturbed.

Stimulated by the personnel testing and selection programs begun during the First World War, social scientists attempted to identify the distinguishing traits of leaders. On these tests leaders scored higher than followers on a wide variety of characteristics, including intelligence and aptitude, personality, task motivation and performance, and social competence (Stogdill, 1974). Despite the great ingenuity displayed in the development of tests to measure these characteristics, however, such instruments have not proved reliably useful in the selection of leaders.

Although the correlations between individual traits and leadership measures are not large, some conclusions may be made. Stogdill (1974) divided the research on this subject into two periods: studies conducted between 1904 and 1947 and studies conducted between 1948 and 1970. The former body of research, he noted, revealed that leaders who participated actively in organizing cooperative tasks and carrying them through to completion were characterized by intelligence, alertness to the needs and motives of others, insight into situations, and such habits as responsibility, initiative, persistence, and self-confidence. The trait studies conducted between 1948 and 1970 indicated that leaders who have the capacity for organizing and expediting cooperative effort are characterized by a strong drive for responsibility and task completion, vigor and persistence in pursuit of goals, venturesomeness and originality in problem solving, a drive to exercise initiative in social situations, self-confidence and a sense of personal identity, willingness to accept the consequences of decisions and actions, readiness to absorb interpersonal stress, readiness to tolerate frustration and delay, ability to influence the behavior of others, and the capacity to structure social systems according to the purpose at hand.

These characteristics seem to differentiate (a) leaders from nonleaders, (b) effective from ineffective leaders, and (c) higher-echelon from lower-echelon leaders. Stogdill (1974) added, however, that when these characteristics are considered singly, they have little diagnostic or predictive significance. In combination they appear to be advantageous to the person seeking the responsibilities of leadership. Stogdill also noted that whether any one person with these characteristics rises to a leadership position depends considerably on chance: One must not only have the traits but also be in the right place at the right time. Perhaps the safest conclusion to draw from the trait and personality studies of leadership is that individuals who have the energy, drive, self-confidence, and determination to succeed will become leaders, because they work hard to get leadership positions.

Simon Bolivar once said, "Man is the weak toy of fortune." The trait theory of leadership gains some support when it is combined with social determinism. The **social de-**

terminism or Zeitgeist theory of history states that historic events are determined by social forces, social movements, and changing social values. **Zeitgeist** means "spirit of the times" or "temper of the times." Leaders simply play out roles designed for them by broad social forces. As Victor Hugo wrote, "there is nothing in this world so powerful as an idea whose time has come." Dean Simonton (1979), for example, analyzed why certain scientists rise notably above their peers and suggested that sheer chance and the influence of the Zeitgeist and previous technological discoveries are more important determinants of scientific eminence than personal traits. The trait and social determinism views are combined in the view that the great person plays a unique and decisive role only when the historical situation permits major alternative paths of development (Hook, 1955). Only when choices exist does the great person influence history.

What makes one person a successful leader, whereas another person fails in the same position? Some leaders (Napoleon, Hitler, Mao Tse-tung) have been able to control the destinies of millions of people. There are, however, at least four problems with trying to identify the traits of leaders: (1) An unlimited number of leadership traits may be identified; (2) different traits may be needed under different conditions; (3) "great" leaders are identified after the fact, but who will become a great leader cannot be predicted ahead of time; and (4) a match between the Zeitgeist and the great person may be required for great leadership to occur. In addition, there has been a biased focus on great men as leaders and a relative inattention to great women. Perhaps the best predictor of leadership success is prior success in leadership roles (Stogdill, 1974).

Besides the extensive research trying to differentiate leaders from nonleaders on the basis of personal attributes, there has been considerable discussion and research on two major traits of some leaders: charisma and Machiavellianism.

Charismatic Leaders

One of the dictionary definitions of **charisma** is "an extraordinary power, as of working miracles." Sometimes charismatic leaders seem to inspire their followers to love and be passionately devoted to them. At other times, charismatic leaders offer their followers the promise and hope of deliverance from distress. Charismatic leaders are saviors who say in essence, "I will make you safe," "I will give you identity," or "I will give your life significance and meaning."

Charisma does not seem to be correlated with any one personality type. The personalities of Alexander, Julius Caesar, George Washington, Robespierre, Bolivar, Sun Yat-sen, and Gandhi were widely different, yet all of these individuals were able to inspire confidence in their followers and to demand from them the sacrifice even of life itself. Garibaldi won the loyalty of his Roman soldiers with an unusual appeal: "What I have to offer you is fatigue, danger, struggle, and death; the chill of the cold night in the fall air, and heat under the burning sun; no lodgings, no provisions, but forced marches, dangerous watchposts, and the continual struggle with the bayonet against batteries—those who love freedom and their country may follow me!" Winston Churchill offered "blood, sweat, and tears" but sustained the faith and courage of millions.

Attempts to define charisma specifically and to measure the degree of charisma possessed by various leaders have failed. In general, however, a **charismatic leader** has (a) an extraordinary power or vision and is able to communicate it to others or (b) unusual powers of practical leadership that will enable him or her to achieve the goals that will alleviate followers' distress. The charismatic leader has a sense of mission, a belief in the social-change movement he or she leads, and confidence in him- or herself as the chosen instrument to lead the movement to its destination. The leader appears extremely self-confident in order to inspire others with the faith that the movement he or she leads will prevail and ultimately reduce their distress.

Machiavellianism

Current theories of leadership ignore not only the irrational aspects of leadership and followership reflected in charisma but also the realities of how power is often handled. If charismatic leaders found social movements and bring them to power, it is the Machiavellian leaders who consolidate and wield the power the charismatic leaders obtain. The essence of **Machiavellian leadership** is believing that (a) people are basically weak, fallible, and gullible, and not particularly trustworthy; (b) others are impersonal objects; and (c) one should manipulate others whenever necessary in order to achieve one's ends.

Niccolo Machiavelli (1469–1527) was a Florentine statesman whose treatise *The Prince* advocated the use of craft, duplicity, and cunning by rulers as political principles for increasing their power and success. He did not originate such an approach. Throughout history there have been theorists who conceived of leadership essentially in terms of the possession and exercise of power for self-enhancement. After analyzing the historical literature on how political leaders should govern, Richard Christie (Christie & Geis, 1970) concluded that Machiavellian leaders who manipulate their followers for political and personal reasons have four characteristics. *First,* they have little emotional involvement in their interpersonal relationships, because it is easier to manipulate others if they are viewed as objects rather than as fellow humans. *Second,* because they take a utilitarian rather than a moral view of their interactions with others, they are not concerned with conventional morality. *Third,* because successful manipulation of followers depends on an accurate perception of their needs and of reality in general, they are not grossly psychopathological. *Finally,* because the essence of successful manipulation is a focus on getting things done rather than on achieving long-term ideological goals, Machiavellian leaders have little ideological commitment.

Trait Theory of Leadership

Strengths	Weaknesses

5.4 *Interpersonal Patterns*

This exercise focuses on your interaction with other members of your group. It may help you think about how you conduct yourself in a group. The procedure is as follows:

1. The class divides into groups of three. Each person fills out the following checklist.
2. Analyze the meaning of the verbs you checked by following the instructions after the checklist.
3. Share with the other two members of your triad the results of the exercise and ask whether they perceive you in the same way or differently.

These twenty verbs describe some of the ways people feel and act from time to time. Think of your behavior in groups. How do you feel and act in groups? Check the five verbs that best describe your behavior in groups as you see it.

_____ acquiesce	_____ coordinate	_____ lead
_____ advise	_____ criticize	_____ oblige
_____ agree	_____ direct	_____ relinquish
_____ analyze	_____ disapprove	_____ resist
_____ assist	_____ evade	_____ retreat
_____ concede	_____ initiate	_____ withdraw
_____ concur	_____ judge	

	High dominance	**Low dominance**
High sociability	advises coordinates directs initiates leads	acquiesces agrees assists concurs obliges
Low sociability	analyzes criticizes disapproves judges resists	concedes evades relinquishes retreats withdraws

Two underlying patterns of interpersonal behavior are represented in the list of objectives: *dominance* (authority or control) and *sociability* (intimacy or friendliness). Most individuals tend either to like to control things (high dominance) or to let others control things (low dominance). Similarly, most persons tend either to be warm and personal (high sociability) or to be somewhat cold and impersonal (low sociability). In the preceding diagram, circle the five verbs you used to describe yourself in group activities. The set of ten verbs—horizontal for the dominance dimension and vertical for the sociability dimension—in which three or more are circled represents your tendency in that pattern of interpersonal behavior.

LEADERSHIP STYLES

Perhaps Benjamin Franklin became a leader through his style of relating to others. Franklin was noted for his charm, conversational skills, humor, wisdom, and kindness. But was Franklin's leadership style the same as George Washington's or Thomas Jefferson's? Even casual observation of leaders in action reveals marked differences in their styles of leadership. *Style* refers to the way in which something is said or done. It is usually contrasted with the *substance* of the statements and actions. The style with which an action is taken carries messages as well as the substance of the action. Style affects its legitimacy and credibility. Leadership may be defined as a style of behavior. Even casual observations of leaders in action reveal marked differences in their styles of leadership. Some leaders seem **autocratic:** They dictate orders and determine all policy without involving group members in decision making. Some leaders seem **democratic:** They set policies through group discussions and decisions, encouraging and helping group members to interact, requesting the cooperation of others, and being considerate of members' feelings and needs. Finally, some leaders take a **laissez-faire** approach: They do not participate in their group's decision making at all. It seems obvious that such differences in leadership style should affect group productivity and the attitudes of group members.

The pioneering study of whether leadership styles do in fact make a difference in group functioning was conducted by Lewin, Lippitt, and White (1939). Although the study has many shortcomings, it demonstrated strikingly that the same group of individuals will behave in markedly different ways under leaders who behave differently. As we have seen in Chapter 1, groups of ten- and eleven-year-olds were run by three adult leaders who adopted each of three leadership styles for a specified period: autocratic, democratic, or laissez-faire. When the groups were under an autocratic leader, they were more dependent on the leader and more egocentric in their peer relationships. When rotated to a democratic style of leadership, the same children evidenced more initiative, friendliness, and responsibility, and continued to work even when the leader was out of the room. Their interest in their work and in the quality of their product was higher. Aggressive acts were more frequent under autocratic and laissez-faire leaders than they were under a democratic leader. Hostility was thirty times as great in the autocratic groups as in either of the other two: Frequently one group member was made the target of hostility and aggression until he or she left the group, and then another member was chosen to perform the same function. Nineteen of twenty members liked the democratic leader better than the autocrat, and seven of ten liked the laissez-faire leader better than the autocrat.

A number of later researchers have investigated the relative impact of democratic and autocratic leaders on group functioning. In reviewing these studies, Stogdill (1974) noted that neither democratic nor autocratic leadership can be advocated for increasing productivity but that members are most satisfied with a democratic style of leadership. Satisfaction with democratic leadership tends to be highest in small, interaction-oriented groups. Other studies have compared permissive, follower-oriented, participative, and considerate leadership styles with restrictive, task-oriented, directive, socially distant, and structured leadership styles. After reviewing the studies in each of these areas, Stogdill (1974) drew the following conclusions:

1. Person-oriented styles of leadership are not consistently related to productivity.
2. Among the work-oriented leadership styles, socially distant, directive, and structured leader behaviors that tend to maintain role differentiation and let members know what to expect are consistently related to group productivity.
3. Among the person-oriented leadership styles, only those providing for member participation in decision making and showing concern for members' welfare and comfort are consistently related to group cohesiveness.
4. Among the work-oriented leadership styles, only the structuring of member expectations is uniformly related to group cohesiveness.
5. All of the person-oriented leadership styles tend to be related to member satisfaction.
6. Only the structuring of member expectations is related positively to member satisfaction among the work-oriented leadership styles.

Initiating group structure by clearly defining one's role as a leader and what one expects from the other members of the group is the single style of leadership that promotes group productivity, cohesiveness, and satisfaction. The most effective leaders may be those who show concern for the well-being and contributions of group members and at the same time structure members' role responsibilities.

The Lewin, Lippitt, and White (1939) study, along with other research conducted by Lewin and his colleagues, helped inspire and initiate the training programs in applied group dynamics conducted for the past thirty years at Bethel, Maine, by the National Training Laboratories Institute of Applied Behavioral Science. Immediately after the Second World War, a group of adult educators and Kurt Lewin and his associates began conducting workshops aimed at developing the leadership competencies of participants. These workshops formed the basis for the explosion of small group methods for personal and organizational change that took place during the 1960s and the growth in the number of consultants concerned with improving the development and planned change of organizations.

The major shortcomings of the style approach to leadership are that (a) different styles are effective under different conditions and (b) an unlimited number of styles may be identified. In certain conditions, autocratic leadership seems more effective (such as when an urgent decision has to be made). In other conditions, a democratic style may be most effective (such as when considerable member commitment to the implementation of the decision needs to be built). There are even conditions in which the laissez-faire style seems best (such as when the group is committed to a decision, has the resources to implement it, and needs a minimum of interference to work effectively). Because different leadership styles seem to be required in different situations, even with the same group, many social scientists have focused on situational approaches to leadership. But before we consider such approaches, two other theories of leadership are briefly discussed.

Style Theory of Leadership

Strengths	Weaknesses

INFLUENCE THEORY OF LEADERSHIP

A leader is a man who has the ability to get other people to do what they don't want to do, and like it.

Harry S. Truman

Leadership is the ability to decide what is to be done, and then to get others to want to do it.

Dwight D. Eisenhower

Leadership appears to be the art of getting others to want to do something that you are convinced should be done.

Vance Packard, *The Pyramid Climbers*

Benjamin Franklin may have been an outstanding leader because he knew how to influence people. Leadership involves influencing other group members. A leader may be defined as a group member who exerts more influence on other members than they exert on him or her. A number of studies have examined the factors affecting the amount of influence a leader has on the attitudes and behaviors of groupmates. Michener and Burt (1975), for example, found that members are more compliant when a leader justifies his demands as being good for the group, has the power to punish members who do not do as he asks, and has a legitimate right to make demands of subordinates. The success or failure of the group does not seem to affect a leader's ability to influence, nor does approval of him by subordinates.

An **influence approach to leadership** implies that there is a reciprocal role relationship between leaders and followers. Without followers there can be no leader, and without a leader there can be no followers. The leader and the followers both give something to and receive something from each other. As Homans stated, "Influence over others is purchased at the price of allowing oneself to be influenced by others" (1961, p. 286). Although leadership may be defined as the successful influencing of other group members, the followers also influence the leader. The leader receives status, recognition, esteem, and other reinforcement for contributing his or her resources to the accomplishment of the group's goal. The followers obtain the leader's resources and ability to structure the group's activities toward the attainment of a goal. The leader provides structure, direction, and resources. The followers provide deference and reinforcement. Because both the leader and the followers control resources that the other desires, they can each influence the other's behavior.

Many studies demonstrate the interdependence of leader and followers. Leaders tend both to talk more than other group members and to receive more communications (Zander, 1979). When a person is reinforced and encouraged by other group members to act as a leader, the person's proportion of talking time increases as his or her perceived leadership status increases (Bavelas, Hostorf, Gross, & Kite, 1965; Zdep & Oakes, 1967). Pepinsky and his associates (1958) demonstrated that individuals who had previously exhibited few leadership behaviors were influenced to behave far more actively by the group's evident support for their assertions; individuals who had previously exhibited many leadership behaviors were affected in precisely the opposite way by the group's evident disagreement with their statements. From these and other studies it may be concluded that (a) the amount of participation and influence of a leader affects how members perceive his or her leadership, and (b) the amount of encouragement and support by followers affects the amount of a person's participation and perceived leadership status.

Viewing leadership as a reciprocal influence between a leader and a set of followers

does not necessarily mean that leadership is based on domination. Hitler, for example, defined leadership as the ability to move the masses (either through persuasion or violence). Ho Chi Minh believed a good leader must learn to mold, shape, and change the people just as a woodworker must learn to use wood. Both views are erroneous. Leaders do not influence through domination and

Influence Theory of Leadership

Strengths	Weaknesses

coercion. Rather, they persuade group members to cooperate in setting and achieving goals. Leadership is thus the art of ensuring that group members work together with the least friction and the most cooperation. This often means that leaders need to persuade and inspire members to follow their views of what needs to be done in order to achieve a group's goals.

ROLE POSITION APPROACH TO LEADERSHIP

Perhaps Benjamin Franklin was known as a leader simply because he was appointed to various leadership positions. A leader may be defined as a person who holds a position of authority. Leadership in organizations begins with the formal role structure that defines the hierarchy of authority. **Authority** is legitimate power vested in a particular position to ensure that individuals in subordinate positions meet the requirements of their organizational role. Because organizations demand that subordinates obey their superiors in performing their roles, a person with authority will influence his or her subordinates. A person who is directly above you in the authority hierarchy, therefore, is your leader.

There are at least three problems with the **role position approach to leadership.** *First*, it is unclear how individuals are appointed to high-authority positions. It does not have to be for leadership ability. *Second*, it does not explain how the leader can engage in nonleadership behaviors and the subordinates can engage in leadership actions. Not all of the appointed leader's actions are leadership behavior. In addition, subordinates can provide leadership. *Third*, the role behavior of subordinates is influenced by outsiders who have no direct authority over them.

Role Position Theory of Leadership

Strengths	Weaknesses

EXERCISE

5.5 *Understanding Your Leadership Actions Questionnaire*

Each of the following statements describes a leadership action. For each statement mark:

5 = I always behave that way   2 = I seldom behave that way
4 = I frequently behave that way   1 = I never behave that way
3 = I occasionally behave that way

WHEN I AM A MEMBER OF A GROUP:

_____ 1. I offer facts and give my opinions, ideas, feelings, and information in order to help the group discussion.

_____ 2. I make sure I understand what other group members say by restating it in my own words. I use good communication skills and help facilitate effective communication among group members.

_____ 3. I give direction to the group by calling attention to the tasks that need to be done and suggesting procedures for completing them. I organize role responsibilities for group members.

_____ 4. I promote the open discussion of conflicts among group members in order to resolve disagreements and mediate when the members seem unable to resolve the conflicts directly.

_____ 5. I tell jokes and make amusing comments in order to make members laugh and to increase the fun we have working together.

_____ 6. I summarize the contributions of group members into one condensed statement and integrate all the diverse actions of members into a unified whole.

_____ 7. I express support, acceptance, and liking for other members of the group and give appropriate recognition and praise when another member has taken a constructive action.

_____ 8. I ask for facts, information, opinions, ideas, and feelings from the other members in order to use all the group's resources to complete the task.

_____ 9. I encourage all members of the group to participate. I try to give them the confidence to contribute actively to the group effort. I let them know I value their contributions.

_____ 10. I ask others to explain the group's answers and conclusions to ensure that they understand the material being discussed by the group.

_____ 11. I give the group energy. I try to get group members excited about achieving our goals.

_____ 12. I observe the way the group is working and use my observations to help discuss how group members can work together better.

SCORING THE LEADERSHIP QUESTIONNAIRE

In order to obtain a total score for task actions and maintenance actions, write the score for each item in the appropriate column and then total the scores for each column (see Figure 5.1).

Task Actions	*Maintenance Actions*
_____ 1. Information and opinion giver	_____ 2. Communication facilitator
_____ 3. Direction and role definer	_____ 4. Interpersonal problem solver
_____ 6. Summarizer	_____ 5. Tension reliever
_____ 8. Information and opinion seeker	_____ 7. Supporter and praiser
_____ 10. Checker for understanding	_____ 9. Encourager of participation
_____ 11. Energizer	_____ 12. Process observer
_____ **Total for Task Actions**	_____ **Total for Maintenance Actions**

Figure 5.1   Task-maintenance grid.

TASK–MAINTENANCE PATTERNS

(6, 6) Only a minimum effort is given to getting the required work done. There is general noninvolvement with other group members. The person with this score may well be saying: "To hell with it all!" Or he or she may be so inactive in the group as to have no influence whatsoever on other group members.

(6, 30) High value is placed on maintaining good relationships within the group. Thoughtful attention is given to the needs of other members. The person with this score helps create a comfortable, friendly atmosphere and work tempo. However, he or she may never help the group do any work.

(30, 6) Getting the job done is emphasized in a way that shows very little concern with group maintenance. Work is seen as important, and relationships among group members are ignored. The person with this score may take an army-drillmaster approach to leadership.

(18, 18) The task and maintenance needs of the group are balanced. The person with this score continually makes compromises between task needs and maintenance needs. Though a great compromiser, this person does not look for or find ways to creatively integrate task and maintenance activities for optimal productivity.

(30, 30) When everyone plans and makes decisions together, all the members become committed to getting the task done as they build relationships of trust and respect.

MATCHING EXERCISE 1

To help you learn the task and maintenance actions, match the following terms with their definitions (answers appear on page 225).

Task Actions

_____ 1. Information and opinion giver
_____ 2. Information and opinion seeker
_____ 3. Direction and role definer
_____ 4. Summarizer
_____ 5. Energizer
_____ 6. Comprehension checker

a. Makes sure all group members understand what other members say.
b. Pulls together related ideas or suggestions and restates them.
c. Offers facts, opinions, ideas, feelings, and information.

Maintenance Actions

---- 7. Encourager of
participation

---- 8. Communication facilitator

---- 9. Tension reliever

---- 10. Process observer

---- 11. Interpersonal problem
solver

---- 12. Supporter and praiser

d. Expresses acceptance and liking for group members.

e. Uses observations of how the group is working to help discuss how the group can improve.

f. Lets members know their contributions are valued.

g. Asks for facts, opinions, ideas, feelings, and information.

h. Asks others to summarize the discussion to make sure they understand.

i. Encourages group members to work hard to achieve goals.

j. Calls attention to tasks that need to be done and assigns responsibilities.

k. Helps resolve and mediate conflicts.

l. Tells jokes and increases the group fun.

MATCHING EXERCISE 2

How Well Do I Understand Functioning (Leadership) Skills?

Match the following statements with goal relationship leadership action they best seem to fill (answers appear on page 225).

Goal Actions

---- 1. Information and
opinion giver

---- 2. Information and
opinion seeker

---- 3. Direction and role definer

---- 4. Summarizer

---- 5. Energizer

---- 6. Comprehension checker

Relationship Actions

---- 7. Encourager of
participation

---- 8. Communication facilitator

---- 9. Tension reliever

---- 10. Process observer

---- 11. Interpersonal
problem solver

---- 12. Supporter and praiser

a. "Helen, my understanding is that you are suggesting that we define the problem before we try to solve it."

b. "How about giving our report on yoga while standing on our heads?"

c. "Three ideas have been suggested. Dale thinks we should play football, Jose thinks we should go to lunch, and Tai believes we should write a story about what we are doing."

d. "I think we should help resolve the conflict between David and Linda."

e. "George Washington was the first president of the United States and, in my opinion, the best one."

f. "Francene has not said anything for the past five minutes. Is there a problem?"

g. "That is an important insight, Roger. It indicates that you have really worked hard on the homework."

h. "Fire up! We can find a good solution. Let's put a little more effort into it."

i. "Frank, explain to us step by step how to solve question 12."

j. "We should first define the problem and second suggest solutions. We can then decide which solution to adopt."

k. "Roger, do you know who the fourth president of the United States was and what he is famous for?"

l. "Helen, I would like to hear what you think about this; you have good ideas."

SITUATIONAL THEORIES OF LEADERSHIP

Perhaps Benjamin Franklin became a renowned leader because he was able to vary his behavior systematically from situation to situation so as to provide the appropriate leadership actions at the appropriate time. Social scientists now believe that leadership skills and competencies are not inherited from one's ancestors, that they do not magically appear when a person is assigned to a leadership position, and that the same style will not provide adequate leadership in every situation. Different situations require different approaches to leadership. To be a leader, you must be able to vary your behavior to provide the functions a group needs at specific times. In other words, **leadership is actions performed by many, not a position held by one.** You are not the leader and I am not the leader; what we do provides leadership. We shall discuss four situational theories in this chapter: the distributed-actions theory, Bales' interaction-process analysis, Fiedler's situational theory, and Hersey and Blanchard's situational theory.

The Distributed-Actions Theory of Leadership

Not the cry, but the flight of the wild duck, leads the flock to fly and follow.

Chinese proverb

The **distributed-actions theory of leadership** emphasizes that certain functions need to be performed if a group is to achieve its goals and maintain effective working relationships among members. A *function* is an action that must take place in order for a group to be effective. At different times, different functions are required. At one time, information may be needed. At another time, the contributions of members may have to be summarized and integrated. Members must engage in the *goal-leadership actions* of contributing, asking for, summarizing, and coordinating information. Members have to structure and direct the group's efforts and provide the energy to motivate members to make the decision.

It does no good to achieve goals successfully if the manner of doing so alienates group members. Members must maintain good relationships while working to achieve goals. They must achieve goals in ways that increase their ability to work together effectively in the future. Members engage in *relationship-leadership actions* when they encourage each other to participate, facilitate communication, relieve tension, and evaluate the emotional climate of the group. They have to discuss how the group's work can be improved, and they have to listen carefully and respectfully to one another.

The distributed-actions theory of leadership includes two basic ideas: (1) Any member of a group may become a leader by taking actions that help the group complete its goals and maintain effective working relationships; (2) any leadership function may be fulfilled by different members performing a variety of relevant behaviors. Leadership, therefore, is specific to a particular group in a particular situation. Under some circumstances an action may be helpful, whereas under other circumstances it may not. When a group is trying to define a problem, for example, providing information about the nature of the problem may be helpful, but when the group is deciding which solution to adopt, giving more information about the nature of the problem may be unhelpful.

To provide leadership, you must have:

1. The flexibility to engage in a wide variety of actions.
2. The ability to determine what behaviors are needed at a particular time in order for the group to function most efficiently.
3. The ability to engage in these behaviors or to get other members to do so.

To be a skilled leader, therefore, you have to have the diagnostic skills to be aware that a given function is needed, be sufficiently flexible to provide the diverse types of actions needed for different situations, and be able to utilize the abilities of other group members in providing the actions needed by the group.

For at least three reasons, the behaviors that fulfill group functions usually should be distributed among group members. *First,* if members do not participate, then their ideas, skills, and information are not being utilized. This reduces the group's effectiveness. *Second,* members become committed to what they help build. Members who participate become more committed to the group than do members who remain silent. *Third,* active members often become worried or annoyed about the silent members and view them as unconcerned about goal achievement. This can create relationship problems within the group.

When you help the group achieve its goals and maintain good working relationships among members, you sometimes help yourself at the same time. Helping the group can clarify your personal identity (Who am I in this group? Where do I fit in?), fulfill personal goals (I am better off when I am a member of a successful group), increase your power and influence (How much power and influence do I have?), and build better relationships with others (How close will we get to each other? Who are my friends?).

The distributed-actions theory of leadership is one of the most concrete and direct approaches available for improving your leadership skills and for improving the effectiveness of the groups to which you belong. You can be taught the diagnostic skills and behaviors that help a group accomplish its goal and maintain effective working relationships among members. There is, however, some criticism of the approach. There are so many different actions members can take to help the group achieve its goals and maintain good relationships that specific ones are hard to pin down. What constitutes leadership, then, depends on the view of the person who is listing the leadership behaviors.

Interaction-Process Analysis

If you put five strangers together and assign them a task that requires them to cooperate, something remarkable but predictable happens: The social interaction among them becomes patterned and a leadership structure emerges. One variable that is consistently related to the emergence of leadership is the amount of talking a group member does. The person who talks the most is the one most likely to emerge as leader (Burke, 1974; Stein & Heller, 1979). The average correlation between participation and leadership is 0.65. Group members attribute leadership qualities to certain behaviors they observe in

Example of a Leader: Harriet Tubman

Harriet Tubman was born a slave about 1820 in Bucktown, Maryland. Her grandparents had been brought from Africa to America sometime after 1725. Very early in life, Harriet developed a rebellious nature, perhaps from the hard work and many beatings she endured. She was determined to be free. At age fifteen she was beaten nearly to death with a two-pound iron counterweight for helping another slave to escape. She never completely recovered, having a dent in her skull and seizures during which she would suddenly fall asleep. In 1849, Harriet escaped to Delaware and then to Pennsylvania. While working in Philadelphia, Harriet became involved with the Underground Railroad, a network of routes, guides, and hiding places that helped runaway slaves reach freedom in the northern states. As early as 1850 she began working as a guide or *conductor* for the railroad, risking her life over and over again to help others gain their freedom. She was given the name Moses for the frequency with which she conducted runaways to the North and was so successful that a reward of $40,000 was offered for her capture. She helped at least 300 slaves escape in all. After the Fugitive Slave Law was passed in 1850, Harriet conducted escaped slaves all the way to Canada. During the Civil War she worked as a nurse, laundress, cook, and spy for the Union army in South Carolina. She spent the rest of her life working to feed and house needy blacks and to gain full freedom for them. She died at about the age of ninety-three on March 10, 1913. She represents a leader whose actions spoke louder than words.

the group: strong participation as a sign of motivation, involvement, willingness to share resources with the group, and seriously trying to contribute to the group's goals (Sorrentino & Boutiller, 1975).

Whether it is a work group, discussion group, learning group, or recreation group, one of the common forms this leadership structure takes is for one person to assume a task-leadership role that includes behaviors oriented primarily to task achievement (such as directing, summarizing, and providing ideas) and another person to assume a social-emotional-leadership role that includes behaviors oriented primarily to the expressive, interpersonal affairs of the group (such as alleviating frustrations, resolving tensions, and mediating conflicts).

Robert Bales (1950, 1952, 1955), in a series of studies in the late 1940s and early 1950s, was among the first to focus on task and social-emotional leadership in his equilibrium theory. His work has been corroborated and extended by Burke (1972). The basic interaction-process theory consists of the following points:

1. When a group has a task to complete, its members engage in task-related behaviors on an unequal basis.
2. The members who are high on task behaviors tend to create some tension and hostility among members who are less committed to the task.
3. There is a need for actions that help maintain effective working relationships among members.

4. Members other than those high on task actions engage in social-emotional actions.

5. These differentiated roles (task and social-emotional) are stabilized and synchronized as the task and social-emotional leaders reinforce and support each other.

When the group has no task to achieve or no commitment to achieve its assigned task, a task leader is not needed and will not appear. Correspondingly, with no commitment to a goal there is no need to maintain relationships among members, and a social-emotional leader will not evolve.

In his research, Bales developed an observational instrument for identifying task and social-emotional behaviors within a small group (Figures 5.2 and 5.3). The instrument consists of several categories that are designed to allow a systematic classification of all the acts of participation in a group. As you can see in Figure 5.2, the categories are polarized: Category 1 is the opposite of category 12, 2 is the opposite of 11, and so on. The first three categories are positive emotions, the last three negative emotions. Categories 7, 8, and 9 request aid, whereas categories 4, 5, and 6 offer it.

Bales' research indicates that positive emotions (categories 1, 2, and 3) are usually expressed more than twice as often as negative emotions (10, 11, and 12). Opinions and information are volunteered much more often (46% of all participant behaviors observed)

Social-Emotional Area: Positive

1. Shows solidarity, raises others' status, gives help, rewards.

2. Shows tension release, jokes, laughs, shows satisfaction.

3. Agrees, shows passive acceptance, understands, concurs, complies.

Task Area: Neutral

4. Gives suggestions, directions, implying autonomy for others.

5. Gives opinions, evaluation, analysis; expresses feelings, wishes.

6. Gives orientation, information, repeats, clarifies, confirms.

Task Area: Neutral

7. Asks for orientation, information, repetition, confirmation.

8. Asks for opinions, evaluation, analysis, expressions of feeling.

9. Asks for suggestions, direction, possible ways of action.

Social-Emotional Area: Negative

10. Disagrees, shows passive rejection, formality, withholds help.

11. Shows tension, asks for help, withdraws, leaves the field.

12. Shows antagonism, deflates others' status, defends or asserts self.

Figure 5.2 Bales' system of categories used in observation.
Source: R. Bales, *Interaction process analysis* (Reading, MA: Addison-Wesley, 1950).

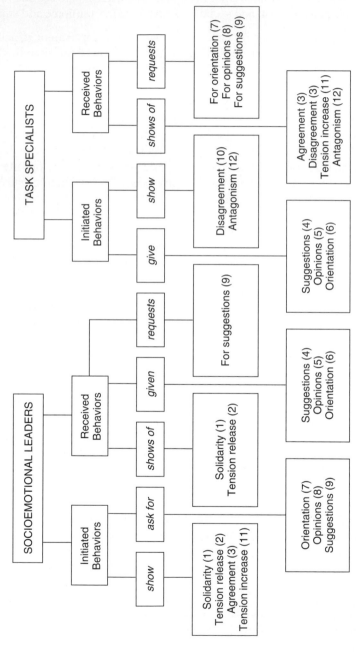

Figure 5.3 How behaviors differ for socioemotional leaders and task specialists. (Numbers in parentheses are category numbers from Bales' interaction-process analysis.)

than asked for (7%). Problem-solving groups tend to progress through three stages: orientation (What is the problem?), evaluation (How do we feel about it?), and control (What should we do about it?). As the discussion moves from the intellectual examination of the problem (the orientation phase) to evaluation and decision (the control phase), emotions are expressed more often.

Bales' observation form may be found in Figure 5.4. Why not try using it to observe a number of group meetings?

Fiedler's Situational Theory of Leadership

Social psychologist Fred Fiedler did a series of studies on leadership (1964, 1967, 1969) in many different situations and groups. Defining a leader's effectiveness in terms of the group's performance in achieving its goals, Fiedler divided leaders into those who were task oriented and those who were maintenance oriented. He found no consistent relationship between group effectiveness and leadership behaviors, because maintenance-oriented leaders were more effective in some situations and task-oriented leaders were more effective in others.

A *task-oriented leader* is effective under two sets of conditions. Under the first, he or she is on very good terms with the group members, the task is clearly structured, and the leader has high authority and power. Under such conditions the group is ready to be directed and is willing to be told what to do. Under the second set of conditions, the leader is on poor terms with group members, the task is ambiguous, and the leader has low authority and power. Under these conditions the leader can also be effective in taking responsibility for making decisions and directing group members. When moderately good or poor relations exist between the leader and the group members, when the leader has a position of moderate authority and power, and when the task is moderately clear, the *maintenance-oriented leader* who emphasizes member participation in decision making seems to be the most effective type of leader.

Fiedler's results imply that the distributed-functions theory of leadership needs to be modified to take into account the situational conditions influencing the impact of leadership style on a group. There are some difficulties with this theory, however. For example, how can a person tell if the situational conditions of leader–member relations, task clarity, and leader power are high, moderate, or low? Almost all group situations fall into the moderate range; in only the most extreme cases are the conditions in the high or low categories. A second difficulty is that although the theory is more complex than the outdated leadership-style theory, which held that a leader should always be democratic, it may not be complex enough. A good leader is always paying attention to the situational conditions that influence the group, modifying his or her behavior to make it effective. Moreover, leader–member relations, task clarity, and leader power may be only three of many different situational factors that group leaders should be aware of.

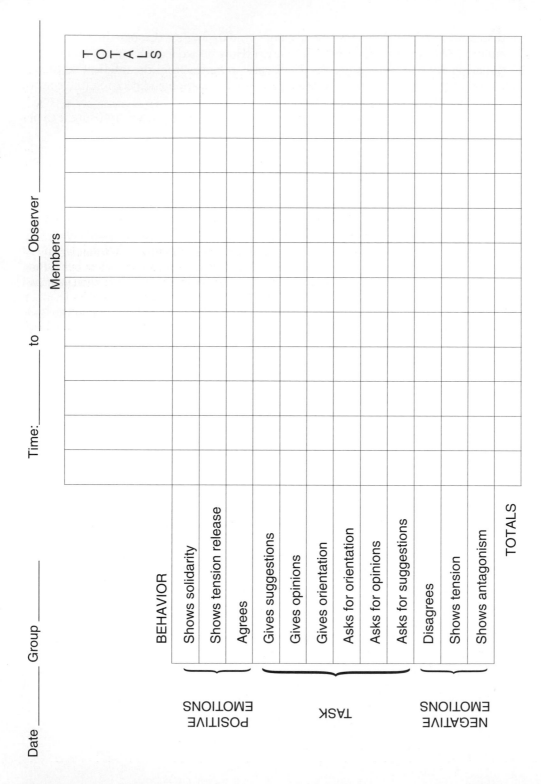

Figure 5.4 Cumulative interaction form.

Source: R. Bales, *Interaction process analysis* (Reading, MA: Addison-Wesley, 1950).

204

5.6 *The Least Preferred Co-worker Scale*

Fiedler (1978) developed an indirect measure of leadership style known as the *Least Preferred Co-worker* (*LPC*) *Scale*. See Figure 5.5. Think of a person with whom you can work least well. This may be someone you work with now or someone you knew in the past. This person need not be the one you liked least well but should be the person you have had the most difficulty working with to get the job done.

Your score will fall somewhere between 16 and 128. To calculate it, add up the numbers you have circled for each of the adjective pairs. If your score is 56 or less, you are a low-LPC leader. The lower your score, the more task oriented you are. If your score is 63 or above, you are a high-LPC leader. The higher your LPC score, the more relationship oriented you are. If your score falls between 56 and 63, you do not fit easily into either category and may call yourself *socioindependent*.

According to Fiedler (1978), people who describe their least preferred co-worker in very negative, rejecting terms are so oriented toward completing the task that it completely determines their perception of co-workers whom they have trouble working with. In effect, they say, "If I cannot work with you, if you frustrate my need to get the job done, then you cannot be good in other respects. You are unfriendly, unpleasant, cold, and nasty." People who describe their least preferred co-workers in positive terms are relationship oriented. In effect, they say, "Even though I cannot work with you, getting the job done is not everything, and I can still see you as friendly, relaxed, and interesting."

Pleasant	: 8 7 6 5 4 3 2 1 :	Unpleasant
Friendly	: 8 7 6 5 4 3 2 1 :	Unfriendly
Rejecting	: 1 2 3 4 5 6 7 8 :	Accepting
Tense	: 1 2 3 4 5 6 7 8 :	Relaxed
Distant	: 1 2 3 4 5 6 7 8 :	Close
Cold	: 1 2 3 4 5 6 7 8 :	Warm
Supportive	: 8 7 6 5 4 3 2 1 :	Hostile
Boring	: 1 2 3 4 5 6 7 8 :	Interesting
Quarrelsome	: 1 2 3 4 5 6 7 8 :	Harmonious
Gloomy	: 1 2 3 4 5 6 7 8 :	Cheerful
Open	: 8 7 6 5 4 3 2 1 :	Guarded
Backbiting	: 1 2 3 4 5 6 7 8 :	Loyal
Untrustworthy	: 1 2 3 4 5 6 7 8 :	Trustworthy
Considerate	: 8 7 6 5 4 3 2 1 :	Inconsiderate
Nasty	: 1 2 3 4 5 6 7 8 :	Nice
Agreeable	: 8 7 6 5 4 3 2 1 :	Disagreeable
Insincere	: 1 2 3 4 5 6 7 8 :	Sincere
Kind	: 8 7 6 5 4 3 2 1 :	Unkind

Figure 5.5 The LPC Scale.
Source: F. Fiedler, Recent developments in research on the contingency model, in L. Berkowitz (Ed.), *Group processes* (New York: Academic Press, 1978).

Hersey and Blanchard's Theory of Situational Leadership

On the basis of studies of leadership conducted at Ohio State University, Paul Hersey and Kenneth Blanchard (1977) concluded that they can classify most of the activities of leaders on two distinct behavioral dimensions: initiation of structure (task actions) and consideration of group members (relationship of maintenance actions). They define **task behavior** as the extent to which a leader engages in one-way communication by explaining what each follower is to do, as well as when, where, and how tasks are to be accomplished. They define **relationship behavior** as the extent to which a leader engages in two-way communication by providing emotional support and facilitating behaviors. According to Hersey and Blanchard, the Ohio State University studies found that some leaders focus mainly on directing task-related activities for their followers, whereas other leaders concentrate on providing emotional support through relationships with their followers. Still other leaders engage in both task and relationship behaviors or in neither. Hersey and Blanchard determined that task and relationship behaviors are two separate dimensions, which can be portrayed as in Figure 5.6.

Hersey and Blanchard's situational-leadership theory assumes that any of the four combinations of leadership behaviors shown in Figure 5.6 may be ineffective or effective, depending on the situation. Which combination of behaviors is appropriate depends on the level of maturity of the group. They define **maturity** as the capacity to set high but attainable goals (achievement motivation), willingness and ability to take responsibility, and the education and/or experience of group members. Maturity is determined only in

Figure 5.6 Situational leadership.
Source: P. Hersey and K. Blanchard, *Management of organizational behavior: Utilizing human resources,* 3rd ed. (Englewood Cliffs, NJ: Prentice-Hall, 1977). Reprinted with permission.

relation to a specific task to be performed. On one task a member may have high maturity, on another task low maturity.

The essence of Hersey and Blanchard's theory is that when group members have low maturity in terms of accomplishing a specific task, the leader should engage in high-task and low-relationship behaviors. When members are moderately mature, the leader moves to high-task and high relationship behaviors and then to high-relationship and low-task behaviors. When group members are highly mature, low-task and low-relationship behaviors are needed. Hersey and Blanchard refer to high-task/low-relationship leadership behavior as **telling,** because it is characterized by one-way communication in which the leader defines the roles of group members and tells them how, when, and where to do various tasks. As the members' experience and understanding of the task increase, so does their task maturity. High-task/high-relationship leadership behavior is referred to as **selling,** because while providing clear direction as to role responsibilities, the leader also attempts through two-way communication and socioemotional support to get the group members to accept and support decisions that have to be made. As group members' commitment to the task increases, so does their maturity. Low-task/high-relationship leadership behavior is referred to as **participating,** because the leader and group members share in decision making through two-way communication and considerable facilitating behavior from the leader, because the group members have the ability and knowledge to complete the task. Finally, low-task/low-relationship leadership behavior is referred to as **delegating,** because the leader allows group members considerable autonomy in completing the task, as they are both willing and able to take responsibility for directing their own task behavior.

ORGANIZATIONAL LEADERSHIP

Whenever anyone asks me (how to be a leader) I tell them I have the secret to success in life. The secret to success is to stay in love. Staying in love gives you the fire to really ignite other people, to see inside other people, to have a greater desire to get things done than other people. A person who is not in love doesn't really feel the kind of excitement that helps them to get ahead and lead others and to achieve. I don't know any other fire, any other thing in life that is more exhilarating and is more positive a feeling than love is.

Army Major General John H. Stanford (Kouzes & Posner, 1987)

On July 15, 1982, Don Bennett, a Seattle businessman, was the first amputee ever to climb Mount Rainier (reported by Kouzes & Posner, 1987). He climbed 14,410 feet on one leg and two crutches. It took him five days. When asked to state the most important lesson he learned from doing so, without hesitation he said, "You can't do it alone."

What did he mean? There were many ways in which others helped him achieve his goal, including his daughter. During one very difficult trek across an ice field in Don Bennett's hop to the top of Mount Rainer, his daughter stayed by his side for four hours and with each new hop told him, "You can do it, Dad. You're the best dad in the world. You can do it, Dad." There was no way Bennett would quit hopping to the top with his daughter yelling words of love and encouragement in his ear. His daughter's encouragement kept him going, strengthening his commitment to make it to the top. The team and the organization are similar. With members of their cooperative group cheering them on, members amaze themselves, their colleagues, and their superiors with what they can achieve.

There is growth and decline. Staying the same is not an option. Growth takes leadership, not management. There is a difference. Some individuals manage, others lead. The difference may be found in the root meanings of *lead* and *manage* (Kouzes & Posner, 1987). The root origin of *lead* is a word meaning "to go," denoting travel from one place to another. Leaders are those who "go first," pioneering unexplored territory and showing others the direction they should take. By comparison, the root origin of *manage* is a word meaning "hand." Managing seems to connote "handling" things by controlling and maintaining the status quo. Managers tend to handle things; leaders tend to get us going somewhere. **The unique role of the leader is to take us on journeys to places where we have never been before.**

The metaphor of the journey may be the most appropriate one for discussing the tasks of leaders. Individuals can manage what now exists, the status quo, or take staff members on a journey to increase their expertise and create a new and better organization.

Perhaps more than anything else, leadership is about the creation of a new way of life within organizations. Leadership is inextricably connected with the process of innovation, of bringing new ideas, methods, or solutions into use. Leaders are agents of change. Change requires leadership, a "prime mover" to push for implementation of strategic decisions. The leader highlights the challenges the organization faces and makes them shared challenges for the staff. **Leaders create a "family" within which staff members care deeply about each other and the mutual vision they are trying to actualize.** Managers get other people to do, but leaders get other people to *want* to do.

Several leadership issues must be faced in order to maximize the productivity of the organization (Johnson & Johnson, 1994; Kouzes & Posner, 1987).

1. How to **challenge the status quo** of the traditional competitive and individualistic models of management.
2. How to **inspire a clear mutual vision** of what the organization should and could be, a clear mission that all members are committed to achieving, and a set of goals that guide members' efforts.
3. How to **empower members through cooperative teamwork.** Doing so enables each member to take action to increase his or her expertise and effectiveness, both technically and interpersonally.
4. How to **lead by example** by (a) using cooperative team procedures and (b) taking risks to increase expertise.
5. How to **encourage the hearts** of members to persist and keep striving to improve their technical and interpersonal expertise.

Challenging the Status Quo

Organizations (and groups) are sites for an inevitable and external conflict. On one side are the forces of maintenance and continuity (i.e., the status quo), which strive to create and sustain the use of orderly and predictable procedures. Opposing them are the forces of innovation and discontinuity, which seek to alter established practices. Both seek the same goal of team and organizational productivity. Both are needed. The creative tension between the two is what powers considered and thoughtful development and change.

These same two forces operate within the individual member. Group members will experience the conflict between the security of the past and the satisfaction of growth in expertise and accomplishment. The status quo side wants to continue what was done in the past. The enhanced expertise side strives for growth, change, and increased competence. Leaving the status quo and risking one's current success against the potential of being even better in the future requires courage.

In challenging the status quo, leaders highlight that **if members are not working to increase their expertise, they are losing their expertise.** Expertise is a process, not an end product. Any person or organization is constantly changing. If expertise is not growing, then it is declining. The minute a person believes he or she is an expert and stops trying to learn more, that person is losing his or her expertise. **Leaders must lead members toward enhanced expertise, not manage for bureaucratic control. The clearest and most direct challenge to traditional competitive and individualistic actions is the adoption of cooperative teams within the organization.** The organization needs to be transformed into an interlocking network of cooperative teams in order to increase productivity, promote more supportive and committed relationships, and increase members' psychological adjustment and self-esteem.

Creating a Shared Vision

The second leadership responsibility is to create a joint vision of what the team or organization should and could be, a clear mission that all members are committed to achieving, and a set of goals that guide members' efforts. To do so, a leader must:

1. Have a vision/dream of what the organization could be.
2. Communicate that vision with commitment and enthusiasm.
3. Make it a *shared* vision that staff members adopt as their own.
4. Make it a rational vision based on theory and research and sound implementation procedures.

Leaders enthusiastically and frequently communicate the dream of the team and the organization as being places where individuals share, help, encourage, and support each other's efforts to achieve and succeed. These are places where *we* dominates *me*, where working together to get the job done creates caring and committed relationships that propel people forward in their mutual search for excellence.

Leaders inspire a shared vision. It is the common vision that creates a basic sense of "sinking or swimming together" (i.e., positive interdependence) among members. Leaders breathe life into the hopes and dreams of others and enable them to see the exciting possibilities the future holds by striving for a common purpose. **The vision and its advocacy, furthermore, has to be rational.** The new practices have to be backed up with knowledge of the relevant research and theory. A person with no followers is *not* a leader, and people will not become followers until they accept a vision as their own. It is the long-term promise of achieving something worthwhile and meaningful that powers an individual's drive toward greater expertise. **You cannot command commitment; you can only inspire it.**

Empowering Members Through Cooperative Teams

The most important of all the five leadership practices is empowering individuals by organizing them into cooperative teams. To be effective, a cooperative team must

be carefully structured to include positive interdependence, face-to-face promotive interaction, individual accountability, social skills, and group processing (Johnson, Johnson, & Holubec, 1998a, 1998b).

The one-word test to detect whether someone is on the road to becoming a leader is *we*. Leaders do not achieve success by themselves. It is not *my* personal best that leaders inspire; it is *our* personal best. The most important thing a leader can do is to organize members so that they work cooperatively with each other for at least two reasons.

The first is to promote committed and caring relationships among organization members. This is achieved through a team approach. Having members work as part of cooperative teams fosters committed and caring relationships. Cooperative efforts result in trust, open communication, and interpersonal support, all crucial ingredients for productivity. When trust is broken by competition, harsh feelings, criticism, negative comments, and disrespect, productivity suffers.

The second is to empower staff members through teamwork. The real world involves working with and through many different people to get the job done. By organizing members into cooperative teams, leaders increase members' confidence that if they exert effort, they will be successful. Teams empower their members to act by making them feel strong, capable, and committed. Being part of a team enables members to innovate, experiment, take risks, and grow professionally.

Leading by Example

One does not improve through argument but through examples. . . . Be what you wish to make others become. Make yourself, not your words, a sermon.

Henri Frederic Amiel

To provide leadership, you will need to model (a) using cooperative procedures and (b) taking risks to increase your technical and interpersonal expertise. You model the way by practicing what you are preaching. **You lead by example.** To do so, you must be clear about your belief in cooperative efforts, you must be able to speak coherently about your vision and values, and your actions must be congruent with your words. **You begin leadership by becoming a role model that exemplifies the orga-**

nizational and leadership values you believe are important. You show your priorities through living your values.

One thing you can count on for certain: **Every exceptional leader is a learner.** The self-confidence required to lead comes from trying, failing, learning from mistakes, and trying again. We are all involved in a continuous process of increasing our technical and interpersonal expertise. By making your own journey to actualize your vision, you model the way for others.

Encouraging the Hearts of Staff Members

Love 'em and lead 'em.

Major General John H. Stanford,
    Commander, U.S. Army

Leaders are vigilant about the little things that make a big difference. Each spring at Verstec, annual bonuses are given to about 2,000 nonmanagerial personnel (Kouzes & Posner, 1987). In a recent year, the president arrived at the celebration dressed in a satin costume, riding atop an elephant, and accompanied by the Stanford Marching Band. The president frequently says, "If you are going to give someone a check, don't just mail it. Have a celebration."

This example may seem extreme. It usually does not take a marching band and an elephant to make organizational members feel appreciated. **What makes a difference to each staff member is to know that his or her successes are perceived, recognized, and celebrated.** Leaders search out "good news" opportunities and orchestrate celebrations. Striving for increased technical and interpersonal expertise is an arduous and long-term enterprise. Members become exhausted, frustrated, and disenchanted. They often are tempted to give up. **Leaders must inspire members to continue the journey by encouraging the heart** (Kouzes & Posner, 1987). Leaders inspire staff members by giving them the courage and hope to continue the quest. This does not require elephants and marching bands (although they are not a bad idea). What it does require is:

1. The recognition of individual contributions to the common vision.
2. Frequent group celebrations of individual and joint accomplishments.

Members do not start the day with a desire to fail. It is the leader's job to show them that they can succeed. **The primary tools for doing so are individual recognition and group celebration.** A leader becomes a master of celebration. Leaders should give out stickers, T-shirts, buttons, and every other conceivable award when members achieve a milestone. One leader sends out cards that have "I heard something good about you" printed at the top. **Leaders find ways to celebrate accomplishments.** If you do not show your appreciation to your members, they are going to stop caring, and then, in essence, you are going to find yourself out of business.

To give individual recognition and have a group celebration requires a cooperative organizational structure. In competitions, to declare one person a winner is to declare all others losers. Group celebrations do not take place in competitive/individualistic organizations. In such environments, praise may be perceived as phony or satirical and recognition may be the source of embarrassment and anxiety about future retaliation by colleagues. **Within cooperative enterprises, however, genuine acts of caring draw people** together and forward. **Love of their work and each other is what inspires many members to commit more and more of their energy to their jobs.** Establishing a cooperative structure and encouraging the development of caring and committed relationships among members may be the best-kept secret of exemplary leadership.

5.7 *The Furniture Factory*

The purpose of this exercise is to give participants an opportunity to observe task-leadership and maintenance-leadership actions within a decision-making group. The procedure is as follows:

1. The class divides into groups of seven. Two members should volunteer to be observers. The task of the observers is to record the frequency of task and maintenance actions within the group. The observation sheets to be used are on pages 213–214.
2. The task of each group is to read and discuss the problem description that follows and rank the five possible solutions on the basis of how effective they would be in ensuring the least resistance to the proposed changes in work procedures. Each member of the group must be willing to sign the group answer sheet, indicating that he or she agrees with the group's ranking and can explain the rationale for ranking the possible solutions in the order in which the group did so.
3. After deciding how the possible solutions are to be ranked, members discuss the nature of leadership within the group. The following questions may be used as a starter:
   a. What leadership actions were present and absent in the group?
   b. What leadership actions did each member engage in?
   c. How do the members feel about their participation in the group?
   d. How might the task effectiveness of the group be improved?
   e. How might the relationships among group members be improved?
4. Each group shares its conclusions with the class.
5. The ranking of possible solutions by experts on organizational change appears on page 586.

PROBLEM DESCRIPTION: FURNITURE FACTORY EXERCISE

Lazy-Days Manufacturing Company is located in a small northern town. This small, family-owned business manufactures school furniture. Because of the opportunities for work available in a larger town located about fifty miles away, Lazy-Days must attract whomever it can and train them to do the job. Most of the 400 workers are women and young people just out of high school. Lazy-Days also hires some physically and mentally disabled adults as part of a special community program.

Until now, Lazy-Days has manufactured school furniture, but because of a fall in the economy, management has realized a dire need to diversify its manufacturing capabilities. After a study of the market, they decided to add showroom display cases as a new product. If well made, this line will bring increased income and security to Lazy-Days Manufacturing.

Because of the difficulties in getting new workers, particularly trained ones, Lazy-Days would like to divert current personnel to the new jobs. However, the current workers are very set in their ways, and are highly resistant to and suspicious of changes at work. The last time changes were needed, workers demanded higher wages and threatened to unionize, and a few key people quit. If the new line is successful, Lazy-Days could raise wages, but this is not possible under current conditions. Available income must be used to help purchase the new equipment and finance necessary remodeling to accommodate it.

Michael Days, president of Lazy-Days, has listed several ways of approaching the workers about the needed changes. He has asked you to decide which alternative to use. As a group, rank these alternatives from 1 to 5 in terms of their effectiveness in bringing about the desired changes with the least resistance from the workers. Number 1 would be the most effective, 2 the next most effective, and so on through 5, the least effective. Remember, your decision can make the difference between the success or failure of Lazy-Days Manufacturing Company.

_____ a. Mr. Days would send a memo to all employees telling them about the needed changes. He would then make the changes and lay off any employees who did not comply.

_____ b. Mr. Days would meet with small groups of employees, explaining the need for the changes and the reasoning behind them. He would then ask everyone to help in designing and implementing the new jobs.

_____ c. Mr. Days would meet with large groups of employees. He would enthusiastically describe the needed changes and present multicolored charts and film clips to make his points dramatically and forcefully. He would then implement the changes.

_____ d. Mr. Days would send a memo to all employees explaining the need for the changes and asking them to go along with the changes for the good of the company.

_____ e. Mr. Days would meet with large groups of employees, explaining the need for the changes and the reasoning behind them. He would then have the employees select representatives to work with him in designing and implementing the new jobs.

Observation Sheet for Task Actions

Actions	Group Members				
Information and opinion giver					
Information and opinion seeker					
Direction and role definer					
Summarizer					
Energizer					
Comprehension checker					

Observation Sheet for Maintenance Actions

Actions	Group Members				
Encourager of participation					
Communication facilitator					
Tension reliever					
Process observer					
Interpersonal problem solver					
Supporter and praiser					

Observation Sheet for Task and Maintenance Actions

Actions	Group Members				
Information and opinion giver					
Information and opinion seeker					
Direction and role definer					
Summarizer					
Energizer					
Comprehension checker					
Encourager of participation					
Communication facilitator					
Tension reliever					
Process observer					
Interpersonal problem solver					
Supporter and praiser					

Leaping the Abyss of Failure

When you look into the abyss, the abyss is looking into you.

Nietzsche

Leaders give organizational members the courage they need to take the risks necessary to increase technical and interpersonal expertise. Members can choose to play it safe in the short run by maintaining the status quo, thereby facing guaranteed long-term failure through obsolescence, atrophy, and burnout. Adherents to the status quo slowly and gradually descend into the abyss of failure. They descend even though they may not always realize it. Managers organize the easy walk down into the abyss of failure along the path of the status quo. Leaders encourage and inspire members to take the difficult leaps toward increased technical and interpersonal competence. They take a leap over the abyss of failure to reach enhanced expertise. Sometimes their leap falls short and they fail. Sometimes they soar high above the abyss to land safely on the other side. Leaders encourage the risk of short-term failure in order to enhance long-term productivity.

WHAT IF YOU DO NOT WANT TO BE A LEADER?

If you follow the following rules carefully, you can be guaranteed never to be a leader:

1. Be absent from group meetings as frequently as possible.
2. When you do attend, contribute nothing.
3. If you do participate, come on strong early in the discussion. Demonstrate your knowledge of everything, including your mastery of big words and technical jargon.

4. Indicate that you will do only what you have to and nothing more.
5. Read the paper or knit during meetings.

5.8 Tower Building

This exercise provides participants with an opportunity to observe leadership behavior in a situation of intergroup competition in which verbal communication is not allowed. Several groups are needed for this exercise, all of which should have at least seven members. The task of each group is to build a tower from supplied materials. A large room is needed so that the groups can work separately (but within sight of one another). The time needed to complete the exercise is approximately one hour. The procedure is as follows:

1. Two judges are selected to determine which tower is (a) the highest, (b) the strongest, (c) the most beautiful, and (d) the cleverest.
2. The class forms groups of at least seven members.
3. Each group selects two of its members to observe leadership in the group. The observers (using the observation sheets on pages 213–214) are to note:
   a. How the group organizes for work.
   b. How decisions are made by the group.
   c. Whether participation and influence are distributed throughout the group or whether a few members dominate.
   d. What task and maintenance actions are needed to improve the functioning of the group.
   e. How the group reacts to winning or losing.
4. Each group receives a box of supplies containing construction paper, newsprint, tape, magazines, crayons, pipe cleaners, scissors, and glue.
5. The groups have twenty minutes to build their towers. This is a *nonverbal exercise: No talking among group members or between groups is allowed.*
6. During the twenty minutes, the judges meet to decide how they will evaluate the towers on the basis of the four criteria given. At the end of the twenty minutes, the judges decide which tower wins and award a box of candy (provided by the person conducting the exercise) to the winning group.
7. The groups meet with their observers and discuss the exercise. All impressions concerning how the group functioned and what leadership patterns were present and absent should be presented and reviewed.

5.9 Selecting a City

The purposes of this exercise are for participants to develop through role playing an understanding of the distributed-actions theory of leadership and to observe task and maintenance actions in a decision-making group. Instructions for the coordinator are as follows:

1. Introduce the exercise by stating the objectives. Then explain the following leadership actions (see pages 196–197 for definitions):
   a. Information and opinion giver
   b. Information and opinion seeker
   c. Direction and role definer
   d. Summarizer
   e. Encourager of participation

    f. Communication facilitator

    g. Process observer

    h. Tension reliever

2. Form groups of eight. Two members from each group should volunteer to be observers.
3. Explain the task-behavior and maintenance-behavior observation form to the observers and instruct them to look for:
   a. What leadership actions are present and absent in the group.
   b. How well participation is distributed among group members.
   c. What specific leadership actions each group member provides.
4. Place a large envelope containing role-playing instruction envelopes in the center of each group; give no further instructions or information.
5. After the exercise has been completed, instruct each group to discuss its experience, using the following questions as starters:
   a. What leadership actions was each member supposed to role play, and how were they carried out?
   b. What leadership actions were present and absent in the group's decision making, and what were the consequences of their presence or absence?
   c. What were the feelings and reactions of the group members?
   d. What conclusions about leadership and group functioning can be drawn from this exercise?
6. Have each group share its conclusions with the class.

ENVELOPE INSTRUCTIONS

Instructions written on the large envelope, which contains all other envelopes:

Enclosed you will find three envelopes containing directions for the phases of this group session. You are to open the first one (labeled Envelope I) at once. Later instructions will tell you when to open the second (Envelope II) and third (Envelope III).

Envelope I contains the following directions:

Directions for Envelope I:

Time allowed: Fifteen minutes

Special instructions: Each member is to take one of the enclosed envelopes and follow the individual role-playing instructions contained in it.

Task: The group is to select a city.

DO NOT LET ANYONE ELSE SEE *YOUR* INSTRUCTIONS!

(After fifteen minutes, go on to the next envelope.)

Envelope II contains the following directions:

Directions for Envelope II:

Time allowed: Five minutes

Task: You are to choose a group chairperson.

(After five minutes go on to the next envelope.)

Envelope III contains the following directions:

Directions for Envelope III:

Time allowed: Ten minutes

Task: You are to evaluate the first phase of this group session.

Special instructions for the second phase: The newly selected chairperson will lead a discussion on the roles and actions of group members in the process of decision making and their feelings and reactions to that process. The discussion should begin with the report of the observers.

(After ten minutes, return the directions to their respective envelopes and prepare for a general discussion of the exercise.)

ROLE-PLAYING INSTRUCTION ENVELOPES FOR PHASE I

Here are the contents of the six individual instruction envelopes to be used in the first phase of the exercise. Each envelope contains an assigned leadership action and a position concerning which city to select. Two of the envelopes also contain special knowledge concerning the selection process.

1. *Leadership Action:* Direction and Role Definer
   Position: Introduce and support Albuquerque. Oppose San Diego.
2. *Leadership Action:* Encourager of Participation
   Position: Introduce and support San Diego. Oppose Albuquerque.
   Special Knowledge: The group is going to select a chairperson later in the exercise. You are to conduct yourself in such a manner that they will select you.
3. *Leadership Action:* Information and Opinion Seeker
   Position: Introduce and support New York City.
4. *Leadership Action:* Summarizer and Process Observer
   Position: Oppose New York City.
5. *Leadership Action:* Communication Facilitator
   Position: When there seems to be a clear polarity in the discussion, suggest a compromise city, such as Minneapolis or Frameswitch, Texas.
6. *Leadership Action:* Tension Reliever
   Position: Support San Diego.
   Special Knowledge: The group is going to select a chairperson later in the exercise. You are to conduct yourself in such a manner that they will select you.
7. (if needed) *Leadership Action:* Any
   Position: Any

Selecting a City Exercise Observation Sheet

	Group Members				
Actions					
Information and opinion giver					
Information and opinion seeker					
Direction and role definer					
Summarizer					
Encourager of participation					
Communication facilitator					
Process observer					
Tension reliever					

5.10 *Are Groups Run by Great Persons?*

The purpose of this exercise is to compare two opposing theories of leadership: the great-person theory and the interaction-process-analysis theory. According to the great-person theory, the leader is the best-liked member of the group and is perceived as being the most important member for achieving the group's goals. The interaction-process-analysis theory suggests that task actions and maintenance actions are ordinarily executed by different persons, so that a group will usually have two complementary leaders. The procedure for the exercise is as follows:

1. Each participant locates a group that has worked together for some time and has a stable structure. The group should be small enough so that every member knows every other member well enough to evaluate them on likability and task ability.
2. Give every member of the group a questionnaire consisting of two items:
   a. Rank the members from best to worst at helping the group complete its tasks.
   b. Rank the members from most to least likable.
3. Construct two sociometric matrices from the group. The task-ability matrix is constructed by:
   a. Listing the names of the group members down the left-hand side of the matrix and across the top of the matrix.
   b. Listing the ranks given by each group member to all other members on task ability in the rows. Each column then represents the rankings received for one member by all the other members of the group.
   c. Compute the mean rank of each member.
4. Repeat this process for the likability rankings.
5. By graphing the mean ranking of the members on the two dimensions (see Figure 5.7), the group can determine which theory holds in that group. If the two sets of rankings correspond, the graph should resemble a straight line, and the great-person theory of leadership is confirmed. If any pattern other than a straight line results, the theory of two complementary leaders or another theory of leadership is supported.

Example of Sociometric Task-Ability Matrix

Members Being Ranked

	John	Sue	Fred	Ralph	Betsy	Helen
John						
Sue						
Fred						
Ralph						
Betsy						
Helen						
Mean Ranking						

Members Doing Ranking

Figure 5.7 Sociometric matrix and graph.

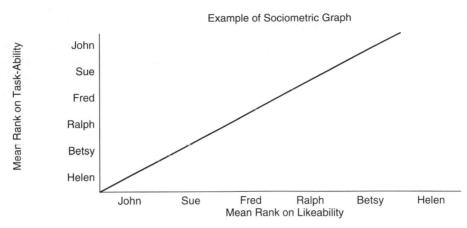

Example of Sociometric Graph

Figure 5.7   *Continued*

6. The class divides into groups of five. Share your graphs with each other. Discuss the following questions:
   a. How do the graphs of the different groups compare with one another?
   b. What overall conclusions concerning group leadership can be drawn from the five graphs?
   c. What have you learned about leadership by analyzing and comparing the leadership patterns of the five groups?

5.11   *Hollow Square*

The Hollow Square Exercise is a problem-solving situation in which you can observe leadership functions. You can see the processes of group planning, the problems of communication between a planning group and an implementing group, and the problems with which an implementing group must cope when carrying out a plan it did not make itself, all of which require effective leadership behavior. The objectives of the exercise are to provide a problem-solving task in which you can observe leadership behavior, to increase your awareness of the problems involved in using a formal hierarchy in group problem solving, and to give you practice in observing groups and in giving the group feedback on your observations.

The exercise is carried out in clusters of ten to twelve persons. Each cluster is divided into three subgroups; four persons are planners, four are implementers, and the rest are observers. The planners decide how they will instruct the implementers to do a task, the implementers carry out the task as best they can, and the observers watch the process of both groups in the two phases. Here is the specific procedure for the coordinator of the exercise:

1. Tell the participants the objectives of the exercise and divide them into four-person planning teams, four-person implementing teams, and observers. Each team goes to a separate room or different parts of a large room (out of earshot) to await instructions.
2. Hand out the appropriate instruction sheets to each team. Give them adequate time to read them; then review them with each team. The observers should be fully briefed first, the planners next, and the implementers last.

3. The planners are given the general diagram sheet and the pieces of the puzzle and are instructed to begin phase I. Each planner is given four pieces of the puzzle. The exact distribution of the pieces is not crucial, but they should not have any labels marked on them. Phase I lasts forty-five minutes. All information the planners need to know is on their briefing sheet. The answer to how the puzzle fits together is on page 586.

4. At the end of phase I the planning team gives the implementing team its instructions. The planners are then prohibited from giving any further help; they must remain silent and uninvolved as the implementing team works.

5. Implementers are to finish the task, phase II, according to their instructions, taking as much time as necessary.

6. When the task is completed, a discussion is held involving all the members of each cluster. This discussion is to include reports from the observers, planners, and implementers, and a comparison of similarities between the exercise and other organizational and group experiences of the members. Questions for the discussion should include:

   a. What leadership functions were present and absent in the planning and implementing teams? What were the consequences of their presence or absence?

   b. What leadership functions were needed for each type of activity?

   c. How could the functioning of each team have been improved?

   d. Were the leadership functions distributed among all the team members? Were participation and influence evenly distributed throughout the team?

   e. How was communication between the planning and implementing teams handled? How could it have been improved?

   f. How did it feel to wait for the planners' instructions, and how did it feel to watch the implementers carry them out?

7. The major points of the discussion should be summarized, with an emphasis on the conclusions about the leadership functions being present, absent, and distributed within the teams. Other types of learning that typically take place during the exercise are:

   a. Planners often place limitations on team behavior that do not appear in the instructions, thereby making their task harder. They could, for example, ask the implementing team to observe their planning meeting.

   b. There is considerable frustration in planning something that others will carry out without your involvement. The commitment to implement a plan is usually built through the planning process, and when the planners cannot put the plan into effect, they often experience frustration.

   c. Planning is so interesting and absorbing that planners can forget what their implementing team is experiencing. Implementers can become anxious because they do not know what the task will be, though this concern does not usually enter the minds of the planners.

   d. Planners often fail to use all the resources at their disposal to solve the problem, such as getting the silent members of the planning team to participate.

   e. Planners can spend so much time planning the task that they do not allow enough time to communicate their plans adequately to the implementers, which results in wasting much of their effort.

   f. In communicating their plan to the implementing team, the planning team often does not take into account the implementers' anxieties, their need to be physically comfortable, and so on. Their preoccupation with giving information under pressure blinds them to the needs of the members of the implementing team, which reduces the effectiveness of the communication.

   g. Implementers usually develop some antagonism or hostility toward their planners while they are waiting for their instructions. These feelings increase if they are given complex instructions in a short amount of time and left confused as they take responsibility for finishing the task.

INSTRUCTION SHEET FOR OBSERVERS

You will be observing a situation in which a planning team decides how to solve a problem and gives instructions to an implementing team. The problem consists of assembling sixteen flat pieces into a square containing an empty square in its middle. The planning team is supplied with a general diagram of the assembled pieces. The planners are *not* allowed to put the puzzle together themselves; they are to instruct the implementing team on how to assemble the pieces in minimum time. You will be silent observers throughout the process. Half of you should observe the planners throughout the entire exercise and half of you should observe the implementers. Observation sheets focusing upon task and maintenance leadership behaviors are provided to help you observe. Make sure you understand the behavioral roles before you begin. Some suggestions for observers are:

1. Each observer should watch the general patterns of leadership behavior.
2. During phase I, consider the following questions:
    a. What kinds of behavior block or help the process?
    b. Are the team members participating equally?
    c. How does the planning team divide its time between planning and instructing?
    d. What group functions are not provided by the group members?
3. During the instructing process, note these behavioral questions:
    a. At the beginning of the instruction, how do the planners orient the implementers to their task?
    b. What assumptions made by the planning team are not communicated to the implementing team?
    c. How effective are the instructions?
    d. Does the implementing team appear to feel free to ask questions of the planners?
    e. What leadership functions are present and absent?
4. During the assembling period, seek answers to the following questions:
    a. How does the implementing team show that instructions were clearly understood or misunderstood?
    b. What nonverbal reactions do planning team members show as they watch their plans being implemented or distorted?
    c. What leadership functions are present and absent?
5. You should each have two copies of the observation sheets, one for phase I and one for phase II.

INSTRUCTION SHEET FOR PLANNERS

Each of you will be given a packet containing four pieces of a puzzle. When all the pieces from all four packets are properly assembled, they will form a large square containing an empty place in the middle. A sheet bearing a diagram of the completed puzzle is provided for your team. Your task is to:

1. Plan how the sixteen pieces distributed among you can be assembled to solve the puzzle.
2. Decide on a plan for instructing your implementing team on how to carry out your plan for putting the puzzle together.
3. Call the implementing team and begin instructing them at any time during the next forty minutes.

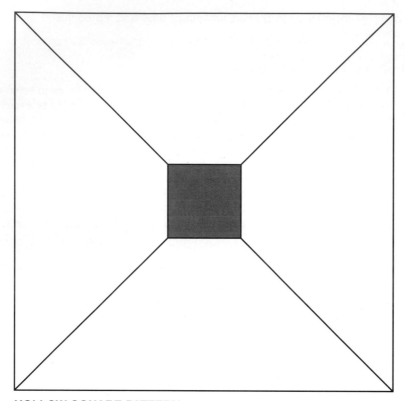

HOLLOW SQUARE PATTERN

4. Give them at least five minutes of instructions; the implementing team must begin assembling the puzzle forty-five minutes from now.

Before you begin, read these rules:

1. During planning:
   a. Keep the pieces from your packet in front of you at all times.
   b. Do not touch the pieces or trade any of them with other persons, either now or during the instruction period.
   c. Do not assemble the square; that is the implementers' job.
   d. Do not mark any of the pieces.
2. During instruction:
   a. Give all instructions in words. Do not show the diagram to the implementers; hide it. Do not draw any diagrams yourselves, either on paper or in the air with gestures. You may give your instructions orally or on paper.
   b. The implementing team must not move the pieces until the signal is given to start phase II.
   c. Do not show any diagram to the implementers.
   d. After the signal is given for the assembly to begin, you may not give any further instructions; stand back and observe. You may not touch the pieces or in any way join in the implementers' work.

INSTRUCTION SHEET FOR IMPLEMENTERS

1. Your team will have the responsibility of carrying out a task in accordance with instructions given you by your planning team.
2. Your task will begin forty minutes from now.
3. Your planning team may call you in for instruction at any time during the next forty minutes.
4. If the planning team does not call you in during the next forty minutes, you must report to it on your own at the end of that time.
5. You may send notes to the planners and they may send notes in reply.
6. Once you have begun the task of assembling the puzzle, your planning team will not be allowed to give you any further instructions. Finish the assigned task as quickly as possible.
7. While you wait for a call from your planning team, do the following:
   a. Individually, write on a piece of paper the concerns you feel while waiting for instructions.
   b. As a group, think of anything that might help you follow instructions or keep you from doing so. Write actions that will help you on one sheet of paper and those that will hinder you on another.
   c. Make notes on how the four of you can organize as a team to receive and follow the instructions.
   d. Keep handy the sheets on which you have written these notes. You may find them useful during the discussion that takes place after you have completed the task.

EXERCISE 5.12 *Other Leadership Exercises*

1. An exercise for an ongoing group is to place the task and maintenance functions singly on 3 × 5-inch cards, shuffle the cards, and deal each member one or two of them face down. During a meeting of the group, each member then practices the task or maintenance function on the card he or she received. There must be at least two observers. After the meeting, the group discusses which functions different members fulfilled and which ones they were trying to fulfill.
2. The class forms groups of six. Each group chooses a leader and then analyzes why it selected that person.
3. Members lie on the floor with their heads toward the center of the group and begin a group fantasy about the qualities of the perfect leader for this group. When the fantasy is over, the group reviews the experience.
4. Working as a group, members paint or draw a picture of the perfect leader for their group. Members then discuss both the process of making the picture and the picture itself.

EXERCISE 5.13 *Your Leadership Behavior*

Now that you have completed some or all of the exercises in this chapter and have read some or all of the information presented, it may be helpful for you again to take stock of your leadership behavior. Here is a procedure for doing so.

1. Describe the task and maintenance actions in which you usually engage.
2. Describe the task and maintenance actions you would like to practice and improve.

3. Ask other members of your group to describe your usual task and maintenance actions and help you decide which ones would be helpful for you to practice.

4. Plan how you can practice being a process observer in order to determine which task and maintenance actions would be most helpful for the group to focus on.

5. Plan how you can encourage other group members to engage in needed task and maintenance actions.

EXERCISE **5.14** *Why I Am a Leader*

Working individually, rank the five theories of leadership from:

1. Most difficult to least difficult to implement.
2. First choice to last choice for your personal plan to improve your leadership abilities.

Form a group of four members. Working cooperatively, rank the five theories, reaching a consensus as to (a) the difficulty to implement and (b) the group's choice to improve members' leadership abilities.

Difficulty	Theory	My Personal Plan
_____	I plan to highlight my genetic superiority to most other people. They will realize I was born to lead and they were born to follow me.	_____
_____	I plan to do things with such great style that I will be the leader of any group to which I belong.	_____
_____	I plan to know how to influence people so skillfully that they will gladly follow me.	_____
_____	I plan to be appointed or elected leader of every group to which I belong.	_____
_____	I plan to learn the goal and relationship skills required for groups to function effectively.	_____

SUMMARY

Small group leadership may be defined in a variety of ways. It has been defined as a set of traits, a personal style, the ability to influence others, a role in an authority hierarchy, or the fulfillment of functions necessary for achieving the group's goals and maintaining effective working relationships among members. Organizational leadership involves a process of challenging the status quo, inspiring a mutual vision, empowering members through teams, leading by example, and encouraging the heart to persist.

The third guideline for creating an effective group is to ensure that leadership and participation are distributed among all group members. All members are responsible for providing leadership. The equalization of participation and leadership ensures that all members are involved in the group's work, committed to implementing the group's decisions, and satisfied with their membership. It also (a) ensures that the resources of every member are fully utilized and (b) increases the cohesiveness of the group.

ANSWERS

Pages 196–197: 1. c; 2. g; 3. j; 4. b; 5. i; 6. h; 7. f, 8. a; 9. 1; 10. e; 11. k; 12. d.
Page 197: 1. e; 2. k; 3. j; 4. c; 5. h; 6. a; 7. 1; 8. i; 9. b; 10. f; 11. d; 12. g.

14 exercises in ch 5

6

Using Power

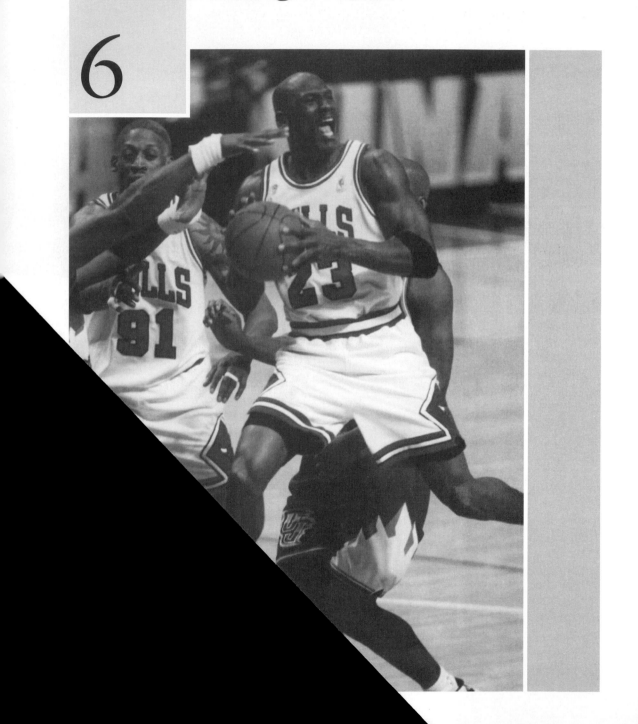

Basic Concepts to Be Covered in This Chapter

In this chapter a number of concepts are defined and discussed. The major ones are listed following. Divide into pairs. Each pair is to (a) define each concept, noting the page on which it is defined and discussed, and (b) ensure that both members of the pair understand the meaning of each concept. Then combine into groups of four. Compare the answers of the two pairs. If there is disagreement, look up the concept in the chapter and clarify it until all members agree on and understand the definition.

Concepts

1. Coercive power
2. Constructive power
3. Deindividuation theory
4. Destructive power
5. Dynamic-interdependence approach to power
6. Expert power
7. Group mind (influences)
8. Group norms
9. Informational power
10. Legitimate power
11. Message effects

12. Neutral power
13. Power
14. Power as relationship variable
15. Reactance
16. Receiver effects
17. Referent power
18. Reward power
19. Social dominance
20. Source effects (credibility, attractiveness)
21. Trait-factor approach to power

6.1 Is Power a Personal or a Relationship Attribute?

EXERCISE

There has been some controversy over whether power is an attribute of a person or an aspect of a relationship between two or more persons. The purpose of this exercise is to structure a critical discussion of the issue. The procedure is as follows:

1. **Assignment of Positions:** The class forms groups of four. Each group is ultimately to write a report summarizing its position:

    Position A: Power is a personal attribute. Some people are naturally born to wield power (and some are not). Because of their innate personality and makeup, they are able to influence others and rise to positions of power.

    Position B: Power is an attribute of a relationship. For power to exist, there must be both an influencer and an influencee. In most situations, who is influencing whom to what degree changes constantly according to who has relevant information and expertise. As circumstances and situations change, the relationship changes and the relative power of group members change.

    The report is to contain the group's overall conclusions and the facts and rationale supporting its position. The supporting facts and rationale may be obtained from this chapter, the entire book, and outside reading.

2. **Preparation Pairs:** Each group divides into pairs. One pair is assigned Position A (power is a personal attribute) and the other pair is assigned Position B (power is an attribute of

a relationship). Each pair reviews the supporting sections of this chapter, the procedure for the exercise, and the guidelines for constructive controversy (p. 34). They prepare a persuasive "best case" rationale for their assigned position that includes as many facts and research findings as possible. Ten minutes are allowed for this phase.

3. **Presentations:** One member of each pair changes chairs. A "personal attribute" person should be seated with a "relationship attribute" person. The personal attribute person has up to three minutes to present the best case possible for the position, being as forceful and persuasive as possible. The relationship attribute person takes notes and asks for clarification of anything that is not fully understood. The relationship attribute person then presents.

4. **Open Discussion** (Refute and Rebut): There is an open discussion of whether power is a personal attribute or an aspect of a relationship. Each side presents as many facts and research findings as it can to support its point of view. Members listen critically to the opposing position and ask for facts supporting any conclusions made by the opponent. Participants should ensure that all the facts supporting both sides are brought out and discussed. The guidelines for constructive controversy should be followed. About ten minutes are allowed for this phase.

5. **Perspective Reversal:** Members of each pair change chairs. The personal attribute person presents in three minutes the best case possible for the relationship attribute position. He or she should be as forceful and persuasive as he or she can and add new arguments or facts if possible. The relationship attribute person then presents the best case possible for the personal attribute position.

6. **Synthesis and Integration:** Participants drop all advocacy and come to their best reasoned judgment about whether power is an attribute of a person or of a relationship. The pair members summarize the information and arguments for each position and come to an agreement. Each pair prepares a short presentation on its conclusion to the rest of the class. Since other groups will have reached other conclusions, each group may need to explain the validity of its position to the class. About ten minutes are allowed for this phase.

7. **Whole Class Discussion:** The coordinator samples the decisions made by the groups of four by having several of them present their position to the class. The class then discusses the similarities and differences among the positions, and the coordinator summarizes what the participants have learned about power and influence.

INTRODUCTION

The price of greatness is responsibility.

Winston Churchill

In Orwell's fable, *Animal Farm,* the livestock of a farm overthrow their human masters and form an egalitarian system. At first, the ideology of the new order is summarized in several simple maxims including, "All animals are equal." As the story unfolds, however, the pigs (who assume the managerial positions on the farm) soon take advantage of their new status and power to bestow all kinds of special treatment on themselves. For instance, they do none of the many arduous chores that are the essence of farm work, and they claim the farm house (which is the most comfortable spot on the farm). Eventually, the swine legitimize their behaviors by formally changing the farm's ideology. They delete six of the seven maxims, retaining only the equality principle, which they qualify with the addendum "But some animals are more equal than others." In Or-

The Image of Power

When you think of power, what images come to mind? Do you think of a football player, a great orator, a semi-truck, or a gun? Write down the images you have when you think of power. Find a partner. Share your images and listen carefully to your partner's images. Then choose the two images most illustrative of the concept *power.*

1.   4.

2.   5.

3.   6.

well's world, the pigs, by assuming superior power and status, come to see themselves as privileged and meriting favorable treatment. What is true for pigs may also be true for humans.

Even though we sometimes do not like to admit it, power is a basic aspect of social life. It can be seized or given up, increased or lost. It can be used for good, evil, or trivial purposes. All relationships—with family, friends, lovers, coworkers—involve power. Yet many persons are unaware of the influence they exert on others, and many are unaware of how necessary and constructive mutual influence is in building effective groups and collaborative relationships. Being skillful in influencing other group members and taking responsibility for such influence are important parts of being a member of a group.

In this chapter we will discuss the nature of power and the constructive and destructive use of power. Direct ways of using power are discussed (Figure 6.1). These include the dynamic-interdependence and the trait-factor perspectives on power, the six bases of power, and the interaction between high- and low-power individuals. Indirect ways of using power are then discussed. These include group norms and the group mind.

Perspectives on Power

Dynamic Interdependence View of Power   Trait-Factor View of Power
   Power exists in relationships   Source effects
   Cooperative versus competitive context   Message effects
   Personal power and goal attainment   Receiver effects

Bases of Power
Reward   Coercive   Legitimate   Referent   Expert   Informational

Unequal Power
High-Power Persons   Low-Power Persons

Indirect Power
Group Norms   Group Mind
   Comforming to group norms
   Implementing group norms

Figure 6.1   The nature of power: Constructive versus destructive use of power.

6.2 *Group Power Exercises*

1. With your classmates, form groups of five. Place all the change the group members have in a hat. Decide who in the group gets all the money. Discuss the experience.

2. Stand next to the walls of the room with your classmates. Each of you chooses a spot in the center of the room in which you would like to sit. At a signal from a coordinator, sit in that spot. Once all of you are settled, discuss your experience with the nearest person.

3. Stand in the circle with your classmates, touching fingertips with the person on either side. Pick a spot in the room to which you would like the group to go. Do not talk. When the signal is given, try to get the group to move to your chosen spot. Discuss what you learned with a partner.

4. Stand in a circle with your classmates. Each member helps with one hand to hold a sheet of paper. No verbal communication is allowed. At the signal, the paper suddenly becomes "power." See what happens and discuss.

5. Pair up with a classmate. Sit in chairs facing each other. You have five minutes to decide, nonverbally, who is going to sit on the floor. At the end of that time, one person must be on the floor. See what happens and discuss.

6. Sit in a circle with your classmates. Each of you closes your eyes and imagines that you live in a small village. You have been handed an important message to deliver to someone in a much more powerful neighboring village. You begin to walk to the other village. You pass a girl on a bridge. You pass a man on a bicycle. You pass a family having a picnic. You hear the sound of birds singing, you see trees moving in the breeze, and you smell the grass and the earth. Rounding a bend, you suddenly come upon a wall. It continues in both directions as far as you can see. The village you need to reach is beyond the wall. For a few minutes, think of what happens. Then open your eyes and share stories of what happened at the wall. Discuss them from the standpoint of power.

7. Sit in a circle with your classmates. Close your eyes and picture the group of which you are a member. In your fantasy, begin a game of follow-the-leader. At first, see yourself as the leader and note what happens among the followers. Now shift leaders and see someone else at the head of the line. Keep going until all the members of your group have had a chance to be the leader. Then open your eyes and discuss the following questions:
   a. What kinds of things did different persons lead the group to do?
   b. What feelings did you imagine among the followers?
   c. How did you picture the group behaving when you were the leader?
   d. Who seemed most natural in the leadership role?
   e. Who seemed least natural in the leadership role?

8. Divide into groups of four with your classmates. Make a picture or collage showing power, using available resources—magazines, pencils, paints, crayons, newspapers, and so forth. At the end of thirty minutes, discuss the picture of each group. If Polaroid cameras are available, instead of making a picture showing power, go out and take a symbolic photograph. Then come back and discuss.

9. This exercise is for a group that has been working together on a task. Arrange yourselves in a line according to how powerful you see yourselves. Before beginning, mark one end of the line as the place for the most powerful person so that all members will know how to arrange themselves. After the line has stabilized, ask if anyone wants to move to a different location. Discuss self-perceptions and perceptions of others. How does your power, as perceived by other members, compare with how you see it? Were there disagreements among members about who is the most powerful? Does the group have certain biases about power, such as the richest person being seen as the most powerful?

WHAT IS POWER?

The fundamental concept in social science is power, in the
same sense in which energy is the fundamental concept in physics.

Bertrand Russell (1938, ch. 1)

The fourth guideline for creating an effective group is to ensure that the use of power is distributed among group members and that patterns of influence vary according to the needs of the group. In order to explicate this guideline, it is first necessary to define *power*. In the vast literature on power in philosophy, history, sociology, political science, anthropology, and psychology, there are many different definitions. Power has been conceived as a quality of the person, the position, the place, the situation, or the relationship. Some individuals are viewed as having power because of their ability to dominate others through their physical prowess, verbal prowess, or charisma. Some positions are viewed as carrying power, such as the presidency of a corporation or the chair of a committee. Some places are viewed as containing power, such as a church, mosque, or Stonehenge. Some persons view situations as determining the level of power of each person, such as when a nurse is giving emergency medical aid to a general. Finally, some view power as a quality of the relationship in which both parties influence the other.

Constructive versus Destructive Use of Power

The use of power may be constructive, destructive, or neutral. The use of power is **constructive** when it enhances the effectiveness of the group, and it is **destructive** when it interferes with group effectiveness (Table 6.1). As discussed in Chapter 1, group effectiveness is determined by the group's success in (a) achieving its goals, (b) maintaining good working relationships among members, and (c) adapting to changing conditions in the surrounding environment (i.e., organization, society, and world). When power is used to enhance the achievement of the group's goals, the quality of relationships among members, and the group's adaptation to its environment, it is constructive or positive. There are also personal benefits. The influence of other group members can enhance one's competencies, improve one's relationships, increase one's psychological health, and promote one's altruistic behaviors. When power is used in ways that interfere with the group's goal achievement, damage the relationships among members, and obstruct adaptation, it is destructive or negative. More specifically, the dimensions on which the constructiveness of the use of power may be determined are (Deutsch, 1962, 1973, 1985):

1. Self-benefit versus other benefit: Power may be wielded for the benefit of oneself, others, or the common good of the group and its environment.
2. Agreement versus nonagreement of others: The use of power may be invited by others or may be imposed on others against their will.

Table 6.1   **The Constructiveness of Power**

	Imposed on Others	**Invited by Others**
Benefits Self	Most destructive	Mislead, swindled, altruism
Benefits Others	Paternalism	Most constructive

What Is Power?

Following are five different views of power. Find a partner. Working cooperatively:

1. Come to agreement on the definition of each view. Ensure that your partner can explain the reasoning for your joint answers.

2. Choose the view of power that is most interesting to the two of you.

	Concept	Definitions
_____	Person	a. Power is a quality of the relationship in which both parties influence the other.
_____	Position	b. Situational factors determine the level of power of each person.
_____	Place	c. Positions contain power, such as the presidency of a corporation or the chair of a committee.
_____	Situation	d. Power is a trait that some individuals have, usually because they were born with it.
_____	Relationship	e. Certain churches, mosques, or ancient sites such as Stonehenge contain power.

In each of these cases, power is defined differently. For the purposes of this chapter, **power** is defined as the capacity to affect the outcomes of oneself, others, and the environment (Coleman & Tjosvold, 2000). The use of power may be direct (within interpersonal interaction) or indirect (through group norms and values). The direct use of power may be examined from two points of view: (a) the dynamic-interdependence perspective and (b) the trait-factor perspective. Before these perspectives are discussed, however, the constructiveness of the use of power will be discussed.

Note that power may be used purposefully or nonpurposefully. Sometimes power is deliberately wielded and sometimes it is an unintended side effect of one's actions. In this chapter, only the purposeful use of power is discussed.

When power is used primarily for self-benefit and/or to force others to do something they do not wish to do, its use tends to be destructive. Correspondingly, the more power is used to benefit other members of the group and its environment, and/or with the agreement and even encouragement of those individuals, the more constructive the use of power tends to be. There are circumstances in which the use of power for self-benefit may be encouraged by others, either because they are misled or because they are willing to sacrifice for the person's well-being. There are also times when the use of power will benefit others but is imposed on them against their will. This signifies a more paternalistic view of the relationship.

Finally, there are conditions under which the use of power may be **neutral** in the sense that it enhances self-benefit without affecting others' benefits either positively or negatively and without needing anyone else's resources. Power is neutral when the individual can achieve his or her goals without being unduly constrained by someone or something else.

The dominant view is that power is negative and destructive. Lord Acton's observation that "Power tends to corrupt, and absolute power corrupts absolutely" is typical of this view. The powerful are viewed as self-serving and tyrannical, and the powerless are viewed as vulnerable and ingratiating. Power is studied in order to control, prevent, or eliminate its destructive use. There are social scientists, however, who believe that power is positive and essential for mutual enhancement and the achievement of mutual goals. Mary Parker Follett ([1924] 1973), for example, believed that power could be developed through co-action to achieve mutual goals, and that doing so would enrich the soul and advance the humanity of every participant. Similarly, Deutsch (1949a and b, 1962) viewed power as an inherent aspect of cooperation and competition, with the success of cooperative efforts dependent on the constructive use of power among collaborators. Their views are best represented in the dynamic-interdependence view of power.

THE DYNAMIC-INTERDEPENDENCE VIEW OF POWER

Coercive power is the curse of the universe; co-active power,
the enrichment and advancement of every human soul.

Mary Parker Follett ([1924] 1973, p. xii).

Dynamic means in a constant state of change; *interdependence* means that each member's actions affect the outcomes of other members. The **dynamic-interdependence approach to power** posits that who is influencing whom to what degree changes constantly as members strive to achieve the group's goals. Members' power is based on expertise, ability, and access to information, not on authority or personality characteristics. The theory is based on two important principles: power exists in relationships, not in individuals, and constructive use of power requires a cooperative context.

Power Exists in Relationships

The first principle of the dynamic-interdependence approach to power is that power exists in relationships, not individuals. It takes two persons for power to exist. A person cannot be an influencer if there is no influencee and vice versa. The use of power is inherent in any relationship. Any two persons who interact influence and are influenced by each other.

When group members work together to achieve mutual goals, the use of power is inevitable, essential, dynamic, and distributed. *First*, power is inevitable—it exists in all relationships. By definition, a group is a cooperative enterprise. In order to achieve their mutual goals, group members must influence and be influenced by each other. Mutual influence goes on continuously as group members act and react and adjust to each other's actions. They take turns talking, modify the expression of their attitudes and beliefs to take into account the reactions of other members, and speed up or slow down their activity to stay coordinated with one another.

Second, the use of power is essential to all aspects of group functioning. Goals cannot be established and communication cannot take place without mutual influence. Leadership cannot exist without using power. Decisions cannot be made unless members influence one another. Controversies and conflicts of interest cannot be managed or resolved without the use of power. Every group member should be aware of his or her power, accept it, and take responsibility for its use.

Third, the use of power is dynamic. The patterns of influence among group members change constantly as the group progresses toward its goals, as the costs (in energy, emotion, time, and so forth) of working together vary, and as alternative relationships and groups become available in which the goals of group members might be better achieved (Cartwright, 1959; Thibaut & Kelly, 1959). If the group members make progress toward achieving their goals and the costs of working together go down, so that no other group would be as rewarding, the ability of members to influence each other increases. If, on the other hand, the group is not making progress toward goal accomplishment, if the costs to group members in terms of emotion and energy are high, and if other groups are available that are more effective and less demanding, the ability of group members to influence each other decreases. In the latter case, members may even terminate their membership and join other groups, thereby reducing to zero the capacity of the original group members to influence and be influenced by them.

Fourth, power is distributed among all group members. Every group member has some influence over other members and over what takes place in the group. Every member has power over the others and is open to influence by every other member. Group members use their power to ensure that (a) the joint goals are achieved and (b) their personal goals (reasons for being a member of the group) are also accomplished.

The dynamic-interdependence approach to power is ideal for describing the exercise of power in groups where individuals are constantly interacting.

Context in Which Power Is Used

The second principle of the dynamic-interdependence approach to power is that the context in which it is used largely determines whether it is constructive or destructive. The context in which power is exerted may be competitive or cooperative.

Dynamic-Interdependence Approach to Power

	Characteristics
Dynamic	Focuses on the changing nature and patterns of influence within a group as members strive to achieve mutual goals rather than on who possesses power.
Holistic	Assumes that power is a complex phenomenon that has to be studied as a whole and cannot be meaningfully broken into components.
Phenomenological	Stresses the immediate experience of group members and the ways they influence each other in the present rather than focusing on members' history and genetic background.
Deductive	Applies and validates theoretical principles concerning the nature and use of power.
Distributed	Stresses that power is distributed among all group members and that every member has some influence over others and over what takes place in the group.
Inevitable	Assumes that power exists in all relationships. In small groups, mutual influence goes on continuously as group members act and react and adjust to each other's actions.
Pervasive	Assumes that the use of power is essential to all aspects of group functioning—goal setting, communication, leadership, decision making, and conflict resolution.

Competitive Context.   In a **competitive context,** power is used to gain advantage and to promote one's own success at the expense of others. Power tends to be viewed as successful influence over another that overcomes the other's unwillingness to perform the desired behaviors. Robert Dahl (1967), for example, states that power involves "an ability to get another person to do something that he or she would not otherwise have done" (p. 158). Such definitions implicitly view power as (Coleman & Tjosvold, 2000):

1. A fixed-pie resource. The amount of power is limited.
2. A zero-sum resource. The more power A has, the less is available for B.
3. A commodity that should be hoarded. Competitors tend to use their power in order to extend it to maximize the power differences between themselves and others. This is known as the *iron law of oligarchy* (individuals in power tend to remain in power) (Michels, 1915/1959). Concepts such as *powerholder* reflect this view that power is a commodity to be obtained and preserved. Power holders often become preoccupied with seeking more and more power (McClelland, 1975, 1985).

4. Acting in a unidirectional way. The dominant person influences the subservient person, not vice versa. There is a division between the powerful and the powerless.

5. Being inherently coercive. The dominant person overcomes the subservient person's reluctance and resistance to engaging in the targeted behavior. Lasswell and Kaplan (1950), for example, describe the exercise of power as "simply the exercise of a high degree of coerciveness" (p. 98).

This view currently dominates the approach to power of most social scientists and power holders. Reliance on dominating strategies of power use, however, has a number of negative consequences, such as the alienation and resistance of those subjected to the influence attempts. This reaction increases the need for continuous scrutiny and control of the less powerful. It also limits the powerholder's ability and willingness to use other types of power that are based on trust and power sharing, such as normative, expert, referent, and reward power.

The resistance to the coercive use of power may be viewed as psychological reactance. **Reactance** is the need to reestablish a person's freedom whenever it is threatened. It is a motivational state that is aroused whenever persons feel that their freedom has been abridged or threatened (Brehm, 1966). Threats to personal freedom motivate persons to take actions that will help them regain their freedom and control, such as seeking to obstruct or negate the powerholder's influence and to sabotage the group's efforts and effectiveness.

The use of coercive power may escalate as it encounters resistance. The more the target of the influence resists, the greater the likelihood that the influencer will shift from a mild to a strong tactic (Gavin, Green, & Fairhurst, 1995; Kipnis, 1984; Michener & Burt, 1975). This, in turn, will generate more resistance. The coercive use of power then escalates to more and more extreme forms.

Cooperative Context.   Four mountain climbers are ascending a rock face in the Italian Alps. Bound together by a rope, they give each other constant instructions on how to proceed: "Use the handhold on the right," "Put a piton in there," "Give me a little more rope," "Belay me." Each member of the team welcomes the suggestions of teammates and responds promptly and competently to the requests.

In a **cooperative context,** power is used to maximize joint benefits and enhance the group's effectiveness. In cooperative situations, people want others to perform effectively and to use their joint resources to promote common goals; therefore, cooperation fosters an orientation toward enhancing mutual power. Members share their resources, apply their competencies, and seek to enhance the resources and competencies of other group members. The more power all members have, the more successful their efforts to achieve the group's goals. Joint power is created and developed out of the interaction among group members and their commitment to achieving their mutual goals. Power is implicitly viewed as (Coleman & Tjosvold, 2000):

1. Expandable. Power is jointly developed and expands as the individuals work together. As the positive interdependence and the ability of members to work together increase, so does the joint power to achieve the group's goals.

2. Something to be shared. Power and resources are shared with others in order to be more effective in achieving mutual goals, out of genuine concern for other group members, and because it is seen as morally right to do so.

3. Acting in a bidirectional way. Every group member influences all others. The more open a member is to the influence of others, the more open they are to the member's attempts to influence them. This more open mode of interaction results in greater learning and integration of new information and discovery of creative ways to improve group effectiveness (Kolb & Coolidge, 1991; Zajonc, 1960). Power differences tend to be minimized as members enhance each other's power in order to achieve their shared goals more effectively.

4. Being inherently noncoercive. In cooperative situations, group members (a) want to be influenced by other members in order to improve their effectiveness and (b) wish to influence other members in order to promote the success of their actions aimed at achieving the group's goals.

Constructive use of power has been largely ignored in the literature. The research that does exist indicates that people with a cooperative cognitive orientation to power are more willing to share resources and involve others in decision making than those with a competitive orientation (Coleman, 1997). Cooperative goals (compared with competitive and individualistic goals) induce higher expectations of assistance, more assistance, greater support, more persuasion and less coercion, and more trusting and friendly attitudes between superiors and subordinates (Tjosvold, 1981, 1985a, 1985b; Tjosvold, Johnson, & Johnson, 1984). Students chosen at random and given the power to participate in classroom decisions, compared to those who were informed of them, spend more time on tasks and demonstrate greater learning (Richter & Tjosvold, 1980). Also, when power holders believe that power is expandable (rather than a limited resource), they develop cooperative relationships with subordinates and provide support and resources to them, especially when subordinates lack the ability rather than the motivation to perform well (Tjosvold, Coleman, & Sun, 1999). Individuals with cooperative goals (compared with individuals with competitive goals) tend to be more open to influence, more positive toward those who exercise power, and more appreciative of the way power is used (Tjosvold, 1996).

The key to the constructive use of power in cooperative situations is inducibility. **Inducibility** is openness to influence (Deutsch, 1949a, 1962). In cooperative situations, if A's actions move B toward his or her goals, it may be expected that B will facilitate A's actions and will be receptive to A's attempts to induce him or her to engage in behavior that will facilitate A's actions. If, for example, your cat is in a tree and will not come down, and a friend brings over a ladder and asks you to help carry it to the tree and set it up, you are quite willing to do so. Your friend's power to induce your help is quite high, as your helping promotes the achievement of your goal. Since in cooperative situations participants are striving to achieve mutual goals, they are open to being influenced by each other. It is inducibility that allows coordination among the members of a cooperative group, as it underlies the norm that members should be receptive to each other's influence attempts and facilitate each other's actions that promote the achievement of the group's goals.

MOBILIZING POWER TO ACHIEVE GOALS

After a severe wind storm, a man attempted to move a tree off his driveway so that he could get his car out of the garage. His neighbor watched as he strained, but the tree did not move. "Are you using all your strength?" asked the neighbor. "Of course I am," replied the man. "Can't you see how I'm straining?" "Are you sure you are using all your strength?" asked the neighbor. "Yes, yes, yes!" replied the man. "No, you are not," said the neighbor. "You haven't asked me to help."

Most groups are formed because the group can accomplish goals that any one individual, working alone, cannot. Members cooperate in achieving the goals. Based on the dynamic-interdependent view of power, each group member (a) has the power to promote or obstruct the goal achievement of other members and (b) is dependent on the assistance of other members to achieve his or her own goals. While power may be viewed as dependence on another's resources, in most situations there is interdependence; each group member is dependent on the resources of the other members. The degree of interdependence among group members determines the power available to be used. Power is almost always bidirectional in groups (each member can influence the others). The interdependence may be symmetrical (members are equally dependent on each other's resources) or asymmetrical (one member is more dependent on the resources of another member than vice versa). In the complexities of group life, power is always asymmetrical on any one issue under one set of conditions. Since the conditions are constantly changing, and since multiple issues are being dealt with at the same time, the power relations among group members are always changing and complex. At any moment, member A may have more power on issue 1 than other members but less power on issues 2 and 3. As members coordinate their actions in working on the issues, the power of members constantly shifts and changes.

The process by which group members mobilize their power in order to accomplish their goals consists of five steps (Figure 6.2):

1. **Determining Your Goals:** The first step in using your power in a group is to clarify your personal goals. **Goals** are desired future states based on wants, needs, and interests. Typically, goals are consciously sought, but some are obtained unconsciously. In order to plan to attain your goals, you must be aware of them, accept them as valuable and worthwhile, and be willing to enlist the aid of other group members to accomplish them.

2. **Determining Your Relevant Resources:** The second step in using your power is to contribute your resources to help achieve the group's and your goals. You must be aware of and accept your resources in order to use them effectively. Moreover, it is only when you know your own resources that you understand (a) what other resources you need to achieve your goals, (b) how you can help other group members achieve their goals, and (c) how the resources of all members may be combined to achieve the group's goals.

3. **Determining Your Needed Coalitions:** The third step in using your power is to assess what coalitions you need to secure the information and resources you need to achieve your goals. Coalitions are formed by (a) identifying the group members who have the information and resources you need, (b) identifying how your information and resources could contribute to their goal accomplishment, and (c) negotiating a mutual support agreement in which each agrees to contribute to the other's success.

4. **Negotiating Mutual Support Contracts:** The fourth step in using your power is to negotiate an agreement with the appropriate group members to mutually support each other's efforts to achieve goals. In planning how resources will be utilized to

Figure 6.2 Mobilizing power to accomplish goals.

help achieve the group's goals, group members often develop formal or informal contracts with one another. The contract usually includes (a) the resources you want from the group members, (b) the resources other group members want from you, and (c) how members will coordinate their efforts so that everyone can accomplish his or her goals. In essence, the contracts are a plan for group members to apply their resources in certain ways to achieve the group's goals.

5. **Implementing the Contracts:** The fifth step in using your power is to carry out the activities necessary to achieve your goals.

EXERCISE 6.3 *Personal Power and Goal Accomplishment*

This exercise gives you an opportunity to experience the process of increasing, step by step, your personal power.

1. Form groups of four.
2. Read step 1 **(Determining Your Goals).** Each person should first state all the goals that he or she might work toward in this group. After everyone has had a say, each member should state which three goals he or she would like the group to accomplish first. Write these goals down and include your name. Then go on to the next step.
3. Read step 2 **(Determining Your Resources).** Determine your resources by creating a list of your skills, talents, abilities, or personal traits that help you function more productively. The object is to increase your awareness of (a) your strengths so that you may more consciously mobilize them to achieve your goals and (b) other resources you need. The procedure for each group is as follows:
   a. Individually, think of all the things you do well, all the things you are proud of having done, and all the things for which you feel a sense of accomplishment. List all your positive accomplishments and your successes.
   b. Share your lists with one another. Then, with the help of the other group members, examine your past successes and identify the personal strengths you used to achieve them. Make a list of these strengths.

    c. After you have all made a list of strengths, give one another feedback about additional strengths. Add to each person's list the qualities, skills, and characteristics he or she has overlooked or undervalued.

    d. Each member should then discuss the question "What might be keeping me from using all my strengths?" The group helps members explore the ways in which they can free themselves from constraints on the use of their strengths.

    e. Review the material on self-acceptance and the acceptance of others in Johnson (2000).

4. Read step 3 **(Determining Your Needed Coalitions).** As a group, look for similarities among your goals. Decide as a group upon the three goals that are most in accord with the personal goals of each member. List them. Review the strengths listed in step 2. Try to determine what resources are needed to accomplish each of the three goals and who has them. In participating in this exercise, you may experience either the frustration of finding little or no compatibility between your own goals and those of the other group members or the rejection of having your resources overlooked, undervalued, or underused. At this point, do not make any formal coalitions with other group members. Limit yourself to determining what coalitions are needed. Then go on to the next step.

5. Read step 4 **(Negotiating Mutual Support Contracts).** Negotiate formal contracts with other group members and form open coalitions. In doing so, focus specifically on (a) what you want from the group members, (b) what the other group members want from you, and (c) what you can exchange so that all members can accomplish their goals. Write down your contracts so that all members can see and read them. In essence, these contracts are a plan for group members to apply their resources cooperatively to achieve the group's goals.

6. Read step 5 **(Implementing the Contracts).** Carry out the actions specified in the contracts.

DISCUSSION

After completing the preceding steps, the groups should discuss their experiences. The following questions may be used to stimulate discussion:

1. What was the outcome of the five steps? To what extent were everyone's goals integrated in the group's goals, and to what extent were everyone's resources committed to the accomplishment of these goals?

2. What are the present reactions and feelings of each group member to the five steps?

3. On the basis of the group's experiences, what conclusions can be drawn about the use of power in a group? Groups should write down their answers. When all groups have finished their discussion, the conclusions should be shared.

THE TRAIT-FACTOR APPROACH TO POWER

One night long, long ago, a princess lay down to sleep on a bed that contained thirteen mattresses. At the bottom of the pile of mattresses had been placed a tiny pea. The princess tossed and turned all night, unable to sleep. This fairy-tale princess was unable to sleep because it is part of the nature of princesses to be disturbed by factors that those of us with mundane natures do not even notice. The princess illustrates the **trait-factor approach to power** and influence, which views the capacity to exert power over other people as a genetically inherited trait or disposition. The princess is credited with hav-

Trait-Factor Approach to Power

	Characteristics
Static	Focuses more on continuity than on change.
Atomistic	Assumes that complex phenomena can be analyzed into component parts.
Historical	Assumes that the cause of present behavior is a function of genetic and experiential factors acting cumulatively over relatively long periods of time.
Inductive	Stresses accounting for empirically observed phenomena more than seeking empirical validation for general theoretical statements.

ing innate dispositions that differentiated her from all other females. Who can deny her divine spark?

The trait-factor approach to power is based on the assumption that a person's traits explain why the person is as he or she is, how the person became so, and why the person stays the same despite circumstances, fortune, and opportunities. Thus, certain individuals are born with the capacity to influence others. Two of the trait-factor approaches to power are the work on power and persuasion and the work on social dominance.

Power and Persuasion

Aristotle dealt at some length in his Rhetoric with the characteristics of an effective influencer and gave detailed advice on the techniques of persuasion. From the trait-factor point of view, influence depends on the characteristics of both the person exerting influence and the person being influenced. The characteristics of the influence attempt itself may also have some importance.

The major post–World War II application of the trait-factor approach to power was the Yale Attitude Change Program, headed by Carl Hovland (Hovland, Janis, & Kelley, 1953; Hovland, Lumsdaine, & Sheffield, 1949; McGuire, 1985). Most of the research in this program focused on the area in which the trait-factor view is strongest—the effects of a single attempt to influence people delivered through the mass media. In situations where a politician is giving a speech to an audience, an announcer is delivering a television commercial, or a health official is warning the public about a health danger, the findings of the Yale Program are quite useful. In each of these situations, the contact between the communicator and the receiver of the communication is brief and not repeated. Moreover, the communication is one-way; there is no interaction between the two parties. Because single instances of one-way communication are essentially static, a trait-oriented theory is quite helpful in analyzing them.

Hovland's wartime studies of propaganda were organized around the question "Who says what to whom with what effect?" Investigators have usually broken this question down into variables relating to the **source** (the characteristics of the communicator), the **message** (the characteristics of the communication), and the **receiver** (the characteristics of the person receiving the message). The exercise of power may thus be seen as a credible and attractive communicator's delivery of an effectively organized message to a vulnerable or influenceable audience. People are more likely to be influenced by individuals whom they perceive to be trustworthy, fairly distributing resources, and treating people with respect (Tyler, 1997; Tyler & Degoey, 1996). Messages are more effective if they are phrased so that they are two-sided, action-oriented, and discrepant with members' current beliefs. The powerholder is more effective if the less powerful individuals have low self-esteem, see their attitudes under modification as peripheral to them, have no forewarning of the influence attempt, role play positions that agree with one's own, are distracted while one is presenting the message, and are not very intelligent. Trait-factor researchers assume that people are rational in the way they process information and are motivated to attend to a message, learn its contents, and incorporate it into their attitudes. The trait-factor approach to influence, however, is weak both logically and empirically in situations where two or more individuals are constantly interacting.

Social Dominance Theory

A theory of power directly based on competition is social dominance theory. **Social dominance** is defined as the ability to control resources. Resources are anything outside the individual essential for survival, growth, and development (Charlesworth, 1996). It is assumed that resources are limited and, therefore, that resource acquisition compels competition among group members as well as among groups and species (Darwin, 1859). A social dominance hierarchy is created when members of a social group vary in their ability to acquire resources (Hawley, 1999). A social dominance hierarchy is not a way of organizing groups; it is an inescapable consequence of differences in individuals' ability to compete. The member's ability to compete successfully for limited resources defines his or her position in the social hierarchy. Dominance hierarchies are created by the adaptive rule of thumb in competitive encounters that "Depending on who your opponent is, assert when you can prevail, yield when you cannot." This rule is seen as diminishing conflict among group members and minimizing the personal costs of interacting with other members.

While young children may compete for resources through physical coercion and force, older persons learn that aggression is unacceptable and adopt other, more socially acceptable, means of obtaining resources, such as persuasion or forming coalitions. An exception may be school bullies, who dominate others through physical and verbal aggression. The intent is to establish dominance (i.e., gain control of resources) while minimizing interpersonal conflict with the other group members. Forming coalitions may be the most successful strategy for acquiring control of resources, as groups of individuals who help each other do better than groups of individuals who do not (Campbell, 1965, 1978; Kropotkin, 1902). Groups, however, are viewed as being composed of self-interested individuals, whose interests include balancing their own needs with the needs of others. Social relationships can be viewed as resources in themselves, because individuals who have social contacts to collaborate with do better than those who do not. Thus, the most adaptive way to acquire resources may be to be a fair player, to consider others, to compromise, and to be an overall good group member.

Being dominant (reflecting relative competitive ability) is assumed to be correlated with health, vigor, productiveness, and reproductive success, presumably because dominant individuals are better able to fulfill their nutritional, social, and security needs than other group members. Thus, the dominant individual within a social hierarchy becomes the focus of attention, admired, liked, viewed as an attractive social partner, and obeyed.

The motivation to dominate others and the ability to do so may be seen as traits that differentially appear in individuals. Social dominance theory, therefore, may be the clearest example of the trait-factor approach to power.

Individual versus Relationship Perspectives

The field of group dynamics is divided between social scientists who focus on individual variables and those who focus on relationship variables. In the individual orientation to human behavior, social scientists search for laws governing the behavior of a single individual and look at the individual's attitudes, personality traits, skills, aptitudes, genes, and other causes of behavior. These causes are often assumed to be static, present at any one moment, and have a physical, often neuropsychological, representation of some kind.

In contrast, relationship scholars seek laws governing individuals' interactions with each other, that is, the influence each person's behavior exerts on his or her partner's behavior. By looking at relationships, they identify dynamics such as conflict, power, love, and cooperation. There is a rhythm displayed in regularities in interaction patterns, and the goal of the relationship perspective is to identify the conditions responsible for that rhythm. A relationship does not reside in the individual; it resides between individuals. The rhythm of a relationship is revealed only over time in specific situations; relationships are inherently temporal rather than static and are influenced by the situation. A relationship's rhythm is not presumed to have a direct representation. Finally, like gravity and electricity, a relationship is invisible; its existence can be discerned only by observing its effects.

Power is one of the most complex relationship variables in group dynamics. The nature of power can only be determined between people, not within people, and the actions of the individuals over time and within certain contexts must be taken into account. There is no doubt that power can have strong effects.

THE BASES OF POWER

On November 1, 1095, Pope Urban II delivered a speech in an open field outside the town of Clermont, France, in which he urged the crowd to arm itself and drive the "wicked race" of pagans from the Holy Land. Moved by the pope's words, the crowd began to yell, "It is the will of God!" Thus began the long series of wars known as the Crusades. Peter the Hermit organized the first Crusade in 1096. All over Europe, huge groups of unarmed men, priests, monks, women, and children became captivated by the

Ranking Bases of Power

Find a partner. Working cooperatively, rank the following bases of power from most to least effective in influencing others. Compare your ranking with the ranking of another pair. Explain the reasoning underlying your ranking and listen to their rationale.

Rank	Base of Power
_____	Ability to deliver positive consequences or remove negative consequences in response to their behavior.
_____	Ability to mete out negative consequences or remove positive consequences in response to the behavior of group members.
_____	Possession of a position in the group or organization (such as president) or special role responsibilities (such as those of an x-ray technician).
_____	Modeling behavioral patterns and personal qualities that others want to imitate out of respect, liking, and wanting to be liked.
_____	Possession of special expertise that is useful in accomplishing the goal and that is not available anywhere else.
_____	Possession of resources or information that is useful in accomplishing the goal and that is not available anywhere else.

promise of salvation, the lure of riches, and the promise of adventure and gathered to begin the trek to Jerusalem. Caught up in their religious fervor, few stopped to contemplate their chances for survival. Almost all of them died. Yet the Crusades lasted until 1291, when the Muslims regained full control of the Holy Land. What gave Pope Urban II the power to launch such a 200-year effort?

According to **social exchange theory,** power is based on the control of valuable resources. If a person controls a resource you want, that person has power over you unless, of course, you have an alternative source for the resource. The type of resource under a person's control determines the basis for the person's power. The **power bases** typically are reward, coercive, legitimate (based on position in a hierarchy), referent, expertise, and informational (French & Raven, 1959; Frost & Stahelski, 1988; Raven, 1992, 1993; Raven & Kruglanski, 1970).

Pope Urban II may have attained his power through the promise of heavenly rewards for participating in a Crusade. A person has **reward power** over other group members if he or she has the ability to deliver positive consequences or remove negative consequences in response to their behavior. Rewards can be higher salaries, food, gold stars, positive feedback, or salvation. A person's power will be greater the more the group members value the reward, the more they believe that the person can dispense the reward (i.e., the powerholder's promises seem credible), and the less their chances appear of getting the reward from someone else. When reward power is used successfully, group members comply with the powerholder's requests, seek out the powerholder, like the powerholder, and communicate effectively with the powerholder. Under certain conditions, however, reward power can backfire. Too many rewards can create the suspicion that group members are being bribed or conned, which tends to result in dislike and/or resistance.

Pope Urban II may have attained his power from the threat of punishment (eternal damnation) if Christians did not participate in the Crusade. A person has **coercive power** over other group members if he or she can mete out negative consequences or remove positive consequences in response to the behavior of group members. Punishments may include physical pain or isolation, withholding money or approval, or eternal damnation. Punishment for a member who fails to get the group to go along with his or her wishes often increases the pressure on group members to engage in the desired behavior. Coercive power frequently causes group members to avoid the person and to like her or him less. Group members may do what the person wants, but they tend to avoid interacting with the person in the future. Only when the use of coercive power brings a conflict into the open to be resolved can it have many positive effects.

Pope Urban II may have attained his power from his position. When a person has **legitimate power,** group members believe the person ought to have influence over them because of his or her position in the group or organization (such as an employer) or because of his or her special role responsibilities (such as those of a police officer). Legitimate authorities are obeyed by members who accept the norms of the group and therefore comply through a sense of duty, loyalty, or even moral obligation. Group members believe it is their duty to follow the commands of a person with legitimate power, even when it means limiting their own behaviors. Individuals have more legitimate power when they are perceived to be trustworthy, distributing resources fairly, and treating people with respect (Tyler, 1997; Tyler & Degoey, 1996). Legitimate power is often used to reduce conflict—when the person with such power plays the role of an arbitrator or a mediator or when those with less power simply conform to the person's wishes.

Pope Urban II may have attained his power because of the desire of Christians to emulate him and win his respect and liking. When a person has **referent power,** group members identify with or want to be like the person and therefore do what he or she wants out of respect, liking, and wanting to be liked. Charismatic leaders have referent power, and they typically use it to demand new obligations that contradict established social norms and require self-sacrifice and united action (Hoffer, 1951; Weber, 1921/ 1946). Generally, the more the person is liked, the more the group members will identify with him or her.

Pope Urban II may have attained his power through his superior skills and abilities resulting from being God's representative on earth. When a person has **expert power,** group members see the person as having some skills and competencies that will be useful in accomplishing the goal and that are not available anywhere else. The more a person is perceived to be an expert, the more influential he or she is within the group (Littlepage & Mueller, 1997). Group members may need to work together for some time before they can clearly assess each other's expertise. Over time, the group becomes more proficient at recognizing and utilizing the strengths of each member (Littlepage, Robison, & Reddington, 1997; Littlepage & Silbiger, 1992) and thereby improving its coordination of efforts and expertise (Goodman & Leyden, 1991). The successful use of expert power results in liking for the person, as group members are convinced of the correctness of the influence attempts. Only if her expertise fosters a feeling of inadequacy in the group members will it have negative effects.

Pope Urban II may have attained his power from his information on the will of God. When a person has **informational power,** group members believe that the person has resources or information (not available anywhere else) that will be useful in accomplishing the goal. Information resources include rational argument, factual data, and logic. The person's power is based on the logic of the person's arguments or the superiority of his or her demonstrated knowledge; it has effects similar to those that result from the use of expert power.

French and Raven (1959) argued that power may be drawn from these six key sources. Pope Urban II was powerful because he could use all six bases of power. Note that it is the *perception* of a group member's power base that affects the behavior of other members, not actual resources. A member can have considerable resources that are unknown or ignored by other group members and therefore have little power over the others. On the other hand, a group member can have few resources but be seen as having many resources and thereby can have a great deal of influence over the other group members.

While resources may create the basis of power, power is still expressed through behavior. Sometimes power is exerted in conversation. How we talk to another person often reflects and reinforces the balance of power between us. Gender relations are no exception. There is evidence that men are more likely to dominate discussions of neutral topics and masculine topics, while women dominate discussions only on traditionally feminine subjects (Brown, Dovidio, & Ellyson, 1990). Men tend to interrupt and touch women more than vice versa (Hall & Veccia, 1990; Major, Schmidlin, & Williams, 1990; West & Zimmerman, 1983), both of which have been interpreted as indicators of greater social power.

Cooperative versus Competitive Context

French and Raven's theory of power bases has been very influential. Researchers, however, have not found a consistent relationship between influence attempts and effectiveness (Falbe & Yukl, 1992; Tjosvold, 1995a; Yukl & Falbe, 1991; Yukl & Tracey, 1992). One reason may be that the context in which the power basis is utilized has not been taken into account. Tjosvold (1995) had undergraduates in a Canadian university participate in a simulation in which (a) power was used to reward or punish and (b) in a cooperative, competitive, or individualistic context. Each participant was told that he or she was an employee of a consulting company that specializes in solving problems of other organizations and would be working with another participant who was assigned the role of manager. All participants were given four chances in a lottery for $50. In one condition, participants were given a reward of four additional chances for their efforts; in another condition, the four chances were taken away. Tjosvold found that participants in a *cooperative context* (compared with participants in a competitive or individualistic context) were more open-minded, felt greater warmth, were more confident in the work relationship, believed more strongly that power was used wisely, and perceived the powerholder as being more likable, fair, and trustworthy. He also found that the use of *power to reward* (rather than to punish) induced more openness and open-mindedness, feelings of acceptance and warmth, the belief that power was used wisely, attraction and positive attitudes toward the manager, and a

Defining Bases of Power

Find a partner and, working cooperatively, match the following bases of power with their definitions. Compare answers with another pair.

_____	1. Reward	a.	Group members believe the person has useful knowledge not available elsewhere.
_____	2. Coercive	b.	Group members believe the person ought to have power because of his or her position or responsibilities.
_____	3. Legitimate	c.	A person can deliver positive consequences or remove negative consequences.
_____	4. Reference	d.	Group members believe the person has special knowledge or skill and is trustworthy.
_____	5. Expert	e.	Group members do what the person wants out of respect, liking, and wanting to be liked.
_____	6. Informational	f.	The person can deliver negative consequences or remove positive consequences.

stronger working relationship. Previously, Tjosvold (1981, 1989, 1990a) had found that even with unequal power, cooperation promoted the exchange of resources and productively completed tasks, competition and individualism created suspicion and a refusal to exchange resources.

CONFLICT MODEL OF SOCIAL INFLUENCE

The French social psychologist Serge Moscovici (1980, 1985a) proposed an intergroup conflict model of social influence in which power defines whether a group is a majority or a minority. He assumes that both majorities and minorities are sources and targets of influence attempts. Majorities tend to use their power to force minorities to yield and conform to the majorities' expectations. Minorities tend to convert majorities to the minorities' position. What defines the majority and minority groups is the amount of power they have. A power majority is a group that has the most control over how important resources are distributed (it may be the numerical minority). A power minority is a group that has little control over the distribution of important resources (it may be a numerical majority). In the United States and Europe, for example, white males (a numerical minority) have traditionally controlled the distribution of top posts in government and industry (they have been the power majority), while Asians and others have been part of the power minorities (Shinagawa, 1997). In Japan, however, pure Japanese are the power majority and white Europeans are the power minority.

6.4   *Unequal Resources*

This exercise gives participants a chance to observe how groups (a) use resources that have been unequally distributed and (b) negotiate to obtain the resources they need. It is conducted with four groups, each having two to four members. If there are enough participants to have more than one cluster of four groups, the coordinator may wish to add the element of competition between as well as within the clusters. The exercise should take less than one hour. The procedure for the coordinator is as follows:

1. Introduce the exercise as an experience with the use of resources needed to accomplish a task that have been distributed unequally among groups. Form the groups. For each cluster, have at least two observers. Groups should be placed far enough away from each other so that their negotiation positions are not compromised by casual observation.

2. Meet briefly with the observers and discuss what they might focus on. Any aspect of negotiation and problem solving can be observed.

3. Distribute an envelope of materials and a copy of the accompanying task sheet to each group. Explain that each group has different materials but that all groups must complete the same tasks. Explain that the groups may negotiate for the use of materials and tools in any way that is agreeable to everyone. Emphasize that the first group to finish all the tasks is the winner. (If clusters are competing, there will be both a group winner and a cluster winner.) Give the signal to begin.

4. When the groups have finished, declare the winner. Then conduct a discussion on using resources, sharing, negotiating, competing, and using power. Ask the observers to participate in the discussion. Then ask each cluster to summarize its conclusions about the use of power that manifested itself during the exercise.

Group Materials

Group 1	Scissors, ruler, paper clips, pencils, two 4-inch squares of red paper, and two 4-inch squares of white paper.
Group 2	Scissors, glue, and two sheets each of gold paper, white paper, and blue paper, each 8 by 11 inches.
Group 3	Felt-tipped markers and two sheets each of green paper, white paper, and gold paper, each 8 by 11 inches.
Group 4	Five sheets of paper, 8 by 11 inches—one green, one gold, one blue, one red, and one purple.

UNEQUAL RESOURCES EXERCISE TASK SHEET

Each group is to complete the following tasks:

1. Make a 3- by 3-inch square of white paper.
2. Make a 4- by 2-inch rectangle of gold paper.
3. Make a 3- by 5-inch T-shaped piece of green and white paper.
4. Make a four-link paper chain, each link in a different color.
5. Make a 4- by 4-inch flag in any three colors.

The first group to complete all the tasks is the winner. Groups may negotiate with each other for the use of needed materials and tools on any mutually agreeable basis.

6.5 *Power Politics*

The objective of this exercise is to examine the dynamics of negotiating for power. Group members with different amounts of power negotiate to form coalitions. The exercise takes one hour. The procedure is as follows:

1. Divide the participants into groups of twelve. Each participant needs a pencil and a pad of paper for writing notes.

2. **Task:** In this exercise, group members are to select a chairperson for the governing board of a political party. Each group member has a different amount of power. It takes 4,000 votes to elect a chairperson. The chairperson cannot be elected unless members form coalitions and vote as a bloc.

3. Each group member receives (a) a copy of the instruction sheet and (b) a slip of paper indicating the number of votes the participant controls (the numbers range from 100 to 1,200 votes). Each group member controls a different number of votes (one member controls 100 votes, one member 200 votes, another member 300 votes, and so on, with one member controlling 1,200 votes). *Do not show your slip of paper with the number of your votes to other group members.*

4. Two rounds of negotiations will take place before the first vote is taken. Each round will last five minutes. During negotiations, members write notes to one another. No verbal communication is permitted. Members may write as many notes to as many other members as they wish. Notes should include the names of the sender and the receiver. These notes are not to be read until the end of the five-minute period.

5. Give the signal to begin round one. At the end of five minutes, stop all note passing and allow members to read their notes.

6. Give the signal to begin round two. The same rules apply. At the end of five minutes, stop all note passing and allow members to read their notes.

7. Ask the group if they are ready to vote on their chairperson. If seven members want to vote, a vote is taken. All voting takes place by secret ballot. On the ballot, write the number of votes you control and to whom you commit them. If the group is not ready to vote or if no one has enough votes to become chairperson, round three begins.

8. Give the signal to begin round three. Group members may negotiate verbally with one another. There are no restrictions on negotiations during this round, which also lasts for five minutes. At the end of round three, call for a vote. The vote is again taken by secret ballot.

9. If no one has enough votes to become chairperson, give the signal to begin round four. Allow a ten-minute free-negotiation period. Then take a final vote.

10. Discuss the experience, using the following questions as guides:
    a. What deals were made? How was power used in making those deals?
    b. What negotiation/influence strategies were used?
    c. What criteria did members use to decide whom to commit their votes to?
    d. What were the feelings and reactions of the members to the experience?
    e. How did it feel to control a small number of votes? How did it feel to control a large number of votes?
    f. What strategies did members use to create allies and develop power blocs?
    h. What conclusions can you draw about the use of power? (Write these down and share them with other groups.)

POWER POLITICS EXERCISE INSTRUCTION SHEET

This is a game of power politics. Your group is to become the governing body of a political party, and you and the other group members must select a chairperson. A member must receive 4,000 votes to become chairperson. This is a crucial decision for the party. The person you elect chairperson will control who gets how much patronage from the party. The chairperson will have one hundred units of patronage to distribute to deserving group members. Group members may negotiate for votes and the distribution of the patronage. One member controls 100 votes, a second controls 200, a third controls 300, and so on, with one member controlling 1,200 votes. The number of votes each member has is written on a slip of paper handed out by the coordinator of the exercise. Keep this slip. *Do not show it to any other group member.* You may commit your votes to any member you wish; you may split your votes among several members if you wish.

POWER AND PROBLEM SOLVING

In the two previous exercises, the resources of the group were distributed unequally among its members. This is the case with most of the problems a group faces. Yet unequal distribution of resources does not mean that members are powerless. Every group member has some power; every member is able to influence other group members in some way. How a group manages power has an important bearing on group effectiveness.

The effectiveness of any group is improved when (a) power is relatively balanced among its members and (b) power is based upon competence, expertise, and information. The ability of the group to solve problems increases as all group members come to believe that they have equal influence on the direction of the group effort and as the group climate becomes relatively free of domination by a few of the most powerful members. When members have equal power, they are more cooperative in their interactions, more responsive to the cooperative initiatives of other members, and more committed to implementing the group decision. Studies have found that even within organizations, the satisfaction of subordinates increases when they believe they can influence particular aspects of the organization's decision making (Tjosvold, 1995a). Unequal power interferes with the trust and communication necessary for managing group conflicts constructively. Thus, the problem-solving ability of a group is improved when the group has dynamic power patterns that in the long run equalize influence among group members.

A group's decisions are invariably of higher quality when power is based on competence, expertise, and relevant information—not on authority or popularity. The problem-solving capacity of many groups is seriously damaged when the member with the most authority is most influential at a time that calls for expertise and accurate information as the bases of power. When power is not distributed equally among group members, or when the use of authority dominates and expertise and informational bases of power are ignored, group effectiveness is undermined. The next exercise deals with the unequal distribution of power and the consequences it can have for both high- and low-power group members.

6.6 *Power to the Animals*

The objective of this exercise is to examine the interaction among groups with different levels of power as they negotiate with one another. The exercise takes two hours. The coordinator should read the accompanying instructions regarding the distribution of marbles and then follow this procedure:

1. Introduce the exercise as one that highlights interaction among groups with unequal power. Divide the class into groups of twelve. Explain that within each group are three mammals, four birds, and five fish; the status of the members in each group is determined by how well they negotiate—for marbles. (Even if there are more than twelve participants in a group, keep the number of mammals under five.) Hand out a copy of the general instructions to every participant.

2. Distribute twelve bags of marbles randomly within each group. Make sure that the members understand their instructions. Give them time to examine the marbles they have been given, warning them not to let other participants see the marbles. Then begin negotiation session 1, which is to last for five minutes.

3. During the negotiation session place on newsprint three headings: "Mammals," "Birds," and "Fish." After five minutes, stop the negotiating and have the participants compute their scores. Take the three highest scores and place them, along with the persons' initials, under the heading "Mammals." (Even if there are more than twelve participants in a group, keep the number of mammals under five.) Place the next four scores, together with the persons' initials, under the heading "Birds." Place the remaining five scores, with the persons' initials, under the heading "Fish." Have each person make a name tag indicating what he or she is and put it on.

4. Begin negotiation session 2. After five minutes, end it and ask for scores. Read just the individual scores, placing the three highest in the Mammals column, the next four in the Birds column, and the next five in the Fish column. Members who change columns on the basis of their score will have to exchange their name tags.

5. Conduct negotiation session 3 in the same way.

6. Conduct negotiation session 4 in the same way.

7. Announce that the mammals now have the authority to make the rules for the exercise and that although anyone else can suggest rules, the mammals will decide which ones will be implemented. Inform the mammals that they may make any rules they wish, such as a rule that all marbles must be redistributed so that everyone has equal points, or a rule that all fish and birds must give mammals the marbles they ask for whether they want to or not. Have the mammals record their rules in writing.

8. After the new rules are established, conduct negotiation session 5. Then allow five minutes for the mammals to discuss and make any rule changes.

9. Repeat this cycle twice. Then give the birds and the fish copies of the list of strategies for influencing a high-power group. The birds and the fish have ten minutes to discuss the strategies and decide which ones to adopt. Then continue with another negotiation session.

10. After a variety of strategies have been tried by the birds and the fish, or when they refuse to continue, conduct a discussion of the experience. The following questions may be used as guides:

   a. What were your feelings and your reactions to the experience?
   b. Are there any parallels between the system set up by the game and the system in which we live?
   c. Would it have made much difference if the members who were fish had been the mammals?
   d. Were the mammals acting with legitimate authority?
   e. Are there any parallels between the exercise and the relations among racial groups, rich and poor, and adults and students?
   f. What negotiation strategies were used?
   g. What feelings arose from the unequal distribution of power? How did it feel to have high power? How did it feel to have low power? How did your experiences compare with the following discussions of high- and low-power group members?
   h. How did the strategies for changing the high-power group work? What contributed to their effectiveness or ineffectiveness?
   i. What conclusions about the use of power can be drawn from your experiences in the exercise?

DISTRIBUTION OF MARBLES

1. The total number of marbles needed is seventy-two (six times the number of group members).

2. The number of green marbles needed is five (the number of mammals plus two).

3. The number of yellow marbles needed is ten (the number of birds plus the number of fish plus one).

4. The number of red, white, and blue marbles needed is fifty-seven, nineteen of each.

Give each participant a bag of six marbles. Five bags are to contain one green marble, one yellow marble, and four marbles randomly selected from the colors red, white, and blue. Three bags are to contain one yellow marble and five marbles randomly selected from the colors red, white, and blue. The remaining four bags are to contain a random assortment of red, white, and blue marbles. These twelve bags are to be distributed at random within each group.

GENERAL INSTRUCTIONS

In this exercise there are three levels of power, based on the marbles in each group. Group members have the chance to progress from one level of power to another by obtaining marbles through negotiation. The three members who get the most power will be declared the winners when the exercise ends. You will be given six marbles each. The scoring system for the marbles is given below. Additional points are awarded if a member is able to get several marbles of the same color.

Color	Points	Number of a Kind	Points
Green	50	4	50
Yellow	25	3	30
Red	15	2	20
White	10	1	10
Blue	5		

For example, a person's total score if she had six green marbles would be 300 (6 × 50) plus 50 (for 6 of a kind), or 350 points. The rules for negotiation are as follows:

1. You have five minutes to improve your score.
2. You improve your score by negotiating with other group members.
3. Members must be holding hands to have an agreement.
4. Only one-for-one trades are legal. Two-for-one or any other combination is illegal.
5. Once a member touches the hand of another member, a marble of unequal value (or color) must be traded. If two members cannot make an agreement, they will have to hold hands for the entire negotiating round.
6. There is no talking unless hands are touching. This rule must be strictly followed.
7. Members with folded arms do not have to negotiate with other members.
8. All marbles must be hidden. This rule must be strictly followed.

STRATEGIES FOR INFLUENCING A HIGH-POWER GROUP

1. Build your own organizations and resources in order to make the low-power group less vulnerable.
2. Form coalitions.
3. Change the attitudes of high-power group members through education or moral persuasion.
4. Use existing legal procedures to bring pressures for change.
5. Search for ways in which to make high-power group members dependent upon the low-power group.
6. Use harassment techniques to increase the high-power group's costs of sticking with the status quo.

UNEQUAL POWER

One of the most common settings for analyzing power is in the relationship between high- and low-power groups. **Power** includes the capacity to affect another person's goal accomplishment. **High power** is the capacity to have considerable influence on another person's goal accomplishment, while **low power** is the capacity to have little influence on another person's goal accomplishment. When the distribution of power is obviously unequal, the potential for its destructive use increases considerably and the overall effectiveness of the group tends to decrease. The use of power has metamorphic effects on both the high- and low-power group members. In discussions of theory and research pertaining to high and low power, the usual reference is to our society rather than to a small problem-solving group. Yet the same dynamics between high-power and low-power persons can be found in a group of any size, even one as large as our society.

High-Power Members

In Greek mythology, the king of Phrygia, Midas, showed unusual kindness to Dionysus's teacher, Silenus. In appreciation, Dionysus offered to grant any wish King Midas wanted to ask. Midas requested that all he touched would turn to gold. When even his food became gold, he implored Dionysus for relief and was directed to bathe in the river Pactolus (which has since had golden sands). His touch returned to normal. King Midas had gained the wisdom to know that the exercise of power does not always turn out the way it is intended.

Life generally seems good for high-power persons. Everything goes right, every problem is easily solved, everyone seems to like and appreciate them and everything they do. High-power persons are typically happy with their situation and tend not to see how much the use of power is involved in their relationships. They are convinced that low-power persons really do like them, that everyone communicates honestly with them, that no one hides information from them, and that they are really seen as nice persons. When this enjoyable world is threatened by dissatisfaction expressed by low-power persons, however, high-power persons tend not to react benevolently. They are hard to move toward cooperation, conciliation, and compromise, and they largely ignore the efforts of their low-power groupmates to increase cooperative problem solving. To them, low-power persons somehow never learn to "know their place"; they insist on "rocking the boat" out of ignorance and spite.

There are at least two strategies that high-power group members use to make it more difficult for low-power members to reduce the differences in power between them (Jones & Gerard, 1967). The first is to institute norms or rules in the group that legitimize their power and make wrong any attempt by others to change the status quo. The first action taken by most groups who attain power is to legitimate its use and to establish regulations and norms that make illegitimate any change in the existing power relationships. For example, in most communities the white power structure has established strong norms about where minority-group members may live, what occupations they may have, and where they must go to school—as well as procedures for making both whites and nonwhites believe that the status quo is legitimate and right. This strategy may be described as the "power-defines-injustice" strategy, or the "might-is-right" strategy.

The second strategy high-power members employ to solidify their position is to make the risk of attempting to change the status quo so great that the low-power members are deterred from trying to do so. They can invoke this strategy by establishing severe penalties against those who might attempt to change the status quo, and by offering the low-power members a variety of benefits or rewards on the condition that they not rebel. Of the two, the second seems to be more effective. The threat of punishment has never worked effectively to deter behavior, but the paternalistic leadership that tries to keep everyone happy has been applied successfully in combatting labor and racial unrest in many parts of the country. This strategy may be defined as the "this-hurts-me-more-than-it-will-hurt-you" strategy or the "if-only-you-would-behave-neither-of-us-would-go-through-this-suffering" strategy.

The *power-devaluation theory* proposed by Kipnis and his colleagues (Kipnis, 1972; Kipnis, Castel, Gergen, & Mauch, 1976; Kipnis, Schmidt, Prince, & Stitt, 1981; Wilkinson & Kipnis, 1978) posits that as a person's power increases, he or she will make more attempts to influence others. As more influence attempts are made, the person comes to believe that he or she controls the other people's behavior and is the causal agent in producing the outcomes. The performances of low-power others are devalued, and the high-power person takes responsibility for any successes associated with the work of others.

Participants who were randomly assigned to central positions in a communication network (the more powerful positions) not only viewed themselves as powerful but also rated themselves as more capable than the participants who were randomly assigned peripheral positions (Stotle, 1978). Tjosvold (1978) notes that high-power group members (a) feel more secure than low-power members, (b) underestimate the low-power members' positive intentions, (c) devalue the low-power person, (d) are inattentive to the communications of low-power persons, (e) are unresponsive to cooperative gestures by low-power members, and (f) attempt to protect their superior power by rejecting demands for change. High-power group members also seem uninterested in learning about the intentions and plans of low-power members (Tjosvold & Sagaria, 1978). High-power individuals tend to make fewer concessions in conflict situations (Lawler & Yoon, 1993), claim a larger share of available resources (Murnighan & Pillutla, 1995), and are less cooperative and more exploitive of the other's cooperation (Lindskold & Arnoff, 1980). High-power individuals tend to be more angered by a lower person's harm than when positions are reversed (Baumeister, Smart, & Boden, 1996). As Aristotle noted, people think it "right that they should be revered by those inferior to them" (384–322 B.C./1991, p. 143), and they find it particularly vexing to be insulted or harmed by someone who should actually treat them with deference.

The Metamorphic Effects of High Power.   In Greek myths, the heroes typically become so arrogant (based on their past accomplishments) that they compare themselves to the gods. Having gained power from their heroic deeds, they seek even more, and in doing so they engender the jealousy of the gods, who engineer their demise. Arachne, for example, believed she could weave better than Athena (goddess of wisdom and weaving). Athena was offended and came to earth, where they had a contest over who could weave the best. Arachne won. In response, Athena turned her into a spider. The point of these myths is that obtaining power results in a metamorphosis that eventually results in the person's downfall.

There is evidence that using power alters the high-power person (Kipnis, Castel, Gergen, & Mauch, 1976). *First,* the desire for power becomes a need in itself, apart from the larger goals that power is intended to fulfill, such as accomplishing the task. *Second,* the ease of using power encourages powerholders to use power to benefit themselves at the expense of those under their power. *Third,* powerholders receive unwarranted positive feedback, even adulation, from others, thereby producing an inflated sense of self-worth. *Fourth,* power may lead to the devaluation of others, reflected in a tendency to see the worst in others. *Fifth,* having an inflated view of themselves may lead powerholders to overstep the bounds of the appropriate use of their power. A recent meta-analysis indicates that as a person's power increases, the performance ratings of others become increasingly negative (effect size = 0.29) and self-evaluations become increasingly positive (effect size = 0.45) (Georgesen & Harris, 1998). High power seems to produce an egocentric or self-serving bias (Harris & Schaubroeck, 1988), resulting in inflated self-evaluations to maintain the benefits of high power, such as employment, promotions, and perks.

One of the most dramatic examples of the tranformative effects of power is the Stanford Prison Study (Haney, Banks, & Zimbardo, 1973; Zimbardo, 1975). Zimbardo conducted a field study to explore the roles of guards and prisoners in a prison situation. From over one hundred applications to participate in the two-week experiment, Zimbardo carefully selected twenty-four participants on the basis of extensive psychological testing to ensure that they were normal and representative of intelligent middle-class male youth. Participants were randomly assigned to be either guards or prisoners. The prisoners were "arrested" by uniformed police, booked, and transported to the mock prison constructed in the basement of the psychology building at Stanford University. The prisoners were dressed in a prison shirt, heavy ankle chain, and stocking cap. Guards wore khaki uniforms, billy clubs, whistles, and reflective sunglasses. The setting was made realistic, with bars on the doors and strict visiting hours for anyone wanting to meet with the prisoners. The guards were simply instructed to keep order. The surprising outcome of this simulation was that it had to be abandoned after only six days because the treatment of the prisoners by the guards was far more aggressive and dehumanizing than had been expected. The guards seemed to enjoy thinking up new ways to degrade prisoners. What makes these findings so shocking is the expectation that normal, bright, young middle-class men would not act in this way.

Status and Power.   High-status positions invoke a sense of privilege (Messe, Kerr, & Sattler, 1992). Occupants of high-status positions come to believe they are entitled to special treatment simply because of the position they hold. Messe and his associates demonstrated that (a) privileged behaviors are a central component of people's role schema for "supervisor," (b) due to this sense of privilege, supervisors expend less effort than subordinates on shared tasks, and (c) occupants of high-status positions act in a privileged manner by taking more than an equal share of the rewards offered to the group.

High status does not always mean high power. Johnson and Allen (1972) investigated the various combinations of status and power and found that having high status and high power in an organization results in an enhanced self-perception that leads to altruistic behavior but disdain for the worker. But when individuals had high status but low power in an organization that rewards high power, Johnson and Allen found that low-power group members who believed they were equal to their high-power peers felt underrewarded and attempted to obtain increased rewards from the group (they deviated from the prescribed norms in order to increase their own rewards). They tended to emphasize the incompetence, uncooperativeness, lack of generosity, and unfairness of the high-power members. They also tended to dislike their high-power peers but expressed respect for low-power individuals.

Power Stereotyping Theory. There is an association between power and stereotyping (Fiske, 1993; Fiske & Morling, 1996). The general premise of *power-stereotyping theory* is that persons in positions of power are especially vulnerable to stereotyping subordinates because they pay less attention to them, perhaps due to (a) lack of cognitive capacity (having high power requires attending to more people and more issues at the same time), (b) viewing subordinates as unimportant because the high-power persons outcomes do not depend on the actions of subordinates, or (c) high-power individuals having a dominant personality trait, which results in their attempting to control their interactions with others to such an extent that they ignore the actions and motivations of others. Regardless of its cause, decreases in attention make powerful individuals more likely to depend on stereotypes in interacting with subordinates.

Final Note. Folklore emphasizes two aspects of high power. The first is, "Power corrupts." High power is believed to result in arrogance and corruption. The second is that the greater a person's power, the more insufficient it is likely to seem, simply because the claims on it increase faster than the power to fulfill them (Halle, 1967). The Ford Foundation, for example, though by far the richest American foundation, is undoubtedly the most inadequately endowed in terms of the expectations it is called on to meet.

Low-Power Members

Low Power Within an Authority Hierarchy. In many social systems, there is an authority system characterized by several levels, such as president, vice presidents, managers, and workers. Most of the members have both high and low power, depending on whether they are interacting with their superiors or subordinates. Authority is power

that is vested in a particular position and viewed as legitimate by the powerholder and by subordinates. Compliance with authoritative requests is a generalized role expectation in organizations. There is no more pervasive law of organization than that the occupants of certain roles shall grant certain kinds of requests from occupants of certain other roles. Authority is usually backed by the power to reward and punish. Thus, it is no surprise that compared to high-power individuals, low-power individuals tend to be more cooperative (e.g., Lindskold & Arnoff, 1980), to make more concessions (e.g., Lawler & Yoon, 1993), to be more compliant in response to threats while negotiating (e.g., Lawler & Yoon, 1993), to yield to superiors when interpersonal conflicts arise (e.g., Kramer, 1996), and to behave less aggressively than those having high power (e.g., Epstein & Taylor, 1967; Ohbuchi & Saito, 1986). All of these behaviors are appropriate within an authority hierarchy and help the social system function effectively.

Authority can be inappropriately used. In 1971, for example, Lt. William Calley was convicted of the premeditated murder of at least twenty-two Vietnamese civilians in March 1968 in what is known as the My Lai massacre. In his defense, Calley declared that he was acting as a good soldier and following orders. One manifestation of authority is a uniform. Even when a stranger is approached on the street and given a directive that has nothing to do with the authority hierarchy ("give that person a dime"), individuals more frequently follow the directive when the person giving the directive is in a uniform (guard or firefighter) (Bickman, 1974; Bushman, 1984).

Low Power Outside of an Authority Hierarchy.   Outside of an authority hierarchy, when the legitimacy of the powerholders is not accepted by low-power group members, low-power individuals tend to resist attempts by powerholders to control them. Tjosvold (1978) notes that low-power members have been found to defy threats, to counterthreaten, to refuse to comply with an influence attempt even when resistance is costly, to dislike high-power members, and to perceive the relationship as competitive. Overall, low-power individuals generally found their relationship with high-power people threatening and debilitating. Low-power individuals were apt to feel frustrated and uncertain about their future goal facilitation because they depended heavily on the unpredictable behavior of the high-power members. These feelings of uncertainty and anxiety provoked (a) increased vigilance and attempts to understand and predict the high-power members' behavior, (b) distorted perceptions of the positive intent of the high-power members toward them, (c) attraction to, mixed with fear of, the high-power members, (d) stifling of criticism of the high-power members, (e) unwillingness to clarify one's position to the high-power members, (f) ingratiation, conformity, flattery, and effacing self-presentations so as to induce the high-power members to like and to reward them, and (g) the expectation of exploitation (low-power members tend to believe that, because they have no retaliatory capability, they are vulnerable and helpless and will be exploited). Low-power members have been found to direct much of their communication and attention to high-power members and to keep on good terms with them.

Low-power individuals often experience psychological reactance, which motivates them to take actions that will help them regain their freedom and control. A variety of strategies for influencing high-power members are available to low-power members (Deutsch, 1969). *First,* low-power members clarify their goals and build cohesiveness for united action. *Second,* low-power members clarify and develop their own resources so that they function independently of the high-power members if necessary. This not only makes low-power members less vulnerable to exploitation, it also provides alternatives that preclude their dependence solely on the high-power members. *Third,* low-power members need to find goals that are important to the high-power members, especially goals the high-power members cannot accomplish without their cooperation. *Fourth,* low-power members can search for attachments with the high-power members that, if made more obvious, could increase the latter's positive feelings toward or outcome dependence on the low-power members. *Fifth*, low-power members can try to change the attitudes of those with high power through education or moral persuasion. *Sixth*, low-power members may try to use existing legal procedures to bring pressures for change. *Finally*, low-power members can use harassment techniques in order to increase the high-power members' costs of maintaining the status quo.

The Metamorphic Effects of Low Power.

Having low power in a situation can change a person. In the Zimbardo (1975) prison experiment, for example, the students randomly assigned to the role of prisoner mostly became withdrawn and depressed and even pressured their fellow prisoners to follow the rules. The rules became increasingly tyrannical and arbitrary, and the guards woke the prisoners in the middle of the night and forced them to stand at attention for hours, locked them in a closet, required them to clear toilets with their bare hands, and censored prisoners' mail. These "prisoners" were young male students at Stanford University who were highly intelligent, healthy psychologically, and from middle to upper-class backgrounds. Yet they still broke down and became passive acceptors of brutal treatment

Relationships Among Low-Power Groups.

Although the relationships between high- and low-power groups have been extensively examined, there has been little research on how low-power groups relate to each other. There are two views. Based on the similarity-attraction hypothesis (Brown, 1984; Byrne, 1971) and on the common-enemy position (Sherif, Harvey, White, Hood, & Sherif, 1961), it is argued that two disadvantaged groups will be attracted to each other. On the other hand, disadvantaged groups may perceive their similar status as a threat to their distinctiveness, which may decrease the integrity of their identity and self-esteem, thus motivating the group to derogate other low-power out-groups to enhance differentiation (Brown, 1984; Turner, 1978).

Rothgerber and Worchel (1997) conducted a set of studies on the relationship between a disadvantaged low-power group and (a) an advantaged high-power group and (b) other disadvantaged low-power groups. They found that disadvantaged groups relate differently to other disadvantaged groups than they do to an advantaged group. They tend to be more sensitive to the actions of a disadvantaged out-group than to the actions of an advantaged out-group. Good fortune for the disadvantaged out-group excites negative behavior toward that group, whereas good fortune for the advantaged group elicits either little response or more positive behavior toward that group. Thus, it seems that low-power groups respond competitively to each other. When the performance of a low-power group increases over time and they may gain more power, other low-power groups may try to restrain their progress and keep them from bettering themselves. This, of course, helps the high-power group keep its power advantage.

Power and Conflict

Power and conflict are interrelated. While power is always present in interpersonal and group interaction, conflict occurs only when a group member wants something to happen and does not have the power to make it happen. No conflict exists when (a) a person wants group members to do something and they want to do it (even when the person does not have the power to influence them to do so) and (b) a person wants group members to do something and has the power to influence them to do it. Conflict does exist when a person wants other group members to do something they do not want to do and the person does not have enough power to overcome their unwillingness. Conflict often ends when the use of power is successful, but conflict is escalated when influence attempts are unsuccessful, that is, when the desire to influence is not matched by the capacity to influence.

Most conflicts concern power directly or indirectly. There are overt conflicts about power, such as those between the haves and the have-nots. Power may also be indirectly involved in conflicts as leverage for achieving one's goals, in maneuvers to maintain the existing balance or imbalance of power in a relationship, or as a symbolic expression of one's identity. The preexisting power relations, the history of relations between parties, the differential access to resources of the parties, or the existing social norms and roles often affect the nature of the issues in the conflict and determine what is perceived to be feasible and fair.

The destructive management of conflict results in fewer and fewer bases of power being effective. Informational power and expertise power are apt to be rejected because each participant sees the other as being untrustworthy and as trying to use expertise for personal gain. Hostility and distrust undermine legitimate power and mutual referent power. Reward power can arouse suspicions of bribery or suggest that one is attempting to increase another's dependence. Only coercive power is left and thus is relied on more and more.

The use of coercive power is destructive for many reasons. It exacerbates the conflict, thereby increasing hostility, resentment, lies, threats, retaliation, revenge, and distrust. Threats often lead to aggression and counterthreats. Coercion and threats can sometimes shorten or control a conflict through behavioral compliance or withdrawal. Coercion decreases the frequency and reliability of communication. The reliance on coercive power results in a separation of high- and low-power groups and a redefinition of behavior by low-power groups. A political uprising is a "crime of violence" from the high-power perspective but a "humanitarian attempt at liberation" from the low-power perspective. The low-power group's revolutionary hero is the high-power group's terrorist. From the high-power perspective, it makes strategic sense to define any act of political rebellion as "aggressive" in order to weaken the opposition. For these and many other reasons, the use of coercive power should be avoided in conflicts.

Revenge.   Interaction between high- and low-power individuals often results in the low-power person's feeling abused and mistreated. Revenge is arguably the driving force behind a large proportion of conflicts. Power asymmetry between parties affects whether revenge will be carried out or suppressed (Heider, 1958; Raven & Kruglanski, 1970; Reider, 1984). In general, people with low power are less likely to take revenge against a more powerful harm-doer (than high-power people are to take revenge against a less powerful harm-doer)—if only because they must fear the consequences of the high-power person's counterrevenge. In the presence of a third party concerned with justice issues, however, upward revenge by low-power participants is greater than downward revenge (high-power participants taking revenge against low-power participants) (Kim, Smith, & Brigham, 1998).

EXERCISE

6.7 *Power Among Summer Students*

The purpose of this exercise is to provide an opportunity for a discussion on how power is used and how leadership is developed in peer groups. It achieves this purpose by examining the interrelationships among ten college students attending summer school and living together in a small dormitory. The procedure is as follows:

1. Form groups of five members. One member volunteers to be an observer. The task of the observer is to record the nature of leadership and power within the group as members complete the task.
2. Each participating group member (four in all) is given the description of two of the college students (ten in all). The group as a whole is given a copy of the Characteristics Chart. The task of the group is to decide by consensus the answers to the following questions. Each member must agree with the answers, be able to explain them, and be confident that every other member can explain the reasoning of the group in arriving at the answers.
   a. Who are the members of each subgroup?
   b. What is the base of power for each subgroup member?
   c. Who is the leader of each subgroup?
   d. What characterizes the interactions among members of different subgroups?

Characteristics of the Summer Students

Characteristics	Virginia	Renee	Pat	Debbie	Janice
Religion	Catholic	Catholic	Nonsectarian	Methodist	Presbyterian
Attendance	Frequent	Occasional	Never	Frequent	Rare
College major	Math	Education	Business mgt	Home ec.	Accounting
Grade average	B	C	A	B	A
Family income	Medium	Medium	Medium	Low	High
Characteristics	**Diane**	**Gail**	**Cindy**	**Cathy**	**Heidi**
Religion	Baptist	Christian	Baptist	Catholic	Baptist
Attendance	Frequent	Occasional	Occasional	Occasional	Frequent
College major	History	Pre-law	Languages	Home ec.	Music
Grade average	B	A	B	C	C
Family income	Medium	High	Medium	Low	Low

3. When the group has come to a consensus about the answers to the questions in step 2, members write a description of power that includes the answers to the following questions. Group members are to agree by consensus to the answers (i.e., their written description of power and influence).
   a. How do the students exert influence on each other?
   b. What bases of power does each student use?
4. When the group has finished step 3, members write a description of leadership that includes answers to the following questions. Each group is to agree by consensus to all the points included in its written description of leadership.

a. What leadership qualities do the students identified as leaders have?
b. How do the leaders of the subgroups exercise their leadership?
5. The groups should share their descriptions of leadership and power with each other in a discussion involving the entire class.

DESCRIPTION OF THE SUMMER STUDENTS

Virginia is a social person who often talks to others. She is quite attractive and dresses well. She dates often. When she has problems, she shares them with Renee or Pat. She sometimes borrows clothes from them. At night she is usually in her room or in Cathy's room. She sometimes sneaks out of the dorm at night and always gets back without being caught. She shares the food and beer that she sneaks into the dorm with Renee, Cathy, and sometimes Janice.

Renee is a fairly attractive, rather insecure person. She smokes and drinks. She dates occasionally, often double-dating with Cathy. She borrows clothes from Virginia and Debbie. At night she is usually in Virginia's or Cathy's room and confides in them. At times she sneaks out of the dorm at night and is helped by Virginia to get back in. She shares food and liquor with Cathy and Virginia.

Pat is a clear-headed person with a perceptive mind. She does not drink and is fairly traditional in her ideas. She is quiet and seldom dates; she never double-dates. She lends clothes to Janice, Virginia, Gail, and Heidi but does not borrow them. She is a good listener and others confide in her, but she does not reciprocate. At night she can be found in her own room, but she is often accompanied by one of the other students.

Debbie is a rather wild person who dates frequently, occasionally double-dating with Janice. She seems mostly interested in boys—her main topic of conversation. She shares clothes with Virginia and Janice, and at night can usually be found in one of their rooms. At times she sneaks out of the dorm at night and is helped to get back in by Virginia. She shares food with Janice, Virginia, and occasionally Cathy. She confides in Janice.

Janice is an outgoing person who is quite attractive and dresses well. She dates often and sometimes double-dates with Debbie. When she has problems, she goes to see Pat. She borrows clothes from Pat or Debbie. At night she is usually in her own room. She is a good talker and is successful in debating most of the other students. She is well versed in clothes, dating, and men and has a lot of spending money. She shares food from home with Debbie, Virginia, and Gail.

Diane is a neat, well-groomed, modest person with strong moral convictions. She seldom dates and does not smoke or drink. She is very active in church work and attends church several times a week. When she has a personal problem, she goes to see Pat or her minister. She lends clothes to Cindy. At night she is usually in her own room. She likes to read and has been known to remind the students about quiet hours, which has caused some resentment from Janice and Renee.

Gail is a wealthy, well-traveled, sophisticated person who seems to relate well to everyone on a casual level. She dates occasionally but never double-dates. She sometimes borrows clothes from Pat, with whom she shares her problems. She is mature and understanding of others but does not seem to form very close friendships. At night she can be found in the rooms of Pat or Diane. She shares food with Diane, Pat, and sometimes Janice.

Cindy is a very shy person who seldom dates. She doesn't smoke or drink. She occasionally goes to a movie with Diane and sometimes with Heidi. At night she can be found in Diane's or Janice's room. She shares food with Diane or Janice. She avoids Renee and Virginia.

Cathy is a rather loud, slightly overweight person. She often swears and is heard telling dirty jokes. She occasionally double-dates with Renee. She likes to smoke and drink. She shares her problems with Virginia and Renee. At night she is in her room or Virginia's room. She shares food with Virginia, Renee, and sometimes Debbie.

Heidi is an overweight person who tries to be friendly with everyone. She goes out of her way to run errands and otherwise tries to please the other students. She does not smoke, drink, or date. She attends movies with Cindy or Diane. She does not dress well, and Pat is the only one who will lend her clothes. At night she is either in her own room or in Pat's or Diane's room. She shares her problems with Pat or Diane. She shares food with Diane, Cindy, Gail, and Pat.

6.8 *Developing Land Areas*

The purpose of this exercise is to examine the consequences of unequal power among nations or individuals. Group members are representatives of large land areas and strive to advance the standard of living of their residents. The materials needed are copies of the game board for each member (or one large one for each group, with six individual markers); one hundred tokens for each group (coins, small strips of paper, etc.); resource cards—five for each member, thirty for each group; six cards for each group, with the land areas written on them; and copies of the rules for each group. Groups need six members each. The procedure for the coordinator is as follows:

1. Introduce the exercise as a game focusing on the consequences of unequal power among nations or individuals. Each person will represent a land area and will attempt to improve the standard of living of his or her area.
2. Form groups of six. On 3- x 5-inch cards, write the names of the following land areas: Asia, Africa and the Middle East, South America, the former Soviet Union, Europe, and North America. Turn the cards face down and mix them. Each member chooses a card to find out which land area he or she will represent.
3. Tokens are distributed to the group members in the following way:
   a. Asia is given 1.
   b. Africa and the Middle East are given 2.
   c. South America is given 2.
   d. Russia and the members of the former Soviet Union are given 8.
   e. Europe is given 13.
   f. North America is given 26.
   Tell the group members that these numbers represent the approximate gross national product of their areas divided by the population. Forty-eight additional tokens are put in the middle as a common bank from which members can draw according to game instructions.
4. Five resource cards marked with the land area are given to each member. These represent the natural resources of the area, and each can either represent one token or can be used as collateral on loans from other land areas. In order to advance to level 7, however, members must possess all their resource cards.
5. Distribute a game board to each member. Members keep track of their progress by covering each square with a token. They must advance sequentially. (Alternative: Make one large game board per group and have members mark their places with representative markers.) Members begin on the square that represents the number of tokens they were initially given.
6. Go over the rules with the class. Give them a few minutes to study their positions; then have them begin.

Game Board for Developing the Land Areas Exercise

Level VII Nirvana	**Self-Sufficiency:** *You can sit back and watch everyone else play or . . .*						
Level VI Secure	31 Secure food	32 Secure homes	33 Secure work	34 Secure health	35 Secure education	36 Secure energy	Buy back resource cards
Level V Specialized	25 Extra food	26 Luxury homes	27 Comfortable work	28 Specialized medicine	29 Specialized education	30 Solar energy	Receive five tokens
Level IV Mass Production	19 Abundant food	20 Large houses	21 Factories	22 Hospitals	23 Higher education	24 Oil energy	Receive four tokens
Level III Mechanized	13 Sufficient food	14 Small houses	15 Mechanized farms	16 Health clinics	17 Basic education	18 Dam energy	Receive three tokens
Level II Basic	7 Subsistence food	8 Basic shelter	9 Rudimentary farming	10 Folk medicine	11 Early education	12 Forest energy	Receive two tokens
Level I Predevelopment	1 Malnutrition	2 Lack of shelter	3 Inefficient farming	4 Disease	5 Folklore	6 Wood gathering	Receive one token

7. After the game, discuss the following questions with the large group:
   a. How did it feel to begin the game with the number of tokens you did?
   b. How did the number of your tokens make a difference in the strategies you used?
   c. How difficult was it to develop an alliance or get a loan? Why?
   d. How many people called "Attack?" How successful was it as a strategy?
   e. What did you learn about the dynamics of unequal power from playing this game?

RULES FOR DEVELOPING A LAND AREA EXERCISE

1. The purpose of this game is to advance your land area as many spaces as you can. You do this by gaining tokens; one token will advance you one space. You must keep all previous spaces filled, although you may go backward (by loaning tokens, for example) as well as forward. If you give as collateral a resource card you have used as a token, you must fill that empty space first.
2. You start out with the number of tokens that represent your land area's approximate wealth (according to the 1980 gross national product divided by population size). That number determines where you will start the game (put all your tokens on your game board to begin). In addition, you will get five resource cards, which represent your area's natural resources. These can be used to add to your position by representing one token or they can be used as collateral for loans from other countries. You can use a resource card you hold from another land area as collateral as one token.
3. There will be ten rounds. Appoint a timekeeper. Starting with Asia and rotating clockwise, you will get three minutes to find a way to increase your tokens. Once you have added tokens, your turn is over. If you are unsuccessful at the end of three minutes, you lose your turn and the round continues. The game ends after ten rounds or if a stalemate develops.

4. You can gain tokens in four ways:
   a. **Progress:** When you fill a line with tokens, you get additional ones from the World Bank according to the number noted at the end of the line. If, in lending or losing tokens, you fall below a line previously passed, you do not have to repay that token. You may collect (or recollect) tokens when you fill that line again. However, if you use resource cards as tokens, you may take them off a space only if you negotiate a loan and must thereby give the card to the lender.
   b. **Form an alliance:** If you and another land area negotiate an alliance, you both get two tokens from the World Bank. You may negotiate an alliance only once with a particular land area.
   c. **Call an attack:** If you call "Attack," each land area that does not hold any of your resource cards or is not in alliance with you must pay you one token. You may call an attack only twice during the game.
   d. **Negotiate a loan:** Any land area can lend tokens to another land area in exchange for a resource card, which serves as collateral and can later be repurchased. The amount of the loan and the repurchase are negotiable.

GROUP NORMS: INDIRECT POWER

"What's it to be? Pizza or hamburgers?" Six friends who had just exited a movie theater were trying to decide what to eat. "Pizza!" immediately said five. "Hamburgers!" Keith answered. In rapid fire, everyone talked to Keith. "We always get pizza." "Pizza is our group's official food." "You can have hamburger on your pizza." "We never eat hamburgers; hamburgers are for kids!" "Don't be a killjoy!" "Okay," said Keith. "Let's get pizza." This scenario occurs many times a day. The majority of a group decides on a particular course of action that another member prefers not to do. The majority reminds the dissenter of group norms designed to pressure and persuade the member to adopt the group perspective. The incident concludes when the member capitulates and conforms to the group's norms.

Group norms often serve as substitutes for the direct use of power among group members (Kelley & Thibaut, 1978). Group members (whether they have high or low power) tend to gain from having mutually acceptable norms that introduce regularity and control into their relationship without making direct interpersonal application of power necessary. The direct use of power requires the expenditure of considerable energy and resources and has numerous costs. Group norms are often implemented to substitute for direct influence procedures. Indirect influence through group norms avoids the resistance and lack of wholehearted cooperation that may result from the direct application of power. Group norms control the behavior of high-power as well as low-power members and set limits on the use of power. Group members give up part of their personal power to the norms to protect themselves from the capricious or inconsistent use of power and the need to constantly check on each other's behavior to make sure everyone is behaving appropriately. Individuals let themselves be influenced by norms in ways that they would never permit themselves to be influenced by others, for norms often take on the characteristics of moral obligations (they have a specific "ought to" and "must" quality). At the very least, conformity to group norms is a requirement for continued membership in the group.

Conforming to Group Norms

*As for conforming outwardly, and living your own life
inwardly, I do not think much of that.*

Henry David Thoreau

A man stands up and faces the group. "My name is Dale," he says. "I am an alcoholic. I have not had a drink for three years, two months, and six days." The group applauds. This is a meeting of Alcoholics Anonymous. One group norm is to take the "first step" and admit that you are an alcoholic. Another group norm is to stay sober one day at a time. Dale has just publicly testified that he is conforming to these normative expectations. The group is giving him support and recognition for doing so. This scenario occurs countless times daily in families, businesses, schools, churches, and all other groups. A group cannot exist, cannot survive, cannot function, and cannot be productive unless most members conform to its norms most of the time.

In our society, conformity has acquired a generally negative connotation. Many people think of conformity as a blind, unreasoning, spineless, weak, slavish adherence to the demands of the majority of peers or authority figures. Even among social psychologists there is a common conception of conformity as agreement with the majority or for the sake of agreement. Conformity to group norms is frequently viewed as a violation of one's principles in order to obtain group acceptance or a selling out of one's individuality in order to get ahead. Much of the research on conformity is based on behaviors such as lying about one's perceptions or beliefs. These pejorative connotations of conformity, however, are inaccurate and are based on a misunderstanding of the complexity of the process of conforming to group norms. Under some conditions, conformity to group norms may violate important values and principles of an individual, and under other conditions, conforming will support these values and beliefs.

Conformity is defined as changes in behavior that result from group influences. The changes include **compliance** (behavioral change without internal acceptance) and **private acceptance** (changes in both behavior and attitudes). Conforming to group norms frequently improves the functioning of a group at no expense to the individual's principles or beliefs. Conforming to a classroom norm that one should provide assistance to classmates, for example, benefits both the group and the students involved.

The classic studies on conformity under group pressure were conducted by Solomon Asch (1956). Asch was born in 1907 in Poland and arrived in the United States at age thirteen. In 1928 he received a B.S. degree from City College of New York. In 1932 he received a Ph.D. degree from Columbia University. He was an unusually independent person, and of him it has often been said that it took the least conforming social psychologists to defend conformity and to point out that an essential feature of social life is the willingness to trust the observations of others. In his experimental studies on conformity, he asked participants to choose which of several lines came closest in length to a line they had just seen (Figure 6.3). There was an obviously right answer. Yet each participant found himself or herself faced with most or all fellow group members (group size ranged from three to fifteen) agreeing on an obviously wrong answer. The participant was thus faced with a conflict: accepting the evidence of his or her own eyes or going along with the group's perception. Sixty-eight percent of the individual estimates remained independent; 32% were deflected part or all of the way to the unanimous judgment of the fellow group members. One fourth of the participants made no concessions to the unanimous majority;

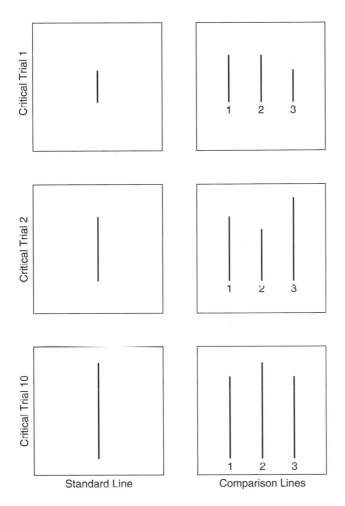

Figure 6.3 The Asch experiments. On twelve of the eighteen trials, the majority of the group members purposely picked the incorrect comparison line. On Critical Trial 1, the standard line was 3 inches long, and Comparison Line 3 was the correct answer. However, the group chose Line 1, which was actually 3¾ inches long. On Critical Trial 2 the correct answer was 1, but the group unanimously answered with 2. Finally, the stimuli used in Critical Trial 10 are also shown; the correct answer in this case was 2, but the group suggested 1.
Source: S. Asch, An experimental investigation of group influence, in *Symposium on preventive and social psychology,* Walter Reed Army Institute of Research (Washington, D.C.: U.S. Government Printing Office, 1957).

one third conformed in half or more of the trials. Whether the majority consisted of three or fifteen members made little difference, as long as it was unanimous. If one other member agreed with the participant, the tendency to err in the direction of the majority estimate dropped from 32% to 10%. If the participant reported his or her estimates secretly, furthermore, the promajority errors were fewer. The results of the Asch experiments were somewhat shocking, as they seemed to indicate that many persons would go along with an erroneous group judgment even when they knew it was false. Most social psychologists reacted to the results of Asch's studies as if they agreed with Thoreau.

In discussing conformity to group norms we must differentiate two dimensions: conformity versus anticonformity and independence versus dependence (Allen, 1965; Hollander & Willis, 1967). The conformers and anticonformers both react to the group norm and base their behavior on it. The conformers agree with the norm, the anticonformers disagree with the norm, and both behave accordingly. An independent person, on the other hand, does not give undue importance to the group norm in making his or her judgment.

Not all behaviors are covered by group norms. Not many groups care what foods their members eat or whether they prefer one type of drink to another. Group norms deal primarily with behavior affecting the accomplishment of the group's task and the ability of the group to maintain itself over time. In general, the more relevant the individual's behavior to the accomplishment of the group's task and the maintenance of the group, the greater the pressures toward conformity. Many years ago, observers in industrial organizations noted that members of male work groups typically established production standards (norms) that were adhered to by most members (Homans, 1950; Roethlisberger & Dickson, 1939). When a worker deviated too much from the standard, he was subjected to ridicule and other sanctions. If the worker produced too much, he was referred to as a "speed king" or a "rate buster"; if he produced too little, the worker was a "chiseler." In their studies of deviation from group norms, Schachter (1951), Emerson (1954), and Schachter and his associates (1954) all found that the more relevant the deviation to the purposes of the group, the greater the rejection of the deviant by the other group members. Festinger (1950) and Allen (1965) concluded that there is greater pressure to conform to task-related norms if goal attainment depends on the coordinated behavior of the group members. Raven and Rietsema (1957) found that the clearer the group goal and the path to the goal are to the group members, the stronger the pressure toward uniformity in task behavior. In general, nonconforming behaviors are accepted if the group members perceive them as potentially improving the group's ability to accomplish its task and maintain itself; they are not accepted if they interfere with group maintenance and task accomplishment.

Implementing Group Norms

There are several ways in which norms can be initiated (Johnson, 1970). One frequent method is for a member to state the norm directly and tell other members to accept it. A member might say, for example, "I think we should express our feelings openly about this topic" and tell other members to do so. Norms can be initiated through modeling, wherein members learn to conform to a group norm by watching others conform. Norms can also be imported from other groups. People usually learn cultural norms of *social responsibility* (you should help someone who is in need of help), *fair play* (don't kick someone when he's down), and *reciprocity* (if someone does you a favor, you should do him or her a favor in return) from others, and these norms can be incorporated into one's own group. All in all, however, perhaps the most effective way of starting group norms is through group discussion.

Johnson (1970) has presented a set of general guidelines for the establishment and support of group norms. Group members will accept and internalize **group norms** when they:

1. Recognize that the norms exist, see the other members accepting and following the norms, and feel some commitment to the norms.
2. See the norms as helping accomplish the goals to which members are committed. It is helpful, therefore, for a group to clarify how conformity to a norm will help goal accomplishment.
3. Feel that they own the norms. They usually establish ownership through their involvement in establishing the norms.
4. Enforce the norms on each other immediately after a violation. Consistent enforcement enhances both understanding of the norms and commitment to them.
5. See appropriate models and examples of conforming to the norms and have a chance to practice the desired behaviors.

6. Import cultural norms that promote goal accomplishment and group maintenance and growth into the group.
7. Perceive that the norms are flexible, so that at any time more appropriate norms can be substituted to increase group effectiveness.

THE GROUP MIND

In 1212 bands of children and young people in Germany and France responded to the Catholic Church's call to reconquer Jerusalem. They began the Children's Crusade, convinced that only the pure in spirit could succeed in taking the Holy Land from the Muslims. In Germany, a boy named Nicholas led the children from town to town, gathering increasing numbers. They walked across the Alps into Italy and then to the sea. The children expected the sea to divide so that they could walk to the Holy Land. It did not. Confused, some returned home and others were sold into slavery. No one knows if any of them reached the Holy Land. Why did thousands of children join the Crusade? Why did their parents let them?

There are unexplained ways in which groups have powerful influences on members. Group members sometimes engage in **collective behavior,** spontaneously performing atypical actions such as in riots, panics, and mass hysteria (the spontaneous outbreak of atypical thoughts, feelings, or actions in a group, including psychogenic illness, common hallucinations, and bizarre actions [Pennebaker, 1982; Phoon, 1982]). In 1903, for example, there was a panic at Chicago's Iroquois Theater. A small fire broke out backstage, and the management tried to calm the audience. When the fire became visible to the crowd, however, the audience stampeded for the exits. Some died by jumping from the fire escapes to the pavement. Many more were killed as fleeing patrons trampled them. Some were burned. Nearly 600 people were killed. From the Crusades to the French Revolution to rock-and-roll concerts, membership in groups and mass hysteria have been associated with each other.

A number of explanations have been proposed to examine such **group influences.** The *first* was the group mind proposed by Le Bon. In 1895 Gustave Le Bon published his classic study *The Crowd* to explain why persons in a mob lose their sense of responsibility. Le Bon argued that people in crowds show "impulsiveness, irritability, incapacity to reason," and "exaggeration of sentiments" (p. 40). Regardless of the qualities of the individuals in the group, once they fall under the "law of the mental unity of crowds," they *all* act in ways that are impulsive, unreasonable, and extreme.

Le Bon believed that three mechanisms contributed to the formation of crowd behavior. The first is anonymity as people feel less responsible for their behavior when they cannot be identified. Crowds create relative anonymity and thus reduce individual responsibility. People then commit acts for which they believe they cannot later be held responsible. The second is contagion as emotional states spread from person to person just as diseases spread. Le Bon was a physician, and so he viewed the collective mind as a kind of disease that began at one point in the crowd and then spread throughout the rest of the crowd. Similarly to the spread of germs from person to person, emotions and behaviors are transmitted from one person to another, resulting in the tendency of group members to behave in very similar ways. The third is suggestibility as crowd members completely accept all suggestions made to them, just as if they were hypnotized.

A *second* possible explanation is convergence theory. According to **convergence theory,** individuals join the group because they possess similar needs and personal characteristics. Crowd action represents the convergence of people with compatible needs, desires, motivations, and emotions. By joining the group, the individual makes possible the satisfaction of these needs, and the crowd situation serves as a trigger for the spontaneous release of previously controlled behaviors. A specific event brings together people who share similar convictions and predispositions. Members bring a common mood to the crowd (as in a protest demonstration). The crowd eventually acts out this mood. Crowd behavior can be predicted, therefore, by identifying the latent tendencies and beliefs of large numbers of people. Although the predisposing features may be latent or virtually unrecognizable, they are the true causes of the formation of both large and small collectives. Convergence theory seeks to identify the latent tendencies in people that cause them to act alike, the circumstances that bring people with such tendencies together, and the kinds of events that cause these tendencies to be released (Freud, 1922; Turner & Killian, 1972/1987, p. 19). Sigmund Freud (1922) believed that people join collectives to satisfy repressed unconscious desires that otherwise would never be fulfilled. In the group situation, control over behavior is transferred to the leader or to other group members, and each person is thus freed from the bonds of restraint and guilt. As a result, formerly repressed needs come to motivate behavior, and atypical actions become more likely.

A *third* explanation is emergent-norm theory. Ralph Turner and Lewis Killian (1972/1987) argue that crowds are quite heterogeneous and do not have "mental unity." Rather, the members all adhere to norms that are relevant to the given situation. Turner and Killian hypothesized that all crowds share a number of elements. Crowds form in ambiguous situations in which the participants' behaviors are unplanned. A sense of urgency characterizes the feelings of their members. As the crowd gets larger, norms are communicated throughout the crowd about appropriate moods, imagery, and actions. The dominant mood, imagery, and actions come to be viewed as right, as those to which the crowd members should conform. A group norm thus emerges. Uniformity ultimately results from the interaction among the initially dissimilar members. Individuals become highly susceptible to suggestions consistent with the emergent norm. As a result, the participants may engage in actions they would ordinarily inhibit.

The *fourth* theory is deindividuation theory. **Deindividuation** is a state of relative anonymity in which group members do not feel singled out or identifiable (Festinger, Pepitone, & Newcomb, 1952). When people cannot be identified, they are more likely to perform antisocial acts. Festinger, Pepitone, and Newcomb argued that people in groups feel themselves to be "submerged in the group" and lose their personal identity, that is, they experience deindividuation. This feeling creates a "reduction of inner restraints" and, in the extreme, atypical actions.

Philip Zimbardo's (1970) **deindividuation theory** attempts to explain the reduction of inner constraints by dividing deindividuation into three interrelated components (inputs, internal changes, outputs):

1. Conditions of deindividuation **(inputs)** include (a) anonymity, (b) reduced responsibility, (c) membership in a large group, and (d) arousal.
2. The state of deindividuation **(internal changes):** a subjective experience in which the individual group members experience "a lowered threshold of normally restrained behavior" based on (a) low self-awareness and (b) altered experiencing.

3. Deindividuated behaviors (**outputs**): extreme, atypical, or polarized actions. Deindividuation can result in a range of positive outcomes, but for the most part it is antisocial behaviors such as violence, destruction, and hostility that are most often discussed.

The conditions of deindividuation *begin* with anonymity, which exists when others cannot identify or single out a person for evaluation, criticism, judgment, or punishment. *Second*, personal responsibility is reduced by the demands for compliance by an authority figure, the separation of the consequences from the act itself, and a diffusion of responsibility among group members. *Third*, the larger the group, the greater the deindividuation. *Finally*, arousal is increased through altered temporal perspective, sensory overload, heightened involvement, and lack of a situational structure.

Individuals, when deindividuated, experience profound changes in emotions, memory, and self-regulation. Deindividuation is experienced by (a) *loss of self-awareness* (minimal self-consciousness, lack of conscious planning, uninhibited speech, and performing

Review of Important Concepts

Match the following concepts with their definitions. Find a partner and compare answers.

_____ 1. Power

_____ 2. High power

_____ 3. Low power

_____ 4. Power majority

_____ 5. Power minority

_____ 6. Norms

_____ 7. Conformity

_____ 8. Compliance

_____ 9. Collective behavior

_____ 10. Deindividuation

a. Prescribed modes of conduct and belief that guide the behavior of group members.

b. Changes in behavior that result from group influences.

c. Behavioral change without internal acceptance.

d. Capacity to affect another person's goal accomplishment.

e. State of relative anonymity, in which group members do not feel singled out or identifiable.

f. Individuals spontaneously perform atypical actions, such as in riots, panics, and mass hysteria.

g. Capacity to have considerable influence on another person's goal accomplishment.

h. Capacity to have little influence on another person's goal accomplishment.

i. Group that has the most control over how important resources are distributed (they may be the numerical minority).

j. Group that has little control over the distribution of important resources (they may be a numerical majority).

uninhibited tasks) and (b) *altered experiencing* (disturbances in concentration and judgment, the feeling that time is moving slowly or rapidly, extreme emotions, a sense of unreality, perceptual distortions, and intense pleasure). People who are deindividuated have lost self-awareness and their personal identity in the group.

Finally, deindividuated behaviors replace reason and order with impulse and chaos. Zimbardo (1975, p. 53) states that the conditions that reduce a person's sense of uniqueness and individuality are the wellsprings of antisocial behaviors, such as aggression, vandalism, stealing, cheating, and rudeness, as well as a general loss of concern for others. The deindividuated person is quite reactive to emotions and situational cues that may lead to uninhibited behaviors and is less concerned with norms, personal punishment, or long-term consequences.

Power can be exercised by the group as a whole. Groups do influence members in profound and powerful ways. Power can be exercised by the group as a whole through such processes as the group mind, converging with people who share similar convictions and predispositions, following norms that emerge in the group, or deindividualization of members. Being influenced by the group is not all bad. While theory and research on group power may be cast in negative ways (e.g., mass hysteria and panic), groups can also encourage members to behave altruistically.

EXERCISE

6.9 *Your Power Behavior*

Now that you have completed this chapter, it may be helpful to focus again on your behavior in exercising power. Form a group of three with two persons who know you well and who have participated with you in some of the exercises in this book. Then complete the following tasks, taking at least two hours to do so.

1. Reflect silently on how each member uses power. Give each other feedback about the animal, song, or book that each member reminds the others of on the basis of how he or she deals with power. Each person explains why he or she chose the animal, song, or book identified.
2. Write down your individual strengths in using power constructively and effectively. Share your lists. Members should add to each other's lists.
3. Write down the individual skills you need to develop in order to use power more constructively and effectively. Share your lists. Members should add to each other's lists.
4. Discuss the feelings each member has in using power and why he or she reacts that way. Help each other think of alternative ways of reacting to the use of power.
5. From magazine pictures and any other materials, build a collage about the way you exercise power. Share the collage with the other members. Add ideas to each other's collages.

SUMMARY

Power is the capacity to affect the outcomes of oneself, others, and the environment. Power is constructive when it enhances group effectiveness and destructive when it interferes with group effectiveness. While the dominant view of power focuses on its potential destructiveness, there are many potential positive outcomes from exerting power. In fact, the positive use of power is essential for group effectiveness.

The dynamic-interdependence approach to influence posits that who is influencing whom to what degree changes constantly as members strive to achieve the group's goals. Power is thus an attribute of an interpersonal relationship in which people are dependent on each other for outcomes and information. In any relationship, the use of power is inevitable, essential, constantly changing, and pervades all aspects of the relationship. To be constructive, power must be used in a cooperative, not a competitive, context. In a competitive context, power tends to be viewed as a limited zero-sum resource that should be accumulated and hoarded, since it is unidirectional and inherently coercive. The coercive use of power creates resistance, reactance, and resentment toward and dislike of the powerholder. In a cooperative context, power is viewed as expandable, sharable, bidirectional, and inherently noncoercive. The key to power in a cooperative context is inducibility, the openness to being influenced by other group members.

The trait-factor approach to influence views power as an attribute of a person. The assumption is that certain individuals are born with a capacity to influence others. Two of the trait-factor approaches to power are the work on power and persuasion and the work on social dominance. The power and persuasion position states that a person exerts power by (a) being credible and attractive, (b) phrasing messages so that they are two-sided, action-oriented, and discrepant with members' current beliefs, and (c) playing on others' low self-esteem and low intelligence, giving them no forewarning of the influence attempt, distracting them during the influence attempt, convincing them that the attitudes being modified are peripheral to them, and having them role play positions counter to their beliefs. Social dominance depends on the ability to control resources. It is assumed that resources are limited and, therefore, resource acquisition compels group members to compete. The member's ability to compete successfully for limited resources defines his or her position in the social hierarchy.

Power may be based on the ability to deliver rewards, the ability to deliver punishments, a legitimate position of authority, being a referent for others, being an expert, and having needed information. When the distribution of power is unequal, both the high- and the low-power person have problems. While the use of power is ever-present in a relationship, it is during conflicts that individuals become most conscious of its use.

Besides the direct use of power, there are indirect ways to exert influence. The primary way is through group norms. When group members conform to normative expectations, they are being influenced. Most power is exerted through indirect means such as group norms. The mass hysteria and panic that are sometimes observed in groups may have their origins in the group mind, converging with people who share similar convictions and predispositions, following norms that emerge in the group, or becoming deindividualized.

You should now have a clear understanding of power and how it can help or hinder a group. You have experienced high- and low-power situations. In the next chapter you will learn how to make effective group decisions.

9 Exercises in Ch 6

Decision Making

7

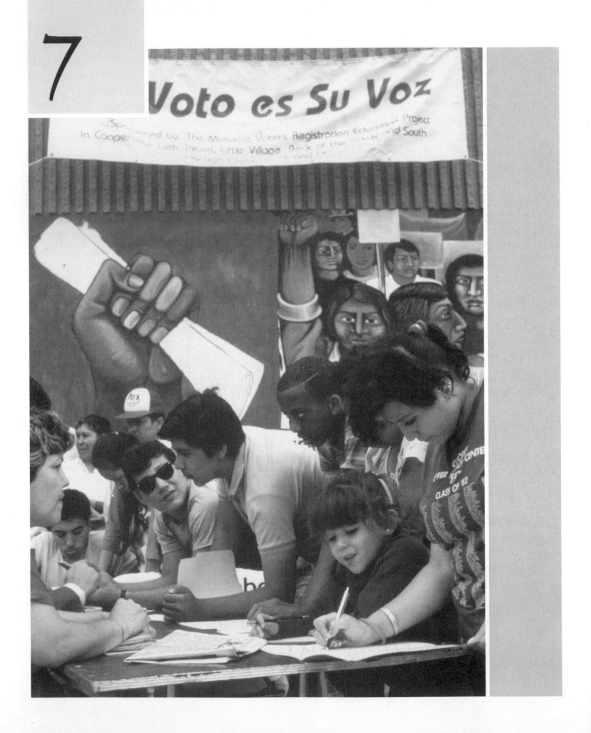

Basic Concepts to Be Covered in This Chapter

In this chapter a number of concepts are defined and discussed. The major ones are listed following. Divide into pairs. Each pair is to (a) define each concept, noting the page on which it is defined and discussed, and (b) ensure that both members of the pair understand the meaning of each concept. Then combine into groups of four. Compare the answers of the two pairs. If there is disagreement, look up the concept in the chapter and clarify it until all members agree on and understand the definition.

Concepts

1. Averaging opinions
2. Concurrence-seeking
3. Consensus
4. Critical evaluation
5. Decision
6. Defensive avoidance
7. Dissonance reduction
8. Effective decision
9. Group polarization
10. Groupthink
11. Majority vote
12. Minority control
13. Vigilance

MAKING EFFECTIVE DECISIONS

Imagine yourself driving down the street. A police officer stops you for a minor traffic violation and then notices that your appearance matches the description of a person who has just robbed a nearby bank. He arrests you and, to your horror, no fewer than six eyewitnesses identify you as the bank robber. You cannot provide a good alibi for the time of the robbery (you were driving around by yourself), and no one pays any attention to your protestations of innocence. The ordeal drags on until the day you go on trial and face your accusers. As the trial begins, you realize that the only barrier between you and a prison sentence is a small group of your peers. The jury members are strangers to one another, chosen randomly from your community, unschooled in legal principles, and unpracticed in group decision making. They hold your fate, your future, your well-being in their hands.

Trial by a jury of peers to determine guilt and innocence has formed the foundation of judicial systems for hundreds of years. As far back as the eleventh century, juries were used both to provide information about the actions of the accused and to weigh the evidence. Gradually, juries evolved into finders of fact who weigh the testimony of each person before deciding if a law has in fact been broken.

A jury is only one of the small groups in our society that have to make vital decisions. Governments, large corporations, military units, and virtually all other social entities entrust their key decisions to groups. As a result, most of the laws, policies, and practices that affect our daily lives (as well as the future course of society) are determined by teams, committees, boards of directors, and similar groups, *not* by single individuals. Many groups exist to make decisions in our society. Thousands of small groups are making most of the vital decisions every day. How good the decisions are depends on how effective the groups are. Groups are continually making decisions, some

---

Individual versus Group Decision Making

Process Gain	Involvement and Commitment
Correct Each Other's Errors	Changed Behavior and Attitudes
Social Facilitation	Type of Task
Risk Taking	Potential Group Productivity

Methods of Decision Making

Decision by Authority Without Group Discussion	Decision by Minority
	Decision by Majority Vote
Decision by Expert	Decision by Consensus
Decision by Averaging Individuals' Opinions	Time and Decision Making
Decision by Authority After Group Discussion	

Essential Components / Hindering Factors

Essential Components	Hindering Factors	
Positive Interdependence	Lack of Group Maturity	
Face-to-Face Promotive Interaction	Dominant Response	
Individual Accountability	Social Loafing	
Social Skills	Free Riding	
Group Processing	Not Being a Sucker	
	Groupthink	Conflicting goals
	Egocentrism of	Homogeneity
	group members	Inappropriate size
	Production blocking	Lack of skills
	Dissonance reduction	
	Lack of Incentives for and Barriers to Contributing	

Considered and Thoughtful Decision Making

Identifying and Defining Problem	Deciding on a Solution
Gathering Information About Problem	Second-chance meeting
Forming Alternative Solutions	Presenting Recommendation to Organization
Force field analysis	Evaluating Success of Implementation
Vigilant analysis	
Barriers	

Problems with Theorizing on Decision Making

Figure 7.1 Overview of the chapter.

as important as whether a peer accused of a crime will live or die, others as ordinary as when and where the group will meet, what course of action it will take toward accomplishing goals, and what procedures it will use in discussions.

The purpose of group decision making is to decide upon well-considered, well-understood, realistic action toward goals every member wishes to achieve. A *group decision* implies that some agreement prevails among group members as to which of several courses of action is most desirable for achieving the group's goals. Making a **decision** is just one step in the more general *problem-solving process* of goal-directed groups—but it is a crucial one. After defining a problem or issue, thinking over alternative courses of action, and weighing the advantages and disadvantages of each, a group will decide which course is the most desirable for them to implement.

Typically, groups try to make their decisions as effectively as possible. There are five major characteristics of an *effective group decision:*

1. The resources of group members are fully utilized.
2. Time is well used.
3. The decision is correct or of high quality.
4. The decision is implemented fully by all the required group members.
5. The problem-solving ability of the group is enhanced or at least not lessened.

A decision is effective to the extent that these five criteria are met; if all five are not met, the decision has not been made effectively.

Not everyone agrees that group decision making is a good idea. For decades social scientists have disagreed over whether individuals or groups make better decisions. The first issue examined in this chapter, therefore, is the comparative effectiveness of individual and group decision making. Second, different methods a group can use to arrive at a decision are explained. Third, the factors that facilitate and hinder an effective group decision are detailed. Finally, a process groups may use to ensure effective decision making is discussed. Figure 7.1 contains an overview to delineate further how these issues are broken down in the chapter.

EXERCISE

7.1 *Individual versus Group Decision Making*

There has been some controversy over whether individual or group decision making is more effective. The purpose of this exercise is to structure a critical discussion of the issue.

1. **Assignment to groups.** Assign participants to groups of four. Each group is to write a short statement summarizing and explaining its position on whether individual or group decision making is more effective.
2. **Assignment to pairs and positions.** Divide each group into two pairs. Pair One is assigned the position that individuals are superior to groups in making decisions and is given Briefing Sheet One. Pair Two is assigned the position that groups are superior to individuals in making decisions and is given Briefing Sheet Two. The procedure and guidelines for constructive controversy may be reviewed (p. 34).
3. **Preparation of positions.** The pairs meet separately. They have ten minutes to prepare a forceful and persuasive three-minute presentation of their position. Anything in this chapter or in the field of decision making may be included in the presentation. Both members of the pair have to be ready to give the presentation.
4. **Presentations of positions.** New pairs are formed consisting of one person from Pair One and one person from Pair Two. Each person presents his or her assigned position. The listener takes notes and asks for clarification of anything that is not fully understood. Each person can present for only three minutes.
5. **Attack and defend discussion.** A ten-minute discussion of the issue is conducted. Each person critically analyzes the opposing position and points out its shortcomings. Each person defends his or her position from the attacks of the opponent. The discussion should focus on theory, research, and facts, not on opinions and impressions.
6. **Reverse perspectives.** Each person has two minutes to summarize the opponent's position and best reasoning. The summary should be complete and accurate.
7. **Joint report.** The pair writes one statement summarizing and explaining its conclusions on whether individual or group decision making is more effective. The best reasoning

from both sides should be synthesized or integrated into a position they both believe is valid. The statement should include theory, research, and facts.

8. **Conclusions and processing.** The pairs join together into a group of four and compare the two statements, writing down three conclusions about what they have learned concerning the relative advantages of individual and group decision making. Finally, each person tells each other group member one thing the person liked about working with him or her.

BRIEFING SHEET ONE: INDIVIDUALS MAKE SUPERIOR DECISIONS

Your position is that individuals make higher-quality decisions than groups. To support your position, use the two quotations below, any material from this chapter that is applicable, and what you know from your outside reading.

> If anything, group membership blunts ethical perception and fetters moral imagination, because we then uncritically and possibly let others think for us. (LaBarre, 1972, p.14)

> When a hundred clever heads join a group, one big nincompoop is the result, because every individual is trammeled by the otherness of others. (Jung, quoted in Illing, 1957, p. 80)

BRIEFING SHEET TWO: GROUPS MAKE SUPERIOR DECISIONS

Your position is that groups make higher-quality decisions than individuals. To support your position, use the following quotation, any material from this chapter that is applicable, and what you know from your outside reading.

> Group operations have two kinds of potential advantage over action by a single individual. One is the caliber of thinking, the range of resources, and the critical scrutiny which enter the problem solving. The other is the willingness with which people carry out decisions they have helped to make. . . . Groups may sometimes be more sane, moderate, well-balanced and wise than their average member. . . . A thoughtful group may make its members more rational, more self-critical, and more ready to revise personal prejudices in the light of objective evidence, than these members would be if they were studying alone. (Watson & Johnson, 1972, pp. 130–131)

INDIVIDUAL VERSUS GROUP DECISION MAKING

Which is more productive, groups or individuals? One of the earliest studies to compare individual and group decision making was conducted by Goodwin Watson (1931). Watson received his bachelor of arts degree from the University of Wisconsin and his masters and doctorate from Columbia University. He taught at Columbia University from 1925 to 1962. In 1970 he founded and became director of the Graduate School of the Union for Experimenting Colleges and Universities. A vigorous, dedicated psychologist, Watson fought against all types of discrimination and challenged the value of standardized intelligence tests. In his 1931 study he used three equivalent forms of an intelligence test, each consisting of nine tasks suited to bright adults. Sixty-eight graduate students participated in the study. Each student took the first test alone; students then joined with one another in groups of four or five to solve the second test cooperatively. The third form of the test was taken by each individual alone. The two individual performances were averaged. The groups had no previous practice in working together and were allowed only ten minutes per task. Eleven of the fifteen groups scored higher than their average member, and six of the fifteen groups scored higher than their best individual performer. The typical group attained a level of intellectual performance of about the seventieth percentile of its members working alone.

Marvin Shaw (1932) conducted a study in which individuals and four-person groups attempted to solve a series of intellectual puzzles. One puzzle had three married couples trying to cross a river in a boat that can hold only three passengers. There were constraints that reflected the sex and marital norms of the day: Only the husbands could row, and no husband would allow his wife to be in the presence of any of the other husbands unless he was also present. Puzzles such as these are called *eureka tasks*; if the correct solution is proposed, it is clear that it is correct (Lorge, Fox, Davitz, & Brenner, 1958). Only three out of twenty-one individuals were able to solve the "husbands and wives" puzzle in Shaw's study, while three of five groups were able to do so.

As a result of studies such as these, Thorndike (1938) concluded that the superiority of group to individual problem solving and decision making had been proved. More recent reviews have also concluded that groups generally learn faster, make fewer errors, recall better, make better decisions, and are more productive, with a higher-quality product than individuals (Baron, Kerr, & Miller, 1992; Davis, 1969; Johnson & Johnson, 1989; Laughlin, 1980). But why are groups superior to individuals (Figure 7.2)? *One explanation (based on the results of Goodwin Watson's study) is that in groups there is process gain; the interaction among group members results in ideas, insights, and strategies that no one member had previously thought of.* Similar to Watson, Barnlund

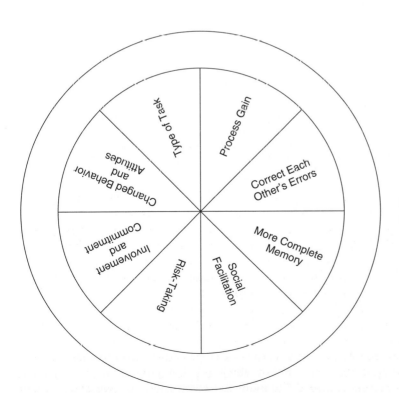

Figure 7.2 Effective group decision making.

(1959) found that after a group discussion, decisions surpassed both the average of the decisions of individual members and the best individual members' answers. Falk and Johnson (1977) and Hall and Williams (1966) found that group discussions led to decisions that none of the participants had thought of before the discussion. Groups discussing problems have been found to derive more crucial insights into how best to solve the problems than do individuals working alone (Johnson, Skon, & Johnson, 1980; Skon, Johnson, & Johnson, 1981). Ames and Murray (1982) even demonstrated that when two young children did not know the basic principles of conservation, by working together cooperatively they spontaneously generated and shared conservation judgments and explanations where none existed on the pretests. The conservation insights were sustained through both immediate and delayed posttests and affected responses to items that were not part of the experimental session. While only 6% of the children working alone gave conservation answers and explanations on the first posttest, 42% of the children in the cooperative condition did so. Overall, it may be concluded that process gain often occurs in groups, as the discussion often stimulates ideas that might not occur to the individual working alone. In a musical jam session, for example, each member responds continuously to the stimulation of others in building a creative product.

Another explanation is that in groups incorrect solutions are more likely to be recognized and rejected. Shaw (1932) concluded that a group is better able to recognize and reject incorrect solutions and suggestions than are individuals working alone. Ziller (1957) concluded that in groups, chance errors and blind spots may be corrected (as it is usually easier to see others' mistakes than one's own) and members can remedy each other's mistakes.

A third explanation is that groups have a more accurate memory of facts and events than do individuals. Bekhterev and DeLange (1924) briefly showed a picture to groups and asked members to write down all the details they could remember. A discussion period followed in which the group tried to reach a consensus about each item. The group decision corrected many of the mistaken recollections of the members. Villasenor (1977) notes that the jurors in a trial remembered far more collectively about the evidence and the testimony than they did individually.

Other reasons why groups may make better decisions than individuals are:

1. Groups provide higher motivation to achieve.
2. Groups make riskier decisions than individuals.
3. Involvement in decision making increases members' commitment to implement the decision.
4. Involvement in group decision making facilitates the changes in behavior and attitudes required to implement the decision.

A discussion of each of these explanations follows. Finally, the issue of whether decision-making groups work up to their potential is examined.

Social Facilitation

Another reason that groups may make better decisions and outperform individuals is that groups provide a cooperative context in which members promote each other's success and give each other assistance. When individuals work alone, the presence of other people may be a source of competitive feelings, fear of being obstructed, and evaluation apprehension. For the past one hundred years, researchers have studied the impact of the presence of other people on individual performance. In social facilitation research, the individual or alone condition typically involves the individual performing in front of an observant experimenter, whereas the group condition involves people working in the presence of co-actors and an experimenter on similar yet independent tasks. The participants in the groups can see and be seen by one another, which produces an implicitly competitive situation (Geen, 1980).

Social facilitation researchers have shown that working in the presence of others improves performance on a variety of tasks such as fishing-reel winding (Triplett, 1898), dressing in familiar clothes (Markus, 1978), recognition of salient stimuli (Cottrell, Wack, Sekerak, & Rittle, 1968), negotiating simple mazes (Hunt & Hillery, 1973), and copying simple material (Sanders & Baron, 1975). On the other hand, they have found that working in the presence of others impairs performance on other tasks, such as solving difficult anagrams (Green, 1977), dressing in unfamiliar clothes (Markus, 1978), recognition of novel stimuli (Cottrell, Wack, Sekerak, & Rittle, 1968), negotiating difficult mazes (Hunt & Hillery, 1973), and copying difficult material (Sanders & Baron, 1975). Thus, having others around us appears to facilitate simple tasks and impair performance on complex ones (Bond & Titus, 1983). Social facilitation and impairment effects, furthermore, occur in a wide range of species. There are a number of explanations for these findings.

Most researchers believe that the underlying reason is that the feeling of competition increases anxiety, evaluation apprehension, and drive, which increases the likelihood that the dominant or most probable response will occur (Baron, Kerr, & Miller, 1992). If the dominant response includes behaviors that lead to successful performance (as in the case of simple tasks), then people do better when in a drive state. If the dominant response primarily includes behaviors that lead to poor performance (as in the case of difficult tasks), then people do worse when in a drive state.

There are a number of theoretical explanations for how social conditions produce drive arousal that then facilitates dominant responding. They involve the mere presence of others, learned drives, and distraction. Zajonc (1965) argued that social facilitation and impairment both occur because we are excited and aroused by the mere physical presence of speciesmates. As a result, we try harder. Cottrell (1972) suggests that the presence of speciesmates elevates drive arousal because, through learning, we have come to associate speciesmates with a variety of rewards and punishments. Social facilitation should occur primarily in competitive or evaluative situations, because such situations have the strongest past associations with rewards and punishments from others. Robert Baron and his associates (1978) proposed that social facilitation occurs because audiences, co-actors, and even bystanders often lead performers into "attentional temptation" in which they are placed in conflict regarding whether to attend to their speciesmates or to the ongoing task. Because the performer wishes to pay attention to more than he or she can manage, the resulting conflict leads to drive arousal and stress, which in turn produce the social facilitation or impairment effects. Distraction during a simple task will actually improve performance if it triggers attentional conflict (Baron, 1986; Sanders, 1981).

All of the preceding theories assume that social conditions produce drive arousal that then facilitates dominant responding. There are three theoretical explanations of social facilitation/impairment that instead focus on self-awareness, self-presentation, and attention. Duval and Wicklund (1972) proposed that social facilitation occurs because (a) audiences or co-actors heighten self-consciousness and (b) self-aware individuals will try harder. Social impairment occurs on difficult tasks because when self-aware people see that they are not succeeding, their motivation drops and they stop trying. Bond (1982) argues that audiences and co-actors affect performance by increasing our concerns about projecting a positive self-image to onlookers. From this self-presentation perspective, social impairment occurs on difficult tasks because initial failures produce embarrassment, which then disrupts performance. Finally, Geen (1976, 1980) suggests that information overload occurs when a person tries to attend to both the task and the audience. When we are bombarded with attentional demands, our focus of attention actually shrinks. On simple tasks that have become more or less automatic, our performance is facilitated because we have to process only a narrow range of cues. On nonautomatic tasks, however, a narrow attentional focus screens out needed cues.

The social facilitation research over the past ninety years has identified a number of conditions under which the presence of others will disrupt an individual's performance. From this work we can conclude that group decision making will be more effective than individual decision making because in groups the cooperation and social support among group members will moderate arousal and reduce competitiveness, evaluation apprehension, fear of punishment, attentional conflicts, fear of making a negative impression on others, fear of embarrassment, and the narrowing of perceptual focus that creates information overload. In other words, the stronger the positive interdependence and the more social support and assistance given in a group, the greater the social facilitation and the less the social impairment. The security of the group, furthermore, encourages members to take risks in forming conclusions and judgments.

Group Polarization

Groups seem to be more secure than individuals in adopting positions that are more liberal or conservative than those originally held by the members (Myers & Lamm, 1976). A group discussion can polarize decisions by causing the group to adopt a position more extreme than the positions individual members held beforehand. When divergent and creative thinking is required and new perspectives are needed, such risk-taking enhances the quality of group decisions.

In 1961 James Stoner (1961), then an MIT graduate student in industrial management, compared risk-taking by individuals and groups for his master's thesis. He wanted to test the commonly held belief that groups were more conservative in their decisions than individuals were. Stoner's procedure, which was followed in dozens of later experiments, posed some decision dilemmas to people by themselves. Each problem described a decision faced by a fictitious person. The subject's task was to advise the person how much risk to take. For example, what advice would you give the person in this item?

> Henry is a writer who is said to have considerable creative talent but who so far has been earning a comfortable living by writing cheap westerns. Recently he has come up with an idea for a potentially significant novel. If it could be written and accepted, it might have considerable literary impact and give a big boost to his career. On the

other hand, if he is not able to work out his idea or if the novel is a flop, he will have expended considerable time and energy without remuneration.

Imagine that you are advising Henry. Please check the *lowest* probability that you would consider acceptable for Henry to attempt to write the novel. Henry should attempt to write the novel if the chances that it will be a success are at least:

—— 1 in 10   —— 4 in 10   —— 7 in 10
—— 2 in 10   —— 5 in 10   —— 8 in 10
—— 3 in 10   —— 6 in 10   —— 9 in 10
—— 10 in 10 (Place a check here if you think Henry should attempt the novel only if it is certain that the novel will be a success.)

After marking their advice on a dozen items similar to this one, subjects would be placed in groups of five or so members to discuss each item and reach a unanimous decision on how much risk the person should take. Much to everyone's surprise, the decisions chosen by the group were by and large riskier than those selected before discussion. The finding was immediately dubbed the **risky shift** phenomenon. Over 300 research studies have since been conducted on this issue. Most of these studies used Stoner's method and found that group decisions were indeed riskier. Other research indicates that group discussion intensifies all sorts of attitudes, beliefs, values, judgments, and perceptions (Myers, 1982).

More recently, researchers have realized that although group discussion often produces a shift in individual opinions, such a shift is not necessarily in the direction of greater risk. It could be in the direction of greater cautiousness (a *caution shift*). If the

initial opinions of the group tend toward conservatism, then the shift resulting from group discussion will be toward a more extreme conservative opinion (Fraser, 1971; Myers & Bishop, 1970). The term **group polarization,** therefore, has replaced the term *risky shift.* When people discuss issues in groups, there is a tendency to polarize decisions by deciding on a more extreme course of action than would be suggested by the average of their individual judgments, but the direction of this shift depends on what was initially the dominant point of view. Groups seem to be more secure than individuals in adopting positions that are more liberal or conservative than those originally held by the members (Myers & Lamm, 1976). See Figures 7.3 and 7.4.

Mr. A., an electrical engineer who is married and has one child, has been working for a large electronics corporation since graduating from college five years ago. He is assured of a lifetime job with a modest, though adequate, salary and liberal pension benefits upon retirement. On the other hand, it is very unlikely that his salary will increase much before he retires. While attending a convention, Mr. A. is offered a job with a small, newly founded company that has a highly uncertain future. The new job would pay more to start and would offer the possibility of a share in the ownership if the company survived the competition of the larger firms.

Imagine that you are advising Mr. A. Listed below are several probabilities or odds of the new company proving financially sound.

Please check the lowest probability that you would consider acceptable to make it worthwhile for Mr. A. to take the new job.

_____ The chances are 1 in 10 that the company will prove financially sound.

_____ The chances are 3 in 10 that the company will prove financially sound.

_____ The chances are 5 in 10 that the company will prove financially sound.

_____ The chances are 7 in 10 that the company will prove financially sound.

_____ The chances are 9 in 10 that the company will prove financially sound.

_____ Place a check here if you think Mr. A. should not take the new job no matter what the probabilities.

Figure 7.3   A choice-dilemma questionnaire item.
Source: M. Wallach, N. Kogan, and D. Bem, Group influence on individual risk taking, *Journal of Abnormal and Social Psychology,* 65 (1962), 75–86.

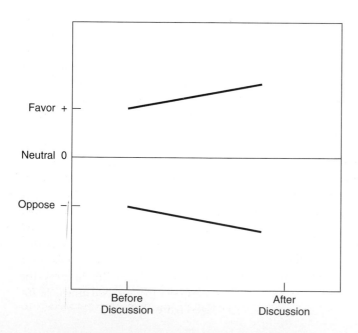

Figure 7.4   The group polarization hypothesis predicts that an attitude shared by group members will usually be strengthened by discussion. For example, if people initially tend to favor risk on a life dilemma question (such as that concerning Henry), they tend to favor it even more after discussion. If initially they tend to oppose risk, they tend to oppose it even more after discussion.

At least three explanations have been given for the group polarization effect:

1. *Normative influences:* Groups may polarize because members want to create a favorable impression on others and, therefore, (a) compare their opinions to those of other group members and (b) modify their opinions to be strong advocates of the group's position. Such normative influence is more likely when the topic concerns values, tastes, and preferences as opposed to factual issues (Laughlin & Early, 1982) or when the situation or topic is ambiguous (Boster & Hale, 1989).

2. *Informational influences:* Groups may polarize because members learn new information that causes them to modify their opinions (Kaplan & Miller, 1987) and members are confronted with persuasive arguments that are (a) compelling (logical and well thought out) and (b) new to some of the group members (Burnstein & Vinokur, 1977; Isenberg, 1986). Research on *information sampling theory* indicates that group members have a strong tendency to discuss primarily the information that they share in common and to fail to mention important information that is known only to single individuals (e.g., Stasser & Titus, 1987). Group members seem reluctant to introduce unique ideas unless they detect some social support for doing so.

3. *Social identification:* Groups may polarize because individuals want to identify with the group and be considered members (Isenberg, 1986; Kaplan & Miller, 1987).

The group polarization effect is limited and even reversed when groups make decisions that have real, binding, costly consequences for all group members (Baron, Roper, & Baron, 1974).

Involvement in Decision Making

There are at least two reasons for involving all group members in the group's decision making. *The first reason is to increase the quality of the decision by fully utilizing the resources of all members.* In general, high involvement in decision making increases the use of the members' resources, which in turn increases the quality of the decision. The more group members participate in making a decision, the more resources are available and, consequently, the higher the quality of the decision. The members responsible for implementing the decision may be especially knowledgeable about what the decision should be and, therefore, should be especially involved in making the decision.

The second reason is to increase members' commitment to implement the decision. Involvement in decision making also tends to increase members' allegiance to the group. One of the most famous research studies of the 1940s dealt with involving workers in decisions about how their work should be conducted. An associate of Kurt Lewin and the personnel manager of a clothing factory teamed up to do a study on overcoming the resistance of workers to changes in their work activities (French & Coch, 1948). The workers in question resisted management's changes in work activities by quitting their jobs, lowering their level of production, and expressing verbal hostility toward the plant and co-workers. French and Coch decided to try out three methods of instituting changes in job duties. One group of workers was simply told about the planned changes in their jobs and what was expected of them; they did not participate in the decision making. The second group appointed representatives from among themselves to meet with management to consider problems involved in changing work methods. All members of the third group met with management, participated actively in discussions, shared many suggestions, and helped plan the most efficient methods for mastering the new jobs. The differences in outcome were dramatic. Average production in the non-participating group dropped 20% immediately and did not regain the prechange level, and 9% of the group quit. Morale fell sharply, as evidenced by marked hostility toward the supervisor, by slowdowns, by complaints to the union, and by other instances of aggressive behavior. The group that participated through representatives required two weeks to recover its prechange output. Their attitude was cooperative, and none of the members quit their jobs. The consequences in the total-participation group were even more positive. Members of this group regained the prechange output after only two days; their output then climbed steadily until it reached a level of about 14% above the earlier average. No one quit, all members of the group worked well with their supervisors, and there were no signs of aggression. Zander and Armstrong (1972), furthermore, found that when work groups in a slipper factory were asked to set their own daily production goals, they tended to aim for goals even higher than the standard set by the manager.

Perhaps the only times decisions should be made by one or a few persons are (a) when the decisions are about matters that do not need committed action by most members of the group, (b) when the decisions are so simple that coordination among group members and understanding of what to do are easy, and (c) when the decisions have to be made quickly.

Changing Behavioral Patterns and Attitudes

It is easier to change individuals formed into a group than to change any of them separately.

Kurt Lewin (1951, p. 228)

Participating in a decision-making discussion within a group can have an impact on a person's subsequent behavior and attitudes. The classic experiments demonstrating this were conducted by Kurt Lewin and his associates. During World War II there was considerable concern in the U.S. government about the reactions of the public to food rationing and the need to promote the use of foods not ordinarily eaten by U.S. citizens. Lewin was persuaded to come to Washington and help. He and his associates conducted a series of experiments to determine what procedures were most effective in changing behavioral patterns and attitudes. More specifically, the studies focused on determining what procedures were most effective in persuading citizens to eat foods they considered undesirable and recommending these to the government. In the first study, Lewin (1943) attempted to encourage housewives to use less popular meat products, such as kidneys and sweetbreads. The subjects were six groups of Red Cross volunteers ranging from thirteen to seventeen members each. Half of the groups were given an interesting lecture arguing for greater use of these meat products, and the other half were led through a group discussion that developed the same arguments as those presented in the lecture. At the end of the group discussion, the group leader asked for a show of hands by those willing to try one of the undesirable meat products. A follow-up survey revealed that only 3% of those in the lecture groups had served one of these meats, whereas 32% of those in the group-decision groups had served them.

A second study was conducted with six groups of housewives, ranging from six to nine members (Radke and Klishurich, 1947). The attempt in this study was to increase the consumption of milk. The groups were temporary and the same person served as both lecturer and group decision leader. Again, an interesting lecture was given to half of the groups, and the other half participated in a group discussion about the use of milk. The groups were followed up after two weeks and again after four weeks. In both cases the increase in the use of milk was greater among those in the group decision situation.

In a third study, an attempt was made to increase babies' consumption of orange juice and cod-liver oil (Radke and Klishurich, 1947). Farm mothers with their first baby either examined interesting materials on the use of orange juice and cod-liver oil or participated in group discussions covering the same material. Again, the group decision procedure was more effective in getting the mothers to use more orange juice and cod-liver oil.

A number of studies have confirmed the findings of Lewin and his associates (Kostick, 1957; Levine & Butler, 1952) and highlighted two causes of the success of group discussion: public commitment to peers to eat the foods and the degree of perceived consensus in the group (Bennett, 1955; Pelz, 1958; Pennington, Haravey, & Bass, 1958). In a related study, Preston and Heintz (1949) compared the impact of participatory and supervisory leadership roles on students' attitudes. The participatory leader was told to be sure that each member of his or her group was considered, to encourage all members to take part in the discussion, to discourage chance methods of decision making, and to complete the group's assigned work in the allotted time. The supervisory leader was instructed not to participate in the discussion and to limit his or her responsibility to seeing that the work was done in the allotted time. The results showed that participatory leadership was more effective than supervisory leadership in changing students' attitudes. Participatory group members also were more satisfied with their group's decision than were members of the supervisory groups, found the task more interesting and meaningful, and rated their group discussions as more friendly and enjoyable.

Overall, the results of these and other studies indicate that if you wish to change people's behaviors and attitudes, you should involve them in group discussions that lead to (a) public commitment to the new behaviors and attitudes and (b) the perception that all members of the group support the new behaviors and attitudes. Participatory leadership may also facilitate changes in behaviors and attitudes.

Type of Task

Whether groups or individuals are more productive may depend on the type of task. If the task is one that allows group members to pool their efforts (such as pulling on a rope in a tug-of-war), groups should do better than individuals (with comparable abilities). But if the task requires extremely precise coordination of action (such as splitting a diamond, driving a car), a well-trained individual will outperform a group. Steiner (1966, 1972) proposed that tasks can be (a) divisible or unitary and (b) maximizing (amount and speed of work) or optimizing (quality of work). On divisible, maximizing, and optimizing tasks, groups tend to do better than individuals. On unitary tasks, comparisons between groups and individuals are more complex. Steiner stated that there are four types of unitary tasks: **disjunctive** (the group score is that of the best individual member), **conjunctive** (the group score is that of the worst individual member), **additive** (the group score is the sum of group members' contributions) and **discretionary** (the group score is any combination of individual efforts the group wants to put together). Baron, Kerr, and Miller (1992) present an interesting illustration of this task taxonomy. Imagine three track groups, each containing four runners competing in the 400-meter run. The finishing times of group A are 46 seconds, 47 seconds, 47 seconds, and 49 seconds. For group B the finishing times are 44 seconds, 45 seconds, 49 seconds, and 53 seconds. For group C the finishing times are 45 seconds, 45 seconds, 46 seconds, and 51 seconds. Which group wins? It depends on how group performance is defined. If the winning group is the group with the first runner to cross the finish line (disjunctive task demands), then group B wins. If every member of the group must cross the finish line before the group has finished the race (conjunctive task demands), then group A is the winner. If the group score is the simple sum of the times of its four runners (additive task demands), then group C wins. Although groups outperform individuals on most tasks, some tasks are better done by individuals.

Potential Group Productivity

A number of psychologists believe that there is one way in which groups are typically inferior to individuals—productivity per person. If, for example, instead of simply comparing groups and individuals on the time needed to reach a solution (which tends to favor groups in most studies), the number of *person-minutes* required were compared (i.e., solution time × size of the group), then individuals solve the problem in fewer person-minutes than groups.

Steiner (1966, 1972) proposed that the most important question is not whether groups are more productive than individuals, but rather if groups are as productive as they should be. He defined a group's *potential productivity* as the group's maximum possible level of productivity at a task and suggested that it depends on two factors—member resources and task demands. He proposed that groups rarely achieve up to their potential because of *process loss* due to *coordination losses* that occur when group members do not organize their efforts optimally and *motivation losses* that occur when members are not optimally motivated. In other words:

Actual Productivity = Potential Productivity – Process Loss

There are problems with Steiner's model. *First,* it implies that there exists a single, unique potential productivity baseline that constitutes an upper boundary on group performance. This is true for certain very simple tasks, but on more complex tasks there is more than one way to define a group's potential productivity. *Second,* Steiner assumes that individuals cannot be more motivated in groups than they are when working individually, but people may have higher motivation levels in some group settings (Hackman & Morris, 1975). It is possible that groups exhibit motivational gains as well as motivational losses (social facilitation research is an example). *Finally,* Steiner seems to assume that individuals are always performing up to their potential. Individuals rarely achieve up to their potential. An individual's potential also depends on the person's resources and the demands of the task. Individuals also can suffer process loss due to lack of motivation.

For many reasons, groups generally make better decisions than do individuals even if the groups do not always work up to their potential. There are, however, a variety of methods of making decisions, and they are not equally effective under all conditions. Certain factors enhance the effectiveness of group decision making, and other factors reduce it. The methods of decision making and the factors that enhance and inhibit group decision-making effectiveness are discussed in the following sections.

EXERCISE

7.2 *The Bean Jar (I)*

The purpose of this exercise is to compare the reactions of group members to the seven methods of decision making discussed in the next section of this chapter. A large jar full of a known quantity of beans is required for the exercise. The procedure for the coordinator is as follows:

1. Set a large jar of beans in front of the participants. You need to know exactly how many beans are in the jar. Inform the participants that they will be asked to estimate how many beans the jar contains.
2. Divide the participants into groups of six. Seven groups are ideal for this exercise. Appoint one member of the group to be the recorder. After the group has made its decision and all group members have completed the postdecision questionnaire (at the end of this exercise), the recorder collects the results and computes a group average for each question by totaling the individual scores for each question and dividing the sum by the number of members in the group.
3. State that each group has to estimate the number of beans the jar contains. Assign one method of decision making to each group. The instructions of each method are as follows:
   a. The member with the most authority makes the decision. One member is appointed leader by the coordinator. This person should exercise control by such means as telling the group how to sit while waiting for the decision to be made and how to use their time while she is deciding. The leader then estimates how many beans are in the jar and announces her decision to the group. All members of the group then complete the postdecision questionnaire.
   b. The member with the most expertise makes the decision. The coordinator appoints the member with the most training in mathematics to be the leader. The expert then considers how many beans are in the jar, makes a decision, and announces it to the group. All group members then complete the postdecision questionnaire.
   c. The opinions of the individual members are averaged. Each member of the group backs away from the group so that he cannot see the answers of other group members and they cannot see his answer. Each member independently estimates the number of beans in the jar without interacting with the other group members. The recorder then asks each member for his estimate, adds the estimates, and divides the sum by the number of members. The resulting number is announced as the group's decision. All group members then complete the postdecision questionnaire.
   d. The member with the most authority makes the decision following a group discussion. One member is appointed leader by the coordinator, and she calls the meeting to order. She asks the group to discuss how many beans are in the jar. When she thinks

she knows how many beans are in the jar, she announces her decision to the group. This is not consensus or majority vote; the leader has full responsibility and makes the decision she thinks is best. All members of the group then complete the postdecision questionnaire.

e. A minority of group members makes the decision. The coordinator appoints an executive committee of two members. The committee meets away from the group to decide how many beans are in the jar. They announce their decision to the group. All group members then complete the postdecision questionnaire.

f. Majority vote. Each group member estimates the number of beans in the jar, and the group then votes on which estimate is to be its decision. When the majority of members agree on an estimate, the group decision is made. All group members then complete the postdecision questionnaire.

g. Consensus. All members of the group participate in a discussion of how many beans are in the jar. Discuss the issue until all members of the group can live with and support the group's estimate. Follow the basic guidelines for consensual decision making given on page 297. When an estimate is agreed on, all members of the group complete the postdecision questionnaire.

4. Collect the results from the postdecision questionnaires and enter them in the summary table. Instruct each group to make four conclusions on what can be learned from these results. Have each group share its conclusions with the class. Then conduct a class discussion on how the conclusions agree or disagree with the material presented in this chapter. Point out the following relationships:

a. The extent to which a member feels understood and influential in the group is related to how well his or her resources are utilized.

b. The extent to which a member is committed to the decision and responsible for its implementation is related to his or her commitment to implement the decision.

c. The extent to which a member is satisfied with his or her participation and the positiveness of the group atmosphere is related to the future problem-solving ability of the group.

5. Note how accurate each group's estimate was. Usually, the more group members are directly involved in the decision making, the better the decision is.

POSTDECISION QUESTIONNAIRE

On a sheet of paper record your answers to the following questions. Then hand the paper to the recorder in your group.

1. How well do you feel your group understood and listened to you?
   Not at all   1 : 2 : 3 : 4 : 5 : 6 : 7 : 8 : 9   Completely

2. How much influence do you feel you had in your group's decision making?
   None   1 : 2 : 3 : 4 : 5 : 6 : 7 : 8 : 9   A great deal

3. How committed do you feel to the decision your group made?
   Very uncommitted   1 : 2 : 3 : 4 : 5 : 6 : 7 : 8 : 9   Very committed

4. How much responsibility do you feel for making the decision work?
   None   1 : 2 : 3 : 4 : 5 : 6 : 7 : 8 : 9   A great deal

5. How satisfied do you feel with the amount and quality of your participation in your group's decision making?
   Very dissatisfied   1 : 2 : 3 : 4 : 5 : 6 : 7 : 8 : 9   Very satisfied

6. Write one adjective that describes the atmosphere in your group during the decision making.

Results of Postdecision Questionnaire

Method of Decision Making	Understanding	Influence	Commitment	Responsibility	Satisfaction	Atmosphere
Decision by authority without discussion						
Expert member						
Average member						
Decision by authority after discussion						
Minority rule						
Majority rule						
Consensus						

METHODS OF DECISION MAKING

Think about the groups to which you belong. How do they make decisions? Do different groups use different methods? Does your family use the same procedure for making decisions that you and your friends do? Among the alternatives that follow, which decision-making method would you prefer for the groups to which you belong? Table 7.1 summarizes the advantages and disadvantages of these decision-making methods.

1. Rely on the person in charge of the group. The designated leader has the responsibility; he or she should also have the power to make the decisions.
2. Postpone making a decision and wait it out. Time takes care of everything; with a little luck, a decision will never have to be made if the group waits long enough.
3. Let the expert make the decision. Give the person with the most expertise in the group the authority to make whatever decision he or she thinks best.
4. Find out what each member thinks, and then choose the most popular alternative. With this method the group does not even have to meet; members are polled individually.
5. Flip a coin, roll the dice, or pick a number out of a hat.
6. Rely on the person in charge of the group to make the decision, but only after the group has thoroughly discussed the issue with that person.
7. Put the decision in the hands of a knowledgeable and qualified committee that will look at the issues, decide what the group should do, and tell the group members its decision.
8. Take a vote and let the majority rule. The issues should be presented to the group, discussed, and then voted on, with the majority deciding.
9. Ask the group next door what it is going to do and then do just the opposite.
10. Obtain a basic agreement among everyone in the group as to what the decision should be. The issues should be thoroughly discussed, with each member participating, until all agree on what the group should do.

Table 7.1 **Advantages and Disadvantages of Decision-Making Methods**

Method of Decision Making	Disadvantages	Advantages
1. Decision by authority without discussion	One person is not a good resource for every decision; advantages of group interaction are lost; no commitment to implement the decision is developed among other group members; resentment and disagreement may result in sabotage and deterioration of group effectiveness; resources of other members are not used.	Applies more to administrative needs; useful for simple, routine decisions; should be used when very little time is available to make the decision, when group members expect the designated leader to make the decision, and when group members lack the skills and information to make the decision any other way.
2. Expert member	It is difficult to determine who the expert is; no commitment to implement the decision is built; advantages of group interaction are lost; resentment and disagreement may result in sabotage and deterioration of group effectiveness; resources of other members are not used.	Useful when the expertise of one person is so far superior to that of all other group members that little is to be gained by discussion; should be used when little membership action is needed to implement the decision.
3. Average of members' opinions	There is not enough interaction among group members for them to gain from each other's resources and from the benefits of group discussion; no commitment to implement the decision is built; unresolved conflict and controversy may damage group effectiveness in the future.	Useful when it is difficult to get group members together to talk, when the decision is so urgent that there is no time for group discussion, when member commitment is not necessary for implementing the decision, and when group members lack the skills and information to make the decision any other way; applicable to simple, routine decisions.
4. Decision by authority after discussion	Does not develop commitment to implement the decision; does not resolve the controversies and conflicts among group members; tends to create situations in which group members either compete to impress the designated leader or tell the leader what they think he or she wants to hear.	Uses the resources of the group members more than previous methods; gains some of the benefits of group discussion.

Table 7.1 **Advantages and Disadvantages of Decision-Making Methods** *(Continued)*

Method of Decision Making	Disadvantages	Advantages
5. Minority control	Does not utilize the resources of many group members; does not establish widespread commitment to implement the decision; unresolved conflict and controversy may damage future group effectiveness; not much benefit from group interaction.	Can be used when everyone cannot meet to make a decision, when the group is under such time pressure that it must delegate responsibility to a committee, when only a few members have any relevant resources, and when broad member commitment is not needed to implement the decision; useful for simple, routine decisions.
6. Majority control	Usually leaves an alienated minority, which damages future group effectiveness; relevant resources of many group members may be lost; full commitment to implement the decision is absent; full benefit of group interaction is not obtained.	Can be used when there is not sufficient time for decision by consensus or when the decision is not so important that consensus needs to be used and when complete member commitment is not necessary for implementing the decision; closes discussion on issues that are not highly important for the group.
7. Consensus	Takes a great deal of time and psychological energy and a high level of member skill; time pressure must be minimal, and there must be no emergency in progress.	Produces an innovative, creative, and high-quality decision; elicits commitment by all members to implement the decision; uses the resources of all members; the future decision-making ability of the group is enhanced; useful in making serious, important, and complex decisions to which all members are to be committed.

There are many ways in which a group can make a decision. We shall take up seven of the major ones. Each decision-making method has its uses and is appropriate under certain circumstances. Each also has its particular consequences for the group's future operation. An effective group understands each method of decision making well enough to choose the method that is best for the

1. Type of decision to be made.
2. Amount of time and resources available.
3. History of the group.
4. Nature of the task being worked on.
5. Kind of climate the group wishes to establish.
6. Type of setting in which the group is working.

Method 1: Decision by Authority Without Group Discussion

In this method the designated leader makes all the decisions without consulting the group members in any way. This method is quite common in organizations. It is efficient in the sense that it can take a short time to execute, but it is not very effective. Even if the designated leader is a good listener who sorts out the correct information on which to base his or her decision, it is still the group that has to act on the decision, and under this method the involvement of the other group members is very small. Furthermore, when the designated leader makes the decision, not all members of the group may understand what it is; they may not, therefore, be able to implement it. If they disagree with it, they may not want to implement it. Under this method, how well the decision is implemented is particularly crucial.

Method 2: Decision by Expert

Group decisions can be made by letting the most expert member in the group decide what the group should do. The procedure for this method is to select the expert, let him or her consider the issues, and then have that person tell the group what the decision is. The group does not discuss the issue, but rather lets the expert decide alone.

There is one major problem with this method: how to tell which member has the most expertise. On most complex issues, individuals disagree as to what the best approach is, and this makes it difficult for them to identify the expert among them. Personal popularity and the amount of power a person has over the group members often interfere with the selection of the most expert member. The classic illustration of this point is the story of the general with a college education and several captains with Ph.D.s in engineering discussing how a bridge should be built. Needless to say, it is the general who designs the bridge, simply because he has the most power. Individuals with a great deal of power are notorious for overestimating their expertise while underestimating the expertise of others. Unless there is a clear and effective way to determine who the expert is, this method does not work very well. Moreover, it too fails to win the involvement of other group members, which is necessary for implementing the decision.

Method 3: Decision by Averaging Individuals' Opinions

This method consists of separately asking each group member his or her opinion and then averaging the results. When the chair of a group, for example, calls each member on the telephone, asks what the member's opinion is, and then takes the most popular opinion as the group's decision, the chair is using the **averaging method.** This procedure is like majority voting, except that the group's decision may be determined by less than 50% of the members (the most common opinion is not necessarily the opinion of more than half of the members), and no direct discussion is held among members as to what decision the group should make.

Because individual errors and extreme opinions tend to cancel themselves out under this method, it is usually a better procedure to follow than the designated leader method (without a group discussion). At least members are consulted. The disadvantage of the method is that the opinions of the least knowledgeable members may annul the opinions of the most knowledgeable members. Letting the most expert member make the decision is always better than using a group average to decide. Although group members are consulted before the decision is made, they are still little involved in the decision making itself. Consequently, their commitment to the decision is not very strong. If implementation of a decision made by this method requires the efforts of all group members, the effectiveness of the decision will probably be slight.

There are group decision-making methods that were created to average group opinions while eliminating or controlling members' interactions with one another. The *Delphi technique* was developed by Dalkey, Helmer, and their colleagues at the Rand Corporation (Dalkey, 1969, 1975). Its original purpose was to improve judgmental forecasting (e.g., economic forecasts and the cost of fringe benefits) by providing practical procedures for eliciting expert opinions. First, members are asked to provide individual estimates for the focal quality, and their opinions are collected and summarized in a way that ensures the anonymity of each member. Then a summary of the members' opinions is circulated among the members. The members are then provided an opportunity to revise their earlier forecasts. This procedure is repeated several times until individual opinions stabilize, that is, members change no more. The median or mean of the set of individual estimates is taken as the final group forecast. Dalkey claimed that the procedure avoided the "biasing effects of dominant individuals, or irrelevant communications, and of group pressure toward conformity" (1969, p. 408).

A *nominal group technique* meeting begins with individual assessment of the focal problem; individuals first generate ideas concerning the issue without any discussion. Each participant then presents personal ideas in a face-to-face group meeting, and these ideas are recorded. After all the ideas are recorded, group discussion begins and is primarily focused on clarifying the stated ideas. Finally, each member evaluates the priorities of these ideas by ranking them, and these rankings are combined mathematically to yield a group judgment (Delbecq, Van de Ven, & Gustafson, 1975).

Both of these methods are based on the assumption that groups are so poorly structured and members are so unskilled that interaction among members is better avoided.

Method 4: Decision by Authority After Group Discussion

Many groups have an authority structure that clearly indicates that the designated leader will make the decisions. Groups that function within organizations, such as businesses and government agencies, usually employ this method of decision making. The group does originate ideas and hold discussions, but it is the designated leader who makes the final decision. Under this method the designated leader calls a meeting of the group, presents the issues, listens to the discussion until he or she is sure of what he or she thinks the decision should be, and then announces his decision to the group.

Listening to a group discussion will usually improve the accuracy of a decision made by the group's leader. The greater the designated leader's skill as a listener, the greater will be the benefits of the group discussion. But although members can become involved in the discussion, they have no part in the decision making, which does not increase the decision's effectiveness. As a result, the group members may tend to either compete to impress the leader or tell the leader what they think he or she wants to hear.

Method 5: Decision by Minority

A minority—two or more members who constitute less than 50% of the group—can make the group's decisions in several ways, some legitimate and some illegitimate. One legitimate method is for the minority to act as an executive committee composed of only a few members, making all but the most important decisions for the group. Another is for the minority to act as a temporary committee that considers special problems and decides what action the group should take. The illegitimate methods involve railroading. For instance, two or more members may come to a quick agreement on a course of action, challenge the rest of the group with a sudden "Does anyone object?" and, if no one replies fast enough, proceed with a "Let's go ahead, then." Or a minority may forcibly recommend a course of action—implying that anyone who disagrees is in for a fight—and then move ahead before other members can consider the issue carefully. We shall focus on the legitimate methods of minority decision making; group members should be able to tell when they are being railroaded.

The minority members who make the decision may be committed to it, but the majority may not only be uncommitted, they may even want to prevent the decision from being implemented. When a few members railroad a decision, furthermore, they seem to assume that persons who are silent agree. But often a majority of group members need more time to organize their thoughts against a proposal, or sometimes members keep silent because they are afraid they are the only ones who disagree. When a group has a large number of decisions to be made and not enough time to deal with them all, decision-making committees can be efficient. This method may also be effective if a large number of decisions do not need member involvement in order to be implemented. In general, however, decision by minority is not a good method of decision making.

Method 6: Decision by Majority Vote

Majority vote is the method of group decision making most commonly used in the United States. Its procedure is to discuss an issue only as long as it takes at least 51% of the members to decide on a course of action. This method is so common in our society—indeed, it is almost a ritual—that it is often taken for granted as the natural way for any group to make decisions. It is certainly one of the methods that is used most often. On the surface, majority voting resembles our election system, but critical differences exist between elections and the use of majority vote in most groups. In our political system, minority rights are carefully protected through the Bill of Rights and the Constitution, and political minorities always have the right to compete on equal terms in the next election in order to become a majority. In most groups, however, minority opinions are not always safeguarded. Thus, majority voting often splits a group into winners and losers, encourages either/or thinking (when there may be other ways of looking at a problem), and fosters blind arguments rather than rational discussion. A majority that has often been outvoted is not contributing its resources toward influencing the decision. This circumstance not only reduces the quality of the decision but often creates coalitions of individuals who resent losing the vote and who try to regroup, pick up support, and overturn the decision. When a task needs the support of everyone in the group, and when the lack of support or sabotage by one or more members could seriously damage the undertaking, a decision by vote can be dangerous. Where commitment by everyone is not essential, of course, a majority vote can serve very well. If majority voting is to be used, however, the group must be sure that it has created a climate in which members feel they have had their day in court and will feel obliged to support the majority decision.

Method 7: Decision by Consensus

Consensus is the most effective method of group decision making, but it also takes the most time. Perfect consensus means that everyone agrees on what the decision should be. Unanimity, however, is often impossible to achieve. There are degrees of consensus, all of which bring about a higher-quality decision than majority vote or other methods of decision making. **Consensus** is commonly defined as a collective opinion arrived at by a group of individuals working together under conditions that permit communications to be sufficiently open—and the group climate to be sufficiently supportive—for everyone in the group to feel that he or she has had a fair chance to influence the decision. When a decision is made by consensus, all members understand the decision and are prepared to support it. That means that all members can rephrase the decision to show that they understand it, that all members have had a chance to tell the group how they feel about the decision, and that those members who continue to disagree or have doubts will nevertheless say publicly that they are willing to give the decision a try for a period of time.

To achieve a consensus, members must have enough time to state their views and, in particular, their opposition to other members' views. By the time the decision is made, they should feel that others really do understand them. Group members, therefore, must listen carefully and communicate effectively. Decisions made by consensus are sometimes referred to as *synergistic* decisions, because the group members working together arrive at a decision of higher quality than the decision they would obtain if each one worked separately. In reaching consensus, group members need to see differences of opinion as a way of (a) gathering additional information, (b) clarifying issues, and (c) forcing the group to seek better alternatives.

The basic guidelines for consensual decision making are as follows:

1. *Avoid arguing blindly for your own opinions.* Present your position as clearly and logically as possible, but listen to other members' reactions and consider them carefully before you press your point.
2. *Avoid changing your mind only to reach agreement and avoid conflict.* Support only solutions with which you are at least somewhat able to agree. Yield only to positions that have objective and logically sound foundations.
3. *Avoid conflict-reducing procedures* such as majority voting, tossing a coin, averaging, and bargaining.
4. *Seek out differences of opinion.* They are natural and expected. Try to involve everyone in the decision because they present a wide range of information and opinions, thereby creating a better chance for the group to hit upon more adequate solutions.
5. *Do not assume that someone must win and someone must lose* when discussion reaches a stalemate. Instead, look for the next most acceptable alternative for all members.
6. *Discuss underlying assumptions,* listen carefully to one another, and encourage the participation of all members.

Consensus is the best method for producing an innovative, creative, and high-quality decision that (a) all members will be committed to implementing, (b) uses the resources of all group members, and (c) increases the future decision-making effectiveness of the group. But it is often difficult to reach (Kerr, Atkin, Stasser, Meek, Holt, & Davis, 1976). Consensus is characterized by more conflict among members, more shifts of opinion, a longer time to reach a conclusion, and more confidence by members in the correctness of their decision (Nemeth, 1977). To reach a consensus, group leaders should encourage all members to participate, encourage differences of opinions to be expressed, and express acceptance of different positions and perspectives (Torrance, 1957). Group leaders should also encourage minority opinions and conflict among members (Maier & Solem, 1952).

Relation Between Time and Decision Making

Every method of decision making takes a different amount of time to carry out. Obviously, methods that involve group discussion take more time than methods that do not. Usually, the more persons involved in the decision making, the longer it will take to reach a decision. Figure 7.5 summarizes the relationship among the number of persons involved, the type of method used, the quality of the decision, and the time needed to arrive at a decision. If the time needed for both making and implementing a decision is considered, however, the time factor becomes less clear. Often the extra time taken to make a consensual decision will greatly reduce the time needed to implement it. Thus, many group authorities insist that if the whole process of decision making and implementation is considered, consensus is the least time-consuming method.

Generally, you are better off making important decisions in groups than having one person make them. This does not mean, however, that there is something magical about having a group make a decision. Some groups have a difficult time making decisions.

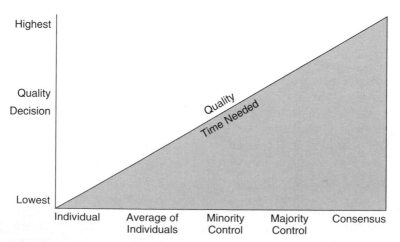

Figure 7.5 Quality of a decision and time needed as a function of the number of decision makers.

Groups can make bad decisions as well as good ones. To help ensure that their group will arrive at effective decisions, members must not only take advantage of the factors that facilitate effective decision making but also pay attention to the factors that may block effective decision making.

FACTORS ENHANCING GROUP DECISION MAKING

Whether a group decision is good or bad depends on how the group is structured. When you want to maximize the likelihood that the group will make a good decision, you need to structure five essential elements into group life: positive interdependence, face-to-face promotive interaction, individual accountability, social skills, and group processing (see Chapter 1). Whenever you want the group to make a good decision or to work productively, make sure the five elements are present.

FACTORS HINDERING GROUP DECISION MAKING

Although groups tend to make higher-quality decisions than individuals working alone, there is nothing magical about groups. There are conditions under which groups function inefficiently and ineffectively. As we saw previously, six of the fifteen groups in the Watson (1931) study made a better decision than their best member. There are a number of possible reasons why more of the groups did not do so. The potential barriers to group decision-making effectiveness are briefly discussed.

Lack of Group Maturity

In the Watson (1931) study and in most of the other studies on group decision making, college students are assigned to groups in which they know none of the other members and in which they stay together for only one hour or so. Such temporary ad hoc groups do not have time to develop enough maturity to function with full effectiveness. Group members need time and experience working together to develop into an effective decision-making group.

Uncritically Giving One's Dominant Response

Poor decisions are often made because group members quickly decide on a solution based on their dominant response and, therefore, do not think of the proper alternatives or do a poor job of evaluating and choosing among the alternatives being considered (Maier & Thurber, 1969). Both Berlyne (1965) and Maier (1970) have theorized that responses are hierarchically arranged and that, when confronted with a problem, individuals may place low probabilities on the correct solution. Dominant responses may be based on (a) physical states such as hunger that affect which stimuli a person attends to (Levine, Chein, & Murphy, 1942; McClelland & Atkinson, 1948); (b) psychological states such as attitudes and beliefs that affect what one perceives (Allport & Postman, 1945; Iverson & Schwab, 1967); (c) general cultural perspectives that lead to distortions in information perceived (Bartlett, 1932); (d) mental sets that cause the same words to have different meanings for different persons (Foley & MacMillan, 1943); (e) expectations that bias how ambiguous events are interpreted (Bruner & Minturn, 1955) and create sensitivity to perceiving some stimuli and not others (Neisser, 1954); (f) fixation on the first reasonable solution thought of (Simon, 1976); (g) laziness that results in failure to analyze available information and fully consider alternative ways of understanding such information (Langer, Blank, & Chanowitz, 1978; Taylor, 1980); and (h) adoption of solutions that have been previously useful (Luchins, 1942).

Social Loafing: Hiding in the Crowd

In certain groups (such as sports groups and combat units) there are factors (such as contagious excitement, strong norms favoring maximal effort, and intense feelings of commitment, loyalty, and obligation) that cause group members to demonstrate levels of motivation and effort far beyond what would be expected from an individual acting alone. During a college basketball game in 1989, for example, Jay Burson, a player on the Ohio State University team, continued to play in a game after he had suffered a broken neck. There are many other examples where people double their efforts or place

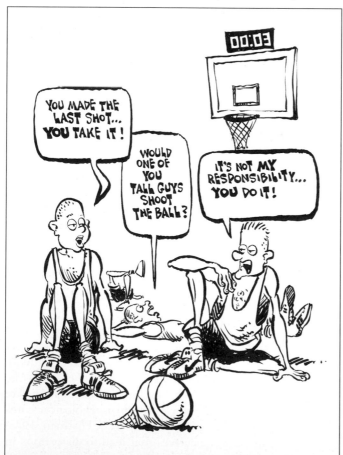

themselves in great jeopardy because of their devotion and loyalty to other group members. Most of the research, however, has focused on how being a group member can lower motivation.

A French professor of agricultural engineering named Max Ringelmann wanted to assess the relative efficiency of humans, oxen, and machinery in pulling and pushing loads. In the course of his investigations, he studied additive tasks by having individuals and groups of two, three, and eight males pull on a rope attached to a pressure gauge (reported in Moede, 1927). Two people, of course, pulled harder than one person. Three people pulled harder than two people. Individuals, on the average, exerted 63 kg of pressure, dyads about 118 kg, triads about 160 kg, and groups of eight about 248 kg of pressure. The intriguing aspect of these findings was that each person added did not increase the performance by 63 kg. Triads, for example, performed only 2.5 times as well as one individual.

The inverse relationship between the number of people in a group and the quality and/or magnitude of individual performance on additive tasks was dubbed the *Ringelmann effect*. Similar results have been observed for groups working on intellectual puzzles (Taylor & Faust, 1952), creativity tasks (Gibb, 1951), and perceptual judgments and complex reasoning (Ziller, 1957).

Ingham, Levinger, Graves, and Peckham (1974) replicated Ringelmann's study to determine if the loss of effort was due to (a) group process problems such as difficulty in coordinating the efforts of group members (on pulling a rope, for example, all persons have to position themselves to get a good hold on the rope, and then they have to pull and pause at the same time) or (b) some group members loafing. They demonstrated that as groups got larger, members pulled less hard at least partially because they were less motivated. A similar replication conducted a few years later used a new task—cheering as loudly as possible (Latané, Williams, & Harkins, 1979). Latané called the decline in motivation *social loafing*. **Social loafing** is a reduction of individual effort when working with others on an additive group task. Additive tasks require the summing together of individual group members' inputs to maximize the group product. Social loafing has been demonstrated on a variety of additive tasks such as rope pulling, shouting, clapping, evaluation of poems and editorials, cheering, cycling, pumping air or water, producing ideas, typing, and detecting signals. It has also been demonstrated in many different cultures, including those of India (Weiner, Pandy, & Latané, 1981), Japan, (Williams & Williams, 1984), and Taiwan (Gabrenya, Wang, & Latané, 1983).

Several situational and social factors appear to have an important impact on the magnitude of the effect. For instance, social loafing has been shown to occur especially when group members lack identifiable contributions (Williams, Harkins, & Latané, 1981); when there is an increased likelihood of redundant efforts (Harkins & Petty, 1982); when there is no cohesiveness among group members (Williams, 1981); when there is lessened responsibility for the final outcome (Petty, Harkins, Williams, & Latané, 1977); when the task is boring, as opposed to challenging, appealing, or involving (Brickner, Harkins, & Ostrom, 1986); when there is no spirit of commitment to the group (Hackman & Walton, 1986); and when group members believe that others are loafing (Zaccaro, 1984). Some four dozen studies show that when individuals working on additive tasks believe that they are lost in a crowd and, therefore, are not accountable and cannot evaluate their own efforts, responsibility is diffused across all group members (see Figure 7.6).

Social loafing seems most likely to occur when individuals or groups have no strong incentive to perform the task. That is, it may be eliminated if group cohesion is sufficiently high (Williams, 1981), the group sets performance goals (Brickner, 1987), and the task is sufficiently involving (Brickner, Harkins, & Ostrom, 1986), attractive (Zaccaro, 1984), or intrinsically interesting (Petty, Cacioppo, & Kasmer, 1985).

When the contribution of each group member is identifiable (Kerr & Brun, 1981; Williams, Harkins, & Latané, 1981) and when the contribution will be evaluated by groupmates and oneself (Harkins, 1987; Harkins & Jackson, 1985; Harkins & Szymanski, 1987; Szymanski & Harkins, 1987), no social loafing tends to occur. An opportunity for group members to evaluate the group's (but not individual members') performance can likewise motivate group members to work (Harkins & Szymanski, 1989).

Social loafing, therefore, seems to be restricted to a fairly narrow range of situations in which the task is additive and evaluation of member or group performance by anyone

Figure 7.6 This chart represents a summary of forty-nine studies involving more than 4,000 participants that disclosed that effort decreases (loafing increases) as the size of the group increases. Each dot represents the aggregate data from one of these studies.

Source: J. Jackson and K. Williams, *A review and theoretical analysis of social loafing* (unpublished manuscript, Fordham University).

is unlikely. In essence, social loafing is related to social facilitation through evaluation apprehension. When people believe that their individual performance is being closely monitored by others, their concern about being evaluated goes up and their performance on simple additive tasks may increase. But when they believe that their efforts are lost in a crowd, their evaluation concerns decrease and social loafing may occur.

Free Riding: Getting Something for Nothing

When one works alone, success or failure is entirely one's own responsibility. When one works in a group, however, the responsibility for the group's success or failure is often shared among group members. In an emergency, for example, the responsibility for helping appears to be diffused among bystanders, such that the larger the group, the less likely it is that any particular individual will provide help (Darley & Latané, 1968; Latané & Nida, 1981). Helping in an emergency is a *disjunctive task*; if one person does it, everyone receives the benefit. Similarly, if you are sharing an apartment with several other people, if one person cleans the apartment, no one else has to do so at that time. On disjunctive tasks, there is the possibility of a *free ride* (Olson, 1965), that is, of benefiting from the work of other group members while doing no work oneself. Under certain conditions, group members are sensitive to the dispensability of their efforts (Kerr, 1983; Kerr & Bruun, 1983). When group members perceive their contributions to be dispensable, such that group success or failure depends very little on whether or not they exert effort, and when that effort is costly, they are less likely to exert themselves on the group's behalf. The opportunity to free ride—to get something for nothing—is not the same as the opportunity to socially loaf—to hide in the crowd.

Motivation Losses Due to Perceived Inequity: Not Being a Sucker

What would you do if you were sharing an apartment and found that you were the only person who cleaned it, that is, everyone else was enjoying the benefits of your cleaning but was making no attempt to help keep the apartment clean? Kerr (1983) labeled the tendency to reduce your efforts when other group members are engaging in free riding the *sucker effect*. He demonstrated that people were willing to reduce their efforts (and thereby their rewards) rather than play the sucker and be exploited by a free-riding partner. This does not mean that everyone has to contribute the same amount to the group's efforts. People generally do not feel like suckers when another group member is trying hard to contribute but is unable to do so (Kerr, 1983; Tjosvold, Johnson, & Johnson, 1981).

Defensive Avoidance and Groupthink

Decision makers are often reluctant to take action; are beset by conflict, doubts, and worry; and struggle with incongruous longings, antipathies, and loyalties. They sometimes seek relief in **defensive avoidance**—procrastinating, rationalizing, or denying responsibility for their own choices. When group decision making is dominated by defensive avoidance, poor decisions are often made. Social psychologist Irving Janis (1971, 1982) analyzed the decision-making procedures that led to several major fiascoes, such as:

1. *Pearl Harbor.* In the weeks preceding the 1941 Pearl Harbor attack, military commanders in Hawaii were fed a steady stream of information about Japan's preparations for attack—somewhere. Then military intelligence lost radio contact with Japanese aircraft carriers, which had begun moving in force straight for Hawaii. Air reconnaissance could have spotted the carriers or at least provided a few minutes of warning of the impending attack. But the commanders decided against such precautions.

2. *Bay of Pigs invasion.* "How could we have been so stupid?" asked President John Kennedy after the 1961 invasion of Cuba by 1,400 CIA-trained Cuban exiles. Nearly all the invaders were soon killed or captured, the United States was humiliated, and Cuba allied itself even more closely with the Soviet Union.

3. *Vietnam War.* From 1964 to 1967 President Lyndon Johnson and his "Tuesday lunch group" of policy advisers escalated the Vietnam War on the assumption that the escalations (U.S. aerial bombardment, defoliation, and search-and-destroy missions) were likely to bring North Vietnam to the negotiating table. The escalation decisions were made despite warnings from government intelligence experts as well as from leaders of nearly all U.S. allies. The resulting disaster cost 56,500 American lives and more than 1 million Vietnamese lives, drove Lyndon Johnson from office, and created huge budget deficits that helped fuel inflation in the 1970s.

Janis (1972, 1982) coined the term *groupthink* to describe the decision-making process in these fiascoes. **Groupthink** is the collective striving for unanimity that overrides group members' motivation to realistically appraise alternative courses of action and thereby leads to (a) a deterioration of mental efficiency, reality testing, and moral judgment and (b) the ignoring of external information inconsistent with the favored alternative course of action. Groupthink leads to **concurrence-seeking**—group members inhibiting discussion in order to avoid any disagreement or arguments, emphasizing agreement, and avoiding realistic appraisal of alternative ideas and courses of action. Quick compromises and censorship of disagreement are characteristic of groups

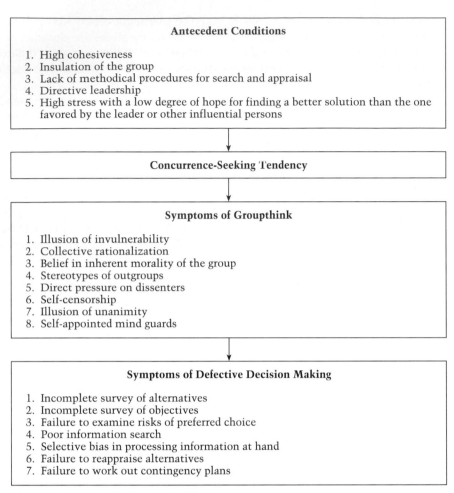

Figure 7.7 A model of groupthink.

dominated by concurrence-seeking. Groupthink is promoted when the group is highly cohesive, when it is insulated from outside criticism, when the leader is directive and dynamic, and when the group does not search for and critically evaluate alternatives (Figure 7.7). Group members rely on shared illusions and rationalizations to bolster whatever option is preferred by the leader. In seeking concurrence and avoiding disagreement, members become trapped in the dynamics of groupthink:

1. *Self-censorship.* Each member minimizes any doubts about the apparent group consensus.
2. *Illusion of unanimity.* Each member assumes that everyone (except oneself) is in agreement. There is a state of pluralistic ignorance in which members falsely assume that the silence of other members implies consent and agreement.
3. *Direct pressure on dissenters.* Anyone expressing doubts is pressured to conform.

4. *Mind guards.* Certain group members try to prevent dissenters from raising objections.

5. *Illusion of invulnerability.* Members develop an illusion of invulnerability, characterized by unwarranted optimism and excessive risk-taking. They often believe that the group is above attack and reproach.

6. *Rationalization.* Group members invent justifications for whatever action is about to be undertaken, thus preventing misgivings and appropriate reconsideration.

7. *Illusion of morality.* Members ignore the ethical consequences of the favored alternative and assume that the group's actions are morally justified.

8. *Stereotyping.* Group members dismiss competitors, rivals, and potential critics as too weak or stupid to react effectively or as too evil to warrant genuine attempts at negotiation. These aspects of groupthink lead to a number of defects in the decision-making process including an incomplete survey of alternatives and objectives, failure to examine the risks of the preferred choice, poor information search, selective bias in processing information, failure to reappraise alternatives, and failure to make contingency plans.

Aldag and Fuller (1993) conducted an extensive review of literature and concluded that most support for groupthink has come from retrospective case studies that have focused on decision fiascoes rather than comparing the decision-making processes associated with good versus bad decisions. Overall, the research does not demonstrate convincingly that groupthink is valid or that groupthink characteristics lead to negative outcomes. Controlled experimental research on the groupthink process has been sparse. Laboratory research shows that high cohesion has generally not produced the poor discussion quality Janis's theory predicts (e.g., Flowers, 1977; Leana, 1985) but that directive leadership results in low-quality group problem solving (e.g., Flowers, 1977). The historical examples that Janis presents have to be viewed with caution because we cannot be certain that contradictory examples have not been overlooked (Longley & Pruitt, 1980). Tetlock (1979), however, did a quantitative content analysis of public statements made by key decision makers and found that for policy decisions Janis had categorized as exemplifying groupthink, decision makers' perceptions of the issue were much more simplistic than they were for decisions that Janis categorized as nongroupthink. Herek, Janis, and Huth (1987) report a negative correlation between the number of groupthink symptoms and the quality of the decision; the greater the groupthink, the more negative was the outcome of the decision. McCauley (1989) did a historical analysis and found that two key groupthink decisions discussed by Janis were characterized by compliance processes that overrode decision makers' serious reservations regarding the group's decision. McCauley's analysis also suggests that directive leadership (stating the leader's views early), homogeneity among group members, and insulation of the group from outside influence are particularly crucial factors in the groupthink process.

Conflicting Goals of Group Members

Members bring to a group a variety of motives. Some may wish, consciously or unconsciously, to sabotage the group effort. Others have self-oriented needs that may interfere with making an effective decision. Members may be competing with one another in ways that reduce their effectiveness in working together. Even when members are genuinely work oriented and anxious to achieve results, they may have different ideas about how to proceed.

Egocentrism of Group Members

A critical aspect of effective decision making is the ability to view the issues being discussed from various points of view. When members egocentrically present their opinions and coldly evaluate the extent to which the information and conclusions of other members agree with their own, competition over whose ideas are going to dominate develops. A number of studies indicate that an egocentric approach to decision making results in lower-quality decisions than an approach emphasizing understanding of other members' perspectives (Falk & Johnson, 1977; Johnson, 1977, 2000). The more members are embedded in their own perspective and the more they refuse to consider the perspectives of others, the lower the quality of the group's decisions will be.

Lack of Sufficient Heterogeneity

Whether a group will be optimally productive depends on how fully the necessary information, skills, and viewpoints are represented. The more homogeneous the participants, the less each member adds to the resources of the others. In general, homogeneous groups make less effective decisions than heterogeneous groups (Johnson, 1980a). The more heterogeneous the group, the more frequent conflict among group members will be (Bass, 1960; Hoffman, 1959), the less willing members will be to accept incorrect responses from each other (Goldman, Dietz, & McGlynn, 1968), and the greater the group productivity (Goldman et al., 1968; Hoffman & Maier, 1961).

Interference or Production Blocking

Because only one person can talk (and be heard by all the others) at any one time, participants in a discussion often have to wait to make their point. Sometimes the delay is so long that the whole course of the discussion has changed before the would-be speaker gets a chance to be heard. He or she may then drop the idea entirely, which deprives the group of information, or may introduce the idea belatedly, which causes the others to backtrack from the issues to which they have moved on. There are times when the participation of one member may interfere with the participation of other members and lower the decision-making effectiveness of the group. When groups are told to generate as many ideas as possible, they usually produce fewer (sometimes less than 50% as many) ideas as nominal groups (Diehl & Stroebe, 1987; Lamm & Trommsdorff, 1973). One of the reasons for this process loss is production blocking; only one group member can talk at any one time.

Inappropriate Group Size

Some decisions require the participation of many persons; other decisions need only one or two individuals. An inappropriate group size may interfere with effective group decision making. There are a number of ways that group size can interfere with group effectiveness. *First, the greater the discrepancy between functional and actual group size, the more ineffective the group will be.* Stephan and Mishler (1952) found that the proportion of active speakers in discussion groups declined with group size. As groups get larger, therefore, only a few of its members are actively trying to solve the problem. The functional size could be much smaller than the actual group size. Bray, Kerr, and Atkin (1978), for example, found that in most instances groups were solving problems about as quickly as the fastest solver when the group size was two. In ten-person groups, considerable process loss is occurring. In groups with more than eight or nine members, a few participants are likely to dominate and others are likely to remain passive (Watson & Johnson, 1972).

Second, the less group members see their efforts as essential for group success, the less effective the group will be. Generally, as the group gets larger and larger, members are less likely to see their own contribution as being important to the group's chances of success (Kerr, 1989; Olson, 1965). Social loafing, therefore, increases as the size of the group increases. The smaller the group, furthermore, the greater the individual accountability (Messick & Brewer, 1983). Morgan, Coates, and Rebbin (1970) found that team performance actually improved when one member was missing from five-person teams, perhaps because members believed that their contributions were more necessary. As group size increases, individual members tend to communicate less frequently, which may reduce the amount of information utilized in arriving at a decision (Gerard, Wilhelmy, & Conolley, 1968; Indik, 1965). Finally, as group size increases, so does the likelihood that individuals will alter their statements to conform to the perceived beliefs of the group (Gerard, Wilhelmy, & Conolley, 1968; Rosenberg, 1961).

Third, generally the greater the complexity of the group structure and the more time it takes to organize joint efforts, the less effective the group will be. A certain amount of time is needed to organize a group that is unnecessary for individuals (Bales & Strodtbeck, 1951). The larger the group, the more time is needed to organize it and coordinate efforts among members.

Fourth, the less the effort of each member, the less effective the group will be. In Ringelmann's (1913) experiment mentioned earlier, in which subjects were supposed to pull on a rope as hard as they could, he found that as group size increased, the average pull per member decreased.

Fifth, the less members identify with the group, the less effective the group will be. Kramer and Brewer (1986) have shown that a strong sense of belonging or social identity leads to cooperative behavior. They suggest that the more you feel part of the group, the less strongly you distinguish between your personal welfare and the group's welfare. Small groups are easier to identify with than large groups.

Sixth, the less members follow the group's norms, the less effective the group will be. Enforcement of group norms requires (a) the ability to monitor members' behavior so that norm violations will be detected and (b) that the social sanctions the group uses to punish norm violation will be salient. Reducing group size makes it easier to monitor members' behavior and increases members' attachment to the group, thereby making rejection by the group more salient (Fox, 1985).

Decision-making groups should be large enough so that the needed resources are present but small enough so that every member's resources are fully utilized, participation is high, acceptance and support by all members is possible, and coordination is easy (Johnson, 1980a). Overall, the larger the group, the harder it is to make it effective, though there are ways to do it. Perhaps the most important way of increasing the effectiveness of large groups is to strengthen the positive interdependence among group members. The larger the group, the stronger positive interdependence has to be. Seta, Paulus, and Schkade (1976) found that for a complex task, larger groups performed worse than smaller groups when given competitive instructions and better when given cooperative instructions. They also found that cooperative groups performed better when they were in close proximity and competitors performed better when they were not in close proximity.

Premature Closure and Dissonance Reduction

Making a decision prematurely and then reducing any dissonance felt by group members can contribute to ineffective decision making. According to the dissonance theory developed by Leon Festinger (1957), anytime one is forced to choose between two attractive options, postdecision dissonance is present. **Cognitive dissonance** exists when a person possesses two cognitions that contradict each other. Dissonance exists, for example, if a group member knows that the group selected one alternative as the most desirable option when other attractive alternatives also exist. Dissonance is assumed to motivate group members to reduce or eliminate it. One way to reduce dissonance is to increase the perceived desirability of the decision made and decrease the perceived desirability of the alternatives that were not adopted. The more difficult or important the decision, the more likely group members are to find reasons to support the choice that was made and to minimize the attractive qualities of the foregone choice. This spreads apart the alternatives so that the one chosen is viewed as more attractive (in comparison with the other alternatives) after the decision than before it. If the group needs to reconsider the decision or reopen the decision making, **dissonance reduction** may interfere with its doing so.

Lack of Relevant Skills Among Members

If group members do not have the needed skills to complete the task and work together effectively, the decisions they make will not be effective. There are two types of relevant skills—those required to complete the task (taskwork skills) and those required to work as part of a group (groupwork skills). Groups with incapable members may often underperform a skilled individual. A skilled lumberjack, for example, could undoubtedly cut, trim, split, and load more timber on his own than any given group of college professors. It is not enough for a group member to know the correct answer to the problem. The member must share the solution with the rest of the group and persuade them to accept it. Factors that may interfere with doing so include the member's status in the group (Torrance, 1954), the confidence the member has in his or her solution, and the amount of his or her participation in the discussion (Thomas & Fink, 1961). In other words, when the most capable members of a problem-solving group are not confident, have low status, or are not talkative, the group is likely to underutilize its resources. If taskwork and groupwork skills are low, the quality of the group's decision making will suffer.

Lack of Individual Incentives for and Barriers to Contributing

Shepperd (1993) concluded after a meta-analysis of the literature that when there are no incentives for contributing, members make little effort to achieve group goals. Correspondingly, there may be barriers that undermine the value of contributing or provide a motive to withhold contributions. When contributing to the group takes time and energy that would better be spent elsewhere or when a person believes his or her contributions are being exploited by others, there is an incentive for not contributing to a group effort.

Summary

Although groups tend to make higher-quality decisions than individuals working alone, there is nothing magical about groups. In order for high-quality decision making to take place within a group, the group needs to work together long enough to mature and to develop effective patterns of interaction among members. Any tendency toward uncritically giving the dominant response to the situation or social loafing needs to be avoided. Conflicting goals of individual members need to be resolved. All members need to participate, have the necessary social skills to present their information, and ensure that it is incorporated into the group's deliberations. Egocentric refusal to consider any ideas but one's own needs to be avoided. Avoidance and suppression of conflict and disagreement must also be avoided. A group needs sufficient heterogeneity among its members to ensure that different viewpoints and resources will be contributed to the discussion. Participation needs to be managed so that all members contribute without interfering with one another's thinking process. The group's size needs to be appropriate to the problem, the problem has to be important to group members, and there needs to be sufficient time to deal with the problem. Power within the group needs to be managed constructively, and members' motivation needs to be sustained. Quick decisions and premature closures need to be avoided.

EXERCISE | 7.3 | *Winter Survival*

The purpose of this exercise is to compare the effectiveness of five different methods of making decisions. Three of the methods do not utilize group discussion; the others do. The methods compared are (1) decision by a designated leader before a discussion, (2) decision by averaging members' opinions, (3) decision by an expert member, (4) decision by a designated leader after a discussion, and (5) decision by consensus. At least four groups of eight to twelve members each should take part. Inasmuch as the results are very predictable, however, fewer groups with fewer members may be used if necessary. The exercise takes approximately two hours. The materials needed are as follows:

Instructions for observers.
A description of the situation and a decision form.
A group summary sheet.
Instructions for groups that decide by consensus.
Instructions for groups whose leader decides.
A summary table.

The coordinator for the exercise should use the following procedure:

1. State that the purpose of the exercise is to compare several different methods of decision making. Set the stage by pointing out that group decision making is one of the most significant aspects of group functioning, that most consequential decisions are made by groups rather than individuals, that though many decisions are routine others are extremely crucial, and that participants in this exercise are now in a situation where the decisions they make as a group may determine whether or not they survive.

2. Divide the participants into groups of approximately eight members—six participants and two observers. Give each group a number or name for purposes of identification, ask the observers to meet at a central place to be briefed, and then distribute the description and decision forms to the participants. Review the situation with the participants, again emphasizing that their survival depends upon the quality of their decision. In half of the groups, designate one person as the leader; in the other groups, make no mention of leadership. Then instruct the participants to complete the decision form quietly and by themselves so that the results indicate their own decisions. They have fifteen minutes to complete the decision form and make a duplicate copy of their ranking. The designated group leaders should write "leader" on their duplicate copy, and all participants must write their group designation on their duplicate copy. At the end of the fifteen minutes, collect the duplicate copies.

3. While the participants are completing their decision forms, brief the observers. Give each a copy of the instructions for observers and copies of the description and the decision form (to orient them to the group task). Review the instructions to make sure the observers understand their task.

4. Distribute one copy of the group summary sheet and the appropriate instruction sheet to each participant. (The groups with a leader receive one instruction sheet and the groups without a leader the other instruction sheet.) Observers should also receive a copy of the instructions for their group. The groups should be placed far enough apart so that they cannot hear each other's discussions or be aware that they have different instructions. The groups have forty-five minutes to decide on a group ranking of the items on the decision form. They are to make a copy of their group ranking with their group designation clearly written on the top.

5. While the groups are working on their rankings, score the individual decision forms in the following way:
   a. Score the net difference between the participant's answer and the correct answer. For example, if the participant's answer was 9 and the correct answer is 12, the net difference is 3. Disregard all plus or minus signs; find only the net difference for each item. (The correct ranking appears in the Appendix.)
   b. Total these scores; the result is the participant's score. The lower the score, the more accurate the ranking.
   c. To arrive at an average member's score, total all members' scores for each group and divide by the number of members.
   d. Put the scores in order from best to worst for each group. This ranking will be used to compare how many members, if any, had more accurate scores than the group's score.
   e. In the summary table that follows the instruction sheets for the groups, enter the average member's score for each group and the score of the most accurate group member. Then, for the groups with a designated leader, enter the score of that person.

6. At the end of forty minutes, give a five-minute warning. After forty-five minutes, instruct the groups to complete their ranking in the next thirty seconds and, with the group number or name clearly marked on the paper, to turn in their group ranking. Quickly score the groups' rankings and enter them in the appropriate place in the summary table. Recruit one or two observers to help if you need them.

7. In a session with all the participants, give the correct ranking and the rationale for each item. The correct ranking and the rationale appear on pages 586–587 in the Appendix. Then explain how the rankings are scored so that each person can determine his or her score.

INSTRUCTION TO OBSERVERS

This exercise looks at the process by which groups make decisions. Crucial issues are how well the group uses the resources of its members, how much commitment to implement the decision is mustered, how the future decision-making ability of the group is affected, and how members feel about and react to what is taking place. As an observer, you may wish to focus on the following issues:

1. Who does and does not participate in the discussion? Who participates the most?
2. Who influences the decision and who does not? How is influence determined (expertise, sex, loudness of voice)?
3. Who is involved and who is uninvolved?
4. What are the dominant feelings of the group members? How would you describe the group atmosphere during the meeting?
5. What leadership behaviors are present and absent in the group? You may wish to use the task-behavior and maintenance-behavior observation sheets on pages 213–214.
6. Why were the members' resources used or not used?

WINTER SURVIVAL EXERCISE: THE SITUATION

You have just crash-landed in the woods of northern Minnesota and southern Manitoba. It is 11:32 A.M. in mid-January. The light plane in which you were traveling crashed on a lake. The pilot and copilot were killed. Shortly after the crash the plane sank completely into the lake, with the pilot's and copilot's bodies inside. None of you is seriously injured, and you are all dry.

The crash came suddenly, before the pilot had time to radio for help or inform anyone of your position. Because the pilot was trying to avoid a storm, you know the plane was considerably off course. The pilot announced shortly before the crash that you were twenty miles northwest of a small town that is the nearest known habitation.

You are in a wilderness area made up of thick woods broken by many lakes and streams. The snow depth varies from above the ankles in windswept areas to knee-deep where it has drifted. The last weather report indicated that the temperature would reach −25°F in the daytime and −40°F at night. There is plenty of dead wood and twigs in the immediate area. You are dressed in winter clothing appropriate for city wear—suits, pantsuits, street shoes, and overcoats.

While escaping from the plane, the several members of your group salvaged twelve items. Your task is to rank these items according to their importance to your survival, starting with 1 for the most important item and ending with 12 for the least important one.

You may assume that the number of passengers is the same as the number of persons in your group and that the group has agreed to stick together.

WINTER SURVIVAL DECISION FORM

Rank the following items according to their importance to your survival, starting with 1 for the most important and proceeding to 12 for the least important.

_____ ball of steel wool   _____ sectional air map made of plastic
_____ newspapers (one per person)   _____ 20 × 20-ft piece of heavy-duty canvas

_____ compass   _____ extra shirt and pants for each survivor
_____ hand ax   _____ can of shortening
_____ cigarette lighter (without fluid) _____ quart of 100-proof whiskey
_____ loaded .45-caliber pistol   _____ family-size chocolate bar (one per person)

INSTRUCTIONS FOR GROUPS WITHOUT A LEADER

This is an exercise in group decision making. Your group is to employ the method of group consensus in reaching its decision. This means that the ranking for each of the twelve survival items *must* be agreed upon by each group member before it becomes a part of the group decision. Consensus is difficult to reach. Therefore, not every ranking will meet with everyone's complete approval. Try, as a group, to make each ranking one with which all group members can at least partially agree. Here are some guidelines to use in reaching consensus:

1. Avoid arguing *blindly* for your own opinions. Present your position as clearly and logically as possible, but listen to other members' reactions and consider them carefully before you press your point.
2. Avoid changing your mind just to reach agreement and avoid conflict. Support only solutions with which you are able to agree to at least some degree. Yield only to positions that have objective and logically sound foundations.
3. Avoid conflict-reducing procedures such as majority voting, tossing a coin, averaging, and bargaining.
4. Seek out differences of opinion. They are natural and expected. Try to involve everyone in the decision process. Disagreements can improve the group's decision because a wide range of information and opinions improves the group's chance to hit on more adequate solutions.

Winter Survival: Group Summary Sheet

Item	Members						Summary
	1	2	3	4	5	6	
Ball of steel wool							
Newspapers							
Compass							
Hand ax							
Cigarette lighter							
.45-caliber pistol							
Sectional air map							
Canvas							
Shirt and pants							
Shortening							
Whiskey							
Chocolate bars							

Summary Table: Accuracy of Decisions

Group	Before Group Discussion			After Group Discussion		Gain or Loss Over Designated Leader's Score	Gain or Loss Over Average Member's Score	Gain or Loss Over Accurate Member's Score	Number of Members Superior to Group Score
	Designated Leader's Score	Average Member's Score	Most Accurate Member's Score	Leader-Group Score	Consensus-Group Score				
1									
2									
3									
4									

5. Do not assume that someone must win and someone must lose when discussion reaches a stalemate. Instead, look for the next most acceptable alternative for all members.
6. Discuss underlying assumptions, listen carefully to one another, and encourage the participation of *all* members—the especially important factors in reaching decisions by consensus.

INSTRUCTIONS FOR GROUPS WITH A LEADER

This is an exercise in how a leader makes decisions after participating in a group discussion. Your group is to discuss what the ranking of the survival items should be, but the final decision rests with the designated leader of your group. At the end of forty-five minutes, your group's leader will hand in what he or she considers to be the best ranking of the items. The role of the group members is to provide as much help as the leader wants in trying to determine how the items should be ranked.

EXERCISE

7.4 *They'll Never Take Us Alive*

This exercise uses the same procedure as the Winter Survival Exercise.

THEY'LL NEVER TAKE US ALIVE RANKING SHEET

In a recent survey, *Dun's Review* lists the most perilous products or activities in the United States based on annual death statistics. Following are fifteen of these death-causing hazards. Your task is to rank them in order of dangerousness according to the number of deaths caused each year. Place 1 by the most dangerous hazard, 2 by the next most dangerous one, and so forth. See page 589 for correct ranking.

_____ swimming	_____ nuclear power	_____ bicycles
_____ railroads	_____ smoking	_____ firefighting
_____ police work	_____ motor vehicles	_____ mountain climbing
_____ home appliances	_____ pesticides	_____ vaccinations
_____ alcohol	_____ handguns	_____ surgery

APPROACHES TO DECISION MAKING

Neither life nor liberty nor sacred honor are safe while the legislature is in session.

Revere's Canon

This country has come to feel the same when Congress is in session as when a baby gets hold of a hammer.

Will Rogers

Involving all group members in the decision making ensures that a considered and thoughtful decision is made that everyone is committed to implementing. Making a considered and thoughtful decision is much harder than it sounds. Many times decisions are made by trying to:

1. *Stay with the status quo.* The decision makers complacently decide to continue whatever they have been doing, clinging to tradition, ignoring information about its ineffectiveness and the risks of losses. This is often a nonrational resistance to change, such as clinging to tradition, inertia and habit, overdependence on authority, illusions of powerlessness, or insecurity about the consequences of the change for oneself.

2. *Change as little as possible.* The decision makers adopt a new course of action that requires as little effort to implement as possible. Lindbloom (1959) notes that decision makers engage in *disjointed incrementalism,* in which decisions differ incrementally from existing policies and, therefore, only small changes ever result.

3. *Delay and avoid making the decision.* The decision makers believe that they are "damned if they change and damned if they don't." Because they believe there are serious risks no matter what they do, they defensively avoid the decision. *Defensive avoidance* is characterized by (a) procrastination (turning attention away from the conflict to other less distressing matters), (b) shifting of responsibility or buck-passing to someone else (enabling them to evade the dilemma and providing them with a handy scapegoat should the decision prove to have undesirable outcomes), or (c) psychological escape by inventing fanciful rationalizations to support one of the choice alternatives (selectively attending to only the good aspects of that alternative and ignoring or distorting negative information about it so that decision makers feel invulnerable to threat and danger) (Mann & Janis, 1983). This last procedure is often known as *groupthink.*

4. *Choose the first likely solution without considering all alternatives.* The decision makers feel pressure to make the decision immediately. Fear and anxiety about the consequences of the decision may result in vacillation, panic, and impulsively seizing a hastily contrived solution without understanding its full implications. The new course of action that requires minimal change, is most salient, or is most strongly advocated is uncritically adopted without much thought. Hoffman (1961) notes that decisions are adopted when they reach a minimum level of support necessary for acceptance. There is a reduced time perspective, reduced memory span, simplistic and repetitive thinking, and cognitive rigidity, all of which lead to a higher value on immediate goals, premature closure, restricted search for alternatives, and less rigorous evaluation of alternatives and their consequences (Mann & Janis, 1983).

5. *Encourage considered and thoughtful decision making in which all major alternatives are given a fair and thorough hearing.* Group members search for relevant information, assimilate it in a relatively unbiased way, and carefully evaluate the major

alternatives before making a choice. Considered and thoughtful decision making can be best achieved by the small-group/large-group decision-making procedure using advocacy subgroups. This procedure is discussed in depth in Chapter 8.

The first four methods are easy but inadequate compared to considered and thoughtful decision making.

CONSIDERED AND THOUGHTFUL DECISION MAKING

Decision making occurs within the context of problem solving. In order to consider the steps in making considered and thoughtful decisions, the whole problem-solving procedure has to be discussed (Johnson & Johnson, 1989).

Identifying and Defining the Problem or Issue

The first step of a decision-making group is to identify and define the problem. A **problem** is a discrepancy or difference between an actual state of affairs and a desired state of affairs. Problem solving requires both an idea about where the group should be and valid information about where it is now. The more clear and accurate the definition of the problem, the easier it is to do the other steps in the problem-solving processes. The group's vision, mission, and goals are relevant to defining the problem. There are three steps in defining the problem:

1. Reaching agreement on what the desired state of affairs is (that is, the group's purposes, goals, and objectives).
2. Obtaining valid, reliable, directly verifiable, descriptive (not inferential or evaluative), and correct information about the existing state of affairs.
3. Discussing thoroughly the difference between the desired and actual state of affairs, because it is from the awareness of this discrepancy that the commitment and motivation to solve the problem is built.

Because problem-solving groups often progress too quickly toward a solution to the problem without first getting a clear, consensual definition of the problem itself, members of the group should see to it that everyone understands what the problem is before trying to assess its magnitude.

Defining a workable problem is often the hardest stage of the problem-solving process. Suggestions for procedures are as follows:

1. List a series of statements about the problem. Describe it as concretely as possible by mentioning people, places, and resources. There should be as many different statements of the problem as the members are willing to give. Write them on a blackboard where everyone can see them. Avoid arguing about whether the problem is perfectly stated.
2. Restate each problem statement so that it includes a description of both the desired and actual state of affairs. Take out alternative definitions that are beyond the resources of the group to solve. Choose the definition that the group members agree is most correct. *The problem should be important, solvable, and urgent.*

3. Write out a detailed description of what group life will be like when the problem is solved. The more detailed and specific the scenario is, the better.

There are a number of potential barriers to identifying and defining problems. *The first is prematurely defining the problem.* The direction a group first takes in defining the problem may keep it from finding a successful solution (Maier, 1930); therefore, the group should be careful not to agree prematurely on the definition of its problem. *The second is a lack of clarity in stating the problem.* Much of the initial effort of groups in solving a problem is directed toward orienting members to what the problem is. This phase is extremely important, and it deserves sufficient time and effort to identify the problem, to define it, and, through this process, to get the members involved in and committed to solving it. Often, groups are doomed to failure when they inadequately define the nature of their problem. *Third, a critical, evaluative, competitive climate* prevents creative and workable solutions from being discovered. A supportive, trusting, cooperative atmosphere is necessary for solving problems successfully. If group members are afraid that other members are evaluating their ideas, effective problem solving is destroyed. *Fourth, if group members have inadequate motivation to solve the problem,* a compelling solution will not be found. Any problem-solving group must have the motivation to solve its problems. If the group members are not motivated, they must be persuaded to see the importance of the problem and the necessity for seeking a solution. Members who leave the work to others clearly lack motivation.

Gathering Information About the Existence of the Problem

The second step in the problem-solving process is diagnosing the existence, magnitude, and nature of the problem. The group must gather valid information. They must then thoroughly discuss and analyze it to ensure that all task force members understand it. The frequency of occurrence of the problem, the magnitude of the forces helping the group to move toward the desired state of affairs, and the forces hindering this movement need to be documented. Determining what forces are acting upon the problem situation is called **force field analysis** (Lewin, 1944; Myrdal, 1944). In force field analysis the problem is seen as a balance between forces working in opposite directions—some helping the movement toward the desired state of affairs and others restraining such movement. The balance that results between the helping and restraining forces is the actual state of affairs—a *quasi-stationary equilibrium* that can be altered through changes in the forces (Figure 7.8).

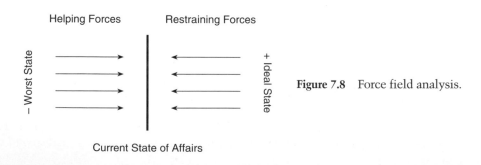

Helping Forces   Restraining Forces

− Worst State   + Ideal State

Current State of Affairs

Figure 7.8   Force field analysis.

The ideal state of affairs toward which the group is working is on the right side and is represented by a plus sign. The worst state of affairs, on the left side of the figure, is represented by a minus sign. The vertical line in the middle signifies the current state of affairs—a middle ground. On any problem numerous forces are at work, some restraining change and others helping change. There are two basic steps for a group to follow in doing a force field analysis:

1. Make up lists of forces by first brainstorming all the helping forces and then all the restraining forces. The list should include all possible forces, whether psychological, interpersonal, organizational, or societal. If a force seems to be a complex of variables, each variable should be listed separately. Critical judgment should be avoided; it is essential that every member's ideas are publicly requested and aired.
2. Rank the forces according to their importance in affecting the present situation. Agree on the most important helping and restraining forces, which may total from three to six each. Rate the important forces according to how easily they can be resolved, and avoid spending time discussing those that the group cannot influence with their current resources.

An example is as follows. The implementation of cooperative learning within a school may be seen as a balance between forces helping teachers implement cooperative learning and restraining teachers from using cooperative learning. The use of cooperative learning is promoted by the teachers' awareness that it will increase student achievement, higher-level reasoning, social skills, self-esteem, and social support. The use of cooperative learning is restrained by teachers habitually using other instructional procedures, being unwilling to commit the time to learn how to use cooperative learning, inherent fear of change, unwillingness to revise their standard lessons, and incomplete understanding of what cooperative learning is (Figure 7.9).

There are two major *barriers* to gathering valid information about the nature and magnitude of the problem. *The first is not getting the needed information.* When information is minimal, the definition of the problem will be inadequate, fewer alternative strategies for the solution will be generated, and potential consequences of those alternatives will not be properly explored. The result is relatively low-grade solutions. Great emphasis must be placed on fact finding in order to solve a problem effectively. *The second barrier is poor communication within the group.* Poor communication

Figure 7.9   Implementing cooperative learning.

among group members has the same effect as lack of information, with the added problem that it makes the implementation of any action that requires coordination among group members difficult. Effective communication among all group members is necessary for effective problem solving.

Unless the problem is defined correctly and specifically, it cannot be adequately understood. And without an accurate and precise understanding of the forces involved, the alternative strategies for solving the problem cannot be formulated.

Formulating and Considering Alternative Solutions

The overall purpose of a decision-making group is to make a free and informed choice of a solution to the problem based on having and understanding the relevant information. To achieve that purpose a cooperative structure must be established, the problem must be accurately identified and defined, and valid information about the existence, magnitude, and nature of the problem must be gathered and organized so that it is easily understood. Once the nature and magnitude of the problem are accurately understood, alternative ways to solve it may be identified.

The third step in problem solving is identifying and analyzing alternative ways to solve the problem. Groups often make poor decisions because they (a) do not think of the proper alternative solutions and/or (b) do a poor job of evaluating and choosing among the alternatives considered. *Systematically evaluating each alternative and analyzing its advantages and disadvantages before making a final decision are the most important steps in effective decision making.* The more explicit the systematic evaluation, the less likely that an alternative will be overlooked or rationalized away. If decision makers do know what the alternatives are and have correctly diagnosed each alternative's advantages and disadvantages, they will not choose a certain course of action unless its advantages are expected to exceed its disadvantages.

Identifying and analyzing alternative ways to solve the problem requires creative, divergent, and inventive reasoning. Such higher-level thinking and analysis comes primarily from intellectual disagreement and challenge (i.e., controversy). Controversy is discussed in Chapter 8. By definition, all decisions involve controversy, as decision making is a choice among alternative courses of action. Controversy is structured within problem-solving groups through the use of advocacy subgroups. In order to participate competently in the controversy process, group members must be able to prepare a position, advocate it, defend it from criticism, critically evaluate the alternative positions, be able to view the problem from all perspectives, and be able to synthesize and integrate the best parts of all solutions.

Force Field Analysis.   Force field analysis is a particularly useful way of specifying alternative strategies for solving a problem. It is based on the assumption that changes in the present situation will occur only as the helping and restraining forces are changed so that the level where they are balancing is altered. *There are two basic methods for changing the equilibrium point between the two sets of forces:* increasing the strength or number of the helping forces and decreasing the strength or number of the restraining forces. Of the two, the preferable strategy is to reduce the strength of or eliminate the restraining forces. Increasing the pressure for change in the present situation by strengthening the helping forces also increases natural resistance to change, reducing the strategy's effectiveness. Restraining forces may be reduced or eliminated without creating resistance. *Reducing the restraining forces, therefore, is usually the more effective of the two strategies.* The fewer the forces acting on the present situation, furthermore, the lower the tension level of the people in the situation.

The two methods are not mutually exclusive. Often you will wish to reduce restraining forces and increase helping forces at the same time. When this can be done, it is very effective. One way of intervening simultaneously with both types of forces is to modify a restraining force so that it becomes a helping force. One of the most successful strategies for changing the direction of a restraining force is to involve the group members who are resisting the desired changes in diagnosing the problem situation and in planning the solutions (Watson & Johnson, 1972). *People enjoy and affirm the changes they make themselves, and they resist changes imposed upon them by others.* Involving resisters in diagnosing and planning change often means a more difficult planning process, but it virtually guarantees that they are committed to the proposed changes. It also helps clear up any misunderstandings and differences of opinion before the strategies are implemented, and it uses the resources of the opposition.

Force field analysis is useful for two reasons. First, it avoids the error of a single-factor analysis of a problem; using it will keep attention on the problem situation until a number of relevant factors are identified. *Second,* by helping to identify a number of problem-related factors, it gives group members several points at which they may intervene in their attempt to produce a change. Because any change is the result of a number of factors, an effective change strategy involves plural actions that are directed toward several of those factors. When the group works to modify several factors at the same time, the possibility is increased that the improvement will be permanent.

In specifying alternative strategies for change, group members should think of as many ways as possible to reduce the forces keeping the group from moving toward the desired state. They should obtain ideas from everyone in the group. If group members do not have many ideas, outside consultants can always be invited to lend assistance. Bringing in an expert who knows a lot about the problem is often extremely helpful at this point. Group members should try to take each restraining force in turn and think of ways to reduce its strength or to eliminate it altogether. Divergent thinking should be encouraged.

Vigilant Analysis.   Janis and Mann (1977) recommend a procedure they believe eliminates defensive avoidance and ensures that each alternative solution is carefully considered. The group systematically evaluates each alternative solution on the basis of four factors:

1. The tangible gains and losses for the group members.
2. The tangible gains and losses for significant others, such as other members of the organization.
3. Members' self-approval or self-disapproval (Will we feel proud or ashamed if we choose this alternative?).
4. The approval or disapproval of the school by significant others (Will important people we are connected with think we made the right decision?).

The group ensures that these four factors are used to analyze each alternative in the following way:

1. A balance sheet is completed for each course of action considered. A balance sheet consists of listing the tangible gains from adopting the alternative on one side and the tangible losses on the other.
2. Each gain or loss is rated in terms of its importance on a 10-point scale from 1 (not important) to 10 (extremely important).
3. After a balance sheet is completed for each alternative course of action, the balance sheets are compared and the alternatives are ranked from "most desirable" to "least desirable."

Using a balance sheet to ensure systematic evaluation provides a high level of satisfaction with a decision, commitment to a decision, and security about the correctness of a decision (Janis & Mann, 1977).

Other procedures for ensuring that high-quality decisions are made by preventing groupthink and by structuring systematic evaluation include the following (Janis and Mann, 1977; Mann and Janis, 1983):

1. *Impartial leadership.* The leader avoids communicating his or her position at the outset so that members cannot adopt it uncritically. By not stating preferences and expectations at the outset and by not advocating specific proposals, the leader allows members to develop an atmosphere of open inquiry and to explore impartially a wide range of policy alternatives.

2. *Critical evaluator role for every member.* Group members are encouraged to express doubts and objections freely. The leader assigns each member the role of critical evaluator, giving high priority to airing objections and doubts and accepting criticism of judgments in order to discourage group members from soft-pedaling their disagreements.

3. *Devil's advocate.* One or more group members are assigned the role of challenging the testimony of all those who support the majority opinion. Members are chosen to represent unpopular positions in the group.

4. *Outside experts.* Outside experts are invited to group meetings and asked to challenge the views of group members.

Barriers. There are a number of barriers to formulating and considering alternative solutions to a problem. *The first is a failure to identify the proper alternative courses of action.* If a course of action is not identified, it cannot be considered and evaluated. *The second is premature elimination of courses of action without proper analysis and evaluation or uninformed and premature choice.* Groups often make poor decisions not because they did not think of the proper alternatives, but because they did a poor job of evaluating and choosing among the alternatives they considered (Maier & Thurber, 1969). For most people, ideas are fragile creations, easily blighted by a chill or even an indifferent reception. As groups proceed in their problem-solving activities, they must avoid the tendency to squelch each idea as it comes along; instead, they should create an atmosphere that supports the presentation and the pooling of a wide assortment of ideas. All alternative solutions should receive a fair hearing. Only then can the group avoid becoming fixated on the first reasonable solution suggested and critically evaluate the worth of all alternatives. *The third is pressures for conformity.* Pressures for conformity and compliance slow down the development of different and diverse ideas. Divergent thinking as well as convergent thinking is necessary for sound problem solving. *The fourth is a lack of inquiry and problem-solving skills.* Some groups may need special training in how to use inquiry and problem-solving methods to advantage. Training may be provided by an expert member of the group, or the group may wish to call in an outside consultant. *The fifth is a lack of procedures to aid analysis and synthesis.* The forces creating the problem must be understood and systematically analyzed in order for new alternatives to be created.

Deciding on a Solution

Once all the possible solutions have been identified and formulated in specific terms, the group needs to select the solution it will implement. Making a decision involves considering possible alternatives and choosing one. The purpose of group decision making is to decide on well-considered, well-understood, realistic action toward goals every member wishes to achieve. Whenever possible, decisions by task forces should be made by consensus. Consensus is not easy to achieve, as it is characterized by more conflict among members, more shifts of opinion, a longer time to reach a conclusion, and more confidence by members in the correctness of their decision. It is, however, worth the time and trouble.

Second-Chance Meeting. Even when decisions are made by consensus, there are times when members fixate on an alternative without thinking through all its consequences. One procedure for ensuring that a decision is not made too hastily is a *second-chance meeting*. Alfred Sloan, when he was chairman of General Motors, once called an executive meeting to consider a major decision. He concluded the meeting by saying,

> Gentlemen, I take it we are all in complete agreement on the decision here. . . . Then I propose we postpone further discussion until our next meeting to give ourselves time to develop disagreement and perhaps gain some understanding of what the decision is all about. (Quoted in Drucker, 1974, p. 472)

After a preliminary consensus on the best alternative, a *second-chance meeting* can be held in which all members are encouraged to express any remaining doubts and criticisms. Second-chance meetings help prevent premature consensus and concurrence-seeking.

Some societies have assumed that under the influence of alcohol there would be fewer inhibitions against expressing residual doubts about a preliminary decision made when everyone was sober. According to Herodotus, the ancient Persians made important decisions twice—first sober and then drunk. According to Tacitus, the Germans in Roman times also followed this practice. In Japan, where an emphasis is placed on harmony and politeness, a decision is frequently reconsidered after work in a bar. *Saki talk* takes place after each person has had a couple of cups of saki and, therefore, is no longer required to be polite. How group members really feel about the decision is then revealed.

Presenting the Recommendation to the Organization

It is not enough to make a decision. All persons who must implement the decision need to be convinced that it is the best thing to do. Thus, the recommended solution has to be clearly communicated to the organization as a whole, and the relevant others must have an opportunity to modify the decision if they are to be committed to implementing it. If the people who must implement the decision are not involved in making it, they will have little or no commitment to help implement it. People tend to affirm, support, and implement decisions they have helped make and to resist implementing decisions imposed on them. The key to this step is to ensure that everyone participates, everyone is involved in making the decision, and, therefore, everyone is committed to implementing the decision once it is made. The *barrier* to effective decision making at this point is inadequate involvement of the individuals who have to implement the decision.

Evaluating the Extent and Success of Implementation

The responsibilities of the group members do not end when the group makes a decision. The decision has to be implemented. *Decision implementation* is a process of taking the necessary actions that result in the execution of the decision. *Decision implementation requires commitment by relevant group members to the decision made.* No decision is worthwhile unless it is implemented. Once the group decides, the next step is to go out and do what members have decided to do.

To evaluate the success of the solution the group has decided to implement, members must determine (a) whether the solution was successfully implemented and (b) what the effects were. The first activity is sometimes called *process evaluation* because it deals with the process of implementing a strategy. The second is called *outcome evaluation* because it involves assessing or judging the consequences of implementing the strategy. Planners should establish criteria for or ways in which to judge the effectiveness of their actions in implementing the strategy and review their progress as each action step occurs. The major criterion for assessing the outcome of an implemented strategy is whether the actual state of affairs is closer to the desired state of affairs than it was before the strategy was carried out. The group documents the extent to which implementation takes place, notes barriers to implementation, and evaluates the success of the decision.

If the group finds that its solution has been successfully implemented, but has failed to substantially change the current situation into the ideal state of affairs, a new solution must be chosen and implemented until the group finds one that is effective. The solution of one set of problems, however, often brings other problems into the open, and in trying out various strategies the group may find that it has not been working to solve the most critical problem in the situation. The final result of the evaluation stage, therefore, should be to show the group what problems have been solved and to what extent, what problems still need to be solved, and what new problems have come up. Evaluation should result in a new definition of a problem, a rediagnosis of the situation, and the beginning of a new problem-solving sequence.

PROBLEMS WITH THEORIZING ON DECISION MAKING

There are at least two major problems with the theorizing and research on decision making in small groups. The *first* is that much of the research has focused on whether the decisions made by groups are of high or low quality. In the real world, many decisions cannot be objectively evaluated in terms of success or failure because their long-term effects cannot be fully measured. To evaluate long-term success or failure, one would need to take into account the negative consequences of the decision made, the positive consequences that would have resulted if each of the other alternatives were adopted as the decision, the positive consequences of the decision, and the negative consequences that would have resulted if each of the other alternatives had been adopted. Obviously, it is difficult if not impossible to quantify these factors.

The *second* problem is that much of the theorizing and research on decision making has assumed that decision makers are completely informed (that they know all the possible courses of action and the potential outcomes of each), infinitely sensitive (they see each alternative in all its complexity), and always rational (they always maximize the outcomes of their action). Real-life decision makers, however, are not always completely informed (they do not or cannot know all courses of action and their potential outcomes), do not understand fully the intricacies of various alternatives, and are rarely completely rational. Real-life decision makers often seem beset by conflicts, doubts, and worries: They struggle with conflicting loyalties, antipathies, and longings and engage in procrastination, rationalization, and denial of responsibility for their decisions. Instead of determining the solution that maximizes their outcomes, many decision makers look only for the alternative that meets a minimal set of requirements (this is called *satisficing*) and make quick decisions (Hoffman, 1961; Simon, 1976). Ineffective groups seem to operate under a variety of decision-making rules, such as "Tell a qualified expert about the problem and do whatever he or she says—that will be good enough" and "Do what we did last time if it worked and the opposite if it didn't work." Real-life decision makers also realize how expensive it is in time, effort, and money to collect and dissect the huge amounts of information a group needs in order to use an ideal form of decision making.

Researchers can alleviate these two problems by studying the process of decision making rather than focusing on quality, and by specifying procedures that encourage real-life decision makers to become more systematic and rational in their decision making.

EXERCISE | **7.5** | ***A Problem Diagnosis Program***

This program is designed to help you in diagnosing a problem that involves people working together in a group. In this program eleven separate steps are presented, each of which contains a complete and separate idea, question, or instruction. Be sure that you understand and complete each step before going on to the next one.

1. Identify the problem you wish to work on. Describe the problem as you now see it.

_____

_____

_____

2. Most problem statements can be rephrased so that they describe two things:
   a. The situation as it is now.
   b. The situation as you would like it to be (the ideal).
   Restate your problem situation in these terms. _____

_____

_____

_____

3. Most problem situations can be understood in terms of the forces that push toward and against change—in other words, helping forces and restraining forces. It is useful to analyze a problem by making lists of the helping and restraining forces affecting a situation. Think about these now and list them. Be sure to list as many as you can, not worrying at this point about how important each one is. Use additional paper if you need to.

Helping	Restraining

4. Review the two lists. Underline those forces that seem to be most important right now and that you think you might be able to influence constructively. Depending on the problem, there may be one specific force that stands out, or there may be two or three helping forces and two or three restraining forces that are particularly important.

5. Now, for each restraining force you have underlined, list some possible courses of action that you might be able to plan and carry out to reduce the effect of the force or to eliminate it completely. Brainstorm. List as many action steps as possible, without worrying about how effective or practical they would be. You will later have a chance to decide which are the most appropriate.

Restraining force A. Possible action steps to reduce this force:

_____

_____

Restraining force B. Possible action steps to reduce this force:

_____

_____

Restraining force C. Possible action steps to reduce this force:

_____

_____

6. Now do the same with each helping force you underlined. List all the action steps that come to mind that would increase the effect of each helping force.

Helping force A. Possible action steps to increase this force:

_____

_____

Helping force B. Possible action steps to increase this force:

_____

_____

Helping force C. Possible action steps to increase this force:

_____

_____

7. You have now listed action steps to change the key forces affecting your problem situation. Review these possible action steps and underline those that seem promising.

8. List the steps you have underlined. Then for each action step list the materials, people, and other resources available to you for carrying out the action.

Action Steps	**Resources Available**

9. Review the list of action steps and resources and think about how each might fit into a comprehensive action plan. Take out those items that do not seem to fit into the overall plan, add any new steps and resources that will round out the plan, and think about a possible sequence of action.

_____

_____

_____

_____

10. Plan a way of evaluating the effectiveness of your action program as it is implemented. Think about this now, and list the evaluation procedures you will use.

_____

_____

_____

_____

11. You now have a plan of action to deal with the problem situation. The next step is for you to implement it.

7.6 The Bean Jar (II)

The purpose of this exercise is to show that the involvement of more persons in the decision-making process affects the accuracy of the decision. The exercise can be done in an hour, and it requires only a large jar full of a known quantity of beans. The procedure for the co-ordinator is as follows:

1. Explain that the exercise focuses on the accuracy of the decisions made by different combinations of individuals. Then set a large jar of beans in front of the participants. You need to know exactly how many beans are in the jar. Tell the participants that they will be asked to estimate how many beans the jar contains.
2. Have each person estimate the number of beans, working alone. Record the estimates.
3. Have each participant pick a partner. Have the two-person teams work out a system for estimating how many beans are in the jar, and record their estimates.
4. Have each pair pick another twosome and have the four-person teams estimate the number of beans. Record their estimates.
5. Have each quartet pick another foursome and have the eight-member groups estimate the number of beans. Record their estimates.
6. Have each octet pick another group and have the sixteen-member groups estimate the number of beans. Record their estimates.
7. Ask for the final estimates and then tell the participants the number of beans in the jar. Have the class form groups of eight and discuss their experience, how they felt during the decision making, and the way they operated in the groups. Finally, ask the groups of eight to form a set of conclusions about the effect that an increasing number of members has on the accuracy of the decision and why the number of members influenced decision accuracy in the way it did. Have each group share its conclusions with the rest of the participants, and then have a class discussion of the conclusions.

7.7 Your Decision-Making Behavior

Before this chapter ends, it might be useful for you to consider your decision-making behavior. How do you usually behave in a decision-making group? How would you like to behave? Here is a closing exercise for you to do in a group with two of your classmates:

1. Throw all your loose change into the center of the group. Decide (using consensus) how to use the money. Then look at the group decision in terms of the behaviors of each member. How did each of you behave? What task and maintenance functions did you your-

self fulfill? How did you feel about your participation? How did your usual behavior reveal itself in the group decision making?

2. Review as a group the task and maintenance functions listed in Chapter 5. Discuss what other functions could be added. Examples are:

   a. *Clarification or elaboration.* Interpret or reflect on ideas or suggestions; clear up confusion; bring up alternatives and new issues before the group; give examples.

   b. *Summarization.* Pull together related ideas; restate suggestions after the group has discussed them.

   c. *Consensus testing.* Check with the group to see how much agreement has been reached; test to see if the group is nearing a decision.

   d. *Communication of feeling.* Express your feelings about the issues the group is discussing and the way in which it is functioning.

   e. *Verification of feeling.* Ask other members how they are feeling; check to see if your perception of their feelings is correct.

   Pick the task and maintenance functions you usually engage in; pick those you would like to perform better. Give one another feedback about each member's behavior.

3. Have you received any feedback on your behavior that has increased your awareness of how you behave? How would you now describe your behavior in decision-making situations?

4. Decide as a group when to end this exercise.

HOW I BEHAVE QUESTIONNAIRE

The purpose of this questionnaire is to help you look at how you behave in a group that is making a decision. Different persons act in different ways when they are members of groups that are making decisions. Moreover, the same person may act differently at different times, depending on the group, the decision to be made, and the circumstances. But, in general, how do you act when a group of which you are a member is making a decision? In each of the following three statements, choose the best description of the way you behave when a group to which you belong is making a decision. Be as objective and honest as you can; the results are for your use only.

1. When my group is making a decision, I

   _____ Passively defer to others.

   _____ Work for a decision that satisfies everyone without worrying about how good it is.

   _____ Look entirely at the merits of the alternatives, without thinking about how the members of the group feel or how satisfied they are.

   _____ Look for alternatives that work, though I might not personally think they are the best.

   _____ Work for a strong, creative decision having a common basis of understanding among group members.

2. When my group is facing a decision, I

   _____ Show little interest in the decision or the other group members.

   _____ Think mostly about how the members of the group are getting along, without worrying about what the decision will be.

   _____ Push for a really good decision and view the other members only as contributors of resources that will help make a better decision.

   _____ Work for good relations among the members and a good solution, though I am willing to sacrifice a little of each to get the job done.

   _____ Avoid compromise and try to get everyone to agree to and be satisfied with a decision that is based upon looking at the situation in a realistic way.

3. When my group is making a decision, I

_____ Wait for the group to tell me what to do and accept what they recommend for me.

_____ Help others participate by giving them moral support and by testing to see if members can agree.

_____ Give information, evaluate how well the group is working toward completing the task, set ground rules for behavior, and see that everyone stays at the task.

_____ Summarize periodically what has been discussed, call for things to be made clearer, and encourage members to compromise.

_____ Help the group think of alternatives, discuss how practical the alternatives are, and work out ways in which the group can come to an agreement.

You can plot this self-assessment on the task–maintenance grid in Figure 5.1 (page 196). Each of the preceding statements can be completed in five possible ways. The first alternative for each statement is a (6,6) response; it shows that this person has little or no interest in either maintaining the group or helping it accomplish its task of making a decision. The second alternative is a (6,30) response, showing that this member emphasizes group maintenance while ignoring the task. The third alternative is a (30,6) response; here the person focuses on getting the task done but ignores group maintenance. The fourth alternative is an (18,18) response, indicating a member who compromises on both task and maintenance in order to reach a decision. The fifth alternative for each question is a (30,30) response; this person tries to achieve a creative, consensual decision, and emphasizes both the task and maintenance functions of the group.

Look at your three responses. Locate each on the task–maintenance grid. Then discuss the results in groups of three, comparing your responses here with those you gave on the leadership surveys in the previous chapter and with the way you would like to act in groups.

SUMMARY

Typically, groups make more effective decisions than do individuals because groups create the possibility for social facilitation, risk-taking, member commitment to the group, appropriate behavioral and attitudinal patterns being adopted, and the likelihood that the task is better done in a group. Once a group is given the responsibility for making the decision, there are seven methods to choose from, ranging from letting the member with the highest authority decide to averaging individual opinions to group consensus. In using the decision-making methods, there are components that must be carefully structured (positive interdependence, promotive interaction, individual accountability, social skills, and group processing) and there are factors that hinder the group's decision-making efforts. The hindering factors include lack of group maturity, taking the dominant response, social loafing, free riding, fear of being a sucker, groupthink, conflicting goals, members' egocentrism, homogeneity, production blocking, inappropriate size, dissonance reduction, and the lack of necessary taskwork and teamwork skills. In order to structure the essential components and avoid the hindering factors, the group has to engage in considered and thoughtful decision making. The steps for doing so are to identify and define the problem, gather the information needed to diagnose it, formulate alternative solutions, decide on the solution to implement, present the group's recommendations to the larger organization (if appropriate), and evaluate the success of the implementation to determine if the problem is now solved.

An essential aspect of decision making is deciding among alternative solutions. To do so effectively, conflict among members' preferences, analyses, conclusions, and theories must be encouraged and resolved constructively. The next chapter focuses on structuring decision-making controversies and ensuring that it leads to creative problem solving.

7 exercises in CH 7.
9   CH 6
14   "   in CH 5
11   "   CH 4
14 in CH 3.   39   PICK 5
                               16
                               65

8

Controversy and Creativity

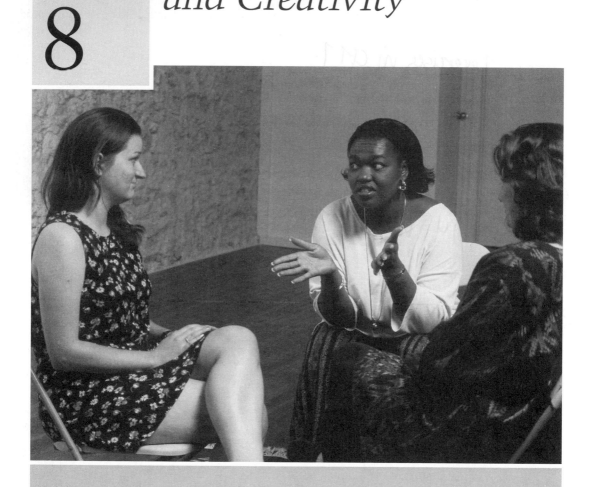

Basic Concepts to Be Covered in This Chapter

In this chapter a number of concepts are defined and discussed. The major ones are listed following. Divide into pairs. Each pair is to (a) define each concept, noting the page on which it is defined and discussed, and (b) ensure that both members of the pair understand the meaning of each concept. Then combine into groups of four. Compare the answers of the two pairs. If there is disagreement, look up the concept in the chapter and clarify it until all members agree on and understand the definition.

Concepts

1. Brainstorming
2. Cognitive perspective
3. Conceptual conflict
4. Concurrence-seeking
5. Controversy
6. Creativity
7. Debate
8. Differentiation of positions
9. Dogmatism
10. Epistemic curiosity
11. Integration of positions
12. Open-mindedness
13. Perspective-taking

EXERCISE

8.1 Controversy: Was Peter Pan Right or Wrong?

Task: In the book *Peter Pan,* a case is made for staying young forever in Never-Never Land. Is this a good idea? Would you like to live in Never-Never Land and never grow up? Write a report on the question "Was Peter Pan right or wrong? Should you grow up or stay a child?" The report should present a position and the reasons why the position is valid.

   Cooperative: Write one report for the group. Everyone has to agree, and everyone has to be able to explain the choice made and why the choice is good.

PROCEDURE

1. **Research and Prepare Your Position:** Your group of four has been divided into two pairs. One pair has been assigned the pro position and the other the con position. With your partner, plan how to present to the other pair the best case possible for your assigned position in order to make sure that it receives a fair and complete hearing. Research your position and get as much information to support it as possible. Make sure that both you and your partner are ready to present.
2. **Present and Advocate Your Position:** Forcefully and persuasively present the best case for your position to the opposing pair. Be as convincing as possible. Take notes and clarify anything you do not understand when the opposing pair presents.
3. **Open Discussion:** Argue forcefully and persuasively for your position, presenting as many supporting facts as you can. Critically evaluate the opposing pair's arguments, challenge their information and reasoning, and defend your position from their attacks. Keep in mind that you need to know both sides to write a good report.
4. **Reverse Perspectives:** Reverse perspectives and present the best case for the opposing position. The opposing pair will do the same. Strive to see the issue from both perspectives simultaneously.

5. **Synthesis:** Drop all advocacy. Synthesize and integrate the best evidence and reasoning from both sides into a joint position on which all members can agree. Then (a) finalize the group report, (b) present your conclusions to the class, (c) individually take the test covering both sides of the issue, and (d) analyze how well you worked together as a group and how you could be even more effective next time.

CONTROVERSY RULES

1. I am critical of ideas, not people. I challenge and refute the ideas of the opposing pair, but I do not indicate that I personally reject them.
2. I remember that we are all in this together. I focus on coming to the best decision possible, not on *winning*.
3. I encourage everyone to participate and to master all the relevant information.
4. I listen to everyone's ideas, even if I don't agree.
5. I restate what someone has said if it is not clear.
6. I first bring out *all* ideas and facts supporting both sides, and then I try to put them together in a way that makes sense.
7. I try to understand both sides of the issue.
8. I change my mind when the evidence clearly indicates that I should do so.

EXERCISE

8.2 *Your Behavior in Controversies (I)*

The purposes of this exercise are to (a) make you more aware of your typical actions when involved in a controversy and (b) make your group more aware of the pattern of members' actions when they are involved in a controversy. The procedure is as follows:

1. Working by yourself, complete the following questionnaire.
2. Using the scoring table, determine (a) your scores and (b) the average of all group members' scores.
3. Engage in a group discussion of (a) the strategies used most frequently during a controversy and (b) how controversies may be managed more constructively.

UNDERSTANDING MY CONTROVERSY BEHAVIOR

Each of the following questions describes an action taken during a controversy. For each question write 5 if you always behave that way, 4 if you frequently behave that way, 3 if you occasionally behave that way, 2 if you seldom behave that way, and 1 if you never behave that way.

_____ 1. When I disagree with other group members, I insist that they change their opinions to match mine.

_____ 2. If someone disagrees with my ideas and opinions, I feel hurt and rejected.

_____ 3. I often infer that persons who disagree with me are incompetent and ignorant.

_____ 4. When others disagree with me, I try to view the issue from all points of view.

_____ 5. I try to avoid individuals who argue with me.

_____ 6. When others disagree with me, I view it as an interesting opportunity to learn and to improve the quality of my ideas and reasoning.

_____ 7. When I get involved in an argument with others, I become more and more certain that I am correct and argue more and more strongly for my own point of view.

_____ 8. When others disagree with my ideas, I get hostile and angry at them.

_____ 9. When I disagree with others, I am careful to communicate respect for them as persons while I criticize their ideas.

_____ 10. I am careful always to paraphrase the thoughts and feelings of others when they present ideas and opinions that are different from mine.

_____ 11. When others disagree with me, I generally keep my ideas and opinions to myself.

_____ 12. When others disagree with me, I encourage them to express their ideas and opinions fully, and seek to clarify the differences between their position and perspective and mine.

_____ 13. I view my disagreements with others as opportunities to see who wins and who loses.

_____ 14. I often insult those who criticize my ideas and opinions.

_____ 15. When another person and I disagree, I carefully communicate that "I appreciate you, I am interested in your ideas, but I disagree with your current position."

_____ 16. When others disagree with me, I keep thinking of my ideas and opinions so that I do not forget them or get confused.

_____ 17. I am careful not to share my ideas and opinions when I think others may disagree with them.

_____ 18. When I disagree with others, I listen carefully to their ideas and opinions and change my mind when doing so is warranted by their information and reasoning.

_____ 19. When others disagree with me, I try to overpower them with my facts and reasoning.

_____ 20. I tend to dislike those who disagree with my ideas and opinions.

_____ 21. When I am disagreeing with and criticizing others' ideas and opinions, I let them know that I like them as persons.

_____ 22. I try to view the situation and issue from my opponent's perspective when involved in a disagreement about ideas and opinions.

_____ 23. I refuse to get into an argument with anyone.

_____ 24. When others disagree with me, I try to clarify the differences among our ideas and opinions, clarify the points of agreement, and seek a creative integration of all our ideas and information.

_____ 25. When others disagree with me, I have to convince them that I am right and they are wrong.

_____ 26. When others disagree with my ideas and opinions, it means that they are angry with me and dislike me.

_____ 27. While I disagree with others, I let them know that I appreciate their ability to present a challenging and thought-provoking position.

_____ 28. When I am involved in an argument, I restate and summarize the opposing positions.

_____ 29. When others disagree with me, I stay very quiet and try to avoid them in the future.

_____ 30. When I am involved in an argument, I never forget that we are trying to make the best decision possible by combining the best of all our facts and reasoning.

SCORING

Write your answer to each question in the space provided and total your answers for each controversy-managing strategy. The higher the total score for each controversy strategy, the more frequently you tend to use that strategy; the lower the total score for each controversy strategy, the less frequently you tend to use it. Add up the scores of all group members for each strategy and divide by the number of members in the group. This will give your group average for each strategy.

Win–Lose	Rejection	Confirmation
_____ 1.	_____ 2.	_____ 3.*
_____ 7.	_____ 8.	_____ 9.
_____ 13.	_____ 14.	_____ 15.
_____ 19.	_____ 20.	_____ 21.
_____ 25.	_____ 26.	_____ 27.
_____ **Total**	_____ **Total**	_____ **Total**
_____ **Group Average**	_____ **Group Average**	_____ **Group Average**

Perspective-Taking	Avoidance	Problem Solving
_____ 4.	_____ 5.	_____ 6.
_____ 10.	_____ 11.	_____ 12.
_____ 16.*	_____ 17.	_____ 18.
_____ 22.	_____ 23.	_____ 24.
_____ 28.	_____ 29.	_____ 30.
_____ **Total**	_____ **Total**	_____ **Total**
_____ **Group Average**	_____ **Group Average**	_____ **Group Average**

*Reverse the scoring on this question by substituting 1 for 5, 2 for 4, and so on.

CONTROVERSY QUESTIONNAIRE

Write your scores in the following spaces. If your score is above 15, it means that you are likely to engage in this strategy. If your score is less than 15, it means that you are not likely to engage in this strategy. Add up the scores of all group members for each strategy and divide by the number of members in the group. This will give you your group average for each strategy.

Constructive Strategy	Your Score	Group Average	Destructive Strategy	Your Score	Group Average
Problem solving	_____	_____	Win–lose	_____	_____
Confirmation	_____	_____	Rejection	_____	_____
Perspective-taking	_____	_____	Avoidance	_____	_____

Procedure

1. Compare your scores for the constructive and destructive strategies.
2. Compare your scores with your actual behavior (as reported by the observer) in the controversy exercise.
3. Discuss the strategies that are difficult for you to engage in.
4. On the basis of the group average scores and the actual behavior of the group members in the controversy exercise, characterize the group's tendencies toward constructive and destructive controversy.

Scoring Criteria: Constructive Scales

If you scored less than 15 on any of the scales, you need to begin consciously practicing the skill several times a day until you (a) have mastered it and (b) have integrated it into your behavioral repertoire. If you scored between 16 and 20 on any of the scales, you need to find more opportunities to use the skill and make it a more automatic response in many situations. If you scored over 21, you should congratulate yourself and keep up the good work.

Scoring Criteria: Destructive Scales

If you have scored over 15, you need to begin consciously to stop engaging in the skill until it is no longer an automatic response. You should replace the destructive actions with constructive ones. If you scored between 10 and 14, you need to reduce your destructive actions and seek opportunities to engage in constructive ones. If you scored less than 10, you should congratulate yourself and keep up the good work.

CONTROVERSY AND DECISION MAKING

Since the general or prevailing opinion on any subject is rarely or never the whole truth, it is only by the collision of adverse opinion that the remainder of the truth has any chance of being supplied.

John Stuart Mill

A large pharmaceutical company had to decide whether to buy or build a chemical plant (*Wall Street Journal,* October 22, 1975). To maximize the likelihood that the best decision was made, the president established two advocacy teams to ensure that both the buy and build alternatives received a fair and complete hearing. An advocacy team is a subgroup that prepares and presents a particular policy alternative to the decision-making group. The buy team was instructed to prepare and present the best case for purchasing a chemical plant, and the build team was told to prepare and present the best case for constructing a new chemical plant near the company's national headquarters. The buy team identified over one hundred existing plants that would meet the company's needs, narrowed the field down to twenty, further narrowed the field down to three, and then selected one plant as the ideal plant to buy. The build team contacted dozens of engineering firms and, after four months of consideration, selected a design for the ideal plant to build. Nine months after they were established, the two teams, armed with all the details about cost, (a) presented their best case and (b) challenged each other's information, reasoning, and conclusions. From the spirited discussion, it became apparent that the two options would cost about the same amount of money. The company, therefore, chose the build option because it allowed the plant to be conveniently located near company headquarters. This procedure represents the structured use of controversy to ensure high-quality decision making.

In almost every meeting room within every organization, people are disagreeing with each other. Whether the organization is a business, an industry, a government agency, a hospital, a school, a law firm, or a family, disagreements occur as decisions are made and problems are solved. Involved participation in such situations means that different ideas, opinions, beliefs, and information will surface and clash. The result is **controversy**—the conflict that arises when one person's ideas, information, conclusions, theories, and opinions are incompatible with those of another person, and the two seek to reach an agreement. Figure 8.1 summarizes this process. Controversies are resolved by engaging in what Aristotle called **deliberate discourse** (i.e., the discussion of the advantages and

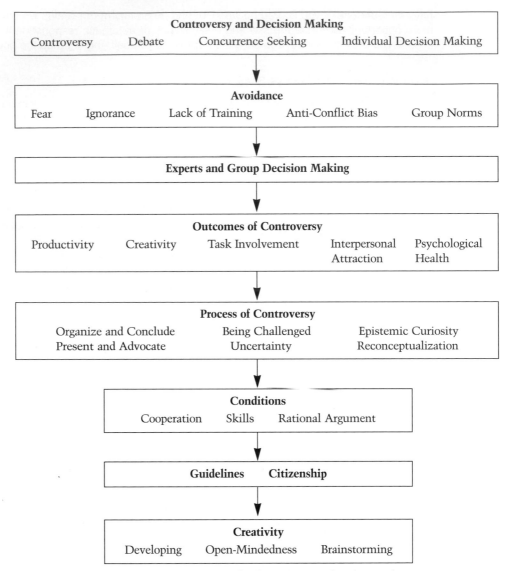

Figure 8.1   Overview of how controversy leads to creative decision making.

disadvantages of proposed actions) aimed at synthesizing novel solutions (i.e., *creative problem solving*). When a group has to make an important decision, the group identifies a number of alternative courses of action and ensures that each alternative the group considers gets a fair and complete hearing by going through the following steps (Johnson, 1970; Johnson & Johnson, 1979, 1989, 1995a; Johnson, Johnson, & Johnson, 1976):

1. *Research and prepare a position.* Each alternative course of action is assigned to a two-person advocacy team. The advocacy teams are given time to research their assigned alternative course of action and find all the supporting evidence

available. They organize what is known into a coherent and reasoned position. They plan how to present their case so that all members of the group understand thoroughly the advocacy pair's position, give it a fair and complete hearing, and are convinced of its soundness.

2. *Present and advocate their position.* Each advocacy pair presents its position forcefully, sincerely, and persuasively. Other group members listen carefully and critically, but with an open mind.

3. *Engage in an open discussion.* Each advocacy pair (a) continues to advocate its position, (b) attempts to refute opposing positions, and (c) rebuts attacks on its position. Each alternative course of action is thus given a trial by fire.

4. *Reverse perspectives:* Advocacy pairs reverse perspectives and present each other's positions. In arguing for the opposing position, group members summarize it in a forceful, sincere, and persuasive way. They add any new information that the opposing pairs did not think to present. They strive to see the issue from all perspectives simultaneously.

5. *Reach a decision through consensus on which course of action to implement.* Group members drop all advocacy and integrate what they know into a reasoned decision to which all members agree. This requires reconceptualizing the issue by synthesizing and integrating the best information and reasoning from all sides. The group's decision then reflects their best reasoned judgment.

Structured controversies are most commonly contrasted with concurrence-seeking, debate, and individualistic decision making. **Debate** exists when two or more individuals argue positions that are incompatible with one another and a judge declares a winner on the basis of who presented his or her position most effectively. An example is when each member of a group is assigned a position on whether more or fewer regulations are needed to control hazardous wastes and an authority declares as the winner the person who makes the best presentation of his or her position to the group.

Concurrence-seeking occurs when members of a group inhibit discussion to avoid any disagreement or arguments, emphasize agreement, and avoid realistic appraisal of alternative ideas and courses of action. An example is when a group is to decide whether more or fewer regulations are needed to manage hazardous waste, with the stipulation that group members are not to argue but rather to compromise quickly whenever opposing opinions are expressed. Most group decision-making situations are dominated by concurrence-seeking (Walton, 1987). Concurrence-seeking is close to the *groupthink* concept of Janis (1982), in which members of a decision-making group set aside their doubts and misgivings about whatever policy is favored by the emerging consensus so as to be able to concur with the other members. The underlying motivation of groupthink is the strong desire to preserve the harmonious atmosphere of the group on which each member has become dependent for coping with the stresses of external crises and for maintaining self-esteem.

Individualistic decision making occurs when isolated individuals independently decide on a course of action without any interaction or consultation with each other; each decision maker comes to his or her decision without interacting with others or discussing the information upon which the decision is based. The processes generated by controversy, debate, concurrence-seeking, and individual decision making are summarized in Table 8.1.

A key to the effectiveness of conflict procedures for promoting learning is the mixture of cooperative and competitive elements within the procedure (Table 8.2). The more the cooperative elements and the fewer the competitive elements, the more constructive the conflict (Deutsch, 1973). Cooperative elements alone, however, do not ensure maximal productivity. There has to be both cooperation and conflict.

Table 8.1 **Controversy, Debate, Concurrence-Seeking, and Individualistic Processes**

Controversy	Debate	Concurrence-Seeking	Individualistic
Categorizing and organizing information to derive conclusions	Categorizing and organizing information to derive conclusions	Categorizing and organizing information to derive conclusions	Categorizing and organizing information to derive conclusions
Presenting, advocating, and elaborating position and rationale	Presenting, advocating, and elaborating position and rationale	Active presentation of position	No oral statement of positions
Being challenged by opposing views	Being challenged by opposing views	Quick compromise on one view	Presence of only one view
Conceptual conflict and uncertainty about the correctness of own views	Conceptual conflict and uncertainty about the correctness of own views	High certainty about the correctness of own views	High certainty about the correctness of own views
Epistemic curiosity and perspective-taking	Epistemic curiosity	No epistemic curiosity	No epistemic curiosity
Reconceptualization, synthesis, integration	Closed-minded adherence to own point of view	Closed-minded adherence to own point of view	Closed-minded adherence to own point of view
High productivity, positive relationships, psychological health and social competencies	Moderate productivity, relationships, psychological health	Low productivity, relationships, psychological health	Low productivity, relationships, psychological health

Table 8.2 **Nature of Decision-Making Procedures**

	Controversy	Debate	Concurrence-Seeking	Individualistic
Positive goal interdependence	Yes	No	Yes	No
Resource interdependence	Yes	Yes	No	No
Negative goal interdependence	No	Yes	No	No
Conflict	Yes	Yes	No	No

Thus, controversy is characterized by both positive goals and resource interdependence as well as by conflict. Debate has positive resource interdependence, negative goal interdependence, and conflict. Within concurrence-seeking there is only positive goal interdependence, and within individualistic learning there is neither interdependence nor intellectual conflict.

Controversies are common within decision-making situations. In the mining industry, for example, engineers are accustomed to addressing issues such as land use, air and water pollution, and health and safety. The complexity of the design of production processes, the balancing of environmental and manufacturing interests, and numerous other factors often create controversy. Most groups waste the benefits of such disputes, but every effective decision-making situation thrives on what controversy has to offer. Decisions are by their very nature controversial, as alternative solutions are suggested and considered before agreement is reached. When a decision is made, the controversy ends and participants commit themselves to a common course of action.

THE AVOIDANCE OF CONTROVERSY

Within most organizations there is considerable conflict that is managed in costly and time-consuming ways. Thomas and Schmidt (1976) found that between 20% and 25% of managers' time is spent dealing directly with conflicts. Janz and Tjosvold (1985) determined in an interview study the cost of interpersonal conflicts in terms of employee time, materials, and project days. Included in their broad definition of conflict was refusing to communicate directly, ignoring advice and suggestions, being uninterested in learning from others, viewing problems from only one's own point view, involving only others that support one's point of view, embarrassing and blaming others, and seeing design flaws but not bringing them up because of wanting others to look bad. They estimated that the cost in employee time and materials for ineffectively managing interpersonal conflicts was about $15,000 (Canadian dollars) per employee per year and over $40,000 per employee per year if project days were taken into account. Conflicts, therefore, are pervasive within most organizations and frequently mismanaged. Managers and other organizational personnel must be trained in the procedures and skills needed to manage conflicts constructively.

If a group is to make effective decisions and solve problems competently, controversies should not only be encouraged and sought out but deliberately structured. Yet too few organizational members seek to stimulate or structure controversy. There are at least three reasons. *First,* too few people understand controversy to be able to accept and utilize it effectively. They know and understand too little of the procedures involved in controversy and the advantages and potentially constructive outcomes that can result from disagreements. *Second,* many people lack the interpersonal skills and competencies needed to stimulate controversy and ensure that it is managed constructively. Although most managerial training programs, for example, spend years providing technical training, the interpersonal skills needed to manage decision-making and problem-solving situations are not systematically and extensively taught.

Third, the discussion of conflicting ideas may not be a standard and common practice within decision-making and problem-solving situations because of the fear and anxiety most people seem to feel in conflict situations. Our society generally believes that conflicts are bad and should be avoided; consequently, many people believe that an effective group is one with no conflicts among members. Many discussions of conflict see it only as causing divorce, separation, psychological distress, social disorder, violence, divisiveness, and even war. The disintegration of many groups and organizations has been blamed on conflict. Within most groups, members try to either shun conflict or crush it. Neither strategy works. Avoidance or force only raises the level of the conflict and becomes part of the problem rather than being the solution.

A healthy group does not suffer from a lack of conflict. Rather, the absence of conflict may signal apathy, lack of interest, noninvolvement, and alienation—not maturity. In a healthy group, conflicts among members are inevitable. Thus, the issue is not whether conflicts can be prevented, but rather how they are managed, for conflicts can have both highly constructive and highly destructive effects on group and organizational functioning. Being able to initiate conflicts and capitalize on their constructive outcomes are essential group and managerial skills. Nowhere is that more true than in decision-making situations.

There are a number of hypotheses as to why conflict is avoided and suppressed in decision-making situations (Johnson, 1970; Johnson & Johnson, 1979, 1989, 1995c; Johnson, Johnson, & Johnson, 1976). *The first hypothesis is that fear blocks group members from engaging in controversies.* Because destructively managed conflicts create divisiveness and hostility, when conflicts occur group members may have some anxiety about whether constructive or destructive outcomes will result. Palmer (1991, 1992), for example, believes that fear of conflict blocks constructive behavior and recommends that group members have the courage to promote intellectual conflict despite their apprehensions about doing so.

The second hypothesis is that ignorance of how to engage in controversy blocks group members from doing so. Until recently there has not been a clear set of procedures that group members can use in a wide variety of decision-making and problem-solving situations. Structured controversy gives group members a clear procedure they can use to structure decisional conflicts in ways that increase the quality of their decision making.

The third hypothesis is that lack of training programs in the effective use of decisional conflict blocks group members from engaging in it. Most group members have not been trained in how to create intellectual conflicts and how to use the conflicts to increase the quality of their decision making and problem solving. Such training programs exist only in a few organizations. As a consequence, most group members do not know how to take advantage of decisional conflicts when they occur.

The fourth hypothesis is that our culture is so anticonflict that group members do not see the promotion of decisional conflicts as a possibility. The view that conflict is a potentially positive and powerful force in decision making and problem solving may be culturally unacceptable. A general feeling in our society is that conflict is bad and should be avoided. Many people, consequently, believe that a well-run group is one in which there are no conflicts among members.

The fifth hypothesis is that group norms may block group members from engaging in intellectual conflicts. Most groups promote getting along and not challenging each other's reasoning. In such a climate, the norms of acceptable behavior may not include creating decisional conflict among members.

The sixth hypothesis is that inertia, the power of the status quo, may be so great that group members just do not try anything new. Group members may choose to play it safe by not disagreeing or challenging groupmates because it is their personal tradition and the tradition of the group.

These six barriers are formidable obstacles to overcome if group members are to utilize the power of conflict during decision making and problem solving.

Experts and Group Decision Making

When two men in business always agree, one of them is unnecessary.

William Wrigley, Jr.

Organizations are filled with individuals who have expertise in their limited areas and must interact and make joint decisions with each other. Important decisions are typically made by small groups of individuals with diverse expertise. To maximize the quality of the decision, expertise must be exchanged. Most important group decisions involve more than one expert and, as Tversky and Kahneman (1981) note, most decision makers are normally unaware of alternative perspectives and frames of reference and of their potential effects on the relative attractiveness of options. Thus, two different experts, with different information and perspectives, can make directly opposing decisions without recognizing the limitations of their frames of reference. The experts do not see the whole world; they see only the part they specialize in. Because they are capable of all sorts of rationalizations about their areas of expertise—mainly in the direction of enhancing its importance—any decision made by a single expert is suspect. Lord, Ross, and Lepper (1979) found that individuals who hold strong beliefs about an issue are apt to examine relevant evidence in a biased manner, accepting confirming evidence at face value and subjecting disconfirming evidence to highly critical evaluation.

When experts with different information and perspectives come together to make a joint decision, conflict and disagreement result. Their points of departure need to be explicitly highlighted so that they will be able to sort out their differences and arrive at a mutually acceptable synthesis. Most decisions have to be made under the condition of uncertainty (the probability of desired outcomes resulting from the alternative course of action is unknown). Individuals with a wide variety of expertise and frames of reference are brought together to make such decisions. Conflict among their ideas, information, opinions, preferences, theories, conclusions, and perspectives is inevitable. Having the skills to manage the controversies constructively and knowing the procedures for exchanging information and perspectives among individuals with differing expertise are essential for organizational effectiveness and growth.

Expertise is not only developed but must be maintained. If experts are not gaining new information and knowledge, not refining their theories and conceptual frameworks, and not challenging their conclusions, they may soon lose their expertise. With the rapid growth of knowledge in almost all fields, individuals can quickly lose their expertise if they do not stay current and push beyond their present levels of understanding. To do so they must generate epistemic curiosity about their field of knowledge, promote their internal conceptual conflict by seeking out different perspectives and theories that contradict their own, adopt new and broader perspectives, and incorporate new information into their conceptual frameworks. Controversy is an essential factor in obtaining and maintaining expertise.

8.3 *Stranded in the Desert*

There is nothing as beautiful as a desert night. And there are few places more dangerous to be stranded than the desert during the night or day. In such a situation, effective decision making is a matter of life or death, and because the emotional content of the arguments over what a stranded group should do will be high, skills in managing controversies constructively are essential. The purpose of this exercise is to examine the dynamics of controversy and its effects on the decision making of a group caught in a survival dilemma. The materials needed for the exercise are a description of the situation, a group decision form, a postdecision questionnaire, a summary table, a constructive controversy checklist, and a controversy observation form. Approximately sixty minutes are needed for the exercise. The procedure for the coordinator is as follows.

1. Introduce the exercise by stating its objective and reviewing the overall procedure and tasks.
2. Divide the class into five groups. Give each group member a Stranded in the Desert Situation Sheet and a copy of the appropriate role-playing instructions. The role-playing instructions for each group are as follows:
   a. *Group 1.* Your position is that the group members have to walk to the nearest ranch if they are to survive. Plan carefully the best procedure for doing so. Select the five or six possessions of the group that are most important for implementing your plan and rank them from 1 (most important) to 5 or 6 (least important).
   b. *Group 2.* Your position is that the group members have to signal search planes and vehicles if they are to survive. Plan carefully the best procedure for doing so. Select the five or six possessions of the group that are most important for implementing your plan and rank them from 1 (most important) to 5 or 6 (least important).
   c. *Group 3.* Your position is that the group members have to protect themselves from the heat of the day and the cold of the night if they are to survive. Plan carefully the best procedure for doing so. Select the five or six possessions of the group that are most important for implementing your plan and rank them from 1 (most important) to 5 or 6 (least important).
   d. *Group 4.* Your position is that the group members must stay by the wrecked minibus and keep physical movement to a minimum if they are to survive. Plan carefully the best procedure for doing so. Select the five or six possessions of the group that are most important for implementing your plan and rank them from 1 (most important) to 5 or 6 (least important).
   e. *Group 5.* Your responsibility is to be observers. The observer's role is to record the nature of each member's participation in the group, using the accompanying obser-

vation form. Each observer needs two copies of this form. Make sure that all members understand the role of the observer and how to use the observation form.

3. Within each group, have participants divide into preparation pairs (one triad if there is an odd number of participants in the group). The preparation pairs are responsible for:
   a. Planning a rationale for their assigned position.
   b. Selecting the five or six possessions of the group that are most important for implementing their plan and ranking them from 1 (most important) to 5 or 6 (least important).
   c. Planning a persuasive presentation of their position and its rationale.

4. Introduce the situation. Have the groups read the description of the situation and their role assignment sheets. Tell them to construct as good a rationale for their position as possible and plan a persuasive presentation of it. Give them fifteen minutes to do so.

5. Form new groups of five by taking one participant from each of the previous groups and placing them together. Each member of the group should be representing a different position (with the exception of the observer).

6. Have the new groups read the situation description and then rank the twelve possessions of the group from 1 (most important for the survival of the group) to 12 (least important). All members must agree on the ranking and be able to explain why each possession is ranked as it is. Give the groups twenty minutes to decide on their ranking.

7. Have participants complete the postdecision questionnaire and give their responses to the group observer. Have the observers determine the group mean for each question while you share the correct/experts' ranking (see page 589 in the Appendix). Have each group score its ranking.

8. Record the results of each group in the Summary Table.

9. Instruct each group to discuss its experience and derive at least four conclusions using:
   a. The decision and questionnaire results.
   b. The information collected by the observers.
   c. The impressions of the group members.
   d. The constructive controversy checklist.

10. Have each group share its conclusion with the entire class.

STRANDED IN THE DESERT SITUATION

You are one of the members of a geology club that is on a field trip to study unusual formations in the New Mexico desert. It is the last week in July. You have been driving over old trails, far from any road, in order to see out-of-the-way formations. At about 10:30 A.M. the specially equipped minibus in which your club is riding overturns, rolls into a twenty-foot ravine, and burns. The driver and the professional adviser to the club are killed. The rest of you are relatively uninjured.

You know that the nearest ranch is approximately forty-five miles east of where you are. There is no closer habitation. When your club does not report to its motel this evening, you will be missed. Several persons know generally where you are, but because of the nature of your outing, they will not be able to pinpoint your whereabouts.

The area around you is rather rugged and very dry. There is a shallow water hole nearby, but the water is contaminated by worms, animal feces and urine, and several dead mice. You heard from a weather report before you left that the temperature would reach 108°F, making the surface temperature 128°F. You are all dressed in lightweight summer clothing, and you all have hats and sunglasses.

While escaping from the minibus, each member of your group salvaged a couple of items; there are twelve in all. Your group's task is to rank these items according to their importance to your survival, from 1 for the most important to 12 for the least important.

You may assume that the number of club members is the same as the number of persons in your group and that the group has agreed to stick together.

STRANDED IN THE DESERT DECISION FORM

Rank the following items according to their importance to your survival, from 1 for the most important to 12 for the least important.

_____ magnetic compass

_____ 20 × 20-ft piece of heavy-duty light blue canvas

_____ book, *Plants of the Desert*

_____ rearview mirror

_____ large knife

_____ flashlight (four-battery size)

_____ one jacket per person

_____ one transparent, plastic ground cloth (6 × 4 ft) per person

_____ .38-caliber loaded pistol

_____ one 2-quart plastic canteen per person, full of water

_____ accurate map of the area

_____ large box of kitchen matches

STRANDED IN THE DESERT: POSTDECISION QUESTIONNAIRE

1. To what extent did other members of the group listen to and understand your ideas?
   Not at all   1 : 2 : 3 : 4 : 5 : 6 : 7 : 8 : 9   Completely
2. How much influence do you feel you had on the group's decision?
   None at all   1 : 2 : 3 : 4 : 5 : 6 : 7 : 8 : 9   A great deal
3. To what extent do you feel committed to and responsible for the group's decision?
   Not at all   1 : 2 : 3 : 4 : 5 : 6 : 7 : 8 : 9   Completely
4. To what extent are you satisfied with your group's performance?
   Very dissatisfied   1 : 2 : 3 : 4 : 5 : 6 : 7 : 8 : 9   Very satisfied
5. How much did you learn about the issue under discussion?
   Nothing at all   1 : 2 : 3 : 4 : 5 : 6 : 7 : 8 : 9   A great deal
6. Write two adjectives describing the way you now feel. _____

Summary Table: Response to Postdecision Questionnaire

Group	Group Score	Understanding	Influence	Commitment	Satisfaction	Learning	Feelings
1							
2							
3							
4							

Determine the group means from the questionnaire responses and record them in the appropriate column, except for the first and last columns. In the Feelings column put representative adjectives from the questionnaire.

CONSTRUCTIVE CONTROVERSY CHECKLIST

_____ 1. There was no winner or loser, only a successful, creative, and productive solution. The cooperativeness of group members should outweigh by far their competitiveness.

_____ 2. Disagreements among members' positions were initiated.

_____ 3. Every member's contributions were listened to, respected, and taken seriously.

_____ 4. Effective communication skills were attended to, respected, and taken seriously.

_____ 5. Issues and problems were viewed from all available perspectives.

_____ 6. Group members criticized ideas and positions, not individuals. Members disagreed with each other while confirming each other's competence.

_____ 7. Group members viewed disagreement as an interesting situation from which something could be learned, not as personal rejection or a sign that they were being perceived as incompetent or ignorant.

_____ 8. There was appropriate pacing of differentiation and integration of members' positions. Differentiation took place first, followed by integration.

_____ 9. Emotions were allowed, and members were encouraged to express them

_____ 10. The rules of rational argument were followed. Members presented organized information to support their positions, reasoned logically, and changed their minds when others presented persuasive and convincing arguments and proof.

_____ 11. The arguments of all members were given equal consideration, regardless of how much formal power a member had.

CONTROVERSY OBSERVATION FORM

Behaviors	Participants				Total
Contributes ideas and opinions					
Asks others for their ideas and opinions					
Emphasizes mutual goals					
Emphasizes win–lose competition					
Asks others for proof, facts, and rationale					
Paraphrases, summarizes					
Criticizes and disagrees with others' ideas					
Criticizes other members as persons					
Differentiates positions					
Integrates positions					
Total					

Insert the name of a group member above each of the columns. Then record how frequently each member engages in each behavior. After the group meeting is over, total the columns and rows.

8.4   *Who Should Get the Penicillin?*

The purpose of this exercise is to examine the dynamics of controversy within a social studies lesson. The materials needed for the exercise are a description of the situation, a briefing sheet for the medical point of view, a briefing sheet for the military point of view, a postdecision questionnaire, a summary table, a constructive controversy checklist, and a controversy observation form. (The last four items are the same as in the previous exercise and are also used in the following three exercises.) Approximately ninety minutes are needed for the exercise. The procedure for the coordinator is as follows:

1. Introduce the exercise by stating its objective and reviewing the overall procedure.
2. Form groups of five members. One member from each group should volunteer to be an observer. The observer's role is to record the nature of each member's participation in the group, using the controversy observation form.
3. Divide the remaining four members of each group into two pairs. Give one pair a copy of the medical viewpoint briefing sheet and the other pair a copy of the military viewpoint briefing sheet.
4. Introduce the situation. Instruct the pairs to build as good a rationale for their assigned position as they can in fifteen or twenty minutes, using the information on the briefing sheet as a guide.
5. Instruct the pairs to meet together as a group of four. The group is to come to a decision that all four members can agree to. The decision should reflect the best reasoning of the entire group. The group discussion should follow these steps:
   a. Each pair presents its position as forcefully and persuasively as it can while the opposing pair takes notes and clarifies anything the two members do not fully understand.
   b. Have an open discussion in which the members of each pair (1) argue forcefully and persuasively for their position, presenting as many facts as they can to support it, and (2) listen critically to the members of the opposing pair, asking them for the facts that support their point of view. This is a complex issue, and members need to know both sides in order to come to a thoughtful decision.
6. Instruct the pairs to reverse their perspectives by switching sides and arguing for the opposite point of view as forcefully and persuasively as possible. Members should see if they can think of any new facts that the opposing pair did not present in support of its position and should elaborate on that position.
7. Instruct the groups to come to a joint decision by:
   a. Summarizing the best arguments for both points of view.
   b. Detailing the facts they know about World War II and the African campaign.
   c. Achieving consensus among the members.
   d. Organizing the rationale supporting the decision that they will present to the rest of the class. They should be ready to defend the validity of their decision to groups who may have come to the opposite decision.
8. Instruct participants to complete the postdecision questionnaire. Then have the observers determine the group mean for each question.
9. Summarize the decision of each group in front of the entire class. Then summarize the results of the postdecision questionnaire, using the summary table.
10. Instruct each group to discuss their experience, using
    a. The decision and questionnaire results.
    b. The information collected by the observers.
    c. The impressions of the group members.
    d. The constructive controversy checklist.

The following questions may help the groups discuss how they managed the controversy:

    a. How did the group manage disagreements among its members? (Use the checklist for constructive controversy as a guide.)

    b. From its experience, what conclusions can the group reach about the constructive handling of controversies?

    c. Did the opinions of the group members change as a result of the group's discussion? Did members gain insight into the other point of view through the perspective reversal procedure? Did members learn anything new about World War II?

    d. What members learn about themselves and other group members? How did each member react to the controversy?

11. Have each group share its conclusions about the constructive management of controversy with the rest of the class.

WHO SHOULD GET THE PENICILLIN EXERCISE SITUATION

In 1943, penicillin, which is used for the prevention of infection, was in short supply among the U.S. armed forces in North Africa. Decisions had to be made on whether to use this meager supply for the thousands of hospitalized victims of venereal disease or for the thousands of victims of battle wounds at the front. If you were a member of a team of medical and military personnel, for whom would you use the penicillin?

    _____ victims of venereal disease

    _____ victims of battle wounds

Share your position and rationale with your group. Stick to your guns unless logically persuaded otherwise. At the same time, help your group achieve consensus on this issue.

BRIEFING SHEET: THE MEDICAL VIEWPOINT— WHO SHOULD GET THE PENICILLIN EXERCISE

Your position is to give the penicillin to the battle-wounded. Whether or not you agree with this position, argue for it as strongly and honestly as you can, using arguments that make sense and are rational. Be creative and invent new supporting arguments. Seek out information; ask members of other groups who may know the answers to your questions. Remember to learn the rationale for both your position and the military position. Challenge the military position; think of loopholes in its logic; demand facts and information that back up its arguments.

1. Our responsibility is to treat the wounded and save as many lives as possible. Without the penicillin many of the wounded will die needlessly. Minor wounds will get infected and become major, life-threatening wounds.

2. Our strategies must be based on the premise that human life is sacred. If one person dies needlessly, we have failed in our responsibility. The soldiers who have sacrificed so much to help us win the war must be treated with all the care, concern, and resources we can muster. Our soldiers must be able to fight harder than the German soldiers.

3. Troop morale is vital. Nothing raises troop morale as much as the men's knowledge that if they are wounded they will receive top-notch medical treatment.

4. Morale at home is vital. People must make sacrifices to produce the goods and materials we need to win the war. Nothing raises morale at home more than knowing that husbands, sons, and brothers are receiving the most effective medical care that is humanly possible. It would be devastating for word to reach the United States that we were needlessly letting soldiers die for lack of medical care.

5. Even though we are at war, we must not lose our humanity. It will do no good to defeat Germany if we become Nazis in the process.
6. At this point the war is going badly in North Africa. Rommel and the German army are cutting through our lines like butter. We are on the verge of being pushed out of Africa, in which case we will lose the war. Rommel must be stopped.
7. Fresh troops and supplies are unavailable. The German submarines control the Atlantic, and we cannot get troop ships or supply ships into African ports. We have to make do with what we have.
8. Penicillin is a wonder drug that will save countless lives if it is used to treat the wounded.

BRIEFING SHEET: THE MILITARY VIEWPOINT—WHO SHOULD GET THE PENICILLIN EXERCISE

Your position is to give the penicillin to the VD patients. Whether or not you agree with this position, argue for it as strongly and honestly as you can, using arguments that make sense and are rational. Be creative and invent new supporting arguments. Seek out information that supports your position. If you do not have needed information, ask members of other groups who may. Remember to learn the rationale for both your position and the medical position. Challenge the medical position; think of loopholes in its logic; demand facts and information that back up its arguments.

1. Our responsibility is to win the war for our country at all costs. If we lose Africa, we will lose Europe to Hitler, and eventually we will be fighting in the United States.
2. Our strategies to win must be based on the premise of the greatest good for the greatest number. We may have to sacrifice soldiers in order to win the war, save our democracy, and free Europe.
3. Troop morale is vital. Our soldiers must be able to fight harder than the German soldiers. Nothing raises troop morale like seeing fresh troops arrive at the front.
4. Morale at home is vital. People must make sacrifices to produce the goods and materials we need to fight the war. Nothing raises morale at home like hearing of battles won and progress being made in winning the war. Victories give our people at home more dedication.
5. At this point, the war is going badly in North Africa. Rommel and the German army are cutting through our lines like butter. We are on the verge of being pushed out of Africa, in which case we will lose the war. Rommel must be stopped at all costs!
6. Penicillin is a wonder drug that will send VD into remission, and within twenty-four hours the VD patients will be free from pain and able to function effectively on the battlefield.

8.5 *Fallout Shelter*

The purpose of this exercise is to provide a decision-making situation in which controversy will occur. The procedure for the exercise is as follows:

1. Form groups of six. One member should volunteer to be an observer. The observer should use the controversy observation form on page 345.
2. Each group member completes the fallout shelter ranking task.
3. The group decides by consensus on the best ranking possible for the fallout shelter items. There should be one ranking for the group; every member should agree with the ranking and be able to explain the rationale behind the ranking of each item.

4. Members complete the postdecision questionnaire. Compute the group means for each question and place them in the summary table.
5. Score the accuracy of the group's ranking by comparing it with the experts' ranking on pages 591–592 in the Appendix. Find the absolute difference between the group's ranking and the experts' ranking for each item and add them together. The lower the score, the more accurate the group's ranking.
6. Using the observer's information, the postdecision questionnaire results, the members' impressions, and the accuracy score for the ranking, discuss the way in which controversy was managed in the group. The constructive controversy checklist and the discussion questions given on pages 344–345 may be helpful. The group should write down its conclusions about the constructive management of controversy.
7. Groups should share their conclusions with the entire class.

FALLOUT SHELTER EXERCISE: RANKING TASK

The possibility of a nuclear war has been announced and the alert signal has been sounded. You and the members of your group have access to a small basement fallout shelter. When the attack warning signal is announced, you must immediately go to the shelter. In the meantime, you must decide what to take with you to help you survive during and after the attack. You are outside the immediate blast areas. The greatest danger facing you is from radioactive fallout. In order to help your decision making, rank the following items in order of their importance to your survival in the shelter (answers on pages 591–592 of Appendix).

____ one large and one small garbage can with lids	____ vaporizing liquid fire extinguisher
____ broom	____ flashlight and batteries
____ containers of water	____ battery-powered radio
____ blankets	____ soap and towels
____ canned heat stove	____ first-aid kit with iodine and medicines
____ matches and candles	____ cooking and eating utensils
____ canned and dried foods	____ Geiger counter
____ liquid chlorine bleach	

OUTCOMES OF CONTROVERSY

*Have you learned lessons only of those who admired you, and were
tender with you, and stood aside for you?
Have you not learned great lessons from those who brace themselves
against you, and disputed the passage with you?*

Walt Whitman

When controversy is suppressed and concurrence-seeking is emphasized, several defects in making decisions will appear. When NASA, for example, decided to launch the space shuttle *Challenger*, engineers at the Morton Thiokol Company (which makes the shuttle's rocket boosters) and at Rockwell International (which manufactures the orbiter) opposed the launch because of dangers posed by the subfreezing temperatures.

The Thiokol engineers feared that the cold would make the rubber seals at the joints between the rocket's four main segments too brittle to contain the rocket's superhot gases. Several months before the doomed mission, the company's top expert had warned in a memo that whether the seal would hold was a "jump ball," and that if it failed, "the result would be a catastrophe of the highest order" (Magnuson, 1986). In a group discussion the night before the launch, the engineers argued for a delay with their uncertain managers and the NASA officials who wanted to launch on schedule. Because the engineers could not prove there was danger, they were silenced (illusion of invulnerability). Conformity pressures were brought to bear on the engineers, such as when one of the NASA officials complained, "My God, Thiokol, when do you want me to launch, next April?" The NASA managers formed a coalition with the Thiokol managers to shut the engineers out of the decision making (illusion of unanimity). Finally, to provide a mindguard, the top NASA executive who made the final decision to launch was never told about the engineers' concerns or about the reservations of the Rockwell officials. Protected from the disagreeable information, he confidently gave the go-ahead to launch the *Challenger* on its tragic flight.

How could such faulty decision making take place? The answer is, because of the lack of controversy. NASA officials never gave the alternative of delaying the launch a fair and complete hearing. Disagreement was stifled rather than utilized. Often in group discussions, if a margin of support for one alternative develops, then better ideas have little chance of being accepted. In mob lynchings, for example, misgivings, if not immediately expressed, were drowned out. Drawing on biased information is evident in some group polarization experiments; often the arguments that surfaced in group discussion tended to be more one-sided than those volunteered by individuals privately. Group discussions can exacerbate the tendency toward overconfidence, thereby heightening an illusion of judgmental accuracy (Dunning & Ross, 1988), and minority opinions can be suppressed. When initially only one member of a six-member group knew the correct answer, in almost 75% of the cases that member failed to convince the others because he or she was not given a fair and complete hearing (Laughlin, 1980; Laughlin & Adamopoulos, 1980). Group decision making often goes wrong because alternatives are not considered carefully, minority opinions are silenced, and disagreement among members' conclusions is suppressed.

Without controversy, group decisions may always be less than optimal. Over the past twenty years there have been more than twenty-three experimental studies on controversy. The nature and results of those studies are summarized in Johnson and Johnson (1989, 1995c). These studies form a solid body of evidence that controversy promotes high productivity and quality of decision making, creativity, task involvement, positive interpersonal relationships, and psychological health.

Productivity and Quality of Decision Making

Compared with concurrence-seeking, debate, and individualistic efforts, controversy typically produces higher group productivity, individual achievement, and quality of decision making (Johnson & Johnson, 1979, 1989, 1995c). In a meta-analysis of the available research, Johnson and Johnson (1989) found that controversy produced greater productivity and higher achievement than did concurrence-seeking (effect size = 0.42), debate (effect size = 0.77), or individualistic efforts (effect size = 0.65) (Table 8.3). Controversy also tends to result in greater ability to transfer learning to new situations and more frequent use of higher-level reasoning strategies. Finally, group members tend to exert more physical and psychological energy in working on the decision when controversy occurs.

Even a minority in a group can have influence over group decision making when they are consistent in their advocacy of their views (Wood, Lundgren, Quelletter, Busceme, & Blackstone, 1994). An interesting real-world example is a study conducted by Dean Tjosvold (1990b) involving airline flight crews. Most air accidents are due to pilot error resulting from the failure of crew members to use their information expeditiously to cope with safety hazards. Tjosvold interviewed twenty-seven pilots, first officers, second officers, and eight flight attendants on how specific incidents that threatened the safety of the airplane were managed. Sixty incidents were provided. Respondents were asked to describe in detail a recent significant air safety problem they managed effectively and one they managed ineffectively. Hierarchical regression analyses indicated that the open discussion of conflicting views and ideas within a cooperative context was a powerful antecedent to using safe procedures expeditiously.

An interesting question concerning controversy and problem solving is what happens when erroneous information is presented by participants. Simply, can the advocacy of two conflicting but wrong solutions to a problem create a correct one? The value of the controversy process lies not so much in the correctness of an opposing position as in the attention and thought processes it induces. More cognitive processing may take place when individuals are exposed to more than one point of view, even if the point of view is incorrect. A number of studies with both adults and children found significant gains in performance when erroneous information was presented by one or both sides in a controversy. Ames and Murray (1982) compared the impact of controversy, modeling, and nonsocial presentation of information on the way nonconserving, cognitively immature children performed on conservation tasks. The children were presented with erroneous information that conflicted with their initial position. Ames and Murray found modest but significant gains in conservation performance. Three children with initial scores of 0 out of 18 scored between 16 and 18 out of 18 on the posttest, and eleven children with initial scores of 0 out of 18 scored between 5 and 15. The authors concluded that conflict *qua* conflict is not only cognitively motivating, but that the resolution of the conflict is likely to be in the direction of correct performance. In this limited way, two wrongs come to make a right.

Table 8.3 Mean Effect Sizes of Controversy on Productivity

Condition	Mean	*sd*	*n*
Controversy/concurrence-seeking	0.42	0.57	49
Controversy/debate	0.77	0.41	20
Controversy/individualistic	0.65	0.32	20
Debate/individualistic	0.36	1.03	3

Creativity

By blending the breath of the sun and the shade, true harmony
comes into the world.

Tao Te Ching

Disagreements and arguments among individuals with diverse information and ideas are important in gaining creative insight. Compared with concurrence-seeking, debate, and individualistic efforts, controversy allows group members to generate more potential solutions, have more creative insights into the problem, view the problem from different perspectives, and reformulate the problem in ways that allow new orientations to emerge (Glidewell, 1953; Hoffman, Harburg, & Maier, 1962a; Johnson & Johnson, 1989, 1995c; Maier & Hoffman, 1964; C. Rogers, 1970a). Controversy increases the number of ideas, quality of ideas, creation of original ideas, use of a wider range of ideas, originality, use of more varied strategies, and the number of creative, imaginative, novel solutions (Bahn, 1964; Bolen & Torrance, 1976; Dunnette, Campbell, & Jaastad, 1963; Triandis, Bass, Ewen, & Mieksele, 1963). Studies further demonstrate that controversy encourages group members to dig into a problem, raise issues, and settle them in ways that show the benefits of a wide range of ideas being used, as well as resulting in a high degree of emotional involvement in and commitment to solving the problems.

Task Involvement

Task involvement refers to the quality and quantity of the physical and psychological energy that individuals invest in their efforts to achieve. Task involvement is reflected in the attitudes participants have toward the task and toward the controversy experience. Individuals who engaged in controversies tended to like the task and procedure better and generally had more positive attitudes toward the experience than did individuals who engaged in concurrence-seeking discussions, individualistic efforts, or debate. Compared with concurrence-seeking, debate, and individualistic efforts, controversy tends to result in greater task involvement, reflected in greater emotional commitment to solving the problem, a stronger feeling of stimulation, and greater enjoyment of the process (Johnson & Johnson, 1989, 1995c). As Samuel Johnson once stated, "I dogmatize and am contradicted, and in this conflict of opinions and sentiments I find delight." Controversy not only creates high involvement in and commitment to solving a problem, it also tends to be enjoyable and exciting.

Interpersonal Attraction Among Participants

It is often assumed that conflict within a group will make it difficult to establish good interpersonal relationships and will promote negative attitudes toward groupmates. It is also assumed that arguing leads to rejection, divisiveness, and hostility among members. Within controversy and debate there are elements of disagreement, argumentation, and rebuttal that could result in individuals disliking each other and could create difficulties in establishing good relationships. The research indicates otherwise (Johnson & Johnson, 1979, 1989, 1995c). Controversy has been found to promote greater liking and social support among group members than do debate, concurrence-seeking, and individualistic efforts. Spirited disagreement and intellectual challenge can bind people in deeper and more meaningful relationships.

Psychological Health and Social Competence

Many components of psychological health are strengthened by participating in academic controversies (Johnson & Johnson, 1989, 1995c). Compared with concurrence-seeking, debate, and individualistic efforts, controversy tends to result in higher task-oriented self-esteem and greater perspective-taking accuracy. Being able to manage disagreements and conflicts constructively enables individuals to cope with the stresses involved in interacting with a variety of other people.

PROCESS OF CONTROVERSY

Difference of opinion leads to inquiry, and inquiry to truth.

Thomas Jefferson

The process by which controversy sparks high-quality decision making, increased productivity, better relationships, increased psychological health, and other positive outcomes for the group is outlined in Figure 8.2. During a constructive controversy, decision makers proceed to do the following (Johnson & Johnson, 1989, 1995c):

1. When individuals are presented with a problem or decision, they form an initial conclusion based on categorizing and organizing incomplete information, their limited experiences, and their specific perspective.
2. When individuals present their conclusion and its rationale to others, they engage in cognitive rehearsal, deepen their understanding of their position, and discover higher-level reasoning strategies.
3. Individuals are confronted by other people with different conclusions based on other people's information, experiences, and perspectives.
4. Individuals become uncertain about the correctness of their views. A state of conceptual conflict or disequilibrium is aroused.
5. Uncertainty, conceptual conflict, and disequilibrium motivate an active search for more information, new experiences, and a more adequate cognitive perspective and reasoning process in hopes of resolving the uncertainty. Berlyne (1965) calls this active search *epistemic curiosity*. Divergent attention and thought are stimulated.
6. As persons adapt their cognitive perspective and reasoning through understanding and accommodating the perspective and reasoning of others, a new, reconceptualized, and reorganized conclusion is derived. Novel solutions and decisions are detected that are, on balance, qualitatively better.

A discussion of each of these premises follows. These premises are illustrated in Figure 8.3.

Step 1: Organizing Information and Deriving Conclusions

In order to make high-quality decisions, individuals have to think of the proper alternatives, do a good job of evaluating them, and choose the most promising one. When individuals are presented with a problem or decision, they form an initial conclusion based on categorizing and organizing incomplete information, their limited experiences,

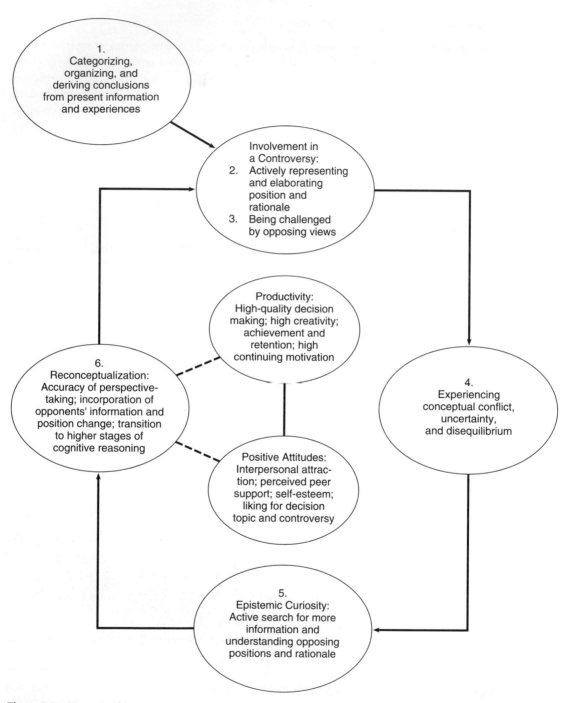

Figure 8.2   Process of controversy.
Source: D. W. Johnson and R. Johnson, *Creative conflict* (Edina, MN: Interaction Book Company, 1987).

Figure 8.3 Illustration of controversy.

and their specific perspective. Individuals organize their current knowledge and experiences, from their own perspective, into a conceptual framework from which they can derive a conclusion (through the use of inductive and deductive logic). The conceptual frameworks formed, however, often lead to inaccurate conclusions because of the limitations of perspective, one's expectations and mental set at the time, a tendency to give one's dominant response to the situation, or fixation on the first seemingly satisfactory solution generated.

Step 2: Presenting and Advocating Positions

Edward R. Murrow, the journalist, said, "To be persuasive we must be believable; to be believable we must be credible; to be credible, we must be truthful." Most students get few opportunities to present and advocate a position. Within a controversy, students present and advocate positions to others who, in turn, are advocating opposing positions. *Advocacy* may be defined as presenting a position and providing reasons why others should adopt it. Decisions and conclusions are then reached through a process of argument and counterargument aimed at persuading others to adopt, modify, or drop positions. Advocating a position and defending it against refutation require engaging in considerable cognitive rehearsal and elaboration, increased understanding of the position, and the discovery of higher-level reasoning processes. Disagreements within a group have been found to provide a greater amount of information and a greater variety of facts, as well as changes in the salience of known information.

Step 3: Being Challenged by Opposing Views

"Has anything escaped me?" I asked with some self-importance.
"I trust there is nothing of consequence that I have overlooked?"
"I'm afraid, my dear Watson, that most of your conclusions were erroneous.
When I said that you stimulated me I meant, to be frank, that in noting
your fallacies I was occasionally guided towards the truth."

Sir Arthur Conan Doyle, *The Hound of the Baskervilles*

In controversy, individuals' conclusions are challenged by the advocates of opposing positions. Members critically analyze each other's positions in attempts to discern weaknesses and strengths. They attempt to refute opposing positions while rebutting the attacks on their position. At the same time, they are aware that they need to learn the information being presented and understand the perspective of the other group members.

The direct evidence indicates that individuals engaged in controversy are motivated to know the others' positions and to develop an understanding and appreciation of them (Johnson & Johnson, 1989, 1995c). Furthermore, hearing opposing views being advocated stimulates new cognitive analysis and frees individuals to create alternative and original conclusions. When contrary information is not clearly relevant to completing the task at hand, it may be ignored, discounted, or perceived in biased ways in favor of supporting evidence. When individuals realize, however, that they are accountable for knowing the contrary information some time in the near future, they tend to learn it. Even being confronted with an erroneous point of view can result in more divergent thinking and generate novel and more cognitively advanced solutions.

Step 4: Conceptual Conflict and Uncertainty

Hearing other alternatives being advocated, having one's position criticized and refuted, and being challenged by information that is incompatible with and does not fit with one's conclusions lead to conceptual conflict and uncertainty. **Conceptual conflict** exists when incompatible ideas exist simultaneously in a person's mind or when information being received does not seem to fit with what one already knows. The greater the disagreement among group members, the more frequently disagreement occurs, the greater the number of people disagreeing with a person's position, the more competitive the context of the controversy, and the more affronted the person feels, the greater the conceptual conflict and uncertainty the person experiences (Johnson & Johnson, 1989, 1995c).

Step 5: Epistemic Curiosity and Perspective-Taking

Macbeth said, "Stay, you imperfect speakers, tell me more." When faced with intellectual opposition within a cooperative context, students will ask each other for more information. Conceptual conflict motivates an active search for more information (called *epistemic curiosity*) in hopes of resolving the uncertainty. **Epistemic curiosity** includes actively (a) searching for more information, (b) seeking to understand opposing positions and rationales, and (c) attempting to view the situation from opposing perspectives.

Step 6: Reconceptualization, Synthesis, Integration

When overt controversy is structured within a problem-solving, decision-making, or learning group by identifying alternatives and assigning members to advocate the best case for each alternative, the purpose is not to choose the best alternative. The purpose is to create a synthesis of the best reasoning and conclusions from among the various alternatives. **Synthesizing** occurs when individuals integrate a number of different ideas and facts into a single position. It is the intellectual bringing together of ideas and facts and engaging in inductive reasoning by restating a large amount of information into a conclusion or summary. Synthesizing is a creative process involving seeing new patterns within a body of evidence, viewing the issue from a variety of perspectives, and generating several ways of integrating the evidence. This requires **probabilistic** (i.e., knowledge is available only in degrees of certainty) rather than **dualistic** (i.e., there is only right and wrong, and authority should not be questioned) or **relativistic thinking** (i.e., authorities are seen as sometimes right, but right and wrong depend on your perspective). The dual purposes of synthesis are to arrive at the best possible decision or solution and to find a position that all group members can agree on and commit themselves to. There is evidence that controversy leads to accuracy of perspective-taking; incorporation of others' information and reasoning into one's own position; attitude and position change; and a transition to higher stages of cognitive reasoning, all of which increase the quality of individuals' reconceptualization, synthesis, and integration.

CONDITIONS DETERMINING THE CONSTRUCTIVENESS OF CONTROVERSY

He that wrestles with us strengthens our nerves, and sharpens our skill.
Our antagonist is our helper.

Edmund Burke, *Reflections on the French Revolution*

Although controversies can operate in a beneficial way, they will not do so under all conditions. As with all types of conflict, the potential for either constructive or destructive outcomes is present in a controversy. Whether there are positive or negative consequences depends on the conditions under which controversy occurs and the way in which it is managed. The key elements include the context in which the controversy takes place, the heterogeneity of participants, the distribution of information among group members, the level of group members' social skills, and group members' ability to engage in rational argument (Johnson & Johnson, 1979, 1989, 1995c).

Cooperative Goal Structure

Deutsch (1973) emphasizes that the context in which conflicts occur has important effects on whether the conflict turns out to be constructive or destructive. There are two possible contexts for controversy: cooperative and competitive. A cooperative context facilitates constructive controversy, whereas a competitive context promotes destructive controversy in several ways (Johnson & Johnson, 1987, 1989):

1. In order for controversy to be constructive, information must be accurately communicated. Communication of information is far more complete, accurate, encouraged, and utilized in a cooperative context than in a competitive context.
2. Constructive controversy requires a supportive climate in which group members feel safe enough to challenge each other's ideas. Cooperation provides a far more supportive climate than competition.
3. In order for controversy to be constructive, it must be valued. Cooperative experiences promote a stronger belief that controversy is valid and valuable.
4. Constructive controversy requires dealing both with feelings and with ideas and information. There is evidence that cooperativeness is positively related and competitiveness is negatively related to the ability to understand what others are feeling and why they are feeling that way.
5. How controversies are defined has a great impact on how constructively they are managed. In a cooperative context, controversies are defined as problems to be solved, whereas in a competitive situation they are defined as win–lose situations.
6. Constructive controversy requires members to recognize both the similarities and differences between their positions. Controversy in a cooperative context identifies more of the similarities between members' positions than does controversy in a competitive context.

In a series of studies, Dean Tjosvold and his associates studied the impact of cooperative and competitive contexts (Tjosvold, 1995a). They found that controversy in a competitive context promoted closed-minded uninterest and rejection of the opponent's ideas and information. Competitors tended to refuse to incorporate any of the opponents' viewpoints into their own position. The increased understanding that resulted from controversy tended to be ignored in favor of a defensive adherence to the competitors' own positions. When competitors were unsure of the correctness of their position, they chose to be exposed to disconfirming information when it could easily be refuted, presumably because such refutation could affirm their own beliefs. Avoidance of controversy results in little interest in or actual knowledge of opposing ideas and information and in making a decision that reflects one's own views only. In a cooperative context, controversy induces feelings of comfort, pleasure, and helpfulness in discussing opposing positions, open-minded listening to the opposing positions, motivation to hear more about the opponent's arguments, more accurate understanding of the opponent's position, and integration whereby both one's own and one's opponent's conclusions and reasoning are synthesized into a final position.

Skilled Disagreement

Controversy requires a complex set of procedures and skills. For controversies to be managed constructively, people need collaborative and conflict-management skills (Johnson, 1991, 2000; Johnson & Johnson, 1989, 1995c). One of the most important skills is the ability to disagree with each other's ideas while confirming each other's personal competence. Disagreeing with others, and at the same time implying that others are incompetent, tends to increase their commitment to their own ideas and their rejection of the other person's information and reasoning. Disagreeing with others while simultaneously confirming their personal competence, however, results in being better liked and in opponents being less critical of others' ideas, more interested in learning about others' ideas, and more willing to incorporate others' information and reasoning into their own analysis of the problem.

Another important skill for exchanging information and opinions within a controversy is **perspective-taking.** More information, both personal and impersonal, is disclosed when one is interacting with a person who is engaging in perspective-taking behaviors, such as paraphrasing, which communicates a desire to understand accurately. Perspective-taking ability increases one's capacity to phrase messages so that they are easily understood by others and to comprehend accurately the messages of others. Engaging in perspective-taking in controversies results in increased understanding and retention of the opponent's information and perspective (Johnson, 1971). Perspective-taking facilitates creative, high-quality problem solving (Falk and Johnson, 1977; Johnson, 1977). Finally, perspective-taking promotes more positive perceptions of the information-exchange process, of fellow group members, and of the group's work. To obtain a creative synthesis of all positions in a controversy, group members must obtain a clear understanding of all sides of the issue and an accurate assessment of the validity and relative merits of each position. In order to do this fully, they must accurately perceive the frame of reference from which the other person is viewing and analyzing the situation and problem.

A third set of skills involves the cycle of **differentiation of positions** and their **integration.** Group members should ensure that there are several cycles of differentiation (bringing out differences in positions) and integration (combining several positions into one new, creative position). Differentiation must precede integration. Differentiation involves seeking out and clarifying differences among members' ideas, information, conclusions, theories, and opinions. It involves highlighting the differences among members' reasoning and seeking to understand fully what the different positions and perspectives are. All different points of view must be presented and explored thoroughly before new, creative solutions are sought. Integration involves combining the information, reasoning, theories, and conclusions of the various group members so that all members are satisfied. After it has differentiated positions, the group needs to seek a new, creative position that synthesizes the thinking of all the members. The group should never try to integrate members' positions before adequate differentiation has taken place. The potential for integration is never greater than the adequacy of the differentiation already achieved. Most controversies go through a series of differentiations and integrations before group members reach a final decision.

Rational Argument

During a controversy, group members have to follow the canons of rational argumentation. Members present their position and its rationale while asking other members for proof that their analyses and conclusions are valid. Rational argumentation includes generating ideas, collecting and organizing relevant information, using inductive and deductive logic, and reaching tentative conclusions based on current understanding. Rational argumentation requires that participants keep an open mind, changing their conclusions and positions when others are persuasive and convincing in their presentation of a rationale, proof, and logical reasoning. The abilities to gather, organize, and present information, to challenge and disagree, and to engage in reason logically are essential for the constructive management of controversies.

STRUCTURING ACADEMIC CONTROVERSIES

In conducting a controversy within a group there are a series of steps to follow.

1. *Propose several courses of action that will solve the problem.* When the group is making a decision, identify several alternative courses of action for the group to follow.

2. *Form advocacy teams.* To ensure that each course of action receives a fair and complete hearing, assign two group members to be an advocacy team to present the best case possible for the assigned position. **Positive interdependence** is structured by highlighting the cooperative goal of making the best decision possible (goal interdependence) and noting that a high-quality decision cannot be made without considering the information that is being organized by the other advocacy teams (resource interdependence). **Individual accountability** is structured by ensuring that each member participates in preparing and presenting the assigned position. Any information discovered that supports the other alternatives is given to the appropriate advocacy pair.

3. *Engage in the controversy procedure.*

   a. Each advocacy team researches its position and prepares a persuasive presentation to convince other group members of its validity. The assigned alternative course of action is thoroughly researched through consultants, relevant articles and books, and experts. Persuasive arguments are organized into a presentation.

   b. Each advocacy team presents without interruption the best case possible for its assigned alternative course of action to the entire group. Other advocacy teams listen carefully, taking notes and striving to learn the information provided.

   c. There is an open discussion characterized by advocacy, refutation, and rebuttal. The advocacy teams give opposing positions a trial by fire, seeking to refute them by challenging the validity of their information and logic. They defend their own position while attempting to persuade other group members of its validity. For higher-level reasoning and critical thinking to occur, it is necessary to probe and push each other's conclusions. Members ask for data to support each other's statements, clarify rationales, and show why their position is the most rational one. Group members refute the claims being made by the opposing teams and rebut the attacks on their own position. They take careful notes on and thoroughly learn the opposing positions. Members follow the rules for constructive controversy. Sometimes a time-out period is needed so that pairs can caucus and prepare new arguments. Members should encourage spirited arguing and playing devil's advocate. Members are instructed to "Argue forcefully and persuasively for your position, presenting as many facts as you can to support your point of view. Listen critically to the opposing pair's position, asking them for the facts that support their viewpoint, and then present counterarguments. Remember, this is a complex issue, and you need to know all sides to make a good decision."

d. Advocacy teams reverse perspectives and positions by presenting one of the opposing positions as sincerely and forcefully as they can. Members may be told, "Working as a pair, present an opposing pair's position as if it were your own. Be as sincere and forceful as you can. Add any new facts you know. Elaborate their position by relating it to other information you have previously learned."

e. All members drop their advocacy and reach a decision by consensus. They may wish to summarize their decision in a group report that details the course of action they have adopted and its supporting rationale. Often the chosen alternative represents a new perspective or synthesis that is more rational than the two assigned. All group members sign the report, indicating that they agree with the decision and will do their share of the work in implementing it. Members may be instructed to "Summarize and synthesize the best arguments for *all* points of view. Reach a decision by consensus. Change your mind only when the facts and the rationale clearly indicate that you should do so. Write a report with the supporting evidence and rationale for your synthesis that your group has agreed on. When you are certain that the report is as good as you can make it, sign it."

f. Group members analyze how well the group functioned and how their performance may be improved during the next controversy.

4. *Implement the decision.* Once the decision is made, all members commit themselves to implement it, regardless of whether they initially favored or opposed the alternative adopted.

GUIDELINES FOR CONSTRUCTIVE CONTROVERSY

There are no rules for making controversies productive, but the following guidelines can help group members argue more constructively and transform disagreement among themselves into a positive experience.

1. *Emphasize your common need to make the best possible decision.* Statements such as "We are all in this together" and "Let's make the best possible decision" should dominate the group, not "I am right and you are wrong." The context in which the controversy takes place should be cooperative, not competitive. The issue is not to establish who has the best answer but to make the best group decision possible by exploring different perspectives and integrating different information.

2. *Look for opportunities to engage in controversy.* Highlight contrasting viewpoints, point out disagreements, and promote challenging tasks. Include diverse people in the group. People who differ in background, expertise, opinions, outlook, and organizational position are likely to disagree.

3. *Prepare the best case possible for your position.* Develop your thesis statement and research the best rationale possible to support it. It is up to you to ensure that your position is seen in its best light. Consult relevant articles, books, and experts to compile information and experiences to support your position. List relevant facts, information, and theories.

4. *Advocate your position forcefully but with an open mind.* Speak up. Make sure everyone listens. It is up to you to ensure that your position gets a fair and complete hearing.

5. *Encourage others to advocate their positions forcefully.* Express a warm, intense interest in all contributions. Every member should share his or her position and ideas in order to get comments and reactions from other members that will help improve the quality of the group's work. Value, respect, and take seriously everyone's contributions. Help all members, regardless of their status, to speak out confidently.

6. *Understand, then challenge, opposing ideas and positions.* Ask questions. Ask for the supporting facts, information, and theories in order to understand the opposing positions more thoroughly. Understanding the statements of another group member is not enough; the frame of reference from which the member is speaking must also be clearly understood. View the issue under discussion from a variety of perspectives. Then point out fallacies in information and logic. Try to refute other members' thesis statements and claims. Group members should be critical of ideas, not of persons. Arguments should concern ideas, not personality traits. Group members should be highly

critical of each other's ideas while at the same time affirming each other's competence and communicating respect and appreciation for the member as a person. Any inference of incompetence or weakness and any hint of rejecting another member should be avoided. Combine personal regard with intellectual challenge. Say, "We are friends," "I am interested in what you have to say." Then say, "I do not agree with you on that point," "I have come to a different conclusion," "I appreciate you, I am interested in your ideas, but I disagree with your current position." Do not say, "You are stupid and ignorant and I do not like you!" Insults or imputations that challenge another member's integrity, intelligence, and motives are to be avoided.

7. *Do not take personally other members' disagreements and rejection of*

your ideas. Other members' disagreements with your ideas and conclusions should be taken as an interesting situation from which something can be learned, not as a personal attack. Do not confuse rejection of your ideas and opinions with personal rejection. Separate the validity of your thinking from your competence and worth as a person.

8. *Ensure that there are several cycles of differentiation and integration.* Differentiation involves bringing out differences in positions, and integration involves combining several positions into one new, creative position. Differentiation must come before integration is attempted.

9. *Put yourself in the other member's shoes.* Controversy is an opportunity to improve the quality of your own reasoning by seeing the issue from a variety of perspectives. Ensure that you understand the perspectives underlying positions as well as their content.

10. *Follow the canons of rational argument.* Generate ideas, collect and organize relevant information, use deductive and inductive logical procedures, and reach tentative conclusions. Avoid premature evaluations.

11. *Synthesize the best ideas from all viewpoints and perspectives.* The end result is a synthesis that is better than any single position advocated. Think creatively until it is discovered.

BEING A CITIZEN IN A DEMOCRACY

The word *democracy* comes from the Greek word *demokratia,* which is a combination of *demos* (people) and *kratos* (rule). Thomas Jefferson believed that rule by the people required free and open discussion in which knowledge is the basis of influence within society, not the person's social rank. American democracy was thus founded on the premise that truth will result from free and open discussion in which opposing points of view are advocated and vigorously argued. Before a decision is made, every citizen is given the opportunity to advocate for his or her ideas. A vote is then taken, and the majority rules. The minority is then expected to go along willingly with the majority because they know that (a) they received a fair and complete hearing and (b) they will have another chance in two or four years. To be citizens in our democracy, individuals need to master the process of advocating one's views, challenging opposing positions, making a decision, and committing oneself to implement the decision made (regardless of whether one initially favored or opposed it).

Summary

Decision making typically involves considering possible alternatives and choosing one. By definition, all decision-making situations involve some conflict as to which of several alternatives should be chosen. Within decision-making groups, that conflict takes the form of controversy. Controversy exists when one individual's ideas, information, conclusions, theories, and opinions are incompatible with those of another, and the two seek to reach an agreement. Such intellectual conflict among individuals may be avoided and suppressed or it may be structured and encouraged. Simply by emphasizing concurrence-seeking, intellectual conflict among group members may be avoided. If it does occur, it may be suppressed by stating that it is against the rules.

Most intellectual conflicts are avoided and suppressed. Yet there is evidence that controversy can be a powerful tool. Conflicts among ideas, conclusions, theories, information, perspectives, opinions, and preferences are inevitable. Such conflicts are (a) an inherent aspect of decision making, problem solving, reasoned judgment, and critical thinking and (b) inevitable. If individuals get intellectually and emotionally involved in cooperative efforts, controversies will occur no matter what participants do. They are critical events that may bring (a) increased learning, creative insight, high-quality problem solving and decision making; (b) closer and more positive relationships; and (c) greater social competence and psychological health. Or they may bring closed minds and poorly conceived decisions, lasting resentment and smoldering hostility, psychological scars, rigidly ineffectual behavior, and a refusal to change or learn.

Controversy begins when your group, faced with a decision that has to be made, assigns the major alternatives to advocacy subgroups and has each subgroup (a) develop its alternative in depth and (b) plan how to present the best case possible for its alternative to the rest of the group. *First,* group members prepare a position to present to the rest of the group based on their current information, experiences, and perspective. *Second,* they present and advocate your position to the rest of the group, who, in turn, are advocating opposing positions. High-quality decisions and conclusions are reached through a process of argument and counterargument aimed at persuading others to adopt, modify, or drop positions. *Third,* group members are confronted by other group members with different positions based on their information, experiences, and perspectives. Members attempt to refute opposing positions while rebutting the attacks on their own position. *Fourth,* faced with these opposing positions, criticisms of your position, and information that is incompatible with and does not fit with their conclusions, they become uncertain as to the correctness of your views. A state of conceptual conflict or disequilibrium is aroused. This results in conceptual conflict, uncertainty, and disequilibrium. *Fifth,* members' uncertainty, conceptual conflict, and disequilibrium motivate an active search for more information, new experiences, and a more adequate cognitive perspective and reasoning in hopes of resolving the uncertainty. Epistemic curiosity, divergent attention, and thought are stimulated. Members search for more information and experiences to support your position, seek to understand the opposition's, and attempt to view the problem from opposing perspectives. This results in a reorganization and reconceptualization of their conclusions.

Finally, members adapt their cognitive perspective and reasoning through understanding and accommodating the perspective and reasoning of others and derive a new, reconceptualized, and reorganized conclusion. Novel solutions and decisions that, on balance, are qualitatively better are detected. The purpose of controversy is not to choose the best of the alternatives. Rather, it is to create a synthesis of the best reasoning and conclusions from all the various alternatives. To do so, members have to keep conclusions tentative, accurately understand opposing perspectives, incorporate new information into their conceptual frameworks, and be willing to change their attitudes and position. This process is repeated until the differences in conclusions among group members have been resolved, a decision is reached, and the controversy has ended.

Controversies tend to be constructive when the situational context is cooperative, there is some heterogeneity among group members, information and expertise are distributed within the group, members have the necessary conflict skills, and the canons of rational argumentation are followed. An essential aspect of controversy is the creativity that is derived from the collision of adverse opinion.

8.6 *The Johnson School*

Form groups of six. Give one set of cards to each group. Each member should take one of the cards. The cards should contain the following statements, one on each card.

1. The strongest coach coached wrestling second.
   Track was a sport coached at the Johnson School.
   Dale offered to recruit cheerleaders for the school.
2. Members of your group have all the information needed to find the answer to the following question (only one answer is correct): *In what sequence did the Johnsons coach the sports taught at their school?* Some of the information your group has is not relevant and will not help your group solve the problem.
3. Frank coached wrestling third.
   The strongest coach had been coaching longer than the other coaches.
   Edye's favorite sport was eating.
4. The strongest coach coached first the sport that David liked the best.
   All coaches coached all the sports.
   Keith preferred telling others what to do rather than doing it himself.
5. Helen had been coaching longer than any of the other coaches.
   David coached basketball third.
   Each coach coached the sport he or she liked best second.
6. Roger preferred to coach golf more than the other sports.
   All coaches preferred or liked one sport above the others.
   All coaches coached at the same time.

Give the following instructions: You have all the information you need to define a problem and solve it. You have twenty to forty minutes. One rule you must follow: Although you may tell your group what is on your card, you may not pass it around for others to read. All communication in the group is to be verbal. I repeat, you may not let others read what is on your card; you may only tell them what it says.

8.7 *Avoiding Controversies*

People often find ingenious methods to keep from having to deal directly with controversies. How do you behave when you want to avoid a dispute? How do the other members of your group behave?

The following exercise is designed to produce feedback about how other group members see your behavior when you want to avoid a controversy. Its objective is for participants to examine their own behavior in controversies and disagreements. Understanding avoidance behavior, or how people avoid responding, can be as helpful as increasing their awareness of constructive behaviors. The procedure for the coordinator is as follows:

1. Introduce the exercise as a chance for each group member to get feedback from other group members on his or her behavior.
2. Tell each group member to place a sheet of paper on the wall with his or her name clearly written at the top.
3. Have group members walk around the room writing down their impressions on the paper of how each of the others behaves when he or she wants to avoid a controversy. You may wish to use the checklist below to trigger ideas.
4. All members should classify themselves according to the checklist below and then read the remarks other group members have written on their sheet.
5. Divide the participants into groups of three and have them discuss the content of the remarks written on their sheets, their own perceptions of their behavior, and the feelings generated by the exercise. Note that although the defenses against directly facing controversy are not helpful to the group and will promote destructive outcomes, they are at times very helpful and have constructive value for the individual. Participants should ask themselves whether there are ways to protect themselves without being harmful to the group.

DEFENSES AGAINST CONTROVERSY

1. *Ostrich:* Deny that the controversy exists; refuse to see the potential or actual disagreement.
2. *Turtle:* Withdraw from the issue and the persons disagreeing with you.
3. *Lemming:* Give in and accept the other person's point of view or ideas.
4. *Weasel:* Rationalize by stating that the issue is not important, that you really don't hold an opposing opinion, that the issue is one on which you have no expertise, and so on.
5. *Gorilla:* Overpower the other members by forcing them to accept your ideas and point of view.
6. *Owl:* Intellectualize about the issue and ideas so that all feelings and emotions are hidden.
7. *Sheep:* Formulate, support, and conform to group norms forbidding the expression of opposition and disagreement in the group.

EXERCISE | **8.8** | *Beliefs About Creativity*

The purpose of this exercise is to provoke a discussion concerning the nature of creativity. The procedure is as follows:

1. Working by yourself, react to the following statements about creativity.
   a. Creativity and intelligence are (1) unrelated, (2) highly related to each other in the sense that creativity promotes cognitive development.
   b. Creativity is a (1) stable trait that some persons are born with and others lack, (2) process of problem solving characterized by an interaction between group members and the challenges of their environment.
   c. Creativity (1) is at the same level across situations—a creative person is creative in every situation—(2) varies a great deal from situation to situation, depending on the problem-solving process being used.
   d. Creativity is something that (1) cannot be taught because it is an inborn trait, (2) can be taught because it is a problem-solving process.

    e. The role of the school is to (1) discover or identify creative students and place them in accelerated programs so that their creativity is utilized, (2) develop creative competencies in all students by providing the needed challenges and teaching them the problem-solving skills necessary for a creative response.

2. Form groups of six and arrive at a group consensus for each question.

3. Compare your group's answers with those of the other groups in the class.

CREATIVITY

One of the most compelling outcomes of decisional and intellectual conflict is creative problem solving. Creative thinking and reasoning, while vitally important to effective groups, is hard to find in the real world and little understood even in the laboratory. **Creativity** is a process of bringing something new into existence, consisting of a sequence of overlapping phases (Johnson, 1979). *First, group members must recognize that a problem exists and it is challenging enough to motivate them to solve it.* For the possibility of creativity to exist, group members need to be aroused to a level of motivation sufficient to sustain problem-solving efforts despite frustrations and dead ends (Deutsch, 1969). This level of motivation, however, cannot be so intense that it overwhelms members or keeps them too close to the problem. The motivation to persist is increased by both controversy and a group tradition supporting the view that with time and effort, constructive solutions can be discovered or invented for seemingly insoluble problems.

Second, group members must gather the necessary knowledge and resources within the group and plan an intense, long-term effort to solve the problem. The more members are immersed in and focused on the problem and the relevant information and circumstances, the greater the likelihood that they will achieve a creative insight.

Third, a cooperative context must be highlighted in order for the necessary level of social support to be achieved within the group. Members must not feel threatened or under too much pressure (Deutsch, 1969; Rokeach, 1960; Stein, 1968). Feeling threatened prompts defensiveness and reduces both tolerance of ambiguity and receptiveness to the new and the unfamiliar. Too much tension leads to stereotyping of thought processes. Feeling threatened and under pressure prevents group members from becoming sufficiently detached from their original viewpoint to be able to see the problem from new perspectives.

Fourth, group members need to seek out different perspectives and different ways of viewing the problem. They then can reformulate it in a way that lets new orientations to a solution emerge. Creative insight usually depends on (a) the availability of diverse information and viewpoints and (b) group members disagreeing and challenging each other's reasoning and perspectives. The more varied the members of a group, the more likely the group will arrive at a creative solution. Both male and female, lower-class and middle-class, white and minority, high-achieving and low-achieving persons should be placed in the same cooperative problem-solving groups to maximize the possibility of finding creative solutions. The members with diverging ideas and perspectives must disagree and challenge each other's reasoning and perspectives. Once diverse ideas and perspectives are available, the exchange of ideas has to be encouraged so that they can be put together into new and varied patterns. Each group member needs the freedom, support, and self-confidence to express him- or herself without being afraid of censure. The resulting conflict among group members will tend to spark new ideas and approaches, broaden the range of available solutions, and produce moments of insight or inspiration by one or more group members. Creative insight is often accompanied by intense emotional experiences of illumination and excitement and leads to the formulation of a tentative solution.

Fifth, group members need to experience an incubation period during which they feel frustration, tension, and discomfort due to their failure to produce an adequate solution to the problem and temporarily withdraw from the issue. In order for group members to derive creative answers to problems they are working on, they must be allowed time to reflect. Instant answers should not be demanded. Creative thinking "is commonly typified by periods of intense application and periods of inactivity" (Treffinger, Speedie, & Brunner, 1974, p. 21). After all sides of a controversy have been presented, group members should be allowed to think about solutions for a day or so before trying to put things together in new and varied patterns.

Sixth, group members formulate a new and unique solution to the problem, elaborate on it and work out the details of implementing it, and test it against reality. If the implementation is successful, group members then give the validated solution to relevant audiences.

DEVELOPING AND FOSTERING CREATIVITY

How do you increase group members' creative thinking? There are no easy answers to this question. From the process perspective, here is a set of procedures that can be used to promote creativity.

1. Reaffirm the cooperative goal of making the best decision possible.
2. Promote controversy among the ideas, opinions, information, theories, and perspectives of group members. Members should promote different points of view, critically analyze each other's information and reasoning, serve as devil's advocates to challenge other members' positions and creative diversity of opinion, and recombine known facts into new combinations and relationships. Members should be enthusiastic about originality in thinking and problem solving,

and become immersed in the perspectives and approaches to approaching and solving the problem.

3. Set aside time for members to reflect on the diverse ideas and perspectives generated by the controversy process. Encourage persistence in solving the problem, no matter how difficult it is. Creative insights come out of struggle, not quick reflection. Creative individuals such as Einstein and Picasso experienced great difficulties before achieving insight.

4. Meet to make final decisions, but do not rush to judgment. Creative insights cannot be hurried.

David and Houtman (1968) are the authors of a book intended to teach creativity. They suggest four methods of generating novel ideas that can be taught: part changing, using a checkerboard figure, using a checklist, and finding something similar. The *part-changing method* involves group members in identifying the parts or attributes of something that might be changed. The following is an example:

> Four qualities of a chair are color, shape, size, and hardness. Invent a new kind of chair by listing fifteen different colors, ten different shapes, five sizes, and five grades of hardness. Try to think of different ideas, and do not worry about whether or not they are any good. Think of different ways to change each part of the chair. Use your imagination.

The *checkerboard method* involves making a checkerboard figure with spaces for entering words or phrases on the vertical and horizontal axes. Different sets of properties or attributes are listed on the axes. Then group members examine the interaction or combination of each pair of things or attributes. For example:

> Your group is to invent a new sport. Place materials and equipment along the top horizontal axis and place the things the players do (such as running, batting, kicking, hanging from their knees) down the side or vertical axis. Then examine the combination of each item on each axis with all the other items on the other axis.

The *checklist method* involves developing and using checklists to make sure that something is not left out or forgotten. David and Houtman suggest a checklist that includes these procedures:

1. Change color.
2. Change size.
3. Change shape.
4. Use new or different material.
5. Add or subtract something.
6. Rearrange things.
7. Identify a new design.

A group can apply this checklist to any object or problem.

The *"find something similar" method* involves encouraging group members to come up with new ideas by thinking of other persons, animals, or social units in the world that perform the same acts the group wants to perform. Here is an example:

> Imagine your city has a parking problem. Find ideas for solving this problem by thinking of how bees, squirrels, ants, shoe stores, clothing stores, and so on store things.

Another technique designed to enhance the creativity of group members is *synectics,* developed by William J. Gordon (1961). Gordon stresses the importance of psychological states in achieving creativity and the use of metaphor in achieving the proper psychological state. He suggests using three interrelated techniques for making the strange appear familiar and the familiar strange:

1. *Personal analogy,* in which persons imagine how it feels to be part of the phenomenon they are studying. Asking them how they would feel if they were an incomplete sentence or if they were Paul Revere's horse are examples.
2. *Direct analogy,* in which group members are asked to think about a parallel situation in order to gain insight into what they are studying. Asking them to describe how a book is like a lightbulb or how a beaver chewing on a log resembles a typewriter are examples.
3. *Compressed conflict,* in which group members are forced to perceive an object or concept from two frames of reference. Asking them to give examples of repulsive attraction or cooperative competition are illustrations.

EXERCISE

8.9 *Creativity*

This problem requires creativity on the part of the group that is attempting to solve it. The class should divide into groups of three. Each group's assignment is to connect all nine dots with only four straight and connected lines. (Answer is on page 592 in the Appendix.)

● ● ●

● ● ●

● ● ●

EXERCISE

8.10 *Joe Doodlebug*

This problem also requires group creativity to solve. It is taken from Rokeach (1960). The procedure for the coordinator is as follows:

1. Have the class divide into groups of three.
2. Hand out copies of the problem sheet and state that it contains all the necessary information. The problem is *why* Joe *has* to take *four* jumps to reach the food, which is only

three feet away. The groups have thirty minutes to come up with an answer. Explain that you will give hints after fifteen, twenty, and twenty-five minutes if the groups have not solved the problem.

3. After fifteen minutes give the first hint, after twenty minutes the second, and after twenty-five minutes the third (see page 592 in the Appendix).

4. At the end of thirty minutes, stop the groups and give them the answer (it appears on page 592 in the Appendix). After clarifying the answer, conduct a discussion of moving outside one's belief system to solve a problem. Then ask the group to discuss how they worked together, listened to each other, handled controversies, and so on.

THE PROBLEM

Joe Doodlebug has been jumping all over the place getting some exercise when his master places a pile of food three feet directly west of him. Joe notices that the pile of food is a little larger than he. As soon as Joe sees all this food, he stops dead in his tracks, facing north. After all his exercise Joe is hungry, and he wants to get the food as quickly as possible. Joe examines the situation and then says, "I'll have to jump four times to get the food." Why does Joe have to take four jumps to get to the food?

Joe Doodlebug, a strange sort of imaginary bug, can and cannot do the following things: (a) He can jump only in four different directions: north, south, east, and west (he cannot jump diagonally, such as southwest); (b) once he starts in any direction, he *must* jump four times in that direction before he can change direction; (c) he can only jump, not crawl, fly, or walk; (d) he cannot jump less than one inch per jump or more than ten feet per jump; (e) Joe cannot turn around.

OPEN VERSUS CLOSED BELIEF SYSTEMS

A key element of creative problem solving is the **open-mindedness** to view the problem from diverse perspectives. When a group member is willing to attend to, comprehend, and gain insight into information, ideas, perspectives, assumptions, beliefs, conclusions, and opinions discrepant from his or her own, the member is *open-minded*. When the member resists such opportunities, the member is *closed-minded* and dogmatic. Group members must be open-minded about different beliefs, opinions, information, ideas, perspectives, and assumptions. The extent to which a member can receive, evaluate, and act on relevant information on its own merits (as opposed to viewing it only from his or her own perspective) defines the extent to which the student is open-minded (as opposed to being closed-minded) (Rokeach, 1960). Without seeing the problem from several perspectives, members will not be able to analyze it and synthesize various ideas to produce creative solutions. Controversy is an essential ingredient in discovering new perspectives on the problem being solved.

How do you tell if a group is open- or closed-minded? *Closed-minded groups* (a) emphasize the differences between what they believe and what they do not believe; (b) deny information that is contrary to what they believe; (c) have contradictory beliefs that go unquestioned; (d) discard as irrelevant the similarities between what they believe and what they reject; and (e) avoid exploring differences in beliefs and distortion of information that does not fit their beliefs. *Open-minded groups* (a) seek out opposing and differing beliefs; (b) discover new beliefs; (c) remember information that disagrees with currently held beliefs; and (d) organize new beliefs that lead to the solution of the problem. Open-mindedness is an important requirement for creative problem solving.

Rokeach (1954, 1960) has developed the concept of dogmatism to categorize persons in terms of the openness or closedness of their belief system. He defines **dogmatism** as "(a) a relatively closed cognitive organization of beliefs and disbeliefs about reality, (b) organized around a central set of beliefs about absolute authority which, in turn, (c) provides a framework for patterns of intolerance toward others." This research indicates that closed-minded persons, compared with open-minded ones (Ehrlich & Lee, 1969; Vacchiano, Strauss, & Hochman, 1968):

1. Are less able to learn new beliefs and to change old beliefs.
2. Are less able to organize new beliefs and integrate them into their existing cognitive systems during problem solving, and thus take longer to solve problems involving new beliefs.
3. Are less accepting of belief-discrepant information.
4. Are more resistant to changing their beliefs.
5. More frequently reject information that is potentially threatening to their perceptions and attitudes.
6. Have less recall of information that is inconsistent with their beliefs.
7. Evaluate information that is consistent with their beliefs more positively.
8. Have more difficulty in discriminating between the information received and its source, so that the status of an authority is confused with the validity of what the authority is stating; in other words, dogmatic persons tend to accept what authorities say as the truth and discount what low-status individuals say as invalid.
9. Resolve fewer issues in conflict situations, are more resistant to compromise, and are more likely to view compromise as defeat.

The creative solution of problems requires open-mindedness. In being open-minded, group members must be willing to give up their current beliefs about the situation and adopt new ones. The new beliefs help them synthesize an unforeseen but effective solution. The replacement of old beliefs with new beliefs is called the *analytic phase* of the problem-solving process. Once new beliefs have superseded the old ones, group members must organize their new beliefs in a way that leads them to the solution of the problem. This organizational step is called the *synthesizing phase* of the problem-solving process.

In solving the Joe Doodlebug problem, for example, group members must first overcome three beliefs, one by one, and replace them with three new beliefs. The *first* belief to be replaced is the facing belief. In everyday life we have to face the food we are to eat. But Joe does not have to face the food in order to eat it; he can land on top of it. The *second* is the direction belief. In everyday life we can change direction at will. But Joe is not able to do this because he must forever face north. The only way Joe can change direction is by jumping sideways and backward. The *third* belief that must be replaced is the movement belief. When we wish to change direction in everyday life, there is nothing to stop us from doing so immediately. But Joe's freedom of movement is restricted by the fact that once he moves in a particular direction (north, south, east, or west), he has to continue four times in that direction before he can change it. Many group members assume that Joe is at the end rather than possibly in the middle of a jumping sequence.

The replacement of old beliefs that limit a group's thinking with new beliefs that enable whole new orientations and perspectives depends on challenging and disconfirming the old beliefs. It is conflict that sparks the cognitive changes that enable creative insight. If group members are to engage in creative problem solving, they must be open-minded and be challenged with opposing positions, which results in seeing the issue from a variety of perspectives, which leads to developing a creative synthesis that solves the problem. Controversy, replacement of old beliefs with new ones, and the synthesis of new beliefs are all essential.

BRAINSTORMING

Problem solving depends on developing divergent views that conflict with each other. Often groups suffer when members do not produce a wide variety of ideas that can be contrasted with each other. Before group members can converge on a creative course of action, they must develop a wide variety of possibilities to be explored. Brainstorming was invented to (a) encourage divergent thinking, (b) produce many different ideas in a short period of time, and (c) ensure the full participation of all group members. **Brainstorming** is a procedure in which group members are asked to produce as many, and as uninhibited, ideas as they possibly can and to withhold criticism in order to optimize creativity. All criticism is withheld in order to reduce evaluation apprehension. The use of free association of ideas is supposed to open new avenues of thought. Brainstorming tends to increase member participation and involvement, generate a lot of ideas in a relatively short period of time, and reduce the need to look for the "right" idea in order to impress authority figures in the group. During brainstorming, the ground rules are:

1. All criticism or evaluation of ideas is ruled out. Ideas are simply placed before the group.
2. Wild ideas are expected in the spontaneity that evolves when the group suspends judgment. Practical considerations are not important at this point. The session is to be freewheeling.
3. The quantity of ideas counts, not their quality. All ideas should be expressed, and none should be screened out by any individual. A large number of ideas will increase the likelihood of the group's discovering good ones.
4. Build on the ideas of other group members when possible. Pool your creativity. Everyone should be free to build on ideas and to make interesting combinations from the various suggestions.
5. Focus on a single problem or issue. Don't skip around to various problems or try to brainstorm a complex multipart problem.

6. Promote a congenial, relaxed, cooperative atmosphere.
7. Make sure that all members, no matter how shy and reluctant to contribute, have their ideas heard.
8. Record all ideas.

After the period of brainstorming, all the ideas are categorized, and the group critically evaluates them for possible use or application. Priorities are selected, and the best ideas are applied.

The rationale for using brainstorming is the belief that many ideas are never born or are quickly stifled due to domineering members, stereotypes of each other's expertise and intelligence, interpersonal conflicts, habitual patterns of uninvolvement and silence, or fear of ridicule or evaluation. It is like a vice president in charge of a group of managers saying, "Those opposed will signify by clearing out their desks, putting on their hats, and saying 'I resign.' "

There is only one problem with brainstorming. Most research suggests that it is less effective than allowing the same number of people to generate ideas on their own, independent of any group experience (Diehl & Stroebe, 1987; Mullen, Johnson, & Salas, 1991). The lack of effectiveness of brainstorming is due in part to production blocking. *Production blocking* reflects the common group norm that only one person is to speak at a given time. This prevents members from blurting out their ideas the moment they think of them, and therefore, the ideas may be forgotten or censored. Groups (compared to isolated individuals), therefore, are at a definite disadvantage in generating a lot of ideas in a short period of time. Yet the use of brainstorming remains widespread. The reasons may be that (a) people enjoy working in groups and are therefore more motivated to produce ideas in a group setting (Stroebe, Diehl, & Abukoumkin, 1992), and (b) the dynamics of group brainstorming create better analysis, adoption, and implementation in later stages of group problem solving.

The thinking of all of us is highly influenced by the thinking of those with whom we talk and otherwise interact. It is almost always possible to be part of a group process that encourages, supports, and rewards our potential for creativity. The ideas of others spark our own. The theory of one group member may help build a much more creative theory by touching off all sorts of new ideas among the rest of the members. Untold amounts of creative problem solving may occur when diversity and controversy are sought and used.

EXERCISE

8.11 *Brainstorming*

The objective of this exercise is to come up with a large number of ideas or solutions to a problem by temporarily suspending criticism and evaluation—in other words, to experience the process of brainstorming. The procedure is as follows:

1. The group reviews the ground rules for brainstorming.
2. The group is presented with a problem: One of the authors of this book has been cast ashore nude on a desert island, with nothing but a glass peace symbol on a leather thong.
3. The group has fifteen minutes to generate ideas as to what can be done with this object.
4. The group has another fifteen minutes to critically select their best ideas.

5. The group discusses how well it applied the rules of brainstorming and what its results were. Was creativity enhanced? Did it help the group to discover interesting ways of using the object?

After initial exposure to brainstorming, a group should pick a specific problem it is working on and apply brainstorming to it to see if new, creative perspectives can be gained. If, however, a second practice session is desired, the following story can be used:

> A small wholesaler in the hinterland of New Mexico called his buyer in Santa Fe and asked him to obtain a large order of pipe cleaners from Mexico. The buyer agreed. He also agreed to advance the wholesaler the money to finance the deal. A month later, just as the shipment of pipe cleaners was arriving, the buyer received a phone call from the wholesaler: His warehouse and outlet store had burned down and there simply was no more business. The buyer was suddenly faced with the prospect of trying to sell 20,000 pipe cleaners.

In one minute, group members should generate as many ideas as possible (with a recorder counting the number of different ideas) for selling pipe cleaners. (A relatively spontaneous group will create approximately twenty-five ideas in little more than a minute. If the group creates fifteen or fewer ideas, it should be given more training in brainstorming.)

In brainstorming a group problem, it is important that the problem be well defined and specific. It must also be a problem that the group has the power to do something about. If possible, the group members should be notified in advance about the issue to be explored so that they will have given some thought to it.

EXERCISE | **8.12** | *Creativity Warm-up*

Have you ever felt in a rut? Have you ever felt embarrassed about sharing new or wild ideas? Have you ever ignored your thinking because you felt it was too far out? Do you ever enjoy letting your imagination and thoughts run wild? Have you ever been so critical of your own thoughts that you could not get started?

Here are six short, enjoyable exercises to loosen up group thinking and warm up group creativity:

1. The group sits in a circle (group size should be limited to eight members or so). The person nearest the window says the first thing that comes to his mind. The statement should be short, no more than a sentence or two. Without pause, the person to his left says what comes to her mind. Her statement must be relevant to something the first person said. The relevance may be of any kind—an association, a contrast, an alternative, a continuation, and so on. The process continues at high speed until at least three rounds have been completed. Members critique the process by discussing the feelings they had during the exercise.

2. The group sits in a circle and identifies a problem or issue. The person nearest the door states his solution. Each subsequent group member (to his left) states his or hers, using as many ideas of previous speakers as possible. The process continues until a plan generally acceptable to all the group members is arrived at. When a member cannot add anything new, he or she passes. Finally, members' reactions to and feelings about the experience are discussed.

3. The group sits in a circle, and a group problem or issue is identified. The first person states her solution to the problem. The next person immediately states what his opposition to the first person's solution is. The third person immediately states her opposition to the

second person's opposition. The process is continued until everyone in the group has spoken at least three times. The emphasis is upon generating creative ideas in arguments. Members' reactions to and feelings about the experience are discussed.

4. The group lies on the floor, members' heads toward the center of the room. The first person begins with a fantasy about what the group could be like. After no more than two or three minutes, the fantasy is passed on to the next group member, who continues it, adding his or her own associations and fantasies. The process continues until everyone has spoken at least three times. Members' reactions to and feelings about the exercise are examined.

5. The group has before it a number of assorted materials, such as clay, water paints, Tinker Toys, magazines, newspapers, and so on. It then creates something out of the materials—a mural, a collage, a design. If more than one group participates, they end the exercise by discussing one another's creations.

6. The group acts out a walk through the woods. Each member takes the leadership role for a while and directs the walk, indicating what he or she is experiencing and seeing. What the members learn about one another, the group, and walking through the woods should be discussed.

EXERCISE

8.13 *Your Behavior in Controversies (II)*

How do you behave in controversies? Has your behavior changed as a result of your experiences connected with this chapter? How would you now describe your behavior?

1. When a difficult decision is to be made
   _____ I seek out people who agree with me and see the situation the same way I do.
   _____ I seek out people who disagree with me and see the situation much differently than I do.

2. When I disagree with other members of my group, I
   _____ Become more and more certain I am right and try to overpower any opposition so that I win by having the final decision reflect what I want to do.
   _____ Present my point of view but listen carefully to everyone else's ideas and change my mind when I am logically persuaded to do so.

3. When other members of the group disagree with my ideas, I
   _____ Feel hurt and rejected.
   _____ Believe they may have important information and insights that may help me better understand the situation.

4. When other group members disagree with me, I
   _____ Try to see the situation from their point of view.
   _____ Am puzzled that they cannot see the situation as accurately and completely as I do.

5. When other members of my group disagree with me, I
   _____ State my position and my feelings so that everything is out in the open.
   _____ Keep quiet and sit the discussion out.

6. When I get involved in an argument, I
   _____ Incorporate other members' ideas into my thinking, try to see the situation from all perspectives, and search for a creative synthesis that is better than my original position.
   _____ Become more and more certain that I am correct and argue more and more strongly for my point of view.

7. Disagreement and arguments among group members are

_____ Constructive because they clear the air and enhance involvement and commitment of group members while improving the creativity and quality of decision making.

_____ Destructive because they lead to dislike, rejection, and defeat.

Compare your answers with the answers you gave to the questionnaire at the beginning of the chapter. Have you changed? How would you now describe your behavior in controversy situations? Write a description of your controversy behavior and share it with two persons who know you well and who have participated in some of the controversy exercises with you. Ask them to add to and modify your self-description.

FINAL NOTE

This chapter focused on the use of the controversy procedure to increase the creativeness and quality of a group decision making. The next chapter focuses on the constructive resolution of conflicts of interest.

9

Managing Conflict of Interests

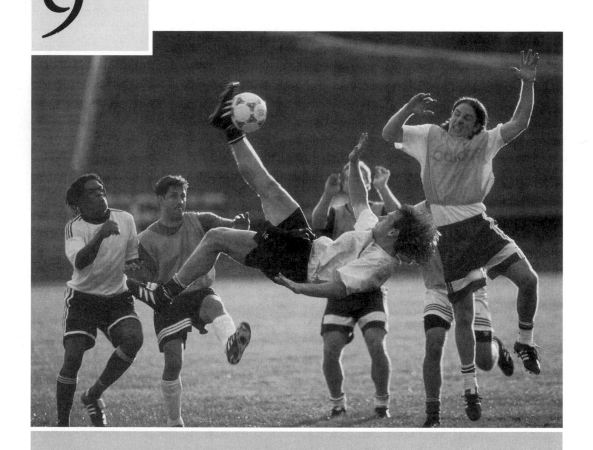

Basic Concepts to Be Covered in This Chapter

In this chapter a number of concepts are defined and discussed. The major ones are listed following. Divide into pairs. Each pair is to (a) define each concept, noting the page on which it is defined and discussed, and (b) ensure that both members of the pair understand the meaning of each concept. Then combine into groups of four. Compare the answers of the two pairs. If there is disagreement, look up the concept in the chapter and clarify it until all members agree on and understand the definition.

Concepts

1. Attribution theory
2. Compromise
3. Conflict of interests
4. Conflict negative group
5. Conflict positive group
6. Dilemma of honesty and openness
7. Dilemma of trust
8. Distributive (win–lose) negotiations
9. Forcing
10. Frustration-aggression process
11. Fundamental attribution error
12. Goal dilemma
13. Integrative, problem-solving negotiations
14. Mediation
15. Negotiation
16. Norm of reciprocity
17. Psychological reactance
18. Self-fulfilling prophecy
19. Smoothing
20. Steps of integrative negotiation
21. Stereotype
22. Superordinate goal
23. Withdrawal

CONFLICT POSITIVE GROUP

Groups can be either conflict negative or conflict positive (Tjosvold, 1991b) (Table 9.1). In a **conflict negative group** conflicts are suppressed and avoided and, when they occur, are managed in destructive ways. In a **conflict positive group** conflicts are encouraged and managed constructively to maximize their potential for enhancing the quality of decision making and problem solving and group life in general. Group members create, encourage, and support the possibility of conflict.

Table 9.1 **Conflict Negative and Conflict Positive Groups**

Conflict Negative Group	Conflict Positive Group
Sees conflict as unitary.	Recognizes different types of conflicts.
Sees conflict as the problem.	Sees conflict as part of the solution.
Avoids, suppresses, contains conflicts.	Seeks out and encourages conflicts.
Believes conflict is inherently destructive.	Believes conflict is potentially constructive.
Sees no value in conflict.	Sees many values in conflict.
Conflicts create anxiety and defensiveness.	Conflicts create excitement, interest, focus.
Individuals try to "win."	Individuals try to "solve the problem."

In order to create a conflict positive group, you must understand:

1. The nature of conflicts of interests.
2. The five strategies most commonly used to manage conflicts of interests.
3. The nature of distributive and integrative negotiations.
4. The steps for using integrative negotiations.
5. The nature of intergroup conflict.
6. How to apply constructive procedures to intergroup conflict.

NATURE OF CONFLICTS OF INTERESTS

Imagine you are part of a group that has just been given five thousand dollars to spend in any way it wishes over the next two weeks. Your group has six members: Jane, Mary, Joe, John, Edythe, and yourself. Jane and Mary want to donate the money to the women's liberation movement. Edythe, John, and Joe want to give a series of parties for all their friends. You want the group to use the money for a college scholarship for your younger brother. Your group is in conflict, and it is more than just a matter of opposing opinions. There is a scarce resource (money) that the group must decide to allocate among the competing needs of the members. Because different members have vested interests in spending the money in different ways, your group has a conflict of interests.

According to the *World Book Dictionary*, a **conflict** is a fight, struggle, battle, disagreement, dispute, or quarrel. A conflict can be as small as a disagreement or as large as a war. Probably the most influential definition is that of Deutsch (1973), who states that a conflict exists whenever incompatible activities occur. An activity that is incompatible with another activity is one that prevents, blocks, or interferes with the occurrence or effectiveness of the second activity. Incompatible activities may originate in one person, between two or more people, or between two or more groups. The word *conflict* is derived from the Latin *conflictus*, meaning a "striking together with force." There are times when group members' needs and preferences "strike together" and produce disruptive effects.

We are all unique individuals with our separate needs and goals, and conflicts of interests result. To understand conflicts of interests, you must first understand what wants, needs, goals, and interests are (Johnson & Johnson, 1995a) (Table 9.2). There are many things each of us want. A **want** is a desire for something. Each person basically has a unique set of wants. A **need** is a necessity for survival. Needs are more universal. Every

Table 9.2 **Understanding Conflicts of Interests**

Concept	Definition
Want	Desire for something.
Need	Universal necessity for survival.
Goal	Desired ideal state of future affairs.
Interests	Potential benefits to be gained by achieving goals.
Conflict of interests	Actions taken by person A to achieve goals that prevent, block, or interfere with actions taken by person B to achieve goals.
Negotiation	Process by which persons who have shared and opposed interests and want to come to an agreement try to work out a settlement.

person needs to survive and reproduce (water, food, shelter, sex), belong (loving, sharing, cooperating), have power, have freedom, and have fun (Glasser, 1984). On the basis of our wants and needs we set goals. A **goal** is an ideal state of affairs that we value and are working to achieve. Our goals are related through social interdependence. When we have mutual goals we are in a cooperative relationship; when our goals are opposed we are in a competitive relationship. Our **interests** are the potential benefits to be gained by achieving our goals.

A **conflict of interests** exists when the actions of one person attempting to maximize his or her needs and benefits prevent, block, interfere with, injure, or in some way make less effective the actions of another person attempting to maximize his or her needs and benefits (Deutsch, 1973). Conflict among interests can be based on (a) differences in needs, values, and goals; (b) scarcities of certain resources, such as power, influence, money, time, space, popularity, and position; or (c) rivalry. **Both because they occur naturally and because they are deliberately created, conflicts of interests are common.** The management of conflicts of interests is an important aspect of maintaining the cooperation among group members that is needed for group effectiveness (Figure 9.1).

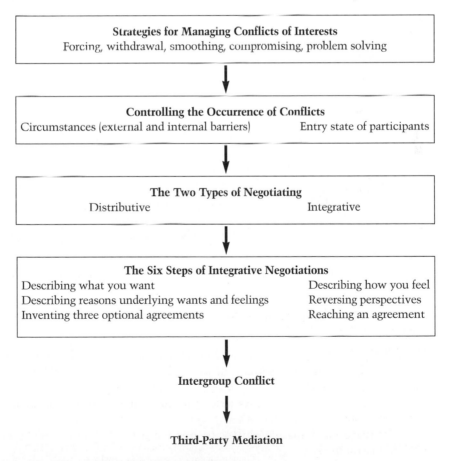

Figure 9.1 Managing conflicts of interests.

CONFLICTS CAN BE DESTRUCTIVE OR CONSTRUCTIVE

When conflicts are managed constructively, they have many desirable outcomes (Deutsch, 1973; Johnson, 1970; Johnson & Johnson, 1995a, 1995c). The Chinese character for crisis represents a combination of the symbol for danger and the symbol for opportunity. Inherent in any conflict is the potential for destructive or constructive outcomes. On the *destructive* side, conflicts can create anger, hostility, lasting animosity, and even violence. Conflicts can result in pain and sadness. Conflicts can end in lawsuits, divorce, and war. Destructively managed conflicts are highly costly to a group, destroying the group's effectiveness, ripping apart relationships, sabotaging work, delaying and decreasing teaching and learning efforts, and devastating individuals' commitment to the group's goals, sense of security, and personal feelings (Janz & Tjosvold, 1985). Poorly managed conflicts result in group members spending time brooding and fighting rather than teaching and learning.

Conflicts, however, carry the potential for many important *positive outcomes.* Conflicts can focus attention on problems that have to be solved and energize and motivate you to solve them. Conflicts can clarify how you need to change. Patterns of behavior that are dysfunctional are highlighted and clarified by conflicts. Conflicts can clarify what you care about and are committed to. You fight over only those wants and goals you value. You fight much more frequently and intensely with people you value and care about. The more committed you are to your goals, and the more committed you are to the other person, the more frequent and intense the conflicts. Conflicts can clarify who you are and what your values are. It is through conflicts that your identity is developed. Conflicts can help you understand who the other person is and what his or her values are. It is through conflicts that the identity of your friends and acquaintances is clarified. Conflicts (a) keep the relationship clear of irritations and resentments and (b) strengthen relationships by increasing your confidence that the two of you can resolve your disagreements. A good conflict may do a lot to resolve the small tensions of interacting with others and increase your confidence that the relationship can survive stress and adversity. A conflict a day keeps depression away. Conflicts can release anger, anxiety, insecurity, and sadness that, if kept inside, make us mentally sick. Conflicts can be fun. Being in a conflict reduces boredom, gives you new goals, motivates you to take action, and stimulates interests. Life would be incredibly boring if there were no conflict. Finally, when conflicts of interests are managed properly, they can help ensure that all group members are committed to implementing the group's decisions and that the group's problem-solving ability does not deteriorate during the decision-making process.

It is not the presence of conflicts, but the way in which they are managed, that determines whether they are destructive or constructive. **Conflicts are constructive to the extent that they:**

1. Result in an agreement that allows all participants to achieve their goals. The agreement maximizes joint outcomes, benefits everyone, and is in all participants' best interests.
2. Strengthen the relationship among participants by increasing their liking, respect, and trust for each other.
3. Increase participants' ability to resolve future conflicts with each other constructively.

9.1 *Your Conflict Strategies*

Different persons learn different ways of managing conflicts. The strategies you use to manage conflicts may be quite different from those used by your friends and acquaintances. This exercise gives you an opportunity to increase your awareness of what conflict strategies you use and how they compare with the strategies used by others. The procedure is as follows:

1. With your classmates, form groups of six. Make sure you know the other members of the group. Do not join a group of strangers.
2. Working by yourself, complete the following questionnaire.
3. Working by yourself, read the accompanying discussion of conflict strategies. Then make five slips of paper. Write the names of the other five members of your group on the slips, one name to a slip.
4. On each slip of paper write the conflict strategy that best fits the actions of the person named.
5. After all group members are finished, pass out your slips of paper to the persons whose names are on them. In turn, you should end up with five slips of paper, each containing a description of your conflict style as seen by another group member. Likewise, each member of your group should end up with five slips of paper describing his or her conflict strategy.
6. Score your questionnaire, using the table that follows the discussion of conflict strategies. Rank the five conflict strategies from the one you use most often to the one you use least often. This will give you an indication of how you see your own conflict strategy. The second most frequently used strategy is your backup strategy, the one you use if your first one fails.
7. After drawing names to see who goes first, one member describes the results of his or her questionnaire. This is the member's view of his or her own conflict strategies. The member then reads each of the five slips of paper on which are written the views of the group members about his or her conflict strategy. Next he or she asks group members to give specific examples of how they have seen him or her act in conflicts. The group members should use the rules for constructive feedback. The person to the left of the first member repeats this procedure, and so on around the group.
8. Each group discusses the strengths and weaknesses of each of the conflict strategies.

HOW YOU ACT IN CONFLICTS

The following proverbs can be thought of as descriptions of some of the different strategies for resolving conflicts. Proverbs state traditional wisdom, and these proverbs reflect traditional wisdom for resolving conflicts. Read each of the proverbs carefully. Using the following scale, indicate how typical each proverb is of your actions in a conflict.

> 5 = very typical of the way I act in a conflict
> 4 = frequently typical of the way I act in a conflict
> 3 = sometimes typical of the way I act in a conflict
> 2 = seldom typical of the way I act in a conflict
> 1 = never typical of the way I act in a conflict

_____ 1. It is easier to refrain than to retreat from a quarrel.
_____ 2. If you cannot make a person think as you do, make him or her do as you think.
_____ 3. Soft words win hard hearts.
_____ 4. You scratch my back, I'll scratch yours.
_____ 5. Come now and let us reason together.
_____ 6. When two quarrel, the person who keeps silent first is the most praiseworthy.

_____ 7. Might overcomes right.

_____ 8. Smooth words make smooth ways.

_____ 9. Better half a loaf than no bread at all.

_____ 10. Truth lies in knowledge, not in majority opinion.

_____ 11. He who fights and runs away lives to fight another day.

_____ 12. He hath conquered well that hath made his enemies flee.

_____ 13. Kill your enemies with kindness.

_____ 14. A fair exchange brings no quarrel.

_____ 15. No person has the final answer, but every person has a piece to contribute.

_____ 16. Stay away from people who disagree with you.

_____ 17. Fields are won by those who believe in winning.

_____ 18. Kind words are worth much and cost little.

_____ 19. Tit for tat is fair play.

_____ 20. Only the person who is willing to give up his or her monopoly on truth can ever profit from the truths that others hold.

_____ 21. Avoid quarrelsome people, as they will only make your life miserable.

_____ 22. A person who will not flee will make others flee.

_____ 23. Soft words ensure harmony.

_____ 24. One gift for another makes good friends.

_____ 25. Bring your conflicts into the open and face them directly; only then will the best solution be discovered.

_____ 26. The best way of handling conflicts is to avoid them.

_____ 27. Put your foot down where you mean to stand.

_____ 28. Gentleness will triumph over anger.

_____ 29. Getting part of what you want is better than getting nothing at all.

_____ 30. Frankness, honesty, and trust will move mountains.

_____ 31. There is nothing so important that you have to fight for it.

_____ 32. There are two kinds of people in the world, the winners and the losers.

_____ 33. When one hits you with a stone, hit him or her with a piece of cotton.

_____ 34. When both give in halfway, a fair settlement is achieved.

_____ 35. By digging and digging, the truth is discovered.

Scoring

Withdrawing	Forcing	Smoothing	Compromising	Problem Solving
_____ 1.	_____ 2.	_____ 3.	_____ 4.	_____ 5.
_____ 6.	_____ 7.	_____ 8.	_____ 9.	_____ 10.
_____ 11.	_____ 12.	_____ 13.	_____ 14.	_____ 15.
_____ 16.	_____ 17.	_____ 18.	_____ 19.	_____ 20.
_____ 21.	_____ 22.	_____ 23.	_____ 24.	_____ 25.
_____ 26.	_____ 27.	_____ 28.	_____ 29.	_____ 30.
_____ 31.	_____ 32.	_____ 33.	_____ 34.	_____ 35.
_____ Total	_____ Total	_____ Total	_____ Total	_____ Total

The higher the total score for each conflict strategy, the more frequently you tend to use that strategy. The lower the total score for each conflict strategy, the less frequently you tend to use that strategy.

CONFLICT STRATEGIES: WHAT ARE YOU LIKE?

Dealing with a conflict of interests is like going swimming in a cold lake. Some people like to test the water, stick their foot in, and enter slowly. Such people want to get used to the cold gradually. Other people like to take a running start and leap in. They want to get the cold shock over quickly. Similarly, different people use different strategies for managing conflicts. Usually, we learn these strategies in childhood so that later they seem to function automatically on a preconscious level. We just do whatever seems to come naturally. But we do have a personal strategy and, because it was learned, we can always change it by learning new and more effective ways of managing conflicts.

When we become engaged in a conflict, we have to take two major concerns into account (Johnson & Johnson, 1995a):

1. **Reaching an agreement that satisfies our needs and meets our goals.** We are in conflict because we have a goal or interests that conflict with another person's goal or interests. Our goal may be placed on a continuum between being of unimportant and being highly important.

2. **Maintaining an appropriate relationship with the other person.** Some relationships are temporary, whereas others are permanent. Our relationship with the other person may be placed on a continuum between being unimportant and being highly important.

The dual concern model of conflict resolution has its origins in Blake and Mouton's (1964) managerial grid and has been articulated by several theorists (Cosier & Ruble, 1981; Filley, 1975; Johnson, 1991; Pruitt & Rubin, 1986; Rahim, 1983; Thomas, 1976). Other labels are sometimes given to the two concerns, such as *concern for self* and *concern for others*.

In a conflict of interests, how you behave depends on how important your goals are to you and how important you perceive the relationship to be. Given these two concerns, there are five basic strategies (Figure 9.2) that may be used to manage conflicts:

1. **The Owl (Problem-Solving Negotiations):** Owls highly value their own goals and relationships. When both the goal and the relationship are highly important to you, you initiate problem-solving negotiations to resolve the conflict. Solutions are sought to ensure that both you and the other person fully achieve your goals and resolve any tensions and negative feelings between the two of you. This strategy requires risky moves, such as revealing your underlying interests while expecting the other to do the same.

2. **The Teddy Bear (Smoothing):** To teddy bears the relationship is of great importance, whereas their own goals are of little importance. When the goal is of no importance to you but the relationship is of high importance, you give up your goals in order to maintain the relationship at the highest quality possible. When you think the other person's interests are much stronger or more important than yours, you smooth and give the other person his or her way.

3. **The Shark (Forcing or Win–Lose Negotiations):** Sharks try to overpower opponents by forcing them to give in. When the goal is very important but the relationship is not, you seek to achieve your goal by forcing or persuading the other to yield. You compete for a win. Tactics used to force the other to yield include

Compromise
Take a chance, such as rolling some dice. Let luck decide who wins.

Compromise **Meet in the middle!**

Compromise
Take turns!

Smooth
Decide who needs it the most. Let that person have it.

Smooth

Give in with humor. Do not laugh at the person. La the problem

Smooth

Apologize. When you do not want to engage in conflict, saying "I'm sorry" will help you find an exit.

Confront

Face the conflict. Negotiate. Think of solutions that give both of you what you want and keep your relationship positive.

High Importance

	4 Smoothing	**5** Confronting
	3	
1	Compromising	**2**
	Withdrawing	Forcing

RELATIONSHIPS

Low Importance   GOALS   High Importance

Seek Help
When all else fails, go see the mediator!

Withdraw
Postpone. Put off discussing the conflict until you both want to resolve it and are in control of your emotions.

Force
Never use force with someone you'll see soon!

Figure 9.2 Conflict Strategies Game.
D. W. Johnson & R. Johnson, *Teaching students to be peacemakers.* (3rd ed.). Edina, MN: Interactive Book Company. Reprinted with permission of the authors.

making threats, imposing penalties that will be withdrawn if the other concedes, and taking preemptive actions designed to resolve the conflict without the other's consent (such as taking a book home that the other insists is his). Tactics to persuade the other to yield include presenting persuasive arguments, imposing a deadline, committing oneself to an "unalterable" position, or making demands that far exceed what is actually acceptable.

4. **The Fox (Compromising):** Foxes are moderately concerned with their own goals and their relationships with others. When both the goal and the relationship are moderately important to you, and it appears that both you and the other person cannot get what you want, you may need to give up part of your goals and sacrifice part of the relationship in order to reach an agreement. Compromising may involve meeting in the middle so that each gets half or flipping a coin to let chance decide who will get his or her way. Compromising is often used when disputants wish to engage in problem-solving negotiations but do not have the time to do so.

5. **The Turtle (Withdrawing):** Turtles withdraw into their shells to avoid conflicts. When the goal is not important and you do not need to maintain a relationship with the other person, you may wish to give up both your goals and the relationship and avoid the issue and the other person. Avoiding a hostile stranger, for example, may be the best thing to do. Sometimes you may wish to withdraw from a conflict until you and the other person have calmed down and are in control of your feelings.

In using these strategies there are five important points to consider. **First, to be competent in managing conflicts, you must be able to engage competently in each strategy.** You need to practice all five strategies until they are thoroughly mastered. You do not want to be an overspecialized dinosaur who can deal with conflict in only one way. Each strategy is appropriate under a certain set of conditions and, based on the dual concerns of one's goals and the relationship with the other person, you choose the conflict strategy appropriate to the situation.

Second, some of the strategies require the participation of the other disputant and some may be enacted alone. You can give up your goals by using withdrawing and smoothing no matter what the other disputant does. When you try to achieve your goals by using forcing, compromising, and problem solving, the other disputant has to participate in the process.

Third, the strategies tend to be somewhat incompatible in the sense that choosing one of them makes choosing the others less likely. Though sometimes used in combination (temporarily withdrawing before initiating problem-solving negotiations), withdrawing implies lack of commitment to one's goals, whereas negotiating implies high commitment to one's goals. Forcing implies low commitment to the relationship, whereas smoothing implies high commitment to the relationship. Essentially, the five strategies are independent of each other, and when you engage in one, the likelihood of your being able to switch effectively to another is not high.

Fourth, certain strategies may deteriorate into other strategies. When you try to withdraw, and the other disputant pursues you and will not allow you to withdraw, you may respond with forcing. When you try to initiate problem-solving negotiations and the other disputant responds with forcing, you may reciprocate by engaging in win–lose tactics. When time is short, problem-solving negotiations may deteriorate into compromising.

Fifth, whether problem-solving or win–lose negotiations are initiated depends on your perception of the future of the relationship. When conflicts arise, potential short-term gains must be weighed against potential long-term losses. When you perceive the relationship as being unimportant, you may go for the win by attempting to force the other person to capitulate. The relationship may be perceived as unimportant because

(a) there will be only one or a few interactions or (b) you are so angry at the other person that only the present matters. When you perceive the relationship as being important, then you will try to solve the problem in a way that achieves the other person's goals as well as your own. The relationship is perceived to be important because it is ongoing and long term or there are strong positive emotions (such as liking and respect) that bond you to the other person.

The shadow of the future looms largest when interactions among individuals are durable and frequent. Durability ensures that individuals will not easily forget how they have treated, and been treated by, each other in the future. Frequency promotes stability by making the consequences of today's actions more salient for tomorrow's dealings. When individuals realize they will work with each other frequently and for a long period of time, they see that the long-term benefits of cooperation outweigh the short-term benefits of taking advantage of the other person. In ongoing relationships, the future outweighs the present so that the quality of the relationship is more important than the outcome of any particular negotiation. In schools, all relationships are long term and, therefore, the shadow of the future is ever present.

Field studies found problem solving to be strongly associated with constructive resolution of conflicts and high organizational performance, whereas forcing the other person to accept one's position was strongly associated with ineffective conflict management (Burke, 1969, 1970; Lawrence & Lorsch, 1967). Experimental studies have found that high concern about both one's own and the other's outcomes produced high joint outcomes; high concern about one's own outcomes but low concern about the other's outcomes tended to result in attempts to dominate and persuade; low concern about one's own outcomes but high concern about the other's outcomes resulted in low joint benefit (Ben-Yoav & Pruitt, 1984a, 1984b; Carnevale & Keenan, 1990; Pruitt & Syna, 1983).

CONTROLLING THE OCCURRENCE OF CONFLICTS

Not everything that is faced can be changed
but nothing can be changed until it is faced.

James Baldwin

When a conflict of interests arises, it is usually advisable to face and resolve it. There are times, however, when you may wish to postpone the occurrence of a conflict. You can control the occurrence of a conflict when you understand (a) the circumstances that brought about the conflict and (b) the entry state of the participants. The circumstances that surround the conflict include both the barriers to beginning negotiations and the events that trigger expressions (Walton, 1987). **Internal barriers** include negative attitudes, values, fears, anxieties, and habitual patterns of avoiding conflict. **External barriers** may include task requirements, group norms for avoiding conflict, pressure to maintain a congenial public image, and faulty perceptions of one's vulnerability and others' strength. Physical separation is a frequently used barrier to the expression of conflicts of interests. Placing members in different locations, avoiding being in the same room with certain other members, and removing a member from the group can all suppress a conflict of interests. A **triggering event** may be as simple as two group members being physically near each other or as complex as two members being in competition. Negative remarks, sarcasm, and criticism on sensitive points are common triggering events, as is the feeling of being deprived, neglected, or ignored. Some events may trigger a destructive cycle of conflict and others may trigger problem solving; group members will want to maximize the latter type of triggering event.

The diagnosis of a conflict involves discovering (a) the barriers to negotiation and (b) what triggers open expression of the conflict. From such knowledge, group members can choose the time and place for negotiations. If an appropriate time is not immediately available, the barriers to expressing the conflict can be increased and the triggering events can be decreased in order to avoid the conflict temporarily. To *avoid* the conflict, you remove the triggering events and build up the barriers to negotiations. To *resolve* the conflict, you increase the frequency of the triggering events and decrease the barriers to negotiations.

The second factor in controlling the occurrence of a conflict is the entry state of the disputants. The **entry state** of a group member is that person's ability to deal constructively with the conflict. Members' level of self-awareness, their ability to control their behavior, their skills in communicating and in other ways being interpersonally effective (Johnson, 2000), their ability to withstand stress, and their ability to incorporate their strengths in constructive conflict behavior are all important aspects of their entry state. Your opponent may be too anxious, defensive, or psychologically unstable to negotiate effectively, or his or her motivation to change may be very low. Group support and consultation can raise the entry state of each participant.

Not every conflict of interest is negotiable. It is a mistake to assume that you can always openly negotiate the resolution of a conflict. There are times when conflicts are better avoided. Usually, however, through careful attention to the entry state of participants and the circumstances that trigger or prevent a conflict, a time optimal for constructive resolution can be chosen.

THE NATURE OF NEGOTIATIONS

Negotiation is woven into the daily fabric of our lives. Many individuals, however, do not know how to negotiate, and those who do often negotiate very poorly. Negotiating with skill and grace is not easy. It must be learned. **Negotiation** is a process by which persons who have shared and opposed interests and want to come to an agreement try to work out a settlement (Johnson & Johnson, 1995a). Negotiations are aimed at achieving an agreement that specifies what each group member gives to and receives from each other. Negotiation may involve *distributive issues*, where one member benefits only if the opponent agrees to make a concession, or *integrative issues*, where the two members are working together to seek a solution that will benefit everyone. You spend a great deal of time negotiating, even when you (a) do not think of yourself as doing so and (b) are not fully aware that negotiations are taking place. You can tell you are negotiating by using the following checklist:

_____ Is there another person involved, and are you dependent on each other for information (about what is a reasonable agreement) and an agreement (you get what you want only if the other person agrees and vice versa)?

_____ Are both cooperative elements (we both wish to reach an agreement) and competitive elements (we both wish the agreement to be as favorable to ourselves as possible) present in the situation?

_____ Are both primary and secondary gains a concern?

_____ Are there contractual norms on how negotiation should be conducted?

_____ Is there a beginning, a middle, and an end?

_____ Do you wish to propose an agreement that is favorable to yourself but not so one-sided that it drives the other away from negotiations?

There are several important points to be made about negotiations. The *first* is that there are three types of interdependence inherent in any negotiations: participation interdependence, outcome interdependence, and information interdependence. **Participation interdependence** requires at least two to negotiate, whether it is two group members, two groups, two organizations, or two nations. You cannot negotiate by yourself. It takes the consent and participation of others. **Outcome interdependence** involves an agreement that can be reached only with the cooperation of the other disputant. Both members must commit themselves to an agreement and, therefore, each is dependent on the other for the outcome. All negotiating is aimed at achieving certain outcomes for oneself, but those outcomes are possible only if the other negotiator agrees to them. **Information interdependence** exists because negotiators are dependent on each other for information about a possible agreement. Such information can be secured in one of two ways: Negotiators can openly and honestly share their preferences, needs, and expectations, or they can deduce what the other wants from his or her behavior during the negotiations. This is a complicated issue because negotiators often do not know what their own expectations should be until they learn what the other negotiator's expectations are. To the point that negotiators know both what the other wants and what is the least the other will accept, they will be able to develop an effective negotiating position. Information interdependence sets up two dilemmas: the dilemma of trust and the dilemma of honesty and openness. The **dilemma of trust** involves a choice about whether to believe the other negotiator. To believe the other negotiator is to risk potential exploitation. Disbelieving the other negotiator reduces the possibility of any agreement being reached. The **dilemma of honesty and openness** involves the risk of either being exploited for disclosing too much too quickly or seriously damaging the negotiating relationship by refusing to disclose information and thereby seeming deceitful or distrusting. Both of these dilemmas are the result of information interdependence.

Second, within any negotiations there are both cooperative and competitive elements. The mixed-motive situation is created by the desire to reach an agreement and the desire to make that agreement as favorable to oneself as possible (Figure 9.3). The two motives can seriously interfere with each other. The balance between the cooperative and competitive elements determines how negotiations are conducted.

Third, both primary and secondary gains must be attended to in negotiations. The **primary gain** is determined by the nature of the agreement: The more favorable the agreement is to a member's short-term goals, the greater the primary gain for him or her. The **secondary gain** is determined by factors influencing the effectiveness of the working relationship between the disputants, the impact of an angry and revengeful person on the quality of one's life, the future effectiveness of the group, and the relatively unimportant benefits to oneself. The more effective the group, the more the member's

Figure 9.3 Integrative negotiations.

long-term goals will be met, and therefore the greater the long-term gain for him or her. Consequently, in negotiating a resolution to a conflict, a group member has to be concerned not only with what is more desirable for him or her in the short term but also with what is most desirable for improving the effectiveness of the group, relationships with group members, and other possible future outcomes.

Fourth, during negotiations **contractual norms** are developed that spell out the ground rules for conducting the negotiations and managing the difficulties involved in reaching an agreement. Two common norms are the **norm of reciprocity** (a negotiator should return the same benefit or harm given him or her by the other negotiator) and the **norm of equity** (the benefits received or the costs assessed by the negotiators should be equal).

Fifth, negotiations have important time dimensions. There is a beginning, a middle, and an end. The strategies and tactics used to initiate negotiations, exchange proposals and information, and precipitate an agreement can be quite different and sometimes contradictory.

Sixth, in negotiations disputants face a **goal dilemma:** how to reach an agreement favorable to oneself but not so one-sided that the other negotiator will refuse to agree. In resolving the goal dilemma, negotiators must decide on a reasonable proposal, one that not only will get the most for themselves but also will have a good chance of being acceptable to the other. Inasmuch as there is rarely any obvious "correct" agreement, each must decide during the negotiations what is a reasonable outcome for oneself and for the other negotiator.

Negotiating skills are one of your keys to success in life. There is no overstating the importance of being able to negotiate well. A survey conducted for Accountemps (a large accounting, bookkeeping, and data processing temporary personnel service that is a division of Robert Half International Inc.) of vice presidents and personnel directors of 100 of the nation's 1,000 largest corporations found that the people who manage America's leading corporations spend over four working weeks a year dealing with the problems caused by employees who cannot resolve their conflicts with each other. In answer to the question "What percent of management time is spent dealing with conflicts among employees?" respondents revealed that executives spend an average of 9.2% of their time or, based on a 40-hour week, 4.6 weeks a year attempting to deal with employee conflicts and the difficulties and disruptions they cause. In addition to taking up valuable management time, employee conflicts can seriously reduce any company's productivity and its ability to compete effectively in the marketplace. Knowing how to negotiate constructive resolutions to conflicts of interests is an essential skill for any career.

9.2 *Making a Profit*

The purpose of this exercise is to give participants an opportunity to negotiate a profit–loss situation so that they may examine the dynamics of bargaining. The exercise can be conducted in less than an hour. The procedure for the coordinator is as follows:

1. Introduce the exercise as an opportunity to study the dynamics of negotiation between two persons with different interests. The negotiation is between a buyer and a seller in a wholesale market. Explain that the exercise has three parts: (a) preparing for negotiations, (b) negotiating, and (c) discussing what happened in negotiations.

2. Divide the class into groups of four. Divide each group into two pairs. Assign one pair the role of buyers and the other pair the role of sellers. Give each pair the appropriate profit schedule (see page 593 in the Appendix). *Their first task is to prepare for negotiations.* Both pair members (a) need to understand the profit schedule so that they know which agreements are most and least profitable for them and (b) be ready to negotiate an agreement that is beneficial to them. On the profit schedule are three commodities (oil, gas, coal). The nine prices for each commodity are represented by the letters A to I. Next to each price is the profit the person would make. The following questions may clarify whether pair members understand the profit schedule:

a. What is your most important commodity? _____

b. What is your least important commodity? _____

c. For price B for coal, what would your profit be? _____

d. For price D for gas, what would your profit be? _____

Make sure participants understand that all communication during negotiations will be verbal only. They cannot show their profit schedules to the opposing negotiator.

3. One member of each pair switches chairs so that a buyer is facing a seller. *The second task is to negotiate one agreement that includes a price for each of the three commodities,* such as AAA, III, or BDC. Each person is expected to make and respond to proposed agreements. They can say anything they want to each other, but they may not show each other their profit schedule. When an agreement is reached, write it down and sign it. Each negotiator then writes down (without asking the other) (a) which commodity was most important to the opponent and (b) which commodity was least important to the opponent.

4. The two pairs combine into a group of four and complete the *third task* by discussing the following questions:

a. What were the agreements reached by the members of the group? Each person writes down: (1) the buyers' total profit, (2) the sellers' total profit, and (3) the joint profit (the buyers' and sellers' profits added together).

b. How did negotiators communicate information about their profit schedule, and how did they learn about the profit schedule of their opponent? Were their perceptions of which commodities were most and least important to their opponent correct? Was information exchange direct (did buyer and seller accurately tell each other their profit schedules)? Or was it indirect (did they deduce each other's profit schedule by comparing each other's responses to different package offers)?

c. Did negotiators try to win (maximize their own profit at the other's expense) or solve the problem (maximize their joint profit)?

d. Did the negotiators make package deals or did they negotiate the commodities one at a time?

e. What conclusions can the group reach about negotiations on the basis of their experience and discussion?

5. Have each group share its conclusions with the rest of the class.

9.3 *Group-Member Excellence*

The objective of this exercise is to examine the dynamics of negotiation among members of the same group. The exercise can be conducted in less than one hour. The procedure for the coordinator is as follows:

1. Divide the class into groups of seven: six participants and one observer. You need at least two groups.

2. For each group, make up six bags of marbles (one for each participating member) consisting of marbles of varied colors (see the following table).

Distribution of Marbles to the Six Negotiators

Member	Red	Blue	Green	White
1	4	3	2	1
2	1	4	3	2
3	2	1	4	3
4	3	2	1	4
5	3	3	2	2
6	2	2	3	3

3. From each group, collect one dollar from each member (excluding the observer). The money will be awarded to group members who negotiate successfully and achieve the assigned goal.
4. Distribute the instructions:
    a. One copy of the general instruction sheet to all group members.
    b. One copy of the observers' instructions to each observer.
    c. Without letting the groups know that they are getting different instructions, give half of the groups a copy of the "win–lose negotiation instructions" and the other half a copy of the "problem-solving negotiation instructions."
5. Meet with the observers to make sure they understand their responsibilities.
6. Distribute a bag of marbles to each group member. Each member has ten marbles. The number of each color varies from member to member.
7. **Negotiations Task:** "*The goal of negotiations is to collect fifteen marbles of the same color.* In addition, for each marble over fifteen you will receive a 10% bonus. Thus, if you turn in eighteen green marbles, you will receive the regular award for fifteen marbles plus 30% more. You may only negotiate with members of your group." Answer any questions members have about the exercise. Announce that participants have ten minutes to achieve the goal. Give the signal to begin.
8. **Self-Monitoring Task:** After ten minutes, announce, "Time is up. Stop negotiating. Write down *two adjectives* that describe your feelings during the negotiations."
9. Determine how many negotiators succeeded in collecting fifteen marbles of the same color. Determine bonuses for collecting more than fifteen. Divide the money accordingly. If no group member collected fifteen marbles, the money goes into a class fund to purchase food for the next class session.
10. **Small Group Analysis:**
    a. In each group the observer reports his or her observations. Members are to discuss and summarize the experience:
       (1) What negotiation strategies were used?
       (2) How did members react to each other's strategies?
       (3) How successful was each strategy?
       (4) How often did coalitions form in which two or more members pooled their marbles and negotiated with other members as a bloc?
       (5) What side agreements were made about the money?
       (6) Did any member collect marbles of two colors in order to be flexible until the last few minutes? What other interesting strategies were used?

    b. Record the adjectives written down by each member.

    c. Summarize (1) members' negotiation strategies, their success, and the reactions of groupmates; (2) members' adjectives; and (3) conclusions group members drew from the experience. Plan how to make a five-minute presentation of your summary to the class as a whole.

11. **Whole Class Analysis:**

    a. Have each group (1) share its instructions for negotiation (problem solving or win–lose) and (2) present a five-minute summary of members' experiences and conclusions. Record the results on the following table.

Group	Problem-Solving Instructions		Win–Lose Instructions	
	# Successful	Adjectives	# Successful	Adjectives
1				
2				
3				
4				
5				
6				
Total				

Conclusions: _____

    b. Ask participants to reflect on the information from all the groups and share their conclusions about the effectiveness of the problem-solving and win–lose strategies. Summarize the major points of the discussion.

12. Have participants read the subsequent sections on negotiation and compare their conclusions about the exercise with the material in those sections.

GENERAL INSTRUCTIONS

Systems for evaluating the performance of group members have many shortcomings. Different members behave in different ways to accomplish their objectives. These variations make most comparisons difficult and unfair. To overcome this problem, we have developed a simulation. All members will participate (except for the observer). From your behavior in this exercise, we will be able to tell if you are a poor, average, good, or excellent group member. The exercise provides an impartial and equal measure of your performance.

You are being issued a bag containing ten marbles of four different colors: red, green, blue, and white. Each negotiator has ten marbles, but different negotiators have different numbers of each color (you may have two white marbles but another member may have four). *Your goal is to collect fifteen marbles of the same color. You will receive a 10% bonus for each marble over the fifteen that you collect.* Thus, if you collect eighteen green marbles, you will receive the regular award for fifteen marbles *plus* 30% more. The money collected will be divided among the group members who succeed in obtaining fifteen or more marbles.

You have ten minutes to negotiate with other members of your group (you may not negotiate with members of the other group).

OBSERVERS' INSTRUCTIONS

As an observer, your task is to obtain as much information about the interaction among group members as possible. Concentrate on:

1. What strategies of negotiation group members are using.
2. How group members are reacting to each other's strategies.
3. How successful the strategies are.

Observations of any other aspect of group behavior will also be helpful. Write down your observations. Make as many observations as possible.

INSTRUCTIONS FOR WIN–LOSE NEGOTIATION

In this exercise your group is to adopt a win–lose negotiation strategy in which each member will try to obtain more marbles of the same color than anyone else. Obviously, some of the members of your group are going to win and some are going to lose. You want to be a winner. Be a tough negotiator. Make extreme opening offers and compromise slowly. Hide as much information from other group members as you can. Trust no one. Say whatever will be helpful in negotiating with the other members. During the negotiations try to achieve the best outcome for yourself, and use your power and skill in any way that helps you do so. Remember, if you keep the other group members from winning, you will increase your own chances of winning.

INSTRUCTIONS FOR PROBLEM-SOLVING NEGOTIATION

In this exercise your group is to adopt a problem-solving negotiation strategy in which members try to find a creative solution to the problem that benefits as many members as possible. In negotiating with other group members, communicate openly and honestly about what you want and try to identify as many ways as possible to maximize joint gain. Search for a rational agreement that ensures both your own and other group members' success. Avoid all threats and deceptions that might destroy trust among group members. The problem is to figure out how as many group members as possible can achieve the goal.

TWO TYPES OF NEGOTIATING

Storms are a natural and unavoidable aspect of Earth's weather system. They range in intensity from rainstorms to hurricanes. Some are accompanied by gentle rain, others by thunder and lightning. Similarly, interpersonal storms are a natural and unavoidable aspect of life within groups that vary in intensity from mild to severe. To resolve them you may wish to negotiate. When you use negotiations to resolve a conflict of interests, you have a choice. You can try to win by acting like a shark and using forcing or distributive procedures, or you can try to solve the problem in a mutually beneficial way by acting like an owl and using integrative or problem-solving procedures. Both are appropriate under certain circumstances (Table 9.3).

Table 9.3   **The Two Types of Negotiating Strategies**

Distributive (Win–Lose)	Integrative (Problem Solving)
Presenting an opening offer very favorable to oneself and refusing to modify that position.	Describing what one wants.
Gathering information about what the other considers a reasonable agreement from the other's opening offer and proposals.	Describing how one feels.
Continually pointing out the validity of one's own position and the incorrectness of the other person's.	Describing reasons underlying wants and feelings.
Using a combination of threats and promises to convince the other person that he or she has to accept one's offer.	Reversing perspectives.
Committing oneself to a position in such a way that if an agreement is to be reached, the other person has to agree to one's terms.	Inventing at least three optional agreements that maximize joint outcomes.
Agreeing if one's benefits are greater than the other's or if no better outcome is available elsewhere.	Choosing one alternative and agreeing to it.

Distributive Negotiations: Win–Lose Negotiations

People . . . are trying to either shun conflict or crush it. Neither strategy is working. Avoidance and force only raise the level of conflict. . . . They have become parts of the problem rather than the solution.

DeCecco and Richards, 1974

When the negotiation is with a person whose continued goodwill and cooperation are not necessary (such as a car salesperson), you negotiate to win (this means that the other person loses). In **distributive negotiations** the goal is to maximize your outcomes while minimizing the other person's outcomes. You try to reach an agreement more favorable to you than to the other person. You go for the win when your wants, needs, and goals are important and you have a temporary, ad hoc relationship with the other person. In some cultures, where bargaining is a way of life, this type of negotiating is both recreation and an art form.

In distributive negotiations a sequence of behavior occurs in which one party presents a proposal, the other evaluates it and presents a counterproposal, the first party replies with a modified proposal, and so on until a settlement is reached (Chertkoff & Esser, 1976; Johnson, 1974; Johnson & Johnson, 1995a; Rubin, Pruitt, & Kim, 1994; Walton & McKersie, 1965). The negotiators use this sequence of behaviors to obtain information that helps resolve the dilemma of goals. On the basis of the other party's opening offer, the proposals one receives, and the counterproposals one offers, a negotiator can obtain an idea of what sort of settlement the person will accept. A common win–lose negotiating pattern is for both negotiators to set a relatively high but tentative goal at first; they can then change it on the basis of the other person's reactions and counterproposals. This sequence of behaviors, which allows one negotiator to assess the second negotiator's points of potential settlement, can also be used to influence the second negotiator's assessment of the first one's points of potential settlement. Through their opening offers and their counterproposals, negotiators can influence each other's expectations of what they consider a reasonable agreement. Ideally, a win–lose negotiator would like to obtain the maximal information about the other's preferences while disclosing the minimal, or misleading, information about his or her own preferences. Helpful hints for engaging in distributive negotiations, therefore, are:

1. **Identify triggering events and barriers to negotiations.** Trigger the conflict at a moment when it is most advantageous to you and least advantageous to your opponent.

2. **Make an extreme opening offer** (if you are willing to pay $1,500, offer $500) to (a) establish a negotiating range skewed in your favor, (b) influence the other's expectations about your anticipated minimal terms (do not let the other person know how much you are willing to pay), (c) change the other's beliefs about his or her minimum terms, and (d) create an impression of toughness. The perception of toughness has considerable influence on determining how far a negotiator thinks he or she can push an opposing negotiator (that is, what terms the opponent will finally agree to).

3. **Compromise slowly** (try to get the other person to compromise first). A slow rate of compromise is aimed at creating an image of toughness and influencing the opponent's expectations of (a) what a reasonable outcome is for him or her and (b) what your expectations of a reasonable outcome are. As the opponent **reconnoiters the negotiating range** for possible points of agreement, he or she seeks information to reduce the uncertainty about what the agreement might be. Every action a negotiator makes affects the opponent's conclusions about what to propose next.

4. **Use threats, promises, and arguments, and stick doggedly to a committed position,** to (a) coerce and entice the opponent to accept your proposal, (b) convince the other person that what he or she wants is unreasonable and unattainable, and (c) change the other's evaluation of how many concessions are required to reach an agreement. A **threat** states that if the other negotiator performs an undesired act, you will harm him or her. A **promise** states that if the other negotiator performs a desired act, you will provide benefits. A **preemptive action** is designed to resolve the conflict without the other's consent (such as taking up residence on a disputed piece of land). A **persuasive argument** is pointing out the validity of your position and the incorrectness of the other's. **Committing oneself to an "unalterable" position** is making it clear that it is the other negotiator who has the last chance of avoiding "no agreement." Plugging your ears until the other negotiator says yes is an example.

5. **Be ready to walk away with no agreement.** Every negotiator is faced with a continual threefold choice of (a) accepting the available terms for agreement, (b) trying to improve the available terms through further negotiation, and (c) discontinuing negotiations without agreement and with no intention of resuming them. If you cannot walk away with no agreement, you must accept what the opponent is willing to give.

For a goal-oriented group a win–lose strategy of negotiation has some fundamental shortcomings. Although it will often result in more favorable primary gains for some group members, the damage it can cause to future cooperation among group members significantly reduces its secondary gains. Because a win–lose strategy emphasizes power inequalities, it undermines trust, inhibits dialogue and communication, and diminishes the likelihood that the conflict will be resolved constructively. Attempts to create cooperative relations between negotiators are more effective if their power is equal (Deutsch, 1973). Walton (1987) notes that **when power is unequally distributed, the low-power person will automatically distrust the high-power person because he or she knows that those with power tend to use it in their own interests.** Usually, the greater the difference in power, the more negative the attitudes toward the high-power person and the less likely the low-power person is to present his or her views in a clear and forceful way. The high-power person, on the other hand, tends to underestimate the low-power person's positive intent and will react with hostility whenever the low-power person tries to reduce his or her power. Even when an agreement is reached, losers have little motivation to carry out the actions agreed upon, resent the winner, and often try to sabotage the agreement. The winner finds it hard to enforce the agreement. Damage to interpersonal relationships results, as winners and losers are often hostile toward each other.

In going for the win, you assume that the relationship is unimportant and has no future. This is often a mistake. There are very few times in your life when you negotiate with someone you will never interact with again. If you go for a win and then have to face the same person the next day, sooner or later the other person will get revenge. In most situations, therefore, you want to try to resolve the conflict by maximizing joint outcomes. A famous example is the dispute between Egypt and Israel. When their leaders sat down to negotiate at Camp David in October 1978, it appeared that they had before them an intractable conflict. Egypt demanded the immediate return of the entire Sinai Peninsula; Israel, which had occupied the Sinai since the 1967 Middle East war, refused to return an inch of this land. Efforts to reach agreement, including the proposal of a compromise in which each nation would retain half of the Sinai, proved completely unacceptable to both sides. As long as the dispute was defined in terms of what percentage of the land each side would control, no agreement could be reached. Once both realized that what Israel really cared about was the security that the land offered, whereas Egypt was primarily interested in sovereignty over it, the stalemate was broken. The two countries were then able to reach an integrative solution: Israel would return the Sinai to Egypt in exchange for assurances of a demilitarized zone and Israeli air bases in the Sinai.

Integrative Negotiations: Negotiating to Solve the Problem

Imagine that you and another person are rowing a boat across the ocean and you cannot row the boat by yourself. Although the two of you may have conflicts about how to row, how far to row, in what direction to row, and so forth, you seek food and water for the other person as well as for yourself. Otherwise, you may perish. Your conflicts become mutual problems that must be solved to both persons' satisfaction. In **integrative negotiations,** the goal is to maximize joint benefits. Maintaining a high-quality relationship with other group members is usually more important than getting your way on any one issue. In a family, for example, ensuring the survival of the family is almost always more important than winning on any one issue. In integrative negotiations, therefore, there is a hardheaded, side-by-side search for a fair agreement that is advantageous to both sides.

In ongoing relationships, conflicts are often resolved by a procedure known as the **one-step negotiation.** Each person (a) assesses the strength of his or her interests, (b) assesses the strength of the other person's interests, and (c) agrees that whoever has the greatest need gets his or her way. Marital satisfaction, for example, has been found to be higher when couples allocated decision-making power such that each person exercises more power on decisions that mattered to that individual (Beach & Tesser, 1993). The one-step negotiation procedure works only if it is reciprocal. Each person should get his or her way half of the time. Ongoing relationships are guided by a **norm of mutual responsiveness** (you help them reach their goals and they help you reach your goals). One-way relationships never last long.

When disputants have to achieve their goals and, therefore, one-step negotiation is not appropriate, they engage in integrative negotiations. There are six basic steps in negotiating a workable solution to a problem that maximizes joint outcomes:

1. Each person explains what he or she wants in a descriptive, nonevaluative way.
2. Each person explains how he or she feels in a descriptive, nonevaluative way.
3. Each person explains the reasons for his or her wants and feelings.
4. Each person reverses perspectives by summarizing what the other person(s) wants and feels and the underlying reasons.
5. The participants invent at least three good optional agreements that would maximize joint outcomes.
6. The participants choose the agreement that seems the wisest and agree to abide by its conditions.

EXERCISE

9.4 *Negotiating Resolutions to Conflicts of Interests*

The purpose of this exercise is to stimulate a discussion on how to negotiate constructive resolutions to conflicts of interests. The procedure is as follows:

1. Form groups of four. Divide each group into two pairs. Assign one pair the role of Chris and the other pair the role of Pat or the instructor. Brief descriptions of several conflicts of interests appear below. Taking one at a time, the pair prepares to role play its assigned character by reading the description of the situation and writing out the answers to the following questions:
   a. What do you want?
   b. How do you feel?
   c. What are your reasons for wanting what you want and feeling as you do?
2. One person from each pair changes chairs. A Chris and a Pat should now be seated together. They role play negotiating an agreement that resolves the conflict. The role play will be more interesting if you overdramatize somewhat.
3. Combine both pairs into a group of four. Each group is to share the agreements negotiated, discuss what made the conflict difficult to resolve, come to a consensus about how it could be managed most constructively, and write out the ideal agreement to be negotiated. Each group shares its solution with the rest of the class.

CONFLICT DESCRIPTIONS

1. Chris enters a large lecture class and takes an aisle chair. Before the class begins, Chris places his or her books on the chair and then leaves to get a drink of water. Upon returning, Chris finds his/her books sitting in the aisle and Pat in the chair. What do you do? Role play the exchange.
2. Chris tells Pat (a friend) in confidence about someone Chris would like to date. The next day, several people comment on it. Chris gets Pat alone to talk about it. What do you do? Role play the exchange.
3. Chris has been sick for several weeks. The science instructor refuses to extend the deadline for Chris' final project. Because Chris cannot finish the project in time, this means that Chris will receive a low grade for the course. Chris believes the instructor is being very unfair. Chris decides to try talking to the instructor again. Role play the exchange.
4. Chris borrows Pat's history book. The next day, when Chris returns the book, it is muddy and the cover is torn. Pat believes that when you borrow something, you are responsible for taking care of it. Pat spends twenty minutes cleaning the book and taping the cover back together. Chris laughs and calls Pat a "neatness freak." What do you do? Role play the exchange.

HAMLET AND HIS FATHER'S GHOST

Using the instructions given above, role play the negotiations between Hamlet and his father's ghost.

Situation

The scene is the battlements of the castle of the king of Denmark. It is midnight, the witching hour. The ghost of Hamlet's father appears and beckons Hamlet to follow him for a private talk. They have a conflict that must be resolved. Find a partner. Flip a coin to see who will be Hamlet and who will be the ghost. Then resolve the conflict using the problem-solving negotiation procedure.

Ghost

I am your father's spirit. Listen to me. If you ever loved me you must avenge my foul, strange, and most unnatural murder. I was not bitten by a poisonous snake. The serpent that bit me now wears my crown. He is an incestuous beast. He seduced your mother, a seemingly virtuous queen. Then, when I was asleep in the garden, he poured poison into my ear. My own brother, your uncle, killed me to gain both my crown and my wife. This is horrible! Horrible! You must kill him! You are my son, and it is your duty to avenge my death. I cannot rest in my grave until my murder is avenged. You must fulfill your obligation and put me to rest. Denmark will not prosper with such a man on the throne. The king must be committed to the welfare of Denmark, not himself. Besides, if he has a son, you will lose your birthright.

Hamlet

I did not know you were murdered. I thought you died of a snake bite. This is a complete surprise to me. The fact that my uncle murdered you is even more of a surprise. I have a relationship with this man. I certainly want justice, but let's not be hasty. Asking me to kill him is a serious request. First, I may be too young and inexperienced to do it right. You would do better to ask one of your generals to do it. Second, killing my uncle could seriously damage my future career options and quality of life. Don't be so bloodthirsty. Think of my future.

Third, this is not the time for me to kill someone. I am a carefree youth. I am in love. I'm still in school. I have years of learning and maturing left before I will be ready to kill someone. Fourth, I would never rest in my grave, and I might even go to hell, if I killed my uncle. Finally, killing my uncle is a complex task. I have to catch him alone doing something wicked so that his soul will go to hell. What use is it if I kill him when he is doing something virtuous and he goes to heaven? This is not one of the usual "walk into the room and stab him" killings. This one is very complex and difficult. I'm not sure I want to do that much work.

THE INTEGRATIVE NEGOTIATING PROCEDURE

Step 1: Describe What You Want (Your Interests)

In describing what you want, you assert your wants and listen carefully to the other person's wants. Describing your wants and goals includes describing (not evaluating) the other person's actions and defining the conflict (a) as a mutual problem and (b) as briefly and specifically as possible.

Describing What You Want.   Negotiating begins when you describe what you want. **Everyone has a perfect right to their wants, needs, and goals** (Alberti & Emmons, 1978). Two of the major mistakes in defining a conflict are to be *aggressive* by trying to hurt the other person or to be *nonassertive* by saying nothing, giving up your interests, and keeping your wants to yourself. You can *assert* your wants, needs, and goals directly to another person in an honest and appropriate way that respects both yourself and the other person. On the other hand, **everyone has a perfect right to refuse to meet your wants and needs or facilitate your goal accomplishment if they see it as destructive to their own interests to do so.** No one has to act against his or her own interests just to please someone else. After asserting your needs and goals, therefore, do not expect the other person to do exactly as you wish. **Do not confuse letting others know what you want with demanding that they act as you think they should.** Providing others with information about your interests is different from trying to force others to act in the ways you wish them to.

Communicating what you want involves taking ownership of your interests by making personal statements that describe your wants and goals (Table 9.4). To clearly communicate your wants and goals to the other person (Johnson, 2003; Johnson & Johnson, 1995a):

1. **Make personal statements** that refer to *I, me, my,* or *mine*.
2. **Be specific** about your wants, needs, and goals and establish their legitimacy.
3. **Acknowledge the other person's goals as part of the problem.** Describe how the other person's actions are blocking what you want. In doing so, separate the behavior from the person. A **behavioral description statement** includes the specific behaviors you have observed and does *not* include any judgment or evaluation or any inferences about the person's motives, personality, or attitudes.

Table 9.4 **Respect for Self and Others**

My Respect for Me	My Respect for You
I Have a Perfect Right To:	**You Have a Perfect Right To:**
My needs and wants	Your wants and needs
Tell you what I want	Tell me what you want
Tell you how I feel	Tell me how you feel
Refuse to give you what you want	Refuse to give me what I want

We Have a Perfect Right to Negotiate with Each Other

4. **Focus on the long-term cooperative relationship.** During most conflicts of interests, you will be discussing the current problems in your relationship. Negotiations within a long-term cooperative relationship include discussing how the relationship can be changed so that the two of you can work together better. During such conversations, you will need to make relationship statements. A **relationship statement** describes some aspect of the way the two of you are interacting with each other. A good relationship statement indicates clear ownership (refers to *I, me, my,* or *mine*) and describes how you see the relationship. "I think we need to talk about our disagreement yesterday" is a good relationship statement.

Furthermore, how you present your proposed agreement has implications for both your commitment to your current position and the response to it by other group members. To persuade others, you may overemphasize the factors that favor your position, and this overattention to positive arguments results in selective retention of position-consistent information. In addition, arguing for your position tends to result in increased commitment to it (Hovland, Janis, & Kelley, 1953) and a belief that you are committed through self-perception (Bem, 1972). If you are too demanding in your presentation, however, your attempts to persuade may boomerang. Jack Brehm (1976; Brehm & Brehm, 1981) demonstrated that persuasive attempts that are viewed as coercive or biased often backfire by causing others to reject what you are saying and increase their commitment to their original positions. This intensification is called **psychological reactance**—the need to reestablish your freedom whenever it is threatened. In one of the Bem studies, for example, two teammates had to choose between two alternatives marked 1-A or 1-B. When the partner stated, "I prefer 1-A," 73% chose it but when the partner stated, "I think we should both do 1-A," only 40% chose it (Brehm & Sensenig, 1966). Similarly, 83% of the members of a group refused to go along with a member who stated, "I think it's pretty obvious that all of us are going to work on task A" (Worchel & Brehm, 1971).

Listening to the Other Person's Wants. Your success as a negotiator depends largely on showing the other person how his or her needs and goals may be met by accepting your proposals. In order to make a persuasive case for your position, you have to understand clearly what the other person's interests (and feelings) are. This requires careful listening and being able to see the situation from the other person's perspective. There is no set of skills more important for negotiating than being a good listener (Johnson, 1991, 2003). **To listen to another person, you must (a) face the person, (b) stay quiet (until your turn comes), (c) think about what the person is saying, and (d) show that you understand.** The key to good listening is paraphrasing. **Paraphrasing** is restating, in your own words, what the person says, feels, and means. This improves communication in several ways. *First,* it helps you avoid judging and evaluating. When you are restating, you are not passing judgment. *Second,* restating gives the sender direct feedback on how well you understand the messages. If you do not fully understand, the sender can add messages until you do. If you are interpreting the message differently from the way he or she intended it, the sender can clarify. Being able to clarify and elaborate is important for making sure that communication is taking place. *Third,* paraphrasing communicates to the sender that you want to understand what he or she is saying. It shows that you care enough to listen carefully, that you are interested, that you take what he or she is saying seriously, and that you want to understand. *Finally,* paraphrasing helps you see the message from the sender's perspective.

Paraphrasing is often a simple restatement of what has been said. At first, it may feel foolish to restate what another person has said. It may feel awkward and unnatural until you get used to doing it. But the speaker will be grateful for a chance to clarify or add to the original statement, and he or she will feel grateful for being understood. Paraphrasing becomes harder when it includes feelings as well as ideas. It is not limited to the words the sender uses. Nonverbal cues are also important.

Often in a conflict it is helpful to follow the **paraphrasing rule** (Johnson, 1971): Before you can reply to a statement, restate what the sender says, feels, and means correctly and to the sender's satisfaction. When you use paraphrasing, there is a rhythm to your statements. The rhythm is "You said . . . ; I say. . . ." First, you say what the sender said (You said). Then you reply (I say). Paraphrasing is often essential in defining a conflict so that a constructive resolution may be negotiated.

Describing the Other Person's Actions.   Imagine that you and a close friend are in a conflict. Your friend believes you have behaved in a very destructive way. You believe your behavior was caused by extenuating circumstances, the actions of other people, and a desire to do the right thing. You conclude that your friend should understand and forgive you. Your friend, however, insists that your behavior was caused by your negative personal characteristics such as poor judgment, irresponsibility, selfishness, a lack of concern, a tendency to show off, and incompetence. You are deeply hurt and counterattack, accusing your friend of being a person of low moral character who is irresponsible and selfish, has poor judgment, and lacks any concern for you. Both you and your friend consider the other's attributions to be unfair and unreasonable and, therefore, the conflict is escalated. Harold Kelley and his associates (Kelley, 1979; Orvis, Kelley, & Butler, 1976) found just such a cycle in a study of 700 conflicts in forty-one marriages.

Conflicts are created and escalated when individuals engage in destructive acts. The harm destructive acts do cannot be easily repaired, no matter how considerate and thoughtful a person is later. Destructive acts are exceptionally detrimental to relationships, whereas constructive acts do not yield commensurately positive consequences (e.g., Billings, 1979; Gottman, 1993; Jacobson & Margolin, 1979; Markman, 1981; Rusbult & Van Lange, 1996). In conflicts, there are two general classes of destructive acts:

1. Directly hurting the other person.
2. Inferring that the other person's actions are the result of dispositional (personality, beliefs, attitudes, and values) factors.

Avoiding directly hurtful actions is always a good idea. More difficult to control, however, are the inferences you make about other people's behavior. Especially in conflicts, there is a tendency to attribute the causes of the opponent's behavior to his or her psychological state (Blake & Mouton, 1962; Chesler & Franklin, 1968; Sherif & Sherif, 1969) while at the same time attributing the causes of your own behavior to situational (environmental) factors. This is known as the **fundamental attribution error** (Ross, 1977; Ross & Nisbett, 1991). Inferences about the causes of behaviors and events are known as *attributions*. **Attribution theory** posits that people continually formulate intuitive causal hypotheses so that they can understand and predict events that transpire in the group (Heider, 1958). Attributions are especially important in conflict, because they influence perceptions of groupmates' motives and intentions (Steiner, 1959) and mediate reactions to groupmates' behaviors (Horai, 1977; Messe, Stollak, Larson, & Michaels, 1979). If attributions are accurate, they help group members understand each other better. If attributions are inaccurate, conflicts become destructive. Like everyone else, opponents want to appear strong and capable to others, and if they believe you are trying to label them as sick, weak, incompetent, or ineffective, they will refuse to negotiate flexibly (Brown, 1968; Pruitt & Johnson, 1970; Tjosvold, 1974, 1977).

During conflicts, attributing the causes of the opponent's behavior often follows a two-step process. *First,* there is an automatic (without conscious awareness) attribution of the causes of the opponent's behavior to dispositional (not situational) causes (Gilbert & Malone, 1995). *Second,* there is a reflective, thoughtful analysis during which the dispositional inferences are qualified with relevant situational information about the context of behavior and the initial dispositional inferences are corrected (Gilbert, McNulty, Giuliano, & Benson, 1992; Reeder, 1993). Whether or not the second step occurs may depend on how constructively the conflict is being managed.

Defining a conflict is like lacing your shoes. If you start out wrong, the whole process is derailed. Separate the person from the problem. Negotiate over issues, not personalities. Avoid personalized attacks. Describe the other's actions toward you.

Defining the Conflict as a Mutual Problem

A house divided against itself cannot stand.

Abraham Lincoln

Two drivers, coming from different directions, are roaring down a one-lane road. Soon they will crash head on. If the two drivers define the situation as a competition to see who will "chicken out," they will probably crash and both will die. If the two drivers define the situation as a problem to be solved, they will tend to see a solution in which they alternate giving each other the right of way. Even simple and small conflicts become major and difficult to resolve when they are defined in a competitive, win–lose way. Even major and difficult conflicts become resolvable when they are defined as problems to be solved.

A conflict defined as a problem to be solved is much easier to resolve constructively than a conflict defined as a win–lose situation (Blake & Mouton, 1962; Deutsch

& Lewicki, 1970). The total benefits for all sides in negotiations are higher than when problem-solving strategies are used (Lewis & Pruitt, 1971). One of the most constructive things you can do in a conflict is to define the conflict as a mutual problem to be solved. Doing so will tend to increase communication, trust, liking for each other, and cooperation. No one tends to lose when you and the other person sit down to solve a mutual problem.

To define a conflict jointly, group members have to use a common language about conflicts. The group language may include such terms as *win–lose, problem solve, confront, beltline,* and *gunnysack* (i.e., to store up grievances for a long time and then unload them all on an offending group member). A common language about conflicts facilitates the identification of constructive and destructive strategies of negotiation. Groups may develop their own vocabulary for describing conflict behaviors and procedures.

Defining the Conflict as Being Small and Specific.   Fred wants to join a baseball game on the playground. "You can't play," Ralph shouts. "We already have our teams!" "You are no longer my friend!" Fred shouts back. "You're selfish and mean! I'll never help you with your homework again!" In defining a conflict, there is an unfortunate tendency to be global and general. Fred is defining the conflict as being one of friendship and gratitude. This creates difficulty in resolving it. He could just as easily have defined the conflict as being one of arriving late or finding a way to make the teams even.

In defining a conflict, the more briefly and specifically it is defined, the easier it is to resolve (Deutsch, Canavan, & Rubin, 1971). Think small. The more global, general, and vague the definition of the conflict, the harder it is to resolve. Defining a conflict as "She always lies" makes it more difficult to resolve than defining it as "Her statement was not true." When it comes to resolving conflicts, small is easy and large is hard.

Step 2: Describe Your Feelings

Many of us in business, especially if we are very sure of our ideas, have hot tempers. My father knew he had to keep the damage from his own temper to a minimum.

Thomas Watson, Jr., Chairman Emeritus, IBM

The second step in negotiating to solve a problem is to describe how you feel. Expressing and controlling your feelings is one of the most difficult aspects of resolving conflicts. It is also one of the most important for several reasons (Johnson, 1996; Johnson & Johnson, 1995a). *First,* many conflicts cannot be resolved unless feelings are openly recognized and expressed. If individuals hide or suppress their anger, for example, they may make an agreement but they keep their resentment and hostility toward the other person. Their ability to work effectively with the other person is damaged, as is their ability to resolve future conflicts constructively. The conflict will tend to recur regardless of what the agreement is. *Second,* it is through experiencing and sharing feelings that close relationships are built and maintained. Feelings provide the cement holding relationships together as well as the means for deepening relationships and making them more effective and personal. *Third*, feelings that are not accepted and recognized can (a) create bias in your judgments, (b) create insecurities that make it more difficult to deal with the conflict in constructive ways, and (c) reduce your control over your behavior. For many reasons it is often best to communicate your feelings directly when conflicts are building.

Fourth, the only way other people can know how you are feeling and reacting is to tell them (see Johnson, 1996, and Johnson & Johnson, 1995a, for specifics). In order to communicate your feelings you must be aware of them, accept them, and be skillful in expressing them constructively.

Step 3: Exchange Reasons for Positions

Once both you and the other person have expressed what you want and how you feel, listened carefully to each other, and jointly defined the conflict as a small and specific mutual problem, you must exchange the reasons for your positions. To do so, both of you have to:

1. Express cooperative intentions.
2. Present your reasons and listen to the other person's reasons.
3. Focus on wants and interests, not positions.
4. Clarify the differences between your and the other's interests before trying to integrate them into an agreement.
5. Empower the other person.

Expressing Cooperative Intentions: Enlarging the Shadow of the Future. One of the most constructive things you can do in resolving a conflict is to highlight the long-term cooperative relationship. This is done in three ways. The *first* is to stress dealing with the conflict in a problem-solving way. Say such things as "This situation means that we will have to work together," or "Let's cooperate in reaching an agreement," or "Let's try to reach an agreement that is good for both of us." The *second* is to state that you are committed to maximizing the joint outcomes. Successful negotiation requires finding out what the other person really wants and needs and showing him or her a way to get it while you get what you want. The *third* is to enlarge the shadow of the future by stating that you are committed to the continuation and success of the joint cooperative efforts. In doing so, you must point out (a) the long-term mutual goals and (b) the ways the two of you will be interdependent for the foreseeable future.

The clear and unambiguous expression of cooperative intentions in negotiations allows you to reach higher-quality agreements in less time. The other person becomes less defensive, more willing to change his or her position, less concerned about who is right and wrong, and more understanding of your views and ideas (Johnson, 1971, 1974; Johnson, McCarty, & Allen, 1976). The other person tends to see you as an understanding and trustworthy person whom he or she can confide in.

The expression of competitive intentions, such as threats and punishments, tends to escalate the conflict (Deutsch & Krauss, 1960, 1962). Imagine that you own a trucking company that carries merchandise over the roads pictured in Figure 9.4. Each time your truck reaches its destination, you earn sixty cents minus the operating cost of

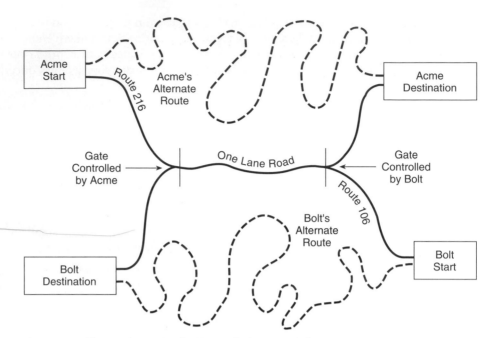

Figure 9.4 The road map in the Deutsch–Krauss trucking game.
Source: M. Deutsch, *The resolution of conflict: Constructive and destructive processes* (New Haven, CT: Yale University Press, 1973). Reprinted with permission.

one cent for each second it takes. Part of the road is one-way. If you encounter a truck going the opposite way, one of you will have to reverse to let the other through. If the other person refuses to back up, you can close a gate at the other end, and then he or she will have to back up and take the alternative route. You can then open the gate for yourself and proceed rapidly to your destination. Describe how you would behave.

Morton Deutsch and Robert Krauss (1960, 1962) used this imaginary situation to determine how the use of threats affects hostility, counterthreats, and unwillingness to compromise. In the unilateral-threat condition, only one participant had a gate. In the bilateral-threat condition, both sides had gates. In the control condition, no gates were present. When no gate was present, the participants learned to alternate in their use of the one-way road and both made a profit of about $1.00. When one participant had a gate, participants lost an average of $2.03 per person, although the participant with the gate lost less than the participant without the gate. When both participants had a gate, each one lost an average of $4.38. Thus, the use of threats was counterproductive, intensifying the destructive aspects of the conflict. In considering the use of threats, you may be advised to remember the advice of Niccolo Machiavelli, an adviser to sixteenth-century Florentine princes:

> I hold it be a proof of great prudence for men to abstain from threats and insulting words toward anyone, for neither . . . diminishes the strength of the enemy; but the

one makes him more cautious and the other increases his hatred of you and makes him more persevering in his efforts to injure you.

Presenting Your Reasons and Listening to the Other Person's Reasons. To say what you want and how you feel is not enough. You must also give your reasons for wanting what you want and feeling as you do. It is not enough to say, "I want to use the computer now and I'm angry at you for not letting me have it." You must also say, "I have an important homework assignment due today and this is my only chance to get it done." Your reasons are aimed at (a) informing the other person and (b) persuading him or her to agree with you.

Many times you will have to ask the other person why he or she has taken a certain position. You may ask a friend to study with you. She may reply "no." Until you understand the reasons for the answer, you will not be able to think creatively of ways for both of you to get what you want. The statement in doing so is, "May I ask why?" If the answer is vague, you add, "Could you be more specific?" or "What do you mean when you say . . . ?" or "I'm not sure I understand." Your tone of voice is as important as the words when you ask these questions. If you sound sarcastic your attempt to understand the other person will backfire.

Once both of you have explained your reasons, either of you may agree or disagree to help the other person reach his or her goals. The decision to help the other person reach his or her goals or keep negotiating is based on two factors:

1. How important your goal is to you.
2. How important the other person's goal is to him or her (based on the reasons he or she presents).

You must listen carefully to the reasons given and decide whether they are valid or not. If you decide that the other person's goals are far more important to him or her than yours are to you, then you may wish to agree at this point. Giving up your goals to help the other person reach his or her goals works only if he or she does the same for you about 50% of the time. This is the one-step negotiation procedure.

If the other person's reasons are not valid, you need to point that out so that he or she can see the inadequacies of his or her proposals. If neither you nor the other person is convinced to give up your own goals in order to fulfill the goals of the other, then the two of you must reaffirm your cooperative relationship and explore each other's reasons at a deeper level.

Focusing on Wants and Interests, not Positions. Susan is usually a compliant student in Mr. Johnson's English class. Today, however, she comes up to Mr. Johnson's desk and states, "I won't do this homework assignment. I don't care what you do to me; I'm not going to do it!" Mr. Johnson, having read this book, immediately recognizes that Susan is presenting a position, and he does not yet know what her needs and wants are. He says, "May I ask why?" In order to negotiate successfully and reach an agreement that satisfies both people, you have to approach the other person on the basis of his or her wants and goals.

The classic example of the need to separate interests from positions is that of two sisters, each of whom wanted the only orange available. One sister wanted the peel of the orange to make a cake; the other wanted the pulp to make orange juice. Their positions ("I want the orange!") were opposed, but their interests were not. Often when conflicting parties reveal their underlying interests, it is possible to find a solution that suits them both.

The heart of negotiations is meeting the goals of the other person while ensuring that your goals are being met. The success of negotiations depends on finding out what the other person really wants and showing him or her a way to get it while you get what you want. For a wise decision, therefore, reconcile wants and goals, not positions. For every want or goal, there usually exist several possible positions that could satisfy it. A common mistake is to assume that because the other person's position is opposed to yours, his or her goals must also be opposed. Behind opposed positions lie shared and compatible goals as well as conflicting ones. To identify the other person's wants and goals, ask "Why?" or "Why not?" and think about his or her choice, and realize that the other person has many different wants and goals.

Focusing on needs and goals rather than positions eliminates many of the traps that cause conflicts to become destructive. One such trap is the aggression that arises from being frustrated by the opponent's refusal to agree with your position. The link between frustration and aggression is one of the oldest social psychological explanations of hostility and physical violence. The **frustration-aggression process** may be summarized in the following way (Berkowitz, 1978). Individuals who are unable to attain their goals because of personal limitations or external influences sometimes experience frustration. This frustration produces a readiness to respond in an aggressive manner, which may boil over into hostility and violence if situational cues that serve as *releasers* are present. Negotiators can become frustrated and, at any sign of belligerence or hostility by others, release verbal and, in some cases, physical violence. What often prevents high levels of frustration is the continual clarification of needs and goals and the search for new positions that let all members reach their goals.

Differentiating Before Integrating.   Conflicts cannot be resolved unless you understand what you are disagreeing about. You must understand the differences between your wants and needs and those of the other person. Only then will you be able to think of ways to satisfy both yourself and the other person so that the conflict can be resolved constructively. Your ability to come up with satisfactory solutions depends on your understanding of how the other person's thoughts, feelings, and needs are different from yours. The more you differentiate between your interests and those of the other person, the better you will be able to integrate them into a mutually satisfying agreement. In discussing a conflict, you try to find the answers to these questions: (a) What are the differences between my wants and needs and those of the other person? (b) Where are our needs and goals the same? (c) What actions of the other person do I find unacceptable? and (d) What actions of mine does the other person find unacceptable?

Empowering the Other Person.   During negotiations it is important that you do not let the other person feel powerless. Shared power and wise agreements go hand in hand. **There are two ways to empower the other person.** The *first* is by being open to negotiations and flexible about the option you like the best. If the other person can negotiate with you, then he or she has power and options. Willingness to negotiate is based on being open to the possibility that there may be a better option available than you now realize. Staying tentative and flexible means that you do not become overcommitted to any one position until an agreement is reached. The *second* is to provide power through choice among options. Generate a variety of possible solutions before deciding what to do. If Susan says to Mr. Johnson, "You have to agree to let me not do my homework," he will feel powerless. If Susan said, "Let's think of three possible agreements, and then choose the one that seems the best," both she and Mr. Johnson feel powerful.

The psychological costs of being helpless to resolve grievances include frustration, anxiety, and friction. When a person is powerless, he or she either becomes hostile and tries to tear down the system or becomes apathetic and throws in the towel. You do not want the other person to do either one. We all need to believe that we have been granted a fair hearing and that we should have the power and the right to gain justice when we have been wronged. If it becomes evident that we cannot gain justice, frustration, anger, depression, and anxiety may result (Deutsch, 1985).

Staying Flexible.   **Stay flexible, changing your position and feelings when persuaded to do so.** Negotiating is a rational process. You are seeking a way to satisfy your needs and reach your goals, and the other person is doing the same. How successful you are in reaching an agreement that is good for you depends on how creatively you can think of alternatives that also are good for the other person. This requires flexibility and a willingness to change your mind when you are persuaded that it is rational to do so. It is very easy and quite common to become trapped in your commitment to a position and close your mind to alternatives. Allan Teger (1980), for example, studied the entrapment process by conducting "dollar auctions." A dollar is auctioned off to the highest bidder with the rule that although the highest bidder gets to keep the dollar, the second highest bidder must pay the amount he or she bid. Thus, if a person bid eighty cents for the dollar and someone else bid ninety cents, the person is trapped in bidding higher to avoid losing the eighty cents. Negotiators need to be vigilant against being trapped by their commitment to old proposals and positions.

Coordinating Motivation to Negotiate in Good Faith.   There are often differences in motivation to resolve a conflict. You may want to resolve a conflict but other group members could care less. Your groupmate may be very concerned about resolving a conflict with you, but you may want to avoid the whole thing. Usually, a conflict cannot be resolved until both persons are motivated to resolve it at the same time. **The motivation to resolve a conflict is based on the costs and gains of continuing the conflict for each person.** The costs of continuing a conflict may be the loss of a friendship, the loss of enjoyment from work, the loss of job productivity, the loss of a friend, or the loss of respect from the other person. The gains for continuing the conflict may be satisfaction in expressing your anger or resentment and the protection of the status quo. By protecting the status quo, you avoid the possibility that things will get worse when the conflict is resolved. Answering the following questions may help you clarify your motivation and the motivation of the other person to resolve the conflict:

1. What do I gain from continuing the conflict?
2. What does the other person gain from continuing the conflict?

3. What do I lose from continuing the conflict?
4. What does the other person lose from continuing the conflict?

A person's motivation to resolve a conflict can be changed. By increasing the costs of continuing the conflict or by increasing the gains for resolving it, the other person's motivation to resolve it can be increased. By changing the costs and gains, you can change both your and the other person's motivation to resolve the conflict.

When the outcomes of negotiations are presented as gains, more concessions are made than when the outcomes are presented as losses. Negotiators who think in terms of losses or costs are more likely to take the risk of losing all by holding out in an attempt to force further concessions from the opponent. A negotiator should try to present information in a way that leads the opposition to see what they have to gain from a settlement.

It is within the exchange of proposals and feelings that the dilemmas of trust and openness arise. The better negotiators understand each other's interests, the better the agreement that can ultimately be achieved. A negotiator faces the dilemmas of whether or not to (a) trust opponents to tell the truth about their interests and (b) tell the truth about his or her own interests to the opposing negotiators. Deutsch (1958, 1960, 1973) used the **Prisoner's Dilemma Game** (PDG) to study the issue of trust within conflict situations. The PDG derives its name from a hypothetical situation studied by mathematical game theorists (Luce & Raiffa, 1957). Imagine that you and your partner have just robbed a bank, hidden the money, and are arrested by police who are sure you are guilty but have no proof. The police's only hope of convicting you is to get you to confess. The officers take you and your partner into separate rooms to question you (Figure 9.5). You are both presented with two alternatives: Confess to the crime or remain silent. If neither of you confesses, you will both be tried on a minor charge that carries the light sentence of one year in prison. If you both confess, each of you will spend five years in prison. If your partner confesses and you do not, your partner will go free but you will get ten years in prison. Conversely, if you confess and your partner does not,

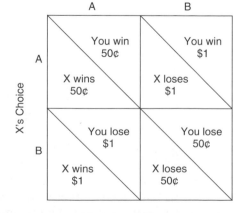

Figure 9.5   The Prisoner's Dilemma Game.

you will go free and your partner will go to prison for ten years. The dilemma for you and your partner is whether to trust the other to remain silent and not exploit your silence if you remain silent. If both you and your partner trust the other to keep silent, both of you will benefit.

To conduct research on trust, Deutsch used the prisoner's dilemma situation in a game format in which pairs of participants were paid according to the combination of their choices (see Figure 9.5). If both choose A, both receive fifty cents. If both choose B, both lose fifty cents. If one chooses A and the other chooses B, the person choosing B wins one dollar and the person choosing A loses one dollar. Although the PDG has been overused in research on conflict, it was a remarkable methodological breakthrough when Deutsch initiated its use. One of its most important uses was by Robert Axelrod (1984) in his studies of the evolution of cooperation (see Chapter 4). What the results of research using the PDG demonstrate is that the pursuit of self-interests by each group member leads to a poor outcome for all. In the long run, only cooperative behavior based on trust ensures the well-being of all group members.

Potential Problems. There are two problems in analyzing underlying interests. *First,* sometimes a person does not understand the interests underlying his or her position and preferences and, therefore, cannot describe them to others. *Second,* disputants may not wish to reveal their interests out of fear that the other will use this information to personal advantage. Revealing one's wants, goals, and interests always carries the risk of having one's vulnerability exploited. A person's interests are often organized into hierarchical trees, with the initial interests discussed being the tip of the iceberg. With more and more discussion, deeper and deeper interests may be revealed.

Step 4: Understand the Other's Perspective

The test of a first-rate intelligence is the ability to hold two opposed ideas in the mind at the same time, and still retain the ability to function.

F. Scott Fitzgerald

To reach a wise agreement, you must have a clear understanding of all sides of the issue, an accurate assessment of their validity and relative merits, and the ability to think creatively to come up with potential solutions that maximize joint outcomes and fulfill the interests of all disputants. To do all this, you must be able to (a) see the conflict from both your own and the other person's perspective and (b) keep both perspectives in mind at the same time. A **perspective** is a way of viewing the world (as well as specific situations) and one's relation to it. **Social perspective-taking** is the ability to understand how a situation appears to another person and how that person is reacting cognitively and emotionally to the situation. The opposite of perspective-taking is **egocentrism,** or being unaware that other perspectives exist and that one's own view of the conflict is incomplete and limited. There are two types of social perspective-taking (Batson, Early, & Salvarani, 1997). The *first* is understanding how another person feels; it creates empathy and evokes altruistic motivation. The *second* is understanding how you would feel if you were the other person; it creates a combination of empathy for the other person and personal distress, and it evokes egoistic motivation. In engaging in perspective-taking, it is important to understand the situation from the other's perspective, not imagine how you would feel if you were the other person.

Engaging in social perspective-taking may be difficult given the following aspects of perspectives. **First, each person has a unique perspective.** Your perspective is developed as a result of the ways in which you respond to your experiences as an infant, child, youth, and adult. Other people have developed their perspectives on the basis of their responses to their life experiences. This means that different people have different perspectives. No two people will see an issue in exactly the same way. Each person will interpret identical events differently.

Second, a person's perspective selects and organizes what the person attends to and experiences. All experiences are interpreted and understood within the perspective from which they are viewed. People tend to see only what their perspective allows them to see. A rich person and a poor person may see a homeless person differently because they have two quite different perspectives. To make the situation worse, people tend to see only what they want to see. Out of a mass of detailed information, people tend to pick out and focus on those facts that confirm their prior perceptions and to disregard or misinterpret those that call their perceptions into question. Each side in a negotiation tends to see only the merits of its case and only the faults of the other side. It is not enough to understand logically how the other person views the problem. If you want to influence the other person, you also need to understand empathetically the power of his or her point of view and to feel the emotional force with which he or she believes in it. You may see on the table a glass half full of water. The other person may see a dirty, half-empty glass about to cause a ring on the mahogany finish. Change a person's perspective and you change what the person attends to and the way the person interprets the events in his or her life. Understand the other's perspective and you change your ability to find integrative solutions to the conflict.

Third, a person can have different perspectives at different times. If you have been lifting hundred-pound bags of cement and someone tosses you a forty-pound bag, it will seem very light. But if you have been lifting twenty-pound bags, the forty-pound bag will seem very heavy. When you are hungry, you notice all the food in a room. When you are not hungry, the food does not attract your attention. As your job role, experiences, assumptions, physiological states, and values change, your perspective will change.

Fourth, the same message can mean two entirely different things from two different perspectives. A teasing comment may be perceived as a sign of friendliness by a coworker or as a sign of hostile insubordination by your boss. Different perspectives may result in the message being given different meanings.

Fifth, misunderstandings often occur because we assume that everyone sees things from our perspective. If we like Italian food, we assume that all our friends like Italian food. If we are interested in sports, we assume that everyone is interested in sports. If we get angry when someone laughs at our behavior, we assume that everyone will get angry when they are laughed at. If we think a teacher is stupid, we are surprised when a peer thinks the teacher is brilliant.

Accurate perspective-taking is one of the most difficult aspects of conflict resolution. It is also one of the most important for a number of reasons (see Johnson & Johnson [1989] for a complete review of the research).

First, perspective-taking improves communication and reduces misunderstandings and distortions by influencing how messages are phrased and received. Negotiators often misunderstand and distort the positions of the others involved in the conflict due to poor communication. The better you understand the other person's perspective, the more able you are to phrase messages so that the other person can easily understand them. If a person does not know what snow is, for example, you do not refer to "corn snow" or "fresh powder." In addition, understanding the other person's perspective helps you understand his or her messages accurately and retain them over time. For example, if the other person says, "That's just great!" the meaning is reversed if you know the person is frustrated. The better negotiators are at perspective-taking, the more information, both personal and impersonal, they disclose.

Second, perspective-taking facilitates the development of creative and high-quality solutions to the joint problem. Understanding a wide variety of perspectives on an issue, seeing the merits of other positions and the shortcomings of your position, incorporating information from other positions into your own, and feeling the emotional force with which others hold their positions all help spark the creativity needed to find integrative solutions to the joint problem.

Third, perspective-taking tends to improve the relationship with the other person. You are more liked and respected when the other person realizes that you are seeing his or her perspective accurately and using it to create potential agreements that benefit both sides equally. You also will tend to have a more positive view of the negotiations.

Fourth, taking the other person's perspective transforms a disputant's motivation from immediate self-interests to long-term concerns about joint outcomes and the well-being of the relationship. Being locked in one's own perspective results in acting on the basis of immediate self-interest (Dehue, McClintock, & Liebrand, 1993; Yovetich & Rusbult, 1994). Adopting the partner's perspective activates broader concerns including joint outcomes and the well-being of the partner and the relationship (Davis, Conklin, Smith, & Luce, 1996; Johnson, 1971). Adopting the other person's perspective results in more positive and less negative emotion and cognition, such as situationally based, less blameful construals of the partner's seemingly destructive acts (Johnson, 1971; Jones & Nesbett, 1972; Regan & Totten, 1975; Storms, 1973). Adopting the perspective of the other person (a) increases positive emotional reactions (caring, affectionate), attributional interpretations (relationship enhancing), and behavior preferences (constructive and active behaviors) and (b) reduces negative emotions (annoyed, bitter), attributions (blaming the partner), and behavioral preferences (destructive and passive behaviors) (Arriaga & Rusbult, 1998).

You ensure that you accurately see the situation from the other person's perspective by (a) asking for clarification or correction to make sure your understanding is accurate (this is called **perception checking**), (b) stating your understanding of the other's wants and needs (i.e., paraphrasing), and (c) presenting the other's position from his or her perspective.

The most effective way to gain insight into the other person's perspective is to play the role of the other person and present the other person's position and reasoning as if you were he or she. Then have the other person do the same. The more involved the two of you get in arguing for the other's position, the more you will understand how the conflict appears from the other person's viewpoint. Such role playing is invaluable in finding solutions that are mutually acceptable. A systematic series of studies on the impact of perspective reversal on the resolution of conflicts has been conducted (Johnson, 1971). The results indicated that skillful role reversal increases cooperative behavior between

Rules to Follow in Taking the Other's Perspective

1. Do not deduce the other person's intentions from your fears. People tend to assume that whatever they fear, the other person intends to do.

2. Do not blame the other person for your problem. Blaming is an easy habit to fall into. Even if blaming is justified, it is counterproductive. It will make the other person defensive and closed-minded.

3. Discuss each other's perceptions.

4. Look for opportunities to act inconsistently with the other person's negative perceptions.

5. Give the other person a stake in the outcome by making sure that he or she participates in the process. Agreement becomes much easier if both people feel ownership of the ideas.

6. Make your proposals consistent with the other person's goals and values, thereby, help him or her save face.

negotiators, clarifies misunderstanding of the other's position, increases understanding of the other's position, and increases one's ability to perceive the issue from the other's frame of reference. Johnson also found that role reversal, skillfully used, can result not only in a reevaluation of the issue and a change of attitude toward it, but also in a perception of the role reverser as a person who tries to understand the other's position, as an understanding person in general, as a person willing to compromise, and as a cooperative and trustworthy person. Temporarily arguing your opponent's position does result in insight into your opponent's perspective and changes your attitudes about the issues being negotiated.

There is nothing more important in resolving conflicts constructively than understanding how the conflict appears from the other person's perspective. Once you can view the conflict from both your own and the other person's perspective, you can find mutually beneficial solutions. You can also communicate to the other person that you really understand his or her thoughts, feelings, and needs. It is usually much easier to resolve a conflict when the other person feels understood. The more skilled you are in seeing things from the other person's point of view, the more skilled you will be in resolving conflicts constructively.

Step 5: Invent Options for Mutual Gain

One completely overcomes only what one assimilates.

Andre Gide

The fifth step of negotiating is to identify several possible agreements. One will rarely do. People have a tendency to agree to the first reasonable solution that is proposed, but doing so shuts off consideration of even more advantageous agreements. Thus, make sure you generate at least three good alternative agreements before deciding on which one to adopt. To invent a number of potential agreements, you must avoid a number of obstacles and you must think creatively.

Avoiding Obstacles.   Inventing options does not come naturally. Not inventing options is the normal state of affairs, even within the easiest negotiations. In most negotiations, five major obstacles inhibit the invention of a number of options:

1. **Judging prematurely.** Nothing is so harmful to inventing options as a critical attitude waiting to pounce on the drawbacks of any new idea. Premature criticism is the first impediment to creative thinking.
2. **Searching for the single answer.** Premature closure and fixation on the first proposal formulated as the single best answer is a sure short circuit of wise decision making.
3. **Assuming a fixed pie.** This inhibits creative thinking. Do not assume that the less for you, the more for me. Rarely, if ever, is this assumption true. Expanding the pie is a key to flexible problem solving. Imagine that you want to see one movie and your date wants to see another one. You also know that your date likes to eat at a certain restaurant. By enlarging the pie to include which restaurant you go to for dinner before going to a movie, an integrative agreement is possible (one person picks the restaurant, the other picks the movie).
4. **Being concerned only with your own immediate needs and goals.** In a relationship, to meet your needs you also have to meet the other person's needs. Shortsighted self-concern leads to partisan positions, partisan arguments, and one-sided solutions.
5. **Defensively sticking with the status quo to avoid the fear of the unknown inherent in change.** Changing creates anxiety about potential new and unknown problems and guilt over ineffective or inappropriate behavior in the past. Many times people try to justify their past actions by refusing to change.

Inventing Creative Options.   Follett (1940) gives an example of a conflict between two people reading in a library room. One wants to open the window for ventilation; the other wants to keep it closed in order not to catch cold. To resolve their conflict, they search for creative options. They finally agree to open a window in the next room, thereby letting in fresh air while avoiding a draft. Finding potential agreements that will maximize joint outcomes often takes creative problem solving. To invent creative options, you need to:

1. **Think of as many options as possible.** The more options exist, the greater the room for negotiations. Find ways to expand the number of options rather than looking for a single answer. One of the keys to wise decision making is selecting from among a large number and variety of options.
2. **Separate the act of inventing options from the act of judging them.** Invent first, judge later.
3. **Gather as much information as possible about the problem.** The more you know about the problem, the easier it is to find solutions.
4. **See the problem from different perspectives and reformulate it in a way that lets new orientations to a solution emerge.** Such a reformulation often produces a

moment of insight by one or both participants. The insight is often accompanied by intense emotional experiences of illumination and excitement and leads to the reformulation of the problem so that solutions emerge.

5. **Search for mutual gains.** There always exists the possibility of joint gain. Look for solutions that will leave the other person satisfied as well. Try to maximize joint outcomes.

6. **Invent ways of making decisions easily.** Give the other person choices that are as painless as possible. If you want a horse to jump a fence, do not raise the fence. Propose agreements that both persons can truly accept.

7. **Test each proposed agreement against reality.** What are its strengths and weaknesses? What does each person gain and lose? How does it maximize joint outcomes?

The types of agreements that help maximize joint outcomes include:

1. **Expanding the pie** by finding ways to increase the available resources. Many conflicts arise from a perceived resource shortage. In such circumstances, integrative agreements can be devised by increasing the available resources.

2. **Package deals** in which parties include several related issues in one agreement. A package deal involving homework, in-class behavior, and helping another student may be easier to reach than trying to negotiate each separately.

3. **Trade-offs** in which two different things of comparable value are exchanged. A student may agree to do his homework if the teacher agrees never to call on him in class.

4. **Tie-ins** in which an issue considered extraneous by the other person is introduced and you offer to accept a certain settlement provided that this extraneous issue will also be settled to your satisfaction.

5. **Carve-outs** in which an issue is separated from a larger context, leaving the related issues unsettled. This is the opposite of a tie-in.

6. **Logrolling** in which each party concedes on his or her low-priority issues that are of high priority to the other person.

7. **Cost cutting** in which one person gets what he or she wants and the other's cost of conceding on those issues is reduced or eliminated.

8. **Bridging the initial positions** by creating a new option that satisfies both parties' interests that is different from what each originally thought he or she wanted. Rubin, Pruitt, and Kim (1994), for example, discuss a married couple in conflict over whether to vacation at the seashore or in the mountains. After some discussion, they identified their interests as swimming and fishing. They then agreed to visit a lake region that was neither at the seashore nor in the mountains but that offered excellent swimming and fishing.

After inventing a number of options, you and the other person will have to agree on which one to try out first. Some realistic assessment of the alternatives then takes place. In trying to decide which alternative to try first, it may help to remember Aesop's fable about the mice in trouble. The mice were saying, "It's terrible, just terrible! We really must do something about it, but what?" The mice were talking about the cat. One by one, they were falling into her claws. She would steal up softly, then spring suddenly, and there would be one mouse less. At last the mice held a meeting to decide what to do. After some discussion a young mouse jumped up. "I know what we should do—tie a bell around the cat's neck. Then we would hear her coming and we could run away fast!" The mice clapped their little paws for joy. What a good idea! Why hadn't they thought of it before? What a clever little fellow this young mouse was! But now a very old mouse, who hadn't opened his mouth during the whole meeting, got up to speak. "Friends, I agree that the plan of the young mouse is very clever indeed. But I should like to ask one question. Which of us is going to tie the bell around the cat's neck?" The moral is that there is no use adopting an option that cannot be implemented by one or both persons.

Once a variety of optional agreements are invented that maximize mutual gain and fulfill the interests of all parties, one of the options is selected to be the initial agreement.

Step 6: Reach a Wise Agreement

I never let the sun set on a disagreement with anybody who means a lot to me.

> Thomas Watson Sr., Founder, IBM

Given that we are all separate individuals with our own unique wants and needs, whenever we interact with others, we will have some interests that are congruent and other interests that are in conflict. It takes wisdom to manage the combination of shared and opposed interests and reach an agreement. **Wise agreements** are those that are fair to all participants, are based on principles, strengthen participants' ability to work together cooperatively, and improve participants' ability to resolve future conflicts constructively. In other words, wise agreements are those that meet the following criteria.

The first requirement for a wise agreement is that the agreement must meet the legitimate needs of all participants and be viewed as fair by everyone involved. In deciding on which option to adopt, keep in mind the importance of shared good feelings, preserving mutual interests, and preserving your shared history. Focus on the long-term relationship to ensure that the agreement is durable. Point out that your long-term survival and happiness should not be jeopardized by any agreement reached. To meet your and the other person's legitimate interests, the agreement should clearly specify the responsibilities and rights of everyone involved in implementing the agreement. This includes:

1. **The ways each person will act differently in the future.** These responsibilities should be stated in a *specific* (tells who does what, when, where, and how), *realistic* (each can do what he or she is agreeing to do), and *shared* (everyone agrees to do something different) way.

2. **How the agreement will be reviewed and renegotiated if it turns out to be unworkable.** This includes (a) the ways in which cooperation will be restored if one person slips and acts inappropriately and (b) the times participants will meet to discuss whether the agreement is working and what further steps can be taken to improve cooperation with each other. You cannot be sure the agreement will work until you try it out. After you have tested it for a while, it is a good idea to set aside some time to talk about how things are going. You may find that you need to make some changes or even rethink the whole problem. The idea is to keep on top of the problem so that the two of you can solve it creatively.

The second requirement for a wise agreement is that it is based on principles that can be justified on some objective criteria (Fisher & Ury, 1981). The objective criteria may be:

1. Everyone has an equal chance of benefiting (such as flipping a coin; one cuts, the other chooses; or letting a third-party arbitrator decide).
2. Fairness (taking turns, sharing, equal use). One way to assess fairness is to list the gains and losses for each person if the agreement is adopted and then see if they balance.
3. Scientific merit (based on theory, tested, evidence indicates it will work).
4. Community values (those who are most in need are being taken care of first).

Evaluate each of the proposed options on the basis of one of these objective criteria. Think through which standards are most appropriate to evaluate the options and make a decision based on principle. The more you do so, the more likely you are to produce a final agreement that is wise and fair.

Using objective criteria to evaluate a possible agreement may result in clarifying what is fair and just from both sides of the issue. Remember King Solomon. One of the first problems the new king was presented with involved two women who both claimed the same baby. They wanted him to decide whose it was. Sitting on his throne, Solomon listened carefully. The two women lived together in the same house. Their babies had been born only three days apart. Then one of the babies died. The first woman said, "This woman's child died in the night. She then arose and took my son from beside me and placed the dead child next to me. When I woke to feed my baby, I found her dead child in my arms." "No!" the other woman cried frantically. "The living child is my son!" Solomon calmly said, "Bring me a sword and bring me the baby. Divide the living child in two and give half to the one and half to the other." Everyone was shocked. "No! Please don't!" screamed the real mother. "She can have the child. Don't kill it!" "No," the other woman said, "let the child be neither mine nor yours, but divide it." "Aha!" said Solomon. "Now I know to whom the child belongs." Then pointing to the woman who had asked that the baby's life be spared, he said, "Give her the living child. She is its mother."

The third requirement for a wise agreement is that the agreement and the process of reaching it strengthen participants' ability to work together cooperatively in the future (the trust, respect, and liking among participants should be increased). All participants in the conflict must remain moral persons who are caring and just. They should see each other as being entitled to caring and justice. When conflicts are resolved constructively, **commitment to the long-term survival of the relationship** is increased. The more committed individuals are to their relationship, the more they inhibit negative emotions (annoyance, bitterness), negative attributions (it is all the other person's fault), and negative behaviors (passiveness, destructive acts) (Arriaga & Rusbult, 1998). Commitment appears to involve the *inhibition* of destructive processes rather than the *activation* of constructive processes. Individuals inhibit destructive patterns of thinking (e.g., do not think bad things about us [Rusbult, Yovetich, & Verette, 1996]), drive away thoughts of tempting alternative relationships (Johnson & Rusbult, 1989), and think in collective terms (e.g., *we, us, our* rather than *I, me, mine* [Agnew, Van Lange, Rusbult, & Langston, 1998]).

The fourth requirement for a wise agreement is that the agreement and the process of reaching it strengthen participants' ability to resolve future conflicts constructively.

Conflicts of interests will recur frequently; each time one is faced and resolved, the procedures and skills used should be strengthened and validated.

It is important that both you and the other person understand which actions trigger anger and resentment in the other. Criticism, put-downs, sarcasm, belittling, and other actions often trigger a conflict. If the two of you understand what not to do as well as what to do, the conflict will be resolved much more easily.

One way to understand how constructive agreements may be reached is to look at a few examples.

1. Roger was a coin collector; his wife, Ann, loved to raise and show championship rabbits. Their income did not leave enough money for both to practice their hobbies, and splitting the cash they did have would not have left enough for either. Solution: Put all the first year's money into the rabbits, and then, after they were grown, use the income from their litters and show prizes to pay for Roger's coins.
2. Edythe and Buddy shared an office but had different work habits. Edythe liked to do her work in silence, whereas Buddy liked to socialize and have the radio on. Solution: On Mondays and Wednesdays Buddy would help keep silence in the office, and on Tuesdays and Thursdays Edythe would work in a conference room that was free. On Fridays the two worked together on joint projects.
3. Keith loved to spend his evenings talking to people all over the world on his ham radio set. His wife, Simone, felt cheated out of the few hours of each day they could spend together. Keith did not want to give up his radio time, and Simone was not willing to forego the time they had together. Solution: Four nights each week, Keith stayed up late and talked to his ham radio friends after spending the evening with Simone. On the following mornings, Simone drove Keith to work instead of having him go with a carpool, which allowed him to sleep later.

TRY, TRY AGAIN

When you fail to negotiate an integrative agreement that is wise, the next step is to start over. To be successful at negotiating in a problem-solving way, you must remember to try again. No matter how far apart the two sides seem, no matter how opposed your interests seem to be, keep talking. With persistent discussion, a viable and wise decision will eventually become clear.

EXERCISE | **9.5** | *Negotiating Within an Organization*

This exercise consists of two situations in which members of the same organization or group have to negotiate a resolution to a conflict of interests. In each situation the basic procedure for the coordinator is the same. The exercise takes less than one hour to complete.

1. Introduce the exercise as one in which the dynamics of negotiation among members of a group become apparent. Divide the class into groups of three (two participants and one observer) for case studies 1 and 2. You need at least two groups. Distribute the

accompanying background sheets and role-playing sheets to the participants and observers. Give each observer one copy of the observers' instructions used in the previous exercise. Without letting the groups know that they are getting different instructions, give half of them copies of the accompanying bargaining instructions and the other half copies of the role-reversal instructions.

2. Meet with the observers to make sure that they understand what they are expected to do.
3. Give them the signal to begin. Groups have up to twenty-five minutes to negotiate an agreement. If they finish before their time is up, note how long it took them to negotiate an agreement and what type of negotiation instructions they had.
4. At the end of twenty-five minutes, announce that the time is up and the negotiations must end. Ask each participant to write on a sheet of paper two adjectives describing his or her feelings during the negotiations and hand the paper to you. Record how many groups negotiated an agreement and which type of instructions (bargaining or role reversal) they had.
5. Ask each group to discuss its experience with its observer. The main topics of the discussion should be the negotiation strategies used, how members reacted to one another's strategies, and how successful the different strategies were. Then, on a sheet of paper, have each group summarize its strategies, how successful they were, how members reacted to them, and any conclusions members can draw about their effectiveness.
6. In a general session have each group share its instructions for negotiation, the strategies its members used, and its conclusions about their effectiveness. You can then reveal how participants with bargaining instructions reacted to the negotiations compared with participants with role-reversal instructions, how many groups with each type of instructions completed the negotiations successfully, and how long it took these groups to do so. Summarize the main points of the discussion.
7. Have the participants read the subsequent sections on negotiation and compare their conclusions with the material in those sections.

NEGOTIATION EXERCISE: CASE STUDY 1

Background

Jim and Chris (a female) both work for a research firm but in different divisions. Chris has been assigned to be project leader of a study, and Jim has been assigned from the other division to work on it. This does not necessarily imply that Chris is Jim's boss. This arrangement has been in effect for about a year and is relatively unsatisfactory to Chris, who would like to have Jim taken off the project. Meetings of the project team are often dominated by arguments between Chris and Jim. As a result, Chris has often held meetings without notifying Jim. Jim and Chris are meeting to see if the conflict between them can be resolved.

Chris

Jim is a know-it-all who is always trying to tell you how to run your project. You do not agree with his approach. Jim comes to meetings, slumps down in a chair, and demands that everyone pay attention to him, even if he is late and they have already started. What he wants to study is not the subject of the research. You cannot stand Jim's voice. He has an extremely grating voice with imperious overtones. He is generally obnoxious. Jim doesn't give others a chance to talk and always interrupts if they do get a chance.

Jim does not care about the project. If he finds something else to do that he likes better, he simply ignores his responsibilities for completing work on the project. The group had to miss one deadline because he chose to do something else, and in the previous report, you had to rewrite a whole section because what he turned in was not adequate. He was busy working on something for the director of the organization just to make a name for himself. Meanwhile, he sacrificed your reputation by causing your project to be late and your group to produce inferior work.

Jim

You do not agree with Chris' approach to the project. Working with her is difficult, because her main emphasis is on something that is not relevant to the real problems. She is ignoring the immediate problems that need to be solved and focusing on future issues that are not yet relevant. You believe you cannot tell her this, because Chris thinks she is better than anyone else around here and only the research she is doing is any good. She is a prima donna who thinks all the other work in the organization except for hers is trash. Consequently, you do not really feel involved in the project, especially because Chris accepts what everyone else on the project is doing but chooses your area to criticize. Occasionally you have worked on other projects. The director, for example, had you working on something more important for the organization for a while. But Chris is not willing to agree that anyone except herself can do anything well.

NEGOTIATION EXERCISE: CASE STUDY 2

Background

Juanita and Richard both work for a research organization. Originally the director of the organization was the leader of a project. Richard was interviewed for a position on that project and hired by the director. Juanita also interviewed Richard and strongly opposed his being hired for the project. Juanita thought Richard wasn't competent to do the job. Five or six months after work on the project began, the director decided that she wanted to be relieved and proposed that Richard and Juanita conduct it jointly. Juanita agreed only reluctantly—with the stipulation that it be made clear that she was not working for Richard. The director consented. They were to have a shared directorship. Within a month Juanita was angry because Richard was behaving as though he was the director of the entire project and she was working for him. Juanita and Richard are meeting to see if the conflict between them can be resolved.

Juanita

Right after the joint-leadership arrangement was reached with the director, Richard called a meeting of the project team without even consulting you about the time or content. He just told you when it was being held and said you should be there. At the meeting Richard reviewed everyone's paper line by line—including yours—thus treating you as just another team member working for him. He sends out letters and signs himself as project director, which obviously implies to others that you are working for him. You are hurt, angry, and determined to reestablish your position as joint director of the project.

Richard

You think Juanita is obsessed by feelings of power and titles. Just because you are project director, or sign yourself that way, doesn't mean that she is working for you. You do not see anything to get excited about. What difference does it make? She is too sensitive about everything. You call a meeting, and right away she thinks you are trying to run everything. Juanita has other things to do—other projects to run—so she does not pay too much attention to this one. She mostly lets things slide. But when you take the initiative to set up a meeting, she starts getting upset about how you are trying to make her work for you.

NEGOTIATION EXERCISE: WIN–LOSE NEGOTIATING INSTRUCTIONS

Win–lose negotiation exists when each person attempts to reach an agreement as more favorable to him- or herself than to the other person. Strategies used to be successful include:

1. Presenting an opening offer very favorable to oneself and refusing to modify that position.
2. Gathering information about what the other considers a reasonable agreement from the other's opening offer and proposals.
3. Continually pointing out the validity of one's own position and the incorrectness of the other person's.
4. Using a combination of threats and promises to convince the other person that he or she has to accept one's offer.
5. Committing oneself to a position in such a way that if an agreement is to be reached, the other person has to agree to one's terms.

NEGOTIATION EXERCISE: ROLE-REVERSAL INSTRUCTIONS

Role reversal is defined as a negotiating action in which one person accurately and completely paraphrases, in a warm and involved way, the feelings and position of the other. It is the expression of a sincere interest in understanding the other person's position and feelings. The basic rule for role reversal is this: Each person speaks up for himself only after he has first restated the ideas and feelings of the other person accurately and to the other's satisfaction. In other words, before one person presents his point of view, it is necessary for him to achieve the other person's perspective and to understand her position and feelings so well that he can paraphrase them accurately and completely. General guidelines for role reversal are as follows:

1. Restate the other person's expressed ideas and feelings in one's own words rather than parroting the words of the other person.
2. Preface your reflected remarks with "You think . . . ," "Your position is . . . ," "You feel . . . ," "It seems to you that . . . ," and so on.
3. Avoid any indication of approval or disapproval in paraphrasing the other person's statements. It is important to refrain from interpreting, blaming, persuading, or advising.
4. Make your nonverbal messages congruent with your verbal paraphrasing. Look attentive, be interested in and open to the other's ideas and feelings, and appear to be concentrating on what the other person is trying to communicate.

In this exercise you are to engage in role reversal during the entire negotiating session and use it to arrive at the solution to the problems you and the other person(s) are facing.

NEGOTIATING IN GOOD FAITH

You can bring your credibility down in a second. It takes a million acts to build it up, but one act can bring it down. . . . People are suspicious because for several thousand years that suspicion was warranted . . . we try very hard not to do things that will create distrust.

Howard K. Sperlich, president, Chrysler Corporation

Everyone has a negotiating reputation. The promises of some people are to be believed; other people rarely keep their commitments. You want to build a reputation of being someone who is honest, truthful, trustworthy, and, therefore, fulfills your promises. You want your word to be good. When your word has not been good in the past, there are at least three strategies you can use to increase your credibility:

1. **Pay your debts.** Do whatever you agreed to do in the past and have not yet done. Once you have fulfilled past promises, your current promise will be more credible.
2. **Use collateral.** The collateral should be something of value, something the other person does not expect you to give up. While being significant enough to be meaningful, the collateral should not be something so outrageous that it is not believable. Promising to give someone $1,000 if you break your word is not believable.
3. **Have a "cosigner" who guarantees your word.** Find someone who trusts you and whom the other person trusts, and have him or her guarantee that you will keep your word.

REFUSAL SKILLS: THIS ISSUE IS NOT NEGOTIABLE

Not all issues are negotiable. Group members must be able to:

1. Know when an issue is and is not negotiable.
2. Be able to say "no" or "I refuse to negotiate this issue."

There are times when group members should not negotiate. Group members must always have the option of saying "no" to negotiations. There are clear reasons for doing so, such as when the issue is illegal, inappropriate, will hurt other people, or it is doubtful whether people can keep their word. There are also unclear reasons, such as intuition, being unsure, not seeing the right option, and having changed one's mind (Table 9.5). You will save considerable time and trouble by not persuading others to make agreements they do not wish to make and not letting others persuade you to agree to something you do not wish to do.

Table 9.5 **Reasons for Saying "No"**

Clear	Unclear
Illegal.	My intuition tells me to say "no."
Inappropriate.	I am not sure.
It will hurt other people.	The right option does not exist.
I will not be able to keep my word.	I have changed my mind.

E X E R C I S E

9.6 *Breaking Balloons*

This exercise demonstrates a nonverbal conflict—which is a complete change from the previous highly verbal activities. The procedure is as follows:

> Each participant is to blow up a balloon and tie it to his or her ankle with a string. Then, when the coordinator gives the signal, the participants are to try to break one another's balloons by stepping on them. The person whose balloon is broken is "out" and must sit and watch from the sidelines; the last person to have an unbroken balloon is the winner. The participants can then discuss their feelings of aggression, defense, defeat, and victory. Strategies for protecting one's balloon while attacking others should be noted. A variation on the exercise is to have teams with different-colored balloons compete against each other.

E X E R C I S E

9.7 *Intergroup Conflict*

This exercise studies the dynamics of intergroup conflict and negotiation among groups with conflicting positions. It takes two hours. The procedure for the coordinator is as follows:

1. Introduce the exercise as an experience in intergroup conflict and negotiation. Divide the participants into four groups of no fewer than six members each and distribute a copy of one of the accompanying instruction sheets to each group. Emphasize that the exercise will determine which group is best.
2. Have each group meet separately to select a negotiator and to develop its proposals on the issue. They have half an hour to do this. At the end of this period, give them the accompanying reaction form and ask them to answer only questions 1, 2, and 5 and to write the name of their group at the top.
3. Have the negotiators meet in the center of the room, each with her group sitting behind her. Give each group representative five minutes to present her group's proposals. After each representative has completed her presentation, have all participants complete the reaction form, answering all questions.
4. Tell the groups to reconvene separately and brief their negotiator on the best way to proceed in a second presentation of their position. The groups have fifteen minutes to confer. At the end of this period they again answer questions 1, 2, and 5 on the reaction form.
5. Have the negotiators again meet in the center of the room, with their groups seated behind them. They have up to half an hour to reach an agreement. Group members can communicate with their negotiator through written notes. At the end of fifteen minutes, stop the negotiations and have everyone again complete the questionnaire. Negotiations then resume, and at the end of the thirty-minute period everyone answers the reaction form for the last time.
6. Conduct a general session in which the results of the questionnaire are presented and discussed. Ask group members how they feel about the experience and then focus upon the experience of the negotiators.
7. Have the groups meet separately to discuss how well they worked together and what the experience was like for them. Develop a list of conclusions about intergroup conflict and write them down.
8. Again conduct a general session, this time to discuss the conclusions reached by each group.

INSTRUCTIONS TO COORDINATOR FOR USE OF THE REACTION FORMS

1. Pick one person in each group—as many assistants as you need—to hand out and collect the reaction forms and to compute the group mean for each question each time the forms are used.
2. Copy the four accompanying charts on a chalkboard or large sheets of paper. After each use of the reaction forms, calculate the group means and place them on the charts, using a different color for each group. The response to question 5 should be listed for use in the discussion sessions. Do not let the participants see the results until the general session in which the results are discussed.
3. In discussing the results of each question, look for certain trends. The response to question 1 should be somewhat high at the beginning, increase after comparison with other group's proposals, and drop off if agreement is reached. If no agreement is reached, it should not drop off. For question 2, look for the "hero–traitor" dynamic: Satisfaction goes up if the negotiator convinces other groups that her proposals are best and goes down if she compromises the group's position. It is often helpful to look at the notes passed to the negotiator to see how the group is reacting. The responses to question 3 should be the reverse of the responses to question 1 (if satisfaction with one's own group's proposal is high, satisfaction with the other groups' proposals is low, and vice versa). This usually amounts to devaluing the other groups' proposals and a loss of objectivity in evaluation. Question 4 usually demonstrates overconfidence in one's own group's proposal, though this sense of superiority gradually slips from an initial high as negotiations progress.

INTERGROUP CONFLICT EXERCISE: TEACHERS' GROUP

You are residents of Engleston, a medium-sized but quickly growing suburban community that is within commuting distance of a large city. Engleston has recently been torn by a number of civil rights demonstrations centering on the issue of school integration. Two of the public schools in Engleston contain approximately 90% of the underprivileged, culturally different white and black children in the community. Moreover, the high school drop-out rate (60%) has shown the inadequacy of the educational program for these youngsters. Acts of vandalism and other forms of juvenile delinquency have been frequent and costly to the town, and most of those responsible are among the drop-outs. Four opposing groups in the community, yours among them, have suggested various solutions to some of these problems. The school board has asked the four groups to get together and settle on a single set of four to six proposals, which it will then implement. As a member of the teachers' group, you are essentially opposed to breaking up the schools in any way. You are interested in creating better schools and are generally in favor of expanding the educational program.

Your group is to submit four to six recommendations for dealing with the problems at a meeting at which your representative and one from each of the other three groups will be present. You and your groupmates may prepare a simple chart of the *main* points you wish to emphasize. Try to make your recommendations original and creative, because it will be to your advantage if the other groups accept your proposals. After the representatives have presented their groups' proposals, they will negotiate a *composite proposal* of four to six points to be presented to the school board.

PARENTS' GROUP

You are residents of Engleston, a medium-sized but quickly growing suburban community that is within commuting distance of a large city. Engleston has recently been torn by a number of civil rights demonstrations centering on the issue of school integration. Two of the public schools in Engleston contain approximately 90% of the underprivileged, culturally different white and black children in the community. Moreover, the high school drop-out rate (60%) has increasingly shown the inadequacy of the educational program for these youngsters. Acts of vandalism and other forms of juvenile delinquency have become frequent and costly to the town, and most of those responsible are among the drop-outs. Four opposing groups in the community, yours among them, have suggested various solutions to some of these problems. The school board has asked the four groups to get together and settle on a single set of four to six proposals, which it will then implement. You are a member of the parents' group. Because Engleston's tax rate is already one of the highest in the state, you favor solutions that will *not* increase your taxes. You feel that teachers and administrators have been lax, and that what is needed is more efficient and immediate use of the present resources. You are absolutely against any busing of students and want all students to attend the school closest to their home.

Your group is to submit four to six recommendations for dealing with the problems at a meeting at which your representative and one from each of the other three groups will be present. You and your groupmates may prepare a simple chart of the *main* points you wish to emphasize. Try to make your recommendations original and creative, because it will be to your advantage if the other groups accept your proposals. After the representatives have presented their groups' proposals, they will negotiate a *composite proposal* of four to six points to be presented to the school board.

CIVIL RIGHTS GROUP

You are residents of Engleston, a medium-sized but quickly growing suburban community that is within commuting distance of a large city. Engleston has recently been torn by a number of civil rights demonstrations centering on the issue of school integration. Two of the public schools in Engleston contain approximately 90% of the underprivileged, culturally different white and black children in the community. Moreover, the high school drop-out rate (60%) has increasingly shown the inadequacy of the educational program for these youngsters. Acts of vandalism and other forms of juvenile delinquency have become frequent and costly to the town, and most of those responsible are among the drop-outs. Four opposing groups in the community, yours among them, have suggested various solutions to some of these problems. The school board has asked the four groups to get together and settle on a single set of four to six proposals, which it will then implement. As a member of the civil rights group, you are totally committed to immediate integration. You believe the schools have to be integrated through immediate busing of students. You feel that reforms generally take place too slowly, and you are extremely dissatisfied with the present situation.

Your group is to submit four to six recommendations for dealing with the problems at a meeting at which your representative and one from each of the other three groups will be present. You and your groupmates may prepare a simple chart of the *main* points you wish to emphasize. Try to make your recommendations original and creative, because it will be to your advantage if the other groups accept your proposals. After the representatives have presented their groups' proposals, they will negotiate a *composite proposal* of four to six points to be presented to the school board.

SCHOOL ADMINISTRATORS' GROUP

You are residents of Engleston, a medium-sized but quickly growing suburban community that is within commuting distance of a large city. Engleston has recently been torn by a number of civil rights demonstrations centering on the issue of school integration. Two of the public schools in Engleston contain approximately 90% of the underprivileged, culturally deprived white and black children in the community. Moreover, the high school drop-out rate (60%) has increasingly shown the inadequacy of the educational program for these young-sters. Acts of vandalism and other forms of juvenile delinquency have become frequent and costly to the town, and most of those responsible are among the drop-outs. Four opposing groups in the community, yours among them, have suggested various solutions to some of these problems. The school board has asked the four groups to get together and settle on a single set of four to six proposals, which it will then implement. As a member of the school administrators' group, you are generally satisfied with the way things are and believe that anything but gradual and carefully planned change would lead to chaos. Moreover, you be-lieve that the complaining has been done chiefly by extremist groups at work in the com-munity. In your opinion, all school policy decisions should be made by your group—and parents, teachers, and community groups should not butt in.

Your group is to submit four to six recommendations for dealing with the problems at a meeting at which your representative and one from each of the other three groups will be present. You and your groupmates may prepare a simple chart of the *main* points you wish to present. Try to make your recommendations original and creative, because it will be to your advantage if the other groups accept your proposals. After the representatives have presented their groups' proposals, they will negotiate a *composite proposal* of four to six points to be presented to the school board.

REACTION FORM

Group _____

1. How satisfied are you with your own group's proposals?
      Very dissatisfied 1 : 2 : 3 : 4 : 5 : 6 : 7 : 8 : 9 Very satisfied
2. How satisfied are you with the negotiator your group has selected?
      Very dissatisfied 1 : 2 : 3 : 4 : 5 : 6 : 7 : 8 : 9 Very satisfied
3. How satisfied are you with the proposals of the other groups?
      Very dissatisfied 1 : 2 : 3 : 4 : 5 : 6 : 7 : 8 : 9 Very satisfied
4. How do you think the final composite proposal will compare with your group's proposals?
      Very inferior 1 : 2 : 3 : 4 : 5 : 6 : 7 : 8 : 9 Very superior
5. Write one adjective describing the way you now feel about what is taking place. _____

CHART A: SATISFACTION WITH OWN GROUP'S PROPOSALS

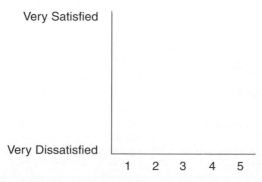

CHART B: SATISFACTION WITH NEGOTIATOR

CHART C: SATISFACTION WITH OTHER GROUPS' PROPOSALS

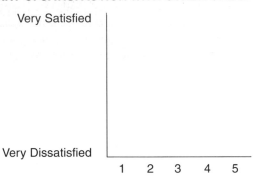

CHART D: SATISFACTION WITH COMPOSITE PROPOSAL

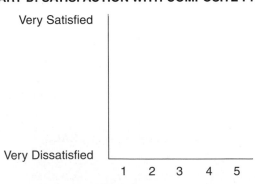

Other Intergroup Conflict Exercises

Other intergroup conflict exercises can easily be created around the general procedure given on page 426. The task can be to state the five most important principles of leadership, the qualities of an effective supervisor, the five most important things for a teacher to know, and so on. The dynamics of intergroup conflict are so predictable that if participants are divided into groups and told to compete, develop their position, and represent that position in negotiations, the dynamics are bound to occur.

INTERGROUP CONFLICT

About 1260 B.C. one of the great intergroup conflicts in history occurred between the powerful Greek king of Sparta (Menelaus) and his allies and Paris from the city of Troy. During the ten-year war, Troy was destroyed and Greece lost some of its greatest warriors and kings. It took another ten years for one of the Greek heroes (Odysseus) to get home. The conflict was over Helen (the most beautiful woman in the world at the time). It began at the wedding of Peleus, a mortal king, and Thetis, an immortal sea nymph. During the ceremony the goddess Eris (goddess of strife and discord) appeared. Angered that she was not invited to the wedding, Eris left a golden apple that she proclaimed would go to the most beautiful goddess. This understandably created a conflict. Hera (supreme goddess of heaven), Athena (goddess of wisdom), and Aphrodite (goddess of love) were all convinced that they were the most beautiful goddess. They began to argue, and the argument raged until Zeus stepped in and ordered Paris, the son of Priam, the king of Troy, to decide. Each of the three goddesses offered Paris a bribe. Hera promised to make him ruler of the entire world if he named her the most beautiful, Athena offered him glory in war, and Aphrodite offered him the most beautiful woman in the world, Helen. Paris chose Aphrodite's offer and named her the most beautiful of the goddesses.

Paris then set sail for Greece to claim his prize. The problem was that Helen was already married to the powerful Greek king of Sparta, Menelaus. Because of Helen's beauty, when Menelaus was courting her, virtually every unmarried Greek male wanted her for his wife. Helen's father, realizing that no matter whom he chose to wed his daughter the others would feel slighted and would very likely seek revenge, consulted Odysseus (who was famed for his cleverness) and made each of Helen's suitors swear an oath (a) that he would defend the marriage no matter who won her hand and (b) if she were ever carried off, they would aid in getting her back.

When Paris arrived at the palace of Menelaus he was given food, shelter, and gifts according to the rules of hospitality. When Menelaus left, however, Paris and Helen, who was irresistibly attracted to him, thanks to Aphrodite, eloped to Troy. When Menelaus returned to find his wife taken, he invoked the oath that the other suitors had taken and began preparations for a huge invasion force to win back Helen. The Trojan War was the result. Not all intergroup conflicts are as famous as the Trojan War. Such deadly intergroup quarrels can also start over trivial reasons. Battles resulting in the death of street gang members, for example, have started from a perceived insult or the intrusion of a member of one gang into an area controlled by another gang.

The tendency to see the world in an "us-versus-them" framework is well documented. If you selected ten people at random and randomly divided them into two groups of five, they would quickly come to value their own group and discriminate in favor of it. There is an **in-group–out-group bias,** in which we hold less favorable views about groups to which we do not belong while holding more favorable opinions about groups to which we do belong (Perdue, Dovidio, Gutman, & Tyler, 1990; Wilder, 1986, 1990). Individuals tend to reward members of their own group at the expense of members of other groups, and they do so in ways that magnify the differences in reward between the two groups. Tajfel and Turner (1979, p. 38) demonstrated a systematic in-group bias in groups where "the mere awareness of the presence of an out-group is sufficient to provoke intergroup competition or discriminatory responses on the part of the in-group." Such social categorization often leads to the **out-group homogeneity bias,** which is the belief that there is less variability among the members of the out-groups than within one's own in-group (Linville, Fisher, & Salovey, 1989).

If such dynamics are found in groups that are minimally differentiated from each other and where members are anonymous, it is hardly surprising that the bias against out-groups would be even stronger when the out-groups have very obvious and salient differences from the in-groups. Three of the dynamics of the in-group–out-group and out-group homogeneity biases are intergroup competition, bias favoring the in-group over the out-groups, and the depersonalization of members of the out-groups. The two theories that discuss the issues most directly are social identity and social categorization theories.

Social identity theory (formulated by Henri Tajfel [1982b] and John Turner [1987]) is based on the hypothesis that individuals seek a positively valued distinctiveness for their own groups compared to other groups to achieve a positive social identity (Figure 9.6). **Social identity** is the individual's knowledge that he or she belongs to certain social groups that have emotional value significant to the individual (Tajfel, 1982). According to social identity theory, people strive to enhance their self-esteem, which has two components: a personal identity and various social identities derived from the groups to which they belong (Tajfel, 1974; Tajfel & Turner, 1986; Turner, Pratkanis, Probasco, & Leve, 1992). Thus, people may boost their self-esteem by viewing their in-groups more favorably than out-groups. In other words, our quest for a positive social identity leads us to inflate the positive aspects of the group to which we belong and belittle groups to which we do not belong (Tajfel, 1974; Tajfel & Turner, 1986; Turner, Pratkanis, Probasco, & Leve, 1992). When a group is successful, members' self-esteem can rise; conversely, when members' self-esteem is threatened, they feel a heightened need for in-group favoritism (attraction to their own group and disparagement of out-groups), which in turn enhances their self-esteem (Crocker & Luhranen, 1990).

Figure 9.6 Social identity theory.

The differentiation between in-groups and out-groups is based on **social categorization.** Social categories function as cognitive "labor-saving devices" by helping you place other people into meaningful categories. While you may use a wide range of categories for classifying people (e.g., male, friend, stranger, Christian, neighbor, political, athlete), two very basic social categorizations are (a) member of my group and (b) member of another group (Hamilton, 1979). **Social categorization theory** is based on the hypothesis that personal and social identity are self-categorizations (Turner & Oakes, 1989) that in themselves are sufficient to create discriminatory intergroup behavior. Social identity is based on differentiating among groups (I am American, male, and Protestant as opposed to Canadian, female, and Catholic) and is assumed to be a more inclusive, superordinate level of abstraction than personal identity in the categorization of the self.

A premise of social identity and social categorization theories is that the process of making categorical distinctions to understand the social world involves minimizing perceived differences within categories and accentuating intercategory differences (Tajfel, 1969). This results in three principles:

1. The **intergroup accentuation principle.** There is assimilation within category boundaries and contrast between categories, such that all members of the in-group are perceived to be more similar to the self than to members of the out-group.
2. The **in-group favoritism principle.** Positive affect (trust, liking) is selectively generalized to fellow in-group members but not to out-group members.
3. The **social competition principle.** Intergroup social comparison is based on perceived negative interdependence (competition) between the in-group and the out group.

There is some evidence that the desire to see oneself as fair-minded can mitigate against discriminating against out-group members (Singh, Choo, & Poh, 1998).

The second premise of social identity and social categorization theories is that because individuals are themselves members of some social categories and not others, social categorization carries with it implicit in-group–out-group (we–they) distinctions resulting in (a) intergroup competition, (b) mutual distrust between the in-group and out-groups, and (c) in-group members receiving preferred treatment (Turner, 1985). Even when social categorizations are imposed on people (given the acceptance and internalization of the categories), members of the in-group are liked more and treated better than members of the out-group. In addition, there is a tendency to depersonalize members of the out-group ("they" are all alike).

It should be remembered that people do not categorize themselves in the same way in every situation. When in Indiana a person may say, "I'm from Muncie," when in California a person may say, "I'm from Indiana," and in Singapore a person may say, "I'm from the United States." As situations change, so do the ways people categorize themselves and others.

Thus, categorization results in competition among groups, social identity, the depersonalization of members of the out-group, and a bias toward the in-group and against the out-group. Social identity and social categorization theories explain how this happens. In order to overcome these effects, a process of decategorization and then recategorization must take place.

Decategorization: Personalizing Interaction

A primary consequence of categorization is the depersonalization of members of out-groups. Members of an out-group tend to be treated as undifferentiated representatives, not as unique individuals. In order to reduce in-group bias and the depersonalization of out-group members, contact among members of the different groups is required. These intergroup interactions should be structured so as to reduce the salience of category distinctions and to promote opportunities to get to know out-group members as individuals (Miller, Brewer, & Edwards, 1985). Contact will be most effective when interactions are highly personalized rather than category based (Brewer & Miller, 1984). Attending to personal characteristics of out-group members tends to disconfirm category stereotypes and decreases the perception of out-groups as homogeneous units.

Recategorization: Building a Common In-Group Identity

Johnson and Johnson (1992a) and Gaertner and his associates (1993) posited that in-group bias and the depersonalization of out-group members can be reduced by structuring the contact among members of different groups so that attention is focused on a superordinate category identification that encompasses both the in-group and the out-group in a single social group representation. Although there may be white Americans, black Americans, Asian Americans, and Hispanic Americans, for example, highlighting the superordinate identity of "American" can unite all citizens into a single social category and identification. Thus, attention to category differences is minimized by creating a new inclusive group identity. This is facilitated by assigning majority and minority members the same role (Bettencourt, Charlton, & Kernahan, in press; Bettencourt & Dorr, 1998). The more individuals perceive the superordinate identity as a single entity, rather than as an aggregate of separate groups, the more positive evaluation of former out-group members becomes.

Note that decategorization and recategorization are not mutually exclusive. Cooperation and superordinate goals promote formation of a common identity. Equal-status, personalized interactions promote decategorization and individuation.

Sherif's Studies of Intergroup Conflict

A number of social scientists have worked to develop an intergroup theory. They include Muzafer Sherif, Robert Blake, and Jane Mouton. Intergroup conflicts also include clashes among cultures and clarifying resulting misunderstandings.

Perhaps the most interesting and best-known studies of intergroup conflict were performed under the direction of Muzafer Sherif (1966). Sherif was born in 1906 in Izmir, Turkey. After attending Izmir International College, he studied at the University of Istanbul, receiving a master's degree in 1928. Awarded a fellowship in national competition for study abroad, he went to Harvard University in 1929, received another master's degree in 1932, and then traveled to Germany, where he attended Kohler's lectures and the University of Berlin. He then taught in Turkey, returned to Harvard to conduct research, and subsequently studied at Columbia University (1934–1936), where he received a Ph.D. degree in 1935. His dissertation was published as a book, *The Psychology of Group Norms* (discussed in Chapter 1). He studied in Paris and taught in Turkey until January 1945, when he returned to the United States. After teaching at both Princeton and Yale, he became director of the Institute of Group Relations at the University of Oklahoma, a position he held from 1949 to 1966. In 1966 he moved to Pennsylvania State University. It was during the years he spent at Oklahoma that he performed his famous research on superordinate goals.

To study intergroup conflict and its resolution, Sherif, his students, and his colleagues ran a summer camp for twelve-year-old boys in the early 1950s. All the boys were strangers to one another prior to attending the camp, so there were no established relationships among them. The camp setting, isolated from outside influences, afforded the experimenters a unique opportunity to manipulate the conditions and circumstances of interaction among the camp members. The investigators were interested in studying intergroup relations, especially the effectiveness of various techniques for reducing hostility between groups. To create intergroup conflict, the experimenters divided the campers into groups and instilled in each group an esprit de corps by such procedures as assigning names like Bull Dogs and Red Devils to the groups and structuring their daily activities so that interdependent, coordinated activity among the group members was necessary for achieving desired goals (the food, for example, needed to be cooked over a campfire and distributed among the group members).

Following the successful development in the camp of two in-groups characterized by mutual good feeling among their members, the experimenters attempted to induce conflict between the two groups by requiring them to participate in competitive activities in which the winning group was rewarded and the losing group was not. For a time the two groups displayed good sportsmanship, but in the course of the competitive activities they became increasingly hostile toward each other. Eventually the two groups were having garbage fights—throwing mashed potatoes, leftovers, bottle caps, and the like—in the dining hall.

Sherif (1966) and his associates next tested several different methods of reducing the conflict between the groups. To find out the effects of social contact between groups on intergroup conflict, Sherif devised several pleasant situations in which members of the rival groups could engage in such contact. These situations included eating together in the same dining room, watching a movie together, and shooting firecrackers in the same area. These contact situations had no effect on reducing intergroup conflict. If anything, they were utilized by members of both groups as opportunities for further name-calling and other forms of conflict. Sherif concluded that contact between groups in pleasant situations does not in itself decrease existing intergroup tension.

The next strategy researched by Sherif (1966) and his associates was the establishment of a common enemy. Sherif demonstrated that it is possible to reduce the hostility between two groups by presenting them with a common enemy against whom they are banded together. He arranged a softball game in which the two groups in conflict were combined to play against a group of boys from a nearby town. The common enemy did bring the two groups of campers together and reduced some of the hostility between them. This approach, however, has little promise for conflict resolution, as it fails to resolve the conflict but only transfers it from two small groups to one larger group. Bringing some groups together against another means larger and more devastating conflicts in the long run.

Sherif (1966) hypothesized that contact between the rival groups would resolve the conflict only when the groups came together to work cooperatively toward goals that were more important to the groups than the continuation of their conflict. Because cooperation toward common goals had been effective in forming the two in-groups, Sherif reasoned, it would be effective in reducing the conflict between the groups. Sherif therefore arranged a series of superordinate-goal situations for the two antagonistic groups of campers to engage in. He defined **superordinate goals** as goals that cannot be easily ignored by members of two antagonistic groups but whose attainment is beyond the resources and efforts of either group alone; the two groups, therefore, must join in a cooperative effort in order to attain the goals. One such goal was to repair the water-supply system, which the experimenters had earlier sabotaged. Another was to obtain money to rent a movie that both groups wanted to see. Still another was to push a truck to get it started after it had suddenly broken down on its way to a camp-out with food. After the campers had participated in a series of such activities, their attitude toward members of the out-group changed; several friendships among members of different groups were formed, members of the rival group were no longer disliked, and the friction between the groups disappeared.

The characteristics of the superordinate goals introduced by Sherif and his associates in their studies were as follows:

1. They were introduced by a more powerful third party (the experimenters).
2. They were perceived by campers to be natural events in no way identified with the third party.
3. They were not perceived by the two groups of campers as being aimed at resolving the conflict.
4. They transcended the conflict situation and restructured the competitive relationship between the groups into a cooperative one.

In most conflict situations, such superordinate goals are not feasible alternatives. A third party, for example, rarely has the power to create goals with the above characteristics. Nor could a participant in a conflict easily create such a goal in an attempt to resolve the conflict.

Although Sherif's studies provide clear documentation that cooperative groups will produce interpersonal attraction even when the individuals start out as enemies, the cooperative goals that were introduced were presented to the campers as "acts of God." Johnson and Lewicki (1969) conducted a study on intergroup conflict in which two types of superordinate cooperative goals were introduced, one appearing to be an act of God and the other introduced by one of the groups engaged in the conflict. The act of God cooperative goal did in fact resolve the intergroup conflict, whereas the opposing group refused to accept the superordinate cooperative goal proposed by one of the parties involved. The opposing group tended to view the superordinate cooperative goal as part of a competitive strategy aimed at furthering the initiating group's vested interests. Thus, to be effective in promoting interpersonal attraction among enemies, cooperative goals may have to be presented by a third party or appear to be natural tragedies or opportunities independent of the parties involved in the conflict.

Sherif's notion of resolving conflicts through the use of superordinate goals is an elaboration of the principle that groups that cooperate with one another to accomplish common goals will have harmonious and friendly relations. Deutsch's (1949a, 1962) theory of cooperation and competition states such a principle, and a number of research studies support the principle's validity (Johnson & Johnson, 1987). Deutsch's theory predicts that even when there is intense hostility between two groups, cooperative action to accomplish goals that are of vital importance to both will result in mutual liking and continued cooperation.

Blake and Mouton Studies of Intergroup Conflict

The more the intergroup conflict is defined as a win–lose situation, the more predictable are the effects of the conflict on the relationships of members within the group, on relationships between the groups, on negotiations between the groups, on the group that wins, and on the group that loses (Blake & Mouton, 1962, 1983). A group in the throes of an intergroup conflict experiences a strong increase in cohesion as members join together to defend their group against defeat. The group becomes more closely knit and gains greater loyalty from its members; members close ranks and put aside some of their conflicts with one another. There is a sharpening and banding together of the in-group power structure as militant leaders take control and group members become more willing to accept autocratic leadership. Maintenance needs become secondary to task needs, and the group becomes more tightly structured and organized. Satisfaction among the members runs high, along with their sense of identification with the group and with its position on the issues in the conflict. At the same time, the opposing group and its positions are belittled and devalued. Conformity is demanded; a "solid front" must be presented.

Between the groups, an attitude of hostility develops. Each sees the other as the enemy. Inaccurate and uncomplimentary stereotypes form. Distortions in perception (Johnson, 2000) increase. Each group sees only the best parts of itself and the worst parts of the other group. Interaction and communication decrease between members of the conflicting groups. Doubt is cast upon the validity of the position of the other group; its position is seen as distinctly inferior to that of one's own group. Group members tend to listen only to what supports their own position and stereotypes. They misperceive and fail to listen carefully to the other group's position. All of these dynamics only intensify the conflict and deepen distrust.

In win–lose negotiations, there are distortions of judgment about the merits of the conflicting positions, with one's own position recognized as *good* and the other group's position assessed as *bad.* Negotiators are relatively blind to points of agreement between their own and the other side's proposals, and they tend to emphasize the differences. The orientation of the negotiators for the two sides is to win for their group, not to reach an agreement that satisfies everyone. This stance inevitably results in the **hero–traitor dynamic:** The negotiator who *wins* is seen as a *hero* and the one who *loses* as a *traitor.* When a neutral third party decides who is right and who is wrong, the winner considers the third party to be impartial and objective; the loser views the third party as biased and thoughtless. Each side sees itself as objective and rational and the other side as unjust and irrational—thereby excluding from the negotiations any elements of genuine objectivity. With the only loyalty being to one's own group's position, the common result of win–lose negotiations is a deadlock. The win–lose strategy can result, of course,

Important Concepts

Demonstrate your understanding of the following concepts by matching the definitions with the appropriate concept. Find a partner. Compare answers.

	Concept	Definition
____	1. Psychodynamic fallacy	a. Seeing every action of members of other groups as a move to dominate, create an advantage, or win.
____	2. Win–lose dynamic	b. The capacity to affect another person's goal accomplishment.
____	3. Hero–traitor dynamic	c. Feeling of discontent aroused by the belief that one fares poorly compared to others.
____	4. Superordinate goals	d. Seeing the motivation for the behavior of members of other groups in terms of personality factors rather than the dynamics of intergroup conflict.
____	5. Power	e. When a person is frustrated but cannot attack the source because of fear or simple unavailability, the person attacks an innocent third party because the party is available and has less power.
____	6. Relative deprivation	f. Goals that cannot be easily ignored by members of two antagonistic groups, but whose attainment is beyond the resources and efforts of either group alone.
____	7. Displaced aggression	g. Antagonism between groups arises from real conflicts of interests and the frustrations these conflicts produce.
____	8. Authoritarian personality	h. Your expectations cause you to behave in a way that provokes behavior from others that confirms your expectations.
____	9. Realistic group conflict	i. Prejudice arises when one group frustrates the other group's goal achievement and the frustrated group reacts with aggression.
____	10. Self-fulfilling prophecy	j. Conflict over basic values occurring among individuals from different cultures.
____	11. Culture clash	k. The negotiator who *wins* is seen as a *hero* and the one who *loses* as a *traitor*.
____	12. Frustration-aggression theory	l. Person characterized by exaggerated submission to authority, rigid conformity to conventional norms, self-righteous hostility, and harsh punitiveness toward anyone considered different.

in the representative being caught in a conflict between his or her own beliefs and perceptions and the mandate given the representative by his or her group.

The group that wins becomes even more cohesive. It also tends to release tension, lose its fighting spirit, and become self-satisfied, casual, even playful. The leadership that was responsible for the victory is consolidated. Although there is high concern for maintenance, there is little tendency to work. Members believe that winning has confirmed the positive stereotype of their group and the negative stereotype of the other group, and that as a result there is little need to reevaluate perceptions or reexamine group operations to learn how to improve them.

The group that loses frequently splinters, seeks the reasons for its defeat, and then reorganizes. Members bring to the surface unresolved conflicts among themselves in an effort to find the reasons for the defeat. Tension increases and the group begins to work even harder. Maintenance concerns abate as task concerns rise in a group effort to recover from defeat. The group often seeks someone to blame for the defeat—the leader, the judges, those who made the rules of the conflict situation, the least conforming members, and so on—and replaces the leadership responsible for the loss. If future victories seem impossible, members may become completely demoralized and assume a defeatist, apathetic attitude toward the group. The losing group tends to learn a great deal about itself because its positive stereotype of itself and its negative stereotype of the other group have been upset by the loss; it has therefore had to reevaluate its perceptions. Consequently, the losing group is likely to reorganize and become more cohesive and effective once it has accepted the loss realistically.

Blake and Mouton (1983) emphasize that those who use this procedure must avoid three basic traps that lead to increased, rather than decreased, conflict. The first to avoid is the **win–lose dynamic**—seeing every action of the other group as a move to dominate, create an advantage, or win. The participants must learn to recognize win–lose attitudes and behaviors and be able to set norms that stress their avoidance. The second trap to avoid is the **psychodynamic fallacy**—seeing the motivation for the behavior of members of another group in terms of personality factors rather than the dynamics of intergroup conflict. It is much easier to blame the conflict on sick, vicious, power-hungry persons than to view the other group's behavior as a predictable result of intense intergroup conflict. The final trap to avoid is the use of a **self-fulfilling prophecy.** For example, one group assumes that the other is belligerent and proceeds to engage in hostile behavior in an attempt to defend itself by mounting a good offense—thereby provoking belligerence on the part of the other group, which confirms the original assumption.

More recent evidence indicates that when third parties decide how to resolve intergroup and cross-cultural conflict (i.e., arbitration), the decision will be evaluated more strongly through judgments about the treatment of disputants (relational concerns) in conflicts within groups and more strongly in terms of the decision's favorability (instrumental concerns) in disputes across groups (Tyler, Lind, Ohbuchi, Sugawara, & Huo, 1998).

EXERCISE

9.8 | *Intergroup Confrontation (I)*

This procedure was developed by Blake and Mouton (1962). It has been used successfully in intergroup conflicts in a variety of organizations for every type of intergroup conflict you can imagine. Its purpose is to change the win–lose orientation to a problem-solving orientation. This exercise takes at least two hours to conduct (Blake and Mouton usually took about twenty hours to use the procedure in actual union–management conflicts).

1. Introduce the exercise as an experience in resolving conflicts between two or more groups. The objective is to change a win–lose to a problem-solving orientation. Discuss

the previous success Blake and Mouton have had with the procedure in difficult union–management conflicts. Use the accompanying descriptions of a union–management conflict to set up a role play that participants can use in the exercise.

2. Each group meets separately and develops on paper (a) how it sees itself as a group and (b) how it sees the other group. Allow the groups at least thirty minutes to complete this task.

3. The two groups come together and share their descriptions. They compare how each side sees itself with how the other group sees it. Often each group sees the other as unreasonable, unethical, and unwilling to cooperate while seeing itself as extraordinarily reasonable, ethical, and cooperative. The differences in the perception of how each group sees the other group are then clarified.

4. The two groups meet separately for twenty minutes to diagnose their present relationship. They should answer such questions as "What problems exist?", "Why aren't the problems being constructively solved?", "What does the other group contribute to the conflict?", and "What does one's own group contribute to the conflict?" The groups should write down this material to share it with the other group.

5. The groups meet together to share their diagnoses. They summarize the key issues causing the conflicts and the main sources of friction. The two groups should keep the integrative, problem-solving negotiation procedure in mind as they plan the next steps in resolving their conflict.

6. The two groups assess their reactions to the exercise and summarize what they have learned about resolving intergroup conflict. Conclusions about preventing intergroup conflict should also be presented and discussed.

UNION–MANAGEMENT CONFLICT

The union in a midsized manufacturing company has asked management for across-the-board increases in pay and fringe benefits. Management has refused to meet these excessive "demands" and has made an offer that the union leadership considers unacceptable. Still without a contract agreement at midnight on the day before the old contract expires, the union has voted to go on strike and remain on strike until a satisfactory agreement is reached. Divide into union and management groups and carry out the above procedure.

Contact Theory

Resolving intergroup conflict is based on the assumption that contact between members of different groups will result in positive relationships and a reduction of **stereotyping** and prejudice. One of the most widely studied intergroup conflicts is that between white and minority individuals. Historically, social scientists believed that sheer ignorance about African Americans and their lives contributed to erroneous and oversimplified racial stereotypes (Myrdal, 1944). Contact was seen as the solution. A wide variety of studies conducted in the 1930s, 1940s, and 1950s indicated that contact was not a straightforward matter. It seemed to be the nature of the contact between members of different ethnic groups, not its frequency, that promoted favorable intergroup attitudes. Researchers studied the effects of actual contact between blacks and whites, utilizing visiting black lecturers in classrooms (Young, 1932), meetings with black professionals (Smith, 1943), school integration (Horowitz, 1936), joint recreational activities in integrated summer camps (Williams, 1948; Yarrow, Campbell, & Yarrow, 1958), voyages of white merchant seamen serving with black seamen (Brophy, 1945), and contact within combat infantry platoons (Mannheimer & Williams, 1949; Star, Williams, & Stouffer, 1965). Many of the earliest research studies used questionnaires in which respondents were asked to note their attitudes toward members of an ethnic group and then to describe the nature and frequency of their contact with members of that group (Allport & Kramer, 1946; Harlan, 1942; MacKenzie, 1948; Rosenblith, 1949). Somewhat later studies were based on postwar occupational and educational desegregation (Gray & Thompson, 1953; Gundlach, 1950; Harding & Hogerge, 1952; Minard, 1952; Reed, 1947; Rose, 1948; Williams & Ryan, 1954) and desegregated residential settings (Deutsch & Collins, 1951; Irish, 1952; Jahoda & West, 1951; Kramer, 1951; Wilner, Walkey, & Cook, 1952, 1955; Winder, 1952). These latter studies indicated that the greater the degree of cooperation growing out of involuntary residential proximity between white and black residents, the more likely the development of friendly ethnic relationships.

We now realize that the issue is not so simple. Sometimes intergroup contact is associated with less prejudice. As these early studies indicated, according to national surveys, having more black friends or more contact with gay men and lesbians is associated with less prejudice (Herek & Capitanio, 1996; Jackman & Crane, 1986). Contact, however, is also correlated with more prejudice. Whites who have had the most contact with illegal immigrants (Espenshade & Calhoun, 1993) and whites living in areas of the South with the largest concentration of African Americans have the most prejudiced political attitudes (Giles & Buckner, 1993; Key, 1949). Thus, contact can either increase or decrease prejudice and discrimination.

Based on these early studies, in 1947 Goodwin Watson published a review of the previous research and writings on intergroup relations. He concluded that contact between members of different ethnic groups was likely to be more effective in changing behavior and attitudes than were such alternative experiences as exposure to correct information or persuasive communication, given that the contact met a number of conditions. The conditions included:

1. Cooperative action to achieve mutual goals (the diverse individuals had to engage in cooperative activities together).
2. Personal interactions among individuals from the different groups.
3. Social norms and authorities favoring equalitarian cross-ethnic contact.
4. Equal-status contact.

In the same year, Williams (1947) published a similar list of conditions for constructive cross-ethnic contact, as did Kenneth Clark in 1953, and in 1954 Gordon Allport published his famous book *The Nature of Prejudice,* in which he identified a similar list of conditions. Stuart Cook followed with a review in 1957.

Between 1950 and 1970 there were approximately forty studies on cross-ethnic interaction (Amir, 1969; Cook, 1969; Stephan, 1978). The reviewers of this research concluded that the evidence on whether cross-ethnic contact resulted in more favorable cross-ethnic attitudes and relationships was inconclusive. Under favorable conditions contact seemed to reduce prejudice, and under unfavorable conditions contact seemed to increase prejudice. The major determinant of whether cross-ethnic contact produced positive attitudes and relationships was cooperative interaction among the individuals involved.

The most recent formulations of contact theory specify that the following conditions must exist for contact to result in a reduction of prejudice, stereotyping, and racism:

1. **Cooperative action to achieve mutual goals.** What largely determines whether interaction results in positive or negative relationships is the context in which the interaction takes place. Rather than requiring members of different groups to compete to see who is best or work individualistically on their own, they must work together to achieve mutual goals. This is the best supported of the conditions. Two meta-analyses indicated that cooperative experiences promote more positive relationships among heterogeneous individuals (Johnson & Johnson, 1989; Johnson, Johnson, & Maruyama, 1983). When people cooperate, they tend to like each other more, trust each other more, be more candid with each other, and be more willing to listen to and be influenced by each other than are people competing or working individualistically (Johnson & Johnson, 1989). In addition, there is considerable evidence that cooperative experiences, compared with competitive and individualistic ones, promote more positive, committed, and caring relationships regardless of differences in ethnic, cultural, language, social class, gender, ability, or other differences (Johnson & Johnson, 1989).

2. **Personal interactions among individuals from the different groups.** In-group members tend to assume that out-group members are all alike. Through intimate, one-on-one interaction, those categories should break down and out-group members should be perceived in more individualized terms (Brewer & Miller, 1984; Marcus-Newhall, Miller, Holtz, & Brewer, 1993; Urban & Miller, 1998; Wilder, 1986). In schools, individual contact among persons from different groups is uncommon. Students associate with members of their own group. Tracking (ability grouping) ensures that white and minority students are separated. Desegregation does not ensure integration. Teachers must create conditions and opportunities for personal interactions among diverse students in order for positive relationships to develop and stereotyping and prejudice to decrease. Such interactions also increase students' sophistication (see the following section).

3. **Support from social norms and authorities.** The social norms, defined in part by relevant authorities, should favor intergroup contact. Norms have a powerful impact on individuals' behavior. Greenberg and Pyszczynski (1986) demonstrated that participants expressed more prejudice after they overheard a confederate utter a racial slur. Blanchard and his associates (1991) demonstrated that college students being interviewed about a racial incident on campus conveyed more racist sentiments after they heard a fellow student do the same. Wilder and Shapiro (1991) demonstrated that participants were more likely to rate an out-group member as "typical" when they were with fellow in-group members than when they were alone.

4. **Equal status of the two groups in the contact situation.** Desegregation situations that provided equal-status contact, as in the army and public housing projects, have been successful (Pettigrew, 1998). When the public schools were desegregated, however, white children came from more affluent families, were better prepared, and were academically more advanced than their black peers (Cohen, 1984).

In addition to these four conditions, recent research has focused on additional conditions that may be required for contact between diverse individuals and groups to have constructive rather than destructive effects. The first is the **salience of social categories.** When category distinctions are highly salient in an intergroup contact situation, group members are more apt to respond in ways that are category-based (Brewer & Miller, 1984; Hong & Harrod, 1988; Oakes, 1987; Tajfel, 1978; Wilder & Shapiro, 1989a, 1989b) and are more biased in their intergroup attitudes (Haunschild, Moreland, & Murrell, 1994; Hong & Harrod, 1988). Three ways to reduce the salience of social categories are:

1. Make shared categories salient. In-group bias is higher when people differ on two real social categories (such as ethnicity and gender) than when they differ on one category but share another (Brewer, Ho, Lee, & Miller, 1987; Commins & Lockwood, 1978; Islam & Hewstone, 1993; Urban & Miller, 1998). Similar results have been found in laboratory studies on nominal group categories (Deschamps, 1977; Deschamps & Doise, 1978; Vanbeselaere, 1987, 1991).
2. Have equal representation of majority and minority members in cooperative groups (Rogers, Hennigan, Bosman, & Miller, 1984; Worchel, Andreoli, & Folger, 1977). Members of numerical minorities are more aware of their social category than are members of numerical majorities (McGuire, McGuire, Child, & Fujioka, 1978; McGuire, McGuire, & Winton, 1979, Mullen, 1983), express more in group bias than do numerical majorities (Brewer, Manzi, & Shaw, 1993; Gerard & Hoyt, 1974; Mullen, Brown, & Smith, 1992; Sachdev & Bourhis, 1984, 1991), and are less accepting of members of other groups (Miller & Davidson-Podgorny, 1987). Groups for whom category salience is high are more biased in their intergroup attitudes (Haunschild, Moreland, & Murrell, 1994; Hong & Harrod, 1988).
3. Create a common identity among majority and minority members (Johnson & Johnson, 1999b). When majority and minority members are assigned the same role, for example, they perceive themselves as sharing a common identity (Bettencourt, Charlton, & Kernahan, in press; Bettencourt & Dorr, 1998).

The second potential addition to contact theory is the **role of intergroup friendship.** In a survey of 3,806 respondents in seven 1988 national probability samples of France, Great Britain, the Netherlands, and West Germany, Pettigrew (1997) found that intergroup friendship is a strong and consistent predictor of reduced prejudice and pro-immigrant policy preferences. The reduction of prejudice among those with diverse friends generalized to more positive feelings about a wide variety of out-groups. There seems to be a benevolent spiral in which intergroup friendship reduces prejudice and, in turn, reduced prejudice increases the likelihood of further intergroup friendships. Similar effects were not found when the individual had an out-group co-worker or neighbor (but not a friend). Herek and Capitanio (1996) found that multiple out-group friends have a strong negative relationship with prejudice. Wright, Aron, McLaughlin-Volpe, and Ropp (1997) found that knowledge that an in-group member had a close relationship with an out-group member results in more positive intergroup attitudes.

Since its original formulation fifty years ago, extensive research has been inspired by contact theory. The research has generally confirmed the theory across a variety of societies, situations, and groups. These include German children in school with Turkish children (Wagner, Hewstone, & Machleit, 1989), the elderly (Caspi, 1984), and the mentally ill (Desforges et al., 1991). The theory has been confirmed by laboratory (e.g., Cook, 1978; Johnson & Johnson, 1989), survey (e.g., Sigelman & Welch, 1993), field (e.g., Johnson & Johnson, 1989; Meer & Freedman, 1966), and archival (e.g., Fine, 1979) research.

There are problems with contact theory. The *first* is that the proliferation of required conditions renders the theory meaningless. As a result of all the diverse research, many social scientists have suggested revisions to contact theory. Some of the revisions have been situational (such as intimacy [Amir, 1976] or salience of social categories [Brewer & Miller, 1984]) and some individual (such as low authoritarianism [Weigel & Howes, 1985]). The danger in contact theory is that too many factors will render it meaningless. Contact theory may become a "grocery list" of necessary conditions rather than a coherent model of attitude and behavior change. The proliferation of conditions may result from social scientists confusing facilitating with essential conditions. Some of the conditions suggested for optimal contact may be catalytic (not essential for harmonious relationships but related to underlying mediating processes). Pettigrew (1997) suggested four broad, encompassing processes: (a) learning about the out-group, (b) empathizing with the out-group, (c) identifying with the out-group, and (d) reappraising the in-group. Some of the conditions proposed as requirements for constructive contact may actually be facilitators of one or more of these processes.

The *second* problem is the need to specify more precisely the mediation of contact effects. Social judgment theory, which is discussed at length in the next chapter, is an attempt to be more specific about the mediators of contact and positive relationships.

The *third* problem is that while contact theory is about interaction among members of diverse groups, it focuses on interpersonal interaction. It needs to refocus on the contact of group with group (Hewstone & Brown, 1986) rather than on contact of individuals from two groups. There is evidence that the perceived collective other is a qualitatively different kind of actor than a perceived individual other. Groups evoke stronger reactions than an individual engaging in the same behavior, and actions by groups and individuals elicit differing preferences for redress (Abelson, Dasgupta, Park, & Banaji, 1998). When observers perceive individuals as part of a cohesive group (as opposed to an aggregate of unrelated individuals), the observers express stereotypic judgments about the individuals and infer that their behavior was shaped by the presence of others (Oakes & Turner, 1986; Oakes, Turner, & Haslam, 1991; Wilder, 1977, 1978b). A racial slur delivered by an individual, for example, provokes a different reaction than a racial slur delivered by a group. Considerably more research is needed on intergroup (as opposed to interpersonal) contact.

Awakening the "Sense of Injustice"

Discrimination against out-groups may be decreased by reducing stereotyping and prejudice. Discrimination may be viewed as a form of injustice (Deutsch, 1985). Removing discrimination, therefore, requires awakening a **sense of injustice** in majority members about their treatment of minority and low-power group members. Deutsch posits that no change in discriminatory practices is possible until a sense of injustice is awakened. To awake the majority's sense of injustice, follow the steps given in the following box.

Awakening a sense of injustice depends on prejudice being more than a uniform set of attitudes and values. Rather than having uniformly negative or positive attitudes toward out-groups, many individuals have conflicting tendencies (Gaertner & Dovidio, 1986; Katz & Hass, 1988; Katz, Wachenhut, & Hass, 1986; McConahay, 1986; Monteith, 1996b). A number of studies, for example, found that approximately 78% of the sam-

How to Awaken a Sense of Injustice

Step 1 Remove the majority's ignorance of the injustices experienced by minorities. Often the majority "insulates" itself from the victims by avoiding contact (living in all-white suburbs) or structuring the contact in ways that prevent the possibility of becoming aware of the discrimination (such as "employee of the month" celebrations). This **insulated ignorance** protects majority-group members from being aware of the consequences of their behavior (Hornstein & Johnson, 1966).

Step 2 Delegitimize the officially sanctioned ideologies and myths that "justify" the injustices (e.g., "The cream rises to the top"). Majority-group members are largely content and tend to have a vested interest in preserving the status quo (which ensures their superior roles and privileges). Awakening a sense of injustice requires majority-group members to become aware of their ideologies, question the ideologies, and decide that ideologies are no longer legitimate.

Step 3 Expose the majority to new ideologies, models, and reference groups that support action to undo the disadvantages of the minorities. Majority-group members must interact with minority-group members, come to understand their perspective and experience, and form a new reference group that includes both majority and minority individuals. The new reference group must support change. The action steps must be clear.

Step 4 Stimulate the hope of the majority that they can effectively reduce injustice. Once victimization has become deeply embedded in social institutions, individual action to overcome it is frequently seen to be futile and costly. There must be hope of success in order for majority-group members to take action.

Step 5 Increase the majority's belief that they will benefit from reducing injustice. This involves (a) reducing the fear of the majority that their new actions will have costly, harmful consequences for them and (b) enhancing the majority's prospect of material and psychic gains from a positive change in their relationships with the minority. Both the majority and the minority must be seen as being better off as a result of decreasing discrimination.

Step 6 Increase the majority's belief that continuation of the old relationship will no longer produce the material benefits and gains the majority has experienced in the past. Thus, continuing the status quo may have costly, harmful consequences for the majority.

pled populations indicated that they should respond with less prejudice than is apparent in their actual responses (Devine, Monteith, Zuwerink, & Elliot, 1991; Monteith, 1996a, 1996b; Monteith, Devine, & Zuwerink, 1993; Zuwerink, Monteith, Devine, & Cook, 1996). This finding held for both highly- and slightly-prejudiced individuals.

Given that many people are highly prejudiced but feel conflicted about it, awakening their sense of injustice will tip the scales in favor of respect and appreciation.

Monteith and Walters (1998) found that many highly prejudiced white individuals feel morally obligated to (a) be less prejudiced and (b) have relatively low-prejudiced personal standards for responding to blacks. These obligations appear to originate from an egalitarian self-image that defines egalitarianism in terms of equality of opportunity. Their belief in the right of every American to have an equal opportunity is more powerful than their prejudices.

EXERCISE | **9.9** | *Intergroup Confrontation (II)*

The following is a conflict resolution procedure for establishing cooperative goals among conflicting groups so that all members are committed to achieving their joint goals (Beckhard, 1969). The objective is to provide a framework for resolving conflicts through highlighting common goals. Beckhard conducts the exercise as a one-day activity, but it can be shortened to a couple of hours when used strictly for learning.

1. Introduce the exercise as an experience in setting cooperative goals among groups in conflict with each other. Emphasize that the exercise is an opportunity for participants to learn how to resolve intergroup conflict. They should be open and honest in the expression of their ideas and feelings. The union–management situation used in the previous exercise can be applied here for role-playing purposes.
2. Divide the participants into groups of four or five and have them meet separately. The task of these conflicting groups is to think of ways in which life would be better for their members and their relationships with other groups. Ask each group to make a list of the ideas and write them down. This phase takes thirty to forty-five minutes.
3. You and the participants categorize the ideas listed.
4. Have the groups complete the following tasks:
   a. Go through the entire list and select three or four items that most affect you and your group. Rephrase the items into goals, determine what actions your group will take to achieve them, and establish a timetable for doing so. Prepare to report your decisions in a general session.
   b. Go through the list again and select those items you think all groups should give highest priority but that your group cannot achieve alone.
5. In a general session, have the groups share the results of their meetings. Combine the lists. The groups should then outline plans of action for implementing their decisions and determine the necessary follow-up procedures. During the discussion they should emphasize intergroup cooperation.
6. Ask the groups to assess their reactions to the exercise and summarize what they have learned about resolving intergroup conflicts. Conclusions about preventing intergroup conflict should also be presented and discussed.

THIRD-PARTY MEDIATION

William Ury often tells a tale of an old gentleman who in his will requested that his estate be divided among his three sons in the following manner: one half to his eldest son, one third to his middle son, and one ninth to his youngest son. When the loving father died, his estate consisted of seventeen camels. The three sons attempted to divide up the estate according to their father's wishes but quickly found that they could not do so without cutting some of the camels into pieces. They argued and argued without agreeing on how to divide the camels. Eventually, a village elder rode up on his own dusty camel and inquired about their problem. The three brothers explained the situation. The elder then offered to make his own camel available if that might help. It did. With eighteen camels, the brothers could solve the problem. The oldest son took nine camels (one-half of eighteen), the middle son chose six more (one-third of eighteen), and the youngest son extracted two camels (one-ninth of eighteen). Nine plus six plus two equals seventeen. Almost before the three brothers knew what had happened, the wise man climbed back onto his own camel and rode off into the setting desert sun.

This story illustrates what a clever and creative mediator can do. A **mediator** is a neutral person who helps two or more people resolve their conflict by assisting them through the steps of problem-solving negotiations so that an agreement is reached that both believe is fair, just, and workable. A mediator does *not* tell disputants what to do, decide who is right and who is wrong, or talk about what he or she would do in such a situation. The mediator is simply a facilitator with no formal power over either disputant. **Mediation** exists, therefore, when a neutral and impartial third party assists two or more people in negotiating a constructive resolution to their conflict. The participants in the conflict who seek mediation are called **disputants.** Mediation is an extension of the negotiation process and is a collection of strategies to promote more efficient and effective negotiations. When mediation has been successful:

1. The conflict will be resolved so that all disputants have benefited.
2. The relationship between the disputants will be as good as or even better than ever.
3. Individuals' negotiating skills and self-confidence in using them will be increased. An important purpose of the mediator is to teach negotiation procedures and skills so that the individuals can manage their conflicts on their own in the future.

When two individuals or groups cannot resolve their conflict constructively, they often seek the help of a mediator. The main difference between negotiating and mediation is that a third party, the mediator, ensures that both parties engage in each step of the problem-solving negotiating process. Mediation is unlikely to be effective when the relationship between the two parties is poor and when resources are scarce. Under such conditions, the likelihood of finding a mutually acceptable compromise is not very high. Conversely, mediation is most likely to be successful when both parties are highly motivated to use the mediation process. In general, disputants are likely to be satisfied with the mediation process, as most studies show satisfaction rates of 75% or higher (Kressel & Pruitt, 1985). Mediation facilitates conflict resolution in the following ways (Raven & Rubin, 1976, p. 462):

1. Reducing emotional upset by giving parties an opportunity to vent their feelings.
2. Presenting alternative solutions by recasting the issues in different or more acceptable terms.
3. Providing opportunities for "graceful retreat" or face saving in the eyes of one's adversary, one's constituency, the public, or oneself.
4. Facilitating constructive communication among parties.

5. Controlling contact between the parties, including such aspects as the neutrality of the meeting site, the formality of the setting, the time constraints, and the number and kinds of people at the meeting.

To be successful, mediators need to possess certain characteristics and adopt particular strategies. Mediators need to be perceived as being trustworthy and able (Rubin, Pruitt, & Kim, 1994). They need to convey an impression of legitimacy, social position, and expertise in order to gain the confidence of both parties and to win acceptance for the proposed solution (Kolb, 1985). Mediators tailor tactics to particular situations. Mediators may lower hostility by being very directive and using humor but being nondirective with inexperienced parties who lack expertise in negotiating (Carnevale & Pegnetter, 1985). When mediation fails, an arbitrator may be brought in. **Arbitration** is a binding settlement of a conflict determined by a disinterested third party.

Mediator Guidelines

A good mediator is impartial, neutral, nonjudgmental, patient, understanding, imaginative, knowledgeable, analytical, respectful, and trustworthy. A mediator acts and talks in ways that show that he or she has these qualities. Some guidelines for doing so are as follows:

1. Listen, don't talk. A mediator cannot listen and talk at the same time. When you do talk, use words and phrases that are impartial and nonjudgmental.
2. Find out the facts. Find out what happened and what must be done to resolve the conflict. Ask each disputant, "What has to happen in order for this conflict to be resolved to your satisfaction?"
3. Analyze what you hear to see if agreement is possible. You must do more than listen. You must think about what is being said so that you can help disputants separate their interests from their positions and think of creative solutions to their problem.
4. Be firm in enforcing the rules. You will not help anyone if you permit disputants to interrupt, insult, or shout at each other. The rules ensure that the procedures are fair.
5. Be patient. Some things take time to resolve.
6. Respect the disputants. They will not participate effectively unless they believe that you respect them.

EXERCISE

9.10 *Your Conflict Behavior*

Having completed this chapter, you may find it helpful to focus again on your behavior in conflict situations. Form a group of three with two persons who know you well and who have participated with you in some of the exercises in this book. Then complete the following tasks, taking at least two hours to do so.

1. Reflect silently on how each member deals with conflict. Give one another feedback about the animal, song, or book that each member reminds the others of on the basis of

how he or she deals with conflict. Each person explains why he or she chose the animal, song, or book in question.

2. Write down your strengths in managing conflicts constructively. Share your lists. Members can add to each other's lists.

3. Write down the skills you need to develop in order to manage conflict more constructively. Share your lists. Members should add to each other's lists.

4. Discuss the feelings each member has in conflict situations and why he or she reacts that way. Help each other think of alternative ways of reacting to conflict situations.

5. From magazine pictures and any other materials, build a collage about the way in which you behave in conflict situations. Share the collage with the other members. Add ideas to each other's collages.

SUMMARY

Group members need to face their conflicts of interests (conflicts promoted by incompatible needs or goals, scarce resources, and competitiveness) and engage in problem-solving (integrative) negotiations to resolve them. There are five basic strategies to manage conflicts of interests: withdrawal, forcing (distributive, win–lose negotiations), smoothing, compromise, and problem solving (integrative negotiations). The more effective the group, the more frequently conflicts of interests will be valued for their potentially constructive outcomes and resolved through problem-solving negotiations. Where problem-solving negotiations fail, another group member needs to mediate. Even in intergroup conflicts, problem-solving negotiations need to be used. When they are resolved constructively, conflicts are an important and indispensable aspect of increasing group effectiveness.

Now that you are acquainted with the dynamics involved in resolving conflicts of interests and have practiced resolving them, you are ready to encounter power. You will do so in the next chapter.

10

Valuing Diversity

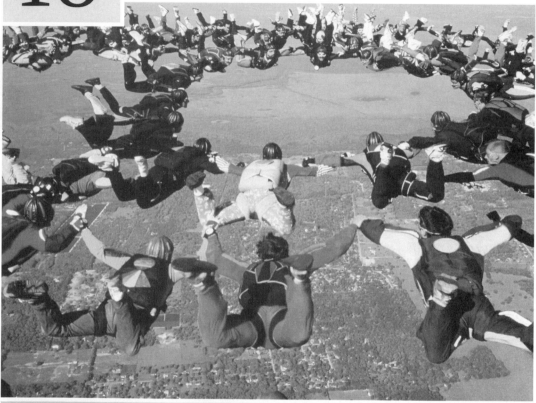

Basic Concepts to Be Covered in This Chapter

In this chapter a number of concepts are defined and discussed. The major ones are listed following. Divide into pairs. Each pair is to (a) define each concept, noting the page on which it is defined and discussed, and (b) ensure that both members of the pair understand the meaning of each concept. Then join with another pair to make a group of four. Compare the answers of the two pairs. If there is disagreement, look up the concept in the chapter and clarify it until all members agree on and understand the definition.

Concepts

1. Ability and skill diversity
2. Blaming the victim
3. Causal attribution
4. Culture clash
5. Demographic diversity
6. Discrimination
7. Ethnocentrism
8. False consensus bias
9. Illusionary correlation
10. Personal diversity
11. Personal identity
12. Prejudice
13. Self-serving attributions
14. Sophistication
15. Stereotype
16. Superordinate identity

EXERCISE

10.1 Diversity: Beneficial or Harmful?

Task: Your tasks are to (a) write a group report on the issue *"Is diversity beneficial or harmful?"* and (b) individually pass a test on the information from both sides of the issue. Your report should provide details of the advantages and disadvantages of diversity. A controversy about the value of diversity is raging. Imagine that you are a committee of the top four officials who are trying to decide whether diversity should be encouraged or discouraged. To ensure that both sides get a complete and fair hearing, you have divided the committee into two groups to present the best case possible for each side of the issue. Your thesis will be either of the following two choices:

_____ Diversity is a resource that has many beneficial influences.
_____ Diversity is a problem that has many harmful influences.

Cooperative: Write one report for the group of four. All members have to agree. Everyone has to be able to explain the choice made and the reasons why the choice is a good one. To help you write the best report possible, your group of four has been divided into two pairs. One pair has been assigned the position that diversity is beneficial, and the other pair has been assigned the position that diversity is harmful.

PROCEDURE

1. **Research and prepare your position:** Your group of four has been divided into two pairs. Each pair is to (a) research its assigned position, (b) organize it into a persuasive argument (thesis, rationale, conclusion), and (c) plan how to present the best case for its position to the other pair.

2. **Present and advocate your position:** Make sure your assigned position receives a fair and complete hearing. Forcefully and persuasively present the best case for your position to the opposing pair. Be as convincing as possible. Take notes and clarify anything you do not understand when the opposing pair presents.
3. **Open discussion (advocate, refute, rebut):** Argue forcefully and persuasively for your position. Critically evaluate and challenge the opposing pair's information and reasoning. Defend your position from attack.
4. **Reverse perspectives:** Reverse perspectives and present the best case for the opposing position. The opposing pair will present your position. Strive to see the issue from both perspectives simultaneously.
5. **Synthesis:** Drop all advocacy. Synthesize and integrate the best information and reasoning from both sides into a joint position on which all group members can agree. Then (a) finalize the group report, (b) plan how to present your conclusions to the class, (c) ensure that all group members are prepared to take the test, and (d) analyze how well you worked together as a group and how you could be even more effective next time.

CONTROVERSY RULES

1. I am critical of ideas, not people. I challenge and refute the ideas of the opposing pair, but I do not indicate that I personally reject the other persons.
2. I remember that we are all in this together, sink or swim. I focus on making the best decision possible, not on winning.
3. I encourage everyone to participate and to master all the relevant information.
4. I listen to everyone's ideas, even if I don't agree.
5. I restate what someone has said if it is not clear.
6. I first bring out all ideas and facts supporting both sides, and then I try to put them together in a way that makes sense.
7. I try to understand both sides of the issue.
8. I change my mind when the evidence clearly indicates that I should do so.

DIVERSITY IS BENEFICIAL

You represent the prodiversity perspective. Your position is: *Diversity is a resource that has many beneficial influences.* Arguments that support your position follow. Summarize the evidence given. Research your position and find as much additional information to support it as possible. Arrange your information into a compelling, convincing, and persuasive argument showing that your position is valid and correct. Plan how to present your assigned position best to ensure that it receives a fair and complete hearing. Make at least one visual to help you present a persuasive case for your position.

1. **Diversity decreases stereotyping and prejudice.** It is only through direct contact and interaction with diverse individuals that stereotypes can be disconfirmed, personal relationships can be built, and prejudice can be reduced.
2. **Diversity increases the positiveness of relationships.** There is evidence that we like people we work with to achieve mutual goals. Positive relationships can lead to acceptance, respect, appreciation, and a commitment to equality.
3. **Diversity renews the vitality of society** by providing a source of energy and creativity. Music, dance, art, literature, and other aspects of culture are enriched and advance by the mixture of different cultural traditions and ways of perceiving the world.

4. **Diversity increases achievement and productivity.** Diverse groups have a wider range of resources available for completing the task and, therefore, tend to have higher achievement and be more productive than homogeneous groups.
5. **Diversity increases creative problem solving.** Diverse groups tend to be more creative in their problem solving than homogeneous groups. The conflicts and disagreements that arise from the different perspectives and conclusions generate more creativity than is available in homogeneous groups.
6. **Diversity fosters growth in cognitive and moral reasoning.** Cognitive and moral growth depend on applying at least two different perspectives to the same issue. Without such diversity, cognitive and moral growth cannot take place.
7. **Diversity fosters perspective-taking** and a broader, more sophisticated view of the world and what happens in it. Without exposure to other perspectives, perspective-taking ability cannot develop. The more able a person is to take a wide variety of perspectives, the more sophisticated the person is. Being sophisticated means that one can see the world, events, and issues from a variety of perspectives. It is through diversity that sophistication is created.
8. **Diversity builds a commitment to American democracy.** It is not possible to value a fully American democracy in a homogeneous environment. The values advocated in the Constitution and the Declaration of Independence can best be understood through the protection of minority rights and the ability of minorities to influence the decisions of the majority.

DIVERSITY IS HARMFUL

You represent the antidiversity perspective. Your position is: *Diversity is a problem that has many harmful influences.* Arguments that support your position follow. Summarize the evidence given. Research your position and find as much additional information to support it as possible. Arrange your information into a compelling, convincing, and persuasive argument showing that your position is valid and correct. Plan how to present your assigned position best to ensure that it receives a fair and complete hearing. Make at least one visual aid to help you present a persuasive case for your position.

1. **Diversity increases stereotyping and prejudice.** Before actual contact takes place, only vague impressions of members of other groups may exist. With actual contact with diverse individuals, stereotypes can be confirmed and prejudice can be strengthened.
2. **Diversity creates interaction strain** (feeling discomfort and uncertainty as to how to behave). Interaction strain inhibits interaction, creates ambivalence, and fosters atypical behavior such as overfriendliness followed by withdrawal and avoidance.
3. **Diversity increases the negativity of relationships.** There is evidence that we like people we see as similar to ourselves and dislike people who seem different. Dislike can lead to rejection, scapegoating, bullying, hostility, and even racism.
4. **Diversity lowers productivity.** Diversity creates difficulties in communication, coordination, and decision making. These difficulties result in spending more time trying to communicate and less time completing the task. Productivity suffers.
5. **Diversity makes life more complex and difficult.** It is so easy to relate to similar people. You never have to stop and think about what to say or do. The more diverse the group, the more you have to monitor your statements and behavior to ensure that you do not inadvertently insult or hurt someone's feelings.
6. **Diversity requires more effort to relate to others.** Even talking to a person from another culture takes more concentration and effort. Accents can be distracting. Phrases can be

unusual. Communicating effectively with diverse individuals takes more effort than with individuals just like yourself.

7. **Diversity can be threatening,** which creates defensiveness, egocentrism, and closed-minded rejection of new information. The more defensive a person is, the more closed-minded and the less receptive to new information the person becomes.

8. **Diversity creates internal dissonance and anxiety** by challenging the standard ways of thinking and doing things. Strange new ways of perceiving the world and completing tasks can create dissonance about one's traditional behavior, and anxiety results. People are calmer and happier when they are with homogeneous peers.

INTRODUCTION

In the story *Beauty and the Beast,* Beauty, to save her father's life, agrees to live in an enchanted castle with the Beast. Although initially very fearful of the Beast and horrified by his appearance, she is able to look beyond his monstrous appearance into his heart. Considering his kind and generous nature, her perception of his appearance changes. She no longer is repelled by the way he looks but instead is drawn to his loving nature. The better she gets to know him, the less monstrous he seems. Finally, finding him dying of a broken heart, she reveals her love for him, which transforms the Beast into a handsome prince. Beauty and the Beast not only live happily ever after, but all those who stumbled into their domain in despair are changed, finding on their departure that their hearts are now filled with goodness and beauty.

This is an often repeated story. Many times we are repelled by those we do not know. Yet after they have become our friends, we do not understand how once they seemed monstrous to us. Nowhere is the story of Beauty and the Beast more apparent than in small groups. For it is in small groups that diversity among individuals is most often faced and eventually valued.

Pluralism and diversity among individuals create an opportunity, but as with all opportunities, there are potentially positive or negative outcomes (Johnson & Johnson, 1989). In other words:

1. **Diversity among group members can result in beneficial consequences,** such as increased achievement and productivity, creative problem solving, growth in cognitive and moral reasoning, increased perspective-taking ability, improved relationships, and general sophistication in interacting and working with peers from a variety of cultural and ethnic backgrounds.

2. **Diversity among group members can result in harmful consequences,** such as lower achievement and productivity, closed-minded rejection of new information, increased egocentrism, and negative relationships characterized by hostility, rejection, divisiveness, scapegoating, bullying, stereotyping, prejudice, and racism.

Whether diversity leads to positive or negative outcomes largely depends on your (Johnson & Johnson, 1989, 1995a, 1995c, 1999b):

1. Recognizing that diversity exists and is a valuable resource.

2. Building a coherent personal identity that includes (a) your own cultural/ethnic heritage and (b) a view of yourself as an individual who respects and values differences among individuals.
3. Understanding the internal cognitive barriers (such as stereotyping and prejudice) to building relationships with diverse peers and working to reduce the barriers.
4. Understanding the dynamics of intergroup conflict (see Chapter 9).
5. Understanding the social judgment process and knowing how to create the process of acceptance while avoiding the process of rejection (see Chapter 3).
6. Creating a cooperative context in which positive relationships among diverse individuals will be built (see Chapter 3). This requires structuring cooperation (as opposed to a competitive or individualistic effort). It is within a cooperative context that diverse individuals develop personal (as opposed to impersonal) relationships.
7. Managing conflicts in constructive ways. This includes:
   a. Intellectual conflicts that are part of decision-making and learning situations (controversy) (see Chapter 8).
   b. Conflicts of interests that are resolved by problem-solving negotiations and mediation (see Chapter 9).
8. Learning and internalizing pluralistic, democratic values.

DIVERSITY

Diversity in America

Most countries are becoming more pluralistic. Historically, the United States always has been pluralistic. Our common culture has been formed by the interaction of various cultures and has been influenced over time by a wide variety of willing (and sometimes unwilling) European, African, and Asian immigrants as well as Native Americans. American music, art, literature, language, food, and customs all show the effects of the integration of diverse cultures into one nation.

The diversity of the United States is still increasing. In the 1980s alone, over 7.8 million people from over 150 different countries and speaking dozens of different languages

Waves of Immigration

Origin	1820–1860	1901–1921	1970–1986
Northern, Western Europe	95%	41%	6%
Southern, Eastern Europe		44	9
Latin America			37
Asia		4	41
North America	3	6	3
Other	2	1	4

Sources: Population Reference Bureau, Bureau of the Census, Immigration and Naturalization Service.

immigrated to the United States. The Carnegie Foundation (1995) notes that from 1980 to 1990 the number of immigrant children increased by 24% and the number of children with limited proficiency in English increased 20%, thereby linguistically isolating those children in households where no one over fourteen speaks English very well. In 1970, 20% of students were from minority groups, whereas in 1992 this percentage had increased to 40%. The percentage of students with disabilities, families in poverty, and suffering from abuse is increasing. There is every reason to expect the diversity of individuals' cultural and experiential backgrounds, knowledge, abilities, and skills to continue to increase in the future.

Sources of Diversity

The major sources of diversity are (a) demographic characteristics, (b) personality characteristics, and (c) abilities and skills. **Demographic diversity** includes culture, ethnicity, language, handicapping conditions, age, gender, social class, religion, and regional differences. North America, for example, is becoming more multicultural and multilingual.

In addition to demographic diversity, individuals can have different **personal characteristics.** Groups can be composed of introverts as well as extroverts and of people who approach problems randomly as well as sequentially. Group members also can have different values, attitudes, opinions, lifestyles, styles of interaction, and commitments. Attitudes, values, and beliefs vary systematically with demographic variables. Age cohorts have had different attitudes toward economic conditions and war, males and females have had different attitudes toward interpersonal relationships, and education has been related to attitudes toward innovation and reduction in prejudice.

Finally, individuals differ in the **abilities and skills** they bring to the group. Experts from a variety of fields, for example, may be brought together to solve a problem or conduct a project. Representatives from design, manufacturing, distribution, and sales departments may form a team to bring a new product to market. Accountants and creative artists may work together to revitalize a neighborhood. It is difficult, if not impossible, to find a productive group whose members do not have a wide variety of abilities and skills.

IMPORTANCE OF MANAGING DIVERSITY

The more voices we allow to speak about one thing, the more eyes, different eyes we can use to observe one thing, the more complete will our concept of this thing, our objectivity, be.

Nietzsche

Utilizing diversity is one of the major challenges facing modern societies. Dealing with diversity is becoming increasingly important for several reasons.

First, we increasingly live in one world. The problems that face each person, each community, and each country cannot be solved without global cooperation and joint action. Changes in the world economy, transportation, and communication are resulting in increased interdependence among individuals, groups, organizations, communities, and societies. The more interdependent the world becomes, the more diverse the membership of any one group will likely be. In a global village, highly diverse individuals are interdependent and, therefore, have to interact and work together.

Second, diversity in most settings is inevitable and, therefore, individuals need the skills to interact effectively with people from a wide variety of backgrounds. For 200,000 years humans lived in small hunting and gathering groups, interacting only infrequently with other nearby small groups. It is only with the recent development of worldwide interdependence and communication and transportation systems that diverse types of individuals have begun to interact, work with, and live next to each other. In North America, Europe, and throughout the world, individuals increasingly interact with people who come from different cultures and ethnic backgrounds, speak different languages, and have grown up in markedly different conditions. In addition, interaction between genders and generations is quite different from what it used to be. Such diversity is relatively new. Diversity among acquaintances, classmates, co-workers, neighbors, and friends is increasingly inevitable.

Third, economically there has been a globalization of business reflected in the increase in multinational companies, co-production agreements, and offshore operations. More and more companies must translate their local and national perspectives into a worldview. Companies that are staffed by individuals skilled in building relationships with diverse types of persons will have an advantage in the global market. A telephone survey of 408 opinion leaders about human resource issues in business (e.g., executives, consultants, faculty), for example, asked respondents to think ahead about the strategic issues that business will face, and found that managing a more diverse workforce was the one issue that was repeatedly mentioned (Sirota, Alpher, & Pfau, 1989).

With increasing interdependence, diversity cannot be avoided or bypassed. Any group may consist of members who are diverse on (a) a large number of personal characteristics and (b) the abilities and skills they contribute to the group's efforts. The diversity of the group's membership may enhance or hinder the performance of the group. Diversity among individuals creates an opportunity, but as with all opportunities, there is the potential for either positive or negative outcomes. **Tomorrow's effective groups (including large groups such as organizations and nations) will be those that have learned to be productive with a diverse membership.** This chapter, therefore, focuses on the ways groups can take full advantage of the positive consequences of diversity and can minimize the potentially negative consequences. The chapter is divided into three sections. *First,* the evidence is reviewed that indicates that diversity in group composition increases productivity on a variety of tasks. *Second,* the difficulties with diversity that have to be faced, such as stereotypes, prejudice, racism, blaming the victim, and culture clash, are discussed. Finally, the practical procedures that groups can use to ensure that diversity is a resource and not a hindrance are presented.

THE VALUE OF DIVERSITY

The research that documents the value of diversity has primarily focused on performance on a variety of tasks. There is also some research examining the impact of diversity on cohesion and conflict, which are determinants of absenteeism, turnover, and satisfaction. Outcomes often are nearly as important as group performance in organizational settings.

Group Composition and Performance on Tasks

How does heterogeneity of group membership affect group performance? Researchers have studied the degree of homogeneity–heterogeneity among members' (a) demographic attributes, (b) personal attributes (including personality, attitudes, values), and (c) abilities and skills (both technical and social). Three types of tasks have been studied: (a) performance on clearly defined production tasks, (b) performance on cognitive or intellective tasks, and (c) creative idea generation and decision making related to ambiguous judgmental tasks (Jackson, 1992; Johnson & Johnson, 1989; McGrath, 1984). The combination of sources of diversity and types of task is presented in Table 10.1 (Jackson, 1992).

Production tasks have objective standards for performance evaluation and require the proficient use of perceptual and motor skills (McGrath, 1984). Haythorn (1968) conducted a comprehensive review of research on group composition and performance tasks, covering studies conducted primarily between 1940 and 1968. Shaw (1981), McGrath (1984), and Driskell, Hogan, and Salas (1987) have conducted subsequent reviews. These reviews indicate that relatively few studies, with mixed results, have assessed the impact of personal attribute composition on performance tasks. Two studies found performance to be higher in groups whose members were homogeneous in personal attributes

Table 10.1 **Group Composition and Types of Tasks**

Types of Diversity Investigated	Types of Tasks
Demographic attributes	Performance on clearly defined production tasks
Personal attributes (personality, attitudes, values)	Performance on cognitive or intellective tasks
Abilities and skills (technical, social)	Creative idea generation and decision making on ambiguous judgmental tasks

(Clement & Schiereck, 1973; Fenelon & Megaree, 1971). Terborg, Castore, and DeNinno (1976), however, found attitude heterogeneity–homogeneity to be unrelated to performance in a longitudinal study of student groups working on land-surveying tasks.

Groups composed of members with heterogeneous technical abilities may do better on production tasks than groups composed of members with homogeneous technical abilities (Jackson, 1992). Pelz (1956) found that more productive scientists and engineers tended to create informal communication networks with dissimilar peers. The productivity among scientists and engineers was positively correlated with their frequency of contact with colleagues whose training and expertise were dissimilar to their own. Such networks resemble loosely structured heterogeneous groups. Voiers (1956) found that heterogeneous abilities facilitated the performance of B-29 bomber crews when the crews could take advantage of the ability heterogeneity by assigning members to those tasks to which they were best suited. Athletic teams with more diverse skills (good offensive and defensive units) have been found to outperform teams with less diverse skills (Jones, 1974).

Intellective tasks are problem-solving tasks with correct answers (McGrath, 1984). Wood (1987) reviewed the research on the impact of sex differences on group performance. He found twelve studies in which objective performance results (accuracy and speed) could be compared for same- versus mixed-sex groups. He found weak support for the conclusion that mixed-sex groups tend to outperform same-sex groups of either males or females. Similar findings have been reported with more complex learning tasks (Johnson, Johnson, Scott, & Ramolae, 1985; Peterson, Johnson, & Johnson, 1991). Laughlin and colleagues (see Laughlin, 1980) have demonstrated that typically in problem-solving groups, "truth supported wins." When heterogeneity increases the probability that the group will contain some members who are capable of determining the correct answer to the problems being solved, mixed-attribute groups should outperform homogeneous groups. For "Eureka" tasks, the group needs only one member with the ability to discover the correct answer. Other studies demonstrated that groups made up of individuals with different ability levels (high, medium, low) outperformed individuals on intellective tasks (Johnson & Johnson, 1989).

Decision-making tasks involve reaching a consensus about the best solution to a problem when the "correct" answer is not known (McGrath, 1984). Research reviews indicate that heterogeneous groups are more likely than homogeneous groups to be creative and to reach high-quality decisions (Fiedler, Meuwese, & Conk, 1961; Filley, House, & Kerr, 1976; Frick, 1973; Hoffman, 1979; Johnson, 1977; Johnson & Johnson, 1989; McGrath, 1984; Shaw, 1981; Torrance, 1961; Webb, 1977). The conclusion holds for a variety of personal attributes, including personality (Hoffman & Maier, 1961), leadership abilities (Ghiselli & Lodahl, 1958), types of training (Pelz, 1956), and attitudes (Hoffman, Harburg, & Maier, 1962b; Triandis, Hall, & Ewen, 1965; Willems & Clark, 1971). Ziller, Behringer, and Goodchilds (1962) created heterogeneity in groups by changing the people who made up the group (open groups) versus groups with stable membership (closed groups). They asked the groups to write cartoon captions. Captions written by the heterogeneous (open) groups were judged to have greater fluency and originality. Pelz and Andrews (1966) also found that groups with fluid membership are likely to be more creative, even when the groups are initially interdisciplinary. They concluded that when scientists of interdisciplinary teams worked closely together on a daily basis, within three years they became homogeneous in their perspectives and approach to solving problems. Although diverse perspectives are potentially advantageous, heterogeneous groups may not always function at an optimal level. Hill (1982) reviewed several studies that found that on creative and decision-making tasks, the performance of interacting groups was less than their potential (as estimated by statistical pooling). Hall and Williams (1966), however, found just the opposite. Furthermore, in a field study of 119 top management teams in the banking industry in six midwestern states, Bantel and Jackson (1989) found that the more heterogeneous (in terms of job expertise) the decision-making teams, the more frequently the bank adopted new, innovative practices.

The ability composition of groups affects their performance on creative and decision-making tasks. Laughlin and Bitz (1975) used a word-association task to compare the performance of groups composed of members with dissimilar ability levels with the performance of individuals whose ability was equivalent to that of the highest-ability group member. They found that the groups outperformed the high-ability individuals. Their findings suggest that high-ability members can benefit from interaction with others who have less ability, perhaps because (a) the high-ability individuals take on the role of teacher, which leads them to sharpen their own thinking, or (b) the questions and inputs of more naive members encourage the more expert members to unbundle the assumptions and rules they automatically use when dealing with issues and problems in which they are experts (Simon, 1979). This unbundling increases the likelihood that unwarranted assumptions are reexamined and decision rules are reexamined for exceptions. Overall, the evidence indicates that when working on complex, nonroutine problems (a situation that requires some degree of creativity), groups are more effective when composed of individuals with diverse types of skills, knowledge, abilities, and perspectives.

The results of the research on group composition and task performance are summarized in Table 10.2. There is little or no research on the impact of heterogeneity of

Table 10.2 **Impact of Group Composition on Outcomes**

Types of Outcomes	Personal Attributes	Abilities and Skills
Production tasks	The few studies found mixed results, so no clear effect of group composition on performance is proved.	The few studies found that heterogeneity of types and levels of ability increases productivity.
Intellective tasks	Overall, there are not enough studies to allow a conclusion to be drawn. Mixed-sex groups may outperform same-sex groups.	Almost no directly relevant research.
Decision-making tasks	Heterogeneous groups out-perform homogeneous groups.	Heterogeneity of ability levels is beneficial.
Cohesion	Heterogeneous groups are some-what less cohesive and have higher turnover rates.	Almost no direct research.
Conflict	More conflicts tend to occur in heterogeneous groups.	Almost no direct research.

demographic attributes on performance of production, intellective, and decision-making tasks. Heterogeneity of membership, both in personal characteristics and in abilities and skills, tends to facilitate performance on creative and decision-making tasks. Heterogeneity of abilities and skills seems to be beneficial for performance tasks. There are too few studies on intellective tasks to allow us to draw a conclusion. Homogeneity of personal characteristics and abilities does not seem to facilitate performance on any of the types of tasks.

Other Outcomes

Absenteeism, turnover, and satisfaction often are nearly as important as group performance to groups and organizations (Nadler, Hackman, & Lawler, 1979; Schmidt, 1974). These outcomes are determined largely by cohesion and conflict. Haythorn (1968) reviewed the evidence and concluded that the effects of *personality heterogeneity–homogeneity* on cohesion depended on a number of factors, including personality characteristics, task characteristics, and extent of interpersonal contact. Bantel and Jackson (1989), in their field study of decision-making teams at 119 banks in six states, found no relationship between team heterogeneity and cohesiveness. Jackson, Brett, Sessa, Cooper, Julin, and Peyronnin (1991), in a follow-up study, found that (a) the demographically homogeneous teams had lower turnover and (b) were more likely to fill vacancies with employees from inside the firm, both of which may indicate higher cohesion. *Turnover* tends to be higher in work groups composed of members who are more diverse with respect to their *ages and years of organizational tenure* (e.g., Jackson et al., 1991; McCain, O'Reilly, & Pfeffer, 1983; O'Reilly, Caldwell, & Barnett, 1989; Wagner, Pfeffer, & O'Reilly, 1984) and who are heterogeneous in terms of *college alma mater, curriculum studied,* and *industry experiences* (Jackson et al., 1991). *Attitude similarity* has been found to be mildly related to group cohesion. There is evidence that people are attracted to others with similar attitudes (Byrne, 1971; Heider, 1958; Newcomb, 1961) and that group members tend to become more similar in their attitudes as they interact over time (Newcomb, 1956). Terborg, Castore, and DeNinno (1976), however, conducted one of the few studies in which attitudes were assessed directly and then used to assemble groups. In their longitudinal investigation of student groups, cohesiveness was assessed at six points in time. At each assessment, cohesiveness was greater in the groups composed of attitudinally similar members, although the magnitude of the effect of attitude similarity on cohesiveness did not approach statistical significance until the last three assessments.

Finally, heterogeneity among group members promotes increased argumentation and **conflict** (Nijhof & Kommers, 1982). Such conflicts can be beneficial for completing complex problem-solving tasks (Cosier, 1981; Janis, 1972; Johnson & Johnson, 1979, 1989, 1992a; Schweiger, Sandberg, & Rechner, 1989; Schwenk, 1983).

Disadvantages of Homogeneity of Membership

Group homogeneity has a number of disadvantages. *First,* homogeneous groups may lack the controversy and clash of perspectives so essential to high-quality decision making and creative thinking. Too many members who think alike and see the world the same way make for a very dull and mediocre group. *Second*, they tend to be risk-avoidant (Bantel & Jackson, 1989) and may, therefore, miss opportunities to increase their productivity. *Third*, they more frequently engage in groupthink (Janis, 1972). *Fourth*, they tend to function best in static situations. They have trouble adapting to changing conditions.

Bringing diverse individuals together does not automatically result in positive outcomes (Johnson & Johnson, 1989). Proximity is a necessary condition for the positive potential of diversity to be realized, but it is not sufficient in itself. What proximity does create is visibility and initial contact. The initial contact is often dominated by **interaction strain** (individuals feel discomfort and uncertainty as to how to behave). Interaction strain inhibits interaction, creates ambivalence, and fosters atypical behavior such as overfriendliness followed by withdrawal and avoidance. Under competitive and individualistic conditions, furthermore, pluralism and diversity may cause problems. Diversity can result in lower achievement due to increased difficulties in communication and coordination. It can create threat, defensiveness, increased egocentrism, and closed-minded rejection of new information. Direct interaction among diverse individuals in competitive situations can create negative relationships characterized by hostility, rejection, divisiveness, scapegoating, bullying, stereotyping, and prejudice.

Conclusions

There are a number of problems with the group composition research. **First, in considering member heterogeneity, it is difficult to determine what attributes are important.** The research has focused on personal attributes (such as personality, attitudes, gender, ethnicity) and skills and abilities. These two categories have been focused on because they can be measured and group members can be selected based on them. It is not clear that they are the variables that affect team performance.

Second, no one attribute is likely to make much difference in the complexity of real work. Thus, multiattribute research may be more important. Instead of studying the impact of gender, ethnicity, age, or cognitive style, studies that track composition along all of these dimensions simultaneously are needed.

Third, organizations employ people to perform a wide variety of both simple and complex tasks that involve perceptual and motor performance, intellective performance, creativity, and judgmental decision making. Groups may be working on a variety of tasks simultaneously, and the tasks that they are doing today may not be the same as those they will work on tomorrow. What tasks a team may have to do at any given time are unpredictable. Over time, the tasks that a group faces are unpredictable; therefore, the safest thing to do is to maximize the heterogeneity in the group.

Fourth, it is difficult to determine what is and is not diversity. What outsiders may define as heterogeneity may not be perceived as such by insiders. Turner (1987), in his discussion of self-categorization theory, argues that many group phenomena (including cohesiveness and cooperation) are influenced by the self-categorizations of group members. Specifically, psychological in-groups form when people perceive themselves to be relatively similar to each other on some dimension(s) and relatively different from comparison others, who are viewed as the out-group. Thus, in order to judge whether a group is heterogeneous or homogeneous with respect to an attribute, it is important to consider how the attribute is distributed among nonteam members.

Fifth, very little is known about precisely how group composition and tasks interact to affect performance. Thus, recommendations cannot be made about the procedures and strategies group members should use to utilize their diversity to improve their productivity. If not enough is known to make recommendations about specific, limited, artificial situations, then in the complex real world, recommendations about using heterogeneous groups are impossible.

Finally, group members are simultaneously both heterogeneous and homogeneous. Each person has hundreds of characteristics and abilities. Members who are homogeneous on one or two attributes are heterogeneous with respect to others. Conversely, members who are heterogeneous with respect to several attributes still share common attributes. It is probably impossible to create a homogeneous group. **Clearly, it is unrealistic to cope with the diversity of people by attempting to completely control the composition of groups.** Instead, we need to find ways to manage groups to ensure that the positive consequences of heterogeneity are maximized and the potentially negative consequences of heterogeneity are minimized.

Because diversity is inevitable and increasing, the choice to avoid diversity does not exist for most people. In school, on the job, and in the community, you will be interacting with people who are different from you in many ways whether you wish to or not. The promise of diversity far outweighs the problems as long as the individuals involved understand how to capitalize on the benefits while avoiding the pitfalls. The greater the understanding of human relations, for example, the more constructive will be the results of diversity.

BARRIERS TO INTERACTING WITH DIVERSE PEERS

Diversity among members is an important resource to be utilized to improve the group's productivity. Doing so may not be easy. There are a number of barriers to interacting effectively with diverse peers (Johnson, 2003; Johnson & Johnson, 1999b). They include stereotyping, prejudice, the tendency to blame the victim, and cultural clashes.

Stereotypes

Stereotypes are everywhere, and everyone has them. Stereotypes are a product of the way the mind stores, organizes, and recalls information. The use of stereotypes cannot be avoided. They are used to describe differences among groups and to predict how others will behave. They reduce complexity, help us make quick decisions, fill in the gaps in what we know, help us make sense out of who we are and what has happened to us, and help us create and recognize the patterns needed to draw conclusions. Unfortunately, stereotypes can also support unfairness and injustice.

The term *stereotype* was first used in the eighteenth century to describe a printing process designed to duplicate pages of type. In the nineteenth century the term *stereotypy* was used by psychiatrists to describe a behavior of persistent repetitiveness and unchanging mode of expression. Modern use of the term *stereotype* originated with Lippmann (1922) in his book, *Public Opinion.* He argues that "there is neither time nor opportunity for intimate acquaintance. Instead we notice a trait which marks a well known type, and fill in the rest of the picture by means of the stereotypes we carry about in our heads" (p. 59). The world is simply too complicated to attend to every detail and, therefore, the perceiver relies on stereotypes to simplify social perception. Katz and Braly (1933) conducted the first classic empirical study of stereotypes and linked them to attitudes and prejudice.

A **stereotype** is a belief that associates a whole group of people with certain traits. Stereotypes (a) are cognitive; (b) reflect a set of related beliefs rather than an isolated bit of information; (c) describe the attributes, personalities, and characters so that groups can be compared and differentiated; and (d) are shared by individuals and groups holding them (Ashmore & Del Boca, 1979). Stereotypes function as simplifiers and organizers of social information. They reduce the complexity of the social environment and make it more manageable. Examples of stereotypes are the following. Women have been stereotyped as being more emotional than men. Men have been stereotyped as being more competitive than women. Tall, dark, and handsome men have been stereotyped as being mysterious. Stereotypes are often influenced by past events. Stereotypes of the Japanese in the 1940s, for example, were heavily influenced by the surprise attack on Pearl Harbor in World War II.

You form stereotypes by (a) categorizing (you sort single objects into groups rather than thinking of each one as unique) and (b) differentiating between in-group (the groups with which you identify) and out-groups. You commonly assume that the members of out-groups are quite similar while realizing that the members of the in-group are quite diverse **(out-group homogeneity effect).** The failure to notice differences among out-group members may result from lack of personal contact with a representative sample of the out-group. A white person, for example, may see all Hispanics as being alike, but someone with a wide variety of Hispanic friends may see little similarity among Puerto Ricans, Cubans, Mexicans, and Argentineans.

An efficient cognitive system does more than simply make things easy for people at all costs. It also distributes limited resources in ways that maximize the informational value gained for the effort expended. There are several reasons why stereotyping is efficient. *First,* the social categorization that precedes stereotyping reduces the amount of information that must be attended to. When you group social stimuli together and treat them as functionally equivalent, you reduce the need to form individualized impressions of each category member (Allport, 1954; Brewer, 1988; Fiske & Neuberg, 1990; Hamilton & Sherman, 1994; Lippmann, 1922). *Second,* stereotypes expand your base of knowledge by allowing you to infer a person's attributes without having to attend carefully to the person's behavior (Brewer, 1988; Fiske & Neuberg, 1990; Hamilton & Sherman, 1994; Medin, 1988; Sherman, 1996). Through the relatively simple act of social categorization, stereotypes allow you to gain a large amount of "functionally accurate" information (Swann, 1984), thus resulting in a beneficial ratio of information gained to effort expended. Stereotypes are particularly useful when processing capacity is constrained, processing resources are scarce, and accurate social perception is difficult to achieve. Stereotypes facilitate the encoding of both stereotype-consistent and stereotype-inconsistent information when processing capacity is low (Sherman, Lee, Bessenoff, & Frost, 1998). The energy saved by encoding stereotype-consistent information is then used to understand stereotype-inconsistent information. Stereotypes may be automatically activated when people experience a threat to their self-image (Spencer, Fein, Wolfe, Fong, & Dunn, 1998).

People who hold strong stereotypes are prone to the **fundamental attribution error.** They attribute negative behavior on the part of a minority-group member to dispositional characteristics and positive behavior by a minority-group member to situational factors, whereas their own negative behavior is attributed to situational causes and their own positive behavior is viewed as dispositional. When a minority-group member acts in an undesirable way, the attribution is "That's the way those people are" or "Those people are born like that." If the minority-group member is seen engaging in desirable behavior, the person holding the stereotype can view the minority person as an exception to the rule or view the minority person's behavior as due to luck, the situational context, or extraordinary motivation and effort.

Stereotypes are perpetuated and protected in four ways. *First,* stereotypes influence what we perceive and remember about the actions of out-group members. The social categories we use to process information about the world control what we tend to perceive and not perceive. Our prejudice makes us notice the negative traits we ascribe to the groups we are prejudiced against. Furthermore, when individuals expect members of an out-group to behave in a certain way, they tend to recall more accurately instances that confirm rather than disconfirm their expectations. Hence, if an out-group is perceived to be of low intelligence, individuals (a) tend to remember instances in which an out-group member was confused in class or failed a test but (b) tend to forget instances in which an out-group member achieved a 4.0-grade-point average or became class valedictorian (Rothbart, Evans, & Fulero, 1979).

There is an association between power and stereotyping (Fiske, 1993; Fiske & Morling, 1996). The general premise is that persons in positions of power are especially vulnerable to stereotyping subordinates because they pay less attention to them. High-power individuals may lack the cognitive capacity to attend to subordinates because having power requires attending to more people and more issues at the same time. High-power individuals may ignore subordinates because the high-power persons' outcomes do not depend on subordinates. High-power individuals may not attend to subordinates because they have a dominant personality trait and may attempt to control their interactions with others to such an extent that they ignore the actions and motivations of others. Regardless of its cause, decreases in attention make powerful individuals more likely to depend on stereotypes in interacting with subordinates.

Second, stereotypes create an oversimplified picture of out-group members. The act of categorization itself leads people to assume similarity among the members of a category. Even when the distinctions between groups are arbitrary, people tend to minimize the differences they see among members of the same group and to accentuate the differences between members of two different groups. When processing information about their in-group and out-groups, people develop relatively simplistic and nonspecific pictures of out-groups. The larger the out-group, the more likely oversimplifications will occur. Individuals, furthermore, do more than simply note the differences between their in-group and the out-groups. They attempt to emphasize the differences and take actions that will discriminate in favor of their own group.

Third, individuals tend to overestimate the similarity of behavior among out-group members. Because out-groups are perceived to be very homogeneous, the actions of one member can be generalized to all.

Why Do Stereotypes Endure?

Following are several reasons why stereotypes persist. Rank them from most important (1) to least important (7). Write down the rationale for your ranking. Find a partner and share your ranking and rationale, listen to his or her ranking and rationale, and cooperatively create a new, improved ranking and rationale. Then find another pair and repeat the procedure in a group of four.

Rank	Reason
	The tendency for people to overestimate the association between variables that are only slightly correlated or not correlated at all (i.e., **illusionary correlation).** Many people, for example, perceive that being poor and being lazy are associated. Any poor person who is not hard at work the moment you notice him or her may be perceived as lazy. Low-power groups can acquire negative traits easily and, once acquired, the stereotype is hard to lose.
	Your prejudice makes you notice the negative traits you ascribe to the groups you are prejudiced against, and you more readily believe information that confirms your stereotypes than evidence that challenges them. People tend to process information in ways that verify existing beliefs. This is known as the **confirmation bias** (the tendency to seek, interpret, and create information that verifies existing beliefs).
	You tend to have a **false consensus bias** by believing that most other people share your stereotypes (see poor people as being lazy). You tend to see your own behavior and judgments as quite common and appropriate, and to view alternative responses as uncommon and often inappropriate.
	Your stereotypes tend to be **self-fulfilling.** Stereotypes can subtly influence intergroup interactions in such a way that the stereotype is behaviorally confirmed. You can behave in ways that elicit the actions you expect from out-group members, thus confirming your stereotype.
	You dismiss individuals who do not match your stereotype as exceptions to the rule or representatives of a subcategory.
	Your stereotypes often operate at an implicit level without your conscious awareness.
	You often develop a rationale and explanation to justify your stereotypes and prejudices.

Fourth, stereotypes can lead to scapegoating. A **scapegoat** is a guiltless but defenseless group that is attacked to provide an outlet for pent-up anger and frustration caused by another group. The term comes from a biblical guilt-transference ritual:

> And Aaron shall lay both his hands upon the head of the live goat, and confess over him all the iniquities of the children of Israel, and all their transgressions in all their sins, putting them upon the head of the goat, and shall send him away by the hand of a fit man into the wilderness. (Leviticus 16:21)

In most instances, if group 1 interfered with group 2, group 2 would respond by retaliating against group 1. If, however, group 1 is extremely powerful, too distant, or too difficult to locate, group 2 may respond by turning its aggression on group 3. Group 3, although in no way responsible for the difficulties group 2 experienced, would nonetheless be blamed and thereby become the target of group 2's aggressive actions. Stereotypes of certain out-groups can create a continual scapegoat that is blamed for all problems and difficulties no matter what their origins.

Stereotypes can be changed. The more personal information you have about someone, the less you stereotype. The more time and energy you have to consider the person's characteristics and behavior, the less you stereotype. The more motivated you are to form an accurate impression of someone, the less you stereotype. The more you perceive the person to be typical of the stereotyped group, the more your interaction will change your stereotypes. What these factors indicate is that in order for stereotypes to change, members of different groups need to interact for prolonged periods of time under conditions where they get to know each other personally and see each other as being typical members of their group.

Stereotypes affect not only those who hold them but also those who are targeted. When a widely known negative stereotype (e.g., poor intellectual ability) exists about a group, it creates for its members a burden of suspicion that acts as a threat. This threat arises whenever individuals' behavior can be interpreted in terms of a stereotype, that is, whenever group members run the risk of confirming the stereotype. Steele and Aronson (1995), in studying **stereotype threat,** found that negative stereotypes about blacks' intellectual ability create a "situational pressure" that distracts black students and depresses their academic performance. They argue that the possibility of being judged by a stereotype can cause so much anxiety that intellectual performance is disrupted. Steele and Aronson suggest that stereotype threat is the reason for the underachievement of black students. Seventy percent of black college students drop out of college (as opposed to about 35% of white students), and the drop-out rate is the highest among black students ranked in the top third by SAT scores. In addition, black students with the highest SAT scores fail more frequently than black students with lower scores and at a rate more than three times that of whites with similar scores. When blacks are placed in achievement situations, the negative stereotypes are activated and black students become more self-conscious and work less efficiently. Similar findings were reported on a study of lower-class individuals (Croizet & Claire, 1998). Stereotype threat is eliminated in programs such as the University of Michigan's Twenty-First Century Program where black and white students are randomly recruited, live together, study together cooperatively, and have personal discussions on social issues.

Prejudice

To know one's self is wisdom, but to know one's neighbor is genius.

Minna Antrim

To be prejudiced means to prejudge. **Prejudice** can be defined as an unjustified negative attitude toward a person based solely on that individual's membership in a group other than one's own. Prejudices are judgments made about others that establish a superiority/inferiority belief system. If one person dislikes another simply because that other person is a member of a different ethnic group, sex, or religion, we are dealing with prejudice.

One common form of prejudice is ethnocentrism. **Ethnocentrism** is the tendency to regard one's own ethnic group, nation, religion, culture, or gender as better or more "correct" than others. The word is derived from *ethnic,* meaning a group united by similar customs, characteristics, race, or other common factors, and *center.* When ethnocentrism is present, the standards and values of our culture are used as a yardstick to measure the worth of other ethnic groups. Ethnocentrism is often perpetuated by **cultural conditioning.** As children we are raised to fit into a particular culture. We are conditioned to respond to various situations as we see others in our culture react.

Stereotypes lead to prejudices. **Racism** is prejudice directed at people because of their ethnic membership. **Sexism** is prejudice directed at a person because of his or her gender. **Ageism** is prejudice against the elderly. There are many other types of "isms."

The concept of race assumes biological differences that are most evident in physical appearances. The evidence indicates that there is only one human race (with many variations). Although race has dubious value as a scientific classification system, it has had real consequences for the life experiences and life opportunities of African Americans. Race is a socially constructed concept that is the defining characteristic for African American group membership. Race has social meaning suggesting one's status within the social system. It introduces power differences as people of different races interact with one another. Racism and prejudice deal with the formation of unfounded and often inaccurate opinions about a group, leading to biased behavior against members of that group. Racism gives individuals permission to treat racial groups differently because it mistakenly assumes that (a) humans may be divided into clearly defined racial groups and (b) these groups vary in capabilities and aptitudes.

Modern Racism and Sexism

Traditionally, in the United States, racism and sexism were expressed through such statements as "Blacks are not as smart as whites" and "Women are too emotional to be good managers." Traditional racism and sexism directly and explicitly contain negative evaluations of minorities and females and use the "natural world order" as a justification ("Nature intended it to be this way").

Beginning with the civil rights movement in the 1960s, however, there has been increasing public pressure to see each person as an individual, not as a member of an ethnic group. This has influenced the way whites talk about minorities. Modern racism is a more subtle form of prejudice in which people appear, on the surface, not to be prejudiced but actually do hold racist attitudes (Dovidio & Gaertner, 1991). Modern racism and sexism camouflage prejudices within more sophisticated principles of meritocracy and justice through such statements as "Blacks and women have gone too far—they are pushing for jobs they do not deserve" (Swim, Aikin, Hall, & Hunter, 1995).

Modern racism and sexism use indirect and implicit negative evaluations of minorities and females and use "protecting cherished social values such as meritocracy from attack by minorities" as a justification. The concept of modern racism posits that if we scratch the apparently nonracist surface of many people, we will find bigotry lurking beneath. Modern racism arises because people can see themselves as being fair, humanitarian, and egalitarian while at the same time holding a somewhat negative view of members of groups other than their own.

Having prejudiced thoughts, however, does not necessarily make you a racist (Devine, Monteith, Zuwerink, & Elliot, 1991). Even those who completely reject prejudice may sometimes experience unintentional prejudice-like thoughts and feelings due to prior learning. In this case, racism is like a lingering bad habit that surfaces despite people's best efforts to avoid it. As with all bad habits, with enough commitment and support, racism can be licked.

Discrimination.   When prejudice is acted on, it is discrimination. **Discrimination** is an action taken to harm a group or any of its members. It is a negative, often aggressive action aimed at the target of prejudice. Discrimination is aimed at denying members of the targeted groups treatment and opportunities equal to those afforded to the dominant group. When discrimination is based on race or sex, it is referred to as *racism* or *sexism*. To reduce your prejudices and use of stereotypes, these steps may be helpful (Johnson, 2000):

1. Admit that you have prejudices (everyone does; you are no exception) and commit yourself to reducing them.
2. Identify the stereotypes that reflect your prejudices and modify them.
3. Identify the actions that reflect your prejudices and modify them.
4. Seek feedback from diverse friends and colleagues about how well you are communicating respect for and valuing of diversity.

Blaming the Victim

It is commonly believed that the world is a just place where people generally get what they deserve. If you win the lottery, it must be because you are a nice person who deserves some good luck. If you are robbed, it must be because you were careless and wanted to be punished for past misdeeds. Any person who is mugged in a dark alley while carrying a great deal of cash may be seen as "asking to be robbed." Most people tend to believe that they deserve what happens to them. Most people also believe that others get what they deserve in the world. It is all too easy to forget that victims do not have the benefit of hindsight to guide their actions.

But what happens when situations appear to be unjust? One method is to blame the victim by convincing ourselves that no injustice has occurred. When someone is a victim of prejudice, stereotyping, and discrimination, all too often he or she is seen as "doing *something* wrong." **Blaming the victim** occurs when we attribute the cause of discrimination or misfortune to the personal characteristics and actions of the victim. The situation is examined for potential causes that will enable us to maintain our belief in a just world. If the victim can be blamed for causing the discrimination, then we can believe that the future is predictable and controllable because we will get what we deserve.

Attribution Theory.   Blaming the victim occurs as we try to attribute a cause to events. We constantly interpret the meaning of our behavior and events that occur in our lives. Many times we want to figure out why we acted in a particular way or why a certain outcome occurred. If we get angry when someone infers we are stupid but not when someone calls us "clumsy," we want to know why we are so sensitive about our intelligence. When we are standing on a street corner after a rainstorm and a car splashes

Errors in Making Decisions About Diverse Others

Making a decision requires gathering information on each major alternative action and inferring from the information which alternative will maximize gain and minimize costs.

Errors in Making Inferences

Relying on small samples	Small samples are highly unreliable.
Relying on biased samples	People often ignore clear information about how typical and representative a sample is.
Underutilization of base-rate information	People tend to pay more attention to a single concrete instance than to valid base-rate information, perhaps because the single concrete instance is vivid and salient and thus more compelling.

Errors from Cognitive Heuristics

Availability heuristic	Estimating the frequency of some event by the ease with which you can bring instances to mind. People tend to overestimate the frequency of events that are easy to remember.
Representativeness heuristic	Seeing how well the information matches some imagined average or typical person in the category; the closer the person is to the prototype, the more likely we are to judge the person to be in the category.

Weighing Information

Positive frame	People avoid risks and opt for the "sure thing."
Negative frame	People take risks to avoid costs.
Postdecision rationalization	The alternative chosen becomes more attractive and the alternatives not chosen become less desirable.

us with water, we want to know whether it was caused by our carelessness, the driver's meanness, or just bad luck. This process of explaining or inferring the causes of events has been termed **causal attribution.** An attribution is an inference drawn about the causes of a behavior or event. Any behavior or event can have a variety of possible causes. We observe the behavior or event and then infer the cause. When our boss criticizes our work, for example, we can attribute his or her behavior to a grouchy mood, being under too much pressure, disliking us, or the sloppiness of our work. Early in childhood we begin observing our own behavior and draw conclusions about ourselves. We seem to have a fundamental need to understand both our own behavior and the behavior of others. In trying to understand why a behavior or event occurred, we generally choose to attribute causes to either of the following:

1. Internal personal factors (such as effort and ability).
2. External situational factors (such as luck, task difficulty, or the behavior/personality of other people).

For example, if you do well on a test, you can attribute it to your hard work and great intelligence (an internal attribution) or to the fact that the test was incredibly easy

Dimensions of Attributions				Success Orientation		
	Stable	**Unstable**			**Stable**	**Unstable**
Internal	Ability	Effort		**Success**	Ability	Effort
External	Task difficulty	Luck		**Failure**	Task difficulty	Luck

(an external attribution). When a friend drops out of school, you can attribute it to a lack of motivation (an internal attribution) or a lack of money (an external attribution).

People make causal attributions to explain their successes and failures. Frequently such attributions are **self-serving,** designed to permit us to take credit for positive outcomes and to avoid blame for negative ones. We have a systematic tendency to claim that our successes are due to our ability and efforts, whereas our failures are due to bad luck, obstructive people, or task difficulty. We also have a systematic tendency to claim responsibility for the success of group efforts ("It was all my idea in the first place, and I did most of the work") and avoid responsibility for group failures ("If the other members had tried harder, this would not have happened").

Attribution theory recommends that students be trained to make self-serving attributions. Students should attribute their academic success to ability and effort and avoid attributing success to luck or other people. Students should attribute academic failures to bad luck or lack of effort and avoid attributing failure to personal factors such as lack of ability.

Attribution theorists assume that how people explain their successes and failures determines how hard they work on subsequent tasks. If minority students, for example, attribute academic failure to lack of ability, it can eventually lead to **learned helplessness** (the feeling that no amount of effort can lead to success) (Seligman, 1975). Learned helplessness is associated with shame and self-doubt. Students with a long history of attributing failure to lack of ability simply make no effort to learn. Teachers should ensure that students (especially minority students) think through why they succeeded or failed and guide them toward the conclusion that their failure is caused by either (a) a lack of effort or (b) using the wrong strategy. The emotions teachers express toward students seem to affect the attributions students make about the causes of their success or failure (Graham, 1991). Teacher sympathy for failure tends to be interpreted as indicating low ability, whereas teacher anger toward failure seems to be interpreted as indicating low effort.

Culture Clash

Another common barrier to interacting effectively with diverse groupmates is cultural clashes. **Culture clash** is conflict over basic values that occurs among individuals from different cultures. The most common form occurs when members of minority groups question the values of the majority. Common reactions by majority-group members when their values are being questioned are feeling:

1. **Threatened:** Their responses include avoidance, denial, and defensiveness.
2. **Confused:** Their responses include seeking more information in an attempt to redefine the problem.

3. **Enhanced:** Their responses include heightened anticipation, awareness, and positive actions that lead to solving the problem. Many cultural clashes develop, ranging from threatening to confusing to enhancing. Once they are enhancing, they are no longer a barrier.

As prejudice, stereotyping, and discrimination are reduced, the tendency to blame the victim is avoided, and cultural clashes become enhancing, the stage is set for recognizing and valuing diversity.

Guidelines for Dealing with Diversity

1. Recognize that diversity among members is ever present and unavoidable.
2. Recognize that the more interdependent the world becomes, the more important it is to be able to work effectively with diverse groupmates.
3. Maximize heterogeneity among members in both personal characteristics and abilities in order to maximize the group's productivity and success.
4. With heterogeneous membership comes increased conflict. Structure constructive procedures for managing conflicts among group members.
5. Identify and eliminate barriers to the utilization of diversity (stereotyping, prejudice, blaming the victim, cultural clashes).
6. Ensure that diversity is utilized as a resource by strengthening the positive interdependence within the group in order to create a context in which diversity is a resource, not a hindrance.
7. Ensure that diversity is utilized as a strength by uniting the personal identities of members of diverse groups. Create a superordinate identity based on a pluralistic set of values. Encourage individuals to develop:
    a. An appreciation for their gender, religious, ethnic, and cultural backgrounds.
    b. An appreciation for the gender, religious, ethnic, and cultural backgrounds of other group members.
    c. A strong superordinate identity of "group member" that transcends the differences among members.
    d. A pluralistic set of values concerning equality, freedom, the rights of individual members, and the responsibilities of group membership.
8. Ensure that diversity is utilized as a strength by fostering personal relationships among members that allow for candid discussions that increase members' sophistication about their differences.
9. Ensure that diversity is utilized as a strength by clarifying miscommunications among diverse group members.

MAKING DIVERSITY AMONG MEMBERS A STRENGTH

Diversity among members is a potential source of creativity and productivity. For group members to capitalize on their differences, they must:

1. Ensure that a high level of positive interdependence exists among group members.
2. Create a superordinate group identity that (a) unites the diverse personal identities of group members and (b) is based on a pluralistic set of values.
3. Gain sophistication about the differences among members through personal relationships that allow for candid discussions.
4. Clarify miscommunications among group members from different cultures, ethnic and historical backgrounds, social classes, genders, age cohorts, and so forth.

Structuring and Strengthening Positive Interdependence

In order to build a superordinant group identity that unites all members and build personal relationships that allow for candid conversations that result in increased sophistication, positive interdependence must be structured into group life and periodically strengthened to remind members that they are engaged in a joint enterprise. **Positive interdependence** exists when group members perceive that they can reach their goals if and only if the other members also do so (Deutsch, 1962; Johnson & Johnson, 1989). Group members must believe that they "sink or swim together" in striving to achieve important mutual goals. Positive interdependence may be structured through mutual goals, joint rewards, shared resources, complementary roles, divisions of labor, and a mutual identity.

Strength through diversity does not automatically occur with proximity. Bringing diverse individuals into the same room does not ensure that constructive results will occur. The discords of diversity are not automatically transformed into a symphony when people are brought face-to-face. Prejudice, stereotyping, and discrimination often increase with proximity. What largely determines whether interaction results in positive or negative relationships is the context in which the interaction takes place. Rather than requiring group members to compete to see who is best or to work individualistically on their own, group members must work together to achieve mutual goals. When people cooperate, they tend to like each other more, trust each other more, are more candid with each other, and are more willing to listen to and be influenced by each other (Johnson & Johnson, 1989). When people compete or work individualistically, liking, trust, influence, and candor tend to decrease. There is considerable evidence that cooperative experiences, compared with competitive and individualistic ones, promote more positive, committed, and caring relationships regardless of differences in ethnic, cultural, language, social class, gender, ability, or other differences (Johnson & Johnson, 1989). The impact of positive interdependence is enhanced when members have equal status and when social norms and authorities promote positive relationships and friendship formation (Allport, 1954; Watson, 1947; Williams, 1947).

Creating a Superordinate Group Identity

Diverse individuals from different gender, religious, social class, ethnic, and cultural backgrounds come together in small group settings. The results will be positive if group members get to know each other, appreciate and value the vitality of diversity, learn how to use their diversity for creative problem solving and enhanced productivity, and internalize a common superordinate identity that binds them all together. In order for group members to actualize the positive potential of their diversity, they must recognize that diversity exists and then learn to value and respect the fundamental differences among them. The goal of managing diversity is not to assimilate all members so that everyone is alike. The goal is for members to work together to achieve mutual goals while recognizing their diversity and valuing and respecting their fundamental differences. Creating an *unum* from *pluribus* is done in four steps.

First, group members develop an appreciation for their historic, cultural, ethnic, and religious background as well as their other important personal characteristics. Members should value and recognize the culture, history, and homeland of their ancestors. A **personal identity** is a consistent set of attitudes that defines "who you are" (see Johnson [2000] for a full discussion on developing a personal identity). An identity helps a person cope with stress, provides stability and consistency to the person's life, and directs what information is attended to, how it is organized, and how it is remembered. A personal

Being an American

Being an American is creedal rather than racial or ancestral. It is our belief that "all [humans] are created equal and endowed by their creator with certain inalienable rights" (i.e., our commitment to the Constitution, Bill of Rights, and Declaration of Independence of the United States) that provides our superordinate identity as Americans. To be an American is to adopt a set of values concerning democracy, freedom, liberty, equality, justice, the rights of individuals, and the responsibilities of citizenship (Johnson & Johnson, 1994). It is these values that form the American creed. The common commitment to equality, justice, and liberty for all unites us as one people, even though we are the descendants of many cultures, races, religions, and ethnic groups. Each cultural group is part of the whole, and members of each new immigrant group, while modifying and enriching our national identity, learn that they are first and foremost Americans. America is one of the few successful examples of a pluralistic society where different groups clashed but ultimately learned to live together by achieving a sense of common nationhood. In our diversity, there has always been a broad recognition that we are one people. Whatever our origins, we are all Americans. It is from the following four steps that the United States creates an *unum* from *pluribus*.

1. I respect, appreciate, and value my religious, ethnic, and cultural background.

2. I respect, appreciate, and value the religious, ethnic, and cultural backgrounds of others.

3. I have a strong superordinate identity as an "American." Being an American is creedal. I believe in the American creed.

4. I have pluralistic values. I value democracy, freedom, liberty, equality, justice, the rights of individuals, and the responsibilities of citizenship.

identity consists of multiple subidentities that are organized into a coherent, stable, and integrated whole. The subidentities include a **gender identity** (fundamental sense of maleness or femaleness), a **cultural identity** (sense of origins and membership in a culture), an **ethnic identity** (sense of belonging to one particular ethnic group), a **religious identity** (sense of belonging to one particular religious group), and so forth. Each of these subidentities should be recognized and valued, and they need to be organized into a coherent, stable, and integrated overall sense of self. Respect for one's subidentities may be the basis for self-respect.

Second, group members develop an appreciation for the historic, cultural, ethnic, and religious backgrounds (and other important personal characteristics) of others. A critical aspect of developing a historical, cultural, and ethnic identity is whether ethnocentricity is inherent in one's definition of oneself. A personal identity that includes one's heritage must be developed in a way that does not lead to rejection of the heritage of other members. There are many situations in which being a member of one group requires the rejection of other groups. There are also many situations in which being a member of one group requires valuing and respect for other groups. Other heritages may be seen as collaborators rather than competitors. The degree to which a person's identity leads to respect for and valuing of others' diversity depends on developing a superordinate identity that subsumes both one's own heritage and the heritage of all other group members. Members need to learn how to express respect for diverse backgrounds and value them as a resource that increases the quality of life and adds to the viability of the group.

Third, encourage members to develop a strong superordinate identity of "group member" that transcends the differences among members. Being a member of a work group is creedal rather than racial or ancestral. The work group unites widely diverse people. In essence, the work group has its own culture that supersedes the individual cultures of members. Members need to learn how to highlight the group's superordinate identity and use it to resolve conflicts based on members' differences.

Fourth, group members adopt a pluralistic set of values concerning democracy, freedom, liberty, equality, justice, the rights of individuals, and the responsibilities of citizenship. All members have a say in how the group operates. All members are free to speak their minds and give their opinions. All members are considered to be of equal value. Every member has the right and responsibility to contribute his or her resources and efforts toward achieving the group's goals. Each member has a right to expect the group to be considerate of his or her needs and wants. All members must at times put the good of the group above their own needs and desires. It is these values that form the group or organizational culture. In the group, members must respect basic human rights, listen to dissenters instead of rejecting them, have freedom of speech, and have open discussion of differences. It is these values that bind group members together. Most groups are or will become a multicultural unit knitted together by a common set of values.

Gaining Sophistication Through Intergroup Relationships

Some people are *sophisticated* about how to act appropriately within many different cultures and perspectives. They are courteous, well-mannered, and refined within many different settings and cultures. Other people are quite *provincial,* knowing only how to act appropriately from their narrow perspective. To become sophisticated, a person must be able to see the situation from the cultural perspective of the other people involved.

Much of the information about different cultural and ethnic heritages and perspectives cannot be attained by reading books and listening to lectures. Only by knowing, working with, and personally interacting with members of diverse groups can individuals really learn to value diversity, utilize diversity for creative problem solving, and work effectively with diverse peers. Understanding the perspective of others from different ethnic and cultural backgrounds requires more than information. It requires the personal sharing of viewpoints and mutual discussion of situations.

To gain the sophistication and skills required to build relationships with diverse peers, you need to develop friendships with persons from a wide variety of cultural, ethnic, social class, and historical backgrounds. There are many aspects of relating to individuals different from you that can be learned only from friends who are candid about misunderstandings you are inadvertently creating. To gain the necessary **sophistication** and skills to relate to, work with, and become friends with diverse peers, you need:

1. **Actual interaction:** Seek opportunities to interact with a wide variety of peers. You do so because you value diversity, recognize the importance of relating effectively to diverse peers, and recognize the importance of increasing your knowledge of multicultural issues.
2. **Trust:** Build trust by being open about yourself and your commitment to cross-cultural relationships and being trustworthy when others share their opinions and reactions with you. Being trustworthy includes expressing respect for diverse backgrounds and valuing them as a resource that increases the quality of your life and adds to the viability of your society.
3. **Candor:** Persuade your peers to be candid by openly discussing their personal opinions, feelings, and reactions with you. There are many events that seem neutral to you that are offensive and hurtful to individuals from backgrounds different from yours. In order to understand what is and is not disrespectful and hurtful, your peers must be candid about their reactions and explain them to you.

If you are not sophisticated and skilled in building relationships with diverse peers, you are in danger of unconsciously colluding with current patterns of discrimination. **Collusion** is conscious and unconscious reinforcement of stereotypic attitudes, behaviors, and prevailing norms. People collude with discriminatory practices and prejudiced actions through ignorance, silence, denial, and active support. Perhaps the only way not to collude with existing discriminatory practices is to build the friendships with diverse peers that allow you to understand when discrimination and prejudice occur.

Clarifying Miscommunications

Imagine that you and several friends went to hear a speaker. Although the content was good, and the delivery entertaining, two of your friends walked out in protest. When you asked them why, they called your attention to the facts that the speaker continually used "you guys" even though half the audience were women, used only sports and military examples, quoted only males, and joked about senility and old age. Your friends were insulted.

Communication is actually one of the most complex aspects of managing relationships with diverse peers. To communicate effectively with people from a different cultural, ethnic, social class, and historical background, you must increase your:

1. **Language sensitivity.** Knowledge of words and expressions that are appropriate and inappropriate in communicating with diverse groups. The use of language can play a powerful role in reinforcing stereotypes and garbling communication. To avoid this, individuals need to heighten their sensitivity and avoid using terms and expressions that ignore or devalue others.
2. **Awareness of stylistic elements of communication.** Knowledge of the key elements of communication style and how diverse cultures use these elements to communicate. Without awareness of nuances in language and differences in style, the potential for garbled communication is enormous when interacting with diverse peers.

Your ability to communicate with credibility to diverse peers is closely linked to your use of language. You must be sophisticated enough to anticipate how your messages will be interpreted by the listener. If you are unaware of nuances and innuendoes contained in your message, then you will be more likely to miscommunicate. The words you choose often tell other people more about your values, attitudes, and socialization than you intend to reveal. Receivers will react to the subtleties conveyed and interpret the implied messages behind your words. The first step in establishing relationships with diverse peers, therefore, is to understand how language reinforces stereotypes and to adjust your usage accordingly.

You can never predict with certainty how every person will react to what you say. You can, however, minimize the possibility of miscommunicating by following some basic guidelines:

1. Use all the communication skills discussed in this book and in Johnson (2000).
2. Negotiate for meaning whenever you think the other persons you are talking with misinterpreted what you said.
3. Use words that are inclusive rather than exclusive such as *women, men,* and *participants.*
4. Avoid adjectives that spotlight specific groups and imply that the individual is an exception, such as *black doctor, woman pilot, older teacher,* and *blind lawyer.*
5. Use quotations, references, metaphors, and analogies that reflect diversity and are from diverse sources—for example, from Asian and African as well as European and American sources.

6. Avoid terms that define, demean, or devalue others, such as *cripple, girl, boy,* and *agitator.*

7. Be aware of the genealogy of words viewed as inappropriate by others. It is the connotations the receiver places on the words that is important, not your connotations. These connotations change over time, so continual clarification is needed. There are "loaded" words that seem neutral to you but highly judgmental to people of diverse backgrounds. The word *lady,* for example, was a compliment even a few years ago, but today it fails to take into account women's

Important Concepts

Demonstrate your understanding of the following concepts by matching the definitions with the appropriate concept. Find a partner. Compare answers.

	Concept		Definition
	1. Prejudice	a.	Belief that associates a whole group of people with certain traits.
	2. Ethnocentrism	b.	An action taken to harm a group or any of its members.
	3. Stereotype	c.	Unjustified negative attitude toward a person based solely on that individual's membership in a group other than one's own.
	4. Illusionary correlation	d.	Attribute the cause of discrimination or misfortune to the personal characteristics and actions of the victim.
	5. Discrimination	e.	Conflict over basic values that occurs among individuals from different cultures.
	6. Blaming the victim	f.	Conscious or unconscious reinforcement of stereotypic attitudes, behaviors, and prevailing norms.
	7. Collusion	g.	Tendency to overestimate the association between variables that are only slightly correlated or not correlated at all.
	8. Scapegoat	h.	Prejudice directed at people because of their ethnic membership.
	9. Racism	i.	Believing that most other people share their stereotypes.
	10. Modern racism	j.	Guiltless but defenseless group that is attacked to provide an outlet for pent-up anger and frustration caused by another group.
	11. False consensus bias	k.	Subtle forms of prejudice in which people appear, on the surface, not to harbor prejudice but actually do hold prejudiced attitudes.
	12. Stereotype threat	l.	Tendency to regard one's own ethnic group, nation, religion, culture, or gender as being more correct than others.
	13. Culture clash	m.	Whenever group members run the risk of confirming the stereotype.

independence and equal status in society and, therefore, is offensive to many women. Words such as *girls* and *gals* are just as offensive.

SUMMARY

In a global village highly diverse individuals interact daily, studying, working, and playing together in small groups. Rapidly growing global interdependence and the increasing emphasis on teamwork result in groups with quite diverse membership. Diversity among members is no longer exceptional or optional; it is the everyday rule. Global interdependence and diversity among team members go hand in hand. With the one comes the other. Diversity among your acquaintances, classmates, co-workers, neighbors, and friends is increasingly inevitable. You will be expected to interact effectively with people with a wide variety of characteristics and backgrounds. Doing so has many advantages. Heterogeneity tends to increase group productivity on a variety of tasks, increase the difficulty of developing cohesive relationships among members, and increase the potential conflict among members. Diversity among members is advantageous, but it is not easy to manage.

Accepting others begins with accepting yourself (see Johnson [2000] for a thorough discussion of self-acceptance). But even for individuals who are quite accepting of themselves and others, there are barriers to building positive relationships with diverse peers. The most notable barriers are prejudice, blaming the victim, and culture clash. Minimizing these barriers makes it easier to recognize that diversity exists and that fundamental differences among people are to be both respected and valued. For group members to capitalize on their differences, they must ensure that a high level of positive interdependence exists among group members (highlight important mutual goals that require cooperative action and develop a common ground on which everyone is co-oriented). They must also create a superordinate group identity that (a) unites the diverse personal identities of group members and (b) is based on a pluralistic set of values, gains sophistication about the differences among members through personal relationships that have sufficient trust to allow for candid discussions, and clarifies miscommunications that arise when group members from different cultures, ethnic and historical backgrounds, social classes, genders, age cohorts, and so forth work together.

EXERCISE

10.2 *Stereotyping*

Once you realize that everyone is socialized to be prejudiced and to stereotype others, you need to clarify just what stereotypes you hold. This exercise is aimed at clarifying (a) what stereotypes you have been taught about other groups, (b) what stereotypes they have been taught about you, and (c) how the process of stereotyping works.

1. Post each word from the following list on sheets of paper around the room:

Male	Roman Catholic	Hispanic American
Teenager	Southern	Deaf
Asian American	Female	Middle income

Native American   Over age 70   Protestant
Blind   African American   Midwestern
Lower income

2. Each participant is to circulate around the room, read the various words, and write one stereotype he or she has heard under each heading. Participants are told not to repeat anything that is already written down. They are not to make anything up. They are to write down *all* the stereotypes they have heard about each of the groups listed.
3. After everyone has finished writing, participants are to read all the stereotypes under each category.
4. Participants discuss:
   a. Their personal reactions.
   b. How accurate the stereotypes of their identities are.
   c. What they have learned about stereotyping others.

EXERCISE 10.3 *Interacting on the Basis of Stereotypes*

Stereotypes are rigid judgments made about other groups that ignore individual differences. The purpose of this exercise is to demonstrate how stereotypes are associated with primary and secondary dimensions of diversity.

1. Divide participants into groups of five. The groups are to role play a discussion of employees of a large corporation of the ways in which the percentage of people of color and women in higher-level executive positions may be increased from 10% to 50%.
2. Give each member of each group a headband to wear with a particular identity written on it for other group members to see. **Group members are not to look at their own headbands.** The five identities are:

   Single mother of two young children, unemployed
   Employee with physical disability   Woman, age 72
   White male, company president   Black female, union official

3. Stop the discussion after ten minutes or so. Then have the groups discuss:
   a. What each person thinks the label on his or her headband was.
   b. Their personal reactions.
   c. The participation pattern of each member—who dominated, who withdrew, who was interrupted, who was influential.
   d. What they have learned about stereotyping others.

EXERCISE 10.4 *Greetings and Goodbyes*

This exercise increases awareness of how different cultural patterns of greetings and goodbyes can create communication problems. The procedure is as follows:

1. Divide the class into groups of four. Divide each group into two pairs, Americans and Lakians (from a fictitious country named Lake). If possible, give each pair something such as colored ribbons or armbands that visually distinguish them from one another.
2. Ask all American pairs to go to one end of the room and all Lakian pairs to go to the other. They receive separate briefings.

3. The participants are to role play that they are business associates who are to engage in an informal discussion of general economic conditions in their countries.

   a. The **American pairs** are instructed to greet their Lakian business associates in the traditional North American fashion. They are to shake hands, say "Good to see you again," talk about the economic conditions of North America for a while, and then say goodbye by shaking hands and waving.

   b. The **Lakian pairs** are instructed to greet their American business associates in the traditional Lakian fashion. They are to give the Americans a warm embrace and then to take and hold their hands for at least thirty seconds. They are to talk about the economic condition of Lake for a while. Then they are to say goodbye by giving the Americans a warm embrace, holding their hands for at least thirty seconds, and telling them how great it was to talk to them.

4. The group of four meets. If they finish the conversation before other groups in the room do, each pair should find another pair from the other country and repeat the experience.

5. The group of four discusses the experience:

   a. What were the cultural differences?

   b. What communication barriers did the cultural differences create?

   c. How did the participants feel during the interchange between the Americans and Lakians?

   d. What are three conclusions about cross-cultural communication that can be drawn from the experience?

The English and their North American counterparts are sometimes seen as being impoverished when it comes to kinesic communication, using words to denote what gesture or tone would express in other cultures. In North America, for example, people are often quite reserved when greeting others. Body contact is avoided. Yet in some Arab countries, men kiss each other on the street when they meet. Nigerian men often walk hand in hand. Italian men embrace warmly and remain touching when engaged in conversation. In some African countries, handshakes may be extended for long periods of time, and a hand on the knee among males is not an offense. All of these differences create potential communication problems when members of different cultures meet.

EXERCISE

10.5 *Time*

This exercise focuses attention on the differences in time and timing in different cultures. The procedure is as follows:

1. Divide the class into groups of four. Divide each group into two pairs, Americans and Pinians (from a fictitious country named Pine). If possible, give each pair something such as colored ribbons or armbands that visually distinguish them from one another.

2. Ask all American pairs to go to one end of the room and all Pinian pairs to go to the other. They receive separate briefings.

3. The participants are to role play that they have an appointment with a photographer at 12:00 to have their picture taken.

   a. The **American pairs** are instructed that the appointment is at 12:00 sharp because the photographer has another appointment at 12:30 in another part of town. The photographer asked them not to be late.

   b. The **Pinian pairs** are instructed that to them time is not important. Today or tomorrow, it does not matter. Twelve o'clock or one o'clock, what difference does it make? Take it easy, have a cup of coffee; why rush?

4. The group of four meets. It is 11:55 in the morning, and it takes five minutes to get to the photographer's studio.
5. The group of four discusses the experience:
    a. What were the cultural differences?
    b. What communication barriers did the cultural differences create?
    c. How did the participants feel during the interchange between the Americans and Pinians?
    d. What are three conclusions about cross-cultural communication that can be drawn from the experience?

Individuals living in industrialized societies are often seen as being "slaves of time." Individuals living in nonindustrialized societies are sometimes seen as being inconsiderate and unreliable. What happens when members of the two cultures meet?

10.6 *Cross-Cultural Communication*

The purpose of this exercise is to increase awareness of how cultural differences can create barriers to communication among group members. The procedure is as follows:

1. Form groups of six and divide each group into three pairs.
2. Each pair is assigned a particular cultural identity based on being a citizen of the country of Winkin, Blinkin, or Nod. Their task is to plan how they will act during the exercise based on the information about their country given on their briefing sheet. The pair is to work together cooperatively to ensure that both members understand how to act appropriately as a citizen of their country. They have ten minutes to prepare.
3. Two triads are formed (one member from each country). Each triad is assigned the task of identifying the ten most important principles of cross-cultural communication. They have fifteen minutes to do so.

CONFIDENTIAL: TO BE SEEN BY WINKIN CITIZENS ONLY

Behavioral Characteristics of the Country of Winkin

1. **Orientation Toward Touch:** Touch as much as possible, stand and sit close to people, and give a long handshake (about fifteen to thirty seconds) when you greet a person.
2. **Orientation Toward Eye Contact:** Look other people in the eyes when you talk to them.
3. **Orientation Toward Disclosure:** You are interested only in yourself, and you love to share yourself with other people. Talk only about yourself and what interests you. Do not listen to other people—they are boring. You do not want to understand other people better; you want them to understand you. Whenever they start talking, you interrupt them and refocus the conversation on yourself.
4. **Orientation Toward Conflict:** You like to argue for the sake of arguing so that people will pay attention to you.
5. **Orientation Toward Helping Others:** You avoid helping people under any circumstances.

CONFIDENTIAL: TO BE SEEN BY BLINKIN CITIZENS ONLY

Behavioral Characteristics of the Country of Blinkin

1. **Orientation Toward Touch:** Do not touch other people. Stand and sit far away from other people. Greet other people by nodding your head—do not shake hands.
2. **Orientation Toward Eye Contact:** Do not look other people in the eyes when you talk to them. If you happen to look a person in the eyes, look for only a split second.
3. **Orientation Toward Disclosure:** You are genuinely interested in other people. You are inquisitive. You get to know other people by asking them questions about what they are interested in. You listen carefully and let other people finish what they are saying before you speak. You never interrupt. You never talk about yourself.
4. **Orientation Toward Conflict:** You are very uncomfortable with conflict and want to avoid it at all costs. You never argue about a point with which you disagree. Instead you change the subject and try to find something else to talk about.
5. **Orientation Toward Helping Others:** You try to help other people (especially in solving a problem) as much as possible.

CONFIDENTIAL: TO BE SEEN BY NOD CITIZENS ONLY

Behavioral Characteristics of the Country of Nod

1. **Orientation Toward Touch:** Touch people only occasionally when you are talking. Stand and sit about an arm's length from a person. Give a short handshake when you are greeting a person.
2. **Orientation Toward Eye Contact:** Look other people in the eyes for only about three seconds at a time when you talk to them.
3. **Orientation Toward Disclosure:** You want to exchange ideas and thoughts. You share your interests and opinions, and you want other people to share theirs with you. You want to talk *with* other people instead of *to* them.
4. **Orientation Toward Conflict:** You seek reasoned judgments. You ignore who is right and who is wrong. You focus on the quality of ideas, seeking a synthesis or integration of different points of view. You listen carefully, add what you want to say, and make an informed judgment based on all positions and perspectives.
5. **Orientation Toward Helping Others:** You help other people only when it benefits you, that is, when it is rational to do so.

4. The group of six discusses the following questions:
   a. How are the two lists different? How are they the same?
   b. How did members react to their assigned roles? Were there any difficulties in enacting them?
   c. What were the communication barriers among the citizens of the three countries? Why did they occur?
   d. How could the communication barriers be avoided or overcome?
   e. What conclusions can be drawn from the exercise?
   f. What applications does the exercise have for everyday life?

10.7 *Merging Different Cultures*

This exercise merges individuals from two different cultures into one group. The procedure for the exercise is as follows:

1. The materials you need to assemble for the exercise are:
   a. Using poster board, construct ten sets of Figure 10.1 for each participant in Atlantis and one set of Figure 10.2 for every participant taking part in the exercise.
   b. One envelope per participant.
   c. One die for each group in Atlantis.
2. Divide the class into citizens of Atlantis and Mu. Assign participants to the society of Mu for every participant assigned to Atlantis. The citizens of Atlantis meet at one end of the room, and the citizens of Mu meet at the other end.
3. At the Atlantis end of the room, assign participants to groups of four and seat each group around a table.
   a. Place enough pieces for ten complete Ts per member in the center of each group (pieces for forty Ts).
   b. Tell the participants:

   > You are a worker in Atlantis who earns his or her living by constructing Ts. A T is formed using four triangles and three squares. Life is hard in Atlantis, so everyone looks out for "number one." You build your Ts by taking pieces from the center of the table. You will take turns in acquiring the shapes. When it is your turn, you acquire shapes by either (a) taking two pieces from the pile or (b) rolling the die (if you roll an even number [2, 4, 6] you can select that number of pieces, but if you roll an odd number [1, 3, 5] you lose that number of pieces from those you have accumulated thus far, including those composing complete Ts). The member with the greatest number of Ts will be declared the wealthiest and will survive. The poorest will perish. You can begin.

4. At the Mu end of the room, a second instructor divides the citizens into groups of four members and seats each group around a table. Their task is to earn their livelihood by constructing Ts. Each citizen of Mu is to form a T using the five pieces as shown in Figure 10.2. The instructor takes the pieces to make up the four Ts for each group and randomly divides the pieces into four envelopes (five pieces in each), making sure that no one envelope contains the correct five pieces for completing a T. One envelope is given to each group member. The instructor tells the participants:

   > You are a worker in Mu who earns his or her living by constructing Ts. Life is hard in Mu, so everyone looks out for everyone else. There are enough pieces among the members of your group to form one complete T for each member, but no one member has the right combination of pieces

Figure 10.1

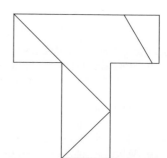

Figure 10.2

to complete his or her T. Mu, however, is a heterogeneous society that does not have a common language. The members of your group, therefore, will not speak to each other. **No verbal communication is allowed.**

Group members must share pieces in order to be successful. You may offer pieces to another group member and accept pieces offered to you by another group member. You cannot offer pieces to more than one person at the same time. You may not ask for a particular piece by pointing, talking, nudging, grimacing, or any other method. When you give a piece to another member, simply hand it to the person without demonstrating how the piece fits into his or her T. You have five minutes to complete this task. You may open your envelopes.

After five minutes, the instructor collects each group's pieces and again places the pieces randomly in the envelopes.

5. The Mu groups repeat the task, except that this time they may use any form of communication they wish. All other rules remain in effect. They have five minutes to complete the task.
6. Bring the Atlantis citizens to join the Mu society. Evenly distribute the citizens of Atlantis among the Mu groups. Add to each group's Ts one additional T for each new member. Take the combined pieces and randomly distribute them in envelopes, one for each member of the integrated groups. Tell the participants:

The citizens of Atlantis are immigrants to Mu. They are to have a part in the work of Mu, and the sooner they learn to earn a livelihood, the better off Mu will be. Members of Atlantis, however, do not speak Mu's language and the meaning of nonverbal gestures in the two societies is quite different. *There will, therefore, be no talking and no nonverbal signaling such as pointing or gesturing.* Your task is to build Ts. The Ts are formed differently from those made in Atlantis. You can begin work.

Stop the groups when all groups have built their Ts or after ten minutes, whichever comes first.
7. Have the groups discuss:
   a. How did the members of each society feel about working in integrated units?
   b. How did the two societies differ?
   c. Why was your group successful or unsuccessful in integrating the two societies?
   d. What conclusions can be drawn about work groups consisting of members from more than one society?

Learning and Discussion Groups

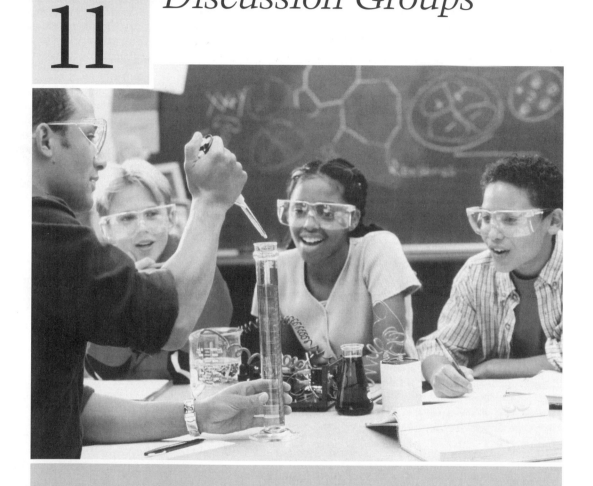

Basic Concepts to Be Covered in This Chapter

In this chapter a number of concepts are defined and discussed. The major ones are listed following. Divide into pairs. Each pair is to (a) define each concept, noting the page on which it is defined and discussed, and (b) make sure that both members of the pair understand the meaning of each concept. Then combine into groups of four. Compare the answers of the two pairs. If there is disagreement, look up the concept in the chapter and clarify it until all members agree on and understand the definition.

Concepts

1. Competitive learning
2. Cooperative base groups
3. Cooperative learning
4. Cooperative school
5. Formal cooperative learning

6. Group processing
7. Individual accountability
8. Individualistic learning
9. Informal cooperative learning
10. Promotive interaction

NATURE OF COOPERATIVE LEARNING

Groups have existed for as long as there have been humans (and even before). Groups have been the subject of countless books. Every human society has used groups to accomplish its goals and celebrated when the groups were successful. It was groups that built the pyramids, constructed the Temple of Artemis at Ephesus, and created the Colossus of Rhodes and the hanging gardens of Babylon. It is obvious that groups outperform individuals, especially when performance requires multiple skills, judgments, and experiences. Many educators, however, overlook opportunities to use groups to enhance student learning and increase their own success.

History of Cooperative Learning

Cooperative learning is an old idea. The Talmud clearly states that in order to learn, you must have a learning partner. In the first century, Quintillion argued that students could benefit from teaching one another. The Roman philosopher Seneca advocated cooperative learning through such statements as *Qui docet discet* (When you teach, you learn twice). Johann Amos Comenius (1592–1679) believed that students would benefit from both teaching and being taught by other students. In the late 1700s Joseph Lancaster and Andrew Bell made extensive use of cooperative learning groups in England, and the idea was brought to America when a Lancastrian school was opened in New York City in 1806. Within the Common School movement in the United States in the early 1800s, there was a strong emphasis on cooperative learning. In the last three decades of the nineteenth century, Colonel Francis Parker brought to his advocacy of cooperative learning enthusiasm, idealism, practicality, and an intense devotion to freedom, democracy, and individuality in the public schools. His fame and success rested on his power to create a classroom atmosphere that was truly cooperative and democratic. Parker's advocacy of cooperation among students dominated American education through the turn of the century. Following Parker, John Dewey promoted the use of cooperative learning groups as part of his famous project method in instruction. In the late 1930s, however, interpersonal competition began to be emphasized in schools, and in the late 1960s, individualistic learning began to be used extensively. In the 1980s, schools once again began to use cooperative learning.

Capitalizing on the Power of Groups

The opportunity to capitalize on the power of groups in schools begins with understanding the answers to the following questions (see Table 11.1):

1. What is cooperative learning?
2. Why use cooperative learning?
3. What are the expected outcomes resulting from cooperative efforts?
4. How do you structure formal cooperative learning?
5. How do you structure informal cooperative learning?
6. How do you structure cooperative base groups?
7. How do you use the three types of cooperative learning in an integrated way?
8. What are the basic elements of cooperative learning that make it work?
9. How do you structure cooperation among faculty and staff to ensure that cooperative efforts are institutionalized throughout school life?

What Is Cooperative Learning?

To understand the nature of cooperative learning, it is necessary to place it within the broader context of social interdependence. **Social interdependence** exists when each individual's outcomes are affected by the actions of others (Deutsch, 1949a; Johnson & Johnson, 1989). Social interdependence may be positive or negative. **Positive interdependence** (cooperation) exists when individuals work together to achieve mutual goals, and **negative interdependence** (competition) exists when individuals work against each other to achieve a goal that only one or a few may attain. **Social independence,** where the outcomes of each person are unaffected by others' actions, is characterized by individualistic actions.

Cooperation is working together to accomplish shared goals. Within cooperative situations, individuals seek outcomes that are beneficial to themselves and to all other group members. **Cooperative learning** is the instructional use of small groups so that students work together to maximize their own and each other's learning. It may be contrasted with **competitive learning** (students work against each other to achieve an academic goal such as a grade of A that only one or a few students can attain) and **individualistic learning** (students work by themselves to accomplish learning goals unrelated to those of the other students). In cooperative and individualistic learning, you evaluate student efforts on a criteria-referenced basis, whereas in competitive learning you grade students on a norm-referenced basis. Although there are limitations on when and where you may use competitive and individualistic learning appropriately, you may structure any learning task in any subject area with any curriculum cooperatively.

Table 11.1 Overview of Chapter: Cooperative Learning

Social Interdependence		
Cooperative	Competitive	Individualistic

Research: Why Use Cooperative Learning		
Effort to achieve	Positive relationships	Psychological health

Five Basic Elements				
Positive interdependence	Individual accountability	Promotive interaction	Social skills	Group processing

Cooperative Learning

Formal Cooperative Learning	Informal Cooperative Learning	Cooperative Base Groups
Make preinstructional decisions	Conduct introductory focused discussion.	Structure opening class meeting to check homework, ensure that members understand academic material, complete routine tasks such as taking attendance.
Explain task and cooperative structure.	Conduct intermittent-pair discussions every ten or fifteen minutes.	Structure ending class meeting to ensure that members understand academic material, homework assignment.
Monitor learning groups and intervene to improve taskwork and teamwork.	Conduct closure-focused discussion.	Members help each other learn between classes.
Assess student learning and process group effectiveness.		Conduct semester- or year-long school or class service projects.

Cooperative School		
Teaching teams	Site-based decision making	Faculty meetings

Constructive Conflict

Students		Faculty	
Academic controversy	Negotiating, mediating	Decision-making controversy	Negotiating, mediating

Civic Values				
Work for mutual benefit, common good	Equality of all members	Trusting, caring relationships	View situations from all perspectives	Unconditional worth of self, diverse others

Within cooperative learning groups, students discuss the material to be learned with each other, help each other to understand it, and encourage each other to work hard. There are three types of cooperative learning groups (see Table 11.2). Cooperative learning groups may be used to teach specific content (**formal cooperative learning groups**), to ensure active cognitive processing of information during a lecture or demonstration (**informal cooperative learning groups**), and to provide long-term support and assistance for academic progress (**cooperative base groups**) (Johnson, Johnson, & Holubec, 1998a, 1998b; Johnson, Johnson, & Smith, 1998). Any assignment in any curriculum for students of any age can be done cooperatively. Each of these types of cooperative learning groups will be discussed in this chapter.

What Is It?

Following are twelve statements. Form a pair and agree on whether each statement reflects a cooperative, competitive, or individualistic situation. Place each statement in the appropriate column in the table.

STATEMENTS

1. Strive for everyone's success.
2. Strive to be better than others.
3. Strive for one's own success only.
4. What benefits oneself does not affect others.
5. Joint success is celebrated.
6. What benefits oneself benefits others.
7. Only one's own success is celebrated.
8. Motivated to help others.
9. What benefits oneself deprives/hurts others.
10. Motivated only to maximize one's own productivity.
11. One's own success and other's failure is celebrated.
12. Motivated to ensure that no one else does better than oneself.

Cooperative	Competitive	Individualistic

Table 11.2 **Types of Cooperative Learning**

Formal Cooperative Learning	Informal Cooperative Learning	Cooperative Base Groups
Completes assignment, lesson, unit, project to maximize own and groupmates' learning.	Discusses assigned questions for a few minutes to focus attention, organize knowledge, set expectations, create mood, ensure cognitive processing and rehearsal, summarize, precue next session, provide closure.	Permanent; lasts for one semester, one year, or several years to ensure that all members make academic progress and develop cognitively and socially in healthy ways.
Teacher Procedure	**Teacher Procedure**	**Teacher Procedure**
Make preinstructional decisions.	Conduct introductory-focused discussion.	Structure opening class meeting to check homework, ensure that members understand academic material, complete routine tasks such as taking attendance, and prepare members for the day.
Explain task and cooperative structure.	Conduct intermittent-pair discussions every ten or fifteen minutes.	Structure ending class meeting to ensure that all members understand academic material, know what homework to do, and are making progress on long-term assignments.
Monitor learning groups and intervene to improve taskwork and teamwork.	Conduct closure-focused discussion.	Members help and assist each other learn between classes.
Assess learning and monitor group effectiveness.		Conduct semester- or year-long school or class service projects.

FORMAL COOPERATIVE LEARNING: BEING "A GUIDE ON THE SIDE"

At age fifty-five, after his defeat by Woodrow Wilson for president of the United States, Teddy Roosevelt took a journey to South America. The Brazilian government suggested that he lead an expedition to explore a vast, unmapped river deep in the jungle. Known as the River of Doubt, it was believed to be a tributary to the Amazon. Roosevelt accepted instantly. "We will go down the unknown river," he declared, and the Brazilian government organized an expedition for the trip. "I had to go," he said later. "It was my last chance to be a boy." Roosevelt, with his son Kermit and a party of eighteen, headed into the jungle. "On February 27, 1914, shortly after midday, we started down the River of Doubt into the unknown," Roosevelt wrote. The journey was an ordeal. Hostile Indians harassed them. Five canoes were shattered and had to be rebuilt. Their food ran short, and valuable equipment was lost. One man drowned when his canoe capsized. Another went berserk, killed a member of the expedition, and then disappeared into the wilderness. Roosevelt, ill with fever, badly injured his leg when he tried to keep two capsized canoes from being smashed against rocks. Unable to walk, he had to be carried. Lying in a tent with an infected leg and a temperature of 105°F, he asked to be left behind. Ignoring his pleas, Kermit brought his father to safety with the help of the other members of the expedition. Teddy Roosevelt barely survived, but he and his companions accomplished their mission. The party mapped the 1,000-mile River of Doubt and collected priceless specimens for the Museum of Natural History. The river was renamed in his honor, the Rio Theodore.

An expedition such as Roosevelt's consists of four phases:

1. You make a series of prejourney decisions about the number of people needed, the materials and equipment required, and the route to be taken.
2. You brief all participants on the goals and objectives of the journey, emphasize that members' survival depends on the joint efforts of all, and describe the behaviors you expect of members of the expedition.
3. You make the journey, carefully mapping the area traveled and collecting the targeted specimens.
4. You report your findings to interested parties, reflect on what went right and wrong with fellow members, and write your memoirs.

Conducting a cooperative lesson is done in the same way. You, the teacher, make a number of preinstructional decisions, explain to students the instructional task and the cooperative nature of the lesson, conduct the lesson, and evaluate and process the results. More specifically, you (Johnson, Johnson, & Holubec, 1994, 1998a):

1. **Make preinstructional decisions.** In every lesson you (a) formulate objectives, (b) decide on the size of groups, (c) choose a method for assigning students to groups, (d) decide which roles to assign to group members, (e) arrange the room, and (f) arrange the materials students need to complete the assignment.
2. **Explain the task and cooperative structure.** In every lesson you (a) explain the academic assignment to students, (b) explain the criteria for success, (c) structure positive interdependence, (d) explain individual accountability, and (e) explain the behaviors you expect to see during the lesson.
3. **Monitor and intervene.** While you (a) conduct the lesson, you (b) monitor each learning group, (c) intervene when needed to improve taskwork and teamwork, and (d) bring closure to the lesson.
4. **Evaluate and process.** You (a) assess and evaluate the quality and quantity of student achievement, (b) ensure that students carefully process the effectiveness of their learning groups, (c) have students make a plan for improvement, and (d) have students celebrate the hard work of group members.

In each class session, teachers must make the choice of being "a sage on the stage" or "a guide on the side." In doing so, they should remember that **the challenge in teaching is not covering the material *for* the students, it's uncovering the material *with* the students.**

PREINSTRUCTIONAL DECISIONS

Specifying the Instructional Objectives

To plan for a lesson, you must know what the lesson is aimed at accomplishing. You need to specify *academic objectives* (based on a conceptual or task analysis) and *social-skills objectives* that detail what interpersonal and small group skills you wish to emphasize during the lesson (Johnson, Johnson, & Holubec, 1994, 1998a). You choose social skills by:

1. Monitoring the learning groups and identifying the specific skills needed to solve the problems students are having in working with each other.
2. Asking students to identify social skills that would improve their teamwork.
3. Keeping a list of social skills you teach to every class. The next one on the list becomes the skill emphasized in today's lesson.
4. Analyzing what social skills are required to complete the assignment.

The most sophisticated way to determine the social skills students need to complete a lesson is to create a flowchart. A **flowchart** is a simple yet powerful visual tool to display all the steps in a process. Creating a flowchart involves six steps (Figure 11.1).

Deciding on the Size of the Group

There is a folk saying about snowflakes. Each snowflake is so fragile and small. But when they stick together, it is amazing what they can do. The same is true for people. When we work together, there is no limit to human ingenuity and potential. For students to work together, they must be assigned to groups. To assign students to groups, you must decide (a) how large a group should be, (b) how students should be assigned to a group, (c) how long the groups will exist, and (d) what combination of groups will be used in the lesson.

Figure 11.1 Creating a flowchart.

> **Group Size Depends on "Team"**
>
> **T** = Time Limits
> **E** = Students' Experience in Working in Groups
> **A** = Students' Age
> **M** = Materials and Equipment Available

Although cooperative learning groups typically range in size from two to four, the basic rule is: *The smaller the better.* There is, however, no ideal size for a cooperative learning group. A common mistake is to have students work in groups of four, five, or six before they have the skills to do so competently. In selecting the size of a cooperative learning group, remember this advice:

1. **With the addition of each group member, the resources to help the group succeed increase.** As the size of the learning group increases, so does (a) the range of abilities, expertise, and skills; (b) the number of minds available for acquiring and processing information; and (c) the diversity of viewpoints.

2. **The shorter the period of time available, the smaller the learning group should be.** If only a brief period of time is available for the lesson, then smaller groups such as pairs will be more effective because they take less time to get organized, they operate faster, and there is more "air time" per member.

3. **The smaller the group, the more difficult it is for students to hide and not do their share of the work.** Small groups increase the visibility of students' efforts and thereby make them more accountable.

4. **The larger the group, the more skillful group members must be.** In a pair, students have to manage two interactions. In a group of three, there are six interactions to manage. In a group of four, there are twelve interactions to manage. As the size of the group increases, the interpersonal and small group skills required to manage the interactions among group members become far more complex and sophisticated.

5. **The larger the group, the less the interaction among members.** The result is less group cohesion, fewer friendships, and less personal support.

6. **The materials available or the specific nature of the task may dictate a group's size.** When you have ten computers and thirty students, you may wish to assign students to groups of three. When the task is to practice tennis, a group size of two seems natural.

7. **The smaller the group, the easier it is to identify any difficulties students have in working together.** Problems in leadership, unresolved conflicts among group members, issues over power and control, tendencies such as sitting back and waiting for others to do the work, and other problems students have in working together are more visible when groups are small. Groups need to be small enough to ensure that all students are actively involved and participating equally.

Assigning Students to Groups

Sic parvis magna (Great things have small beginnings).
                    Sir Francis Drake's motto

There is no ideal group membership. What determines a group's productivity is not who its members are, but rather how well the members work together. There may be times when you will use cooperative learning groups that are homogeneous in ability to teach specific skills or to achieve certain instructional objectives. Generally, however, there are advantages to heterogeneous groups in which students come from diverse backgrounds and have different abilities, experiences, and interests:

1. Students are exposed to a variety of ideas, multiple perspectives, and different problem-solving methods.
2. Students generate more cognitive disequilibrium, which stimulates learning, creativity, and cognitive and social development.
3. Students engage in more elaborative thinking, give and receive more explanations, and engage in more frequent perspective-taking in discussing material, all of which increase the depth of understanding, the quality of reasoning, and the accuracy of long-term retention.

To make groups heterogeneous, you assign students to groups using a random or stratified random procedure. **The easiest and most effective way to assign students to a group is randomly.** You divide the number of students in your class by the size of the group desired. If you wish to have groups of three and you have thirty students in your class, you divide thirty by three. You have students number off by the result (e.g., ten). Students with the same number find each other (all 1's get together, all 2's get together,

LITERARY CHARACTERS	GEOGRAPHICAL AREAS
Give students cards with the names of characters in the literature they recently have read. Ask them to group with characters from the same story, play, or poem. Examples are Romeo and Juliet; Captain Hook, Peter Pan, and Wendy; and Hansel, Gretel, Witch, and Stepmother.	List a number of countries or states and have students group themselves according to most preferred to visit. Variations include grouping according to least preferred to visit, similar in terms of climate, similar in geological features, having the same exports, and so forth.
MATH METHOD	**STATES AND CAPITALS**
There are endless variations to the math method of assigning students to groups. The basic structure is to give each student a math problem and ask him or her to (a) solve the problem, (b) find the classmates whose problem has the same answer, and (c) form a group. This may vary from simple addition in the first grade to complex equations in high school classes. Thus, to form a group of three, you may distribute the following three equations throughout the class: $(3 + 3 = \underline{\quad})$, $(4 + 2 = \underline{\quad})$, $(5 + 1 = \underline{\quad})$.	To assign students to groups of two or four, divide the number of students in the class by two $(30 \div 2 = 15)$. Pick a geographic area of the United States and write on a set of cards the names of fifteen states. Then on another set of cards write the names of their capital cities. Shuffle the cards and pass them out to students. Then have the students find the classmate who has the matching state or capital. To form groups of four, have two adjacent states and their capitals combine.

and so forth). A related procedure is *stratified random assignment*. This is the same as random assignment except that you choose one (or two) characteristics of students (such as reading level, learning style, task orientation, or personal interest) and make sure that one or more students in each group have that characteristic. A modified stratified random procedure is to assign students to groups by *preferences*. Have students write their favorite sport to participate in on a slip of paper. Then have them find groupmates who like to participate in the same sport. Variations include favorite food, celebrity, skill, car, president, animal, vegetable, fairy tale character, and so forth.

Teacher-selected groups can be either homogeneous or heterogeneous. When students select their own groups, they usually form homogeneous ones.

For additional methods of assigning students to groups, as well as a variety of team-building and warm-up activities, see R. Johnson, Johnson, Scott, and Ramolae (1985).

Length of Group Life.   A common question is, "How long should cooperative learning groups stay together?" The type of cooperative learning group you use determines one answer to this question. Base groups last for at least one year and ideally for several years. Informal cooperative learning groups last for only a few minutes or at most one class period. For formal cooperative learning groups there is no simple answer to this question. Groups usually stay together to complete a task, unit, or chapter. During a course, every student should work with every other classmate.

Using Combinations of Cooperative Learning Groups.   In many lessons, you will want to use a combination of formal and informal cooperative learning groups as well as base groups. You will use groups of more than one size in any one lesson. You will need ways to assign students to new groups quickly. You will need procedures for making transitions among groups, moving students from pairs to fours to pairs to threes and so forth.

Assigning Roles to Ensure Interdependence

In planning the lesson, you think through the actions that need to occur to maximize student learning. **Roles** prescribe what other group members expect from a student (and therefore what the student is obligated to do) and what that person has a right to expect from other group members who have complementary roles. There is a progression for using roles to structure cooperative efforts:

1. Do not assign roles until students get used to working together.
2. Assign only very simple roles to students, such as forming roles or the roles of reader, recorder, and encourager of participation. Rotate the roles so that each group member plays each one several times.
3. Add to the rotation a new role that is slightly more sophisticated, such as that of a checker for understanding. You assign the functioning roles at this point.
4. Over time, add formulating and fermenting roles that do not occur naturally in the group, such as that of an elaborator. Students typically do not relate what they are learning to what they already know until you specifically train them to do so.

The social skills represented by the roles should be taught like a spiral curriculum, with a more complex version of the skill taught every year.

Solving and Preventing Problems in Working Together. At times there are students who refuse to participate in a cooperative group or who do not understand how to help the group succeed. You can solve and prevent such problems when you give each group member a specific role to play. Assigning appropriate roles may be used to:

1. Reduce problems such as one or more members' making no contribution or one member dominating the group.
2. Ensure that vital group skills are enacted in the group and that group members learn targeted skills.
3. Create interdependence among group members. You structure **role interdependence** by assigning each member complementary and interconnected roles.

Arranging the Room

The design and arrangement of classroom space and furniture communicates what is appropriate behavior and what learning activities will take place. Desks in a row communicate a different message and expectation than desks grouped in small circles. Spatial

Importance of Classroom Design

Form a pair. Rank order the following outcomes of classroom design from most important (1) to least important (9).

	Students' academic achievement. The way in which interior space is designed influences the amount of time students spend on task and other variables affecting achievement.
	Students' visual and auditory focus. The way in which interior space is designed creates overall visual order, focuses visual attention, and controls acoustics.
	Students' participation in learning groups and activities. Classroom design influences the patterns of student (and teacher) participation in instructional activities, the emergence of leadership in learning groups, and the patterns of communication among students and between students and teacher.
	Opportunities for social contact and friendships among students.
	Learning climate. The design of interior space affects students' and teachers' feelings (such as comfort, enjoyment, well-being, anger, depression) and general morale. Good spatial definition helps students feel secure by delineating structured learning areas.
	Classroom management. Spatial definition prevents discipline problems by defining how and where students work, how to interact with others, and how to move through the classroom.
	Students' ease of access to each other, teachers, learning materials.
	Students' ability to make quick transitions from one group to another.
	Teacher's movement from group to group to monitor student interaction carefully during the lesson.

design also defines the circulation patterns in the classroom. *Circulation* is the flow of movement into, out of, and within the classroom. It is movement through space. You determine what students see, when they see it, and with whom students interact by the way you design your classroom.

No single classroom arrangement will meet the requirements of all lessons. Reference points and well-defined boundaries of work spaces are needed to move students from rows to triads to pairs to fours to rows. Color, form, and lighting (a) focus students' visual attention on points of emphasis in the classroom (the learning group, you, instructional materials) and (b) define the territorial boundaries of work spaces. You define boundaries by:

1. **Using labels and signs** that designate areas.
2. **Using colors** to attract visual attention and define group and individual spaces, as well as different storage areas and resource centers.
3. **Taping lines** on the floor or wall to define the different work areas.
4. **Using mobiles and forms** (such as arrows) taped on the wall or hanging from the ceiling to direct attention or designate work areas.
5. **Using lighting** to define specific work areas. Directed light (illuminating part of the room while leaving other areas dim) intensifies and directs students' attention. Brightly lit areas can draw people to the areas and suggest activity. More dimly lit areas surrounding the lighted ones become area boundaries. As the activity in the classroom changes, the lighting could also change.
6. **Moving furniture** to define work and resource areas. Even tall plants, when placed in pots with wheels, can be moved to provide spatial boundaries.
7. **Displaying group work** to designate work spaces. If a cooperative group is to remain together for a period of several days or weeks, members may wish to build a poster or collage that designates their work area.

You can use many of these same procedures to control the level of noise in the classroom.

Planning the Instructional Materials

The types of tasks students are required to complete determine what materials are needed for the lesson. You, the teacher, decide how materials are to be arranged and distributed among group members to maximize their participation and achievement. Usually, you will wish to distribute materials to communicate that the assignment is to be a joint (not an individual) effort. You create:

1. **Materials interdependence** by giving each group only one copy of the materials. The students will then have to work together in order to be successful. This is especially effective the first few times the group meets. After students are accustomed to working cooperatively, teachers can give a copy of the materials to each student.
2. **Information interdependence** by arranging materials like a jigsaw puzzle so that each student has part of the materials needed to complete the assignment. Each

group member can receive different books or resource materials to be synthesized. Such procedures require that every member participate in order for the group to be successful.

3. **Independence from outside enemies** by structuring materials into an intergroup tournament format and having groups compete to see who has learned the most. Such a procedure was introduced by DeVries and Edwards (1973). In the Teams-Games-Tournament format, students are divided into heterogeneous cooperative learning teams to prepare members for a tournament in which they compete with the other teams. During the intergroup competition, the students individually compete against members with about the same ability level from other teams. The team whose members do the best in the competition is pronounced the winner by the teacher.

STRUCTURING THE TASK AND COOPERATIVE STRUCTURE

Explaining the Academic Task

At this point you have planned your lesson by making the preinstructional decisions and preparations. The next step is to tell your class (a) what to do to complete the assignment and (b) how to do it (Johnson, Johnson, & Holubec, 1994, 1998a). The steps are explained in Figure 11.1.

Explaining Criteria for Success

While explaining to students the academic task they are to complete, you need to communicate the level of performance you expect. Cooperative learning requires criterion-based evaluation. *Criterion-referenced* or *categorical judgments* are made by adopting a fixed set of standards and judging the achievement of each student against these standards. A common version of criterion-referenced grading involves assigning letter grades on the basis of the percentage of test items answered correctly. Or you might say, "The group is not finished until every member has demonstrated mastery." Sometimes improvement (doing better this week than one did last week) may be set as the criterion of excellence. To promote intergroup cooperation, you may also set criteria for the whole class to reach. "If we as a class can score over 520 words correct on our vocabulary test, each student will receive 2 bonus points."

Grade	Percent Correct
A	95–100
B	85–94
C	75–84
D	65–74
F	Less than 64

Structuring Positive Interdependence

Positive goal interdependence exists when a mutual or joint goal is established so that individuals perceive that they can attain their goals if and only if their groupmates attain their goals (Johnson & Johnson, 1992a, 1992b). Members know that they cannot succeed unless all other members of their group succeed. Positive interdependence is the heart of cooperative learning. Without positive interdependence, cooperation does not exist. Students must believe that they are in a "sink or swim together" learning situation.

First, you structure positive goal interdependence. Every cooperative lesson begins with positive goal interdependence. To ensure that students think **"We, not me,"** you (the teacher) say to students:

> You have three responsibilities. You are responsible for learning the assigned material. You are responsible for making sure that all other members of your group learn the assigned material. And you are responsible for making sure that all other class members learn the assigned material.

Second, you supplement positive goal interdependence with other types of positive interdependence (such as reward, role, resource, or identity interdependence). Positive reward interdependence, for example, may be structured by providing group rewards— "If all members of your group score above 90% on the test, each of you will receive 5 bonus points." Usually, the more ways positive interdependence is structured in a lesson, the better.

Structuring Individual Accountability

In cooperative groups, everyone has to do his or her fair share of the work. **An underlying purpose of cooperative learning is to make each group member a stronger individual in his or her own right.** You hold all group members accountable to learn the assigned material and help other group members learn by:

1. Assessing the performance of each member.
2. Giving the results to the individual and the group to compare to preset criteria. The feedback enables members to (a) recognize and celebrate efforts to learn and contributions to groupmates' learning, (b) provide immediate remediation and any needed assistance or encouragement, and (c) reassign responsibilities to avoid any redundant efforts by members.

Individual accountability results in group members knowing that they cannot "hitchhike" on the work of others, loaf, or get a free ride. Ways of ensuring **individual accountability** include keeping the group size small, giving an individual test to each student, giving random individual oral examinations, observing and recording the frequency with which each member contributes to the group's work, having students teach what they know to someone else, and having students use what they have learned on different problems.

Structuring Intergroup Cooperation

You can extend the positive outcomes resulting from cooperative learning throughout the whole class by structuring intergroup cooperation. You establish class goals as well as group and individual goals. When a group finishes its work, you encourage members to find other groups that (a) are not finished and help them understand how to complete the assignment successfully or (b) are finished and compare answers and strategies.

Specifying Desired Behaviors

When you use cooperative learning, you must teach students the small group and interpersonal skills they need to work effectively with each other. In cooperative learning groups, students must learn both academic subject matter (taskwork) and the interpersonal and small group skills required to work as part of a group (teamwork). Cooperative learning is inherently more complex than competitive or individualistic learning because students have to engage simultaneously in taskwork and teamwork. If students do not learn the teamwork skills, then they cannot complete the taskwork. The greater the members' teamwork skills, the higher will be the quality and quantity of their learning. You define the needed teamwork skills operationally by specifying the behaviors that are appropriate and desirable within learning groups.

Three rules of thumb in specifying desired behaviors are as follows. **Be specific.** Operationally define each social skill. **Start small.** Do not overload your students with more social skills than they can learn at one time. One or two behaviors to emphasize for a few lessons is enough. **Emphasize overlearning.** Having students practice skills once or twice is not enough. Keep emphasizing a skill until the students have integrated it into their behavioral repertoires and do it automatically and habitually.

MONITORING AND INTERVENING

The only thing that endures over time is the law of the farm: I must prepare
the ground, put in the seed, cultivate it, water it, then gradually nurture
growth and development to full maturity . . . there is no quick fix.

Stephen Covey

Once the students begin working in cooperative learning groups, the teacher's role is to monitor students' interaction and intervene to help students learn and interact more skillfully (Johnson, Johnson, & Holubec, 1994, 1998a).

Monitoring Students' Behavior

Your job begins in earnest when the cooperative learning groups start working. Resist the urge to get a cup of coffee or to grade papers. You observe the interaction among group members to assess students' (a) academic progress and (b) appropriate use of interpersonal and small group skills.

Observations can be formal (with an observation schedule on which frequencies are tallied) or anecdotal (informal descriptions of students' statements and actions). Based on your observations, you can then intervene to improve students' academic learning and/or interpersonal and small group skills. Remember, **students respect what we inspect.** To **monitor** means to check continuously. Monitoring has four stages:

1. **Preparing to observe** the learning groups by deciding who will be the observers, what observation forms to use, and training the observers.
2. **Observing** to assess the quality of cooperative efforts in the learning groups.
3. **Intervening when necessary** to improve a group's taskwork or teamwork.
4. **Having students assess the quality of their own participation** in the learning groups to encourage self-monitoring, having groups assess the level of their effectiveness, and having both individuals and groups set growth goals.

In monitoring cooperative learning groups, there are a number of guidelines for teachers to follow:

1. Plan a route through the classroom and the length of time spent observing each group so that all groups are observed during a lesson.
2. Use a formal observation sheet to count the number of times you observe appropriate behaviors being used by students. The more concrete the data, the more useful the data are to you (the teacher) and to students.
3. Initially, do not try to count too many different behaviors. At first you may wish simply to keep track of who talks. Your observations should focus on positive behaviors.
4. Supplement and extend the frequency data with notes on specific student actions. Especially useful are descriptions of skillful interchanges that can be shared with students later and with parents in conferences or telephone conversations.
5. Train and utilize student observers. Student observers can obtain more complete data on each group's functioning and may learn important lessons about appropriate and inappropriate behavior.
6. Allocate sufficient time at the end of each group session for discussion of the data gathered by the observers.

Providing Task Assistance

Cooperative learning groups provide teachers with a "window" into students' minds. Through working cooperatively, students make hidden thinking processes overt and subject to observation and commentary. From carefully listening to students explain to each other what they are learning, you can determine what students do and do not understand. Consequently, you may wish to intervene to clarify instructions, review important procedures and strategies for completing the assignment, answer questions, and teach task skills as

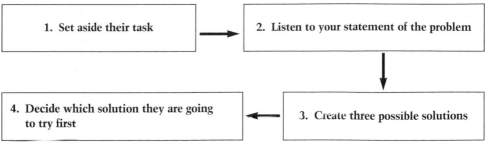

Figure 11.2 When to intervene.

necessary. In discussing the concepts and information to be learned, you should make specific statements, such as "Yes, that is one way to find the main idea of a paragraph," not "Yes, that is right." The more specific statement reinforces the desired learning and promotes positive transfer by helping the students associate a term with their learning. Metacognitive thought may be encouraged by asking students (a) "What are you doing?", (b) "Why are you doing it?", and (c) "How will it help you?"

Intervening to Teach Social Skills

Cooperative learning groups provide teachers with a picture of students' social skills. The social skills required for productive group work are discussed in detail, along with activities that may be used in teaching them, in Johnson (1991, 2003). While monitoring the learning groups, you may intervene to suggest more effective procedures for working together or reinforce particularly effective and skillful behaviors. Choosing when to intervene is part of the art of teaching. In intervening, ask group members to follow the steps of Figure 11.2.

Providing Closure to the Lesson

You provide closure to a lesson by having students summarize the major points in the lesson, recall ideas, and identify final questions for the teacher. Students should be able to summarize what they have learned and to understand how they will use it in the future.

EVALUATING LEARNING AND PROCESSING INTERACTION

Assessing the Quality and Quantity of Learning

The quality and quantity of student learning should be regularly assessed and occasionally evaluated using a criterion-referenced system. This is covered in depth in *Meaningful and Manageable Assessment Through Cooperative Learning* (Johnson & Johnson, 1996a). Cooperative learning, furthermore, provides an arena in which *performance-based assessment* (requiring students to demonstrate what they can do with what they know by performing a procedure or skill), *authentic assessment* (requiring students to

Assessment Procedures

Form a pair. Rank order each of the following columns from most important to you (1) to least important to you.

What Is Assessed	Procedures	Ways Cooperative Learning Helps
_____ Academic learning	_____ Goal setting	_____ Additional sources of labor
_____ Reasoning strategies	_____ Testing	_____ More modalities in assessment
_____ Skills, competencies	_____ Compositions	_____ More diverse outcomes
_____ Attitudes	_____ Presentations	_____ More sources of information
_____ Work habits	_____ Projects	_____ Reduction of bias
	_____ Portfolios	_____ Development of rubrics
	_____ Logs, journals	_____ Implement improvement plan

demonstrate the desired procedure or skill in a real-life context), and *total quality learning* (continuous improvement of the process of students helping teammates learn) can take place. A wide variety of assessment formats may be used, and students may be directly involved in assessing each other's level of learning and then providing immediate remediation to ensure that all group members' learning is maximized.

Processing How Well the Group Functioned

When students have completed the assignment, or at the end of each class session, students describe what member actions were helpful (and unhelpful) in completing the group's work and make decisions about what behaviors to continue or change. Group processing occurs at two levels—in each learning group and in the class as a whole. There are four parts to processing:

1. **Feedback.** You ensure that each student and each group and the class receives (and gives) feedback on the effectiveness of taskwork and teamwork. Feedback given to students should be descriptive and specific, not evaluative and general (Johnson, 2000).
2. **Reflection.** You ensure that students analyze and reflect on the feedback they receive. You avoid questions that can be answered "yes" or "no." Instead of asking, "Did everyone help each other learn?" you should ask, "How frequently did each member (a) explain how to solve a problem and (b) correct or clarify other members' explanations?"
3. **Improvement goals.** You help individuals and groups set goals for improving the quality of their work.
4. **Celebration.** You encourage the celebration of members' hard work and the group's success.

Summary

Any assignment in any subject area may be structured cooperatively. In using formal cooperative learning, the teacher makes a number of preinstructional decisions, explains to students the task and the cooperative goal structure, monitors the groups as they work, intervenes when it is necessary, and then evaluates and helps groups process. In addition to formal cooperative learning, teachers use informal cooperative learning and cooperative base groups.

INFORMAL COOPERATIVE LEARNING GROUPS

There are times when teachers need to lecture, show a movie or videotape, give a demonstration, or have a guest speaker. In such cases, informal cooperative learning may be used to ensure that students are active (not passive) cognitively (Johnson, Johnson, & Holubec, 1994, 1998b). **Informal cooperative learning** (Figure 11.3) consists of having students work together to achieve a joint learning goal in temporary, ad hoc groups that last from a few minutes to one class period. Their *purposes* are to focus student attention on the material to be learned, set a mood conducive to learning, help organize in advance the material to be covered in a class session, ensure that students cognitively process the material being taught, and provide closure to an instructional session. Informal cooperative learning groups also ensure that misconceptions, incorrect understanding, and gaps in understanding are identified and corrected and that learning experiences are personalized. They may be used at any time, but are especially useful during a lecture or direct teaching.

During lecturing and direct teaching, the instructional challenge for the instructor is to ensure that students do the intellectual work of organizing material, explaining it, summarizing it, and integrating it into existing conceptual networks. This may be achieved by having students do the advance organizing, cognitively process what they are learning, and provide closure to the lesson. Breaking up lectures with short cooperative processing periods will give you slightly less lecture time but will help counter what is proclaimed

Figure 11.3   Informal cooperative learning.

Purposes of Informal Cooperative Learning

Form a pair. Rank order the following purposes of informal cooperative learning from most important (1) to least important (7).

	Focuses student attention on the material to be learned.
	Sets a mood conducive to learning.
	Helps cognitively organize in advance the material to be covered in a class session.
	Ensures that students cognitively process the material being taught.
	Provides closure to an instructional session.
	Allows for identifying and correcting misconceptions, incorrect understanding, and gaps in comprehension.
	Personalizes learning experiences.

as the main problem of lectures: "The information passes from the notes of the professor to the notes of the student without passing through the mind of either one."

USING INFORMAL COOPERATIVE LEARNING

The following procedure will help you plan a lecture that keeps students more actively engaged intellectually (Johnson & Johnson, 1999a; Johnson, Johnson, & Holubec, 1998b). It entails having *focused discussions* before and after the lecture (i.e., bookends) and interspersing *pair discussions* throughout the lecture. Two important aspects of using informal cooperative learning groups are to (a) make the task and the instructions explicit and precise and (b) require the groups to produce a specific product (such as a written answer). The procedure is as follows.

1. **Introductory focused discussion:** Assign students to pairs. The person nearest them will do. You may wish to require different seating arrangements for each class period so that students will meet and interact with a number of other students in the class. Then give the pairs the cooperative assignment of completing the initial (advance organizer) task. Give them only four or five minutes to do so. The discussion task is aimed at promoting *advance organizing* of what the students know about the topic to be presented and *establishing expectations* about what the lecture will cover.
2. **Intermittent focused discussions:**
   a. Lecture segment 1: Deliver the first segment of the lecture. This segment should last for ten to fifteen minutes. This is about the length of time a motivated adult can concentrate on a lecture. For unmotivated adolescents, the time may be shorter.

    b. Pair discussion 1: Give the students a discussion task focused on the material you have just presented that may be completed within three or four minutes. Its purpose is to ensure that students are actively thinking about the material being presented. The discussion task may be to (a) give an answer to a question posed by the instructor; (b) give a reaction to the theory, concepts, or information being presented; or (c) relate material to past learning so that it gets integrated into existing conceptual frameworks (i.e., elaborate the material being presented). Discussion pairs respond to the task in the following way:

      (1) Each student formulates his or her answer.

      (2) Students share their answer with their partner.

      (3) Students listen carefully to their partner's answer.

      (4) Pairs create a new answer that is superior to each member's initial formulation through the process of association, building on each other's thoughts, and synthesizing.

    Randomly choose two or three students to give thirty-second summaries of their discussions. **It is important that students are randomly called on to share their answers after each discussion task. Such individual accountability** ensures that the pairs take the tasks seriously and check each other to ensure that both are prepared to answer.

    c. Lecture segment 2: Deliver the second segment of the lecture.

    d. Pair discussion 2: Give a discussion task focused on the second part of the lecture.

    e. Repeat this sequence of lecture segment and pair discussion until the lecture is completed.

3. **Closure-focused discussion:** Give students an ending discussion task lasting for four to five minutes to summarize what students have learned from the lecture. The discussion should result in students integrating what they have just learned into existing conceptual frameworks. The task may also point students toward what the homework will cover or what will be presented in the next class session. This provides closure to the lecture.

Informal cooperative learning ensures that students are actively involved in understanding what they are learning. It also provides time for instructors to gather their wits, reorganize notes, take a deep breath, and move around the class listening to what students are saying. Listening to student discussions can give instructors direction and insight into how well students understand the concepts and material being taught.

    In the following sections, more specific procedures for the initial focused discussion, the intermittent pair discussions, and the closure-focused discussion will be given.

NATURE OF BASE GROUPS

Committed relationships do not develop in a few hours or even a few days. They develop from spending long hours working together in which group members depend on and support each other. In schools, therefore, it is important that some of the relationships built

Base Groups

Types	Functions	Nature
Class (meet at the beginning and ending of each session or week)	Provide academic support to members	Heterogeneous in membership
School (meet at the beginning and ending of each day or week)	Provide personal support to members	Meet regularly (daily, biweekly)
	Manage class routines and administrative requirements	Last for duration of class, year, or until graduation
	Personalize class and school experience	Ensure all members are making good academic progress

through cooperative learning groups are long term. School has to be more than a series of temporary encounters that last for only a few minutes, a class period, an instructional unit, or a semester. Students could be assigned to permanent cooperative base groups (Johnson & Johnson, 1999; Johnson, Johnson, & Holubec, 1998b).

Cooperative base groups are long-term, heterogeneous cooperative learning groups with stable membership. Members' primary responsibilities are to (a) provide each other with support, encouragement, and assistance in completing assignments; (b) hold each other accountable for striving to learn; and (c) ensure that all members are making good academic progress. Typically, cooperative base groups (a) are heterogeneous in membership (especially in terms of achievement motivation and task orientation), (b) meet regularly (e.g., daily or biweekly), and (c) last for the duration of the class (a semester or a year) or preferably until the students graduate.

Types of Base Groups

There are two ways in which base groups may be used. The *first* is to have a base group in each course. Class base groups stay together only for the duration of the course. The *second* is to organize all students within the school into base groups and have the groups function as an essential component of school life. School base groups stay together for at least a year and preferably for four years or until all members graduate. The agendas of both types of base groups can include:

1. **Academic support tasks:** Base group members encourage each other to master course content and complete all assignments. Members check to see what assignments each member has and what help he or she needs to complete them. The group discusses assignments; answers any questions about assignments; provides information about what a member missed; and plans, reviews, and edits papers. Members can prepare each other to take tests and go over the questions missed afterward. Members can share their areas of expertise (such as art or computers) with each other. Above all, members monitor each other's academic progress and make sure that all members are achieving.

2. **Personal support tasks:** Base group members listen sympathetically when a member has problems with parents or friends, have general discussions about life, give each other advice about relationships, and help each other solve nonacademic problems. Base groups provide interpersonal relationships that personalize the course.

3. **Routine tasks:** The base group provides a structure for managing course procedures such as taking attendance and homework.

4. **Assessment and evaluation tasks:** The base group provides a structure for assessing and evaluating student academic learning. Many of the more complex and important assessment procedures can best be used in the context of cooperative learning groups.

Forming Base Groups

Group size: Four (or three)
Assigning students: Random assignment to ensure heterogeneity
Arranging the room: Providing a permanent place for each group to meet
Preparing materials: Standard forms students use at each meeting; group file folders
Assigning roles: Runner, explainer, accuracy checker, encourager

Class Base Groups

The larger the class and the more complex the subject matter, the more important it is to have class base groups. The base groups meet at the beginning and end of each class session or (if the class session is fifty minutes or less) at the beginning of the first class session each week and at the end of the last class session each week. The members of base groups should exchange phone numbers and information about schedules, as they may wish to meet outside of class. All members are expected to contribute actively to the group's work, strive to maintain effective working relationships with other members, complete all assignments and assist groupmates in completing their assignments, and indicate agreement with the base group's work by signing the weekly contract. At the beginning of each session students meet in base groups to perform these **opening tasks:**

1. Greet each other and check to see that no member of their group is under undue stress. Members ask: "How are you today?" and "Are we all prepared for class?"

2. Complete the next task for the membership grid. This helps members get to know each other better. The task is to answer such questions as "What is the best thing that has happened to you this week?", "What is your favorite television show?", and "Who is your favorite music group?"

3. Pick up their file folders with an attendance sheet, a feedback form, and their assignments from the previous class session (with the instructor's comments). The group members record their own attendance by writing the date and their initials in the *Attendance* section of the folder. They pass out the assignments from the previous class session and discuss any comments the instructor has made.

4. Check to see if members have completed their homework or need help in doing so. Members ask: "Did you do your homework?" and "Is there anything you did not understand?" If extensive help is needed, an appointment is made.

5. In addition to the homework, members review what each member has read and done since the last class session. Members should be prepared to (a) give a succinct

Base Group Agendas

Opening Tasks	Closing Tasks
Greeting and welcome	Review and clarify assignments
Relationship- and group-building task	Discuss what was learned
Check homework	Discuss applications of learnings
Review progress: ongoing assignments	Celebrate members' hard work

summary of what they have read, thought about, and done; (b) share resources they have found; and (c) share copies of assignments they have completed.

6. Students collect each member's work, record it in their *Base Group Progress Report Sheet,* and place the assignments in their file folder. The file folder is returned to the instructor's desk. Periodically, the base groups may be given a checklist of academic skills and assess which ones each member needs to practice.

Generally, class base groups are available to support individual group members. If a group member arrives late or must leave early on occasion, the group can provide information about what that student missed. Group members may assist one another in writing required papers and completing other assignments. They can discuss assigned work, plan papers, review each other's progress, and edit each other's work. Questions regarding the course assignments and class sessions may be addressed in base groups.

The class session closes with students meeting in base groups. **Closing tasks** may be:

1. Ensure that all members understand the assignments. Find out what help each member needs to complete the assigned work.
2. Summarize at least three things members learned in today's class session.
3. Summarize how members will use/apply what they have learned.
4. Celebrate the hard work and learning of group members.

School Base Groups

At the beginning of their freshman year (or any academic year), students should be assigned to base groups. Base groups should stay together for at least a year and ideally for four years (or until members graduate). Class schedules should be arranged so that members of base groups are assigned to as many of the same classes as possible. In essence, the computer is programmed to assign base groups to classes (whenever possible) rather than individuals.

When base groups meet twice each week (perhaps first thing on Monday and last thing on Friday), they discuss the academic progress of each member, provide assistance to each other, and hold each member accountable for completing assignments and progressing satisfactorily through the academic program. The **meeting on Monday morning** refocuses the students on school, provides any emotional support required after the weekend, reestablishes personal contact among base group members, and helps students set their academic goals for the week (what is still to be done on assignments that are due and so forth). Members should carefully review each other's assignments and ensure that members have the necessary assistance. In addition, they should hold each other accountable for succeeding academically. The **meeting on Friday afternoon** helps students review the week, set academic goals for the weekend (what homework has to be done before Monday), and share weekend plans and hopes.

INTEGRATED USE OF ALL THREE GOAL STRUCTURES

The third step in increasing your expertise in using cooperative learning is to use all three goal structures in an integrated way. While the dominant goal structure within any classroom should be cooperation (which ideally would be used about 60% to 70% of the time), competitive and individualistic efforts are useful supplements. Competition may be used for an enjoyable change of pace during an instructional unit that is predominantly structured cooperatively, and individualistic learning is often productive when the information learned is subsequently used in a cooperative activity. The integrated use of cooperative, competitive, and individualistic learning is described in Johnson and Johnson (1999a) and in Johnson, Johnson, and Holubec (1998b).

Example of Integrated Use of Cooperative Learning

An example of the integrated use of cooperative learning procedures is as follows. Students arrive at class and meet in their **base groups** to welcome each other, complete a self-disclosure task (such as answering the question "What is each member's favorite television show?"), check each student's homework to make sure all members understand the academic material and are prepared for the class session, and tell each other to have a great day.

The teacher then begins a lesson on the limitations of being human. To help students cognitively organize in advance what they know about the advantages and disadvantages of being human, the teacher uses **informal cooperative learning.** The teacher asks students to form a triad and ponder the question "What are five things you cannot do with your human limitations that a Billion-Dollar Being might be designed to do?" Students have four minutes to do so. In the next ten minutes, the teacher explains that although the human body is a marvelous system, we (like other organisms) have very specific limitations. We cannot see bacteria in a drop of water or the rings of Saturn unaided. We cannot hear as well as a deer or fly like an eagle. Humans have never been satisfied in being so limited and, therefore, we have invented microscopes, telescopes, and our own wings. The teacher then instructs students to turn to the person next to them and answer the questions "What are three limitations of humans?", "What have we invented to overcome them?", and "What other human limitations might we be able to overcome?"

Formal cooperative learning is used in this lesson. (For the Billion-Dollar Being lesson, see *Topics in Applied Science*, Jefferson County Schools, Golden, Colorado.) The teacher has the thirty-two students count off from 1 to 8 to form groups of four randomly. Group members sit so that they can face each other and the teacher. Each member is assigned a role: researcher/runner, summarizer/timekeeper, collector/recorder, and

Types of Cooperative Learning

Form a pair. In the spaces provided, write out the definition of each type of cooperative learning in your own words.

Formal	Informal	Base Groups

technical adviser (role interdependence). Every group gets one large 2 × 3-foot piece of paper, a marking pen, a rough draft sheet for designing the Being, an assignment sheet explaining the task and the cooperative goal structure, and four student self-evaluation checklists (resource interdependence). The **task** is to design a Billion-Dollar Being that overcomes the human limitations thought of by the class and the group. The group members are to draw a diagram of the Being on the scratch paper and, when they have something they like, transfer it to the larger paper. The teacher establishes **positive goal interdependence** by asking for one drawing from the group that all group members contribute to and can explain. The **criterion for success** is to complete the diagram in the thirty-minute time limit. The teacher ensures **individual accountability** by observing each group to ensure that members are fulfilling their roles and that any one member can explain any part of the Being at any time. The teacher informs students that the **expected social skills** to be used by all students are encouraging each other's participation, contributing ideas, and summarizing. He or she defines the skill of encouraging participation and has each student practice it twice before the lesson begins. While students work in their groups, the teacher **monitors** by systematically observing each group and intervening to provide academic assistance and help in using the interpersonal and small group skills required to work together effectively. At the end of the lesson, the groups hand in their diagrams of the Billion-Dollar Being to be assessed and **evaluated.** Group members then **process** how well they worked together by identifying actions each member engaged in that helped the group succeed and one thing that could be added to improve their group next time.

The teacher uses **informal cooperative learning** to provide closure to the lesson by asking students to meet in new triads and write out six conclusions about the limitations of human beings and what we have done to overcome them.

At the end of the class session, the **cooperative base groups** meet to review what students believe is the most important thing they have learned during the day, what homework has been assigned, what help each member needs to complete the homework, and to tell each other to have an enjoyable afternoon and evening.

Integrated Use of All Types of Cooperative Learning for Fifty-Minute Session

Step	Activity	Time (in minutes)
1	Welcome and opening base group meeting	10
2	Choice 1: Direct teaching, informal cooperative learning	35
3	Choice 2: Work in formal cooperative learning groups	35
4	Choice 3: Direct teaching, formal cooperative learning groups	35
5	Choice 4: Academic controversy	35
6	Closing base group meeting	5

Weekly Schedule for Fifty-Minute Class Sessions

Session 1		Session 2		Session 3	
Time	Activity	Time	Activity	Time	Activity
15	Base group meeting	5	Base group meeting	5	Base group meeting
30	Lecture with informal CL	35	Formal CL groups work on assignment or controversy	15	Formal CL groups work on assignment
5	Base group meeting	5	Base group meeting	10	Lecture with informal CL
				15	Base group meeting

Integrated Use of All Types of Cooperative Learning for Ninety-Minute Session

Step	Activity	Time
1	Opening base group meeting	10
2	Direct teaching with informal cooperative learning	25
3	Work on assignment in formal cooperative learning	40
4	Direct teaching with informal cooperative learning	10
5	Closing base group meeting	5

THE COOPERATIVE SCHOOL

W. Edwards Deming, Joseph Juran, and other founders of the quality movement have stated that over 85% of the behavior of members of an organization is directly attributable to the organization's structure, not the nature of the individuals involved. Your classroom is no exception. If competitive or individualistic learning dominates your classroom, your students will behave accordingly, regardless of whether you have temporarily put them in cooperative groups. If cooperative learning dominates your classroom, your students will behave accordingly and a true learning community will result.

The issue of cooperation among students is part of a larger issue of the organizational structure of schools (Johnson & Johnson, 1994). For decades schools have functioned as mass-production organizations that divided work into component parts (first grade, second grade; English, social studies, science) to be performed by teachers who are isolated from their colleagues and work alone, in their own room, with their own set of students, and with their own set of curriculum materials. Students can be assigned to any teacher because students are considered to be interchangeable parts in the education machine. By using cooperative learning, the majority of the time you are changing the basic organizational structure of your classroom to a team-based, high-performance one. In other words, cooperation is more than an instructional procedure. It is a basic shift in organizational structure that will affect all aspects of classroom life.

In a **cooperative school,** students work primarily in cooperative learning groups, teachers and building staff work in cooperative teams, and district administrators work in cooperative teams (Johnson & Johnson, 1994). The organizational structures of the classroom, school, and district are then congruent. Each level of cooperative teams supports and enhances the other levels.

A cooperative school structure begins in the classroom with the use of cooperative learning the majority of the time (Johnson & Johnson, 1994). Work teams are the heart of the team-based organizational structure, and cooperative learning groups are the primary work teams. Cooperative learning is used to increase student achievement, create more positive relationships among students, and generally improve students' psychological well-being. Having teachers advocate cooperation to their students, furthermore, changes their own attitudes toward working collaboratively with colleagues.

The second level in creating a cooperative school is to form collegial teaching teams, task forces, and ad hoc decision-making groups within the school (Johnson & Johnson, 1994). Teacher teams are just as effective as student teams. The use of cooperation to structure faculty and staff work involves (a) collegial teaching teams, (b) school-based decision making, and (c) faculty meetings. Just as the heart of the classroom is cooperative learning, the heart of the school is the collegial teaching team. **Collegial teaching teams** are small cooperative groups (two to five teachers) whose purpose is to increase teachers' instructional expertise and success (Johnson & Johnson, 1994).

A school-based decision-making procedure is implemented through the use of two types of cooperative teams (Johnson & Johnson, 1994). A **task force** considers a school problem and proposes a solution to the faculty as a whole. The faculty is then divided into **ad hoc decision-making groups** and considers whether to accept or modify the proposal. The decisions made by the ad hoc groups are summarized, and the entire faculty then decides on the action to be taken to solve the problem.

The third level in creating a cooperative school is to implement administrative cooperative teams within the district (Johnson & Johnson, 1994). Administrators are organized into collegial teams to increase their administrative expertise, as well as task forces and ad hoc decision-making groups.

Willi Unsoeld, a mountain climber and philosopher, gave this advice as the secret to survival to all those who set off to climb a mountain: "Take care of each other and share your energies with the group. No one must feel alone, cut off, for that is when you do not make it." The same may be said for everyone entering a school.

SUMMARY

In this chapter we have seen that there are three types of social interdependence: competitive, individualistic, and cooperative. Of the three, cooperation tends to promote the highest achievement, most positive relationships, and greatest psychological health. In order to harness the power of cooperation, however, it is necessary to know what makes it work and apply those elements with discipline and diligence. As with Sandy Koufax, natural talent is not enough to make a great teacher. Being well trained in how to use cooperative learning and unusually well disciplined in structuring the five basic elements in every lesson are also necessary. The five essential components are positive interdependence, individual accountability, promotive interaction, social skills, and group processing. By structuring these five elements into lessons, teachers can create formal cooperative learning lessons, informal cooperative learning lessons, and cooperative base groups. Repetitive lessons and procedures may be turned into cooperative scripts. Cooperative learning takes place within an organizational context. If the organizational context emphasizes mass production of educated students, it works against the use of cooperative learning. If the organizational context is a team-based, high-performance structure, then it encourages and supports the use of cooperative learning. In a high-performance school, the five basic elements of cooperation are used to structure teaching teams, faculty meetings, and site-based decision making. Finally, the long-term success of cooperative efforts depends on members having frequent conflicts that are managed constructively.

12

Leading Growth and Counseling Groups

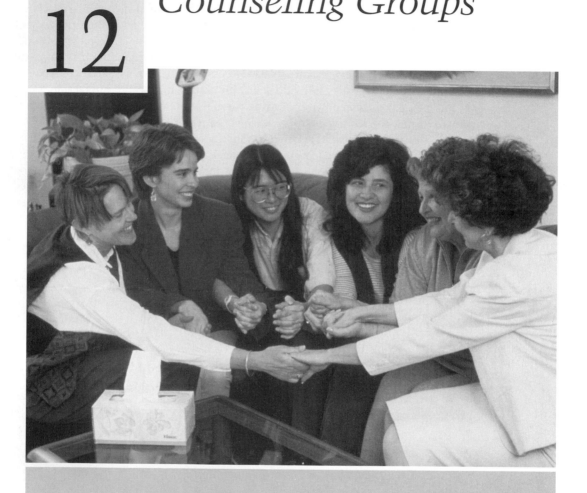

Basic Concepts to Be Covered in This Chapter

In this chapter a number of concepts are defined and discussed. The major ones are listed following. Divide into pairs. Each pair is to (a) define each concept, noting the page on which it is defined and discussed, and (b) make sure that both members of the pair understand the meaning of each concept. Then combine into groups of four. Compare the answers of the two pairs. If there is disagreement, look up the concept in the chapter and clarify it until all members agree on and understand the definition.

Concepts

1. Counseling and therapy groups
2. Growth groups
3. Interpersonal effectiveness
4. Intuition
5. Psychological health
6. Reactance
7. Self-actualization
8. Self-defeating behaviors
9. Self-enhancing behaviors
10. Self-help groups

INTRODUCTION

Groups are uniquely suited to help persons grow and change in constructive ways. There are a wide variety of therapeutic groups aimed at achieving many different goals. What they have in common is an emphasis on members changing toward increased psychological health, happiness, effectiveness, and competence. There are a number of therapeutic events that promote the achievement of these goals. Individuals may change (a) by themselves in isolation from others, (b) in dyads (such as with a counselor, therapist, minister, or friend), or (c) in small groups (such as growth, counseling, or therapy groups). Groups, however, have several unique powers that make them the ideal setting for personal change. Facilitators of growth and counseling groups need to create the conditions for promoting therapeutic events and capitalizing on the unique power of groups.

TYPES OF THERAPEUTIC GROUPS

Millions of Americans have participated or are participating in groups aimed at personal growth, therapeutic change, or self-help (Figure 12.1). **Growth groups** focus on emotional growth, improved interpersonal relationships, and group skills. They include T-groups, encounter groups, human relations training groups, and structured growth groups. **Counseling and therapy groups** focus on increased psychological adjustment and health. They include psychoanalytic groups, Adlerian groups, psychodrama groups, Gestalt groups, cognitive-behavioral groups, existential groups, person-centered groups, rational-emotive groups, reality groups, and interpersonal therapy groups. **Self-help groups** focus on overcoming or coping with life stresses, such as addiction or illness. There are an enormous number of self-help groups. In all three areas, there is both a demand for small group experiences and an expansion of the types of group experiences available.

Types of Therapy Groups		
Growth Groups	Therapy Groups	Self-Help Groups
Unique power of groups	Importance of disclosing emotions	
Leading growth and therapy groups	Conceptualizing, feelings, intuition	
Becoming a facilitator	Growth groups and anxiety, costs	
Costs of participating in groups	Comparative effectiveness	

Figure 12.1   Growth and therapy groups.

Goals

Growth, counseling, and self-help groups have similar, overlapping goals. They seek to achieve these goals through different processes. While the diversity of the groups precludes a full listing of their goals, generally the groups seek goals such as:

1. Decreasing self-defeating patterns and increasing self-enhancing patterns of behavior and attitudes. Many individuals have developed behavior patterns and attitudes that create and sustain negative and self-destructive consequences and ultimately lead to a more painful and troubled life. They often join groups to identify these self-defeating and self-destructive patterns and change them to patterns that promote the ability to maintain themselves, grow, and flourish.
2. Increasing psychological health and decreasing psychological pathology. **Psychological health** is the ability to be aware of and manage effectively one's interdependent interactions with others (Johnson, 1980b; Johnson & Johnson, 1989).
3. Increasing the ability to build and maintain humanizing relationships. **Humanizing relationships** reflect the qualities of kindness, mercy, consideration, tenderness, love, concern, compassion, responsiveness, and friendship.
4. Increasing self-actualization. **Self-actualization** is the psychological need for growth, development, and utilization of potential (Maslow, 1954). A self-actualizing person will be moving toward the full use of his or her talents, capacities, and potentialities. Self-actualization involves both self-development and self-utilization: One develops potentialities and then uses them in order to actualize oneself.
5. Increasing interpersonal effectiveness. **Interpersonal effectiveness** is the extent to which the consequences of a person's behavior match his or her intentions (Johnson, 2003). When two participants interact, for example, they are seeking to achieve certain consequences. When their behavior results in the consequences they want, their interpersonal effectiveness is high; when the consequences are not what they want, their interpersonal effectiveness is low. Interpersonal effectiveness depends on mastering interpersonal and small group skills. All the group skills discussed in this book and the interpersonal skills discussed in Johnson (2003) are relevant to interpersonal effectiveness.

When participants join a growth, therapy, or self-help group, they and the group's facilitator have a set of goals for the group. If the goals of the participants and those of the group facilitator do not completely overlap, the two must negotiate a set of goals that they can mutually commit themselves to achieving. When participants and the facilitator have different goals, the goals may initially be cooperative (working to achieve the participants' goals facilitates the accomplishment of the facilitator's goals and vice versa) or competitive (working to achieve the participants' goals interferes with the accomplishment of the facilitator's goals and vice versa). For the group to be successful, the facilitator and the participants need to negotiate mutual goals.

Growth Groups

T-Groups.   Broadly speaking, the term *T-group* (sometimes known as *laboratory-training* or *sensitivity-training group*) refers to the more conservative, more traditional growth group in which the primary emphasis is on studying the development of the group and the relationships among group members (Watson & Johnson, 1972). Small group discussions (involving eight to ten members) are conducted in which the primary (almost exclusive) source of information for learning is the behavior of the group members themselves. The discussions are almost exclusively confined to what is happening in the group, not what happened in the past histories of the participants. It is associated with the National Training Laboratories in Bethel, Maine, and Washington, D.C.

T-groups originated from an accident that occurred in the presence of a brilliant and creative social psychologist who was quick to appreciate the potential utility of what was taking place (Marrow, 1969). In 1946, Kurt Lewin was asked to conduct a workshop to explore the use of small groups to train community facilitators to strengthen democracy at the grass-roots level. The participants were educators, public officials, and social scientists. They met in small groups focused on the development of democratic facilitators. The small groups were observed by several of Lewin's graduate students (one of whom was Morton Deutsch), who met in the evenings to discuss the dynamics of the group discussions they had observed during the day. One evening, two of the participants asked if they could sit in and listen while the graduate students discussed their observations. Much to everyone's surprise, Lewin said, "Yes." By chance, the observers were discussing an episode that involved one of these participants. As the discussion progressed, the participant became more and more agitated until she interrupted and disagreed with the observers' interpretations. She then proceeded to give her version of the episode. The resulting discussion proved to be very involving and enlightening. The next night, all fifty of the participants showed up and enthusiastically joined in the discussion, frequently disagreeing with and clarifying the interpretations of the trained observers. The participants had sources of information not available to the observers—the participants' intentions.

Lewin and his students grasped the significance of the evening discussions. They concluded that a group engaged in a problem-solving discussion can benefit enormously by taking time out to discuss its own dynamics or *group process*. After a time, what evolved was a group whose purpose was to study its own development and dynamics. The initial name, *sensitivity-training* (as the experience sensitized participants to the impact of their behavior on others) or *laboratory-training groups*, was eventually shortened to *training group* and then to *T-group*. After Lewin's death in 1947, the National Training Laboratory of Applied Behavioral Science (NTL) was organized by Lewin's colleagues and students at the Research Center for Group Dynamics, the National Education Association, and the Office of Naval Research. T-groups became part of larger "laboratories" or workshops that originally were three weeks long in the 1940s and early 1950s, then two weeks long in the late 1950s, and finally one week long in the 1960s. Since the late 1940s, countless educators, executives, managers, and social scientists have participated in programs offered by NTL at Bethel, Maine, and other training centers. T-groups are a key component of many organizational development interventions (Burke & Day, 1986).

Generally, participants in a T-group learn about the way they interact with others while providing leadership, making group decisions, striving to influence what the group does, resolving conflicts, setting group norms, and so forth. They also learn how others see them, how their behavior affects the other participants, and how they are affected by other participants' actions. They learn how to communicate more effectively, how to understand their own feelings and the feelings of other people, and how to build and maintain relationships with others. Many times participants seek answers to specific questions: "Why do I have difficulties getting along with other people?", "Why is it so hard for me to make friends?", "How can I handle my anger?", "Why do I have such difficulty trusting people?", "Why am I so powerless in most groups?" and so forth. Because of its power as an inductive method of teaching group dynamics, because it involves learning through experience, and because of the personal learning and emotional experiences generated by examination of the interaction among members, the use of T-groups mushroomed, probably being used most frequently in the 1960s.

The traditional difference between T-groups and counseling groups is that in a T-group the facilitator and the other participants do not attempt to interpret participants' motives or probe their past experiences. Instead, they focus on behavior in the group and reactions of the others participants to the behavior.

Encounter Groups. This distinction became blurred in the 1960s with the advent of encounter groups. Promoted by psychotherapists such as Carl Rogers (1970b), encounter groups emphasized participants accepting and trusting their feelings, accepting their most personal qualities, and being more open in interacting with others. Participants are encouraged to encounter each other "authentically" by displaying their emotions, thoughts, and worries. The facilitator displays unconditional positive regard and helps participants experience and express their intense feelings. Role playing and other exercises may be used to help participants experience and express feelings such as caring, loneliness, helplessness, and anger. In encounter groups, individuals are encouraged to explain their present behavior in terms of past experiences and to seek healing for past hurts.

Human Relations Training Groups. Human relations training groups focus on increasing members' competence in interacting effectively with individuals from diverse ethnic and cultural backgrounds. Small groups with members from diverse backgrounds study their own interactions and work to build effective relationships with each other. In human relations training groups, interactions among diverse individuals may be experienced and studied simultaneously. Group members tend to develop insights into cultural differences and the ways in which constructive relationships among diverse individuals may be built and maintained.

Structured Growth Groups. Structured growth groups focus on specific interpersonal problems or skills. Exercises may be used to help participants practice the targeted behaviors and skills. Assertiveness training, which focuses on teaching individuals the difference between being aggressive, passive, and assertive, is an example. Participants may engage in exercises in which they practice saying "No" to each other. All of the exercises in this book are examples. Countless organizations all over the world use structured growth groups in their workshops and seminars. They usually follow the format of skills training discussed in Chapter 2.

Counseling and Therapy Groups

Counseling and therapy groups are very powerful tools for solving problems and helping individuals change in positive ways. There are many different types of therapy groups.

Psychoanalytic Groups. Psychoanalytic groups focus on the inner conflicts underlying psychological problems. Since Freud believed that most people avoid confronting their conflicts by repressing them, during group sessions participants are encouraged to discuss their memories, fears, fantasies, and dreams in order to gain insight into their unconscious. The group facilitator may offer interpretations of the participants' free associations to promote insights and take advantage of transference (the tendency of participants to transfer the emotions they feel for their parents to the therapist). In such groups, the therapist dominates, working with each participant, with the other group members observing. Jungian groups, on the other hand, may focus more on dreams.

Adlerian Group Psychotherapy. Alfred Adler contended that based on children's early recognition of their dependence on adults, people often feel inferior with regard to others. The feeling of inferiority motivates them to strive for mastery, superiority, power, and ultimately, perfection. Social forces primarily motivate people as they search for significance. Thus, neuroses are socially determined and are best cured in social contexts such as therapy groups. Striving to overcome inferiority results in a move toward cooperative social living to overcome aloneness and weakness (Richardson & Manaster, 1997). Sonstegard, Dreikurs, and Bitter (1982) and Sonstegard and Bitter (1998) outline four stages of group counseling: (a) building cohesion, (b) assessing each member's psychological health and functioning, (c) helping each member increase self-understanding and gain insights, and (d) helping each member reorient him- or herself by seeing new ways of behaving and making new choices that may be made.

Psychodrama. Moreno (1932/1953) developed therapy groups in which participants acted out past emotional experiences as psychodramas. Two assumptions of Moreno are that (a) physically acting out traumatic past events is more involving than passive discussion of them and (b) the dramatic enactment helps group members overcome their reluctance to discuss intimate and upsetting issues.

Gestalt Group Therapy. Gestalt group therapy is based on the assumption that humans should be treated as total persons. Fritz Perls (1969), who is generally recognized as the founder of Gestalt therapy, emphasized (a) the integration of mind and body;

(b) increased clarity about one's wants, values, and goals; (c) greater awareness of oneself, especially one's feelings and one's impact on others; and (d) resolution or completion of unfinished business. A person is not whole until past experiences (interpersonal conflicts that still upset, the death of a relative or friend that still hurts, a past failure that still sparks regret) are resolved in some way. Generally, the problems are unresolved because individuals repress their emotions. For people to reach their potential, they have to complete their unfinished business by getting in touch with their feelings and resolving their interpersonal problems. In many cases, resolving a problem is difficult because the other person (such as a parent) has died. To solve such problems and to uncover repressed feelings, Perls recommends procedures such as the *empty-chair method* (in which the participant imagines his or her parent sitting in the empty chair and has a conversation with the imagined person) and the *reversal experiment* (in which a person role plays a side of him- or herself rarely or never expressed). Perls viewed therapy as a process by which negative identifications with significant others are replaced with positive identification with the therapist. The facilitator of a Gestalt therapy group works with one member at a time, with the other members observing the process. One by one, each participant is placed in the "hot seat" and works through his or her unfinished business.

Cognitive-Behavioral Group Psychotherapy. Cognitive-behavioral group psychotherapy applies the behavior theories of Skinner (1953, 1971) and the social learning theories of Bandura (1977) to engineer changes in behavior without concern for the origins of the ineffective actions or the psychodynamics of the person. Individuals decide how they wish to change, and through procedures such as modeling, rehearsal, feedback, and reinforcement they develop more effective behavioral patterns. Group members learn self-management skills to control their lives and deal effectively with problems (Watson & Tharp, 1997).

Existential Group Psychotherapy. Existential group psychotherapy helps participants confront the basic "givens" or ultimate concerns of existence: death (conflict between the awareness of the inevitability of death and the wish to continue to be), freedom (conflict between groundlessness and desire for structure), existential isolation (conflict between awareness of one's absolute isolation and the wish for protection, closeness, and desire to be a part of the larger whole), and meaninglessness (conflict between the apparent meaninglessness of life and the desire for a life with meaning). Existential therapy assumes that all individuals are free to choose what to make of their circumstances and, therefore, they are responsible for their choices and actions. Each person is the architect of his or her life. Group members are encouraged to take responsibility for their lives (rather than being passive victims of circumstances), discover alternative ways of dealing with their problems, and choose the path they wish to follow (thus becoming the authors of their lives). In doing so they resolve their concerns about death, freedom, isolation, and meaning.

Person-Centered Group Psychotherapy. Developed by Carl Rogers, the person-centered approach to group psychotherapy assumes that human beings tend to move toward wholeness and self-actualization and that they can find their way without much direction from the group facilitator. The facilitator creates a healing climate in the group by being caring, empathetic, understanding, accepting, nonpossessively warm, and genuine. Group members will then drop their defenses and work toward meaningful goals. There is a basic trust in the person's ability to move forward if the appropriate conflicts for fostering growth are present.

Rational-Emotive Behavior Group Psychotherapy. Rational-emotive behavior group psychotherapy is based on the assumption that at a very early age individuals learn "shoulds," "oughts," and "musts" that are translated into irrational assumptions held on a preconscious level and that result in self-defeating beliefs and behaviors (Ellis, 1996, 1997). An irrational assumption is a belief that makes you depressed, anxious, or upset most of the time. An example of such an irrational assumption is "I must be loved, liked, and approved of by everyone all the time or I will be absolutely miserable and will feel totally worthless." Obviously, everyone will not love you all the time and, therefore, this assumption will inevitably result in depression and disappointment. To combat such an irrational assumption, a person must (a) become aware of the irrational assumption being made and (b) engage in an internal debate to replace it with a new, more constructive one.

Reality Group Psychotherapy. Reality therapy is based on the assumptions that (a) humans are motivated to fulfill their basic needs for survival, love and belonging, power, freedom, and fun and (b) each person chooses how to fulfill these needs in his or her current relationships (Glasser, 1998). The emphasis is on controlling one's own behavior to better meet one's needs in one's current relationships. Thus, in the group, members talk about their current behavior and how to become more effective. Group members explore their needs, examine the effectiveness of their current behavior in meeting their needs, identify the aspects of their behavior they wish to change, and plan how to do so.

Interpersonal Group Psychotherapy. Interpersonal group psychotherapy is based on the assumption that many psychological problems result from problems in relationships (Johnson & Matross, 1977; Yalom, 1995). Depression, anxiety, and personality disorders may be due to problems in relationships with romantic partners, friends, or family members. Individuals need to correct self-defeating, unsuccessful, and ineffective patterns of behavior. The group is used as a social microcosm in which members interact similarly to how they generally behave outside the group. Self-defeating patterns of behavior become apparent in the group, are identified, and are corrected within the group. The new, self-enhancing patterns of behavior are then generalized to relationships outside of the group.

Self-Help, Mutual-Support Groups

Self-help or **mutual-support groups** are voluntary groups whose members meet to exchange social support and aid in order to solve a common problem (Goodman & Jacobs, 1994). Individuals join self-help groups because they face a common predicament, problem, or concern that causes them to bond psychologically. The price for membership is usually not money, but rather (a) admitting that one shares the common problem,

(b) reciprocal helping, and (c) commitment to follow the recovery or treatment program advocated by the group. A member is required to (a) admit, face, and try to solve his or her problem, (b) both give help to other members and receive help from them, and (c) adhere to the recovery or treatment program specified in the group's doctrine (such as the 12-Step Program advocated by Alcoholics Anonymous). While there are many differences among support groups, most are self-governing, with members, not "experts," determining the group's procedures. In order to conduct an Alcoholics Anonymous group, for example, one must be an alcoholic. An academic researcher on addiction who had never been an alcoholic would not be accepted as a facilitator.

The variety of self-help groups is enormous. Self-help groups exist for almost every major stress-related, psychological, and medical problem. If you have an addiction to alcohol, other drugs, sex, or any other activity, support groups are available. If you have lost a child or a spouse or a friend, there is a grief-oriented support group for you. If you have cancer, heart problems, diabetes, or any other major medical condition, support groups exist. If you are dying, support groups are available. The number of such groups is proliferating, primarily because members believe that their needs are not being met by existing educational, social, or health agencies. Goodman and Jacobs (1994) estimate that as many as 8 million people in the United States alone belong to self-help groups.

THE UNIQUE POWER OF GROUP EXPERIENCES

Some persons seek isolation and privacy while they try to think through their problems and decide how to improve their relationships. Others seek out a friend or a counselor and discuss their problems and plans in a dyad. Groups, however, have several unique

advantages over solitary contemplation and dyadic discussion for those who want to grow, develop, change, and heal. Their unique capacities are largely due to the more heterogeneous, complex social setting that groups provide. The greater number of relationships available in the group provides richness and potential for learning, growth, change, and healing that are not possible in a dyad or a solitary situation.

Supportive Community

Groups generate a sense of community, belonging, caring, support, acceptance, and assistance. There are so many benefits from being part of a supportive community that encourages change and growth that it would take an entire book to discuss them. Membership in a supportive group strengthens one's identity as a person who is growing and changing, eases the pain associated with therapeutic exploration, encourages risk taking in achieving growth goals, reduces neurotic distress, increases hope, reduces depression and loneliness, increases self-esteem, improves one's problem-solving ability, and increases the feeling of validation (Cline, 1999; Johnson & Johnson, 1989). Each member's confidence in his or her ability to grow and change tends to increase as the other group members commit themselves to assisting and supporting the member in doing so. The power of the authenticating affirmation of diverse peers gives groups far more influence over individuals' growth and health than solitary contemplation or dyad interaction.

Hope

Groups can inculcate hope and decrease demoralization. A person's sense of hope may be one of the best predictors of mental health and adjustment, and a person's sense of demoralization may be an accurate predictor of psychological problems (Snyder, Cheavens, & Sympson, 1997). To be *demoralized* is to be disheartened, bewildered, confused, disordered, and deprived of courage. The demoralized person feels isolated, hopeless, and helpless. Group situations can generate events that inspire hope, the feeling that one can change, and the belief that one can influence the causes of one's problems. Seeing other group members who have successfully grappled with problems or who have changed as a result of their participation in the group is one such event. The more hope an individual has, the more ways the individual can identify to reach personal goals and the more confident the person is that he or she can engage in the actions necessary to reach the goals.

Microcosm of Real World

Groups provide a microcosm of the real world. Participants eventually create in a growth or therapy group the same interpersonal dynamics they have always been involved in by behaving as they do in their relationships outside of the group. Maladaptive interpersonal behavior is revealed in a setting where it can be changed. Groups provide a remedial environment for the solution of personal and interpersonal problems. It is within relationships that people learned maladaptive patterns of behaving and thinking. It is within groups that people may learn constructive patterns of behaving and reasoning. Growth and therapy groups enable participants to work on their problems immediately by taking corrective steps in their relationships with other members. In addition, strengths and positive interpersonal behavior will be revealed in a setting in which they can be enhanced. In creating a microcosm of the outside world, groups provide an arena for participants to interact freely with others, help them to identify and understand what goes wrong and right in their interactions, and ultimately enable them to change maladaptive patterns and use their strengths more effectively.

Induce and Reduce Powerful Feelings

Groups can induce and then reduce powerful feelings. Not only may the relationship with the facilitator re-create emotions felt toward authority figures, but also relationships with other group members may re-create emotions felt toward siblings and schoolmates.

The wider variety of persons and the more diverse interpersonal events that take place within a group enable the group to induce a wide range of powerful emotions. Growth and therapy groups provide an environment in which participants may experience previously terrifying and deeply upsetting feelings with a new sense of acceptance. By finding that the previously feared feelings are not overwhelming or that the feared consequences do not occur, the participant can have a corrective emotional experience. Experiencing and discussing emotions in a supportive and caring environment usually reduces them and decreases their influence on participants' future behavior and thinking.

Perspective Taking

Groups provide a setting in which participants' egocentrism may be decreased and their perspective-taking ability and empathy increased. With psychological problems comes egocentrism. A depressed or panicked person is focused on him- or herself. Such egocentrism is reduced when group members focus on other members' problems and experience a variety of responses to their actions. Through exchanges of ideas about problems and solutions within a supportive context where group members feel understood and accepted, members will be more aware of and open to other perspectives. Group facilitators may also structure perspective-reversal situations in which participants switch positions and argue each other's point of view or take the perspective of a significant person outside of the group, such as a mother, boss, or spouse. As the ability of a group member to take the other members' perspectives and feel empathy for their plight grows, his or her egocentrism decreases and the ability to solve personal problems increases.

Multiple Sources of Feedback

Groups provide multiple sources of feedback. The availability of immediate information about how one is perceived by peers is unique to the group situation. Each group member uses the other members as a mirror to reflect back reactions to the member's actions. While people usually have an accurate view of themselves (they see themselves as others see them), there are times when others see them quite differently than they see themselves. The other group members become a resource used by a group member to understand him- or herself. The other group members, due to their differing perspectives, will perceive the actions and experiences of each member in a variety of ways. The resulting reactions and feedback provide a rich source for understanding oneself and reframing one's experiences.

Multiple Sources of Social Comparison

Groups provide multiple sources of social comparison for participants. Such comparisons cause members to realize that their problems are universal. Each group member realizes that his or her problems are not unique, but rather a common human experience shared by other members. Yalom (1995) notes that many people secretly believe that they are unique in their wretchedness, that they alone have certain frightening or unacceptable problems, thoughts, impulses, and fantasies. The disconfirmation of the feeling of uniqueness is a powerful source of relief. When individuals feel threatened, confused, or stressed, they often affiliate with others who face similar problems or troubling events (Schachter, 1959), and they tend to feel better about themselves and have a more positive mood after doing so (Frable, Platt, & Hoey, 1998). Group members often compare their feelings, perceptions, attitudes, and behavior with those of their groupmates. Such comparisons occur naturally within a group and facilitate the discovery of possible new ways of feeling, perceiving, and behaving. In a growth or therapy group, members may make *downward social comparisons* (comparing themselves with someone who has even more severe problems) to raise self-esteem and reduce stress (Gibbons & Gerrard, 1989; Wood, Taylor, & Lichtman, 1985) and they may make *upward social comparisons* (comparing themselves with someone who is coping effectively with the problem) to identify ways to improve their own coping (Buunk, 1995; Collins, 1996; Taylor & Lobel, 1989).

Vicarious Learning

Groups provide the opportunity for vicarious learning. Members can view their groupmates modeling constructive behavior and attitudes that the members wish to master. Social learning theory posits that people can acquire new attitudes and behaviors by observing others' actions (Bandura, 1977). Observing other group members resolve conflicts, build trust, and give each other assistance can provide clear guidelines for how the member should behave in the future. There is evidence that members of groups that emphasize explicit modeling of constructive behavior improve more than do members of groups that only discuss the problematic behavior (Falloon, Lindley, McDonald, & Marks, 1977).

Require Wide Variety of Social Skills

Groups promote the learning and use of a wide variety of social skills and competencies. A group is the ideal setting in which to increase a person's expertise in using interpersonal and small group skills. Expertise is built by engaging in an action, receiving feedback on its effectiveness, engaging in a modified action, receiving feedback, and so on. Having experimented with new behavior patterns in the group, the participants will feel able to engage in the new behaviors in the outside world. Groups provide a setting in which problem areas can be identified, new patterns of behavior can be tried out under low-risk conditions, feedback can be attained from others, and the effectiveness of the new behaviors can be determined. Listening to others discuss their problems and helping them experiment with more constructive ways of behaving and thinking, for example, requires social skills and competencies that may never be required in a dyadic relationship. Participants in therapeutic groups stress interpersonal learning as being one of the most helpful results of their participation (Kivlighan & Mullison, 1988; Kivlighan, Multon, & Brossart, 1996).

Influence Behavior and Attitudes

Groups are powerful influences on the behavioral and attitudinal patterns of members. Factors that have been demonstrated to impact patterns of behavior and attitudes include internalizing group norms, publicly committing oneself to engage in new behaviors, viewing credible models, identifying with other group members, being confronted with personalized information, discussing information with peers, and teaching what one has learned to others (see Chapter 6). In a growth or therapy group, the emphasis is on the mastery and adoption of more constructive ways of behaving and thinking.

Helping Others

Groups provide opportunities for participants to understand and help their peers. By working to understand others in the group and by caring for the personal struggles that other members are going through, group members gain in a variety of ways. *First,* helping others reduces egocentrism and focuses attention and energy on others (rather than away from others). *Second,* helping others results in personal change (Franko, 1987). Alcoholics Anonymous, for example, states that the best way to remain sober is to target one's energy outward by helping others remain sober (Saffer & Galinsky, 1989). *Third,* in helping other group members, participants build self-esteem, self-insight, and increased interpersonal competence. Participants may feel needed and helpful. *Fourth,* helping others provides an important opportunity for engaging in altruistic behavior that may be absent from members' daily lives. *Fifth,* a person who can help others is psychologically healthy. Helping others in itself is a sign of health and self-actualization. *Finally,* change is promoted by accepting the help and support of others. In some cases, the help is from external sources such as a higher being (12-Step Program). In other cases, the help is from other group members. While being helped, members benefit from personalized learning, social approval in a supportive climate, and observing others struggle with similar problems.

Resources for Gaining Self-Insight

Groups provide greater resources for obtaining insight into oneself. Change is promoted by reframing past experiences and current problems so that a new social reality emerges. Group members gain a deeper understanding of themselves through other members' reactions to their behavior and disclosures, revealing their problems for the group to analyze, the feedback they receive from groupmates, and their reactions to other members' actions and problems. Groups provide a variety of perspectives and reactions that stimulate insight into and understanding of one's problems and behavior. The other group members become an avenue used by the individual to understand him- or herself. In addition, a group adds to any insight achieved by a member through its consensual validation of the insight. By providing labels for the member's thoughts, feelings, and experiences, and by helping the member reflect on his or her interactions with them, the other group members help the member understand his or her actions. In general, group members who value self-understanding tend to benefit the most from being in a therapeutic group (Butler & Fuhriman, 1983b).

Cognitive Learning

Groups increase the quantity and quality of cognitive learning (Johnson & Johnson, 1989). Many types of growth, therapy, and self-help groups emphasize the learning of specific cognitive frameworks as part of positive change. Both increased understanding of oneself and the conscious implementation of increased competencies depend on cognitive learning. In their classic study of growth groups, Lieberman, Yalom, and Miles (1973) found that it was self-disclosure involving some sort of cognitive mastery or understanding, not self-disclosure in itself, that was related to positive change.

IMPORTANCE OF DISCLOSING EMOTIONS

Change is promoted by experiencing and expressing positive and negative emotions about the actions of other group members and about important life events. The therapeutic and growth value of such self-disclosure depends, of course, on group members responding with acceptance, support, and caring. *First,* change is promoted by experiencing intense positive and negative emotions, whether or not they are expressed. Events within the group may unleash emotions participants have been previously unable or unwilling to experience. Participants may find that such feelings are not overwhelming or that the feared consequences do not occur. Participants may learn to accept the feelings they were previously afraid of, and a corrective emotional experience may result even when the feelings are not overtly expressed.

Second, expressing emotions and describing emotional experiences tends to unify group members and increase their commitment to each other and to the group (Corey & Corey, 1992; Leichtentritt & Shechtman, 1998). It also deepens the group's intimacy and trust, which in turn makes further self-disclosures possible (Kaul & Bednar, 1986; Noonan & Johnson, 1972; Roark & Sharah, 1989; Tschuschke & Dies, 1994). Self-disclosure to a group of peers is quite different from self-disclosure to one other person. It feels less dramatic and is less anxiety-laden to reveal private information to a single person than to a group. The significance of self-disclosure is not what is disclosed, but rather the response of other members to what one has said. There may be stages of self-disclosure that groups move through (Altman & Taylor, 1973). In the *orientation stage,* members focus on superficial topics and avoid disclosing anything too personal or provocative. They form general impressions of each other and strive to present a good impression of themselves. In the *exploratory affective stage,* members discuss their personal attitudes and opinions on a moderate level but avoid disclosing strongly held emotions or intimate details about themselves. In the *affective stage,* only a few topics are avoided. Positive and negative feelings are expressed toward each other's actions. In the *stable exchange stage,* all personal feelings are shared. Members express feelings that they had previously blocked and thereby unburden themselves of emotional restraint.

Third, expressing previously hidden strong emotions may be cathartic. Venting strong emotions can free individuals from the tension and strain of keeping the emotions suppressed.

Fourth, beneficial change is promoted by observing other group members having significant emotional experiences. Other members' emotional experiences may clarify issues for a participant, who may then use the experiences in his or her own problematic areas.

Fifth, disclosing strong emotional experiences to a supportive and caring group can have considerable therapeutic effects, not the least of which is the realization that one's problems are shared by others and that there is hope of feeling better. Secrets often promote dysfunctional patterns of behavior and feeling. As long as strong emotional experiences are hidden, a person may believe that he or she is uniquely troubled or that no one else could possibly understand what he or she is going through. Revealing one's secrets can result in the discovery that one's problems are universal and that other group members have struggled with similar experiences. Self-disclosure can be therapeutic when participants discover that no one is shocked by their deeply hidden secrets that have always made them feel ashamed, guilty, depressed, or angry. When several members of a group engage in self-disclosure on similar problems, they feel considerable relief when they discover that they are not the only ones who have reacted the way they have and who experience the feelings they do. There are times when discovering the similarities in their experiences, reactions, actions, and feelings reassures participants that they are normal. They are freed from anxiety-producing feelings when no one is shocked or horrified by their problems.

Sixth, in self-help groups especially, disclosure by more senior members may result in identification and reduced isolation for newer group members (Mullan, 1992).

Finally, self-disclosure provides participants with insight into their problems. To communicate their emotions and experiences to other group members, they must first organize and think through their experiences. New insights into one's problems and the dynamics of the situations being discussed tend to emerge from such reconceptualizations and from the experience of listening to oneself communicate one's emotions and experiences to others.

LEADING A GROWTH GROUP

While participation in a growth, therapy, or self-help group may result in significant health-producing experiences, skilled group facilitation is needed to guide the process. Group facilitators need several sets of complex skills:

1. Establishing the conditions for (a) experiencing and disclosing emotions and (b) modifying participants' patterns of behavior and attitudes.

2. Being a resource expert on group dynamics, experiential learning, and the approach to growth being emphasized, and defining and diagnosing the problems of participants.
3. Teaching needed interpersonal and small group skills.
4. Modeling the constructive use of small group and interpersonal skills.
5. Ensuring that members have opportunities for self-disclosure and experimentation with new attitude and behavior patterns.
6. Ensuring that members are provided with constructive confrontations and feedback.
7. Promoting corrective or reparative emotional experiences within the group.
8. Guiding problem solving within which participants can address their concerns.
9. Establishing and enforcing a contract with participants.
10. Carrying out the executive functions of the group.

Establishing Conditions for Participant Change

This set of skills consists of establishing the conditions for change in order for group members to (a) become aware of their ineffective and self-destructive patterns of behavior and attitudes, (b) change to more effective and self-enhancing patterns of behavior and attitudes, and (c) stabilize the new patterns of behavior and attitudes so that they become automatic habit patterns. Establishing the conditions for change is discussed in detail in Johnson (1980b). Examples of the conditions are as follows:

1. A strong sense of positive interdependence and commitment to the group's goals, whether the goals are for self-actualization or for psychological healing (see Chapter 3). The mutual goals focus on three levels of activity: maximizing one's own growth, maximizing the growth of the other group members, and contributing to the common good (such as helping create a supportive, caring, and therapeutic environment). Self-help groups in particular have a strong sense of shared identity, often creating a sense of shared suffering among members (Lieberman, 1993). Meetings of Alcoholics Anonymous, for example, begin with each member publicly stating, "I am an alcoholic." This ritual asserts the group identity as focusing on a shared problem.
2. A sufficient level of trust among group members to ensure that participants feel free to take risks (see Chapter 3). Trust is built by (a) great openness and sharing (being trusting) and (b) strong acceptance, support, and cooperativeness (being trustworthy). A group facilitator models both and ensures that group members do likewise.
3. Encouragement and opportunities for members to increase their self-awareness and self-disclose, experiment with new patterns of behaving and thinking, and give and receive feedback.
4. Reduction of participants' egocentrism and the encouragement of their viewing problems and behavior patterns from a variety of perspectives.
5. Hope and optimism that members will increase their control over themselves and their lives.

6. Positive identification with groupmates who have the skills and competencies the member needs in order to solve the problems he or she is experiencing.

7. A supportive group climate characterized by empathy, acceptance, genuineness, spontaneity, and egalitarianism (Gibb, 1961; Rogers, 1961). A supportive climate is believed to promote personal disclosures that are therapeutic in themselves.

Being a Resource Expert

The resource expertise a facilitator needs varies with the type of group. Almost universally, however, facilitators need expertise in (a) group dynamics, (b) experiential and inquiry learning methods, (c) the approach to growth and therapy being used in the group (T-group, encounter group, psychoanalytic, Adlerian, Gestalt, and so forth), and (d) diagnosing personal and interpersonal problems.

Expertise in Group Dynamics. Group facilitators need to be experts in group dynamics (see Chapter 1). First and foremost, a growth or therapy group needs to be an effective group and, therefore, facilitators need a thorough understanding of group dynamics. All the skills discussed in this book are needed and useful. In a growth or therapy group, the facilitator must be able to create clear, operational, mutual goals that members are committed to achieving, promote clear and accurate communication of ideas and feelings among group members, ensure that participation and leadership are distributed among group members, ensure that all members have equal access to power based on expertise and access to information, flexibly match decision procedures with situational needs, promote constructive controversy to promote creative problem solving and critical thinking, and ensure that conflicts are faced and resolved constructively. Regardless of the type of growth or therapy group, the group has to be effective if members are to learn, change, and actualize.

Expertise in Experiential Learning. Group facilitators need to be experts in experiential and inquiry methods of learning (see Chapter 2). Almost all types of growth and therapy groups emphasize inquiry into the experiences of the group members. Learning from experience in interacting with other group members and inquiring into the interaction among group members are fundamental to all approaches to growth and therapy groups. Group facilitators need expertise in helping participants become aware of their action theories, engage in behavior aimed at improving their own and other group members' effectiveness, assess the consequences of and obtain feedback on their behavior, reflect, and modify and refine their action theories.

Expertise in the Approach to Health and Growth. Group facilitators need to be experts in the approach to growth or to the therapy that is being used in the group. The resulting conceptual frameworks are used to interpret events within the group and to reinterpret life events. There is wide diversity among facilitators in terms of the theories being used to promote growth and health. For some it may be the literature on skill training; for others it may be the theories of Freud, Adler, or Rogers. Whatever approach is being used, the facilitator presents conceptual frameworks that enable group members to understand more fully the personal and interpersonal dynamics they are involved in and gain insight into their own behavior and attitudes. In their classic study on growth groups, Lieberman, Yalom, and Miles (1973) found that the most effective facilitators had a great ability to present conceptualizations that gave meaning to the members' experiences. This ability was the most important variable in promoting member learning that they found in their study. Thus, a facilitator should have a solid knowledge of one of the social sciences (such as psychology or sociology) and the ability to use his or her knowledge and expertise to help the members understand what they are experiencing.

Expertise in Diagnosis. Group facilitators need to be able to diagnose the personal and interpersonal problems experienced by the members during group sessions. To make such diagnoses, the facilitator applies a conceptual framework based upon theory and research to the behavior of the group members. Such conceptualizations are especially useful to members after the group experience has ended, when they are able to use them to understand more fully their day-to-day interpersonal and group situations.

A fundamental activity of facilitators of growth and therapy groups is creating meaning for participants. A facilitator creates meaning by (a) labeling feelings and events that participants undergo, (b) influencing the attributions of causation made by group members, and (c) providing meaning to experiences occurring within the group. Comfort may be given when the facilitator can help a participant label a physiological reaction as "anxiety" or a reaction as a "defense mechanism." Such labeling not only increases members' self-understanding, it also reduces their fear and anxiety concerning emotional and interpersonal experiences and provides them with cognitive tools that they can use in future situations.

In helping participants understand their feelings and experiences, the facilitator must be careful about the way in which he or she attributes the causes of their problems and must pay attention to the resulting sense of personal control experienced by participants (Johnson & Matross, 1977). A participant's problems may be attributed to something within the participant (internal causation) or something outside of the participant (external causation). Causes may also be viewed as stable (incapable of change) or unstable (capable of change). Depending on the problem and the situation, a facilitator may wish to help the participant view a problem as having stable external causes or unstable internal causes. When a person is deeply depressed about a perceived failure, for example, the facilitator may wish to help that person focus on the external unstable causes of the failure. But when a group member succeeds, the facilitator may wish to emphasize the internal stable causes of the success in order to improve the person's self-esteem.

In discussing events that take place within the group, facilitators may wish to define members' actions as reflecting high personal control and sense of freedom. A belief that one is in control of one's life makes the world more predictable and one's experiences more positive. One of the reasons for severe depression following a major illness such as a heart attack is assumed to be the feeling that one has lost control over one's life (Glass, 1977). A belief in one's control over events affects performance on tasks (Glass & Singer, 1973), judgments of the pleasantness of one's surroundings and mood (Rodin, Solomon, & Metcalf, 1978), the positiveness of reactions (Glass, 1977), how active, sociable, and vigorous a person is (Langer & Rodin, 1976), and general health and length of life (Rodin & Langer, 1977). The group facilitator will usually want to define and diagnose participants' problems in ways that maximize their sense of control over their lives.

Group facilitators should also define participants' problems in ways that maximize their sense of freedom in solving them. The loss of control or of freedom of choice tends to result in psychological reactance (Brehm, 1966; Brehm & Brehm, 1981). **Reactance** is a motivational state that is aroused whenever persons feel that their freedom has been abridged or threatened. Threats to personal freedom motivate persons to take actions that help them regain their freedom and control. This motivation to regain freedom can be used to change self-defeating to self-enhancing attitudes and behavior. Being placed in a dependent position, on the other hand, can lead to a significant drop in later performance when one is asked to behave independently on one's own.

Teaching Social Skills and Constructive Patterns of Behavior and Reasoning

One of the major keys to decreasing **self-defeating behavior** and increasing **self-enhancing behavior** is improving participants' group and interpersonal skills (see Chapter 2). The problems of group members often exist because the members lack social skills or are unable to utilize them effectively. Social skills may be taught experientially by recognizing what works and does not work in interacting with other group members. Interpersonal and group skills may also be taught directly through exercises like the ones contained in this book. Leading growth groups requires the capacity to facilitate the social-skill learning of the participants. Group facilitators need to be able to explain what the skill is and why it is important, create opportunities for members to practice the skill, ensure that feedback is received on how well the skill was enacted, and create ongoing opportunities for members to practice the skill until they perfect it.

Modeling Social Skills and Constructive Behavior

To explain the nature of a social skill, it is always helpful to demonstrate it. To encourage group members to self-disclose and experiment with new behavior, it is helpful for facilitators to model such actions. Social-learning theory (Bandura, 1977) emphasizes the importance of modeling desired behaviors and then reinforcing group members for imitating the model. Modeling involves demonstrating particular behaviors while the group members observe. Modeling is often followed by rehearsal, where group members practice the targeted skills themselves, either through role playing or with each other. A willingness to model targeted skills means that the facilitator actively participates in the group and interacts with other group members. Activeness on the part of the facilitator is preferable to passiveness (which, when it pertains to members, is associated with anxiety, dissatisfaction, silence, poor attendance, discontinuance, and lack of learning), except when the activeness turns into domination (Bierman, 1969). In order to model desired skills, the facilitator has to be proficient in their use.

Ensuring Opportunities for Self-Disclosure and Experimentation

Many of the important experiences in growth groups come directly from participants' self-disclosures and experimentation with new patterns of thinking and behaving. An important function of the group facilitator, therefore, is to ensure that opportunities to do so are present in the group. In a supportive group, interacting with other group members and disclosing how one is feeling and reacting results in feeling validated, confirmed as a person, better understood, helped, satisfied, and less isolated.

Providing Constructive Feedback and Confrontations

The group facilitator must be able to make sure that members are provided with constructive feedback and that no destructive feedback is exchanged among members. **Helpful feedback** is the sharing, upon request, of a description of how one person sees another person's behavior and its consequences, and a description of how the observer is reacting to the other person's behavior. Not all feedback is helpful. **Destructive feedback** is an evaluation of the recipient's nature and worth as a person that is forced on the recipient (e.g., "You are really ugly, and no one would ever be attracted to you"). In addition to ensuring that feedback among group members is constructive rather than destructive, a group facilitator may encourage constructive confrontations. A **confrontation** is a deliberate attempt to help another person examine the consequences of some aspect of his or her behavior; it is an invitation to engage in self-examination. A confrontation originates from a desire to involve oneself more deeply with the person one is confronting, and it is intended to help the person behave in more fruitful or less destructive ways. In ensuring that feedback and confrontations are constructive, it is helpful to differentiate among (a) the behavior being observed, (b) the conceptual framework the observer is using, and (c) the inferences and interpretations made about the person engaging in the behavior. A group facilitator should never let group members confuse these three elements. The actual behavior being observed should be the same for all group members (assuming that the observations are valid), but the conceptual frameworks used to understand the behavior and to make interpretations and inferences about it can be widely disparate.

Promoting Reparative Emotional Experiences

The facilitator needs to be able to promote corrective or reparative emotional experiences in the group. Highly personalized and relevant learning often arouses emotions. High levels of caring, support, commitment, anger, frustration, and anxiety are found in most growth and therapy group experiences. A facilitator may stimulate emotional reactions by promoting feedback, confronting group members, supporting the experimentation with alternative behaviors, problem solving, supporting self-disclosure, and expressing warmth and support for the members of the group. The most effective facilitators in the Lieberman, Yalom, and Miles (1973) study engaged in a moderate amount of emotionally stimulating behavior. Though emotional experiences do not mean that learning will take place, genuine learning is often accompanied by emotionality. The facilitator needs to be certain that the members not only experience deep emotion but also are helped to reflect on and analyze the experience in ways that give it meaning for the future.

Guiding Problem Solving

The group facilitator will wish to help participants clarify their current attitude and behavior patterns, determining how those patterns are affecting the participants' feelings and interactions with others, strengthening constructive patterns of attitudes and behaviors, and changing destructive patterns that lead to self-defeating cycles of behavior and cause such feelings as guilt, depression, anxiety, fear, anger, and resentment. Encouraging participants to actively take the perspectives of others with whom they are involved, communicating warmth and understanding, highlighting the conflict between desired consequences and actual behavior and thinking, and initiating problem-solving discussions are all ways in which a group facilitator may facilitate participants' mastery of more self-enhancing patterns of attitudes and behaviors (Johnson & Matross, 1977). In such a problem-solving process, it may be important to bring in information about the person's past behavior and feelings as well as his or her behavior and feelings in the group (Lieberman, Yalom, & Miles, 1973).

Establishing and Maintaining a Contract

It is sometimes useful for a facilitator to have a clear contract with participants concerning their responsibilities as group members. The contract might provide, for example, that members are (a) to be completely open to the group about both past and current behavior, (b) to take responsibility for themselves once they enter the group and not blame others or circumstances for their predicaments, and (c) to get involved with the other group members and cooperate in increasing their learning. When an explicit contract is made, the facilitator becomes the "keeper of the contract" and should ensure that it is enforced.

Carrying out Executive Functions

A facilitator may have a variety of executive functions to carry out. These include organizing the group, arranging for facilities in which it is to meet, providing it with needed materials, and evaluating its success (all of which require a range of administrative and evaluative skills).

CONCEPTUAL FRAMEWORKS, FEELINGS, AND INTUITION

Effective facilitators utilize their conceptual frameworks, feelings, and intuition in an integrated way. They utilize conceptual frameworks to understand the dynamics of events taking place in the group, plan interventions, and give explanations of what has taken place. It is through conceptualizing what is happening within the group and among its members that the facilitator usually derives effective interventions. It is through the facilitator's communication of his or her conceptualizations, furthermore, that much of the learning of members takes place. A conceptual framework is a way of looking at members' behavior and connecting it to a pattern that makes the behavior understandable. The knowledge now available in the social sciences provides facilitators with explicit conceptual frameworks that can be used to help members learn from their experiences.

Feelings often are an important source of information about what is happening within the group and what sorts of problems are occurring among members. Feelings, however, are not infallible. They are susceptible to bias, distortion, and misunderstanding, especially in situations where the person is threatened, defensive, anxious, or tense. Moreover, all people have their blind spots, and in certain situations, or under certain conditions, their feelings can be a reflection of their own fears and anxieties rather than of what is actually taking place in the group. It is important, therefore, for facilitators to "calibrate" themselves on the validity and reliability of their feelings in different situations and in response to different types of events.

Highly experienced facilitators may intervene in a group on the basis of their intuition. **Intuition** is a preconscious process in which the person does not know how the conclusions were determined. Intuitive thinking characteristically does not advance in careful, well-defined steps; the person has an emotional and cognitive reaction to the total situation and arrives at an answer. Intuition results from an immersion in the group process and from a strong identification with and empathy for what is occurring among group members. The more familiar facilitators are with the issues that concern the group, the greater the likelihood of their intuitions being correct. The overuse of intuition by facilitators may be problematic because (a) intuitions are inferences that cannot be proven, (b) facilitators may overrate the validity of their personal observations, (c) the history of medicine and clinical psychology gives overwhelming evidence of the folly of treatments based on intuition (e.g., for several centuries it was intuitively obvious that the insane were possessed by demons, and that all diseases were in the blood and, therefore, a sick person could be cured by being bled), (d) interventions based on intuitions can become self-fulfilling (the actions of a facilitator whose intuition is wrong may set in motion certain dynamics that create the very situation the facilitator is trying to correct), (e) usually there is little basis for determining if the intuition is right or wrong, and (f) intuition represents an internal logic based on one's culture and frame of reference (intuitive judgments about another culture or another frame of reference can be very misleading). Experience in calibrating one's intuitive abilities is needed because one may find that one's intuition, like one's emotions, is sound on certain types of issues but misleading on others.

BECOMING A FACILITATOR

Being skilled in conducting inquiry and experiential learning activities does not mean that a person is qualified to conduct growth or therapy groups. A person interested in being a facilitator should answer four basic questions.

"Do I have adequate training in a social science?" A facilitator should have a background in an applied social science (such as social psychology) that emphasizes interpersonal relations and group dynamics. Ideally, one should have a basic knowledge of personality theory, psychopathology, group processes, and interpersonal dynamics. Ideally, the person should be connected with some organization, institution of higher education, or other agency that confirms his or her professional status.

"How much experience have I had as a participant and a facilitator in growth groups?" Lakin (1972) recommends that before a person can legitimately function as a facilitator, he or she should participate in a three-year training sequence somewhat like this:

1. Participate as a member in at least two growth groups.
2. Observe meetings of at least five growth groups and meet after the sessions with their facilitator to discuss the interactions of members and other relevant processes.
3. Co-lead five groups with experienced facilitators.
4. Lead five groups as the sole facilitator, but be observed and discuss with the observer one's functioning as a facilitator.
5. Undergo either psychotherapy or some equivalent sustained experiential self-study.
6. Be evaluated by well-qualified local facilitators who not only focus on your general fitness of character and your preparation, but also review with care evaluations others have made of you and their recommendations.
7. Keep up-to-date by periodically becoming involved in local seminars, supervision by more experienced professionals, and discussions of the ethics of the facilitator's role and function.

"What is my personal level of sensitivity, self-awareness, self-understanding, and self-actualization?" In addition to training, a person who wishes to be a facilitator should work to become self-aware, self-understanding, and sensitive to the needs of others. Maslow (1962) states that a need-deficient person tends to see others in terms of the ways in which they can be of use; the self-actualized person, who is freer and more disinterested, is able to see others as unique persons with their own problems who can be helped in various ways by various means.

"Am I certified by a professional organization?" There are many professional organizations that to some extent certify members as being competent as growth group facilitators. Most states license or certify practicing psychologists. A serious facilitator will take the time and trouble to become certified by a professional organization or licensed by his or her state.

GROWTH GROUPS AND PARTICIPANT ANXIETY

There has been concern that growth groups may create levels of anxiety that are potentially damaging psychologically. This concern has not been supported by evidence. To determine how anxious college students were before and after participating in a growth group, Johnson, Kavanagh, and Lubin (1973), in two separate studies, compared the anxiety level of participants in a growth group with their anxiety level before and after taking a final examination in a course in group dynamics. They found that participants' anxiety at the beginning of the growth group was less than that experienced before a final examination, and that participants' anxiety after the growth group was over was considerably less than that experienced after a final examination. Participating in a growth group, then, seems less stressful than taking course examinations.

COSTS OF GROWTH AND THERAPY GROUPS

Growth and therapy groups have costs as well as benefits. The groups usually require the commitment of considerable time and energy by their members. Members may be expected to become involved with people they might not ordinarily seek out. A small percentage of participants may have negative experiences or find the groups unhelpful. Thus, some group members may drop out because the group does not seem beneficial enough, and a few individuals may feel like casualties and withdraw because they feel significantly harmed by the group experience. Both dropouts and casualties tend to be rare if the facilitator is skilled.

COMPARATIVE EFFECTIVENESS

While groups are very powerful tools that can be used to promote considerable positive growth and change, there is little evidence to indicate that one type of group is more effective than another. In the classic study by Lieberman, Yalom, and Miles (1973), in which 206 students at Stanford University were randomly assigned to eighteen different types of growth and therapy groups, no one group approach was found to be superior to the others. Fuhriman and Burlingame (1994a), in a review of 700 group therapy studies and 7 meta-analyses of the research, concluded that group methods are quite effective but that no one method is more effective than others. McRoberts, Burlingame, and Hoag (1998), in a review of twenty-three studies, concluded that group psychotherapy was quite effective, but no more so than individual therapy. Bednar and Kaul (1994), however, concluded that group treatments were more effective than no treatment, placebo or nonspecific treatments, or other recognized psychological treatments. These research results are not definitive due to the methodological difficulties of comparing one treatment with another.

SUMMARY

Growth, therapy, and self-help groups are both a major trend and standard practice. They are significant health-promoting vehicles. Millions of Americans participate in groups aimed at personal growth, therapeutic change, or self-help. Growth, counseling, and self-help groups have similar overlapping goals of (a) decreasing self-defeating patterns of behavior and increasing self-enhancing ones, (b) increasing psychological health and decreasing psychological pathology, (c) increasing humanizing relationships, (d) increasing self-actualization, and (e) increasing interpersonal effectiveness. The types of growth groups include T-groups, encounter groups, human relations training groups, and structured growth groups. Counseling and therapy groups include psychoanalytic groups, Adlerian groups, psychodrama groups, Gestalt groups, cognitive-behavioral groups, person-centered groups, existential groups, rational-emotive groups, reality groups, and interpersonal therapy groups. There are an enormous number of self-help groups.

The greater number of relationships available in the group provides richness and potential for learning, growth, change, and healing not possible in a dyad or a solitary situation. The unique capacities of groups include (a) providing a supportive community within which to change, (b) increasing hope and decreasing demoralization, (c) creating a microcosm of the real world, (d) inducing and reducing powerful feelings, (e) increasing perspective-taking and decreasing egocentrism, (f) providing multiple sources of feedback, (g) providing multiple sources of social comparison, (h) providing multiple sources of vicarious learning, (i) requiring the use of a wide variety of social skills, (j) powerfully influencing behavioral and attitudinal patterns, (k) providing opportunities for helping others, (l) providing resources for self-insight, and (m) increasing cognitive learning.

One important influence on personal change is the experiencing and expression of positive and negative emotions toward the actions of other group members and about important life events. Both experiencing and expressing emotions can have therapeutic effects. Disclosing emotional experiences can decrease a sense of uniqueness and instill hope that one's problems can be solved. Expressing strong emotions can be cathartic. Observing other group members express their emotions can be beneficial. When emotions

are disclosed by more experienced group mem
sult. Finally, emotional self-disclosure often p
  While participation in a growth, therapy,
health-producing experiences, a skilled grou
While there is evidence that all sorts of gro
one approach seems to be more effective t

13

Team Development, Team Training

Basic Concepts to Be Covered in This Chapter

In this chapter a number of concepts are defined and discussed. The major ones are listed following. Divide into pairs. Each pair is to (a) define each concept, noting the page on which it is defined and discussed, and (b) ensure that both members of the pair understand the meaning of each concept. Then combine into groups of four. Compare the answers of the two pairs. If there is disagreement, the members look up the concept in the chapter and clarify it until all members agree on and understand the definition.

Concepts

1. High-performance organizational structure	4. Pareto chart
2. Mass-production organizational structure	5. Team
	6. Team building
3. Organizational development	7. Team training
	8. Total quality management

INTRODUCTION

The Killer Bees is a boys' high school basketball team from Bridgehampton, New York (a small, middle-class town on Long Island). Bridgehampton High School's total enrollment has declined since 1985 from sixty-seven to forty-one, with fewer than twenty boys attending the school. There have never been more than seven players on the team. Yet, since 1980 the Killer Bees have amassed a record of 164 wins and 32 losses, qualified for the state championship playoffs six times, won the state championship twice, and finished in the final four two other times. None of their players was ever really a standout. Not one of the Killer Bees went on to the pros, and the team was never tall. Although every Killer Bee graduated and most went on to college, few had the talent to play ball in college. To win against bigger, supposedly more talented opponents, the Killer Bees had to be the ultimate in versatility, flexibility, and speed. Their game was team basketball.

How did the Killer Bees become so successful with so few players and so little talent? There were a number of factors. The *first* is that they had a richness and depth of purpose that eludes most teams. Their mission was more than winning basketball games. They were committed to (a) bringing honor and recognition to their community, (b) protecting and enhancing their legacy, and (c) one another. *Second*, the community backed the team. Fathers, brothers, and cousins had played on earlier teams, and mothers, sisters, and aunts cheered the team on relentlessly. *Third*, being a member of the Killer Bees was its own reward. No college scholarships awaited the players. The pros were not interested. No high-paying jobs were waiting. All the reward came from membership in a unique, inspiring, high-performance team. What resulted was team members adopting an incredible work ethic and a focus on skill development (starting in

543

preschool, they practiced 365 days a year), and a focus on playing as part of a team, not as individuals.

Teams such as the Killer Bees have been defined as a small group of people so committed to something larger than themselves that they will not be denied (Katzenbach & Smith, 1993). It is the potential for such performances that makes teams the key to successful organizations.

Teams typically exist within an organizational context. In organizations, many different types of teams are used. To improve organizational performance, the performance of each team must improve. There are three major ways of doing so: (1) carefully forming, structuring, and nurturing teams; (2) using teams to train organizational members; and (3) implementing team-building programs. To ensure that teams continuously improve the quality of their work, team members must know how to assess their performance and must implement total quality management.

WHAT IS A TEAM?

Productivity through people.

Singapore management philosophy

To use teams and be a team member, you need to know what is and is not a team. Placing people in the same room and calling them a team does not make them one. Aggregates are not groups. To use teams effectively, you first have to know what is and is not a group (see Chapter 1). To be a team, you first have to be a group. In many cases the concepts *small group* and *team* are used interchangeably in the group dynamics literature, even within the same research study. But not all groups are teams. Teams are just one type of small group. You must know what groups are teams and what groups are not teams. A team is *not* just a number of people working together. Committees, task forces, departments, and councils are groups, but they are not necessarily teams. Groups do not become teams simply because that is what someone calls them. No matter how often it is called one, the entire membership of any large and complex organization is *never* a team.

A **team** is a set of interpersonal interactions structured to achieve established goals. More specifically, a team consists of two or more individuals who (a) are aware of their positive interdependence as they strive to achieve mutual goals, (b) interact while they do so, (c) are aware of who is and is not a member of the team, (d) have specific roles or functions to perform, and (e) have a limited life span of membership. Teams can be placed along a continuum according to the amount of collaboration (integration and role differentiation) required (Dyer, 1987). At one end of the continuum are teams such as golf teams, that are composed of a set of individual performers whose individual efforts are combined into a team score. At the other end are teams such as football teams, where division of effort is meshed into a single coordinated result and where the whole is more than and different from the sum of its parts.

In a field study conducted on actual ongoing work teams, Katzenbach and Smith (1993) distinguished between teams and other forms of working groups in organizations (Table 13.1). They interviewed hundreds of people in more than fifty different teams in thirty different companies to discover what differentiates various levels of team performance, where and how teams work best, and how to enhance the effectiveness of teams. In a *working group* interdependence is low and accountability focuses on individual members, not on the group as a whole. The product of a working group is the sum of all the work produced by its members. Members do not take responsibility for results other than their own. Members do not engage in tasks that require the combined work of two or more members. In meetings, members share information and make decisions that help each person do his or her job better, but the focus is always on individual performance.

Table 13.1 **Working Groups versus Teams**

Working Groups	**Teams**
A strong, clearly focused leader is appointed.	Shared leadership responsibilities exist among members.
The general organizational mission is the group's purpose.	A specific, well-defined purpose exists that is unique to the team.
Individual work provides the only products.	Team and individual work develop products.
Effectiveness is measured indirectly by the group's influence on others (e.g., financial performance of business, student scores on a standardized examination).	Effectiveness is measured directly by assessing team work products.
Individual accountability alone is evident.	Both team and individual accountability are evident.
Individual accomplishments are recognized and rewarded.	Team celebration occurs. Individual efforts that contribute to the team's success are also recognized and celebrated.
Meetings are efficiently run and last for short periods of time.	Meetings have open-ended discussions that include active problem solving.
In meetings members discuss, decide, and delegate.	In meetings members discuss, decide, and perform real work together.

A *team*, on the other hand, is more than the sum of its parts (Katzenbach & Smith, 1993). A team's performance includes team work products that require the joint efforts of two or more members as well as individual work products. Teams not only meet to share information and perspectives and make decisions, they produce discrete work products through members' joint efforts and contributions. The focus is primarily on team accountability. Team members hold themselves and each other accountable for doing high-quality work. Katzenbach and Smith (1993) emphasize that for a real team to exist, there must be a compelling team purpose that is distinctive and specific to the small group and that requires its members to roll up their sleeves and accomplish something beyond individual end products.

TYPES OF TEAMS

Teams may be classified in an infinite number of ways. Three of the most common are discussed here. One way to classify teams is by the setting in which they are used. Teams are primarily found within work, sports, and learning situations. A *work team* is a set of interpersonal interactions structured to (a) maximize members' proficiency and success in doing their jobs and (b) coordinate and integrate each member's efforts with those of the other team members. A *sports team* is a set of interpersonal interactions structured to (a) maximize members' athletic performance and (b) coordinate and integrate each member's efforts with those of the other team members. A *learning team* is a set of interpersonal interactions among peers of equal status structured to (a) maximize each member's acquisition of knowledge and skills and (b) coordinate and integrate each member's efforts with those of the other team members.

A second way to classify teams is by how they may be used in an organization. Three of the most common uses are as follows:

1. *Problem-solving teams* are teams consisting of five to twelve volunteers, hourly and salaried, drawn from different areas of a department. Problem-solving teams meet one to two hours a week to discuss ways of improving quality, efficiency, and the work environment. They are off-line discussion groups that have no power to reorganize work or enlarge the role of workers in the production process. Problem-solving teams have been found to reduce costs and improve product quality, but to have little effect on how work is organized or how managers behave. Consequently, they have tended to fade away. They were first implemented on a small scale in the 1920s and 1930s and, based on Japanese quality circles, were adopted more widely in the late 1970s.

2. *Special-purpose teams* are teams whose duties include such things as designing and introducing work reforms and new technology, meeting with suppliers and customers, and linking separate functions. In organizations that have unions, special-purpose teams have been used to facilitate collaboration between labor and management on operational decisions at all levels. Special-purpose teams involve work in decisions at ever higher levels, creating an atmosphere for quality and productivity improvements. The teams create a foundation for self-managing work teams. Special-purpose teams

were implemented in the 1980s as the next step after problem-solving teams. They are still spreading, especially in companies with unions.

3. *Self-managing teams* are teams of five to fifteen employees who produce an entire product or provide an entire service. Team members learn all tasks and rotate from job to job. The teams take over managerial duties, including work and vacation scheduling, the ordering of supplies and materials, and the hiring of new members. Self-managing teams can increase productivity 30% or more and substantially raise quality. They fundamentally change the way work is organized, giving employees control over their jobs, wiping out tiers of managers, and tearing down bureaucratic barriers between departments. A flatter organization results. Self-managing teams were used by a few companies in the 1960s and 1970s and rapidly spread in the mid- to late 1980s. They appear to be the wave of the future.

Another view classifies teams in three ways (Katzenbach & Smith, 1993): teams that recommend things, teams that make or do things, and teams that run things.

1. *Teams that recommend things* include task forces, project groups, and audit, quality, or safety groups asked to study and solve particular problems (Katzenbach & Smith, 1993). Teams that recommend things almost always have predetermined completion dates. Their two most critical issues tend to be (a) getting off to a fast and constructive start and (b) giving their recommendations to the people who have to implement them in an effective way. Not inducing commitment in the implementers is almost always the problem that stymies teams that recommend things. Involving the implementers in the process early and often is an effective strategy. Such involvement may take many forms, including participating in interviews, helping with analyses, contributing and critiquing ideas, and conducting experiments and trials. At a minimum, anyone responsible for implementation should receive a briefing on the task force's purpose, approach, and objectives at the beginning of the effort. They should also receive regular reviews of the team's progress.

2. *Teams that make or do things* need to have a relentless focus on performance (Katzenbach & Smith, 1993). In deciding where team performance might have the greatest impact, top management should concentrate on the organization's critical delivery points, that is, places in the organization where the cost and value of the company's products and services are most directly determined.

3. *Teams that run things* tend to be rare, especially in large, complex organizations. Despite the fact that many leaders refer to the group reporting to them as a team, few groups of executives really are. Teams at the top are the most difficult to create, but at the same time they are the most powerful when they work well. Often teams at the top are not needed; working groups are adequate for the performance challenge at hand and present fewer risks. At this level, trust is low and destructive conflict tends to be high. Work groups may be less risky and easier to manage. In addition, teams that run things often find it difficult to formulate a purpose that is distinctive and specific to the team as opposed to the total organizational mission. The organizational mission and the purpose of the team at the top should not be confused. When there are real teams at the top, they tend to be small and informal, mostly having two or three members.

Electronically Linked Teams

Sometimes teams are formed that cannot meet face-to-face. Through the use of modern electronic methods (such as e-mail, bulletin boards, and computer conferences), teams can be created whose members are widely separated geographically. In an electronically networked team, members can be anywhere in the world. Meetings require only that members be at their terminals. Communication between meetings can be asynchronous and extremely fast in comparison with telephone conversations and interoffice mail. Participation is more equalized and less affected by prestige and status (McGuire, Kiesler, & Siegel, 1987; Siegel, Dubrovsky, Kiesler, & McGuire, 1986). Electronic communication, however, relies almost entirely on plain text for conveying messages, text that is often ephemeral, appearing on and disappearing from a screen without any necessary tangible artifacts. It becomes easy for a sender to be out of touch with his or her audience. It is easy for the sender to be less constrained by conventional norms and rules for behavior in composing messages. Communicators can have a greater sense of anonymity, detect less individuality in others, feel less empathy, feel less guilt, be less concerned over how they compare with others, and be less influenced by social conventions (Kiesler, Siegel, & McGuire, 1984; Short, Williams, & Christie, 1976). Such influences can lead to both more honesty and more "flaming" (name-calling and epithets).

Although electronic communication has many positive features, face-to-face communication has a richness that electronic communication may never match. Mehrabian (1971) believed that 93% of people's intent was conveyed by tone of voice and facial expression. Harold Geneen, the former head of ITT, believed that his response to requests was different in face-to-face interactions than through teletype. "In New York, I might read a request and say no. But in Europe, I could see that an answer to the same question might be yes . . . it became our policy to deal with problems on the spot, face-to-face" (cited in Trevino, Lengel, & Draft, 1987). For this and other reasons (such as lack of effective groupware), teams may be most effective when they use face-to-face rather than electronic interaction. Teams at one site, furthermore, may be electronically linked with other teams at other sites.

The organizational context has profound influences on the success of the team and the actions of team members.

ORGANIZATIONAL CONTEXT

Most teams exist within an organizational context. W. Edwards Deming, J. Juran, and others have stated that over 85% of the behavior of members of an organization is directly attributable to the organization's structure, not the nature of the individuals involved (Walton, 1985). The organizational context in which teams work shapes the behavior of team members by presenting opportunities and constraints. One organizational context, for example, may offer members the opportunity to be included on a number of teams, whereas another organizational context may constrain members from interacting with anyone else. There are basically two organizational contexts—a mass-production organizational structure and a team-based, high-performance organizational structure (Johnson & Johnson, 1989). The **mass-production organizational structure** is designed to drive down the unit costs of long runs of standardized products. In a mass-production organization, an authority hierarchy is rigidly imposed and work is divided into small component parts performed by individuals who work separately from and in competition with other members. The **team-based, high-performance organizational structure** is designed to promote teams that focus on continuous improvement in quality. Organizations may be easily conceptualized as a hierarchy of work teams or "families" that are tied together by linking individuals who are leaders in one team but peer-group members at the next highest organizational level (Figure 13.1). These individuals are known as *linking pins* (Likert, 1961). Unlike many other organizational theories, Likert's model emphasizes group concepts such as group goals, leadership, and group responsibility rather than individual concepts such as personal motivation and responsibility. Small groups of motivated individuals are the secret to organizational productivity.

Two important aspects of the organizational context are the degree of interdependence structured among members and social support. The greater the interdependence among organization members, the more positive the relations among divisions, departments, teams, and individuals in an organization (Brett & Rognes, 1986). The greater the social support in an organization, the higher performing the teams (Baldwin & Ford, 1988; Sundstrom, Perkins, George, Futrell, & Hoffman, 1990).

Although there is general agreement that organizational contexts greatly influence the behaviors of individuals and groups, there are few research studies that articulate how contextual influences operate. One study that attempted to do so focused on the collision of a Pan Am 747 and a KLM 747 on the ground at Tenerife Airport that killed 583 people (Weick, 1990). Weick's analysis of the Tenerife air disaster emphasized contextual factors for cockpit and air-traffic-control crews that interrupted their routines and created such stress that the crews (a) fell back on their most familiar and well-rehearsed response routines and (b) acted as individuals rather than as a team. The high level of stress caused diminished cognitive information-processing capabilities, leading to the "omission of important cues for task performance and an increase in cognitive inefficiency" (Weick, 1990, p. 578). As a result, the flight and air-traffic-control crews made the wrong responses, leading to the deadly crash. Weick suggests that a major contributor to the wrong response patterns was that under a high level of stress, crew members acted as individuals, ignoring the need to coordinate their actions with fellow team members.

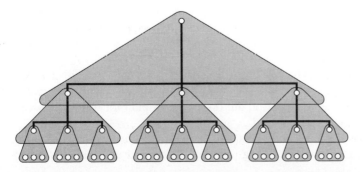

Figure 13.1 The linking-pin model of organizational structure.

Organizational Development

Our people's hard work is our most important resource.

Japanese management philosophy

Organizational contexts are not static; they develop and change. Sometimes the changes are planned. **Organizational development** is the use of diagnosis and intervention procedures to promote effective interpersonal, group, and intergroup behavior within the organization. **Organizational effectiveness** is the extent to which the organization achieves its goals with the use of minimal resources. In doing so the organization has to achieve its goals, maintain effective cooperation among members, and adapt to the external environment. Organizational effectiveness depends on members (a) having the *interpersonal and small group skills* and *personal attitudes* (i.e., commitment to the team and the organization, caring about colleagues, and caring about reliability and the quality of one's work) and *technical competencies* needed to be effective contributors to the organization and (b) committing high levels of *psychological energy* to their work. The commitment of psychological energy and the use of teamwork and taskwork competencies may be encouraged by both the organizational structure and the organizational culture.

Typically referred to as simply *OD*, organizational development utilizes the action research methodology pioneered by Kurt Lewin to improve the effectiveness of organizations. First, the vision and goals of the organization are clarified and their cooperative nature is emphasized. Second, the action research methodology is implemented through the following steps:

1. *Diagnosis.* Diagnosis involves three steps:

   a. *Building a normative theory* of how the team or organization should be functioning. Normative theories focus on such factors as cooperation, communication, leadership, decision making, and conflict resolution. Each chapter of this book presents such theories. Without knowledge of what effective leadership consists of, for example, a diagnosis of how effective the leadership of a group or organization is cannot take place.

   b. *Measuring current team or organizational functioning* by collecting data through interviews, observations, and questionnaires and by diagnostic group sessions.

   c. *Analyzing and organizing the data* so that discrepancies between observed and ideal performance and the causes for the discrepancies can be identified.

2. *Feedback.* The data are reported to those organizational members from whom the data were obtained to highlight the discrepancies between the ideal and actual functioning (i.e., problems) of various teams, work groups, departments, and the organization as a whole.

3. *Discussion and planning.* The problems identified by the data are analyzed, and the implications for improving the effectiveness of the relevant work groups and departments within the organization are discussed. A plan for improving organizational effectiveness is developed.

4. *Action.* The plan is implemented. Structural supports for the new behaviors and procedures are generated by changing role definitions and group norms. Inter-

ventions can be made on the individual (skill training or attitude change), group (modifying group structure and procedures), or intergroup (intergroup problem solving) levels.

5. *Rediagnosis.* New data are collected to determine if the plan (a) was implemented and (b) solved the problem. If not, the cycle is repeated.

This process should become continuous and ongoing within most teams and organizations.

EXERCISE

13.1 *Team Structure*

Task: Below are three ways of organizing a team. Describe the way team members would interact within each structure and predict the resulting productivity, morale, social support, and professional self-esteem.

Cooperative: One answer from the three of you, everyone must agree, and everyone must be able to explain.

Individual Accountability: One member of your group will be chosen randomly to explain the group's answers.

Expected Behaviors: Everyone participates.

Criterion for Success: Thoughtful answers that have a clear supporting rationale spelled out in detail.

SITUATION 1: MERIT PAY FOR THE BEST TEAM MEMBER

Your organization has decided to implement a competitive merit-pay system for employees. One hundred merit points are given to each team within the organization. You, the manager, are told to rank the team members from best to worst in job performance and divide the bonus points among the team members accordingly. A team member could receive all one hundred points or no points, depending on how his or her job performance is rated for that year. The more merit points given to one team member, the fewer available for the other team members.

To implement this system, criteria on which the team members are to be evaluated have to be determined. On the basis of the selected criteria, team members are ranked from most successful to least successful. The most outstanding member of the team receives fifty merit points, the first runner-up receives thirty points, and the second runner-up receives twenty points. The rest of the team members receive no merit points.

SITUATION 2: MERIT PAY FOR OUTSTANDING INDIVIDUAL EFFORTS

Your organization has decided to implement an individualistic merit-pay program for employees. You, the manager, are told to determine how many merit points each of your team members should receive. You decide to reward team members on the basis of how successful they have been this year. All team members who have demonstrated success will receive a merit bonus.

To implement this system, you set criteria for excellent, good, average, poor, and terrible performance. You evaluate the success of each team member. All excellent members are given twenty merit points, good members are given ten merit points, average members are given five merit points, poor members are given one merit point, and terrible members are given no merit points.

SITUATION 3: MERIT PAY FOR OUTSTANDING GROUP EFFORTS

Your organization decides to implement a cooperative merit-pay program for employees. You, the manager, are told to determine how many merit points each of your team members should receive on the basis of how successful their team has been.

To implement the program, you organize all subordinates into teams. You then set criteria for excellent, good, average, poor, and terrible team performance. You evaluate the success of each team. Each member of the excellent teams is given twenty merit points, members of good teams are given ten merit points, members of average teams are given five merit points, members of poor teams are given one merit point, and members of terrible teams are given no merit points.

EXERCISE

13.2 *The Cooperative Team Scenario*

A responsibility of team leaders and members is to provide a vision of what the team will be like when the desired changes have been implemented. This vision must be clear and precise.

1. Working individually, write:
   a. Your personal vision of what you hope the team will be.
   b. Your perception of the team's mission.
   c. The immediate goals your team is working to achieve.
   d. The unique talents, skills, competencies, and perspectives you bring to the team's work.
2. Form a triad. Working cooperatively, share your views of the team's mission and goals and come to a consensus as to what the mission and goals of the team should be.
3. In your triad:
   a. Write a detailed, behaviorally oriented scenario that describes what you would expect to see, hear, and feel if most team members acted cooperatively most of the time. Include how interaction and relationships among team members would be affected. This description should be a personalized, realistic, and attainable description of what you are committed to achieving.
   b. It may be helpful to describe the team's *mission,* specify the *environmental demands* on your team, describe the current *response* to these demands, and then describe how cooperative efforts by team members will *contribute* to achieving the team's mission and responding to the current and future demands on your team.
   c. This is a *cooperative* effort. Form a group of three and write one description from the three of you. Everyone must contribute to the description, agree with it, and be able to explain it. Each will need his or her own copy of the scenario. Each will be *individually accountable* to present the group's scenario to another person. Plan how to do so effectively.

EXERCISE

13.3 *Degree of Interdependence*

Task: Decide which team analogy best describes your team and why.
Cooperative: Form groups of three. Agree on one answer and rationale. Everyone must agree, and everyone must be able to explain the group's answer and reasoning.
Individual Accountability: One member of your triad will be selected randomly to present the group's answer and rationale.

Criterion for Success: A reasoned answer backed up by examples and information.
Expected Behaviors: Everyone participates and contributes ideas, analyses, and examples.

TEAMS

1. **Golf Team:** Members all function independently of each other, working to achieve as high an individual score as possible, so that when individual scores are combined into team scores, their team wins.
2. **Baseball Team:** Members are relatively independent of one another and, although all members are required to be on the field together, they virtually never interact all at the same time.
3. **Football Team:** Members are divided into three subteams—offense, defense, and special teams. When the subteam is on the field, every player is involved in every play, but each has a set of specialized skills required by his or her individual position. The teamwork required is centered in the subteam, not the total team.
4. **Basketball Team:** All members play on the team as a whole. Every player is involved in all aspects of the game, offense and defense, and all must pass, run, guard, and shoot. When a substitute comes in, all must play with the new person. True teamwork is like a basketball team where division of effort is meshed into a single coordinated result—where the whole is more than, and different from, the sum of the individual parts.

13.4 *Roman Army*

THE REORGANIZATION OF THE ROMAN ARMY

As a popular and successful general, Caius Marius had been elected consul of the Roman republic five times. In 102 B.C., at the height of his popularity, he reorganized the Roman army—a reform that had been needed for about 50 years. The structural reorganization was relatively simple. The Roman legion consisted of about 6,000 men. Marius divided them into 60 centuries (100 men), each under a centurion. He grouped each century into 10 cohorts, and he had the heads of the cohorts report directly to the general of the legion. This division made the army more efficient, but the real organization was based on changes in society.

Before the reorganization, the army was based on the draft, and under the Roman constitution the draft applied only to citizens who owned a certain amount of property. But over time, the rich landowners, merchants, and others who were eligible no longer had either the aptitude or the taste for military service. The draft was kept, but Marius allowed the poor and unemployed to volunteer. Soon the reluctant farmers and merchants disappeared from the army. The volunteers were those who saw service under a successful general as a prospect for adventure or escape from poverty.

Then the army began to supply equipment for the soldiers instead of having each individual furnish his own. This meant fewer distinctions based on wealth and ensured that both equipment and training were more standardized.

The bulk of the volunteers were farm laborers or small farmers so heavily in debt that they were in danger of losing their farms. In addition to the prospect of prizes from a successful campaign, a general in search of recruits could promise that, if the army were disbanded, the soldiers would be given an allotment of land. Thus, the new Roman army gave more prominence to generals with established reputations whose names would bring in recruits.

The common soldier began to shift allegiance from the republic or the senate to the general. The senate might back down or delay on promises, but the soldiers could count on their generals to fight political battles for them. This made it almost impossible for one general to take an army from another or to remove another general from command.

Thus, the army fell more and more under the control of the generals. In turn, the generals became servants of their own armies. They could not retire from public life if their own army were disbanded, because they had to fulfill the promises by which they had obtained volunteers.

Although the Roman soldier respected the constitution, the armies would not hesitate to support their generals against the government if the generals had good reason for attacking it. In 51 B.C., approximately fifty years later, Julius Caesar and Pompeius Magnus (Pompey) began a political struggle. In 50 B.C. Pompey violated the constitution, and Caesar's soldiers enthusiastically followed him. Caesar crossed the Rubicon and invaded Italy, and the civil war began. It ended in 44 B.C., with Caesar being voted a perpetual dictator. This was the beginning of the downfall of the Roman republic.*

Source: Edgar F. Huse, *The modern manager* (St. Paul, MN: West Publishing, 1979), pp. 58–59, as adapted from G. Ferrero, *The greatness and decline of Rome* (London: Heinemann, 1909), and F. Marsh, *A history of the Roman world* (New York: Barnes & Noble, 1963).

QUESTIONS

1. Draw an organization chart based on the reorganized Roman army described in this case.
2. What social changes were particularly instrumental in changing the Roman army? How did socioeconomic conditions play a role in these changes?
3. Given hindsight, could the army have been reorganized differently and, perhaps, more effectively?
4. What does this case say about interactions between organizations and their environments?

BUILDING PRODUCTIVE TEAMS

The Plains Indian people, known to whites as the Cheyenne, Crow, and Sioux, are truly the Painted Arrow, the Little Black Eagle, and the Brother People. They follow the *Medicine Wheel Way* (Storm, 1972). Each of the stones within the Medicine Wheel represents one of the many things of the universe. All things are organized within the Medicine Wheel, and all things are equal within it. All things within the Medicine Wheel know of their harmony with every other thing, except for humans. Finding harmony involves recognizing the uniqueness of each person and his or her unity within the Medicine Wheel.

The Medicine Wheel Way states that each person is unique in all ways but one. There is only one thing that all people possess equally, and that is loneliness. The only way we can overcome our loneliness is through touching others. The Medicine Wheel Way begins with touching others. Touching others means to be to each other a gift, as is the buffalo. Touching others means nourishing each other so that all may grow. Through touching others we find our place within the universe and are in harmony with all other things within the universe. We touch others by joining a team and seeing the unity of all members. We are all separate and unique individuals. We are all part of a larger harmony working with each other.

The Plains Indians are not the only ones who believe in unique individuals seeking harmony within a team. Personal productivity in most cases cannot take place without team productivity. A person cannot stand alone. He or she needs a team. Each person needs to be:

1. A unique and valued individual success in his or her own right.
2. Part of a successful (and great) team effort.

The combination of unique individuals who combine into a team fuels productivity. Team productivity depends on ensuring that a clear cooperative structure underlies team efforts and teaching team members the group skills (discussed in this book) they need to be contributing members. In other words, this whole book is about building productive teams. Clear cooperative goals, effective communication, good leadership, effective decision making, constructive conflict management, and positive use of power are all essential (refer back to Figure 1.4 on page 36).

It takes a team to get extraordinary things done. The productivity of teams is not a simple function of team members' technical competencies and task abilities. Productivity is not guaranteed simply by team members being interested in attaining the team's goals. It takes more than just placing several people in the same room and telling them to work together to create a team effort. Successful team performance requires careful structuring of cooperation among team members.

Using a sales team as an example, there are three ways that relationships among team members may be structured. *First*, members of the sales team can *compete* with each other to see who is best. They could be ranked from highest to lowest in terms of sales for the month and be given bonuses accordingly. The person who sells the most, for example, would receive a bonus of $500, the second-best salesperson $300, and the third-best salesperson $100. The rest receive no bonus. When a sales staff competes, they will work against each other to be the best. Because helping a competitor reduces one's own chances of winning, the salespersons will be tempted to hide potential customers from colleagues. A salesperson who has more promising leads than he or she can personally follow up on in the near future, for example, will be motivated to hide that information from colleagues in order to lower their sales and thereby increase his or her own chances of being the top salesperson. The more one person sells, the less likely it is that others will receive a bonus.

Second, members of the sales team can work *individually* to achieve up to a preset level. In this case, each salesperson will be striving to meet a personal sales quota. A salesperson will receive $500 for selling over $5,000 of products, $300 for selling over $3,000 of products, and $100 for selling $1,000 of products. Everyone can succeed or everyone can fail, and the efforts of the salespeople are independent. The number of sales one person makes has no positive or negative influence on the success of others.

Third, team members can work *cooperatively* to maximize the productivity of the team. Team members each receive a $500 bonus if the total sales of all members reach $50,000, a $300 bonus if their total sales reach $30,000, and a $100 bonus if their total sales reach $10,000. When a sales team works cooperatively, members combine their efforts to maximize the sales of all members. Success depends not only on how many sales one member makes but also on the sales of all other members. The more successful one's teammates, the more successful one is. A salesperson who has more promising leads than he or she can personally follow up on in the near future, for example, will be motivated to share that information with colleagues in order to increase their sales and thereby increase the overall performance of the team.

Teams structured cooperatively will be more productive than teams structured competitively or individualistically. As was discussed in Chapter 3, the more cooperative the team, the greater the productivity, the more committed team members are to each other, and the greater are members' social competencies. The positive results derived from cooperative efforts, however, do not happen automatically. The careful structuring of five essential components (positive interdependence, face-to-face interaction, individual accountability, interpersonal and small group skills, and group processing) is required (Johnson & Johnson, 1989).

If high-quality products and services are to be created, organizations are well advised to use teams. Teams are the basic unit of performance for most organizations. In order to understand the essential role of teams in modern organizations, six issues must be discussed. The *first* is the evidence concerning the effectiveness of teams. The *second* is forming, structuring, and nurturing teams so that they are effective. The *third* is the importance of using teams to train team members in the skills and procedures they need to do their job (taskwork skills) and the skills and procedures they need to coordinate their efforts with other team members (teamwork skills). The *fourth* is the possibility of providing team-building experiences to increase the team's effectiveness. *Fifth*, the ways in which teams may measure their effectiveness are outlined. *Finally*, the point of carefully structuring teams, training team members, and building team effectiveness is to deliver high-quality products and services to customers.

RESEARCH ON TEAM EFFECTIVENESS

There are hundreds of studies on team effectiveness. Several meta-analyses have been conducted to summarize what we know from all this research. Johnson and Johnson (1992b) conducted a meta-analysis on the effectiveness of teams (compared to individuals working competitively or individualistically) for adults (individuals eighteen years of age and older). The studies were divided into those using individual productivity as the measure of success and those using team productivity as the measure of success. Over 120 studies were found that compared team versus individual work on individual productivity. Overall, working in teams resulted in higher individual productivity than did working competitively or individualistically (effect sizes of 0.54 and 0.51, respectively). These results held true for verbal, mathematical, and procedural tasks. Over fifty-seven studies compared team and individual work on team productivity. Overall, working in teams resulted in higher team productivity than did having team members work competitively or individualistically (effect sizes of 0.63 and 0.94, respectively). These results also held true for verbal, mathematical, and procedural tasks. Working in teams was also found to promote more positive relationships and social support among members as well as greater psychological health, self-esteem, and social competencies.

Freeberg and Rock (1987) conducted a meta-analysis on 117 studies of team performance. To be included, the study had to measure team performance as a single entity (rather than the individual performances of team members). An overall mean effect size of 0.42 (sd = 0.43, range = – 0.48 to – 0.99) was found. Almost all the studies were conducted in a laboratory, used college students as subjects, and used very small groups (two to four members), and 50% of the studies were unpublished. More important influences on team productivity were prior experience doing the task, practice, complexity of the task, the way the task was structured, task load, amount of interaction among team members, degree of coordination among team members, and amount of cooperation among team members. Cooperation was an especially important influence on team productivity, both in its direct effects and through mediating processes (such as coordination and cohesion). Team variables were found to be more powerful influences on team productivity than were individual characteristics of members, such as their ability to do the task.

Zhining Qin (Qin, Johnson, & Johnson, 1995) identified sixty-three studies conducted between 1929 and 1989 examining the relative success of cooperative and competitive efforts on individual problem solving. She found that members of cooperative teams outperformed individuals who worked competitively on linguistic, non-linguistic, well-defined, and ill-defined problems.

The productivity of teams, however, is not a simple function of team members' technical competencies and task abilities. To be productive, teams (like all groups) must ensure that members perceive strong positive interdependence, interact in ways that promote each other's success and well-being, be individually accountable, employ their small team skills, and process how effectively the team has been working.

Because teams are effective, they must be formed, structured, and nurtured. Nurturing teams includes training and retraining members as well as engaging in team-building procedures to ensure that their effectiveness keeps improving.

FORMING, STRUCTURING, AND NURTURING TEAMS

The strength of the wolf is in the pack.

Rudyard Kipling

Teams and performance go hand in hand. Motorola relied heavily on teams to produce the world's lightest, smallest, and highest-quality cellular phones with only a few hundred parts versus over a thousand for the competition. Ford relied heavily on teams to produce its Taurus model. General Motors relied heavily on teams to produce its Saturn model. At 3M teams are critical to meeting the company's goal of producing half of each year's revenues from product innovations created in the prior five years. General Electric has made self-managing teams a centerpiece of its new organizational approach. Modern tasks often impose greater mental and physical demands than one person can satisfy in isolation or that working groups can meet from the piecemeal efforts of semi-isolated members. It takes a team effort to be successful in completing demanding and dynamic tasks. *There is, however, a basic discipline that makes teams work.* The role of top management includes the ability to recognize a team's unique potential to deliver results, deploy teams when they are the best tool for the job, and foster the basic discipline that teams need to be effective. There are at least three issues to consider in *forming teams.*

1. *Keep the size of teams small.* The larger the group, (a) the smaller the percentage of individuals contributing to its efforts and (b) the more anonymous members feel, which often leads to less task involvement and less sense of responsibility for the team's success. Virtually all effective teams found by Katzenbach and Smith (1993) ranged between two and twenty-five people. The majority of the effective teams had fewer than ten members. Small size is a pragmatic guide (but not an absolute necessity) for success. Large numbers of people have trouble interacting constructively as a group. Doing real work together is even more difficult. Ten people are far more likely than fifty to work through their differences and develop a common set of goals that are specific enough for members to hold themselves jointly accountable for the results. Large groups confront more complex constraints on sharing the viewpoints needed to build a team. They face difficult logistical issues, such as finding the physical space and time to meet.

2. *Select team members on the basis of their (a) expertise and skills and (b) potential for developing new expertise and skills, not on the basis of their position or personality.* No team succeeds without all the expertise and skills needed to meet its purpose and performance goals. As obvious as this sounds, it is a common failing in potential teams. Usually, teams are heterogeneous, with members who have expertise in different areas. Skill requirements fall into two categories: taskwork skills and teamwork skills. Selecting members with the right mix of skills is not easy. Most teams figure out the skills they will need after they are formed. When team members are chosen for their current skills, the right mix may not be present because it is difficult to know in advance what skills the team will require to achieve its mission. Members' potential for improving existing skills and developing new ones, therefore, should also be considered.

3. *Bring together the resources the team will need to function, such as space, materials, information, time lines, support personnel, and so forth.* Careful planning and preparation are needed to form a team.

Once a team has been formed, it must be *structured* and *nurtured.* Procedures for doing so include the following.

1. *Present the team with its mission, structure positive interdependence among team members, and engage in the process of redefining the mission into goals specific to the team.* Successful teams need a compelling purpose and must know that members sink or swim together. They must operationalize their goals in terms of measurable tasks. Through this process members become committed to the team and gain ownership of its goals. Team members need to believe that the team has urgent and worthwhile purposes. The more urgent and meaningful the rationale, the more likely it is that the team will live up to its performance potential.

2. *Have frequent and regular meetings that provide opportunities for team members to interact face-to-face and promote each other's success.* Team members must spend a lot of time together, scheduled and unscheduled, especially in the beginning. Creative insights as well as personal bonding require impromptu and casual interactions as much as analyzing spreadsheets and interviewing customers. Katzenbach and Smith (1993) found that successful teams gave themselves the time to learn to be a team. This time need not always be spent together physically; electronic, fax, and phone time can also count as time spent together.

3. *Pay particular attention to first meetings.* Initial impressions always mean a great deal (Katzenbach & Smith, 1993). When the team first gathers, members monitor the signals given by teammates to confirm, suspend, or dispel assumptions and concerns. They pay particular attention to those in authority, such as the team leader and any executives who set up, oversee, or otherwise influence the team. What such leaders do is more important than what they say. If the senior executive leaves the team kickoff to take a phone call ten minutes after the session has begun and never returns, the members get the message.

4. *Establish clear rules of conduct.* All effective teams develop rules of conduct at the outset to help them achieve their purpose and performance goals (Katzenbach & Smith, 1993). The most critical initial rules pertain to (a) attendance (no interruptions to take phone calls), (b) discussion (no sacred cows), (c) confidentiality (the only things to leave this room are what we agree on), (d) analytic approach (facts are friendly), (e) end-product orientation (everyone gets assignments and does them), (f) constructive confrontation (no finger pointing), and (g) contributions (everyone does real work).

5. *Ensure accountability by directly measuring the progress of the team in achieving its goals and plot it on a quality chart.* There has to be a way of measuring both team performance and the contributions of each member. The team must be accountable for achieving its goals. Each member must be accountable for contributing his or her share of the work.

6. *Show progress.* Establish a few challenging tasks the team can complete early on. Measuring results and establishing early successes help a team to congeal.

7. *Expose the team to new facts and information that help it redefine and enrich its understanding of its mission, purpose, and goals.* Teams err when they assume that all the information needed was present at the beginning of their work or exists in the collective experience and knowledge of their members.

8. *Provide training to enhance both taskwork and teamwork skills.* As the team progresses in achieving its goals, new skills will become relevant. Members need to sharpen their existing skills and gain new ones in order to keep the team progressing toward its goals.

9. *Have frequent team celebrations and seek opportunities to recognize members' contributions to team success.* Celebrations and honest, positive feedback are powerful tools in helping to shape new behaviors critical to team performance. There are many ways to recognize and reward team performance beyond direct compensation. Ultimately, the satisfaction shared by a team in its own performance becomes the most cherished reward.

10. *Ensure frequent team-processing sessions.* The team needs to examine how effectively it is working and discuss ways to improve its effectiveness regularly.

Teams need to be formed, maintained, and nurtured in ways that build team commitment and increase team and individual accountability.

Building Team Commitment

Groups that become real teams are relentlessly focused on performance results. It is from the focus on performance that member commitment is built, and common commitment is the essence of a team. With it, members become a powerful unit of collective performance; without it, they perform as individuals. Ensuring that members jointly commit themselves to achieve the team's goals involves a multistep process (Katzenbach &

Smith, 1993). *First, top management gives the team an initial task, problem, or assignment.* This provides the basic direction for the team's efforts. *Second, the team reframes the assignment into a mutual purpose to which all members can commit themselves.* The common purpose often relates to being on the cutting edge, being first, or revolutionizing the product or service produced by the team. The team shapes its purpose by putting its own "spin" on the demands, opportunities, timing, and approach specified by top management. *Third, the mutual goals are operationalized into a series of distinctive, unique, and specific performance goals that are measurable,* such as increasing sales by 50%. The overall goals and subgoals have to highlight the joint efforts required by team members, that is, the positive interdependence among group members (see Chapters 3 and 4). Team members become confused, pull apart, and revert to mediocre performance when (a) the team fails to establish specific performance goals or (b) the team's activities do not relate directly to the team's overall goals. Compelling mutual goals become a powerful engine of performance.

Teams develop direction, momentum, and commitment through this three-step process of working to shape meaningful purposes and goals from the general mission assigned. The combination of purpose and specific goals is essential to team performance. Each depends on the other to remain relevant and vital. Clear performance goals help a team keep track of progress and hold itself accountable; the broader and nobler aspirations in a team's purpose supply both meaning and emotional energy. The best teams invest a tremendous amount of time and effort exploring, shaping, and agreeing on a purpose that belongs to them both collectively and individually (Katzenbach & Smith, 1993). This purposing activity continues throughout the life of the team. Failed teams rarely develop clear, cooperative goals that give them a common purpose.

Transforming broad directives into specific and measurable performance goals provides a firm foundation for teams. Specific team performance goals should do the following (see Chapter 4; Katzenbach & Smith, 1993):

1. *Help to define work products that are different both from the organization-wide mission and from individual job objectives.* What results is a collective effort of team members to make something specific happen. Simply gathering from time to time to make decisions, by contrast, will not sustain team performance.

2. *Facilitate clear communication and constructive conflict among team members.* The clarity of the goal allows teams to resolve conflicts among members on the basis of what will facilitate the achievement of the team's goals. When goals are ambiguous or nonexistent, communication tends to break down and conflicts tend to be resolved in destructive ways.

3. *Allow teams to measure their progress and focus on getting results.*

4. *Have a leveling effect on power and status.* When a small group of people participating in Outward Bound, for example, challenge themselves to get over a wall, their respective titles fade into the background. The teams that succeed evaluate what and how each individual can best contribute to the team's goal. Teams that fail assign responsibilities on the basis of a person's status or personality.

5. *Allow a team to achieve small wins while pursuing broader purposes.* Small wins build commitment and give members the tenacity to overcome the inevitable obstacles to productive work.

6. *Be compelling symbols of accomplishment that motivate and energize.* They challenge team members to commit themselves to make a difference. Drama, urgency, and a healthy fear of failure combine to drive teams that have their collective eye on an attainable but challenging goal. It is the team's challenge—nobody but the team can make it happen.

Individual and Team Accountability

There are two levels of accountability that must be structured into teams. The team must be accountable for achieving its goals. Each member must be accountable for contributing his or her share of the work. The team must succeed, and all team members must contribute in concrete ways to the team's success and do equivalent amounts of real work.

Mutual accountability cannot be coerced any more than people can be made to trust one another. The procedure for ensuring that team members hold each other accountable for doing their fair share of the work is as follows. *First, the team has to be clear about its purpose and goals and be able to measure its progress toward achieving them.* In order for the team and each member to be accountable, it has to be clear what they are accountable for. *Second, positive interdependence is structured among group members.* Accountability begins with team members believing that they sink or swim together (positive goal interdependence) and ends with team members believing that they must hold each other accountable for doing their best to help the team achieve its goals (Katzenbach & Smith, 1993). The stronger the positive interdependence, the greater the mutual accountability among members. When a team shares a common purpose, mutual accountability grows as a natural counterpart.

Third, team members discuss how the purpose of the team may be translated into specific and measurable goals and how the goals may be accomplished. Accountability arises from the time, energy, and action invested in team discussions aimed at figuring out what the team is trying to accomplish and how best to get it done. Team members candidly explore who is best suited to each task as well as how individual roles will be integrated. Accountability is not about threats or fear of what will happen to members if they do not do their work. At its core, accountability is about the sincere promises members make to themselves and teammates. Accountability is experienced as a sense of personal responsibility to do one's best to help the team succeed.

While a team needs to know how well it is doing and what the contributions of each member are, team accountability may be more important than individual accountability. When Bell of Canada, for example, began monitoring the speed of its operators as a group rather than individually, not only did productivity remain high but the operators themselves also claimed both that their services improved and that they liked their job more (Bernstein, 1991).

When people work together toward a common objective, trust and commitment follow. Consequently, teams enjoying a strong common purpose and approach inevitably hold themselves responsible, both as individuals and as a team, for the team's performance. This sense of mutual accountability produces the rich rewards of mutual achievement in which all members share.

USE OF TEAMS IN TRAINING PROGRAMS

Teams are the heart of effective training programs (Johnson & Johnson, 1992b). Members of organizations have to be trained and continuously retrained throughout their career. The ultimate aim of training is procedural learning, that is, for trainees to be competent in performing a job such as operating and maintaining machines and equipment, conducting an interview, using a computer, piloting aircraft, or being an air-traffic controller. What is learned in a training program has to be transferred to the actual job situation and then maintained for years.

There are a number of reasons why teams are useful in training programs. *First,* in order to be proficient at a job, individuals must understand conceptually what they are supposed to do. When team members explain to each other what they are learning, the material is learned better, retained longer, and transferred to actual job situations more frequently. In addition, team members develop shared mental models of how they are supposed to perform their jobs. *Second,* team members can provide each other with appropriate feedback that individuals learning alone cannot receive. *Third,* team members can encourage and motivate each other to try hard to learn. *Fourth,* doing a job well requires that trainees develop a number of relevant attitudes and values as well as learn how to do the job. Personal commitment to do the job well, liking for the job, and wanting to increase one's skills continuously are all attitudes that affect job performance. Such attitudes are better learned in groups than individually. *Finally,* learning how to do a job well affects one's view of oneself. A professional identity is adopted along with the job. This new identity is shared with other team members and with future colleagues, who make up a community of practice. Such socialization is facilitated when teammates are enthusiastically adopting the new identity.

In order to maximize the performance of teams, individuals need to be trained to do their jobs and to function effectively as part of a team. This training can take place prior to their membership in the team or concurrently while they work as part of the team. In addition, a team as a whole can receive training through **team-building** procedures. The result of carefully structuring teams, training team members, and building team effectiveness is high-quality products and services delivered to customers.

TEAM BUILDING

The Minnesota Timberwolves faced their first year as an NBA professional team with an emphasis on playing as a team. A game such as basketball requires elaborate teamwork if played with any degree of expertise. Each play must be practiced again and again until the athletes function as a single unit, and a desire for personal success must be transformed into a desire for group success. Practices are designed to foster team spirit, formulate group goals, identify weaknesses in team play, build a desire for group success, and strive for better and better cooperation and integration. What is apparent on a basketball team is that the productivity of teams is not a simple function of team members' technical competencies and task abilities. Team goals must be set, work patterns structured and practiced, a desire for team success built, and a sense of team identity developed. Although technical superstars are a great asset, unless all members pursue team success over their own personal stardom, the team suffers. *There is no place for "lone rangers" on a team.* Individual members must learn how to coordinate their actions, identify any strains and stresses in working together, and continuously improve the integration of their efforts.

In order to improve the effectiveness of ongoing work teams, they may be given team-building experiences. Team building takes place at the job site. **Team building** emphasizes the analysis of work procedures and activities of ongoing work teams to improve team productivity, the quality of the relationships among members, the level of members' social skills, and the ability of the team to adapt to changing conditions and demands. The intent of the interventions is to increase long-term team effectiveness by improving the process of members working together. That is, team building focuses more on improving teamwork than on improving taskwork.

Most team-building interventions are typically based on an **action research** model of data collection, feedback, and action planning (Beckhard, 1969; Beer, 1976). Team procedures and activities are analyzed, changes are planned to improve productivity and effectiveness, the changes are implemented, and their success is assessed to see if further changes are needed. Team members are typically involved in diagnosing and planning change. The assumption is that involving team members is more likely to result in favorable consequences than imposing change. This action research model of intervening is commonly focused on (a) goal setting that clarifies the team's goals and the positive goal interdependence among members, (b) improving the interpersonal competence of members, (c) redefining and negotiating the role responsibilities of each member, and

(d) identifying problems interfering with effective teamwork and taskwork (Argyris, 1964; Beer, 1980; Buller & Bell, 1986; Dyer, 1987).

ASSESSING QUALITY OF WORK

To improve quality, the process by which the work is completed is carefully examined so that errors can be eliminated (error-proofing the process), the process can be streamlined to make it simpler (reducing complexity), and the sources of variation can be reduced or eliminated. The stage is then set for continuously improving the process by which the team does its work. Continuous improvement is based on gathering data and displaying it so that informed decisions can be made. To assess the quality of work, two major questions have to be answered:

1. *What should we measure?* The customer is the only one who can define what quality means for a given product or service.
2. *How can we measure it?* Measurement methods should be simple, realistic, and easy for everyone involved to use and understand.

Data-based decision making demands a systematic approach supported by practical tools. Seven of the most widely used tools are:

1. Flowchart
2. Cause-and-effect diagram
3. Check sheet
4. Pareto chart
5. Run chart
6. Scatter diagram
7. Histogram

Flowcharts, cause-and-effect diagrams, check sheets, and Pareto charts are most useful when the team is trying to learn about the process and narrow the focus of the improvement process. Later, tools like run charts, scatter diagrams, and histograms can help provide a clearer picture of how the process is operating over time.

Flowchart

In order to understand how the team actually does its work, the team needs to draw a picture of the work process. The **flowchart** is a simple yet powerful visual tool to display all the steps in a process (Figure 13.2). Flowcharts are used when teams need to identify deviations between the actual and the ideal path for a given process. The flowchart is often the first tool used to begin a process improvement project. It can also be used to describe the flow of people, material, and information within a designated work space. The level of detail will vary based on the needs of the team. Even without significant detail, flowcharts can help identify gaps, duplication, and other potential problems. A flowchart is created by (a) clearly defining the boundaries of the process (exactly where the process starts and stops, what the inputs and outputs are, who the customers are), (b) identifying all the steps the process actually follows (what the key steps are, who

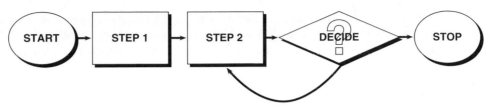

Figure 13.2 Flowchart.

is involved, who does what, when), (c) drawing the steps in sequence, (d) drawing a second flowchart that identifies all the steps the process should follow if everything worked right, and (e) comparing the two charts.

Cause-and-Effect Diagram

A **cause-and-effect diagram** represents the relationship between some effect (the problem being studied) and its possible causes (Figure 13.3). It is used to explore systematically cause-and-effect relationships so that the most likely causes of a problem or effect can be identified. Developed by Kauru Ishikawa, this charting technique is also referred to as a *fishbone diagram* due to its appearance when completed. A cause-and-effect diagram is usually drawn with the effect or problem on the right side of the diagram. The major causes or influences are drawn to the left of the effect. For every effect there are likely to be several major categories of causes. Any category that helps team members think creatively can be used. Examples of common categories include person-power, machinery, methods, materials, measurements. A cause-and-effect diagram is created by (a) defining the problem or effect clearly, (b) drawing a horizontal line or arrow pointing to the effect (on the right), (c) determining the major categories of possible causes (use generic terms), (d) for each major category, drawing a single line that branches off from the horizontal line, (e) thinking of possible causes in each category, (f) adding each cause as a branch of the appropriate category (ask questions like "Why?" or "Why does this

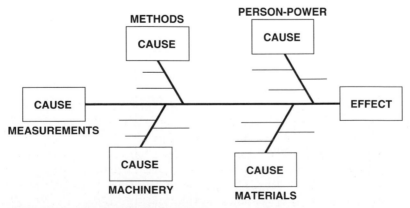

Figure 13.3 Cause-and-effect diagram.

happen?"), (g) identifying and circling the most basic (root) causes (start by looking for causes that appear repeatedly), and (h) using a check sheet to gather data to verify the most likely root cause(s). Use a Pareto chart to display the data collected.

Check Sheet

A **check sheet** is an easy-to-understand form used to answer the question "How often are certain events happening?" (Figure 13.4). Check sheets help a team tally and count the number of times an event is observed in a specified time period or amount of product. Check sheets start the process of translating opinions into facts. They are simple to construct and interpret. They help identify patterns in the data (such as the number of errors made per day). In constructing a check sheet, make sure that all columns are clearly labeled and that there is enough space to enter data. A check sheet is created by (a) defining exactly what event is being observed (everyone has to be looking for the same thing), (b) determining the time period during which the data will be collected (hours to weeks), (c) designing the form and making sure that all team members can use it, (d) collecting data consistently and honestly (ensure that sufficient time is made available to gather the data), and (e) looking for patterns both during and after the data-gathering effort.

Pareto Chart

The **Pareto chart** is a vertical bar chart that helps teams separate the vital few problems and causes from the trivial many. It takes its name from the Italian economist Vilfredo Frederico Damaso Pareto (1848–1923). While studying the unequal distribution of income, Pareto found that 80% of the wealth was controlled by only 20% of the population. His findings have been generalized into the *Pareto principle (80/20 rule)*, which states that 80% of the trouble comes from 20% of the problems. The Pareto chart is used to display the frequency and relative importance of problems, causes, or conditions in order to choose the starting point for process improvement, to monitor progress, or to identify root causes of a problem. Pareto analysis allows the team to take data from

EVENT	TIME PERIOD (days, weeks, months)			TOTAL
	1	2	3	
ERROR A	//	/	///	6
ERROR B	////	///	//	9
ERROR C		//	///	5
ERROR D	///////	////	////	14
ERROR E	///	///	/	7
TOTAL	15	13	13	41

Figure 13.4 Check sheet.

Table 13.2 **Days Absent During June**

Name	Days Absent	Percent of Total Days Absent
David	10	40
Keith	8	32
Helen	4	16
Edythe	2	8
Frank	1	4
Total	25	100

basic tools (like check sheets and interviews) and present them in a simple bar-graph format. The steps in developing a Pareto chart are as follows:

1. List the condition(s) or cause(s) you wish to monitor. Absenteeism is the condition used in our example.
2. Collect the raw data on the number of times the condition occurred within a predetermined period of time. In our example, the data are the number of days absent during a thirty-day period and the names of the employees.
3. Rank the various conditions or causes from highest to lowest (most absent to least absent—Table 13.2).
4. Under the horizontal axis, write the causes in descending order (the most important cause to the left and the least important to the right). In our example, we find David on the left, with ten absences, and Frank on the right, with only one absence (Figure 13.5).
5. On the left-hand vertical axis, list the measurement scale (total number of days absent).
6. On the right-hand vertical axis, note the percentage scale (the total number of absences must equal 100%).
7. Plot the data in a vertical bar graph and then draw a line for the cumulative frequencies. An example deals with the number of times each member of a team

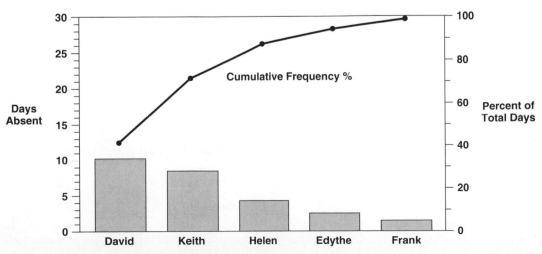

Figure 13.5 Pareto chart: Days absent from work in June per person.

of workers was absent during the month of June (see Table 13.2). Figure 13.5 shows that David, Keith, and Helen make up 88% of the absences among them. An intervention may be planned for David and Keith and perhaps also for Helen.

A Pareto diagram is an extension of the cause-and-effect diagram in that the causes are not only identified but also listed in order of their occurrence. The advantages of the Pareto diagram are that it can be used to analyze almost anything, it is easy to do, and it is easy to understand. The disadvantage is that only quantifiable data can be used in constructing it.

Run Chart

A **run chart** is a line graph used to monitor the behavior of a selected characteristic over time (Figure 13.6). A chart provides teams an opportunity to identify changes in the average performance of a characteristic. Run charts are used to examine data for trends or patterns that occur over time. By displaying the behavior of a specific characteristic over time, the run chart shows meaningful shifts in the average. A run chart is constructed by plotting data points on an *x–y* axis in chronological order. Measurement data are represented on the vertical (*y*) axis, and time or sequence is represented on the horizontal (*x*) axis. A marked point indicates the measurement taken at one point in time. A run chart is created by (a) marking off the time period to be used along the horizontal axis (i.e., hours, days, weeks), (b) entering the unit of measurement along the left vertical axis, (c) entering the historical data as they become available (continue to update the chart and the average), and (d) looking for unusual patterns in the position of the data points relative to the average.

Figure 13.6 Run chart.

Figure 13.7 Scatter diagram.

Scatter Diagram

A **scatter diagram** displays the cause-and-effect relationship between two process variables or characteristics (Figure 13.7; Table 13.3). It is used to display what happens to one variable when another variable changes. Whereas a run chart lets you track one characteristic over time, a scatter diagram lets you observe the relationship between the two variables. A scatter diagram can indicate only the existence of a possible relationship (and its strength); it cannot prove it. Its main use is to test the hypothesis that two variables are related (such as the amount of training received and error rates). A scatter diagram is usually constructed with the horizontal axis representing the measurement values for the possible-cause variable and the vertical axis representing the measurement values for the possible-effect variable. A scatter diagram is created by (a) collecting paired samples that may be related (the more data points the better), (b) constructing a data sheet, and (c) plotting the data on the

Table 13.3 Relationship Between Amount of Training and Error Rate

Sample	Variable 1 (Hours of Training)	Variable 2 (Errors)
1	4	6
2	8	4
3	10	5
4	16	2
5	6	8

chart by placing an *x* on the chart at each point the paired data intersect (circle repeated data points). The ways in which the points are scattered about the chart will tell you if the two variables are related. A randomly scattered pattern suggests that they are un-related. If the pattern moves from bottom left to top right, a positive correlation most likely exists. If the pattern moves from top left to bottom right, a negative correlation most likely exists. The more the cluster of data points resembles a straight line, the stronger the relationship.

Histogram

A **histogram** (history diagram) shows how continuous measurement data are clustered and dispersed (Figure 13.8). It is used when the distribution and spread of data need to be displayed. Histograms show the frequency of an occurrence and the dispersion be-tween the highest and lowest values. By displaying measurement data across a range of values (spread), the team can learn about the process's ability to meet specifications, whether the distribution is centered in the right place, and whether the data points are evenly balanced or skewed. When large quantities of data are collected and simple tab-ulation does not provide easy analysis, histograms are useful. A histogram consists of a series of equal-width columns of varying height. The horizontal axis represents the range of data, and the vertical axis represents the number of data points in each inter-val. Each column represents an interval within the range of data. Because interval size is constant, so are the column widths. Because column height represents the number of data points that occur within a given interval, column heights will vary accordingly. The number of intervals (columns) determines how much of a pattern will be visible. A histogram is created by:

1. Collecting the data to be analyzed.
2. Counting the number of data points to determine the size of the data set (*n*).
3. Determining the range (*R*) by subtracting the smallest values from the largest.
4. Determining the number of classes (*K*) to use (such as fewer than 50 data points = 5–7 classes, 50–100 data points = 6–10 classes, 100–250 data points = 7–12 classes, and more than 250 data points = 10–20 classes).

Interval / Range / Spread (Measurement Data)

Figure 13.8 Histogram.

5. Determining class width or interval size (H) by dividing the range (R) by the number of classes (K) ($H = R/K$).

6. Determining class boundaries for each interval by (a) finding the lowest-value data point (this is the start point for the first class boundary) and (b) finding the second class boundary by adding the class width (H) to the previous boundary's start point.

7. Making sure that each data point can fit in one and only one class (the endpoint of each interval must always be slightly less than the start point of the next class).

8. Counting and recording the number of data points that fall within each class or interval.

9. Drawing a column above each class (horizontal axis) reflecting the appropriate frequency of occurrences.

10. Analyzing the distribution and its implications.

TOTAL QUALITY MANAGEMENT

We don't seek to be one thousand percent better at any one thing.
We seek to be one percent better at one thousand things.

Jan Carlzon, president, Scandinavian Air Systems

In a mass-production organizational structure, quality is determined by inspecting the final product to see if it is adequate or needs improvement. In a team-based, high-performance organizational structure, quality is determined by examining the process by which the product is created to determine if the process can be improved. A **process** is made up of all the tasks, organized in a sequence, that contribute to the accomplishment of one particular outcome, such as producing a product or filling an order. Flowcharts are used to display all the steps in a process. Perhaps the most profound change in improving quality is the focus on processes rather than on products. **Total quality management (TQM)** refers to the use of teams to continuously improve the processes by which the product or service is produced. It requires the formation, training, and development of effective teams, a way to identify processes and measure their effectiveness, the creation of a desire to continuously improve the processes, and a focus on the customer. In other words, *where before companies sold a product, now they concentrate on being better at their processes than any other company in the world.*

The name most closely associated with TQM is W. Edwards Deming. Deming was born in Sioux City, Iowa. A statistician by profession, he formed many of his theories during World War II, when he taught industries how to use statistical methods to improve the quality of military production. Deming taught the Japanese his theories of quality control and continuous improvement following the war, and he is now widely credited (along with J. Juran and others) with laying the groundwork for Japan's economic boom. Deming's great insight was that management tends to look on what goes wrong (in an organization) as the fault of individual people, not the system. Deming (along with Juran) believes in the *85/15 rule*, which states that 85% of the problems can be corrected only by changing systems (structures, practices, rules, expectations, and traditions that are largely determined by management) and less than 15% of the problems can be solved by individual workers. When problems arise, therefore, management should look for causes in the system and work to remove them before casting blame on workers.

To give some guidance to managers on how to eliminate systemic causes of problems, Deming formulated fourteen principles. Managers were to (a) create constancy of purpose for the improvement of products and services; (b) adopt the new philosophy of total quality and continuous improvement; (c) cease dependence on mass inspection; (d) end the practice of awarding business based on the price alone; (e) improve constantly and forever the system of production and service; (f) institute training on the job; (g) institute leadership; (h) drive out fear; (i) break down barriers between staff areas; (j) eliminate slogans, exhortations, and targets for the workforce; (k) eliminate numerical quotas; (l) remove barriers to pride of workmanship; (m) institute a vigorous program of education and self-improvement; and (n) take action to accomplish the transformation.

TQM is also based on a focus on the customer and the continuous improvement of organizational and team processes. Staying close to the customer to satisfy the customer's needs and anticipate the customer's wants is a fundamental aspect of TQM. L. L. Bean is famous for the statement "A customer is the most important person ever in this office, either in person, by mail, or over the phone. A customer is not dependent on us; we are dependent on him. A customer is not an interruption of our work; he is the purpose of it. We are not doing a favor by serving him; he is doing us a favor by giving us the chance to do so. Nobody ever won an argument with a customer." J. Juran stated that all products, goods, and services should be judged on the basis of their fitness for use by the customer. The customer thus is not the point of sale; the customer is part of the design and production process. In the 1970s and 1980s, for example, American industry lost the battle for the hearts and pocketbooks of many consumers because non-American competitors were producing products that met or exceeded consumers' expectations for quality, whereas many American companies were producing standardized goods of mediocre quality in large batches at low cost. Most companies that changed realized that quality begins and ends with the customer.

A focus on quality begins with absolute commitment to meeting the needs of the customer by listening to customers and designing products and services that meet or exceed their expectations. Producing quality products, however, is not enough to stay competitive in today's world economy. Quality includes continuously improving all the organizational processes that lead to customer satisfaction. Continuous improvement demands examination of how the work gets done, not simply the end result. Continuous improvement leads to quality that is taken for granted. The major premise of continuous improvement is that everything an organization does can be improved by:

1. Involving everyone, from the boardroom to the mailroom, in a daily search for *incremental* improvements.
2. Providing everyone with the training, techniques, and authority they need to identify and fix problems.
3. Setting high-performance targets and measuring results.
4. Focusing the company's strategic vision on the needs of its customers.

Despite the early involvement of Americans such as Deming and Juran in the quality revolution, virtually all of the most important innovations in continuous improvement were made in Japan. Kaoru Ishikawa placed the focus on the customer and the responsibility for continuous improvement on every member of the organization. At Toshiba, for example, workers average around forty suggestions per year, and over 95% of the suggested improvements find their way into a product or service. Taiichi Ohno originated the manufacturing concept of *just in time,* whereby materials and components arrive at a factory or workstation at precisely the moment they are needed for use (no sooner and no later).

Ohno was also fanatically committed to the total elimination of waste. He believed that all waste contributes to higher costs and lower quality. To avoid wasting people, he grouped workers in teams and gave the teams the responsibility to determine how best to accomplish their missions. Of special importance for team members are (a) systematically tracing errors back to their root causes and fixing the problems upstream at their source and (b) developing personal networks throughout the organization so that team members are able to work with everyone else and understand their jobs in an organizational context. Ohno's goals included motivating workers to work smarter, to be more productive, and to do the right things right.

The work of people like Deming, Juran, Ishikawa, Ohno, and many others has resulted in a set of procedures for using TQM.

TQM Procedure

How does TQM work? There are six steps. *The first step in making TQM work is to form a team. Nothing can get done in TQM without a team.* Teams have to be formed, trained, and developed. Kinlaw (1991), for example, concluded that (a) team development must precede all other kinds of improvement initiatives and (b) teams, more than executive leadership, cultural change, TQM training, or any other strategy, account for most major improvements in organizations. Team development must be strategically placed at the center of TQM and must form the hub around which other elements (customer satisfaction, supplier performance, measurement and assessment) revolve. Teams are the primary units of performance in organizations. They are the most direct sources of continuous improvement.

The second step is to select a process (subsystem) for improvement. The team needs a specific, definable process to work on. There are four questions the team asks about the process selected: (1) How significant is the process (guard against investing more time and energy in a particular subsystem than makes sense)? (2) What is the potential payoff for working on it? (3) Is it a minor modification of the status quo or a meaningful change? and (4) Is it of realistic size (can the team actually study and improve the process)?

The third step is to define the system clearly, using tools such as flowcharts and cause-and-effect diagrams. The team cannot improve a process until the process has been defined. The best way to define the process is to draw a picture of it.

The fourth step is to develop a design for gathering information about the process to analyze its effectiveness. There are three parts to this step. *First,* quantifiable factors (such as time) have to be identified. If it cannot be counted, it cannot be improved (conversely, to be able to improve it, you must be able to count it). *Second,* a design for gathering the relevant data has to be developed. This includes specifying what data will be collected, who will collect them, when, and how. *Finally,* the data have to be analyzed and portrayed in a way that team members (and other organizational members) can easily understand.

The fifth step is to generate an improvement theory or plan based on the analysis of the data collected. The theory or plan specifies how the process has to be modified or replaced in order to improve the quality of the team's work. The plan is then implemented in a few settings. The implementation is carefully evaluated (more data are gathered). If the modified process works, it is fully adopted. If it does not work, it is redesigned and tried out again on a small basis.

The sixth step is to institutionalize the changes that work and the continuous improvement process. Ensure that there is no backsliding (reverting to the old practices) by taking new data samples forever, analyzing them, revising the theory or plan, revising the process, and so forth.

DEALING WITH PROBLEM BEHAVIORS IN TEAMS

A General Electric (GE) Company plant in Salisbury, North Carolina, typically changes product models a dozen times a day by using a team system to produce lighting panel boards. This plant has increased productivity by a remarkable 250% compared with GE plants that produced the same products in 1985. The success of GE and other companies in using teams, however, does not mean that teams are problem free. Sooner or later, all teams have to deal with one or more members whose actions are causing the team problems. Problem behaviors may result from obstacles to effective team functioning. *The first obstacle is lack of team maturity.* Groups ordinarily require some time to develop and stabilize their patterns of working. *The second obstacle is the team's history.* Norms rooted in past practice can sometimes adversely influence team members' current behavior. *The third obstacle is the mixed motives of team members.* Individuals' motives are almost never purely cooperative. In varying degrees, members may desire team success, but at the same time each member may also desire to have his or her own interests satisfied. Each person may wish to be a star in order to secure individual rewards as well as contribute to the team's success. *Finally, obstructive individual behaviors may interfere with team effectiveness.* Despite good intentions, some people talk too much, argue too often, intimidate others, wander from the topic, become unnecessarily obsessed over detail, acquiesce too soon, stubbornly resist, and generally behave in a very human fashion, complete with neurotic and nonneurotic foibles that obstruct group functioning.

When individuals first start working in teams, they sometimes engage in unhelpful behaviors. Whenever inappropriate member behavior occurs, the team leader's first move should be toward strengthening the perceived interdependence within the work situation. Four of the most common behavioral problems are passive uninvolvement, active uninvolvement, independence, and taking charge.

Passive Uninvolvement

When members are turning away from the team, not participating, not paying attention to the team's work, saying little or nothing, showing no enthusiasm, or not bringing their work or materials, other members may wish to:

1. Rearrange materials so that each team member has information the others need. If the passive and uninvolved member does not voluntarily contribute his or her information, the other team members will actively involve the member.
2. Divide up roles and assign to the passive, uninvolved member a role that is essential to the team's success.
3. Reward the team on the basis of its average performance, which will encourage other team members to derive strategies for increasing the problem member's involvement.

Active Uninvolvement

When a member is talking about everything but work, leaving the team, attempting to sabotage the team's work by giving wrong answers or destroying the team's product, refusing to do work, or refusing to work with another team member, team leaders may wish to give a reward that this member or team finds especially attractive and structure the task so that all members must work steadily and contribute in order for the team to succeed and attain the reward. Assigning the member a specific role to fulfill, making the member a team observer with high accountability to collect data about team functioning, and sitting in on the team-processing session and confronting the member are other possibilities.

Independence

When you see a team member working alone and ignoring the team discussion, you may wish to:

1. Limit the resources of the team. If there is only one set of materials or one piece of equipment for the team, the member will be unable to work independently.
2. Rearrange materials so that the member cannot do the work without the other members' information. To complete the task, the independent member must interact and collaborate.

Taking Charge

When one team member is doing all the work, refusing to let other members participate, ordering other members around, bullying other members, or making decisions for the team without checking to see if the other members agree, team leaders may wish to:

1. Rearrange resources so that the task cannot be completed without the staff member's encouraging others to participate and listening carefully to the other members' contributions.

2. Assign roles so that other team members have the most powerful and dominant roles.

3. Reward the team on the basis of the lowest two performances by team members. This will place pressure on the person taking charge to encourage and help other members learn the material and complete the task.

Teams Are Not Everything

All the research indicates that teams will become the primary unit of performance in high-performance organizations. But that does not mean that teams will crowd out individual opportunity and a formal hierarchy and process. Rather, teams will enhance existing structures without replacing them. An opportunity to use teams exists anywhere in an organization. Every organization, furthermore, faces specific performance challenges for which teams are the most practical and powerful vehicle at management's disposal.

SUMMARY

A *team* is a set of interpersonal interactions structured to achieve established goals. Teams may be differentiated from small groups and from working groups. A team's performance includes team work products that require the joint efforts of two or more members as well as individual work products. Teams may be classified in a number of ways, such as by the setting in which they are used (work, sports, learning), their use in an organization (problem solving, special purpose, self-managing), or what they do (recommend, make or do something, run things). Through the use of modern electronics (such as e-mail, bulletin boards, and computer conferences), teams can consist of individuals who are widely separated geographically. Teams exist within organizational contexts that greatly influence their effectiveness by presenting opportunities and constraints. A general estimate is that over 85% of the behavior of members of an organization is directly attributable to the organization's structure, not the nature of the individuals involved. There are basically two organizational contexts—a mass-production organizational structure and a team-based, high-performance organizational structure. The team-based organizational structure is considered to be the wave of the future because of the relationship between teams and productivity. A number of meta-analyses have found that under a wide range of conditions teams are more effective than individuals working by themselves. The productivity of teams is not a simple function of team members' technical competencies and task abilities. To be productive, teams (like all groups) must ensure that members perceive strong positive interdependence, interact in ways that promote each other's success and well-being, be individually accountable, employ their small team skills, and process how effectively the team has been working.

If high-quality products and services are to be created, organizations are well advised to use teams. Teams are the basic unit of performance for most organizations. Teams need to be formed, carefully structured to be effective, and nurtured. Nurturing teams includes training and retraining members on both taskwork and teamwork skills as well as engaging in team-building procedures to ensure that their effectiveness keeps improving. The point of carefully structuring teams, training team members, and building team effectiveness is to deliver high-quality products and services to customers. Implementing TQM procedures involves focusing on the process by which work gets done rather than on inspecting the finished product or service. Teams have to be able to draw flowcharts of the way they work and measure their productiveness. Finally, no matter how carefully teams are formed and developed, there are problem behaviors that must be dealt with. Through progressively refining procedures and continuously improving members' teamwork skills and the team's procedures, the problems can be solved.

14 *Epilogue*

I am cast upon a horrible, desolate island; void of all hope of recovery.
I am singled out and separated, as it were, from all the world, to be
miserable. I am divided from mankind, a solitary; one banished from
human society. I have no soul to speak to or to relieve me.

Daniel Defoe (1908, p. 51)

When Robinson Crusoe was cast up on the shore of a tropical island, the lone survivor of a shipwreck, he had everything he needed for a comfortable life. He had more than adequate food, the climate was ideal, and the setting was beautiful. Although he was thankful for being alive, he cursed his solitary life. He was emotionally miserable because he was no longer a member of any human group.

Humans are small group beings. We always have been and we always will be. The ubiquitousness of groups and the inevitability of being in them make groups one of the most important factors in our lives. As the effectiveness of our groups goes, so goes the quality of our lives. Quite often groups are not very effective. To create an effective group, you need to follow a set of guidelines.

GUIDELINES FOR CREATING EFFECTIVE GROUPS

Guideline 1

The first guideline is to establish clear, operational, relevant group goals that create positive interdependence and evoke a high level of commitment from every member. Groups exist for a reason. People join groups to achieve goals they are unable to achieve by themselves. To be effective, goals must be clear so that all members understand the nature of the goals, the goals must be operational so that members understand how to achieve them, the goals must be relevant to members' needs so that they commit themselves to achieve the goals, and the goals must create positive interdependence among members. There are hundreds of studies indicating that group effectiveness, group cohesion, and the well-being of members depend on members believing that they sink or swim together. If clear and operational positive goal interdependence is not established in a group, then all the following guidelines become meaningless.

Guideline 2

Once positive goal interdependence has been established, group members must communicate with each other to coordinate their efforts. The second guideline, therefore, is to establish effective two-way communication so that members can express their ideas and feelings accurately and clearly. Communication is the basis for human interaction and group functioning. Members must send and receive messages effectively in order to exchange information and transmit meaning. Barriers to open and accurate communication, such as competition among members, must be minimized. Two-way communication is required for effective group work.

Guideline 3

The third guideline is to ensure that leadership and participation are distributed among all group members. All members are responsible for providing leadership. The equalization of participation and leadership ensures that all members are involved in the group's work, committed to implementing the group's decisions, and satisfied with their membership. It also (a) ensures that the resources of every member are fully utilized and (b) increases the cohesiveness of the group. Leadership is discussed in Chapter 5.

Guideline 4

The fourth guideline for creating an effective group is to ensure that the use of power is distributed among group members and that patterns of influence vary according to the needs of the group as members strive to achieve their mutual goals. Members' power is based on expertise, ability, and access to information, not on authority or personality characteristics. In order to implement this guideline, there are two important principles: (1) Power exists in relationships, not individuals, and (2) for power to be constructive, the context in which it is used has to be cooperative. This dynamic-interdependent view of power assumes that (a) power inevitably exists in all relationships, (b) the use of power is essential to all aspects of group functioning, (c) the use of power is dynamic in that who is influencing whom to what degree changes constantly as the group proceeds in working to achieve its goal, and (d) power is distributed among all group members. Power is discussed in Chapter 6.

Guideline 5

The fifth guideline is to match flexibly decision-making procedures with the needs of the situation. There are many different ways groups can make decisions. There must be a balance between the availability of time and resources (such as members' skills) and the method of decision making used. Another balance must be struck among the size and seriousness of the decision, the commitment needed to put it into practice, and the method used for making the decision. The most effective way of making a decision is usually by consensus (unanimous agreement). Consensus promotes distributed participation, the equalization of power, productive controversy, cohesion, involvement, and commitment. Decision making is discussed in Chapter 7.

Guideline 6

The sixth guideline is for group members to engage in controversy by disagreeing with and challenging each other's conclusions and reasoning, thus promoting creative decision making and problem solving. In order to make effective decisions, members must present the best case possible for each major alternative course of action and subject all other alternatives to critical analysis. Controversies (conflicts among opposing ideas and conclusions) promote involvement in the group's work, quality and creativity in decision making, and commitment to implementing the group's decisions. The controversy procedure ensures that minority opinions are accepted and used. Such intellectual conflict results in more creative, effective decisions. Controversy and creativity are discussed in Chapter 8.

Guideline 7

The seventh guideline is for group members to face their conflicts of interests (conflicts promoted by incompatible needs or goals, scarce resources, and competitiveness) and engage in problem-solving (integrative) negotiations to resolve them. There are five basic strategies to manage conflicts of interests: withdrawal, forcing (distributive, win–lose negotiations), smoothing, compromise, and problem solving (integrative negotiations). The more effective the group, the more frequently conflicts of interests will be valued for their potentially constructive outcomes and resolved through problem-solving negotiations. Where problem-solving negotiations fail, another group member needs to mediate. Even in intergroup and cross-ethnic conflicts, problem-solving negotiations need to be used. When they are resolved constructively, conflicts are an important and indispensable aspect of increasing group effectiveness. Conflicts of interests are discussed in Chapter 9.

LEARNING GROUP SKILLS

To ensure that groups are effective, members must be extremely competent in using small group skills. Humans are not born with these skills; they must be developed. You have completed a variety of experiences aimed at increasing your group knowledge and skills. It is hoped that you are now a more effective group member. It is hoped that you are able to apply your increased skills and knowledge in a variety of groups and under a variety of conditions. You may wish to repeat many of the exercises in this book to reinforce your knowledge and to reread much of the material to gain a more complete understanding of how to utilize group skills. There are, however, two concluding exercises that may be helpful in applying the material covered in this book to the memberships you hold in groups.

EXERCISE

14.1 *Terminating a Group*

The goals of this exercise are to (a) complete any unfinished business in a group, (b) relive and remember the positive group experiences the group has had, (c) synthesize what group members have received from being part of the group, and (d) describe and express constructively group members' feelings about the termination of the group. The theme of the exercise is that although every group ends, the things you as a member have given and received, the ways in which you have grown, and the skills you have learned all continue with you. Terminating relationships may be sad, but the ways in which you have grown within your relationships with other group members can be applied to group situations in the future. Here is the procedure for the group to follow in the exercise:

1. Discuss the topic "Is there anything that needs to be resolved, discussed, dealt with, or expressed before the group ends?"

2. Discuss these questions: "What have been the most significant experiences of the group?", "What have I gotten out of being a member of the group?", "How has being a part of this group facilitated my growth as a person?", "What skills have I learned from being in this group?" As alternatives to a discussion, group members might make a painting, a collage, or a poem describing their experiences.

3. Discuss how you feel about the group's completing its activities and what feelings you want to express about the termination. Personal styles of handling the dissolution of a group may be discussed. If you cannot discuss this issue, the following alternatives may generate a productive discussion:

    a. Each of you in turn says goodbye to the group and leaves. Each of you then spends five minutes thinking about your feelings and returns to express anything you wanted to but did not express before.

    b. Each of you shows nonverbally how you felt when you first joined the group and then shows nonverbally how you feel now.

4. As a closing exercise, stand in a circle close together. You are all to imagine that you have the magical power to give anything you wish to another group member. You are then to give the person on your right a parting gift, each taking a turn so that everyone in the group can hear what the gifts are. Examples of what individuals might give are moonbeams, a flower, a better self-concept, an ability to commit oneself to a relationship, comfort with conflict, more empathy with others, the perfect love affair, and so on. When giving the gift, extend your hands as if actually passing something to the other person.

5. Have a group hug.

EXERCISE 14.2 *Self-Contract*

Write a description of yourself as a group member. Mention all the strengths and skills you can think of, and mention the areas in which you need to increase your skills. Then make a contract with yourself to make some changes in your life; the contract can involve starting something new, stopping something old, or changing some present aspect of your life. It should involve applying your group skills to the actual group situations you are now facing, or working to develop certain skills further. It may involve joining new groups and terminating old group memberships. In making the contract, pick several group memberships you now have and set a series of goals concerning how you will behave to increase your effectiveness and satisfaction as a group member. Write the contract down, place it in an envelope, address the envelope to yourself, and open it three months later.

Answers

1.3: Saving the World from Dracula: Answer Key

The following ranking was made on the basis of information in Bram Stoker's novel *Dracula* (New York: Tom Doherty Associates, 1989).

The first concern is to protect the parties in your group from Dracula. If you cannot stay alive, you cannot succeed. Therefore, the first two items are:

1. *The human ability to work together cooperatively.* Vampires are solitary creatures who cannot join forces with each other. The major advantage of humans is that they can cooperate in defending themselves and in carrying out coordinated attacks on a vampire. Humans have the power of cooperation. Vampires do not.

2. *The cross, holy water, communion wafer.* Vampires are made helpless by the power of Christianity. These three holy objects repel all vampires and protect the holder. An experienced and intelligent vampire such as Count Dracula, however, could find ways to get around holy objects in the hands of an isolated individual. These holy objects, therefore, are much more powerful when used by a group. Another use of the communion wafers (the host) is to seal a vampire in his or her coffin or prevent the vampire from returning to that coffin. Because they immobilize vampires, these holy objects have both a defensive and an offensive function.

There are other ways to protect yourself from vampires that are of little use in destroying Dracula. A vampire, for example, cannot enter your home unless invited. You could stay at home and not let anyone in. Vampires cannot pass swiftly running water. You could surround yourself with running water.

The second concern is to neutralize Dracula's strengths and exploit his weaknesses.

3. *Branch of wild rose:* The branch of the wild rose seals a vampire's coffin so that the vampire cannot leave or enter it. If the branch can be placed on Dracula's coffin before it is opened, it will neutralize all of Dracula's powers by confining him in the coffin. Since vampires have to return to their coffins every day, they are always vulnerable to being sealed in their graves.

4. *Table detailing sunrise and sunset in Transylvania:* The vampire's powers exist only at night. During the day Dracula loses all of his powers (except that he can change shape at exactly noon, sunrise, or sunset).

The third concern is to be able to destroy Dracula after he is neutralized. There are several ways to destroy Dracula (and any other vampire). Vampires can be destroyed only during the day. They must be denied access to their coffin (difficult, since any coffin that has earth from the vampire's grave works and since vampires tend to hide coffins in many different places in case one is found by their enemies) or confined in their coffin while one of two procedures is carried out. In this case, Dracula is already in his coffin, so the second way of destroying him is the best.

5. *Oak stake:* Vampires may be destroyed by driving an oak stake through their bodies and removing their hearts.

6. *Ax and garlic:* Vampires may be destroyed by cutting off their heads and filling their mouths with garlic.

The fourth concern is to find Count Dracula. When Dracula has been located and the scientists are protected against his attacks, they have the means to neutralize his powers. The next step is to destroy or contain him by resealing him in his coffin.

7. *Tickets to travel to Dracula's castle (plane to Budapest, train to Transylvania, car to castle):* In order to destroy Dracula, you must travel to his castle. While this is the first thing you would do, it is not the most important. Unless you are protected, can immobilize Dracula, and can destroy him, it makes no sense to travel to where he is.

8. *Map of Dracula's castle and key to his crypt:* Once you arrive at Dracula's castle, you cannot rely on the archaeologists to assist you. Since they do not believe in vampires, they

will try to prevent you from destroying Dracula. You need to know all the ways to get to Dracula's crypt and be able to open it when you arrive.

9. High-intensity flashlights are needed to find your way through the castle and crypt.

There are a number of items that are useless or unneeded.

10. *44-magnum revolver:* This could be used to fight off wolves, bats, humans, and other creatures under Dracula's control. It will have no effect on Dracula and therefore is ranked very low.

11. *A collapsible steel cage:* This is of no use in containing or destroying Dracula and, therefore, is not needed.

12. *Herbs mixed by a witch at midnight under a full moon:* These have no effect on vampires. It is a waste of space to carry them.

3.6: Broken Squares Exercise: Directions for Making a Set of Squares

For each five-member group you will need a set of five envelopes containing pieces of cardboard that have been cut in different patterns and that, when properly arranged with pieces from some of the other four envelopes, will form five squares of equal size. To prepare a set, cut out five cardboard squares of equal size, approximately 6 × 6 inches. Place the squares in a row and make them as below, penciling the letters "a," "b," "c," and so on lightly so that they can later be erased.

The lines should be so drawn that when the pieces are cut out, all pieces marked "a" will be ex-

actly the same size, the pieces marked "c" will be the same size, and the pieces marked "f" will be the same size. By using multiples of 3 inches, several combinations will be possible that will enable participants to form one or two squares, but one combination is possible that will form five squares 6 × 6 inches.

After drawing the lines of the 6- × 6-inch squares and labeling them with the lowercase letters, cut each square as marked into smaller pieces to make the parts of the puzzle.

Mark the five envelopes "A," "B," "C," "D," and "E" and distribute the cardboard pieces among them as follows:

Envelope A has pieces i, h, e.
Envelope B has pieces a, a, a, c.
Envelope C has pieces a, j.
Envelope D has pieces d, f.
Envelope E has pieces g, b, f, c.

Erase the penciled letter from each piece and write on it instead its appropriate envelope letter. This relabeling will make it easy, when a group has completed the task, to return the pieces to the proper envelope for later use.

3.7: Goal Structures Exercise: Answers

Squares: 40
Biangles: 11
Triangles: 18

4.2: Bewise College Problem: Solution

Name	Background	Education Degree	Teaching Experience	Public Relations Experience	Fund-Raising Experience	Administrative Experience
David Wolcott	African American	Master's	13 years	None	None	8 years
Roger Thornton	Upper-class family	B.A., master's	7 years	9 years; politician	None	16 years
Edythe Constable	Community center director	None	8 years	2 years	4 years	7 years
Frank Pierce	Neighborhood center worker; community relations	Master's	None	14 years	None	14 years
Helen Johnson	Childhood in slums	B.A., master's	4 years	5 years	2 years	15 years
Keith Clement	Volunteer work: author of book	B.A.	5 years	13 years	10 years	None

Andrews College is the smallest college in the state, and therefore, it had a completely black American student body in 1982.

As is evident from the table, all candidates but Helen Johnson are disqualified because they lack one of the qualifications outlined in the data sheets.

4.3: Solstice-Shenanigans Mystery: Solution

The Solstice-Shenanigans Mystery Exercise appears on page 148. The painting by Artisimisso was stolen by Mr. Handsome, who took it with him when he left the party at 9:50. He took the painting because he was a kleptomaniac.

4.4: Liepz and Bounz Exercise: Solution

The Liepz and Bounz Exercise is on page 150. David jogged from Farmland to Muncie in one (5/5) jumpz.

4.6: Square Arrangement I: One-Way Communication

Instructions: Study the arrangement. With your back to the group members, instruct them on how to draw the squares. Begin with the top square and describe each in succession, taking particular note of the placement of each in relation to the preceding one. No questions allowed.

4.6: *Square Arrangement II: Two-Way Communication*

Instructions: Study the arrangement shown. Facing the group, instruct the members on how to draw the squares. Begin with the top square and describe each in succession, taking particular note of the placement of each in relation to the preceding one. Answer all questions from participants and repeat your description if necessary.

5.7: *Furniture Factory Exercise: Solution*

The more directly Mr. Day involves the workers in the change, the more likely they are to support the change.

a. 5
b. 1
c. 3
d. 4
e. 2

5.11: *Hollow Square Exercise*

7.3: *Winter Survival Exercise*

BACKGROUND INFORMATION FOR COORDINATOR

None of the information here should be given to participants until after they have completed the decision-making parts of the exercise. Mid-January is the coldest time of the year in Minnesota and Manitoba. The first problem the survivors face, therefore, is to preserve their body heat and protect themselves against its loss. This problem can be solved by building a fire, minimizing movement and exertion, using as much insulation as possible, and constructing a shelter.

The participants have just crash-landed. Many individuals tend to overlook the enormous shock reaction this has on the human body, and the death of the pilot and copilot increases the shock. Decision making under such conditions is extremely difficult. Such a situation requires a strong emphasis on the use of reasoning, not only for making decisions but also for reducing the fear and panic every survivor would naturally feel. Shock is manifested in feelings of helplessness, loneliness, and hope-lessness as well as in fear. These feelings have brought about more fatalities than perhaps any other cause in survival situations. Through the use of reasoning, hope for survival and the will to live can be generated. Certainly the state of shock means that the movement of the survivors should be at a minimum and that an attempt to calm them should be made.

Before taking off, a pilot always has to file a flight plan. The flight plan contains the vital information regarding the flight, such as the course, speed, estimated time of arrival, type of aircraft, and number of persons on board. Search-and-rescue operations would begin shortly after the failure of the plane to appear at its destination at its estimated time of arrival.

The twenty miles to the nearest known town is a long walk even under ideal conditions, particularly if one is not used to walking such distances. Under the circumstances of being in shock, being dressed in city clothes, and having deep snow in the woods and a variety of water barriers to cross, to attempt to walk out would mean almost certain death from freezing and exhaustion. At temperatures of –25°F to –40°F, the loss of body heat through exertion is a very serious matter.

Once the survivors have found ways to keep warm, their immediate problem is to attract the attention of search planes and search parties. Thus, all the items the group has salvaged must be assessed for their value in signaling the group's whereabouts.

Winter Survival Exercise: Answer Key

Item	Experts' Ranking	Your Ranking	Difference Score
Ball of steel wool	2		
Newspapers (one per person)	8		
Compass	12		
Hand ax	6		
Cigarette lighter (without fluid)	1		
Loaded .45-caliber pistol	9		
Sectional air map made of plastic	11		
20 X 20-ft piece of heavy-duty canvas	5		
Extra shirt and pants for each survivor	3		
Can of shortening	4		
Quart of 100-proof whiskey	10		
Family-size chocolate bar (one per person)	7		
Total			____

EXPLANATION OF ANSWER KEY

The following ranking of the survivors' items was made on the basis of information provided by Mark Wanvig and Roger Johnson and supplemented by Rutstrum (1973). Wanvig was an instructor in survival training for three years in the reconnaissance school in the 101st Division of the U.S. Army and later an instructor in wilderness survival for four years at the Twin City Institute for Talented Youth. Johnson is a national expert on environmental education.

1. *Cigarette lighter* (*without fluid*). The gravest danger facing the group is exposure to the cold. The greatest need is for a source of warmth, and the second greatest need is for signaling devices. This makes building a fire the first order of business. Without matches, something is needed to produce sparks to start a fire. Even without fluid, the cigarette lighter can be used to produce sparks. The fire will provide not only warmth but also smoke for daytime signaling and firelight for nighttime signaling.
2. *Ball of steel wool.* To make a fire, the survivors need a means of catching the sparks made by the cigarette lighter. Steel wool is the best substance with which to catch a spark and support a flame, even if it is a little wet.
3. *Extra shirt and pants for each survivor.* Clothes are probably the most versatile items one can have in a situation like this. Besides adding warmth to the body, they can be used for shelter, signaling, bedding, bandages, string when unraveled, and tinder to make fires. Even maps can be drawn on them. The versatility of clothes and the need for fires, signaling devices, and warmth make these items third in importance.
4. *Can of shortening.* This item has many uses—the most important being that a mirrorlike signaling device can be made from the lid. After shining the lid with the steel wool, the survivors can use it to produce an effective reflector of sunlight. A mirror is the most powerful tool they have for communicating their presence. In sunlight, a simple mirror can generate five to seven million candlepower. The reflected sunbeam can be seen beyond the horizon. Its effectiveness is somewhat limited by the trees, but one member of the group

could climb a tree and use the mirror to signal search planes. If the survivors had no other means of signaling than this, they would still have a better than 80% chance of being rescued within the first twenty-four hours.

Other uses for this item are as follows: The shortening can be rubbed on exposed areas of the body, such as the face, lips, and hands, for protection from the cold. In extreme cases, it could be eaten in small amounts. When melted into an oil, the shortening is helpful in starting fires. When soaked into a piece of cloth, melted shortening will produce an effective candlewick. The can is useful in melting snow to produce drinking water. Even in winter, water is important, as the body loses water in many ways, such as through perspiration, respiration, and shock. This water must be replenished, because dehydration affects one's ability to make clear decisions. The can is also useful as a cup.

5. *Twenty by twenty-foot piece of heavy-duty canvas.* The cold makes some form of shelter necessary. The canvas can be part of a shelter, protecting the survivors from the wind and possible snow. Spread on a frame and secured, it could make a good tent as well as a ground cover. Rigged as a wind screen, it could hold heat. Its squareness, contrasting with the surrounding terrain, might also be spotted in an air search, and this makes it an important signaling device.

6. *Hand ax.* The survivors need a continuous supply of wood in order to maintain the fire. The ax is useful for obtaining wood and for clearing a sheltered campsite, cutting boughs for ground insulation, and constructing a frame for the shelter.

7. *Family-size chocolate bars (one per person).* To gather wood for the fire and to set up signals, the survivors need energy. The chocolate will supply the energy to sustain them for some time. Because it contains mostly carbohydrates, it supplies energy without making digestive demands upon the body.

8. *Newspapers (one per person).* The newspaper can be used for starting a fire. It will also serve as an insulator: When rolled up and placed under the clothes around a person's legs and arms, it provides dead-air space for extra protection from the cold. The survivors can use the paper for recreation by reading it,

memorizing it, folding it, or tearing it. They can roll it into a cone and yell through it as a signal device. They can also spread it around an area to help signal a rescue party.

9. *Loaded .45-caliber pistol.* The pistol provides a sound-signaling device. (The international distress signal is three shots fired in rapid succession.) There have been numerous cases of survivors going undetected because they were too weak to make a loud enough noise to attract attention. The butt of the pistol can be used as a hammer. The powder from the shells will assist in fire building. By placing a small bit of cloth in a cartridge emptied of its bullet, one can start a fire by firing the gun at dry wood on the ground. At night the muzzle blast of the gun is visible, and this provides another means of signaling.

The pistol's advantages are counterbalanced by its dangerous disadvantages. Anger, frustration, impatience, irritability, and lapses of rationality may increase as the group waits to be rescued. The availability of a lethal weapon is a substantial danger to the group under these conditions. Although the pistol could be used for hunting, it would take a highly skilled marksman to kill an animal with it. Even then the animal would have to be transported through the snow to the crash area, which would probably consume more energy than would be advisable.

10. *Quart of 100-proof whiskey.* The only uses of the whiskey are as an aid in fire building and as a fuel. A torch could be made from a piece of clothing soaked in the whiskey and attached to an upright pole. The danger of whiskey is that someone might try to drink it when it is cold. Alcohol takes on the temperature it is exposed to, and a drink of it at −30°F would freeze a person's esophagus and stomach and do considerable damage to the mouth. Drinking it warm would cause dehydration. Alcohol, furthermore, mixes badly with cold because it dilates the blood vessels in the skin. This results in chilled blood being carried back to the heart, which in turn chills the heart and contributes to a rapid loss of body heat. An intoxicated person is much more likely to develop hypothermia than a nonintoxicated person. The bottle may be used to store heated water.

11. *Compass.* Because the compass may also encourage some survivors to try to walk to the nearest town, it too is a dangerous item. The only redeeming feature of the compass is the possible use of its glass top as a reflector of sunlight to signal search planes, but this would be the least effective of the potential signaling devices available. That it might tempt survivors to walk away from the crash site makes it the least desirable of the twelve items.

12. *Sectional air map made of plastic.* This item is dangerous because it will encourage individuals to attempt to walk to the nearest town—thereby condemning them to almost certain death.

7.4: *They'll Never Take Us Alive Exercise: Answer Key*

Item	Experts' Ranking	Your Ranking	Difference Score
Swimming	5		
Railroads	7		
Police work	11		
Home appliances	9		
Alcohol	2		
Nuclear power	12		
Smoking	1		
Motor vehicles	3		
Pesticides	15		
Handguns	4		
Bicycles	8		
Firefighting	10		
Mountain climbing	13		
Vaccinations	14		
Surgery	6		
Total			____

8.3: *Stranded in the Desert Exercise: Scoring, Key*

Item	Experts' Ranking	Your Ranking	Difference Score
Magnetic compass	12		
20- by 20-ft piece of heavy-duty canvas	7		
Book, *Plants of the Desert*	10		
Rear-view mirror	1		
Large knife	5		
Flashlight (four-battery size)	8		
One jacket per person	2		
One transparent plastic ground cloth (6 × 4 feet) per person	4		
Loaded .38-caliber pistol	9		
One 2-quart plastic canteen full of water per person	3		
Accurate map of the area	11		
Large box of kitchen matches	6		
Total			____

Score your group's ranking by finding the absolute difference between your ranking and the experts' ranking. An absolute difference is found by recording the difference between the two rankings while ignoring all plus or minus signs. After finding all the absolute differences, sum them. The lower your total score, the more accurate your ranking.

STRANDED IN THE DESERT: RATIONALE FOR EXPERTS' RANKING

The group has just been through a traumatic situation that has had a shocking impact on all members. The fact that your advisor and the driver were killed would increase the shock reaction. Most, if not all, members of your group need to receive treatment for shock. Five of the more important problems for your group are as follows (Nesbitt, Pond, & Allen, 1959). One vital problem for the group members is dehydration from exposure to the sun, from bodily activity (causing perspiration and respiration), and from the hot, dry air circulating next to the skin. To prevent dehydration the group members should (a) remain calm to reduce loss of moisture through respiration, (b) wear as many clothes as you can to reduce the loss of moisture through perspiration and having the dry desert air circulate next to your skin (by wearing sufficient clothes to keep the desert air away from your skin, you can lengthen your survival time by at least a day), (c) stay in the shade, (d) minimize movement, especially during the day, and (e) drink as much water as you can. Any activity that increases heartbeat, respiration, and perspiration will speed up dehydration. Taking care to remain calm and in the shade, the group could probably survive for three days without water. The need for clothes makes the jackets important. The need for shade makes the canvas important. To survive you must keep your body properly hydrated, either with adequate water or by keeping body heat production down and keeping desert heat (from sun, air, and ground reflection) out. Once the jackets are on and the sunshade is up, everyone should be as calm and inactive as possible.

Another vital problem is signaling search parties of your whereabouts so that you can be rescued. The items that may be used to signal your presence are the mirror, the canvas, the flashlight, the revolver, and a fire (matches). The mirror is the most important signaling device the group has. As Nesbitt, Pond, and Allen (1959) state, "A signal mirror is the best, the simplest, the most important piece of survival equipment ever invented for the desert." In sunlight the mirror can generate five to seven million candlepower of light, which may be seen beyond the horizon. It pays to flash the mirror at the horizon even when no plane is in view; search planes have turned toward a mirror flash even when the survivors have neither seen nor heard them. The canvas, when spread out to make a shelter, not only can reduce the temperature underneath it by as much as 20°F, but can also be easily spotted from the air because it contrasts with the terrain. The flashlight provides a reliable and quick night signaling device. The pistol is an important sound signaling device, because speech becomes seriously impaired due to dehydration. In the desert setting there have been numerous occurrences of searchers not detecting the people they were looking for because the survivors could not make loud enough noises to attract the searchers' attention. There are important disadvantages to having the revolver in the hands of a group member who may become hysterical due to the trauma of the situation or delusional due to dehydration. Finally, building a fire at night and using smoke columns during the day will help attract the attention of searchers. "A column of smoke by day, a pillar of fire by night" is a biblical quotation worth remembering for desert signaling.

The third major problem is obtaining as much drinkable water as possible. The water you have in your canteens is enough to keep you rational for a while but not enough to extend your survival time. That is, the water in the canteens is enough to hold off the effects of dehydration for a while; without water, within twenty-four hours you can expect to have impatience, nausea, and sleepiness interfere with rational decision making. The only way to obtain purified water to drink from the shallow hole nearby is to build a solar still. The still is built by stretching the ground cloths a few inches above the waterhole and tilting them so that they drain into the canteens. The knife is helpful in cutting the stakes necessary to arrange the ground cloths. When the sun shines through the plastic onto the water, condensation forms on the underside of the plastic. The moisture is distilled and purified water.

The fourth problem is protecting yourself from the cold at night. Although the desert is hot during the day, it gets cold at night. The jackets become important to protect the group members from the cold, as do the matches (to build a fire) and the canvas (to provide a shelter).

The fifth problem is gathering food if the group is not rescued in the first few days. It is important not to eat protein, as it takes considerable water to digest protein and flush out the waste products. The book on plants will be helpful in obtaining food. Hunting for animals, furthermore,

would cause dehydration and would do far more harm than good.

If the group decides to walk out, traveling at night, all members will probably be dead by the second day. They will have walked less than thirty-three miles during the two nights. If group members decide to walk during the day, they will probably be dead by the next morning, after walking less than twelve miles. For the group to walk out, having just gone through a traumatic experience that has had a considerable impact on the body, having few if any members who have walked forty-five miles before, and having to carry the canvas and wear the jackets to prevent dehydration would be disastrous. One further fact of great importance: Once the members start walking, they will be much harder to spot by search parties. The compass and the map, therefore, are not helpful to the group's survival.

8.5: *Fallout Shelter Exercise:* Answers*

_1_ Containers of water. (The average person would need at least 1 quart of liquid per day. Each person should be allowed to drink according to need because studies have shown that nothing is gained by limiting the liquids below the amount demanded by the body. Two weeks is probably the maximum time needed to stay in the shelter. After that, other sources of water could be found.)

_2_ Canned and dried foods. (Enough food should be on hand to feed everyone for two weeks, if possible. However, most people can get along on about half as much food as usual and can survive for several days without any food. Therefore, this is not as important as the water.)

_3_ One large and one small garbage can with lids. (Next to water and food, the most important concern is sanitation. Poor sanitation will attract diseases and vermin. The small garbage can can be used as a toilet, and the large garbage

can can be used to store garbage and human wastes until they can be taken outside and buried. Burial of the garbage is important to prevent spread of disease by rats or insects.)

_4_ First-aid kit and iodine and medicines. (Useful if anyone gets hurt or falls ill; should include medicine for anyone with chronic illness. The iodine can be used to sterilize water.)

_5_ Battery-powered radio. (Useful for obtaining information about what is happening outside the shelter and for information on when it is safe to come out. Useful for contact with outside world.)

_6_ Soap and towels. (Useful and important for sanitation.)

_7_ Liquid chlorine bleach. (Useful for sprinkling in the toilet to control odors and germs; it could also be used to sterilize any water that has become cloudy and might contain bacteria.)

_8_ Matches and candles. (Would help illuminate the shelter and thus make it more comfortable, particularly because there is not likely to be any natural source of light or electricity available.)

_9_ Blankets. (Would be used for heat and comfort; would be of important but moderate use.)

10 Flashlight and batteries. (Useful for illumination.)

*This exercise is based on information in *Protection in the nuclear age* (Washington, D.C.: Department of Defense, Civil Defense Preparedness Agency, February 1977).

<u>11</u> Cooking and eating utensils. (Useful in preparing and serving foods but not essential.)

<u>12</u> Broom. (Useful for brushing radioactive fallout off anyone who had to leave the shelter for emergency reasons before he or she reentered.)

<u>13</u> Canned heat stove. (Useful if a heat supply is needed. However, it can be used only if there is adequate ventilation for the fumes; it could be dangerous.)

<u>14</u> Geiger counter. (Unnecessary. It could be used to check the level of radiation outside the shelter to determine when it is safe to emerge, but the same information and more can be obtained from the radio. Also, fallout particles are visible and the radiation from them is given off quickly, so danger from radiation could be reduced by waiting twenty-four to forty-eight hours after the large particles have stopped falling.)

<u>15</u> Foam fire extinguisher. (Useful for fighting fires outside the shelter but could not be used within the shelter because of danger from the fumes.)

8.6: The Johnson School Exercise: Solution

The following Johnsons coached the sports in the order listed.

1. Frank coached golf, basketball, wrestling, and track.
2. Roger coached basketball, golf, track, and wrestling.
3. David coached wrestling, track, basketball, and golf.
4. Helen coached track, wrestling, golf, and basketball.

8.9: Creativity Problem: Solution

The solution of this problem is based upon the creative insight of going outside the obvious boundaries of the dots.

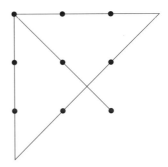

8.10: Joe Doodlebug Exercise: Hints

1. Joe does not always have to face the food in order to eat it.
2. Joe can jump sideways and backward as well as forward.
3. Read the problem again: Joe was moving east when the food was presented.

Joe Doodlebug Exercise: Solution

At the moment Joe's master set down the food, Joe had already jumped once to the east. He therefore has to jump sideways three times more to the east and once sideways back to the west, landing on top of the food. He can now eat.

9.2: *Making a Profit Exercise: Buyer Profit Sheet*

Oil		Gas		Coal	
Price	**Profit**	**Price**	**Profit**	**Price**	**Profit**
A	$4,000	A	$2,000	A	$1,000
B	3,500	B	1,750	B	875
C	3,000	C	1,500	C	750
D	2,500	D	1,250	D	625
E	2,000	E	1,000	E	500
F	1,500	F	750	F	375
G	1,000	G	500	G	250
H	500	H	250	H	125
I	0	I	0	I	0

The nine prices for each commodity are represented by the letters A to I. Next to each price is the profit you would make for each commodity if you sold it at that price.

You can say anything you wish during negotiations, but you may *not* show this profit sheet to the buyer you are negotiating with.

Making a Profit Exercise: Seller Profit Sheet

Oil		Gas		Coal	
Price	**Profit**	**Price**	**Profit**	**Price**	**Profit**
A	$ 0	A	$ 0	A	$ 0
B	125	B	250	B	500
C	250	C	500	C	1,000
D	375	D	750	D	1,500
E	500	E	1,000	E	2,000
F	625	F	1,250	F	2,500
G	750	G	1,500	G	3,000
H	875	H	1,750	H	3,500
I	1,000	I	2,000	I	4,000

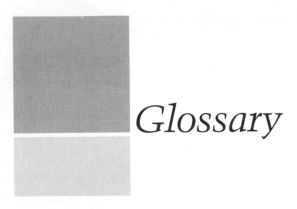

Glossary

Ability and skill diversity: A measure of the variation within a group determined by the different abilities and skills that each individual brings to the group.

Acceptance: The communication of high regard toward others and their contributions to the group's work.

Action research: The use of the scientific method in solving research questions that have significant social value.

Action theory: Theory as to what actions are needed to achieve a desired consequence in a given situation.

Additive tasks: Tasks for which group productivity represents the sum of individual members' efforts.

Ageism: Prejudice against the elderly.

Aggregate: Collection of individuals who do not interact with one another.

Arbitration: A form of third-party intervention in negotiations in which the recommendations of the person intervening are binding on the parties involved.

Assimilation: Changing a message to fit it into your own cognitive frameworks and perspective.

Attractiveness: An important determinant of the ability of a communicator to influence an audience; the following factors are determinants of attractiveness: cooperativeness and goal facilitation, physical appearance, liking, similarity, competence, warmth, and familiarity and propinquity.

Attribution theory: A social-psychological explanation of how individuals make inferences about the causes of behaviors and events.

Authority: Legitimate power vested in a particular position to ensure that individuals in subordinate positions meet the requirements of their organizational role.

Autocratic leader: A leader who dictates orders and determines all policy without involving group members in decision making.

Averaging opinions: A method of group decision making in which each group member contributes their own opinion and a decision is made based on averaging the results.

Bargaining: See **Negotiation.**

Blaming the victim: Attributing the cause of discrimination or misfortune to the personal characteristics and actions of the victim.

Brainstorming: A procedure in which group members are asked to produce as many, and as uninhibited, ideas as they possibly can and to withhold criticism in order to optimize creativity.

Cathexis: The investment of psychological energy in objects and events outside of oneself.

Cause-and-effect diagram: Visual representation of the relationship between some effect (the problem being studied) and its possible causes.

Channel: The means of sending a message to another person, such as sound and sight.

Charisma: An extraordinary power, as of working miracles.

Charismatic leader: A person who has (a) an extraordinary power or vision and is able to communicate it to others or (b) unusual powers of practical leadership that will enable him or her to achieve the goals that will alleviate followers' distress.

Check sheet: Form used to record the frequency with which certain events are happening.

Coercive power: The group leader's control over positive and negative consequences for other group members.

Cognitive dissonance: Possessing two cognitions that contradict each other. The theory developed by Leon Festinger predicts that dissonance is uncomfortable and that a person will seek to reduce it.

Cognitive perspective: An individual's mental interpretation of a situation based on his or her knowledge, understanding, and experiences.

Cognitive structure: A set of principles and processes that organizes cognitive experience.

Cohesion: All the forces (both positive and negative) that cause individuals to maintain their membership in specific groups. These include attraction to other group members and a close match between individuals' needs and the goals and activities of the group. The attractiveness that a group has for its members and that the members have for one another.

Collusion: The conscious and unconscious reinforcement of stereotypic attitudes, behaviors, and prevailing norms.

Communication: A message sent by a person to a receiver (or receivers) with the conscious intent of affecting the receiver's behavior.

Communication networks: Representations of the acceptable paths of communication between persons in a group or organization.

Competition: A negative correlation among group members' goal attainments; when group members perceive that they can obtain their goals if and only if the other members with whom they are competitively linked fail to obtain their goal.

Compliance: Behavior in accordance with a direct request. Behavioral change without internal acceptance.

Compromise: The process of giving up part of the goal(s) and sacrificing part of a relationship in order to reach an agreement; employed when both the goal and relationship are of moderate importance.

Conceptual conflict: The uncertainty that results from having one's position criticized and refuted and being challenged by information and conclusions that are incompatible with one's own conclusions.

Concurrence-seeking: Situation where members of a decision-making group inhibit discussion to avoid any disagreement or arguments and emphasize agreement; there is a suppression of different conclusions, an emphasis on quick compromise, and a lack of disagreement within the group.

Conflict: The occurrence of incompatible activities.

Conflict of interests: When the actions of one person attempting to maximize his or her needs and benefits prevent, block, interfere with, injure, or in some way make less effective the actions of another person attempting to maximize his or her needs and benefits.

Conflict negative group: A group in which conflicts are suppressed and avoided and, when they occur, are managed in destructive ways.

Conflict positive groups: A group in which conflicts are encouraged and managed constructively in order to maximize their potential to enhance the quality of decision making, problem solving, and group life.

Conformity: Changes in behavior that result from group influences. Yielding to group pressures when no direct request to comply is made.

Confrontation: The direct expression of one's view of the conflict and one's feelings about it and, at the same time, an invitation to the opposition to do the same.

Conjunctive tasks: Tasks for which group productivity is determined by the effort or ability of the weakest member.

Consensus: A collective opinion arrived at by a group of individuals working together under conditions that permit communications to be sufficiently open and the group climate to be sufficiently supportive for everyone in the group to feel that he or she has had a fair chance to influence the decision.

Content: The subject that is being discussed within a group.

Contingency theory of leadership: A theory suggesting that effectiveness of leaders is determined both by characteristics of leaders and by several situational factors.

Contractual norms: Statements that spell out the rules to be observed and the penalties for violating them.

Control: When the person being influenced behaves as the one who influences intends.

Controversy: The situation that exists when one group member's ideas, information, conclusions, theories, and opinions are incompatible with those of another, and the two seek to reach an agreement.

Cooperation: A positive correlation among individuals' goal attainments.

Cooperative goal structure: A positive correlation among group members' goal attainments; when group members perceive that they can achieve their goal if and only if the other members with whom they are cooperatively linked obtain their goal.

Creativity: A process consisting of overlapping phases that brings something new into existence.

Credibility: The perceived ability and motivation of a communicator to know valid information and communicate this information without bias.

Critical path method: Identifying the final goal and working backward to detail what must happen (tasks and subgoals) before it is achieved, what resources must be allocated, what the timetable for accomplishing each subgoal should be, and who should have what responsibilities.

Culture clash: Conflict over basic values among individuals from different cultures.

Debate: Situation where group members present the best case for positions that are incompatible with one another and a winner is declared on the basis of who presented the best position.

Decision: The selection of one of multiple options.

Decision making: Obtaining some agreement among group members as to which of several courses of action is most desirable for achieving the group's goals. The process through which groups identify problems in achieving the group's goals and attain solutions to them.

Decision-making tasks: Tasks that require consensus about the best solution to a problem when the correct answer is not known.

Defensive avoidance: The process of procrastinating, rationalizing, or denying the responsibility for choices in order to deal with doubts, conflict, and worry regarding a decision.

Defensive behavior: Behavior that occurs when a person feels threatened or anticipates a threat.

Deindividuation: A psychological state characterized by reduced self-awareness and major shifts in perception. It is encouraged by certain external conditions (e.g., anonymity) and enhances the performance of wild, impulsive forms of behavior.

Delegating: A low-task–low-relationship behavior in which the leader allows group members considerable autonomy in completing a task.

Deliberate discourse: When the advantages and disadvantages of proposed actions are discussed in order to resolve controversy.

Delusion of individualism: When individuals believe that (a) they are separate and apart from all other individuals and, therefore, (b) others' frustration, unhappiness, hunger, despair, and misery have no significant bearing on their own well-being.

Democratic leader: A leader who sets policies through group discussion and decision, encouraging and helping group members to interact, requesting the cooperation of others, and being considerate of members' feelings and needs.

Demographic diversity: A measure of the variation within a group determined by properties of the group members such as age, sex, culture, ethnicity, and language.

Deutsch, Morton: Social psychologist who theorized about cooperative, competitive, and individualistic goal structures.

Differentiation of positions: Seeking out and clarifying differences among members' ideas, information, conclusions, theories, and opinion.

Dilemma of honesty and openness: The risk of either being exploited for disclosing too much too quickly or seriously damaging the negotiating relationship by refusing to disclose information and thereby seeming to be deceitful or distrusting.

Dilemma of trust: Choice between believing the other negotiator and risking potential exploitation or disbelieving the other negotiator and risking no agreement.

Discretionary tasks: Tasks for which the group score is any combination of individual efforts the group wants to put together.

Discrimination: Action taken to harm a group or any of its members.

Disjunctive tasks: Tasks for which group performance is determined by the most competent or skilled member.

Disputants: The participants in the conflict who seek mediation.

Dissonance reduction: The process by which an individual or group attempts to rationalize a decision.

Distributed-actions theory of leadership: The performance of acts that help the group to complete its task and to maintain effective working relationships among its members.

Distributive justice: The rewards of group success are distributed among group members in proportion to their contributions.

Distributive (win–lose) negotiations: In this type of negotiation the goal is to maximize your outcomes while minimizing the other person's outcomes.

Dogmatism: A relatively closed organization of beliefs centered around absolute authority that provide patterns of intolerance toward others.

Dualistic thinking: A type of thinking based on the premise that there is only one right and one wrong answer and that authority should not be questioned.

Dynamic-interdependence view of power: Any two persons who interact constantly and are influenced by each other.

Effective communication: When the receiver interprets the sender's message in the same way the sender intended it.

Effective decision: A decision that is made when the group resources are fully utilized, time is well used, the decision is correct and of high quality, the decision is implemented fully by all required group members, and the problem-solving ability of the group is enhanced and maintained.

Effective group: A group whose members commit themselves to the common purpose of maximizing their own and each other's success.

Egocentrism: Embeddedness in one's own viewpoint to the extent that one is unaware of other points of view and of the limitations of one's perspectives.

Epistemic curiosity: An active search for more information in hope of resolving the uncertainty caused by conceptual conflict.

Equality distribution of benefits: A system in which all group members benefit equally from success.

Equality system of distributive justice: All rewards are distributed equally among group members.

Equity or merit view of distributing rewards: A basic rule of distributive justice and equity theory: In a just distribution, rewards will be distributed among individuals in proportion to their contributions. In other words, those members who contribute the most to the group's success should receive the greatest benefits.

Ethnocentrism: Tendency to regard one's own ethnic group, nation, religion, culture, or gender as better or more correct than others.

Evaluation apprehension: Concern over being evaluated by others. Such concern may increase arousal and may play an important role in social facilitation.

Experiential learning: Generating an action theory from your own experiences and then continually modifying it to improve your effectiveness.

Expert power: When group members believe the leader has special knowledge or skill and is trustworthy.

Expertise: A person's proficiency, adroitness, competence, and skill.

External barriers: Task requirements, group norms for avoiding conflict, pressure to maintain a congenial public image, and faulty perceptions of one's vulnerability and others' strength.

False consensus bias: A belief (often false) that most other people think and feel very much as we do, such as sharing our stereotypes (e.g., believing that poor people are lazy).

Feedback: Information that allows individuals to compare their actual performance with standards of performance.

Flowchart: Visual tool to display all steps in a process.

Force field analysis: Portraying the problem as a balance between forces working in opposite directions—some helping the movement toward the desired state of affairs and others restraining such movement. The balance that results between the helping and restraining forces is the actual state of affairs—a *quasistationary equilibrium* that can be altered through changes in the forces.

Forcing: The process of attempting to achieve a goal by causing the other(s) to yield; employed when the goal is of much greater importance than a personal relationship.

Forewarning: Informing the audience of the communicator's intention of converting them to his or her point of view before the delivery of the message.

Frustration-aggression process: Frustration due to the inability to achieve one's goals produces a readiness to respond in an aggressive manner that may boil over into hostility and violence if situational cues that serve as releasers are present.

Fundamental attribution error: The attribution of the causes of others' behaviors to personal (disposition) factors and the causes of one's own behavior to situational (environmental) factors. In explaining the causes of the others' behavior, the attributor overestimates the causal importance of personality, beliefs, attitudes, and values and underestimates the causal importance of situational pressures. The opposite is done in explaining the causes of one's own behavior.

Gatekeeper: Person who translates and interprets messages, information, and new developments to groupmates. Also called *opinion leader*.

Goal: A desired situation toward which people are working; a state of affairs that people value.

Goal dilemma: The problem of reaching an agreement favorable to oneself but not so one-sided that the other negotiator will refuse to agree.

Goal structure: The type of social interdependence specified among individuals as they strive to achieve their goals.

Great person theory of leadership: A theory suggesting that all great leaders share key traits that equip them for positions of power and authority.

Group: Two or more individuals in face-to-face interaction, each aware of his or her membership in the group, each aware of the others who belong to the group, and each aware of positive interdependence as they strive to achieve mutual goals.

Group cohesion: The mutual attraction among group members and the resulting desire to remain in the group.

Group composition: The demographic properties, personal traits, and abilities and skills that characterize a group.

Group dynamics: The area of social science that focuses on advancing knowledge about the nature of group life. The scientific study of behavior in groups to advance our knowledge about the nature of groups, group development, and the interrelations between groups and individuals, other groups, and larger entities.

Group effectiveness: Success by the group in (a) achieving its goals, (b) maintaining good working relationships among members, and (c) developing and adapting to changing conditions to improve its ability to achieve (a) and (b).

Group efficacy: The expectation of successfully obtaining valued outcomes through the joint efforts of the group members.

Group goal: A future state of affairs desired by enough members of a group to motivate the group to work toward its achievement.

Group influence: The impact of groups on their members.

Group polarization: The tendency of group members to shift toward more extreme positions than those held initially as a function of group discussion. Formerly referred to as the *risky shift* phenomenon.

Group processing: Reflecting on a group session to (a) describe what member actions were helpful and unhelpful and (b) make decisions about what actions to continue or change.

Group structure: A stable pattern of interaction among group members created by a role structure and group norms.

Groupthink: The tendency of members of highly cohesive groups led by dynamic leaders to adhere to shared views so strongly that they totally ignore external information inconsistent with these views.

Group-to-individual transfer: When individuals who learned within a cooperative group demonstrate mastery on a subsequent test taken individually.

Hawthorne effect: A change in behavior that occurs when individuals know they are being observed by researchers.

Hero–traitor dynamic: The negotiator who wins is seen as a hero, and the one who loses is perceived to be a traitor.

Hidden agendas: Personal goals that are unknown to all the other group members and are at cross-purposes with the dominant group goals.

High-performance group: A group that meets all effective group criteria and outperforms all reasonable expectations, given its membership. Most groups are unable to achieve this level of development.

High-performance organizational structure: A hierarchy of work teams that are tied together by linking individuals who are leaders in one team but peer-group members at the next highest organizational level; designed to promote teams that focus on continuous improvement in quality.

Histogram: Visual representation of the frequency with which continuous measurement data are clustered and dispersed across a range of values.

Illusionary correlation: Association perceived between two unrelated factors, such as being poor and being lazy, usually leading to stereotypes.

Independent variable: The variable manipulated by the researcher in an experiment; the causal factor in a cause-and-effect relationship.

Individual accountability: Assessing the quality and quantity of each member's contributions and giving the results to all group members.

Individualistic decision making: When isolated individuals independently decide on a course of action without any interaction or consultation with each other.

Individualistic efforts: No correlation among individuals' goal attainments.

Individualistic goal structure: When group members perceive that obtaining their goal is unrelated to the goal achievement of other members.

Individuation: Maintaining a sense of unique individual identity.

Inducibility: Openness to influence.

Influence: Using power to change another person in a desired direction.

Influence leader: A person who exerts more influence on other group members than they exert on him or her.

Information interdependence: Dependence on others for information about their preferences, needs, and expectations so that an agreement can be reached.

Informational power: When the group leader has informational resources that are useful in accomplishing the goal and are unavailable anywhere else.

Initiating structure: Clearly defining one's role as leader and what one expects from the other members of the group.

Integrative negotiation: A type of negotiation in which the goal is to maximize joint benefits.

Intellective tasks: Problem-solving tasks with correct answers.

Interdependence: In a given set of individuals, an event that affects one member is likely to affect all.

Interest: Need, goal, benefit, profit, advantage, concern, right, or claim.

Internal barriers: Negative attitudes, values, fears, anxieties, and habitual patterns of avoiding conflict.

Interpersonal communication: A message sent by a person to a receiver with the conscious intent of affecting the receiver's behavior.

Laissez-faire leader: A leader who does not participate in a group's decision making at all.

Language sensitivity: The knowledge of words and expressions that are appropriate in communicating with diverse groupmates.

Leader: An individual in a group who exerts the greatest influence on other members.

Leadership: The process through which leaders exert their influence on other group members.

Leadership styles: The different ways in which a leader may operate.

Legitimate power: Power derived from group members' belief that leader should have influence over them because of special role responsibilities (such as police officer) or position in the group (such as employer).

Level of aspiration (LOA): The compromise between ideal goals and more realistic expectations. A concept developed primarily by Kurt Lewin to explain how people set and revise goals for themselves and their groups. Generally, individuals enter situations with an ideal outcome in mind but revise their goals upward after success and downward after failure.

Leveling: Making a message shorter, more concise, and more easily grasped and told. The reciprocal of sharpening.

Lewin, Kurt: Father of group dynamics; social psychologist who originated field theory, experimental group dynamics, and applied group dynamics.

Machiavellian leadership: Leadership based on the beliefs that (a) people are basically weak, fallible, and gullible, and not particularly trustworthy; (b) others are impersonal objects; and (c) one should manipulate others whenever it is necessary to achieve one's ends.

Majority vote: A method of group decision making in which an issue is discussed only as long as it takes at least 51% of group members to decide on a course of action.

Manipulation: The managing or controlling of others by a shrewd use of influence for one's own purposes and profit.

Mass-production organizational structure: An authority hierarchy is rigidly imposed and work is divided into small competent parts performed by individuals who work separately from and in competition with other members; designed to drive down the unit of costs of long runs of standardized products.

Means interdependence: The second major category of interdependence. The ways in which mutual group goals and rewards are to be accomplished (includes resource, role, and task interdependence).

Mediation: A form of third-party intervention in negotiations in which a neutral person recommends a nonbinding agreement.

Mediator: A neutral person who helps two or more people resolve their conflict by assisting them with problem-solving negotiations to reach an agreement that both parties believe is fair, just, and workable.

Member maturity: The capacity to set high but attainable goals, willingness and ability to take responsibility, and adequate education/experience, all with regard to specific task.

Merit distribution of benefits: A system in which the rewards of group success are contingent upon performance and contribution.

Message: Any verbal or nonverbal symbol that one person transmits to another; the subject matter being referred to in a symbolic way (all words are symbols).

Meta-analysis: A method of statistically combining the results of a set of independent studies that test the same hypothesis and using inferential statistics to draw conclusions about the overall result of the studies.

Minority control: A method of group decision making in which less than 50% of group members determine the group's course of action.

Modern racism: A more subtle form of prejudice in which people appear on the surface not to harbor prejudice, but who do in fact hold racist attitudes.

Need: A necessity for survival.

Need distribution of benefits: A situation in which the group members who are most in need of the rewards receive a disproportionate amount of them. A rule suggesting that individuals receive a share of available rewards reflecting their current needs.

Negotiation: A process by which persons who want to come to an agreement try to work out a settlement by exchanging proposals and counterproposals.

Noise: Any element that interferes with the communication process.

Nonoperational goals: Goals that are abstract in that the specific steps required to accomplish them are indiscernible; often used to describe broad, long-range goals.

Norm of equity: Norm specifying that the benefits received or the costs assessed by the negotiators should be equal.

Norm of reciprocity: Norm that a negotiator should return the same benefit or harm given him or her by the other negotiator; "an eye for an eye and a kiss for a kiss" is an example of a norm of reciprocity.

Norms: The rules or expectations that specify appropriate behavior in the group; the standards by which group members regulate their actions.

Observation procedures: Aimed at describing and recording behavior as it occurs. From the behavior of group members, an observer can make inferences about the way in which the group is functioning.

One-way communication: One group member giving instructions and making announcements to other group members who are not allowed to communicate with him or her.

Open-mindedness: The ability to listen to, comprehend, and gain insight from information, ideas, perspectives, assumptions, beliefs, conclusions, and opinions different from one's own.

Openness: The sharing of information, ideas, thoughts, feelings, and reactions to the issue the group is pursuing.

Operational goals: Goals for which specific steps to achievement are clear and identifiable.

Opinion leader: See **Gatekeeper.**

Oppositional interaction: Occurs as individuals discourage and obstruct each other's efforts to achieve.

Organizational development: The use of diagnosis and intervention procedures to promote effective interpersonal, group, and intergroup behavior within the organization.

Organizational effectiveness: The extent to which the organization achieves its goals with the use of minimal resources.

Outcome dependence: Dependence on others to agree to one's proposals in negotiations. Because all parties must commit themselves to an agreement, each is dependent upon the others for the outcome.

Outcome interdependence: When the goals and rewards directing individuals' actions are positively correlated; that is, if one person accomplishes his or her goal or receives a reward, all others with whom the person is cooperatively linked also achieve their goals or receive a reward.

Paraphrasing: Restating in your own words what the person says, feels, and means.

Pareto chart: Form of vertical bar chart that is used to display the frequency and relative importance of problems, causes, or conditions in order to choose the starting point for process improvement.

Participant-observer: A person who is skilled enough to both participate in group work and observe the group process at the same time; analysis of the group process and functioning by a participating member of the group.

Participating: A low-task–high-relationship behavior characterized by sharing of decision making through two-way communication and facilitating behavior from leader.

Participation interdependence: The understanding that it takes two to negotiate—whether it is two group members, two organizations, or two nations.

Performance tasks: Tasks that can be completed only through the proficient use of perceptual and motor skills.

Personal diversity: A measure of the variation within a group determined by the differences in personalities and working and learning styles of group members.

Personal identity: One's perceptions of self, a function of a variety of factors such as age, sex, culture, ethnicity, language, abilities, skills, and so forth.

Perspective-taking: The establishment of a position on an issue based on information, understanding, and experiences.

Persuasive argument: An attempt to point out the validity of your position and the incorrectness of the other's opinion.

Positive goal interdependence: When members perceive that they can achieve their goals if, and only if, all other members of their group also attain their goals.

Positive interdependence: The perception that one is linked with others in such a way that success is impossible without them (and vice versa) and that the group effort must be coordinated in order to complete a task.

Power: The ability to influence and control others while resisting their influence and control.

Preemptive action: A type of conflict resolution designed to resolve the conflict without the other person's consent (such as taking up residence on a disputed piece of land).

Prejudice: An unjustified negative attitude toward a person based solely on that individual's membership in a group other than one's own.

Prisoner's Dilemma Game: Non–zero sum game used by Deutsch and others to investigate trust and conflict.

Probabilistic thinking: A type of thinking based on the premise that knowledge is available only in degrees of certainty.

Problem: A discrepancy or difference between an actual state of affairs and a desired state of affairs.

Procedural learning: Learning conceptually what the skill is, when it should be used, how to engage in the skill, and practicing the skill while eliminating errors until an automatic level of mastery is attained.

Process: An identifiable sequence of events taking place over time.

Process consultation: An organizational-development procedure of analyzing group functioning by an observing expert.

Process gain: When new ideas, solutions, or efforts are generated through group interaction that are not generated when persons work individually.

Process goals: The sequence of events instrumental in achieving outcome goals.

Process loss: Losses in members' performance due to their participation in the group.

Process observation: The act of simultaneously participating in group work and observing group processes for the purpose of assessing group function.

Production tasks: Problem-solving tasks that have objective standards for performance evaluation and require the proficient use of perceptual and motor skills.

Promise: The statement that if you do as I want, I will engage in an act that will benefit you. A negotiator stating that if the other performs a desired act the negotiator will make sure the other receives benefits.

Promotive interaction: When individuals encourage and facilitate each other's efforts to complete tasks and achieve in order to reach the group's goals.

Pseudogroup: A group whose members have been assigned to work together but who have no interest in doing so.

Psychodynamic fallacy: Seeing the motivation for the other's behavior in terms of personality factors rather than the dynamics of intergroup conflict.

Psychological health: The ability to develop, maintain, and appropriately modify interdependent relationships with others to succeed in achieving goals.

Psychological reactance: The need to reestablish one's freedom whenever it is threatened.

Racism: Prejudice directed at people because of their ethnic membership.

Reactance: People's need to reestablish their freedom whenever it is threatened.

Receiver: The person at whom the message is aimed.

Recurring-phase theories: These theories specify the issues that dominate group interaction and that occur over and over again.

Reference group: A group people identify with, compare their attitudes to, and use as a means to evaluate those attitudes.

Referent power: Power based on the group members' identification with, attraction to, or respect for the powerholder.

Relationship actions: Consideration of group members' ideas and feelings before implementing an action.

Relativistic thinking: A type of thinking based on the premise that authorities are sometimes right and sometimes wrong but that right and wrong depend on your perspective.

Resistance: The psychological force aroused in a person that keeps him or her from being influenced.

Resource attractor: An attribute (such as ability or training) that tends to attract other resources because it gives the possessor an advantage in a competition for these other resources.

Reward power: Power based on the power holder's control over the positive and negative reinforcements desired by other group members.

Risky shift: See **Group polarization.**

Role: A set of expectations defining appropriate behaviors associated with a position within a group. The part played by a member of a group. Rules or understandings about the tasks that persons occupying certain positions within a group are expected to perform.

Role conflict: When the demands of one role are incompatible with the demands of another.

Role playing: A tool for bringing a specific skill and its consequences into focus, and thus vital for experiential learning; a way in which one can experience concretely the type of interaction under examination. An imaginary life situation is set up in which one acts and reacts in terms of assumptions one is being asked to adopt based on the character one is asked to play.

Role-position approach to leadership: A set of expected behaviors associated with a position within a hierarchial group.

Rule of self-direction: A belief that people should be free to decide for themselves how they want to guide their lives.

Run chart: Line graph used to monitor the behavior of a selected characteristic over time.

Scapegoat: A guiltless but defenseless group that is attacked to provide an outlet for pent-up anger and frustration caused by another group.

Scatter diagram: Displays the cause-and-effect relationship between two process variables or characteristics.

Self-efficacy: The expectation of successfully obtaining valued outcomes through personal effort; the expectation that if one exerts sufficient effort, one will be successful.

Self-fulfilling prophecy: A set of actions that provokes the other to engage in behavior that confirms one's original assumptions. An example is assuming that the other is belligerent and then proceeding to engage in hostile behavior, thereby provoking the other into belligerent actions, which confirms the original assumption.

Self-regulation: The ability to act in socially approved ways in the absence of external monitors.

Selling: A high-task–high-relationship behavior characterized by two-way communication and socioeconomic support to get group members to believe in decisions that have been made.

Sender: The communicator.

Sender credibility: The attitude the receiver has toward the perceived trustworthiness of the sender's statement.

Sequential-stage theories: These theories specify the typical order of the phase of group development.

Sexism: Prejudice directed at a person because of his or her gender.

Sharing: Offering your materials and resources to others in order to help them move the group toward goal accomplishment.

Sharpening: Selective perceiving and remembering of a few high points of a message while most of the rest is forgotten. The reciprocal of leveling.

Situational approach to leadership: The view that the members of a group most likely to become leaders are those who can best help it to reach its major goals.

Small group: Two or more individuals in face-to-face interaction, each aware of positive interdependence as they strive to achieve mutual goals, each aware of his or her group membership, and each aware of the others who belong to the group.

Smoothing: The process of giving up a goal in order to maintain a relationship at the highest quality possible; employed when the relationship is of much greater importance than personal goals.

Social dependence: The outcome of one person is affected by the actions of a second person, but not vice versa.

Social determinism: The view that historic events are determined by social forces, social movements, and changing social values; see **Zeitgeist.**

Social exchange: A form of social interaction in which participants exchange something of value. What they exchange can range from specific goods or services to information, love, and approval.

Social facilitation: The enhancement of well-learned responses in the presence of others. Effects on performance resulting from the presence of others.

Social independence: When individuals' outcomes are unaffected by each other's actions.

Social interaction: Patterns of mutual influence linking two or more persons.

Social interdependence: When individuals share common goals and each individual's outcomes are affected by the actions of the others.

Social loafing: A reduction of individual effort when working with others on an additive group task.

Socioemotional activity: Behavior that focuses on interpersonal relations in the group.

Sociometry: A measurement procedure developed by Moreno that is used to summarize graphically and mathematically patterns of interpersonal attraction in groups.

Status: The degree to which an individual's contribution is crucial to the success and prestige of the group, how much power that individual has, and the extent to which the person embodies some idealized or admired characteristic.

Steps of integrative negotiating: (1) Each person explains what he or she wants in a descriptive, nonevaluative way. (2) Each person explains how he or she feels in a descriptive, nonevaluative way. (3) Each person explains his or her reasons for wanting what he or she wants and for feeling the way he or she does. (4) Each person reverses perspectives by summarizing what the other person(s) wants and feels and the reasons underlying those wants and feelings. (5) The participants invent at least three good optional agreements that would maximize joint outcomes. (6) The participants choose the agreement that seems wisest and agree to abide by its conditions.

Stereotype: Set of cognitive generalizations that summarize, organize, and guide the processing of information about members of a particular group.

Substitutability: Part of Deutsch's theory of interdependence. When the actions of one person replace the actions of another.

Superordinate goals: Goals that cannot be easily ignored by members of two antagonistic groups, but whose attainment is beyond the resources and efforts of either group alone; the two groups, therefore, must join in a cooperative effort in order to attain the goals.

Superordinate identity: Group identity that transcends the personal, gender, ethnic, and religious identities of group members.

Support: The communication to others that you recognize their strengths and believe in their ability to manage productively the situation they are in.

Survey-feedback method: An organizational development procedure that focuses on describing the current state of the organization through surveys or interviews and then sharing this descriptive information through feedback.

Synthesizing: Integrating a number of different positions containing diverse information and conclusions into a new, single, inclusive position that all group members can agree on and commit themselves to.

Task actions: The initiation of structure to achieve a goal.

Team: A set of interpersonal relationships structured to achieve established goals.

Team building: The analysis of work procedures and activities to improve productivity, relationships among members, the social competence of members, and the ability of the team to adapt to changing conditions and demands.

Team training: Teaching team members the taskwork and teamwork skills that optimize efficiency, effectiveness, and improvement.

Telling: High-task–low relationship leadership behavior characterized by one-way communication between leader and other group members.

Theory: A set of interrelated hypotheses or propositions concerning a phenomenon or set of phenomena.

Threat: The statement that unless you do as I say, I will engage in an act that will harm you. One individual informing another that negative actions will follow if the recipient of the threat does (or does not) behave in some manner. A negotiator stating that unless the other agrees to the proposed settlement, the negotiator will make sure the other is harmed.

Total quality management: Use of teams to continuously improve the processes by which the product or service is produced.

Traditional work group: A group whose members agree to work together, but see little benefit from doing so.

Trait approach to leadership: The belief that inborn traits determine the leadership ability of an individual.

Trait factor view of power: The belief that influence is a function of the characteristics of the person exerting the influence, the person receiving the influence, and the influence attempt itself.

Transactional approach to leadership: An approach suggesting that leadership involves a complex social relationship between leaders and followers in which each exerts influence on the other.

Triggering event: An event (such as two group members being in competition or the expression of criticism on a sensitive point) that triggers the occurrence of a conflict.

Trust: Perception that a choice can lead to gains or losses, that whether you will gain or lose depends on the behavior of the other person, that the loss will be greater than the gain, and that the person will likely behave so that you will gain rather than lose.

Trusting behavior: Being self-disclosing and openly accepting and supportive of others.

Trustworthy behavior: Expressing acceptance, support, and cooperative intentions.

Two-way communication: A reciprocal process in which each member starts messages and tries to understand the other members' messages.

Unitary task: One that cannot be divided into subtasks. One person has to complete the entire task.

Vigilant analysis: A decision-making procedure that ensures that each alternative solution is considered to eliminate the possibility of defensive avoidance.

Vision: An ideal and unique image of the future used to clarify the missions and goals of the group.

Want: A desire for something.

Win–lose dynamic: Seeing every action of the other as a move to dominate.

Withdrawal: The process of giving up goals and a relationship in order to avoid conflict caused by the issue and interactions with the other person.

Zeitgeist: Spirit or temper of the times.

References

Abelson, R., Dasgupta, N., Park, J., & Banaji, M. (1998). Perceptions of the collective other. *Personality and Social Psychology Review, 2*(4), 243–250.

Achenbach, T., & Edelbrock, C. (1981). Behavioral problems and competencies reported by parents of normal and disturbed children aged four through sixteen. *Monographs of the Society for Research in Child Development, 46*(1, Serial No. 188).

Agnew, C., Van Lange, P., Rusbult, C., & Langston, C. (1998). Cognitive interdependence: Commitment and the mental representation of close relationship. *Journal of Personality and Social Psychology, 74,* 939–954.

Alberti, R., & Emmons, M. (1978). *Your perfect right.* San Luis Obispo, CA: Impact Publishers.

Allen, V. (1965). Situational factors in conformity. In L. Berkowitz (Ed.), *Advances in experimental social psychology* (Vol. 2, pp. 133–175). New York: Academic Press.

Allport, F. (1924). *Social psychology.* Boston: Houghton Mifflin.

Allport, G. (1954). *The nature of prejudice.* Cambridge, MA: Addison-Wesley.

Allport, G., & Kramer, B. (1946). Some roots of prejudice. *Journal of Psychology, 22,* 9–39.

Allport, G., & Postman, L. (1945). The basic psychology of rumor. *Transactions of the New York Academic Sciences,* Series II, *8,* 61–81.

Altman, L., & Churchman, A. (Eds.). (1994). *Human behavior and the environment: Advances in theory and research, place attachment* (Vol. 12). New York: Plenum.

Altman, L., & Taylor, D. (1973). *Social penetration: The development of interpersonal relationships.* New York: Holt, Rinehart, & Winston.

Ames, G., & Murray, F. (1982). When two wrongs make a right: Promoting cognitive change by social conflict. *Developmental Psychology, 18,* 894–897.

Amir, Y. (1969). Contact hypothesis in ethnic relations. *Psychological Bulletin, 71,* 319–352.

———. (1976). The role of intergroup contact in change in prejudice and ethnic relations. In P. Katz (Ed.), *Towards the elimination of racism* (pp. 245–308). New York: Pergamon.

Archer-Kath, J., Johnson, D. W., & Johnson, R. (1994). Individual versus group feedback in cooperative groups. *Journal of Social Psychology, 134*(5), 681–694.

Argyris, C. (1964). *Integrating the individual and the organization.* New York: Wiley.

Aristotle (384–322 B.C./1991). *The art of rhetoric* (H. C. Lawson-Tancred, Trans.). New York: Penguin Books.

Aronson, E., Blaney, N., Stephan, C., Sikes, J., & Snapp, M. (1978). *The jigsaw classroom.* Beverly Hills, CA: Sage.

Arriaga, X., & Rusbult, C. (1998). Standing in my partner's shoes: Partner perspective taking and reactions to accommodative dilemmas. *Personality and Social Psychology Bulletin, 24*(9), 927–948.

Asarnow, J., & Callan, J. (1985). Boys with peer adjustment problems: Social cognitive processes. *Journal of Consulting and Clinical Psychology, 53,* 80–87.

Asch, S. (1951). Effects of group pressure upon the modification and distortion of judgments. In H. Guetzkow (Ed.), *Groups, leadership, and men* (pp. 177–190). Pittsburgh: Carnegie Press.

———. (1952). *Social psychology.* New York: Prentice-Hall.

———. (1956). Studies of independence and conformity: A minority of one against a unanimous majority. *Psychological Monographs, 70,* 416.

———. (1957). An experimental investigation of group influence. In *Symposium on preventive and social psychiatry* (pp. 17–24). Walter Reed Army Institute of Research. Washington, DC: U.S. Government Printing Office.

Ashmore, R., & Del Boca, F. (1979). Sex stereotypes and implicit personality theory: Toward a cognitive-social psychological conceptualization. *Sex Roles, 5,* 219–248.

Axelrod, R. (1984). *The evolution of cooperation.* New York: Basic Books.

Babchuk, N., & Good, W. (1951). Work incentives in a self-determined group. *American Journal of Sociology, 16,* 679–687.

Bahn, C. (1964). *The interaction of creativity and social facilitation in creative problem solving.* (Doctoral dissertation, Columbia University.) Dissertation Abstracts International. (University Microfilms No. 65-7499). V24, 57.

Balderston, G. (1930). *Group incentives, some variations in the use of group bonus and gang piece work.* Philadelphia: University of Pennsylvania Press.

Baldwin, T., & Ford, J. (1988). Transfer of training: A review and directions for future research. *Personality Psychology, 41,* 63–105.

Bales, R. (1950). *Interaction process analysis.* Reading, MA: Addison-Wesley.

———. (1952). Some uniformities of behavior in small social systems. In G. Swanson, T. Newcomb, & E. Hartley (Eds.), *Readings in social psychology* (pp. 437–446). New York: Holt.

———. (1953). The equilibrium problem in small groups. In T. Parsons, R. Bales, & E. Shils (Eds.), *Working papers in the theory of action* (pp. 111–162). Glencoe, IL: Free Press.

———. (1955). How people interact in conferences. *Scientific American, 192,* 31–35.

———. (1965). The equilibrium problem in small groups. In A. Hare, E. Borgatta, & R. Bales (Eds.), *Small groups: Studies in social interaction* (pp. 444–476). New York: Knopf.

Bales, R., & Slater, P. (1955). Role differentiation in small decision-making groups. In T. Parsons & R. Bales (Eds.), *The family, socialization, and interaction process* (pp. 159–306). Glencoe, IL: Free Press.

Bales, R., & Strodtbeck, F. (1951). Phases in group problem solving. *Journal of Abnormal and Social Psychology, 46,* 485–495.

Banas, P. (1988). Employee involvement: A sustained labor/management initiative at the Ford Motor Company. In J. Campbell & R. Campbell (Eds.), *Productivity in organizations: New perspectives from industrial and organizational psychology* (pp. 388–416). San Francisco: Jossey-Bass.

Bandura, A. (1969). *Principles of behavior modification.* New York: Holt, Rinehart & Winston.

———. (1977). *Social learning theory.* Englewood Cliffs, NJ: Prentice-Hall.

Bantel, K., & Jackson, S. (1989). Top management and innovations in banking: Does the composition of the top team make a difference? *Strategic Management Journal, 10,* 107–124.

Barnlund, D. (1959). A comparative study of individual, majority and group judgment. *Journal of Abnormal and Social Psychology 58,* 55–60.

Baron, R. (1986). Distraction-conflict theory: Progress and problems. In L. Berkowitz (Ed.), *Advances in experimental social psychology* (Vol. 19, pp. 1–40). New York: Academic Press.

Baron, R., Kerr, N., & Miller, N. (1992). *Group process, group decision, group action.* Pacific Grove, CA: Brooks/Cole.

Baron, R., Moore, D., & Sanders, G. (1978). Distraction as a source of drive in social facilitation research. *Journal of Personality and Social Psychology, 36,* 816–824.

Baron, R., Roper, G., & Baron, P. (1974). Group discussion and the stingy shift. *Journal of Personality and Social Psychology, 30,* 538–545.

Bartlett, F. (1932). *Remembering.* Cambridge: Cambridge University Press.

Bass, B. (1960). *Leadership, psychology, and organizational behavior.* New York: Harper & Row.

———. (1982). Individual capability, team performance, and team productivity. In E. Fleishman & M. Dunnette (Eds.), *Human performance and productivity: Human capability assessment* (pp. 179–232). Hillsdale, NJ: Erlbaum.

Batson, C., Early, S., & Salvarani, G. (1997). Perspective taking: Imagining how another feels versus imagining how you would feel. *Personality and Social Psychology Bulletin, 23*(7), 751–758.

Baum, A., Singer, J., & Baum, C. (1982). Stress and the environment. *Journal of Social Issues, 37*(1), 4–35.

Baumeister, R., Smart, L., & Boden, J. (1996). Relation of threatened egotism to violence and aggression: The dark side of high self-esteem. *Psychological Review, 103,* 5–33.

Bavelas, A. (1942). Morale and training of leaders. In G. Watson (Ed.), *Civilian morale* (pp. 143–165). Boston: Houghton Mifflin.

———. (1948). A mathematical model for group structures. *Applied Anthropology, 7*, 16–30.

Bavelas, A., Hostorf, A., Gross, A., & Kite, W. (1965). Experiments on the alteration of group structure. *Journal of Experimental Social Psychology, 1*, 55–70.

Beckhard, R. (1969). *Organizational development.* Reading, MA: Addison-Wesley.

Bednar, R., & Kaul, T. (1994). Experiential group research: Can the cannon fire? In S. Garfield & A. Bergin (Eds.), *Handbook of psychotherapy and behavior change* (4th ed., pp. 631–663). New York: Wiley.

Beer, M. (1976). The technology of organization development. In M. Dunnette (Ed.), *Handbook of industrial and organizational psychology* (pp. 937–994). Chicago: Rand McNally.

———. (1980). *Organization change and development: A systems view.* Glenview, IL: Scott, Foresman.

Bekhterev, W., & DeLange, M. (1924). Die ergebnisse des experiments auf dem gebiet der kollektiven reflexologie. *Zeitschrift fur Angewandte Psychologie, 24*, 305–344.

Bem, D. (1972). Self-perception theory. In L. Berkowitz (Ed.), *Advances in experimental social psychology* (Vol. 6, pp. 2–62). New York: Academic Press.

Ben-Yoav, O., & Pruitt, D. (1984a). Resistance to yielding and the expectation of cooperative future interaction in negotiation. *Journal of Experimental Social Psychology, 20*, 323–353.

———. (1984b). Accountability to constituents: A two-edged sword. *Organizational Behavior and Human Performance, 34*, 282–295.

Bennett, E. (1955). Discussion, decision, commitment and consensus in "group decision." *Human Relations, 8*, 251.

Berger, J., Rosenholtz, S., & Zelditch, M. (1980). Status organizing processes. *Annual Review of Sociology, 6*, 479–508.

Berkowitz, L. (1978). Whatever happened to the frustration-aggression hypothesis? *American Behavioral Scientist, 32*, 691–708.

Berlyne, D. (1965). Curiosity and education. In J. Krumboltz (Ed.), *Learning and the educational process* (pp. 67–89). Chicago: Rand McNally.

Bernstein, A. (1991, April). Quality is becoming job one in the office, too. *Business Week*, 52–56.

Bettencourt, B., Charlton, K., & Kernahan, C. (in press). Numerical representation of groups in cooperative settings: Social orientation effects on ingroup bias. *Journal of Experimental Social Psychology.*

Bettencourt, B., & Dorr, N. (1998). Cooperative interaction and intergroup bias: Effects of numerical representation and cross-cut role assignment. *Personality and Social Psychology Bulletin, 24*(12), 1276–1293.

Bickman, L. (1974). The social power of a uniform. *Journal of Applied Social Psychology, 4*, 47–61.

Bierman, R. (1962a). Comprehension of points of commonality in competing solutions. *Sociometry, 25*, 56–63.

———. (1962b). The intergroup dynamics of win–lose conflict and problem-solving collaboration in union–management relations. In M. Sherif (Ed.), *Intergroup relations and leadership* (pp. 232–281). New York: Wiley.

———. (1969). Dimensions for interpersonal facilitation in psychotherapy in child development. *Psychological Bulletin, 72*, 338–352.

Bion, W. (1961). *Experiences in groups.* New York: Basic Books.

Bird, C. (1940). *Social psychology.* New York: Appleton-Century-Crofts.

Blake, R., & Mouton, J. (1962). The intergroup dynamics of win–lose conflict and problem-solving collaboration in union–management relations. In M. Sherif (Ed.), *Intergroup relations and leadership* (Vol. 5, pp. 94–140). New York: Wiley.

———. (1964). *The managerial grid.* Houston, TX: Gulf.

———. (1983). Lateral conflict. In D. Tjosvold & D. W. Johnson (Eds.), *Productive conflict management: Perspectives for organizations* (pp. 91–149). Edina, MN: Interaction.

Blanchard, F., Lilly, T., & Vaughn, L. (1991). Reducing the expression of racial prejudice. *Psychological Science, 2*, 101–105.

Blau, P. (1954). Co-operation and competition in a bureaucracy. *American Journal of Sociology, 59*, 530–535.

Bloch, S., Browning, S., & McGrath, G. (1983). Humor in group psychotherapy. *British Journal of Mediation Psychology, 56*, 89–97.

Bolen, L., & Torrance, E. (1976, April). *An experimental study of the influence of locus of control, dyadic interaction, and sex on creative thinking.* Paper presented at the annual meeting of the American Educational Research Association, San Francisco.

Bond, C. (1982). Social facilitation: A self-presentational view. *Journal of Personality and Social Psychology, 42*, 1042–1050.

Bond, C., & Titus, L. (1983). Social facilitation: A meta-analysis of 241 studies. *Psychological Bulletin, 94,* 265–292.

Bonner, H. (1959). *Group dynamics: Principles and applications.* New York: Ronald Press.

Boster, F., & Hale, J. (1989). Responsive scale ambiguity as a moderator of the choice shift. *Communication Research, 16*(4), 532–551.

Botkin, B. (1957). *A treasury of American anecdotes.* New York: Random House.

Bray, R., Kerr, N., & Atkin, S. (1978). Group size, problem difficulty, and group performance on unitary disjunctive tasks. *Journal of Personality and Social Psychology, 36,* 1224–1240.

Brehm, J. (1966). *A theory of psychological reactance.* New York: Academic Press.

———. (1976). Responses to loss of freedom: A theory of psychological reactance. In J. Thibaut, J. Spence, & R. Carson (Eds.), *Contemporary topics in social psychology* (pp. 241–273). Morristown, NJ: General Learning Press.

Brehm, S., & Brehm, J. (1981). *Psychological reactance: A theory of freedom and control.* New York: Academic Press.

Brehm, J., & Sensenig, J. (1966). Social influence as a function of attempted and implied usurpation of choice. *Journal of Personality and Social Psychology, 4,* 703–707.

Brett, J., & Rognes, J. (1986). Intergroup relations in organizations. In P. Goodman (Ed.), *Designing effective work groups* (pp. 202–236). San Francisco: Jossey-Bass.

Brewer, M. (1988). A dual process model of impression formation. In T. Srull & R. Wyer, Jr. (Eds.), *Advances in social cognition* (Vol. 1, pp. 1–36). Hillsdale, NJ: Erlbaum.

———. (1991). The social self: On being the same and different at the same time. *Personality and Social Psychology Bulletin, 17,* 475–482.

———. (1996). Managing diversity: The role of social identities. In S. Jackson & M. Ruderman (Eds.), *Diversity in work teams* (pp. 47–68). Washington, DC: American Psychological Association.

———. (1997). The social psychology of intergroup relations: Can research inform practice? *Journal of Social Issues, 33*(1), 197–211.

Brewer, M., Ho, H., Lee, J., & Miller, N. (1987). Social identity and social distance among Hong Kong schoolchildren. *Personality and Social Psychology Bulletin, 13,* 156–165.

Brewer, M., Manzi, K., & Shaw, J. (1993). Ingroup identification as a function of depersonalization, distinctiveness, and status. *Psychological Science, 4,* 88–92.

Brewer, M., & Miller, N. (1984). Beyond the contact hypothesis: Theoretical perspectives on desegregation. In N. Miller & M. Brewer (Eds.), *Groups in contact: The psychology of desegregation* (pp. 281–302). Orlando, FL: Academic Press.

Brickner, M. (1987). *Locked into performance: Goal setting as a moderator of the social loafing effect.* Paper presented at the annual meeting of the Midwestern Psychological Association, Chicago.

Brickner, M., Harkins, S., & Ostrom, T. (1986). Effects of personal involvement: Thought-provoking implications for social loafing. *Journal of Personality and Social Psychology, 51,* 763–769.

Bronowski, J. (1973). *The ascent of man.* Boston: Little, Brown.

Broome, R., & Fullbright, L. (1995). A multistage influence model of barriers to group problem solving: A participant-generated agenda for small group research. *Small Group Research, 26,* 25–55.

Brophy, J. (1945). The luxury of anti-Negro prejudice. *Public Opinion Quarterly, 9,* 456–466.

Brown, B. (1968). The effects of the need to maintain face on interpersonal bargaining. *Journal of Experimental Social Psychology, 4,* 107–122.

Brown, C., Dovidio, J., & Ellyson, S. (1990). Reducing sex differences in visual displays of dominance: Knowledge is power. *Personality and Social Psychology Bulletin, 16,* 358–368.

Brown, R. (1984). The role of similarity in intergroup relations. In H. Tajfel (Ed.), *The social dimension* (Vol. 2, pp. 603–623). Cambridge: Cambridge University Press.

Bruner, J., & Minturn, A. (1955). Perceptual identification and perceptual organization. *Journal of Genetic Psychology, 53,* 21–28.

Buller, P., & Bell, C. (1986). Effects of team building and goal setting on productivity: A field experiment. *Academy of Management Journal, 29,* 305–328.

Burke, P. (1972). Leadership role differentiation. In C. McClintock (Ed.), *Experimental social psychology* (pp. 514–546). New York: Holt, Rinehart & Winston.

———. (1974). Participation and leadership in small groups. *American Sociological Review, 39,* 832–842.

Burke, R. (1969, July). Methods of resolving interpersonal conflict. *Personnel Administration,* 48–55.

———. (1970). Methods of resolving superior–subordinate conflict: The constructive use of subordinate differences and disagreements. *Organizational Behavior and Human Performance, 5,* 393–411.

Burke, R., & Day, R. (1986). A cumulative study of the effectiveness of managerial training. *Journal of Applied Psychology, 71,* 232–245.

Burnstein, E., & Vinokur, A. (1977). Persuasive argumentation and social comparison as determinants of attitude polarization. *Journal of Experimental Social Psychology, 13,* 315–332.

Bushman, B. (1984). Perceived symbols of authority and their influence on compliance. *Journal of Applied Social Psychology, 14,* 501–508.

Butler, T., & Fuhriman, A. (1983a). Curative factors in group therapy: A review of the recent literature. *Small Group Behavior, 14,* 131–142.

———. (1983b). Level of functioning and length of time in treatment variables influencing patients' therapeutic experience in group psychotherapy. *International Journal of Group Psychotherapy, 33,* 489–505.

Buunk, B. (1995). Comparison direction and comparison dimension among disabled individuals: Toward a refined conceptualization of social comparison under stress. *Personality and Social Psychology Bulletin, 21,* 316–330.

Byrne, D. (1971). *The attraction paradigm.* New York: Academic Press.

Campbell, D. (1965). Ethnocentric and other altruistic motives. In D. Levine (Ed.), *Nebraska symposium on motivation.* Lincoln: University Nebraska Press.

———. (1978). On the genetics of altruism and the counterhedonic components in human culture. In L. Wispe (Ed.), *Altruism, sympathy, and helping* (pp. 58–84). New York: Academic Press.

Cantrell, V., & Prinz, R. (1985). Multiple perspectives of rejected, neglected, and accepted children: Relation between sociometric status and behavioral characteristics. *Journal of Consulting and Clinical Psychology, 53,* 884–889.

Cantril, H. (1940). *The invasion from Mars: A study in the psychology of panic.* Princeton: Princeton University Press.

———. (1941). *The psychology of social movements.* New York: Wiley.

Carlopio, J. (1996). Construct validity of a physical work environment satisfaction questionnaire. *Journal of Occupational Health Psychology, 1,* 330–344.

Carnegie Foundation. (1995). *Report of the Carnegie task force on learning in the primary grades.* New York: Author.

Carnevale, P., & Keenan, P. (1990). *Frame and motive in integrative bargaining: The likelihood and the quality of agreement.* Paper presented at the third annual meeting of the International Association for Conflict Management, Vancouver, British Columbia.

Carnevale, P., & Pegnetter, R. (1985). The selection of mediation tactics in public sector disputes: A contingency analysis. *Journal of Social Issues, 41*(2), 65–81.

Cartwright, D. (1959). A field theoretical conception of power. In D. Cartwright (Ed.), *Studies in social power.* Ann Arbor: University of Michigan Press.

———. (1968). The nature of group cohesiveness. In D. Cartwright & A. Zander (Eds.), *Group dynamics: Research and theory* (3rd ed., pp. 91–109). New York: Harper & Row.

Cartwright, D., & Zander, A. (Eds.). (1968). *Group dynamics: Research and theory* (3rd ed.). New York: Harper & Row.

Caspi, A. (1984). Contact hypothesis and inter-age attitudes: A field study of cross-age contact. *Social Psychology Quarterly, 47,* 74–80.

Cattell, R. (1951). New concepts for measuring leadership, in terms of group syntality. *Human Relations, 4,* 161–184.

Charlesworth, W. (1996). Co-operation and competition: Contributions to an evolutionary and developmental model. *International Journal of Behavioral Development, 19,* 25–39.

Chertkoff, J., & Esser, J. (1976). A review of experiments in explicit bargaining. *Journal of Experimental Social Psychology, 12,* 464–487.

Chesler, M., & Franklin, J. (1968, August). *Interracial and intergenerational conflict in secondary schools.* Paper presented at the annual meeting of the American Sociological Association, Boston.

Christie, R., & Geis, F. (1970). *Studies in Machiavelianism.* New York: Academic Press.

Clark, K. (1953). Desegregation: An appraisal of the evidence. *Journal of Social Issues, 9*(4), 2–8.

Clement, D., & Schiereck, J. (1973). Sex composition and group performance in a visual signal detection task. *Memory and Cognition, 1,* 251–255.

Cline, R. (1999). Communication in social support groups. In L. Frey (Ed.), *Handbook of group communication theory and research* (pp. 516–538). Thousand Oaks, CA: Sage.

Cohen, E. (1984). Talking and working together: Status, interaction and learning. In P. Peterson, L. Wilkinson, & M. Hallinan (Eds.), *The social context of instruction: Group organization and group processes* (pp. 171–187). New York: Academic Press.

Cohen, S., & Weinstein, N. (1981). Nonauditory effects of noise on behavior and health. *Journal of Social Issues, 37*(1), 36–70.

Coie, J., & Kupersmidt, J. (1983). A behavioral analysis of emerging social status in boys' groups. *Child Development, 54,* 1400–1416.

Coleman, P. (1997). Psychological resistance to and facilitation of power-sharing in organizations. Dissertation Abstracts.

———. (2000). Power and conflict. In M. Deutsch & P. Coleman (Eds.), *The handbook of conflict resolution: Theory and practice* (pp. 108–130). San Francisco: Jossey-Bass.

Coleman, P., & Tjosvold, D. (2000, July). Positive power: Mapping the dimensions of constructive power relations. Paper presented at the Social Interdependence Theory Conference, Silver Wind Farm, Minnesota.

Collins, B. (1970). *Social psychology.* Reading, MA: Addison-Wesley.

Collins, N. (1996). Working models of attachment: Implications for explanation, emotion, and behavior. *Journal of Personality and Social Psychology, 71,* 810–832.

Cook, S. (1957). Desegregation: A psychological analysis. *American Psychologist, 12,* 1–13.

——. (1969). Motives in a conceptual analysis of attitude-related behavior. In W. Arnold & D. Levine (Eds.), *Nebraska symposium on motivation.* Lincoln: University of Nebraska Press.

——. (1978). Interpersonal and attitudinal outcomes in cooperating interracial groups. *Journal of Research in Developmental Education, 12,* 87–113.

Corey, M., & Corey, G. (1992). *Groups: Process and practice* (4th ed.). Pacific Grove, CA: Brooks/Cole.

Cosier, R. (1981). Dialectical inquiry in strategic planning: A case of premature acceptance? *Academy of Management Review, 6,* 643–648.

Cosier, R., & Ruble, T. (1981). Research on conflict handling behavior: An experimental approach. *Academy of Management Journal, 24,* 816–831.

Cottrell, N. (1972). Social facilitation. In C. McClintock (Ed.), *Experimental social psychology* (pp. 185–236). New York: Holt.

Cottrell, N., Wack, D., Sekerak, G., & Rittle, R. (1968). Social facilitation of dominant responses by the presence of an audience and the mere presence of others. *Journal of Personality and Social Psychology, 9,* 245–250.

Cox, C. (1926). *The early mental traits of three hundred geniuses.* Stanford, CA: Stanford University Press.

Crocker, J., & Luhranen, R. (1990). Collection self-esteem and ingroup bias. *Journal of Personality and Social Psychology, 58,* 60–67.

Croizet, J., & Claire, T. (1998). Extending the concept of stereotype threat to social class: The intellectual under-performance of students from low socioeconomic backgrounds. *Personality and Social Psychology Bulletin, 24*(6), 588–594.

Dalkey, N. (1969). An experimental study of group opinion: The Delphi Method. *Futures, 1*(3), 408–426.

——. (1975). Toward a theory of group estimation. In H. Linstone & M. Turoff (Eds.), *The Delphi method: Techniques and applications* (pp. 236–257). Reading, MA: Addison-Wesley.

Darley, J., & Latané, B. (1968). Bystander intervention in emergencies: Diffusion of responsibility. *Journal of Personality and Social Psychology, 8,* 377–383.

Darwin, C. (1859). *The origin of species.* London: John Murray.

David, G., & Houtman, S. (1968). *Thinking creatively: A guide to training imagination.* Madison: Wisconsin Research and Development Center for Cognitive Learning.

Davis, J. (1969). *Group performance.* Reading, MA: Addison-Wesley.

DeCecco, J., & Richards, A. (1974). *Growing pains: Uses of school conflict.* New York: Aberdeen Press.

——. (1975). Civil war in the high schools. *Psychology Today, 9,* 51–81.

DeFoe, D. (1908). *The life and strange surprising adventures of Robinson Crusoe.* Boston: Houghton Mifflin.

Delbecq, A., Van de Ven, A., & Gustafson, D. (1975). *Group techniques for program planning.* Glenview, IL: Scott, Foresman.

Dension, D., & Sutton, R. (1990). Operating room nurses. In J. Hackman (Ed.), *Groups that work (and those that don't): Creating conditions for effective teamwork* (pp. 293–308). San Francisco: Jossey-Bass.

Deschamps, J. (1977). Effect of crossing category membership on quantitative judgment. *European Journal of Social Psychology, 22,* 189–195.

Deschamps, J., & Doise, W. (1978). Crossed category memberships in intergroup relations. In H. Tajfel (Ed.), *Differentiation between social groups: Studies in the social psychology of intergroup relations* (pp. 141–158). New York: Academic Press.

Desforges, D., Lord, C., Ramsey, S., Mason, J., Van Leeuwen, M., West, S., & Lepper, M. (1991). Effects of structured cooperative contact on changing negative attitudes toward stigmatized social groups. *Journal of Personality and Social Psychology, 60,* 531–544.

Deutsch, M. (1949a). A theory of cooperation and competition. *Human Relations, 2,* 129–152.

——. (1949b). An experimental study of the effects of cooperation and competition upon group process. *Human Relations, 2,* 199–231.

——. (1958). Trust and suspicion. *Journal of Conflict Resolution, 2,* 265–279.

——. (1960). The effects of motivational orientation upon trust and suspicion. *Human Relations, 13,* 123–139.

———. (1962). Cooperation and trust: Some theoretical notes. In M. R. Jones (Ed.), *Nebraska Symposium on Motivation* (pp. 275–320). Lincoln: University of Nebraska Press.

———. (1969). Conflicts: Productive and destructive. *Journal of Social Issues, 25,* 7–43.

———. (1973). *The resolution of conflict.* New Haven, CT: Yale University Press.

———. (1975). Equity, equality, and need: What determines which value will be used as the basis of distributive justice? *Journal of Social Issues, 31,* 137–149.

———. (1979). Education and distributive justice: Some reflections on grading systems. *American Psychologist, 34,* 391–401.

———. (1985). *Distributive justice: A social psychological perspective.* New Haven, CT: Yale University Press.

Deutsch, M., Canavan, D., & Rubin, J. (1971). The effects of size of conflict and sex of experimenter upon interpersonal bargaining. *Journal of Experimental Social Psychology, 7,* 258–267.

Deutsch, M., & Collins, M. (1951). *Interracial housing: A psychological evaluation of a social experiment.* Minneapolis: University of Minnesota Press.

Deutsch, M., & Krauss, R. (1960). The effect of threat upon interpersonal bargaining. *Journal of Abnormal and Social Psychology, 61,* 181–189.

———. (1962). Studies of interpersonal bargaining. *Journal of Conflict Resolutions, 6,* 52–76.

Deutsch, M., & Lewicki, R. (1970). "Locking in" effects during a game of chicken. *Journal of Conflict Resolution, 14,* 367–378.

Devine, P., Monteith, M., Zuwerink, J., & Elliot, A. (1991). Prejudice with and without compunction. *Journal of Personality and Social Psychology, 60,* 817–830.

DeVries, D., & Edwards, K. (1973). Learning games and student teams: Their effects on classroom process. *American Educational Research Journal, 10,* 307–318.

———. (1974). Student teams and learning games: Their effects on cross-race and cross-sex interaction. *Journal of Educational Psychology, 66,* 741–749.

Diehl, M., & Stroebe, W. (1987). Productivity loss in brainstorming groups: Toward solution of a riddle. *Journal of Personality and Social Psychology, 53,* 497–509.

———. (1991). Productivity loss in idea-generating groups: Tracking down the blocking effect. *Journal of Personality and Social Psychology, 61,* 392–403.

Diesing, P. (1962). *Reason in society.* Urbana: University of Illinois Press.

Dodge, K. (1983). Behavioral antecedents of peer social status. *Child Development, 54,* 1386–1389.

Dodge, K., Coie, J., & Bakke, N. (1982). Behavior patterns of socially rejected and neglected preadolescents: The roles of social approach and aggression. *Journal of Abnormal Child Psychology, 10,* 389–409.

Dovidio, J., & Gaertner, S. (1991). Changes in the expression and assessment of racial prejudice. In H. Knopke, R. Norrell, & R. Rogers (Eds.), *Opening doors: Perspectives on race relations in contemporary America* (pp. 119–148). Tuscaloosa: University of Alabama Press.

Driskell, J., Hogan, R., & Salas, E. (1987). Personality and group performance. In C. Hendrick (Ed.), *Group processes and intergroup relations* (pp. 91–112). Newbury Park, CA: Sage.

Drucker, P. (1974). Multinationals and developing countries: Myths and realities. *Foreign Affairs, 53,* 121–134.

Dunnette, M., Campbell, J., & Jaastad, K. (1963). The effect of group participation on brainstorming effectiveness of two industrial samples. *Journal of Applied Psychology, 47,* 30–37.

Dunning, D., & Ross, L. (1988). *Overconfidence in individual and group prediction: Is the collective any wiser?* Unpublished manuscript, Cornell University, Ithaca, NY.

Durkheim, E. (1897, 1966). *Suicide.* New York: Free Press.

———. (1898). *The rules of sociological method.* New York: Free Press.

———. (1953). Individual and collective representations. In D. F. Pocock (Trans.), *Sociology and philosophy.* New York: Free Press. (Reprinted from *Revue de Metaphysique,* 1898, 6, 274–302.)

Duval, S., & Wicklund, R. (1972). *A theory of objective self awareness.* New York: Academic Press.

Dyer, W. (1987). *Team building: Issues and alternatives.* Reading, MA: Addison-Wesley.

Ehrlich, H., & Lee, D. (1969). Dogmatism, learning, and resistance to change: A review and a new paradigm. *Psychological Bulletin, 71*(4), 249–260.

Elder, G. (1975). Age differentiation and the life course. *Annual Review of Sociology, 1,* 165–190.

Ellis, A. (1996). *Better, deeper, and more enduring belief therapy: The rational emotive behavior therapy approach.* New York: Brunner/Mazel.

———. (1997). The evolution of Albert Ellis and rational emotive behavior therapy. In J. Zeig (Ed.), *The evolution of psychotherapy: The third conference* (pp. 69–82). New York: Brunner/Mazel.

Emerson, R. (1954). Deviation and rejection: An experimental replication. *American Sociological Review, 19,* 688–693.

Epstein, S., & Taylor, S. (1967). Instigation to aggression as a function of degree of defeat and perceived aggressive intent of the opponent. *Journal of Personality, 35,* 265–289.

Espenshade, T., & Calhoun, C. (1993). An analysis of public opinion toward undocumented immigration. *Population Research and Policy Review, 12,* 189–224.

Falbe, C., & Yukl, G. (1992). Consequences for managers of using single influence tactics and combination of tactics. *Academy of Management Journal, 35,* 638–652.

Falk, D., & Johnson, D. W. (1977). The effects of perspective-taking and egocentrism on problem solving in heterogeneous and homogeneous groups. *Journal of Social Psychology, 102,* 63–72.

Falloon, I., Lindley, P., McDonald, R., & Marks, I. (1977). Social skills training of out-patient groups: A controlled study of rehearsal and homework. *British Journal of Psychiatry, 131,* 599–609.

Fay, B. (1929). *Benjamin Franklin: The apostle of modern times.* Boston: Little, Brown.

Fenelon, J., & Megaree, E. (1971). Influence of race on the manifestation of leadership. *Journal of Applied Psychology, 55,* 353–358.

Festinger, L. (1950). Informal social communication. *Psychological Review, 57,* 271–292.

———. (1954). A theory of social comparison processes. *Human Relations, 7,* 117–140.

———. (1957). *A theory of cognitive dissonance.* Evanston, IL: Row, Peterson.

Festinger, L., Pepitone, A., & Newcomb, T. (1952). Some consequences of deindividuation in a group. *Journal of Abnormal and Social Psychology, 47,* 382–389.

Festinger, L., Schachter, S., & Back, K. (1950). *Social pressures in informal groups: A study of human factors in housing.* New York: HarperCollins.

Fiedler, F. (1964). A contingency model of leadership effectiveness. In L. Berkowitz (Ed.), *Advances in experimental social psychology* (Vol. 1, pp. 149–190). New York: Academic Press.

———. (1967). *A theory of leadership effectiveness.* New York: McGraw-Hill.

———. (1969). Style of circumstance: The leadership enigma. *Psychology Today, 2*(10), 38–46.

———. (1978). The contingency model and the dynamics of leadership. *Advances in Experimental Social Psychology, 12,* 59–112.

Fiedler, R., Meuwese, W., & Conk, S. (1961). An exploratory study of group creativity in laboratory tasks. *Acta Psychologie, 18,* 100–119.

Filley, A. (1975). *Interpersonal conflict resolution.* Glenview, IL: Scott, Foresman.

Filley, A., House, R., & Kerr, S. (1976). *Managerial process and organizational behavior.* Glenview, IL: Scott, Foresman.

Fine, G. (1979). The Pinkston settlement: An historical and social psychological investigation of the contact hypothesis. *Phylon, 40,* 229–242.

Fisher, R., & Ury, W. (1981). *Getting to yes: Negotiating agreement without giving in.* Boston: Houghton Mifflin.

Fiske, S. (1993). Controlling other people: The impact of power on stereotyping. *American Psychologist, 48,* 621–628.

Fiske, S., & Morling, B. (1996). Stereotyping as a function of personal control motives and capacity constraints: The odd couple of power and anxiety. In R. Sorrentino & E. Higgins (Eds.), *Handbook of motivation and cognition: Vol. 3. The interpersonal context* (pp. 322–346). New York: Guilford Press.

Fiske, S., & Neuberg, S. (1990). A continuum of impression formation, from category-based to individuating processes: Influences of information and motivation on attention and interpretation. In M. Zanna (Ed.), *Advances in experimental social psychology* (Vol. 23, pp. 1 74). New York: Academic Press.

Flowers, M. (1977). A laboratory test of some implications of Janis's groupthink hypothesis. *Journal of Personality and Social Psychology, 35,* 888–896.

Foley, J., & MacMillan, F. (1943). Mediated generalization and the interpretation of verbal behavior: V. Free association as related to differences in professional training. *Journal of Experimental Psychology, 33,* 299–310.

Follet, M. (1940). Constructive conflict. In H. Metcalf & L. Urwick (Eds.), *Dynamic administration: The collected papers of Mary Parker Follet* (pp. 30–49). New York: Pitman (originally published in 1924).

———. (1973). Power. In E. Fox & L. Urwick (Eds.), *Dynamic administration: The collected papers of Mary Parker Follett* (pp. 50–75). New York: Pitman (originally published in 1924).

Fox, D. (1985). Psychology, ideology, utopia, and the commons. *American Psychologist, 40,* 48–58.

Frable, D., Platt, L., & Hoey, S. (1998). Concealable stigmas and positive self-perceptions: Feeling better around similar others. *Journal of Personality and Social Psychology, 74,* 909–922.

Frank, M. (1984). *A comparison between an individual and group goal structure contingency that differed in the behavioral contingency and performance-outcome components.* Unpublished doctoral thesis, University of Minnesota, Minneapolis, MN.

Frankfort, H., Frankfort, H., Wilson, J., & Jacobson, T. (1949). *Before philosophy.* Baltimore: Penguin.

Fraser, C. (1971). Group risk-taking and group polarization. *European Journal of Social Psychology, 1,* 493–510.

Freeberg, N., & Rock, D. (1987). *Development of a small-group team performance taxonomy based on meta-analysis.* Princeton, NJ: Educational Testing Service, Final Report to the Office of Naval Research.

Freeman, E. (1936). *Social psychology.* New York: Holt.

French, J. (1941). The disruption and cohesion of groups. *Journal of Abnormal Social Psychology, 36,* 361–377.

———. (1951). Group productivity. In H. Guetzkow (Ed.), *Groups, leadership and men* (pp. 44–55). Pittsburgh: Carnegie Press.

French, J., & Coch, L. (1948). Overcoming resistance to change. *Human Relations, 1,* 512–532.

French, J., & Raven, B. (1959). The basis of social power. In D. Cartwright (Ed.), *Studies in social power* (pp. 150–167). Ann Arbor: University of Michigan Press.

Freud, S. (1922). *Group psychology and the analysis of the ego.* London: Hogarth.

Frick, F. (1973). *Study of peer training with the Lincoln Training System* (AFATC Report KE 73-116). Harrison, MS: Keesler Air Force Base.

Frost, D., & Stahelski, A. (1988). The systematic measurement of French and Raven's bases of social power in workgroups. *Journal of Applied Social Psychology, 18,* 375–389.

Fuhriman, A., & Burlingame, G. (1994a). Group psychotherapy: Research and practice. In A. Fuhriman & G. Burlingame (Eds.), *Handbook of group psychotherapy. An empirical and clinical synthesis* (pp. 3–40). New York: Wiley.

———. (Eds.). (1994b). Handbook of group psychotherapy: An empirical and clinical synthesis. New York: Wiley

Gabbert, B., Johnson, D., & Johnson, R. (1986). Cooperative learning, group-to-individual transfer, process gain, and the acquisition of cognitive reasoning strategies. *Journal of Psychology, 120,* 265–278.

Gabrenya, W. K., Wang, Y., & Latané, B. (1983). Social loafing in cross-cultural perspective: Chinese on Taiwan. *Journal of Cross Cultural Psychology, 14*(3), 368–384.

Gaertner, S., & Dovidio, J. (1986). The aversive form of racism. In J. Dovidio & S. Gaertner (Eds.), *Prejudice, discrimination, and racism* (pp. 61–89). New York: Academic Press.

Gaertner, S., Dovidio, J., Anastasio, P., Bachman, B., & Rust, M. (1993). The common ingroup identity model: Recategorization and the reduction of intergroup bias. In W. Stroebe & M. Hewstone (Eds.), *European review of social psychology* (Vol. 4, pp. 1–26). Chichester, England: Wiley.

Gardin, J., Kaplan, K., Firestone, I., & Cowan, G. (1973). Proxemic effects on cooperation, attitude, and approach-avoidance in a prisoner's dilemma game. *Journal of Personality and Social Psychology, 27,* 13–18.

Gavin, M., Green, S., & Fairhurst, G. (1995). Managerial control strategies for poor performance over time and the impact on subordinate reactions. *Organizational Behavior and Human Decision Processes, 63,* 207–221.

Geen, R. (1976). Test anxiety, observation, and range of cue utilization. *British Journal of Social and Clinical Psychology, 15,* 253–259.

———. (1980). The effects of being observed on performance. In P. Paulus (Ed.), *Psychology of group influence* (pp. 61–97). Hillsdale, NJ: Erlbaum.

Georgesen, J., & Harris, M. (1998). Why's my boss always holding me down? A meta-analysis of power effects on performance evaluations. *Personality and Social Psychology Review, 2*(3), 184–195.

Gerard, H., Wilhelmy, R., & Conolley, E. (1968). Conformity and group size. *Journal of Personality and Social Psychology, 8*(1), 79–82.

Ghiselli, E., & Lodahl, T. (1958). Patterns of managerial traits and group effectiveness. *Journal of Abnormal and Social Psychology, 57,* 61–66.

Gibb, J. (1951). The effects of group size and of threat upon certainty in a problem-solving situation. *American Psychologist, 6,* 324.

———. (1961). Defensive and supportive climates. *Journal of Communication, 11,* 141–148.

Gibbons, F., & Gerrard, M. (1989). Effects of upward and downward social comparison on mood states. *Journal of Social and Clinical Psychology, 8,* 14–31.

Gilbert, D., & Malone, P. (1995). The correspondence bias. *Psychological Bulletin, 117,* 21–38.

Gilbert, D., McNulty, S., Giuliano, T., & Benson, J. (1992). Blurry words and fuzzy deeds: The attribution of obscure behavior. *Journal of Personality and Social Psychology, 62,* 18–25.

Glass, D., & Singer, J. (1973). Experimental studies of uncontrollable and unpredictable noise. *Representative Research in Social Psychology, 4*(1), 165–183.

Glass, G. (1977). Integrating findings: The meta-analysis of research. In L. Schulman (Ed.), *Review of research in education* (Vol. 5, pp. 351–379). Itasca, IL: Peacock.

Glasser, W. (1984). *Control theory.* New York: Harper & Row.

———. (1998). *Choice theory: A new psychology of personal freedom.* New York: HarperCollins.

Glidewell, J. (1953). *Group emotionality and productivity.* Unpublished doctoral dissertation, University of Chicago, Chicago, IL.

Goldman, M., Dietz, D., & McGlynn, A. (1968). Comparison of individual and group performance related to heterogeneous-wrong responses, size, and patterns of interaction. *Psychological Reports, 23*(2), 459–465.

Goodman, G., & Jacobs, M. (1994). The self-help, mutual-support group. In A. Fubriman & G. Burlingame (Eds.), *Handbook of group psychotherapy: An empirical and clinical synthesis* (pp. 489–526). New York: Wiley.

Goodman, P., & Leyden, D. (1991). Familiarity and group productivity. *Journal of Applied Psychology, 76,* 578–586.

Gordon, K. (1924). Group judgments in the field of lifted weights. *Journal of Experimental Psychology, 7,* 398–400.

Gordon, W. (1961). *Synectics.* New York: Harper & Row.

Gottman, J. (1993). The roles of conflict engagement, escalation, and avoidance in marital interaction: A longitudinal view of five types of couples. *Journal of Consulting and Clinical Psychology, 61*(1), 6–15.

Gouran, D., & Hirokawa, R. (1996). Functional theory and communication in decision-making and problem-solving groups: An expanded view. In R. Hirokawa & M. Poole (Eds.), *Communication and group decision making* (2nd ed., pp. 53–80). Thousand Oaks, CA: Sage.

Graham, S. (1991). A review of attribution theory in achievement contexts. *Educational Psychology Review, 3,* 5–39.

Gray, J., & Thompson, A. (1953). The ethnic prejudices of white and Negro college students. *Journal of Abnormal and Social Psychology, 48,* 311–313.

Green, D. (1977). The immediate processing of sentences. *Quarterly Journal of Experimental Psychology, 29,* 135–146.

Greenberg, J., & Pyszczynski, T. (1986). Persistent high self-focus after failure and low self-focus after success: The depressive self-focusing style. *Journal of Personality and Social Psychology, 50,* 1039–1044.

Gundlach, R. (1950). The effect of on-the-job experience with Negroes upon social attitudes of white workers in union shops. *American Psychologist, 5,* 300.

Hackman, J., & Morris, C. (1975). Group tasks, group interaction process and group performance effectiveness: A review and proposed integration. In L. Berkowitz (Ed.), *Advances in experimental social psychology* (Vol. 8, pp. 47–99). New York: Academic Press.

Hackman, J., & Oldham, G. (1980). *Work redesign.* Reading, MA: Addison-Wesley.

Hackman, J., & Walton, R. (1986). Leading groups in organizations. In P. Goodman (Ed.), *Designing effective work groups* (pp. 72–119). San Francisco: Jossey-Bass.

Hall, J., & Veccia, E. (1990). More "touching observations": New insights on men, women, and interpersonal touch. *Journal of Personality and Social Psychology, 59,* 1155–1162.

Hall, J., & Williams, M. (1966). A comparison of decision making performance in established and ad hoc groups. *Journal of Personality and Social Psychology, 3,* 214–222.

Halle, L. J. (1967, June). Overestimating the power of power. *The New Republic,* 15–17.

Halpern, D. (1995). *Mental health and the built environment: More than bricks and mortar?* London: Taylor & Francis.

Hamilton, D. (1979). A cognitive-attributional analysis of stereotyping. In L. Berkowitz (Ed.), *Advances in experimental social psychology* (Vol. 12, pp. 53–84). New York: Academic Press.

Hamilton, D., & Sherman, J. (1994). Stereotypes. In R. Wyer, Jr., & T. Srull (Eds.), *Handbook of social cognition* (2nd ed., Vol. 2, pp. 1–68). Hillsdale, NJ: Erlbaum.

———. (1996). Perceiving person and groups. *Psychological Review, 103,* 336–355.

Haney, C., Banks, C., & Zimbardo, P. (1973). Interpersonal dynamics in a simulated prison. *International Journal of Criminology and Psychology, 1,* 69–97.

Harding, J., & Hogerge, R. (1952). Attitudes of white department store employees toward Negro co-workers. *Journal of Social Issues, 8,* 18–28.

Hare, A. (1976). *Handbook of small group research* (2nd ed.). New York: Free Press.

Harkins, S. (1987). Social loafing and social facilitation. *Journal of Experimental Social Psychology, 23,* 1–18.

Harkins, S., & Jackson, J. (1985). The role of evaluation in eliminating social loafing. *Personality and Social Psychology Bulletin, 11,* 457–465.

Harkins, S., & Petty, R. (1982). The effects of task difficulty and task uniqueness on social loafing. *Journal of Personality and Social Psychology, 43,* 1214–1229.

Harkins, S., & Szymanski, K. (1987). Social loafing and self-evaluation with an objective standard. *Journal of Experimental Social Psychology, 24,* 354–365.

———. (1989). Social loafing and group evaluation. *Journal of Personality and Social Psychology, 56,* 934–941.

Harlan, H. (1942). Some factors affecting attitude toward Jews. *American Sociological Review, 7,* 816–827.

Harris, M., & Schaubroeck, J. (1988). A meta-analysis of self-supervisor, self-peer, and peer-supervisor ratings. *Personnel Psychology, 41,* 43–62.

Hartig, T., Mang, M., & Evans, G. (1991). Restorative effects of natural environment experience. *Environment and Behavior, 23,* 3–26.

Hastorf, A., & Cantril, H. (1954). They saw a game. *Journal of Abnormal and Social Psychology, 49,* 129–134.

Haunschild, P., Moreland, R., & Murrell, A. (1994). Sources of resistance to mergers between groups. *Journal of Applied Social Psychology, 24,* 1150–1178.

Hawley, P. (1999). The ontogenesis of social dominance: A strategy-based evolutionary perspective. *Developmental Review, 19,* 97–132.

Haythorn, W. (1968). The composition of groups: A review of the literature. *Acta Psychologica, 28,* 97–128.

Heider, F. (1958). *The psychology of interpersonal relations.* New York: Wiley.

Herek, G., & Capitanio, J. (1996). "Some of my best friends": Intergroup contact, concealable stigma, and heterosexuals' attitudes toward gay men and lesbians. *Personality and Social Psychology Bulletin, 22,* 412–424.

Herek, G., Janis, I., & Huth, P. (1987). Decision-making during international crises: Is quality of process related to outcome? *Journal of Conflict Resolution, 31,* 203–226.

Hersey, P., & Blanchard, K. (1977). *Management of organizational behavior: Utilizing human resources* (3rd ed.). Englewood Cliffs, NJ: Prentice-Hall.

Herzog, T., & Bosley, P. (1992). Tranquility and preference as affective qualities of natural environment. *Journal of Environmental Psychology, 12,* 115–127.

Hewstone, M., & Brown, R. (Eds.). (1986). *Contact and conflict in intergroup relations.* Oxford: Basil Blackwell.

Hill, G. (1982). Group versus individual performance: Are $n + 1$ heads better than one? *Psychological Bulletin, 91,* 517–539.

Hill, W., & Gruner, L. (1973). A study of development in open and closed groups. *Small Group Behavior, 4,* 355–381.

Hoffer, E. (1951). *The true believer.* New York: Harper & Row.

Hoffman, L. (1959). Group problem solving. In L. Berkowitz (Ed.), *Advances in experimental social psychology* (Vol. 2, pp. 99–132). San Diego, CA: Academic Press.

———. (1961). Conditions for creative problem solving. *Journal of Psychology, 52,* 429–444.

———. (1979). Applying experimental research on group problem solving to organizations. *Journal of Applied Behavioral Science, 15,* 375–391.

Hoffman, L., Harburg, E., & Maier, N. (1962a). Differences and disagreement as factors in creative problem solving. *Journal of Abnormal and Social Psychology, 64,* 206–214.

———. (1962b). Quality and acceptance of problem solutions by members of homogeneous and heterogeneous groups. *Journal of Abnormal and Social Psychology, 64,* 206–214.

Hoffman, L., & Maier, N. (1961). Quality and acceptance of problem solutions by members of homogeneous and heterogeneous. *Journal of Abnormal and Social Psychology, 62*(2), 401–407.

Hollander, E., & Willis, R. (1967). Some current issues in the psychology of conformity and nonconformity. *Psychological Bulletin, 68,* 62–76.

Homans, G. (1950). *The human group.* New York: Harcourt, Brace.

———. (1961). *Social behaviors: Its elementary forms.* New York: Harcourt, Brace & World.

———. (1974). *Social behavior: Its elementary forms* (rev. ed.). New York: Harcourt Brace Jovanovich.

Hong, O., & Harrod, W. (1988). The role of reasons in the in-group bias phenomenon. *European Journal of Social Psychology, 18,* 537–545.

Hook, S. (1955). *The hero in history.* Boston: Beacon Press.

Hopper, R. (1950). The revolutionary process. *Social Forces, 28,* 270–279.

Horai, J. (1977). Attributional conflict. *Journal of Social Issues, 33*(1), 88–100.

Hornstein, H., & Johnson, D. W. (1966). The effects of process analysis and ties to his group upon the negotiator's attitudes toward the outcomes of negotiations. *Journal of Applied Behavioral Science, 2,* 449–465.

Horowitz, E. (1936). The development of attitude toward the Negro. *Archives of Psychology* (Whole No. 194).

Horwitz, M. (1954). The recall of interrupted group tasks: An experimental study of individual motivation in relation to group goals. *Human Relations, 7,* 3–38.

Hovland, C., Janis, I., & Kelley, H. (1953). *Communication and persuasion.* New Haven, CT: Yale University Press.

Hovland, C., Lumsdaine, A., & Sheffield, F. (1949). *Experiment on mass communication.* Princeton, NJ: Princeton University Press.

Howells, L., & Becker, S. (1962). Seating arrangement and leadership emergence. *Journal of Personality and Social Psychology, 64,* 148–150.

Hunt, P., & Hillery, J. (1973). Social facilitation in a coaction setting: An examination of the effects over learning trials. *Journal of Experimental Social Psychology, 9,* 563–571.

Hwong, N., Caswell, A., Johnson, D. W., & Johnson, R. (1993). Effects of cooperative and individualistic learning on prospective elementary teachers' music achievement and attitudes. *Journal of Social Psychology, 133,* 53–64.

Illing, H. (1957). C. Jung on the present trends in group psychotherapy. *Human Relations, 10,* 77–84.

Indik, B. (1965). Organization size and member participation: Some empirical tests of alternative explanations. *Human Relations, 18*(4), 339–350.

Ingham, A., Levinger, G., Graves, J., & Peckham, V. (1974). The Ringelmann effect: Studies of group size and group performance. *Journal of Experimental Social Psychology, 10,* 371–384.

Irish, D. (1952). Reactions of Caucasian residents to Japanese-American neighbors. *Journal of Social Issues, 8,* 10–17.

Isenberg, D. (1986). Group polarization: A critical review and meta-analysis. *Journal of Personality and Social Psychology, 50,* 1141–1151.

Islam, M., & Hewstone, M. (1993). Intergroup attributions and affective consequences in majority and minority groups. *Journal of Personality and Social Psychology, 64,* 936–950.

Iverson, M., & Schwab, H. (1967). Ethnocentric dogmatism and binocular fusion of sexually and racially discrepant stimuli. *Journal of Personality and Social Psychology, 7,* 73–81.

Jackman, M., & Crane, M. (1986). "Some of my best friends are black . . . " Interracial friendship and whites' racial attitudes. *Public Opinion Quarterly, 50,* 459–486.

Jackson, J., & Williams, K. (1985). Social loafing on difficult tasks: Working collectively can improve performance. *Journal of Personality and Social Psychology, 49,* 937–942.

———. (1986). *A review and theoretical analysis of social loafing.* Unpublished manuscript, Fordham University, New York, NY.

Jackson, S. (1992). Team composition in organizational settings: Issues in managing an increasingly diverse work force. In S. Worchel, W. Wood, & J. Simpson (Eds.), *Group process and productivity* (pp. 138–173). Newbury Park, CA: Sage.

Jackson, S., Brett, J., Sessa, V., Cooper, D., Julin, J., & Peyronnin, K. (1991). Some differences make a difference: Interpersonal dissimilarity and group heterogeneity as correlates of recruitment, promotion, and turnover. *Journal of Applied Psychology, 76,* 675–689.

Jacobson, N., & Margolin, G. (1979). *Marital therapy: Strategies based on social learning and behavior exchange principles.* New York: Brunner/Mazel.

Jahoda, M., & West, P. (1951). Race relations in public housing. *Journal of Social Issues, 7,* 132–139.

James, N., & Johnson, D. W. (1983). The relationship between attitudes toward social interdependence and psychological health within three criminal populations. *Journal of Social Psychology, 121,* 131–143.

James, S., & Johnson, D. W. (1988). Social interdependence, psychological adjustment, orientation toward negative life stress, and quality of second marriage. *Journal of Social Psychology, 128*(3), 287–304.

Janis, I. (1971). Groupthink. *Psychology Today, 5*(6), 43–46, 74–76.

———. (1972). *Victims of groupthink.* Boston: Houghton Mifflin.

———. (1982). *Groupthink* (revised and enlarged edition of *Victims of groupthink*). Boston: Houghton Mifflin.

Janis, I., & Mann, L. (1977). *Decision making.* New York: Free Press.

Janz, T., & Tjosvold, D. (1985). Costing effective vs. ineffective work relationships: A method and first look. *Canadian Journal of Administrative Sciences, 2,* 53–51.

Johnson, D. W. (1970). *The social psychology of education.* New York: Holt, Rinehart & Winston.

———. (1971). Role reversal: A summary and review of the research. *International Journal of Group Tensions, 1,* 318–334.

———. (1973). *Contemporary social psychology.* Philadelphia: Lippincott.

———. (1974). Communication and the inducement of cooperative behavior in conflicts. *Speech Monographs, 41,* 64–78.

———. (1977). Distribution and exchange of information in problem solving dyads. *Communication Research, 4,* 283–298.

———. (1978). *Human relations and your career.* Englewood Cliffs, NJ: Prentice-Hall.

———. (1979). *Educational psychology.* Englewood Cliffs, NJ: Prentice-Hall.

———. (1980a). Group processes: Influences on student–student interaction on school outcomes. In J. McMillan (Ed.), *Social psychology of school learning* (pp. 123–168). New York: Academic Press.

———. (1980b). Attitude modification methods. In F. Kanfer & A. Goldstein (Eds.), *Helping people change* (pp. 51–88). New York: Pergamon Press.

———. (1991). *Human relations and your career* (3rd ed.). Englewood Cliffs, NJ: Prentice-Hall.

———. (2003). *Reaching out: Interpersonal effectiveness and self-actualization* (8th ed.). Boston: Allyn & Bacon.

Johnson, D. W., & Allen, S. (1972). Deviation from organizational norms concerning the relations between status and power. *Sociological Quarterly, 13,* 174–182.

Johnson, S., & Johnson, D. W. (1972). The effects of others' actions, attitude similarity, and race on attraction towards the other. *Human Relations, 25,* 121–130.

———. (1974). Instructional goal structure: Cooperative, competitive, or individualistic. *Review of Educational Research, 44,* 213–240.

———. (1978). Cooperative, competitive, and individualistic learning. *Journal of Research and Development in Education, 12,* 3–15.

———. (1979). Conflict in the classroom: Controversy and learning. *Review of Educational Research, 49,* 51–70.

———. (1981). Effects of cooperative and individualistic learning experiences on interethnic interaction. *Journal of Educational Psychology, 73,* 454–459.

———. (1983). The socialization and achievement crisis: Are cooperative learning experiences the solution? In L. Bickman (Ed.), *Applied social psychology annual 4* (pp. 119–164). Beverly Hills, CA: Sage.

———. (1987). *Creative conflict.* Edina, MN: Interaction Book Company.

———. (1989). *Cooperation and competition: Theory and research.* Edina, MN: Interaction Book Company.

———. (1990). Cooperative learning: Warm-ups, grouping strategies and group activities (2nd ed.). Edina, MN: Interaction Book Company.

———. (1992a). *Positive interdependence: The heart of cooperative learning.* Edina, MN: Interaction Book Company.

———. (1992b). *Positive interdependence: The heart of cooperative learning* (video). Edina, MN: Interaction Book Company.

———. (1994). *Leading the cooperative school* (2nd ed). Edina, MN: Interaction Book Company.

———. (1995a). *Teaching students to be peacemakers* (3rd ed.). Edina, MN: Interaction Book Company.

———. (1995b). *My mediation notebook* (3rd ed.). Edina, MN: Interaction Book Company.

———. (1995c). *Creative controversy: Intellectual challenge in the classroom* (3rd ed.). Edina, MN: Interaction Book Company.

———. (1996a). *Meaningful and manageable assessment through cooperative learning.* Edina, MN: Interaction Book Company.

———. (1997). *Learning to lead teams: Developing leadership skills.* Edina, MN: Interaction Book Company.

———. (1999a). *Learning together and alone: Cooperative, competitive, and individualistic learning* (6th ed.). Boston: Allyn & Bacon.

———. (1999b). *Human relations: Valuing diversity.* Edina, MN: Interaction Book Company.

Johnson, D. W., Johnson, R., Buckman, L., & Richards, P. (1986). The effect of prolonged implementation of cooperative learning on social support within the classroom. *Journal of Psychology, 119,* 405–411.

Johnson, D. W., Johnson, R., & Holubec, E. (1994). *Nuts and bolts of cooperative learning.* Edina, MN: Interaction Book Company.

———. (1998a). *Cooperation in the classroom* (7th ed.). Edina, MN: Interaction Book Company.

———. (1998b). *Advanced cooperative learning* (5th ed.). Edina, MN: Interaction Book Company.

Johnson, D. W., Johnson, F., & Johnson, R. (1976). Promoting constructive conflict in the classroom. *Notre Dame Journal of Education, 7,* 163–168.

Johnson, D. W., Johnson, R., & Krotee, M. (1986). The relation between social interdependence and psychological health on the 1980 U.S. Olympic ice hockey team. *Journal of Psychology, 120*(3), 279–291.

Johnson, D. W., Johnson, R., & Maruyama, G. (1983). Interdependence and interpersonal attraction among heterogeneous and homogeneous individuals: A theoretical formulation and a meta-analysis of the research. *Review of Educational Research, 53,* 5–54.

Johnson, D. W., Johnson, R., Ortiz, A., & Stanne, M. (1991). Impact of positive goal and resource interdependence on achievement, interaction, and attitudes. *Journal of General Psychology, 118*(4), 341–347.

Johnson, R., Johnson, D. W., Scott, L., & Ramolae, B. (1985). Effects of single-sex and mixed-sex cooperative interaction on science achievement and attitudes and cross-handicap and cross-sex relationship. *Journal of Research in Science Teaching, 22*, 207–220.

———. (1998). Active learning: Cooperation in the college classroom (2nd ed.). Edina, MN: Interaction Book Company.

Johnson, D. W., Johnson, R., Stanne, M., & Garibaldi, A. (1990). Impact of group processing on achievement in cooperative groups. *Journal of Social Psychology, 130*, 507–516.

Johnson, D. W., Kavanagh, J., & Lubin, B. (1973). Tests, *t*-groups, and tension. *Comparative Group Studies, 4*, 81–88.

Johnson, D. W., & Lewicki, R. (1969). The initiation of superordinate goals. *Journal of Applied Behavioral Science, 5*, 9–24.

Johnson, D. W., Maruyama, G., Johnson, R., Nelson, D., & Skon, L. (1981). Effects of cooperative, competitive, and individualistic goal structures on achievement: A meta-analysis. *Psychological Bulletin, 89*, 47–62.

Johnson, D. W., & Matross, R. (1977). The interpersonal influence of the psychotherapist. In A. Gurman & A. Razin (Eds.), *Effective psychotherapy: A handbook of research* (pp. 395–432). Elmsford, NY: Pergamon Press.

Johnson, D. W., McCarty, K., & Allen, T. (1976). Congruent and contradictory verbal and nonverbal communications of cooperativeness and competitiveness in negotiations. *Communication Research, 3*, 275–292.

Johnson, D. W., & Noonan, P. (1972). Effects of acceptance and reciprocation of self-disclosures on the development of trust. *Journal of Counseling Psychology, 19*, 411–416.

Johnson, D. W., & Norem-Hebeisen, A. (1977). Attitudes toward interdependence among persons and psychological health. *Psychological Reports, 40*, 843–850.

Johnson, D. W., Skon, L., & Johnson, R. (1980). The effects of cooperative, competitive and individualistic goal structures on student achievement on different types of tasks. *American Educational Research Journal, 17*, 83–93.

Johnson, D. W., & Rusbult, C. (1989). Resisting temptation: Devaluation of alternative partners as a means of maintaining commitment in close relationships. *Journal of Personality and Social Psychology, 57*, 967–980.

Jones, E., & Gerard, H. (1967). *Foundations of social psychology.* New York: Wiley.

Jones, E., & Nesbett, R. (1972). The actor and the observer: Divergent perceptions of the causes of behavior. In E. Jones, D. Kanouse, H. Kelley, R. Nisbett, S. Valins, & B. Weiner (Eds.), *Attribution: Perceiving the causes of behavior* (pp. 79–94). Morristown, NJ: General Learning Press.

Jones, M. (1974). Regressing group on individual effectiveness. *Organizational Behavior and Human Performance, 11*, 426–451.

Kaplan, M., & Miller, C. (1987). Group decision making and normative versus information influence: Effects of type of issue and assigned decision rule. *Journal of Personality and Social Psychology, 53*, 306–313.

Katz, D., & Braly, K. (1933). Racial stereotypes of 100 college students. *Journal of Abnormal and Social Psychology, 28*, 280–290.

Katz, I., & Hass, R. (1988). Racial ambivalence and American value conflict: Correlational and priming studies of dual cognitive structures. *Journal of Personality and Social Psychology, 55*, 893–905.

Katz, I., Wachenhut, J., & Hass, R. (1986). Racial ambivalence, value duality, and behavior. In J. Dovidio & S. Gaertner (Eds.), *Prejudice, discrimination, and racism* (pp. 35–60). New York: Academic Press.

Katzenbach, J., & Smith, D. (1993). *The wisdom of teams.* Cambridge, MA: Harvard Business School Press.

Kaul, T., & Bednar, R. (1986). Experiential group research: Results, questions, and suggestions. In S. Garfield & A Bergin (Eds.), *Handbook of psychotherapy and behavior change* (3rd ed., pp. 671–714). New York: Wiley.

Kelley, H. (1979). *Personal relationships.* Hillsdale, NJ: Erlbaum.

Kelley, H., & Stahelski, A. (1970). Social interaction basis of cooperators' and competitors' beliefs about others. *Journal of Personality and Social Psychology, 16*, 66–91.

Kelley, H., & Thibaut, J. (1978). *Interpersonal relations: A theory of interdependence.* New York: Wiley.

Kerr, N. (1983). The dispensability of member effort and group motivation losses: Free-rider effects. *Journal of Personality and Social Psychology, 44*, 78–94.

———. (1989). Illusions of efficacy: The effects of group size on perceived efficacy in social dilemmas. *Journal of Experimental Social Psychology, 35*, 287–313.

Kerr, N., Atkin, R., Stasser, G., Meek, D., Holt, R., & Davis, J. (1976). Guilt beyond a reasonable doubt: Effects of concept definition and assigned decision rule on the judgments of mock jurors. *Journal of Personality and Social Psychology, 34*, 282–294.

Kerr, N., & Bruun, S. (1981). Ringelmann revisited: Alternative explanations for the social loafing effect. *Personality and Social Psychology Bulletin, 7*, 224–231.

———. (1983). The dispensability of member effort and group motivation losses: Free-rider effects. *Journal of Personality and Social Psychology, 44,* 78–94.

Key, V. (1949). *Southern politics in state and nation.* New York: Knopf.

Keyton, J. (1999). Relational communication in groups. In L. Frey, D. Gouran, & M. Poole (Eds.), *The handbook of group communication theory and research* (pp. 192–222). Thousand Oaks, CA: Sage.

Kiesler, S., Siegel, J., & McGuire, T. (1984, October). Social psychological aspects of computer-mediated communication. *American Psychologist, 39*(10), 1123–1134.

Kim, S., Smith, R., & Brigham, N. (1998). Effects of power imbalance and the presence of third parties on reactions to harm: Upward and downward revenge. *Personality and Social Psychology Bulletin, 24*(4), 353–361.

Kinlaw, D. C. (1991). *Developing superior work teams: Building quality and the competitive edge.* Lexington, MA: Lexington Books.

Kipnis, D. (1972). Does power corrupt? *Journal of Personality and Social Psychology, 24,* 33–41.

———. (1984). The use of power in organizations and in interpersonal settings. *Applied Social Psychology Annual, 5,* 179–210.

———. (1987). Psychology and behavioral technology. *American Psychologist, 42,* 30–36.

Kipnis, D., Castell, J., Gergen, M., & Mauch, D. (1976). Metamorphic effects of power. *Journal of Applied Psychology, 61,* 127–135.

Kipnis, D., Schmidt, S., Prince, K., & Stitt, C. (1981). Why do I like thee: Is it your performance or my orders? *Journal of Applied Psychology, 66,* 324–328.

Kivlighan, D., & Mullison, D. (1988). Participants' perception of therapeutic factors in group counseling: The role of interpersonal style and stage of group development. *Small Group Behavior, 19,* 452–468.

Kivlighan, D., Multon, K., & Brossart, D. (1996). Helpful impacts in group counseling: Development of a multidimensional rating system. *Journal of Counseling Psychology, 43,* 347–355.

Kolb, D. (1985). To be a mediator: Expressive tactics in mediation. *Journal of Social Issues, 41*(2), 11–26.

Kostick, M. (1957). An experiment in group decision. *Journal of Teacher Education, 8,* 67–72.

Kouzes, J., & Posner, B. (1987). *The leadership challenge.* San Francisco: Jossey-Bass.

Kramer, G. (1951). *Residential contact as a determinant of attitudes toward Negroes.* Unpublished doctoral dissertation, Harvard University, Cambridge, MA.

Kramer, R. (1996). Divergent realities and convergent disappointments in the hierarchic relation: Trust and the intuitive auditor at work. In R. Kramer & T. Tyler (Eds.), *Trust in organizations: Frontiers of theory and research* (pp. 216–245). Thousand Oaks, CA: Sage.

Kramer, R., & Brewer, M. (1986). Social group identity and the emergence of cooperation in resource conservation dilemmas. In H. Wilke, D. Messick, & C. Rutte (Eds.), *Experimental social dilemmas* (pp. 205–234). Frankfurt am Main: Verlag Peter Lang.

Krauss, R., & Deutsch, M. (1966). Communication in interpersonal bargaining. *Journal of Personality and Social Psychology, 4,* 572–577.

Kressel, K., & Pruitt, D. (1985). Themes in the mediation of social conflict. *Journal of Social Issues, 41*(2), 179–198.

Kropotkin, P. (1902). *Mutual aid: A factor of evolution.* London: Doubleday.

LaBarre, W. (1972). *The ghost dance.* New York: Delta.

Lakin, M. (1972). *Interpersonal encounter: Theory and practice in sensitivity training.* New York: McGraw-Hill.

Lamm, H., & Trommsdorff, G. (1973). Group versus individual performance on tasks requiring ideational proficiency (brainstorming): A review. *European Journal of Social Psychology, 3,* 361–388.

Langer, E., Blank, A., & Chanowitz, B. (1978). The mindlessness of ostensibly thoughtful action: The role of "placebic" information in interpersonal interaction. *Journal of Personality and Social Psychology, 36,* 635–642.

Langer, E., & Rodin, J. (1976). The effects of choice and enhanced personal responsibility for the aged: A field experiment in an institutional setting. *Journal of Personality and Social Psychology, 34*(2), 191–198.

Latané, B., & Nida, S. (1981). Ten years of research on group size and helping. *Psychological Bulletin, 89,* 308–324.

Latané, B., Williams, K., & Harkins, S. (1979). Many hands make light the work: The causes and consequences of social loafing. *Journal of Personality and Social Psychology, 37,* 822–832.

Latham, G., & Baldes, J. (1975). The "practical significance" of Locke's theory of goal setting. *Journal of Applied Psychology, 60,* 122–124.

Laughlin, P. (1980). Social combination processes of cooperative problem-solving groups on verbal intellective tasks. In M. Fishbein (Ed.), *Progress in social psychology* (Vol. 1, pp. 127–155). Hillsdale, NJ: Erlbaum.

Laughlin, P., & Adamopoulos, J. (1980). Social combination processes and individual learning for six-person cooperative groups on an intellective task.

Journal of Personality and Social Psychology, 38, 941–947.

Laughlin, P., & Bitz, D. (1975). Individual versus dyadic performance on a disjunctive task as a function of initial ability level. *Journal of Personality and Social Psychology, 31,* 487–496.

Laughlin, P., & Early, P. (1982). Social combination models, persuasive arguments theory, social comparison theory and choice shift. *Journal of Personality and Social Psychology, 42,* 273–280.

Lawler, E., & Yoon, J. (1993). Power and the emergence of commitment behavior in negotiated exchange. *American Sociological Review, 58,* 465–481.

Lawrence, P., & Lorsch, J. (1967). *Organization and environment: Managing differentiation and integration.* Cambridge, MA: Harvard University, Division of Research, Graduate School of Business Administration.

Leana, C. (1985). A partial test of Janis's groupthink model: Effects of group cohesiveness and leader behavior on defective decision making. *Journal of Management, 11,* 5–17.

Leavitt, H. (1951). Some effects of certain communication patterns on group performance. *Journal of Abnormal and Social Psychology, 46,* 38–50.

Le Bon, G. (1895). *The crowd: A study of the popular mind* (2nd ed). London: T. Fisher Unwin.

Leichtentritt, J., & Shechtman, Z. (1998). Therapist, trainee, and child various response modes in child group therapy. *Group Dynamics: Theory, Research, and Practice, 2,* 36–47.

Levine, J., & Butler, J. (1952). Lecture vs. group decision in changing behavior. *Journal of Applied Psychology, 36,* 29–33.

Levine, R., Chein, I., & Murphy, G. (1942). The relation of the intensity of a need to the amount of perceptual distortion: A preliminary report. *Journal of Psychology, 13,* 283–293.

Levinger, G. (1980). Toward the analysis of close relationships. *Journal of Experimental Social Psychology, 16,* 510–544.

Lew, M., Mesch, D., Johnson, D. W., & Johnson, R. (1986a). Positive interdependence, academic and collaborative-skills group contingencies and isolated students. *American Educational Research Journal, 23,* 476–488.

———. (1986b). Components of cooperative learning: Effects of collaborative skills and academic group contingencies on achievement and mainstreaming. *Contemporary Educational Psychology, 11,* 229–239.

Lewin, K. (1935). *A dynamic theory of personality.* New York: McGraw-Hill.

———. (1943). Forces behind food habits and methods of change. *Bulletin of the National Research*

Council, 108, 35–65 (Washington, DC: National Research Council: Committee on Food Habits).

———. (1944). Dynamics of group action. *Educational Leadership, 1,* 195–200.

———. (1948). *Resolving social conflicts.* New York: Harper.

———. (1951). *Field theory in social science.* New York: Harper.

Lewin, K., Dembo, T., Festinger, L., & Sears, P. (1944). Level of aspiration. In J. Hunt (Ed.), *Personality and the behavior disorders* (pp. 333–378). New York: Ronald Press.

Lewin, K., & Grabbe, P. (1945). Conduct, knowledge, and acceptance of new values. *Journal of Social Issues, 1,* 56–64.

Lewin, K., Lippitt, R., & White, R. (1939). Patterns of aggressive behavior in experimentally created "social climates." *Journal of Social Psychology, 10,* 271–299.

Lewis, H. (1944). An experimental study of the role of the ego in work. I. The role of the ego in cooperative work. *Journal of Experimental Psychology, 34,* 113–126.

Lewis, H., & Franklin, M. (1944). An experimental study of the role of the ego in work. II. The significance of task-orientation in work. *Journal of Experimental Psychology, 34,* 195–215.

Lewis, S., & Pruitt, D. (1971). Organization, aspiration level, and communication freedom in integrative bargaining. *Proceedings of the 79th Annual Convention of the American Psychological Association, 6,* 221–222.

Lieberman, M. (1993). Self-help groups. In H. Kaplan & M. N. Sadock (Eds.), *Comprehensive group psychotherapy* (3rd ed., pp. 292–304). Baltimore: Williams & Wilkins.

Lieberman, M., Yalom, I., & Miles, M. (1973). *Encounter groups: First facts.* New York: Basic Books.

———. (1980). Group methods. In F. Kanfer & A. Goldstein (Eds.), *Helping people change* (pp. 433–485). New York: Pergamon Press.

Likert, R. (1961). *New patterns of management.* New York: McGraw-Hill.

Lindbloom, D. (1959). The science of muddling through. *Public Administrative Review, 15,* 79–88.

Lindskold, S., & Arnoff, J. (1980). Conciliatory strategies and relative power. *Journal of Experimental Social Psychology, 16,* 187–198.

Linville, P., Fisher, G., & Salovey, P. (1989). Perceived distribution of the characteristics of in-group and out-group members: Empirical evidence and a computer simulation. *Journal of Personality and Social Psychology, 57,* 165–188.

Lippmann, W. (1922). *Public opinion.* New York: Harcourt, Brace, Jovanovich.

Lissner, K. (1933). The resolution of needs by substitutive acts: Studies of action and affect psychology, edited by K. Lewin. *Psychologische Fortung, 18,* 27–87.

Littlepage, G., & Mueller, A. (1997). Recognition and utilization of expertise in problem-solving groups: Expert characteristics and behavior. *Group Dynamics: Theory, Research, and Practice, 1,* 324–328.

Littlepage, G., Robison, W., & Reddington, K. I. (1997). Effects of task experience and group experience on group performance, member ability, and recognition of expertise. *Organizational Behavior and Human Decision Processes, 69,* 133–147.

Littlepage, G., & Silbiger, H. (1992). Recognition of expertise in decision-making groups: Effects of group size and participation patterns. *Small Group Research, 23,* 344–355.

Longley, J., & Pruitt, D. (1980). Groupthink: A critique of Janis's theory. In L. Wheeler (Ed.), *Review of personality and social psychology* (Vol. 1). Beverly Hills, CA: Sage.

Lord, C., Ross, L., & Lepper, M. (1979). Biased assimilation and attitude polarization: The effects of prior theories on subsequently considered evidence. *Journal of Personality and Social Psychology, 37*(11), 2098–2109.

Lorge, I., Fox, D., Davitz, J., & Brenner, M. (1958). A survey of studies contrasting the quality of group performance and individual performance, 1920–1957. *Psychological Bulletin, 55,* 337–372.

Luce, R., & Raiffa, H. (1957). *Games and decisions.* New York: Wiley.

Luchins, A. (1942). Mechanization in problem solving: The effect of Einstellung. *Psychological Monographs, 54* (Whole No. 248).

MacKenzie, B. (1948). The importance of contact in determining attitudes toward Negroes. *Journal of Abnormal and Social Psychology, 43,* 417–441.

Magnuson, E. (1986, March 10). A serious deficiency: The Rogers Commission faults NASA's flawed decision-making process. *Time,* 40–42.

Mahler, W. (1933). Substitution acts of a different degree of reality. Students of action and affect psychology, edited by K. Lewin. *Psychologishe Fortschung, 18,* 27–89.

Maier, N. (1930). Reasoning in humans. *Journal of Comparative Psychology, 10,* 115–143.

———. (1950). The quality of group decisions as influenced by the discussion leader. *Human Relations, 3,* 155–174.

———. (1970). *Problem solving and creativity in individuals and group.* Belmont, CA: Brooks/Cole.

Maier, N., & Hoffman, L. (1964). Financial incentives and group decision in motivating change. *Journal of Social Psychology, 64,* 369–378.

Maier, N., & Solem, A. (1952). The contribution of a discussion leader to the quality of group thinking: The effective use of minority opinions. *Human Relations, 5,* 277–288.

Maier, N., & Thurber, J. (1969). Innovative problem-solving by outsiders: A study of individuals and groups. *Personal Psychology, 22*(3), 237–249.

Major, B., Schmidlin, A., & Williams, L. (1990). Gender patterns in social touch: The impact of setting and age. *Journal of Personality and Social Psychology, 58,* 634–643.

Mann, L., & Janis, I. (1983). Decisional conflict in organizations. In D. Tjosvold & D. Johnson (Eds.), *Productive conflict management* (pp. 16–45). New York: Irvington.

Mann, R. (1959). A review of the relationship between personality and performance in small groups. *Psychological Bulletin, 56,* 241–270.

Mannheimer, D., & Williams, R. (1949). A note on Negro troops in combat. In S. Stouffer, E. Suchman, L. DeVinney, S. Star, & R. Williams (Eds.), *The American soldier* (Vol. 1, pp. 596–601). Princeton, NJ: Princeton University Press.

Marcus-Newhall, A., Miller, N., Holtz, R., & Brewer, M. (1993). Cross-cutting category membership with role assignment: A means of reducing intergroup bias. *British Journal of Social Psychology, 32,* 124–146.

Markman, H. (1981). Prediction of marital distress: A 5-year follow-up. *Journal of Consulting and Clinical Psychology, 49,* 760–762.

Markus, H. (1978). The effect of mere presence on social facilitation: An unobtrusive test. *Journal of Experimental Social Psychology, 14,* 389–397.

Marrow, A. (1957). *Making management human.* New York: McGraw-Hill.

———. (1969). *The practical theorist: The life and work of Kurt Lewin.* New York: Basic Books.

Maslow, A. (1954). *Motivation and personality.* New York: Harper & Row.

———. (1962). *Toward a psychology of being.* Princeton, NJ: Van Nostrand.

Matsui, N., Kakuyama, T., & Onglateo, M. (1987). Effects of goals and feedback on performance in groups. *Journal of Applied Psychology, 72*(3), 416–425.

McCain, B., O'Reilly, C., & Pfeffer, J. (1983). The effects of departmental demography on turnover. *Academy of Management Journal, 26,* 626–641.

McCauley, C. (1989). The nature of social influence in groupthink: Compliance and internalization. *Journal of Personality and Social Psychology, 57,* 250–260.

McClelland, D. (1975). *Power: The inner experience.* New York: Irvington.

———. (1985). How motives, skills, and values determine what people do. *American Psychologist, 40,* 812–825.

McClelland, D., & Atkinson, J. (1948). The projective expression of needs: I. The effect of different intensities of the hunger drive on perception. *Journal of Psychology, 25,* 205–222.

McConahay, J. (1986). Modern racism, ambivalence, and the modern racism scale. In J. Dovidio & S. Gaertner (Eds.), *Prejudice, discrimination, and racism* (pp. 91–125). New York: Academic Press.

McDavid, J., & Harari, H. (1968). *Social psychology: Individuals, groups, societies.* New York: Harper & Row.

McGrath, J. (1984). *Groups: Interaction and performance.* Englewood Cliffs, NJ: Prentice-Hall.

McGuire, T., Kiesler, S., & Siegel, J. (1987). Group and computer-mediated discussion effects in risk decision making. *Journal of Personality and Social Psychology, 52,* 917–930.

McGuire, W. (1964). Inducing resistance to persuasion. In L. Berkowitz (Ed.), *Advances in experimental social psychology* (Vol. 1, pp. 192–232). New York: Academic Press.

———. (1969). The nature of attitudes and attitude change. In B. Lindsey & E. Aronson (Eds.), *Handbook of social psychology* (Vol. 3, pp. 136–314). Reading, MA: Addison-Wesley.

———. (1985). Attitudes and attitude change. In G. Lindzey & E. Aronson (Eds.), *The handbook of social psychology* (3rd ed., Vol. 2, pp. 233–346). New York: Random House.

McGuire, W., McGuire, C., Child, P., & Fujioka, P. (1978). Salience of ethnicity in the spontaneous self-concept as a function of one's ethnic distinctiveness in the social environment. *Journal of Personality and Social Psychology, 36,* 511–520.

McGuire, W., McGuire, C., & Winton, W. (1979). Effects of household sex composition on the salience of one's gender in the spontaneous self-concept. *Journal of Experimental Social Psychology, 15,* 77–90.

McRoberts, C., Burlingame, G., & Hoag, M. (1998). Comparative efficacy of individual and group psychotherapy: A meta-analysis. *Group Dynamics: Theory, Research, and Practice, 2,* 101–117.

Medin, D. (1988). Social categorization: Structures, processes, and purposes. In R. Wyer, Jr., & T. Srull (Eds.), *Handbook of social cognition* (2nd ed., Vol. 2, pp. 1–68). Hillsdale, NJ: Erlbaum.

Meer, B., & Freedman, E. (1966). The impact of Negro neighbors on White house owners. *Social Forces, 45,* 11–19.

Mehrabian, A. (1971). *Silent messages.* Belmont, CA: Wadsworth.

Mesch, D., Johnson, D. W., & Johnson, R. (1988). Impact of positive interdependence and academic group contingencies on achievement. *Journal of Social Psychology, 128,* 345–352.

Mesch, D., Lew, M., Johnson, D. W., & Johnson, R. (1986). Isolated teenagers, cooperative learning and the training of social skills. *Journal of Psychology, 120,* 323–334.

———. (1993). Effects of cooperative learning on isolated teens. In J. Cohen & M. Fish (Eds.), *Handbook of school-based interventions* (pp. 404–405). San Francisco: Jossey-Bass.

Messe, L., Kerr, N., & Sattler, D. (1992). "But some animals are more equal than others": The supervisor as a privileged status in group contexts. In S. Worchel, W. Wood, & J. Simpson (Eds.), *Group process and productivity* (pp. 203–223). Newbury Park, CA: Sage.

Messe, L., Stollak, G., Larson, R., & Michaels, G. (1979). Interpersonal consequences of person perception in two social contexts. *Journal of Personality and Social Psychology, 37,* 369–379.

Messick, D., & Brewer, M. (1983). Solving social dilemmas: A review. In L. Wheeler & P. Shaver (Eds.), *Review of personality and social psychology* (Vol. 4, pp. 11–44). Newbury Park, CA: Sage.

Michels, R. (1915/1959). *Political parties: A sociological study of the oligarchical tendencies of modern democracy.* New York: Dover.

Michener, H., & Burt, M. (1975). Components of "authority" as determinants of compliance. *Journal of Personality Psychology, 31,* 606–614.

Milgram, S. (1974). *Obedience to authority.* New York: Harper & Row.

Miller, N., Brewer, M., & Edwards, K. (1985). Cooperative interaction in desegregated settings: A laboratory analogue. *Journal of Social Issues, 41*(3), 63–79.

Miller, N., & Davidson-Podgorny, G. (1987). Theoretical models of intergroup relations and the use of cooperative teams as an intervention for desegregated settings. In C. Hendrick (Ed.), *Annual review of personality and social psychology: Group processes and intergroup relations* (Vol. 9, pp. 23–39). Newbury Park, CA: Sage.

Mills, T. (1967). *The sociology of small groups.* Englewood Cliffs, NJ: Prentice-Hall.

Minard, R. (1952). Race relationships in the Pocahontas coal field. *Journal of Social Issues, 8,* 29–44.

Mitchell, T., & Silver, W. (1990). Individual and group goals when workers are interdependent: Effects on task strategies and performance. *Journal of Applied Psychology, 75*(2), 185–193.

Moede, W. (1920). *Experimentelle massenpsychologie.* Leipzig: S. Hirzel.

———. (1927). Die richtlinien der leistungs-psychol-gie. *Industrielle Psychotechnik, 4*, 193–207.

Monteith, M. (1996a). Affective reactions to preju-dice-related discrepant resonses: The impact of standard salience. *Personality and Social Psychol-ogy Bulletin, 22*, 48–59.

———. (1996b). Contemporary forms of prejudice-related conflict: In search of a nutshell. *Personality and Social Psychology Bulletin, 22*, 416–473.

Monteith, M., Devine, P., & Zuwerink, J. (1993). Self-directed versus other-directed affect as a conse-quence of prejudice-related discrepancies. *Journal of Personality and Social Psychology, 64*, 198–210.

Monteith, M., & Walters, G. (1998). Egalitarianism, moral obligation, and prejudice-related personal standards. *Personality and Social Psychology Bul-letin, 24(2)*, 186–199.

Moreland, R., & Levine, J. (1982). Socialization in small groups: Temporal changes in individual-group relations. In L. Berkowitz (Ed.), *Advances in experimental social psychology* (Vol. 15, pp. 137–192). New York: Academic Press.

———. (1988). Group dynamics over time: Develop-ment and socialization in small groups. In J. Mc-Grath (Ed.), *The social psychology of time* (pp. 151–181). Newbury Park, CA: Sage.

Moreno, J. (1932/1953). *Who shall survive? Founda-tions of sociometry, group psychotherapy, and so-ciodrama* (2nd ed.). Beacon, NY: Beacon House.

Morgan, B., Coates, G., & Rebbin, T. (1970). *The effects of Phlebotomus fever on sustained perfor-mance and muscular output* (Tech. Rep. No. ITR-70-14). Louisville, KY: University of Louisville, Performance Research Laboratory.

Moscovici, S. (1980). Toward a theory of conversion behavior. In L. Berkowitz (Ed.), *Advances in exper-imental social psychology* (Vol. 15, pp. 209–239). New York: Academic Press.

———. (1985a). Innovation and minority influence. In S. Moscovici, G. Mugny, & E. Van Avermaet (Eds.), *Perspectives on minority influence* (pp. 9–51). Cam-bridge: Cambridge University Press.

———. (1985b). Social influence and conformity. In G. Lindzey & E. Aronson (Eds.), *The handbook of social psychology* (3rd ed., Vol. 2, pp. 347–412). New York: Random House.

Mullan, F. (1992). Rewriting the social contract in health. In A. Katz, H. Hedrick, D. Isenberg, L. Thompson, T. Goodrich, & A. Kutscher (Eds.), *Self-help: Concepts and applications* (pp. 61–67). Philadelphia: Charles Press.

Mullen, B. (1983). Operationalizing the effect of the group on the individual: A self-attention perspec-tive. *Journal of Experimental Social Psychology, 19*, 295–322.

Mullen, B., Brown, R., & Smith, C. (1992). Ingroup bias as a function of salience, relevance, and status: An integration. *European Journal of Social Psy-chology, 22*, 103–122.

Mullen, B., Johnson, C., & Salas, E. (1991). Produc-tivity loss in brainstorming groups: A meta-analytic integration. *Basic and Applied Social Psychology, 12*, 3–25.

Murnighan, J., & Pillutla, M. (1995). Fairness versus self-interest: Asymmetric moral imperatives in ultimatum bargaining. In R. Kramer & D. Mes-sick (Eds.), *Negotiation as a social process* (pp. 240–267). Thousand Oaks, CA: Sage.

Myers, D. (1978). The polarizing effects of social comparison. *Journal of Experimental Social Psy-chology, 14*, 554–563.

———. (1982). Polarizing effects of social interaction. In H. Brandstatter, J. Davis, & G. Stocker-Kreich-gauer (Eds.), *Group decision making*. New York: Academic Press.

———. (1987). *Social psychology* (2nd ed). New York: McGraw-Hill.

Myers, D., & Bishop, G. (1970). Discussion effects on racial attitudes. *Science, 169*, 778–789.

Myers, D., & Lamm, H. (1976). The group polariza-tion phenomenon. *Psychological Bulletin, 83*, 602–627.

Myers, R. (1969). *Some effects of seating arrange-ments in counseling*. Unpublished doctoral disser-tation, University of Florida, Gainesville.

Myrdal, G. (1944). *An American dilemma: The Negro problem and modern democracy*. New York: Harper.

Nadler, D., Hackman, J., & Lawler, E. (1979). *Manag-ing organizational behavior*. Boston: Little, Brown.

Neisser, U. (1954). On experimental distinction between perceptual process and verbal re-sponse. *Journal of Experimental Psychology, 47*, 399–402.

Nemeth, C. (1977). Interaction between jurors as a function of majority vs. unanimity decision rules. *Journal of Applied Social Psychology, 7*, 38–56.

———. (1986). Differential contributions of majority and minority influence. *Psychological Review, 93*, 23–32.

Nemeth, C., & Wachtler, J. (1974). Creating the per-ceptions of consistency and confidence: A neces-sary condition for minority influence. *Sociometry, 37*, 529–540.

Nesbitt, P., Pond, A., & Allen, W. (1959). *The survival book*. New York: Funk & Wagnalls.

Newcomb, T. (1943). *Personality and social change*. New York: Dryden.

———. (1956). The prediction of interpersonal at-traction. *American Psychologist, 11*, 575–586.

———. (1961). *The acquaintance process.* New York: Holt, Rinehart, & Winston.

Nijhof, W., & Kommers, P. (1982, July). *Analysis of cooperation in relation to cognitive controversy.* Paper presented at the International Conference on Cooperation in Education, Provo, UT.

Oakes, P. (1987). The salience of social categories. In J. Turner, M. Hogg, P. Oakes, S. Reicher, & M. Wetherell (Eds.), *Rediscovering the social group: A self-categorization theory* (pp. 117–141). Oxford: Basil Blackwell.

Oakes, P., & Turner, J. (1986). Distinctiveness and the salience of social category memberships: Is there an automatic perceptual bias toward novelty? *European Journal of Social Psychology, 16,* 325–344.

Oakes, P., Turner, J., & Haslam, S. (1991). Perceiving people as group members: The role of fit in the salience of social categorizations. *British Journal of Social Psychology, 30,* 125–144.

Ohbuchi, K., & Saito, M. (1986). Power imbalance, its legitimacy, and aggression. *Aggressive Behavior, 12,* 33–40.

Olson, M. (1965). *The logic of collective action: Public goods and the theory of groups.* Cambridge, MA: Harvard University Press.

O'Reilly, C., Caldwell, D., & Barnett, W. (1989). Work group demography, social integration, and turnover. *Administrative Science Quarterly, 34,* 21–37.

Ortiz, A., Johnson, D. W., & Johnson, R. (1996). Effects of positive goal and resource interdependence on individual performance. *Journal of Social Psychology, 136*(2), 243–249.

Orvis, B., Kelley, H., & Butler, D. (1976). Attributional conflict in young couples. In J. Harvey, W. Ickles, & R. Kidd (Eds.), *New directions in attribution research* (Vol. 1). Hillsdale, NJ: Erlbaum.

Ovisiankina, M. (1928). Investigations on the psychology of action and affection. VI. The resumption of interrupted acts, edited by K. Lewin. *Psychologische Forschung, 18,* 302–389.

Palmer, P. (1991). The courage to teach. *National Teaching and Learning Forum, 1*(2), 1–3.

———. (1992, March/April). Divided no more. *Change,* 11–17.

Pelz, D. (1956). Some social factors related to performance in a research organization. *Administrative Science Quarterly, 1,* 310–325.

———. (1958). Some factors in "group decision." In E. Maccoby, T. Newcomb, & E. Hartley (Eds.), *Readings in social psychology* (pp. 212–218). New York: Holt.

Pelz, E., & Andrews, F. (1966). *Scientists in organizations.* New York: Wiley.

Pennebaker, J. W. (1982). Social and perceptual factors affecting symptom reporting and mass psychogenic illness. In M. J. Colligan, J. W. Pennebaker, & L. R. Murphy (Eds.), *Mass psychogenic illness: A social psychological analysis* (pp. 139–153). Hillsdale, NJ: Erlbaum.

Pennington, D., Haravey, F., & Bass, B. (1958). Some effects of decision and discussion on coalescence, change, and effectiveness. *Journal of Applied Psychology, 42,* 404–408.

Pepinski, P., Hemphill, J., & Shevitz, R. (1958). Attempts to lead, group productivity, and morale under conditions of acceptance and rejection. *Journal of Abnormal and Social Psychology, 57,* 47–54.

Pepitone, A. (1952). *Responsibility to the group and its effects on the performance of members.* Unpublished doctoral dissertation, University of Michigan, Ann Arbor.

Pepitone, E. (Ed.). (1980). *Children in cooperation and competition.* Lexington, MA: Lexington Books.

Perdue, C., Dovidio, J., Gutman, M., & Tyler, R. (1990). Us and them: Social categorization and the process of intergroup bias. *Journal of Personality and Social Psychology, 59,* 475–486.

Perls, F. (1969). *Gestalt therapy verbatim.* Lafayette, CA: Real People Press.

Peterson, R., Johnson, D. W., & Johnson, R. (1991). Effects of cooperative learning on perceived status of male and female pupils. *Journal of Social Psychology, 13,* 717–735.

Pettigrew, T. (1997). Generalized intergroup contact effects on prejudice. *Personality and Social Psychology Bulletin, 23*(2), 173–185.

Petty, R., Cacioppo, J., & Kasmer, J. (1985). *Individual differences in social loafing on cognitive tasks.* Paper presented at the annual meeting of the Midwestern Psychological Association, Chicago.

Petty, M., Harkins, S., Williams, K., & Latané, B. (1977). Effects of group size on cognitive effort and evaluation. *Journal of Personality and Social Psychology, 3*(4), 579–582.

Phoon, W. H. (1982) Outbreaks of mass hysteria at workplaces in Singapore: Some patterns and modes of presentation. In M. J. Colligan, J. W. Pennebaker, & L. R. Murphy (Eds.), *Mass psychogenic illness: A social psychological analysis* (pp. 21–31). Hillsdale, NJ: Erlbaum.

Poole, M. (1998). The small group should be the fundamental unit of communication research. In J. Trent (Ed.), *Communication: Views from the helm in the 21st century* (pp. 94–97). Boston: Allyn & Bacon.

———. (1999). Group communication theory. In L. Frey, D. Gouran, & M. Poole (Eds.), *The handbook of group communication theory and research* (pp. 37–70). Thousand Oaks, CA: Sage.

Preston, M., & Heintz, R. (1949). Effects of participatory vs. supervisory leadership on group judgment.

Journal of Abnormal and Social Psychology, 44, 345–355.

Pruitt, D., & Johnson, D. (1970). Mediation as an aid to face saving in negotiation. *Journal of Personality and Social Psychology, 14,* 239–246.

Pruitt, D., & Rubin, J. (1986). *Social conflict.* New York: Random House.

Pruitt, D., & Syna, H. (1983). Successful problem solving. In D. Tjosvold & D. W. Johnson (Eds.), *Conflict in organizations* (pp. 62–81). New York: Irvington.

Putallaz, M. (1983). Predicting children's sociometric status from their behavior. *Child Development, 54,* 1417–1426.

Putnam, J., Rynders, J., Johnson, D. W., & Johnson, R. (1989). Collaborative skills instruction for promoting positive interactions between mentally handicapped and nonhandicapped children. *Exceptional Children, 55,* 550–557.

Qin, A., Johnson, D. W., & Johnson, R. (1995). Cooperative versus competitive efforts and problem solving. *Review of Educational Research, 65*(2), 129–143.

Radke, M., & Klisurich, D. (1947). Experiments in changing food habits. *Journal of the American Dietetics Association, 23,* 403–409.

Rahim, M. (1983). A measure of styles of handling interpersonal conflict. *Academy of Management Journal, 26,* 368–376.

Raven, B. (1992). A power/interaction model of interpersonal influence: French and Raven thirty years later. *Journal of Social Behavior and Personality, 7,* 217–244.

———. (1993). The origins of power: Origins and recent developments. *Journal of Social Issues, 49,* 227–251.

Raven, B., & Kruglanksi, A. (1970). Conflict and power. In P. Swingle (Ed.), *The structure of conflict* (pp. 69–110). New York: Academic Press.

Raven, B., & Rietsema, J. (1957). The effects of varied clarity of group goal and group path upon the individual and his relation to his group. *Human Relations, 10,* 29–44.

Raven, B., & Rubin, J. (1976). *Social psychology: People in groups.* New York: Wiley.

Rawls, J. (1971). *A theory of justice.* Cambridge, MA: Harvard University Press.

Reed, R. (1947). Accommodation between Negro and white employees in a west coast aircraft industry, 1942–1944. *Social Forces, 26,* 76–84.

Reeder, G. (1993). Trait–behavior relations and dispositional inference. *Personality and Social Psychology Bulletin, 19,* 586–593.

Regan, D., & Totten, J. (1975). Empathy and attribution: Turning observers into actors. *Journal of Personality and Social Psychology, 32,* 850–856.

Richardson, F., & Manaster, G. (1997). Back to the future: Alfred Adler on freedom and commitment. *Individual Psychology: The Journal of Adlerian Theory, Research, & Practice, 53*(3), 286–309.

Riess, M. (1982). Seating preferences as impression management: A literature review and theoretical integration. *Communication, 11,* 85–113.

Riess, M., & Rosenfeld, P. (1980). Seating preferences as nonverbal communication: A self-presentational analysis. *Journal of Applied Communications Research, 8,* 22–30.

Ringelmann, M. (1913). Research on animate sources of power: The work of man. *Annales de L'Instite National Agronomique, 2e, serietome* XII, 1–40.

Roark, A., & Sharah, H. (1989). Factors related to group cohesiveness. *Small Group Behavior, 20,* 62–69.

Rodin, J., & Langer, E. (1977). Long-term effects of a control-relevant intervention with the institutionalized aged. *Journal of Personality and Social Psychology, 35,* 897–902.

Rodin, J., Solomon, J., & Metcalf, J. (1978). Role of control in mediating perceptions of density. *Journal of Personality and Social Psychology, 36*(9), 988–999.

Roethlisberger, F., & Dickson, W. (1939). *Management and the worker.* Cambridge, MA: Harvard University Press.

Roff, J., & Wirt, R. (1984). Childhood aggression and social adjustment antecedents of delinquency. *Journal of Abnormal Child Psychology, 12*(1), 111–126.

Rogers, C. (1961). *On becoming a person: A therapist's view of psychotherapy.* Boston: Houghton Mifflin.

Rogers, E., & Shoemaker, F. (1971). *Communications and innovations.* New York: Free Press.

Rogers, M., Hennigan, K., Bosman, C., & Miller, N. (1984). Intergroup acceptance in classroom and playground settings. In N. Miller & M. Brewer (Eds.), *Groups in contact: The psychology of desegregation* (pp. 187–212). Orlando, FL: Academic Press.

Rokeach, M. (1954). The nature and meaning of dogmatism. *Psychological Review, 61,* 194–204.

———. (1960). *The open and closed mind.* New York: Basic Books.

———. (1968). *Beliefs, attitudes, and values.* San Francisco: Jossey-Bass.

Rose, A. (1948). Race relations in a Chicago industry. In M. Rose (Ed.), *Studies in the reduction of prejudice.* Chicago: American Council on Race Relations.

Rosenberg, L. (1961). Group size, prior experience, and conformity. *Journal of Abnormal and Social Psychology, 63*(2), 436–447.

Rosenblith, J. (1949). A replication of "some roots of prejudice." *Journal of Abnormal and Social Psychology, 44,* 470–489.

Ross, L. (1977). The intuitive psychologist and his shortcomings: Distortions in the attributional process. In L. Berkowitz (Ed.), *Advances in experimental social psychology* (Vol. 10, pp. 174–220). New York: Academic Press.

Ross, L., & Nisbett, R. (1991). *The person and the situation.* New York: McGraw-Hill.

Rothbart, M., Evans, M., & Fulero, S. (1979). Recall for confirming events: Memory processes and the maintenance of social stereotypes. *Journal of Experimental Social Psychology, 15,* 343–355.

Rothgerber, H., & Worchel, S. (1997). The view from below: Intergroup relations from the perspective of the disadvantaged group. *Journal of Personality and Social Psychology, 73,* 1191–1205.

Rotter, J. (1971). Generalized expectancies for interpersonal trust. *American Psychologist, 26,* 443–452.

Rubin, J., Pruitt, D., & Kim, S. (1994). *Social conflict.* New York: McGraw-Hill.

Rusbult, C., & Van Lange, P. (1996). Interdependent processes. In E. Higgins & A. Kruglanski (Eds.), *Social psychology: Handbook of basic principles* (pp. 564–596). New York: Guilford Press.

Rusbult, C., Yovetich, N., & Verette, J. (1996). An interdependence analysis of accommodation processes. In G. Fletcher & J. Fitness (Eds.), *Knowledge structures in close relationships: A social psychological approach* (pp. 63–90). Mahwah, NJ: Erlbaum.

Rutstrum, C. (1973). *The new ways of the wilderness.* New York: Collier.

Sachdev, I., & Bourhis, R. (1984). Minimal majorities and minorities. *European Journal of Social Psychology, 14,* 35–52.

———. (1991). Power and status differentials in minority and majority group relations. *European Journal of Social Psychology, 21,* 1–24.

Sanders, G. (1981). Driven by distraction: An integrative review of social facilitation theory and research. *Journal of Experimental Social Psychology, 17,* 227–251.

Sanders, G., & Baron, R. (1975). The motivating effects of distraction on task performance. *Journal of Personality and Social Psychology, 32,* 956–963.

Sarachek, G. (1968). Greek concepts of leadership. *Academy of Management Journal, 11,* 39–48.

Schachter, S. (1951). Deviation, rejection, and communication. *Journal of Abnormal and Social Psychology, 46,* 190–207.

Schachter, S., Ellertson, N., McBride, D., & Gregory, D. (1951). An experimental study of cohesiveness and productivity. *Human Relations, 4,* 229–238.

Schachter, S., Nuttin, J., Demonchaux, C., Maucorps, P., Osmer, Diedrich, Duijker, Hubertur, Rommetveit, Ragnar, Israel, & Joachim. (1954). Cross-cultural experiments on threat and rejection. *Human Relations, 7,* 403–439.

Schein, E. (1969). *Process consultation.* Reading, MA: Addison-Wesley.

Schmidt, W. (1974). Conflict: A powerful process for (good and bad) change. *Management Review, 63,* 4–10.

Schultz, W. (1958). *FIRO: A three dimensional theory of interpersonal behavior.* New York: Rinehart.

———. (1966). *The interpersonal underworld.* Palo Alto, CA: Science and Behavior Books.

Schweiger, D., Sandberg, W., & Rechner, P. (1989). Experiential effects of dialectical inquiry, devil's advocacy, and consensus approaches to strategic decision making. *Academy of Management Journal, 32,* 722–745.

Schwenk, C. (1983). Laboratory research on ill-structured decision aids: The case of dialectical inquiry. *Decision Sciences, 14,* 140–144.

Seashore, S. (1954). *Group cohesiveness in the industrial work group.* Ann Arbor, MI: Institute for Social Research.

Seligman, M. (1975). *On depression, development, and death.* San Francisco: Freeman.

———. (1988). Boomer blues. *Psychology Today, 22,* 50–55.

Selman, R. (1981). The development of interpersonal competence: The role of understanding in conduct. *Departmental Review, 1,* 401–422.

Seta, J., Paulus, P., & Schkade, J. (1976). Effects of group size and proximity under cooperative and competitive conditions. *Journal of Personality and Social Psychology, 34,* 47–53.

Shambaugh, P. (1978). The development of the small group. *Human Relations, 31,* 283–295.

Shaw, M. (1932). A comparison of individuals and small groups in the rational solution of complex problems. *American Journal of Psychology, 44,* 491–504.

———. (1964). Communication networks. In L. Berkowitz (Ed.), *Advances in experimental social psychology* (Vol. 1, pp. 111–147). New York: Academic Press.

———. (1976, 1981). *Group dynamics: The psychology of small group behavior.* New York: McGraw-Hill.

Shepperd, J. (1993). Productivity loss in performance groups: A motivation analysis. *Psychological Bulletin, 113*(1), 67–81.

Sherif, M. (1936). *The psychology of group norms.* New York: Harper.

———. (1966). *In common predicament*. Boston: Houghton Mifflin.

Sherif, M., Harvey, O., White, B., Hood, W., & Sherif, C. (1961). *Intergroup conflict and cooperation: The robber's cave experiment*. Norman: University of Oklahoma Press.

Sherif, M., & Sherif, C. (1956). *An outline of social psychology*. New York: Harper & Row.

———. (1969). *Social psychology*. New York: Harper & Row.

Sherman, J. (1996). Development and mental representation of stereotypes. *Journal of Personality and Social Psychology, 70*, 1126–1141.

Sherman, J., Lee, A., Bessenoff, G., & Frost, L. (1998). Stereotype efficiency reconsidered: Encoding flexibility under cognitive load. *Journal of Personality and Social Psychology, 75*(3), 589–606.

Shinagawa, L. (1997). *Atlas of American diversity*. Thousand Oaks, CA: Sage.

Short, J., Williams, E., & Christie, B. (1976). *The social psychology of telecommunications*. London: Wiley.

Siegel, J., Dubrovsky, V., Kiesler, S., & McGuire, T. (1986). Group processes in computer-mediated communication. *Organizational Behavior and Human Decision Processes, 37*, 157–187.

Sigelman, L., & Welch, S. (1993). The contact hypothesis revisited: Black–White interaction and positive racial attitudes. *Social Forces, 71*, 781–795.

Simon, H. (1976). *Administrative behavior: A study of decision-making processes in administrative organization* (3rd ed.). New York: Free Press.

———. (1979). *The science of the artificial* (2nd ed.). Cambridge, MA: Massachusetts Institute of Technology Press.

Simonton, D. (1979). Multiple discovery and invention: *Zeitgeist*, genius or chance? *Journal of Personality and Social Psychology, 37*, 1603–1616.

Singh, R., Choo, W., & Poh, L. (1998). In-group bias and fair-mindedness as strategies of self-presentation in intergroup perception. *Personality and Social Psychology Bulletin, 24*(2), 147–162.

Sirota, Alper, & Pfau, Inc. (1989). *Report to respondents: Survey of views towards human resources policies and practices*. New York: Author.

Skinner, B. (1953). *Science and human behavior*. New York: Macmillan.

———. (1971). *Beyond freedom and dignity*. New York: Knopf.

Skon, L., Johnson, D. W., & Johnson, R. (1981). Cooperative peer interaction versus individual competition and individualistic efforts: Effects of the acquisition of cognitive reasoning strategies. *Journal of Educational Psychology, 73*, 83–92.

Slavin, R. (1986). *Using student team learning*. Baltimore: Center for Research on Elementary and Middle Schools, Johns Hopkins University.

Smith, C., & Powell, L. (1988). The use of disparaging humor by group leaders. *Southern Speech Communication Journal, 53*, 279–292.

Smith, F. (1943). *An experiment in modifying attitudes toward the Negro* (Teachers College Contributions to Education, 887). New York: Columbia University Press.

Smith, K., Johnson, D. W., & Johnson, R. (1982). Effects of cooperative and individualistic instruction on the achievement of handicapped, regular, and gifted students. *Journal of Social Psychology, 116*, 277–283.

Smith, M. (1945). Social situation, social behavior, and social group. *Psychological Review, 52*, 224–229.

Snyder, C., Cheavens, J., & Sympson, S. (1997). Hope: An individual motive for social commerce. *Group Dynamics: Theory, Research, and Practice, 1*, 107–118.

Sommer, R. (1967). Small group ecology. *Psychological Bulletin, 67*, 145–152.

Sonstegard, M., Dreikurs, R., & Bitter, J. (1982). The teleanalytic group counseling approach. In G. Gazda (Ed.), *Basic approaches to group psychotherapy and counseling* (3rd ed., pp. 507–551). Springfield, IL: Charles C Thomas.

Sorrentino, R., & Boutillier, R. (1975). The effect of quantity and quality of verbal interaction on ratings of leadership ability. *Journal of Experimental Social Psychology, 11*, 403–411.

Spencer, S., Fein, S., Wolfe, C., Fong, C., & Dunn, M. (1998). Automatic activation of stereotypes: The role of self-image threat. *Personality and Social Psychology Bulletin, 24*(11), 1139–1152.

Star, S., Williams, R., & Stouffer, S. (1965). Negro infantry platoons in white companies. In H. Proshansky & B. Seidenberg (Eds.), *Basic studies in social psychology* (pp. 680–684). New York: Holt, Rinehart & Winston.

Stasser, G., & Titus, W. (1987). Effects of information load and percentage shared information on the dissemination of unshared information during discussion. *Journal of Personality and Social Psychology, 53*, 81–93.

Steele, C., & Aronson, J. (1995). Stereotype threat and the intellectual test performance of African Americans. *Journal of Personality and Social Psychology, 69*, 797–811.

Stein, M. (1968). *The creative individual*. New York: Harper & Row.

Stein, R., & Heller, T. (1979). An empirical analysis of the correlations between leadership status and participation rates reported in the literature. *Journal of Personality and Social Psychology, 37,* 1993–2002.

Steiner, I. (1959). Human interaction and interpersonal perception. *Sociometry, 22,* 230–235.

———. (1966). Models for inferring relationships between group size and potential group productivity. *Behavioral Science, 11,* 273–283.

———. (1972). *Group process and productivity.* New York: Academic Press.

———. (1974). Whatever happened to the group in social psychology? *Journal of Experimental Social Psychology, 10,* 94–108.

Steinzor, B. (1950). The spatial factor in face-to-face discussion groups. *Journal of Abnormal and Social Psychology, 45,* 552–555.

Stephan, F., & Mishler, E. (1952). The distribution of participation in small groups: An exponential approximation. *American Sociological Review, 17,* 598–608.

Stephan, W. (1978). School desegregation: An evaluation of predictions made in *Brown vs. Board of Education. Psychological Bulletin, 85,* 217–238.

Stogdill, R. (1959). *Individual behavior and group achievement.* New York: Oxford University Press.

———. (1974). *Handbook of leadership.* New York: Free Press.

Stoner, J. (1961). *A comparison of individual and group decisions involving risk.* Unpublished master's thesis, Massachusetts Institute of Technology, Boston.

Storm, H. (1972). *Steven arrows.* New York: Ballantine Books.

Storms, M. (1973). Videotape and the attribution process: Reversing actors' and observers' points of view. *Journal of Personality and Social Psychology, 27,* 165–175.

Stotle, J. (1978). Power structure and personal competence. *Journal of Social Psychology, 38,* 72–83.

Strodtbeck, F., & Hook, L. (1961). The social dimensions of a twelve man jury table. *Sociometry, 24,* 397–415.

Stroebe, W., Diehl, M., & Abukoumkin, G. (1992). The illusion of group effectivity. *Personality and Social Psychology Bulletin, 18,* 643–650.

Sundstrom, E., Perkins, M., George, J., Futrell, D., & Hoffman, D. (1990, April). *Work-team context, development, and effectiveness in a manufacturing organization.* Paper presented at the Fifth Annual Conference of the Society for Industrial and Organizational Psychology, Miami.

Swann, W. (1984). Quest for accuracy in person perception: A matter of pragmatics. *Psychological Review, 91,* 457–477.

Sweeney, J. (1973). An experimental investigation of the free-rider problem. *Social Science Research, 2,* 277–292.

Swim, K., Aikin, K., Hall, W., & Hunter, B. (1995). Sexism and racism: Old fashioned and modern prejudices. *Journal of Personality and Social Psychology, 68,* 199–214.

Szymanski, K., & Harkins, S. (1987). Social loafing and self-evaluation with a social standard. *Journal of Personality and Social Psychology, 53,* 891–897.

Tajfel, H. (1969). Cognitive aspects of prejudice. *Journal of Social Issues, 25,* 79–87.

———. (1974). Social identity and intergroup behavior. *Social Science Information, 13,* 65–93.

———. (1978). Social categorization, social identity, and social comparison. In H. Tajfel (Ed.), *Differentiation between social groups* (pp. 61–76). London: Academic Press.

———. (1981). *Human groups and social categories.* Cambridge: Cambridge University Press.

Tajfel, H., & Turner, J. (1979). An integrative theory of intergroup conflict. In W. Austin & S. Worchel (Eds.), *Psychology of intergroup relations* (pp. 33–47). Monterey, CA: Brooks/Cole.

———. (1986). The social identity theory of intergroup relation. In S. Worchel & W. Austin (Eds.), *Psychology of intergroup relations* (pp. 7–24). Chicago: Nelson-Hall.

Taylor, D., & Faust, W. (1952). Twenty questions: Efficiency in problem solving as a function of size of group. *Journal of Experimental Psychology, 44,* 360–368.

Taylor, S. (1980). The interface of cognitive and social psychology. In J. H Harvey (Ed.), *Cognition, social behavior, and the environment* (pp. 189–211). Hillsdale, NJ: Erlbaum.

Taylor, S., & Lobel, M. (1989). Social comparison activity under threat: Downward evaluation and upward contacts. *Psychological Review, 96,* 569–575.

Teger, A. (1980). *Too much invested to quit.* New York: Pergamon.

Terborg, J., Castore, C., & DeNinno, J. (1976). A longitudinal field investigation of the impact of group composition on group performance and cohesion. *Journal of Personality and Social Psychology, 34,* 782–790.

Terman, L., & Odor, M. (1947). *The gifted child grows up.* Stanford, CA: Stanford University Press.

Tetlock, P. (1979). Identifying victims of groupthink from public statements of decision makers. *Journal of Personality and Social Psychology, 37,* 1314–1324.

Thibaut, J., & Kelly, H. (1959). *The social psychology of groups.* New York: Wiley.

Thomas, E., & Fink, C. (1961). Models of group problem solving. *Journal of Abnormal and Social Psychology, 63,* 53–63.

Thomas, K. (1976). Conflict and conflict management. In M. Dunnette (Ed.), *Handbook of industrial and organizational psychology* (pp. 889–935). Chicago: Rand McNally.

Thomas, K., & Schmidt, W. (1976). A survey of managerial interests with respect to conflict. *Academy of Management Journal, 19,* 315–318.

Thorndike, R. (1938). On what type of task will a group do well? *Journal of Abnormal Social Psychology, 30,* 409–413.

Tjosvold, D. (1974). Threat as a low-power person's strategy in bargaining: Social face and tangible outcomes. *International Journal of Group Tensions, 4,* 494–510.

———. (1977). Low-power person's strategies in bargaining: Negotiability of demand, maintaining face, and race. *International Journal of Group Tensions, 7,* 29–42.

———. (1978). Alternative organizations for schools and classrooms. In D. Bar-Tal & L. Saxe (Eds.), *Social psychology of education: Theory and research* (pp. 275–298). Washington, DC: Hemisphere.

———. (1981). Unequal power relationships within a cooperative or competitive context. *Journal of Applied Social Psychology, 11,* 137–150.

———. (1982). Effects of approach to controversy on superiors' incorporation of subordinates' information in decision making. *Journal of Applied Psychology, 67,* 189–193.

———. (1985a). The effects of attribution and social context on superiors' influence and interaction with low performing subordinates. *Personnel Psychology, 38,* 361–376.

———. (1985b). Power and social context in superior–subordinate interaction. *Organizational Behavior and Human Decision Processes, 35,* 281–293.

———. (1986). *Working together to get things done.* Lexington, MA: Lexington Books.

———. (1989). Interdependence and power between managers and employees: A study of the leader relationship. *Journal of Management, 15,* 49–62.

———. (1990a). Power in cooperative and competitive organizational contexts. *Journal of Social Psychology, 130,* 249–258.

———. (1990b). *The team organization: Applying group research to the workplace.* New York: Wiley.

———. (1991a). *Team organization.* New York: Wiley.

———. (1991b). *The conflict-positive organization.* Reading, MA: Addison-Wesley.

———. (1993). Experiencing a given base of power as a reward or punishment. *Psychological Reports, 73,* 178.

———. (1995a). Cooperation theory, constructive controversy, and effectiveness: Learning from crisis. In R. Guzzo & E. Salas (Eds.), *Team effectiveness and decision making in organizations* (pp. 79–112). San Francisco: Jossey-Bass.

———. (1995b). Effects of power to reward and punish in cooperative and competitive contexts. *Journal of Social Psychology, 135*(6), 723–736.

Tjosvold, D., & Johnson, D. W. (1978). Controversy within a cooperative or competitive context and cognitive perspective-taking. *Contemporary Educational Psychology, 3,* 376–386.

———. (1982). *Productive conflict.* New York: Irvin.

Tjosvold, D., Johnson, D. W., & Johnson, R. (1981). Effect of partner's effort and ability on liking for partner after failure on a cooperative task. *Journal of Psychology, 109,* 147–152.

Tjosvold, D., & Sagaria, D. (1978). Effects of relative power of cognitive perspective-taking. *Personality and Social Psychology Bulletin, 4,* 256–259.

Torrance, E. (1954). Some consequences of power differences in decision making in permanent and temporary three-man groups. *Research Studies, State College of Washington, 22,* 130–140.

———. (1957). Group decision-making and disagreement. *Social Forces, 35,* 314–318.

———. (1961). Can grouping control social stress in creative activity? *Elementary School Journal, 62,* 391–394.

Treffinger, D., Speedie, S., & Brunner, W. (1974). Improving children's creative problem solving ability: The Purdue creativity project. *The Journal of Creative Behavior, 8,* 20–29.

Trevino, L., Lengel, R., & Draft, R. (1987). Media symbolism, media richness, and media choice in organizations: A symbolic interactionist perspective. *Communication Research, 14,* 553–574.

Triandis, H., Bass, A., Ewen, R., & Mieksele, E. (1963). Teaching creativity as a function of the members. *Journal of Applied Psychology, 47,* 104–110.

Triandis, H., Hall, D., & Ewen, R. (1965). Member heterogeneity and dyadic creativity. *Human Relations, 18,* 33–55.

Triplett, N. (1898). The dynamogenic factors in pacemaking and competition. *American Journal of Psychology, 9,* 507–533.

Tschuschke, V., & Dies, R. (1994). Intensive analysis of therapeutic factors and outcome in long-term inpatient groups. *International Journal of Group Psychotherapy, 44,* 185–208.

Tuckman, B. (1965). Developmental sequence in small groups. *Psychological Bulletin, 63,* 384–399.

Tuckman, B., & Jensen, M. (1977). Stages of small group development revisited. *Group and Organizational Studies, 2,* 419–427.

Turner, J. (1978). Social comparison, similarity and ingroup favoritism. In H. Tajfel (Ed.), *Differentiation between social groups* (pp. 235–250). London: Academic Press.

———. (1985). Social categorization and the self-concept: A social cognitive theory of group behavior. In E. Lawler (Ed.), *Advances in group processes* (Vol. 2, pp. 77–122). Greenwich, CT: JAI Press.

———. (1987). *Rediscovering the social group: A self-categorization theory.* New York: Basil Blackwell.

Turner, J., & Oakes, P. (1989). Self-categorization theory and social influence. In P. Paulus (Ed.), *Psychology of group influence* (2nd ed., pp. 233–275). Hillsdale, NJ: Erlbaum.

Turner, M., Pratkanis, A., Probasco, P., & Leve, C. (1992). Threat, cohesion, and group effectiveness: Testing a social identity maintenance perspective on groupthink. *Journal of Personality and Social Psychology, 63,* 781–796.

Turner, R., & Killian, L. (1972/1987). *Collective behavior* (3rd ed.). Englewood Cliffs, NJ: Prentice-Hall.

Tversky, A., & Kahneman, D. (1981). The framing of decisions and the psychology of choice. *Science, 211,* 453–458.

Tyler, T. (1997). The psychology of legitimacy: A relational perspective on voluntary deference to authorities. *Personality and Social Psychology Review, 1,* 323–345.

Tyler, T., & Degoey, P. (1996). Trust in organizational authorities: The influence of motive attributions on willingness to accept decisions. In R. Kramer & T. Tyler (Eds.), *Trust in organizational authorities* (pp. 331–356). Thousand Oaks, CA: Sage.

Tyler, T., Lind, E., Ohbuchi, K., Sugawara, I., & Huo, Y. (1998). Conflict with outsiders: Disputing within and across cultural boundaries. *Personality and Social Psychology Bulletin, 24*(2), 137–146.

Urban, L., & Miller, N. (1998). A theoretical analysis of crossed categorization effects: A meta-analysis. *Journal of Personality and Social Psychology, 74,* 894–908.

Vacchiano, R. B., Strauss, P. S., & Hochman, L. (1968). The open and closed mind: A review of dogmatism. *Psychological Bulletin, 71*(4), 261–273.

Vanbeselaere, N. (1987). The effects of dichotomous and crossed social categorizations upon intergroup discrimination. *European Journal of Social Psychology, 17,* 143–156.

———. (1991). The different effects of simple and crossed categorization: A result of the category differentiation process or of differential category salience? In W. Stroebe & M. Hewstone (Eds.), *European review of social psychology* (Vol. 2, pp. 143–156). Chichester, UK: Wiley.

Villasenor, V. (1977). *Jury: The people vs. Juan Corona.* New York: Bantam Books.

Vinton, K. (1989). Humor in the workplace: It is more than telling jokes. *Small Group Research, 20,* 151–166.

Voiers, W. (1956). *Bombing accuracy as a function of the group-school proficiency structure of the B-29 bomb team.* (Research Report AFDTRC-TN-56-4.) Lackland Air Force Base, TX: Air Force Personnel and Training Research Center.

Von Mises, L. (1949). *Human action: A treatise on economics.* New Haven, CT: Yale University Press.

Wagner, U., Hewstone, M., & Machleit, U. (1989). Contact and prejudice between Germans and Turks. *Human Relations, 42,* 561–574.

Walton, R. (1969). *Interpersonal peacemaking.* Reading, MA: Addison-Wesley.

———. (1985). From control to commitment in the workplace. *Harvard Business Review, 63,* 76–84.

———. (1987). *Managing conflict.* Reading, MA: Addison-Wesley.

Walton, R., & McKersie, R. (1965). *A behavioral theory of labor negotiations.* New York: McGraw-Hill.

Warriner, C. (1956). Groups are real: A reaffirmation. *American Sociological Review, 21,* 349–354.

Watson, G. (1928). Do groups think more effectively than individuals? *Journal of Abnormal and Social Psychology, 23,* 328–336.

———. (1931). Do groups think more effectively than individuals? In G. Murphy & L. Murphy (Eds.), *Experimental social psychology.* New York: Harper.

———. (1947). *Action for unity.* New York: Harper.

Watson, G., & Johnson, D. W. (1972). *Social psychology: Issues and insights* (2nd ed.). Philadelphia: Lippincott.

Webb, N. (1977). *Learning in individual and small group setting* (Tech. Report No. 7). Stanford, CA: Stanford University, School of Education, Aptitude Research Project.

Weber, M. (1921/1946). The sociology of charismatic authority. In H. Gert & C. Mills (Trans. & Eds.), *From Max Weber: Essay in sociology* (pp. 245–252). New York: Oxford University Press.

Weick, K. (1990). The vulnerable system: An analysis of the Tenerife air disaster. *Journal of Management, 16,* 571–593.

Weigel, R., & Howes, P. (1985). Conceptions of racial prejudice. *Journal of Social Issues, 41*(3), 117–138.

Weincr, N., Pandy, J., & Latané, B. (1981). *Individual and group productivity in the United States and India.* Paper presented at the annual meeting of the American Psychological Association, Los Angeles.

West, C., & Zimmerman, D. (1983). Small insults: A study of interruptions in cross-sex conversations between unacquainted persons. In B. Thorne, C. Dramarge, & N. Henley (Eds.), *Language, gender, and society* (pp. 102–117). Rowley, MA: Newbury House.

Wheeler, R., & Ryan, F. (1973). Effects of cooperative and competitive classroom environments on the attitudes and achievement of elementary school students engaged in social studies inquiry activities. *Journal of Educational Psychology, 65,* 402–407.

Whyte, W. F. (1943). *Street corner society.* Chicago: University of Chicago Press.

Wiggam, A. (1931). The biology of leadership. In H. Metcalf (Ed.), *Business leadership.* New York: Pitman.

Wilder, D. (1977). Perception of group, size of opposition, and social influence. *Journal of Experimental Social Psychology, 13,* 253–268.

———. (1978a). Perceiving persons as a group: Effects on attributions of causality and beliefs. *Social Psychology, 41,* 13–33.

———. (1978b). Reduction of intergroup discrimination through individuation of the out-group. *Journal of Personality and Social Psychology, 36,* 1361–1374.

———. (1986). Social categorization: Implications for creation and reduction of intergroup bias. *Advances in Experimental Social Psychology, 19,* 291–355.

———. (1990). Some determinants of the persuasive power of in-groups and the out-groups: Organization of information and attribution of independence. *Journal of Personality and Social Psychology, 59,* 1202–1213.

Wilder, D., & Shapiro, P. (1989a). Effects of anxiety on impression formation in a group context: An anxiety-assimilation hypothesis. *Journal of Experimental Social Psychology, 25,* 481–499.

———. (1989b). Role of competition-induced anxiety in limiting the beneficial impact of positive behavior by an out-group member. *Journal of Personality and Social Psychology, 56,* 60–69.

———. (1991). Facilitation of outgroup stereotypes by enhanced ingroup identity. *Journal of Experimental Social Psychology, 27,* 431–452.

Wilkinson, I., & Kipnis, D. (1978). Interfirm use of power. *Journal of Applied Psychology, 63,* 315–320.

Willems, E., & Clark, R. (1971). Shift toward risk and heterogeneity of groups. *Journal of Experimental and Social Psychology, 7,* 304–312.

Williams, D. (1948). The effect of an interracial project upon the attitudes of Negro and white girls within the YWCA. In A. Rose (Ed.), *Studies in the reduction of prejudice.* Chicago: American Council of Race Relations.

Williams, K. (1981). Developmental characteristics of a forward roll. *Research Quarterly for Exercise and Sport, 51*(4), 703–713.

Williams, K., Harkins, S., & Latané, B. (1981). Identifiability as a deterrent to social loafing: Two cheering experiments. *Journal of Personality and Social Psychology, 40,* 303–311.

Williams, K., & Williams, K. (1984). *Social loafing in Japan: A cross-cultural development study.* Paper presented at the annual meeting of the Midwestern Psychological Association, June, Chicago.

Williams, R. (1947). *Reduction of intergroup tension: A survey of research on problems of ethnic, racial, and religious group relations,* Bulletin 57. New York: Social Science Research Council.

———. (1964). *Strangers next door.* Englewood Cliffs, NJ: Prentice-Hall.

Williams, R., & Ryan, M. (Eds.). (1954). *Schools of transition: Community experiences in desegregation.* Chapel Hill: University of North Carolina Press.

Wilner, D., Walkley, R., & Cook, S. (1952). Residential proximity and intergroup relations in public housing projects. *Journal of Social Issues, 8,* 45–69.

Winder, A. (1952). White attitudes toward Negro–white interaction in an area of changing racial composition. *American Psychologist, 7,* 330–331.

Wolfe, J., & Box, T. (1988). Team cohesion effects on business game performance. *Simulation and Games, 19*(1), 82–98.

Wolman, B., & Stricker, G. (Eds.). (1983). *Handbook of family and marital therapy.* New York: Plenum.

Wood, J., Taylor, S., & Lichtman, R. (1985). Social comparison in adjustment to breast cancer. *Journal of Personality and Social Psychology, 49,* 1169–1183.

Wood, W. (1987). Meta-analytic review of sex differences in group performance. *Psychological Bulletin, 102,* 53–71.

Wood, W., Lundgren, S., Quelletter, J., Busceme, S., & Blackstone, T. (1994). Minority influence: A meta-analytic review of social influence processes. *Psychological Bulletin, 115*(3), 323–345.

Worchel, S., Andreoli, V., & Folger, R. (1977). Intergroup cooperation and intergroup attraction: The effect of previous interaction and outcome on combined effort. *Journal of Experimental Social Psychology, 13,* 131–140.

Worchel, S., & Brehm, J. (1971). Direct and implied social restoration of freedom. *Journal of Personality and Social Psychology, 18,* 294–304.

Worchel, S., Coutant-Sassic, D., & Grossman, M. (1992). A developmental approach to group dynamics: A model and illustrative research. In S. Worchel, W. Wood, & J. Simpson (Eds.), *Group process and productivity* (pp. 181–202). Newbury Park, CA: Sage.

Wright, J. (1979). *On a clear day you can see General Motors.* New York: Avon.

Wright, S., Aron, A., McLaughlin-Volpe, T., & Ropp, S. (1997). The extended contact effect: Knowledge of cross-group friendships and prejudice. *Journal of Personality and Social Psychology, 73*(1), 73–90.

Yager, S., Johnson, D. W., & Johnson, R. (1985). Oral discussion, group-to-individual transfer, and achievement in cooperative learning groups. *Journal of Educational Psychology, 77,* 60–66.

Yalom, I. (1995). *The theory and practice of group psychotherapy* (4th ed.). New York: Basic Books.

Yarrow, M., Campbell, J., & Yarrow, L. (1958). Interpersonal dynamics in racial integration. In E. Maccoby, T. Newcomb, & E. Hartley (Eds.), *Readings in social psychology* (pp. 623–635). New York: Holt, Rinehart, & Winston.

Young, D. (1932). *American minority people: A study in racial and cultural conflicts in the United States.* New York: Harper.

Yovetich, N., & Rusbult, C. (1994). Accommodative behavior in close relationships: Exploring transformation of motivation. *Journal of Experimental Social Psychology, 30,* 138–164.

Yukl, G., & Falbe, C. (1991). Importance of different power sources in downward and lateral relations. *Journal of Applied Psychology, 76,* 416–423.

Yukl, G., & Tracey, J. (1992). Consequences of influence attempts used with subordinates, peers, and the boss. *Journal of Applied Psychology, 77,* 525–535.

Zaccaro, S. (1984). Social loafing: The role of task attractiveness. *Personality and Social Psychology Bulletin, 10,* 99–106.

Zajonc, R. (1965). Social facilitation. *Science, 149,* 269–272.

Zander, A. (1971). *Motives and goals in groups.* New York: Academic Press.

———. (1974). Team spirit vs. the individual achiever. *Psychology Today, 8*(6), 64–68.

———. (1977). *Groups at work.* San Francisco: Jossey-Bass.

———. (1979). The psychology of group process. *Annual Review of Psychology, 30,* 417–451.

Zander, A., & Armstrong, W. (1972). Working for group pride in a slipper factory. *Journal of Applied Social Psychology, 2,* 293–307.

Zander, A., & Medow, H. (1963). Individual and group levels of aspiration. *Human Relations, 16,* 89–105.

Zdep, S., & Oakes, W. (1967). Reinforcement of leadership behavior in group discussion. *Journal of Experimental Social Psychology, 3,* 310–320.

Ziller, R. (1957). Group size: A determinant of the quality and stability of group decision. *Sociometry, 20,* 165–173.

Ziller, R., Behringer, R., & Goodchilds, J. (1962). Group creativity under conditions of success or failure and variations in group stability. *Journal of Applied Psychology, 46,* 43–49.

Zimbardo, P. (1970). The human choice: Individuation, reason, and order versus deindividuation, impulse, and chaos. In W. Arnold & D. Levine (Eds.), *Nebraska symposium on motivation* (pp. 237–307). Lincoln: University of Nebraska Press.

———. (1975). Transforming experimental research into advocacy for social change. In M. Deutsch & H. Hornstein (Eds.), *Applying social psychology* (pp. 33–66). Hillsdale, NJ: Erlbaum.

Zuwerink, J., Monteith, M., Devine, P., & Cook, D. (1996). Prejudice towards Blacks: With and without compunction? *Basic and Applied Social Psychology, 18,* 131–150.

Index

Page numbers followed by *t* or *f* indicate tables or figures respectively.

PHOTO CREDITS

Ch. 1: Steve Sly/The Image Bank
Ch. 2: Lawrence Migdale
Ch. 3: Getty/Stone
Ch. 4: Will Faller
Ch. 5: Corbis
Ch. 6: AP/Wide World Photos
Ch. 7: Tony Stone
Ch. 8: Bob Daemmrich/Stock Boston
Ch. 9: Mark Gamba/The Stock Market
Ch. 10: Tom Sanders/The Stock Market
Ch. 11: Jim Cummins/Corbisstockmarket
Ch. 12: David Young-Wolff/PhotoEdit
Ch. 13: Nathan Bilow/Allsport Concept-Getty Images
Epilogue: Ariel Skelley/Corbisstockmarket